ALSO BY MICHAEL HILTZIK

A DEATH IN KENYA
The Murder of Julie Ward

DEALERS OF LIGHTNING
Xerox PARC and the Dawn of the Computer Age

THE PLOT AGAINST SOCIAL SECURITY
How the Bush Plan Is Endangering Our Financial Future

COLOSSUS
The Turbulent, Thrilling Saga of the Building of Hoover Dam

THE
NEW
DEAL

A MODERN HISTORY

MICHAEL HILTZIK

FREE PRESS

New York London Toronto Sydney New Delhi

*f*P
Free Press
A Division of Simon & Schuster, Inc.
1230 Avenue of the Americas
New York, NY 10020

First Free Press hardcover edition September 2011

FREE PRESS and colophon are trademarks of Simon & Schuster, Inc.

For information about special discounts for bulk purchases, please contact
Simon & Schuster Special Sales at 1-866-506-1949 or
business@simonandschuster.com.

The Simon & Schuster Speakers Bureau can bring authors to your live event.
For more information or to book an event contact the Simon & Schuster
Speakers Bureau at 1-866-248-3049 or visit our website at
www.simonspeakers.com.

Photo on page vii: FDR delivering his first Fireside Chat, from the collections
of the Franklin D. Roosevelt Presidential Library and Museum.

Photo insert credits: 1: Franklin D. Roosevelt Library; 2, 4, 6, 7, 9, 10, 11,
12, 13, 14, 15, 16, 17, 18, 21, 22, 23, 26, 28, 29: Library of Congress; 3: AP;
5, 27: Bettman/Corbis; 8: Tennessee Valley Authority; 19, 20: Public Works
Administration; 24, 25: Collection of the Supreme Court of the United States

Manufactured in the United States of America

1   3   5   7   9   10   8   6   4   2

Library of Congress Cataloging-in-Publication Data

Hiltzik, Michael A.
The New Deal : a modern history / Michael Hiltzik.
p. cm.
Includes bibliographical references and index.
1. New Deal, 1933–1939. 2. United States—Politics and government—1933–1945.
3. United States—Economic conditions—1918–1945. 4. Depressions—1929—
United States. I. Title.
E806.H557 2011
973.917—dc22
2011011367

ISBN 978-1-4391-5448-9
ISBN 978-1-4391-5895-1 (ebook)

To Deborah, Andrew, and David

I do not look upon these United States as a finished product. We are still in the making.

—Franklin Roosevelt, February 23, 1936

I am an old campaigner, and I love a good fight.

—Franklin Roosevelt, October 26, 1936

CONTENTS

PART THREE: RETURN TO EARTH

THE
NEW
DEAL

THE LONG WINTER

"I PLEDGE MYSELF TO a new deal for the American people."

Samuel I. Rosenman always claimed that he gave those words little thought when, holed up in a dining room of the executive mansion in Albany, New York, and fortified by a rough meal of boiled frankfurters and a pot of coffee, he scribbled them on a scrap of paper.

At that moment he was convinced they never would be uttered aloud. It was the early morning of July 1, 1932. In Chicago, the Democratic National Convention had completed its third ballot for the nomination for president. Rosenman's candidate, New York Governor Franklin D. Roosevelt, was still eighty-eight votes short of the required two-thirds majority. Rosenman, who was Roosevelt's speechwriter, a charter member of his Brain Trust, and an old personal friend, had been drafting the governor's acceptance speech intermittently for months. The body of the speech had reached its final form several days earlier. All that remained to be drafted was the peroration, that uplifting oratorical coda pinned to the end of every well-crafted speech. Rosenman had set aside the peroration for last, and during the frenetic first days of the convention left it undone.

Seeking a respite from the long, numbing sequence of nominating and seconding speeches coming over the radio, Roosevelt had tried his own hand at a closing. But constant interruptions by phone from the convention floor ruined his concentration. He read his effort aloud to his gathered aides. "We unanimously said it was terrible, so he sadly tore it up," Rosenman recalled. The next day Rosenman took up the task again as an antidote to his own restlessness. His spirits were weighed down by the thought that

1

all his work would likely be in vain, for the nomination seemed to be drifting further away with every inconclusive ballot.

Rosenman never specified the source of the term *new deal,* but it was certainly in the air. His fellow Brain Truster Ray Moley had used it in a covering note to a package of informational memos he had given Rosenman to pass on to Roosevelt in May. (Moley had written that Herbert Hoover's promise of imminent prosperity "is not the pledge of a new deal; it is the reminder of broken promises.") The term also was part of the title of a series in the *New Republic* by the economic commentator Stuart Chase, which began appearing on June 29, the eve of the convention, and continued through July. In the four installments of "A New Deal for America," Chase argued that the Great Depression had been caused by overinvestment in industrial plants and production during the 1920s. He surveyed possible remedies, rejecting violent revolution or the dictatorship of big business in favor of a "third road": central regulation leading to a "progressive revision of the economic structure, avoiding an utter break with the past."

In his memoirs Rosenman credited neither source, but both usages were certainly known to him and perhaps recorded in his subliminal memory. After all, several other phrases from Moley's cover letter made it into the acceptance speech almost verbatim. And Chase was a sort of orbiting satellite in the Roosevelt universe, if not a member of the inmost circle of advisors; it was he who had discovered and recruited for Roosevelt's economic team a progressive-minded Utah banker named Marriner Eccles, whom Roosevelt would later appoint governor of the Federal Reserve. Chase's view of overinvestment as a cause of the Depression had become Roosevelt campaign orthodoxy, as had his recommendation for overhauling rather than demolishing the nation's existing financial structure.

Roosevelt, who was handed the scrap of paper with Rosenman's drafted peroration before leaving Albany for Chicago, told him it seemed "all right" without remarking on the phrase "new deal." When he delivered the speech from the convention floor on July 2, Roosevelt gave the words a modest cadential stress, but no more than he did to several other phrases in the text that might have served just as well as a clarion call—a "new chance," for example, or a "new order" or a "new time."

The elevation of this casual phrase into a unifying label for Franklin Roosevelt's peacetime domestic policy was an accident of history. The next day's newspapers treated the peroration with indifference. The *New York Times* did not quote the "new deal" phrase at all in the front-page convention report by its distinguished Washington editor, Arthur Krock; the *Los Angeles Times* slightly misquoted its context. But the *New York World-Telegram* published a drawing by its editorial cartoonist, Rollin Kirby, depicting a farmer staring up at a plane passing overhead with the words "New Deal" emblazoned on its wings. This was "the first indication that a popular phrase had been coined," Rosenman reflected. "Within a short time it became a commonplace—the watchword of a fighting political faith."

On the afternoon before Inauguration Day, Rexford Guy Tugwell was weighed down with a sense of foreboding.

Earlier in the day, Tugwell had boarded the train carrying President-elect Franklin Roosevelt along with several other original members of the Brain Trust, the team of old friends and newly recruited academics who had schooled the youthful governor of New York in the intricacies of national policy and joined him on the long road to nomination and electoral victory in 1932. The traveling party had assembled at the President-elect's town house on Sixty-Fifth Street in Manhattan, then crossed the Hudson River and headed for the Baltimore & Ohio Railroad terminal in Jersey City in a parade of limousines.

This was the first of many displays of ostentation during the inauguration weekend that Tugwell would find jarring, given the economic misery all about him. For the moment he chose to submit to routine—"amenities had to be observed," he told himself. After all, this was the President-elect's choice: Roosevelt personally had ended the debate in his circle over whether to hold an inaugural gala complete with parades and balls, vetoing the idea of toning down the festivities lest the change in plans add to the nation's anxiety.

After the train left the station, Roosevelt called the members of his party one by one back to his car, the last one on the special. When Tugwell's turn came, the professor from Columbia expected to be drawn into a discussion of the agriculture crisis, which was his particular expertise and the subject of his portfolio in his new job as an undersecretary of agriculture. Instead he found Roosevelt in a contemplative mood. As the industrial countryside of the Delaware River Valley flashed past, Roosevelt remarked to Tugwell on the profusion of smokeless factory chimneys, yet another sign of economic paralysis.

Then Roosevelt's mood shifted abruptly, and they were on to a discussion of student life at the University of Pennsylvania, where Tugwell had studied twenty years before. At length Tugwell was dismissed to make his way forward to his own compartment, marveling not for the first time at his boss's ability to maintain such composure in the face of the horrific responsibilities he would be assuming in less than twenty-four hours.

Over the many months they had worked together Tugwell had become familiar with Roosevelt's even temper, his supreme self-confidence. Not so Henry A. Wallace, the ascetic, mystical Iowa farmer who would be Tugwell's immediate superior as secretary of agriculture, who came wandering back from his own audience with Roosevelt in a lather. Every compartment on the train, he fumed, seemed to be consumed with frivolous revelry: "It's incredible. The country is in ruins and we seem to be on a kind of Sunday picnic."

Tugwell tried to explain to the outraged Wallace that Roosevelt's apparent cheer stemmed from his knowledge that everything that could be done in the next few weeks was already in process—emergency proclamations had been drafted, bills readied for introduction at a special session of Congress, speeches penciled out.

Yet he could not help but share some of Wallace's misgivings. In the four months since the election, the country's condition had steadily deteriorated—then, in the last two weeks, it had taken a sickening plunge down, as though pitched over the rim of a waterfall. One by one, governors had ordered their states' crippled banks closed. On the very eve of the inauguration, the last lights winked out in Illinois and New York. "The economy was seized with an incurable illness much as an individual is," Tugwell would recall of those dark days. "And the economic doctors had no more helpful advice than medical doctors have when faced with approaching death."

The crisis had exposed the vacuity of Republican economic orthodoxy. But Tugwell wondered whether it might not also expose the limitations of the Wilsonian progressivism motivating Franklin Roosevelt and many members of his inner circle—that marriage of antimonopoly regulation and laissez-faire economic policy that owed so much to Wilson's intellectual guide, Louis D. Brandeis, and the latter's aversion to "bigness" in business and government alike. "The old stuff seemed inadequate," Tugwell wrote. "Desperate illness calls for something more." During the campaign he had preached that the federal government would have to assume an unprecedented role in delivering relief to the destitute and stern discipline to the business community, which had played a central role in the disaster and resisted taking responsibility. The New Deal would live up to his expectations in the first respect, but not the second.

The revelers aboard the inaugural train were not immune from feeling the paralyzing effect of the Depression. Many of them, prevented from withdrawing cash from their shuttered banks before embarking, would be unable to pay their hotel bills in Washington. And they were the privileged, with paying jobs in the new administration. What of the others, millions of others, with no pocket money and no prospects, food and shelter receding out of reach? These were the millions waiting for Franklin Roosevelt's train to arrive.

The presidential election campaign of 1932 had resembled a sporting contest between adversaries playing toward a preordained conclusion. In June the Democrats had gone into their national convention in Chicago confident that their nominee would be presumptively the next president. After prevailing in the ferocious battle for the nomination, Roosevelt promptly electrified the party with his superb sense of drama, breaking tradition by flying to Chicago to deliver an acceptance speech to the convention in person. (By cobwebbed custom, a party's nominee would be offered the honor by a delegation of party elders, weeks after the fact.)

Hoover had been renominated by a dispirited party facing eclipse. A "Dump Hoover" movement launched by Harold L. Ickes, an insurgent progressive Republican from Chicago, failed for lack of a candidate willing to take up the colors. Shortly after the Republican convention, Hoover announced that he would consider it beneath the dignity of his office to campaign actively for reelection.

Circumstances conspired to change his mind. First and foremost were Roosevelt's remorseless attacks on Hoover's record. These started with the Chicago acceptance speech, in which FDR evoked the figure of the forgotten man, "forgotten in the political philosophy of the last years." (This personage had first appeared in a radio speech by FDR in April, as "the forgotten man at the bottom of the economic pyramid.") The attacks would continue up to the eve of election, when Roosevelt castigated the fiscal administration of the Hoover White House as "a veritable cancer in the body politic and economic."

Then there was Hoover's political maladroitness—or as he preferred to view it, his ill luck. The leading example was the attack he ordered on July 28 on the bedraggled remnants of the Bonus Army, encamped in the dismal

Anacostia Flats of Washington, D.C. The bonus marchers had come east to appeal for early payment of the stipend Congress had voted for veterans of the Great War, which stipend was not scheduled for redemption until 1945. Instead of a hearing they got a rout by cavalry forces under General Douglas MacArthur (whose staff aide, Major Dwight D. Eisenhower, looked on in dismay). News of the army's gassing and trampling of civilians—the slain including an infant born during the march—dominated the front pages. In Albany, Governor Roosevelt monitored radio reports of the carnage with his friend and advisor Felix Frankfurter. "Well, Felix," he said, "this elects me."

A third factor forcing Hoover to the hustings was his conviction that Roosevelt was not merely an adversary from across the political divide, but a dangerous radical seducing voters with his appeals to "class antagonisms." Hoover's view of the campaign as a cataclysmic battle with the nation's fate hanging in the balance led him to muse openly but vaguely about using his powers of state to stop Roosevelt and save the republic. Such talk led his aides to wonder whether the pressures of the campaign had unhinged the President. Secretary of State Henry L. Stimson wrote in his diary: "He has wrapped himself in the belief that the state of the country really depended on his reelection."

Hoover's disdain for Roosevelt may have been encouraged by widespread doubts about FDR's character and depth. Among progressive opinion makers Roosevelt was viewed as a wealthy dilettante playacting at liberal politics. "He makes excellent speeches about 'the forgotten man,'" wrote Bruce Bliven, managing editor of the *New Republic*, "but he is no spokesman for that man by any blood brotherhood. . . . [T]o me he seems rather the good fellow who talks in terms of restitution to the poor, but would not do anything which would seriously hurt the rich."

No one expressed these misgivings more acidly than Walter Lippmann, America's leading public intellectual. "Mr. Roosevelt is a highly impressionable person, without a firm grasp of public affairs and without very strong convictions," Lippmann wrote in a historic misreading of the Rooseveltian character in January 1932. "Franklin D. Roosevelt is no crusader. He is no tribune of the people. He is no enemy of entrenched privilege. He is a pleasant man who, without any important qualifications for the office, would very much like to be President."

But then Lippmann found scarcely more to impress him about Hoover, whom he judged singularly inept at the "hurlyburly" of politics. The presidency was the first public office Hoover ever sought, and he won it easily. His campaign had been built, Lippmann observed, around his contrived image as "the master organizer, the irresistible engineer, the supreme economist." Confronted by the reality of a disobedient Congress and Depression rather than prosperity, he revealed himself to be a political leader utterly without political skills, "paralyzed by his own inexperience in the very special business of democracy."

Once drawn into campaigning for reelection, Hoover acted within strict limits. After delivering his acceptance speech on August 11 at a small garden party at the White House—not, like Roosevelt, to a cheering convention audience of thousands—he made only eight more formal speeches, the first not until October 4. Roosevelt, by contrast, could deliver that many formal speeches in a single weeklong campaign swing, and almost never let a whistle-stop go by without addressing the crowd.

Though the New Deal would mark a major watershed in the federal government's approach to economic and social issues, a change of such magnitude was only intermittently telegraphed by the Roosevelt campaign. More often, the candidate's policy stance seemed flexible and only vaguely progressive. This was partially the result of what Raymond Moley, a Columbia professor who served as chief speechwriter during the campaign, called his "abundant hospitality to novel ideas." Moley did not consider this a positive trait. "There is a lot of autointoxication of the intelligence that we shall have to watch," he wrote his sister early in the campaign. "A typical approach to a big problem is 'so and so was telling me yesterday.' . . . So far as I know he makes no effort to check up on anything that I or anyone else has told him."

Some of the equivocation in Roosevelt's campaigning reflected his understanding that politics was often less about substance than presentation, and that audiences always were less bothered by paradox and contradiction than they were impressed by self-confidence. This was brought home to Moley when he presented Roosevelt with two drafts of a speech articulating diametrically opposed approaches to tariff policy. "Roosevelt read the two through with seeming care," Moley recalled. "Then he left me speechless by announcing that I had better 'weave the two together.'"

And some reflected Roosevelt's natural Dutch conservatism. "A practical streak in him caused him to lean upon orthodoxy when grappling with the immediate problems before him," Moley related. "He had been an economical governor of New York. Measurably, he believed in free enterprise." For economic advice he relied on a small circle of conservative Democrats with business backgrounds or distinctly probusiness leanings, including Texas banker Jesse H. Jones, Pennsylvania industrialist Will Woodin, and a young Arizona congressman named Lewis Douglas. All three would play important roles in the new administration.

It is important to understand the delicate political calculus involved in laying out a novel economic program. As the economist John Kenneth Galbraith would later observe, the economic orthodoxy of the era was "all on Mr. Hoover's side. . . . The cranks, crackpots, eccentrics, and the vaguely irresponsible talked about cutting loose from gold, having a big bond issue to alleviate unemployment, of the need for some kind of national planning." Such thinking would become central to New Deal economics, but during the campaign Roosevelt trod a careful path between the orthodox and the heterodox. Wisely so, Galbraith concluded: had he cast his lot with the cranks, "his contemporary reputation as a man of economic sense would have suffered." On the other hand, had he accepted uncritically the respectable ideas of "the men of established reputation, his views would not have been different from those of Mr. Hoover."

For an explicit preview of the improvisational character of the New Deal, one had to reach back to May 1932, and FDR's commencement speech at Oglethorpe University in Atlanta, one month before the Democratic convention. "The country needs and, unless I mistake its temper, the country demands bold, persistent experimentation," he said then. "It is common sense to take a method and try it; if it fails, admit it frankly and try another. But above all, try something."

Yet the Oglethorpe address was unique, in that it was drafted without any input from the Brain Trust. Rather, it arose from a dare Roosevelt issued to a clutch of newspapermen who had joined him on a picnic in Warm Springs, FDR's rural Georgia hideaway. The newspapermen, among them Ernest K. Lindley of the *New York Herald Tribune,* were ribbing Roosevelt for his overly cautious campaigning.

"If you boys don't like my speeches, why don't you take a hand at drafting one yourselves?" Roosevelt shot back.

As drafted by Lindley, the result was what Samuel I. Rosenman termed "a kind of watchword for the New Deal program." More directly than any other Roosevelt speech of that period, it outlined the dismal effects of years of plutocratic rule, focused on the inequality of income and opportunity that characterized the Twenties, and called for "social planning." It was a newspaperman's aspirational road map for the future administration of a President Franklin Roosevelt.

Such candid idealism sneaked into only a few subsequent speeches. One was crafted by Adolf Berle, a brilliant liberal economist and charter Brain Truster, for delivery September 23 at the Commonwealth Club of San Francisco. Berle's view that the domination of the U.S. economy by a shrinking cadre of industrial barons had stifled opportunity for the average American was the theme of his magisterial work *The Modern Corporation and Private Property,* coauthored with Gardiner C. Means and published early in 1932. "We are now providing a drab living for our own people," read the words he set down for Roosevelt. "Put plainly, we are steering a steady course toward economic oligarchy, if we are not there already." The speech stopped short of proposing outright government control over the corporate sector. But it did call for a "re-appraisal of values" guided by "enlightened administration," the aim being to ensure that the "princes of property" work hand in hand with government leadership to advance the public interest. It was very inspiring, yet still rather vague.

In stark contrast was a speech on government economy FDR delivered a few weeks later in Pittsburgh. This one was drafted by a new member of the campaign team, Hugh S. Johnson, a businessman and former West Pointer whose flair for political invective was a byword. It pulsed with the joy of attack on the profligacy of Hoover's four years of deficit spending: "The air is now surcharged with Republican death-bed repentance on the subject of economy, but it is too late." Johnson's brio, however, led Roosevelt to blunder into an unwisely specific pledge to "reduce the cost of current Federal Government operations by 25 percent." Tugwell, regretting having joined in the campaign team's effusive praise of Johnson's draft, later termed it "a piece of unforgivable folly."

Indeed, whenever President Franklin Roosevelt proposed federal budgets reliant on deficit spending—as he would do every year—Republicans would punish him by quoting from the Pittsburgh speech. In 1936, as he prepared to return to Pittsburgh to speak for the first time in four years, he asked Sam Rosenman to work up "a good and convincing explanation for it." Rosenman reread the original and reported back that he could think of only one suitable answer to FDR's critics: "The only thing you can say about that 1932 speech is to deny categorically that you ever made it."

But that was no help to voters in 1932, who could only wonder uneasily what course Roosevelt would pursue in office. It is significant that so penetrating an observer as Marriner Eccles, the Utah banker who would become Roosevelt's Federal Reserve Board chairman, was perplexed by the spectacle of the conservative Hoover basing his campaign on the unprecedented dynamism of his public works spending and banking relief while the ostensibly progressive Roosevelt castigated him for his spendthrift ways. Eccles reflected: "The campaign speeches often read like a giant misprint, in which Roosevelt and Hoover speak each other's lines."

The Kansas newspaperman William Allen White distilled the mixture of doubt and hope that greeted Roosevelt's landslide victory on November 8, 1932, in a letter to Theodore Roosevelt, Jr., the former president's eldest son, early in the new year. "Your distant relative is an X in the equation," White wrote. "He may develop his stubbornness into courage, his amiability into wisdom, his sense of superiority into statesmanship. Responsibility is a winepress that brings forth strange juices out of men."

Politically maladroit as a fully empowered president, Herbert Hoover proved no more adept as a lame duck. Part of the problem was the length of the lame-duck period. The interregnum between administrations would be shortened from four months to about ten weeks by the newly ratified Twentieth Amendment. But the change would not become effective until the 1936 election. In the meantime, Lippmann observed, "no one has power and no one has responsibility. The President is virtually without influence. The President-elect is without authority. So power is divided among the leaders of factions, no one of whom is strong enough to govern, though almost every one of them is strong enough to stop every one else from governing."

Compounding the difficulty, Hoover was ungracious in defeat. He believed he had broken the back of the Depression by June 1932, and that the economic recovery would have continued thereafter had business leaders and the public not become spooked by the prospect of a Roosevelt presidency. The recovery had been stymied, Hoover maintained, by a vicious circle in which fears of Roosevelt's policy intentions bred stagnation, which perversely got blamed on his own administration and caused his defeat at the polls. "The rest of the world turned to recovery in July, 1932, and only the United States marched in the opposite direction with the election of 1932," he wrote later. "With the ominous election returns from Maine on September 14th [Maine traditionally held an early election to beat the onset of winter], the country began to realize that Roosevelt would win. . . . The prices of commodities and securities immediately began to decline, and unemployment increased."

More likely, the July 1932 upturn was merely another in a series of false recoveries that had bedeviled economic prognosticators for more than a year. Although fewer banks failed in the second half of the year (635) than in the first (818), the financial sector was far from stable. Jesse Jones, who as head of the Reconstruction Finance Corporation pumped more than $400 million into banks across the country in that half year, likened the process to stamping out brush fires. "We were far from being out of the woods," he recalled. "Like a fire department we were on all around the clock."

Stock prices ticked up in August from another sickening plunge earlier in the summer, but by the end of the year they were again bumping along the bottom, averaging less than half their 1926 values—in some industrial sectors, such as steel and textiles, only about 25 percent. Even if one wished to take the optimistic view that the economy had stabilized, there could be no doubt about its fragility.

Hoover believed that the nation's only salvation lay in his ability to maneuver Roosevelt away from the "radical and collectivist" tenets of the New Deal and back toward his own traditionalist policies. This effort started only five days after the election. While still en route back to Washington from his California home, Hoover sent the President-elect an urgent telegram. "Our government is now confronted with a world problem of major importance to this nation," the wire stated tendentiously. The issue was a request by the British and French to postpone $125 million in war debt payments due December 15. Hoover's telegram proposed a meeting with Roosevelt to draft a joint response.

Roosevelt's camp treated the overture warily. Given that the $10 billion in loans America had made to the Allied powers had been an irritant in international relations for more than a decade, Hoover's urgency seemed contrived. His proposal for joint action threatened to commit the incoming administration to the policies of the old and to entangle foreign affairs and domestic politics in a way that could only complicate the New Deal's recovery plans.

Hoover's wire caught Roosevelt at an inconvenient moment, bedridden with the flu and looking ahead to a rest in Warm Springs. Cautiously the President-elect agreed to drop in at the White House on his way south. But he specified that a solution to the Europeans' request "rests upon those now vested with executive and legislative authority," in other words, Hoover. Hoover's reaction was a sour one. "I did not like the ring of this disavowal of any responsibility," he recollected.

The meeting that followed on November 22 did little to reduce each side's disdain for the other. Hoover, who was waiting in the Red Room of the White House with Treasury Secretary Ogden Mills, expected the President-elect to be accompanied by a Democratic second of suitable dignity and experience, such as the venerable Senator Carter Glass of Virginia. Instead Roosevelt showed up with Ray Moley, who was struck by the "bristling formality" of the occasion and Hoover's habit of fixing his gaze upon the United States seal woven into the crimson rug, rather than on his successor.

Yet Moley was also spellbound by Hoover's mastery of the complex debt issue. Hoover held the floor for nearly an hour, laying out the history entwining the financial interests of Britain, France, Germany, and the United States in laborious detail without consulting a single scrap of notepaper. "On this subject," Moley conceded, "we were in the presence of the best-informed man in the world." Roosevelt remained silent except to interject an occasional question from note cards prepared in advance.

The meeting adjourned in mutual disagreement, with all possibility of a joint communiqué dashed. Hoover conceived a lower regard for his successor than ever. As Secretary of State Stimson recorded in his diary, Hoover complained that he and Mills "had spent most of their time in educating a very ignorant, and as he expressed it, a well-meaning young man." Despite Hoover's attempt to communicate a sense of emergency to FDR, the war debt issue would remain unresolved until 1940, when it became wrapped up in the lend-lease arrangements associated with a new European war.

Hoover's second effort to inveigle Roosevelt into endorsing his own policies also began inopportunely. On February 18, Roosevelt was enjoying the "Inner Circle" banquet of New York's City Hall newspapermen. This was an annual affair at which the press corps gently tweaked by song and skit New York's mayor and governor, who were invariably in attendance. Shortly before midnight a Secret Service agent placed a buff-colored envelope in the President-elect's hands. Roosevelt inconspicuously scanned its contents, and without changing expression passed it under the table to Moley. The aide was surprised to find himself holding a handwritten letter from Hoover—evidently scribbled hastily, for it was addressed to "President Elect Roosvelt."

It opened, "My Dear Mr. President-Elect: A most critical situation has arisen in the country of which I feel it is my duty to advise you confidentially." What followed was an oddly circuitous text referencing "the state of the public mind . . . a steadily degenerating confidence in the future which has reached the height of general alarm," but alluding only tangentially to the crisis at hand. As song and raillery went on around him, Moley managed to divine the letter's terrible import, which was that the American banking system was on the brink of collapse. "The breaking point had come," he concluded.

The condition of the banks had never been far from the minds of policy makers since the crash of 1929, but it had ebbed and flowed. The crisis had peaked in 1931, when 2,298 banks failed. But it moderated in January 1932 when Congress, at Hoover's urging, established the Reconstruction Finance Corporation as the clearinghouse for more than $3 billion in government capital assistance.

To use Jones's imagery, the RFC was constantly putting out fires. A major flare-up in June 1932, the near failure of the Central Republic Bank of Chicago because of its heavy exposure to the collapsed utility empire of Samuel Insull, had to be doused with an emergency RFC loan of $90 million. The loan was negotiated over the weekend of June 25 as delegates swarmed into Chicago for the Democratic convention, which would shortly nominate Franklin Roosevelt. Jones, himself a delegate, shuttled between the convention hotel and the bank's headquarters, each time making his way through throngs of "frantic, rumor-spreading depositors . . . milling about every bank entrance in La Salle, Clark, and Dearborn Streets."

The loan saved the bank, but at the price of political controversy, for the institution's chairman was Charles Dawes, a former Republican vice president and, until ten days earlier, the RFC chairman. By introducing the odor of favoritism into the agency's work, the Dawes rescue prompted Democrats in Congress to demand that the recipients of all RFC loans be made public. Bankers and policy makers considered this a lethal misjudgment, for it would undermine public confidence even in banks that had been saved and would discourage weakened banks from seeking timely help in the future.

But the fundamental causes of the renewed runs on banks across the country in the winter of 1933 were continued high unemployment and foreclosures on homeowners and farmers. Nowhere was the crisis as acute as in Detroit, the hub of industrial America. Its residential neighborhoods and commercial streets had been abandoned by tens of thousands of furloughed autoworkers, leaving behind derelict homes and patronless shops. Two giant holding companies controlled almost all Detroit's banks—the Union Guardian Group, in which the Ford family was a major investor, and the Detroit Bankers Company. Both were relentlessly hammered by runs draining as much as $3 million a week from their vaults. In mid-January the board of the Union Guardian, which had received $15 million from the RFC in July, bluntly informed federal bank examiners that without another loan of $50 million the group would collapse.

An examination of its books revealed an institution in worse trouble than anyone suspected. Exactly how much worse was a matter of great confusion in Washington and Detroit, because there was no agreement on the value of the stock certificates and other assets owned by the group. Should they be steeply marked down to panic levels, as the Federal Reserve advocated? Or priced liberally on the expectation "that normal times would come again," as the Treasury Department maintained? The answer was elusive, but it soon became clear that even under the most generous evaluation, the RFC could not justify contributing more than $37 million.

Hoover assigned Treasury Undersecretary Arthur Ballantine and Commerce Secretary Roy D. Chapin to appeal to Henry Ford to rescue his family's banking group. Their proposal was for Ford to subordinate his company's $7.5 million in deposits at Guardian, in effect converting the deposits into an open-ended loan to the group. But when they entered Ford's office on February 13—the Monday of a long Lincoln's Birthday holiday—the mogul crisply rejected the plan. As Henry's son Edsel later informed Congress, his father was "quite incensed" at the idea that, after he had contributed more than $10 million over the previous three years to prop up the banks, he should be asked now to do more. (In truth, over the years the Fords and other investors had been paid millions of dollars in dividends by the holding company even while the subsidiary banks were losing money.) Ford bewildered Ballantine and Chapin with a long harangue to the effect that the request to help the bank was a plot against him, cooked up by unidentified enemies.

Informed that his refusal to help would mean the failure of Guardian Trust and rattle all the other major banks in Michigan, Ford replied that, if so, on the very next morning he would withdraw the $25 million his company had on deposit at the First National Bank of Detroit. A startled

Ballantine told him that would mean the closing of every bank in the state of Michigan. The resources of millions of Michigan families hung in the balance.

"All right then, let us have it that way," Ford replied. A thoroughgoing disaster would have a cleansing effect, putting people back to work a little sooner. "Let the crash come. Everything will go down the chute. But I feel young. I can build up again."

Ford's rebuff provoked a final round of frenetic activity in Washington. In the hope of turning over a trump card, Hoover induced Senator James Couzens of Michigan to telephone Ford.

The overture was doomed to fail. Couzens had been a partner in the founding of Ford Motor Company in 1903, and had launched many of the company's most successful operational initiatives. Chief among these was the five-dollar daily wage for assembly line workers, which he implemented over Ford's vehement objections, and which more than paid for itself by virtually eliminating labor turnover and creating a new class of potential consumers. But the partners' relationship, never a warm one, was shattered over Ford's opposition to America's entry into the Great War. Couzens moved into politics. In 1919 he sold Henry Ford his stake in the company, for which he had paid $2,500, for $28 million.

Couzens was not a supporter of an RFC rescue of the Guardian Group—indeed, he had threatened to "denounce from the housetops" any effort to commit the RFC to a loan on insufficient collateral. Ford, as it happened, agreed with Couzens on this one issue. After being told of his former partner's opposition to a government bailout of any banks but those certifiably strong and sound, he remarked, "For once in his life, Jim Couzens is right."

Couzens did believe, however, that Ford had a duty to save Guardian. He agreed to make one last attempt to make Ford see reason. At 8 P.M. Monday, he called his old partner from Jones's office at the RFC. "Those two old roosters were scrupulously polite to each other but frigid," recalled Jones, who was listening on an extension. Yet Couzens, perhaps seized by a vision of his home state teetering on the brink of ruin, suddenly made a strikingly public-spirited overture, offering personally to put up half the collateral needed to back the RFC loan—$6.9 million in cash—if Ford would put up the other half. Ford turned him down.

From there things careened swiftly into the abyss. At 1 A.M., Michigan Governor William Comstock declared an eight-day bank holiday, shuttering 550 state and national banks, freezing $1.5 billion in deposits to businesses and families—including more than $42 million that Henry Ford had been prepared to withdraw from the First National and his own Guardian National Bank the moment those institutions opened their doors Tuesday morning. The moratorium merely deferred a solution to the crisis. If the banks were not saved, Chapin warned Couzens, "we shall have a riotous Detroit and prostrate Michigan facing us."

Five days later, Hoover delivered his handwritten letter to Franklin Roosevelt, warning that the nationwide banking system was on the brink.

Had Hoover intended his approach to be spurned, he could not have done a better job of it. His letter dripped with condescension—and not by inadvertence: Hoover would later acknowledge that he had made it "unduly long" because he "feared from the lack of understanding of such questions which [Roosevelt] had displayed in our earlier interviews . . . that he did not fully grasp the situation."

But it was Hoover who did not fully grasp the situation, and had not for more than a year. Convinced that the banks would eventually right themselves, he had opposed the enactment of strong regulatory and remedial measures throughout 1932. Although he portrayed himself during the campaign and in his memoirs as a strong advocate of banking reform, the evidence is otherwise: a reform bill sponsored by Senator Carter Glass of Virginia foundered in Congress on the "ill-concealed hostility of the White House," recounted one of Glass's advisors, the Columbia University banking expert H. Parker Willis.

Hoover's letter to Roosevelt blamed the conflagration in the banking sector, indeed the continued economic slump in general, on derelictions by the Democratic Congress and on the President-elect's failure to steady the nation's nerves. His proposed remedy was Hooverite to the core: Roosevelt should make a series of reassuring statements. Specifically he should disavow any intention to pursue an inflationary policy (meaning that he should commit to keeping the United States on the gold standard), promise to balance the budget "even if further taxation is necessary," and press congressional leaders to end the publicizing of RFC loans. "Otherwise," Hoover warned, "the fire will spread."

As Hoover informed Republican Senator David A. Reed of Pennsylvania a few days after writing Roosevelt: "I realize that if these declarations be made by the President-elect, he will have ratified the whole major program of the Republican Administration; that is, it means abandonment of 90% of the so-called new deal. But unless this is done, they run a grave danger of precipitating a complete financial debacle. . . . [T]hey have had ample warning—unless, of course, such a debacle is part of the 'new deal.'"

Only someone who thought Roosevelt a gullible pushover could have expected him to take these recommendations seriously. Some of them involved policies that Hoover had failed to implement even in the full bloom of his own presidential authority; far from upholding the principle of a balanced budget, for example, Hoover in his last two full years in office had presided over a combined deficit exceeding $3 billion.

As for his plea that Roosevelt disavow inflation, the President-elect's refusal to do so already had cost him his first choice for Treasury secretary, Carter Glass, who had insisted on an anti-inflationary Treasury policy as a condition to accepting the post. Some Roosevelt advisors believed that Hoover's anti-inflation stance, especially his staunch defense of the gold standard, had exacerbated the Depression in the United States, as it placed the country at a disadvantage compared to Great Britain and other European states that abandoned gold earlier. Roosevelt was disinclined to commit himself to the same error. He failed to respond to Hoover's letter for twelve days. Whether the reason was pique, strategic calculation, or oversight has never been established. But it surely signaled that the new president could not be intimidated by the old.

Meanwhile, the Detroit virus spread across the country. Cleveland's banks were tottering within days; in Ohio, the only thriving trade seemed to be the one in passbooks for accounts at banks that had restricted withdrawals, put up for sale by account holders desperate for ready cash: one could buy a passbook for an account at, say, Home Savings & Loan of Youngstown for 50 cents on the dollar and use it to pay off a loan at the same bank at full value—thus achieving a 50 percent discount. Local newspapers listed the going rates for each bank's accounts next to their stock market quotes.

Gold and currency were draining out of bank vaults by hundreds of millions of dollars a week. At the end of February, money in circulation—a measure of hoarding—reached a record $6.03 billion, a figure that literally ran off the Federal Reserve chart, which stopped at $6 billion. The record was destined to be shattered in each of the next three weeks.

The American people were in the throes of agony. The steel and textile industries were at a virtual standstill. Construction contracts were disappearing. The output of coal plummeted, despite the grip of winter. The nation's most august business leaders trooped before a Senate investigating committee to acknowledge that they had no immediate answer to the crisis or, worse, to mouth tattered old nostrums. "Balance budgets," advised the investment sage Bernard Baruch. "Sacrifice for frugality and revenue. Cut governmental spending—cut it as rations are cut in a siege. Tax—tax everybody for everything. But take hungry men off the world's pavements and let people smile again."

Civil unrest stirred in the farm belt. Bankers appeared at farm foreclosure sales at their peril: In Bowling Green, Ohio, the auction of implements owned by a bankrupt farmer ended when the crowd marched a finance company representative out of sight to certain lynching. (He was rescued by the sheriff.) At a foreclosure auction in Perry, Iowa, 1,500 neighbors showed up in such intimidating humor that the holder of the $2,500 note collected only $45.05. John Andrew Simpson, president of the National Farmers Union, informed the Senate Committee on Agriculture, "The biggest and finest crop of revolutions you ever saw is sprouting all over this country right now."

Signs of an era staggering to its anxious end were everywhere. Six days before the inauguration the Spanish ambassador threw a farewell dinner for Treasury Secretary Mills—"a dinner of the Old World as I fear we will never see it again," recollected an American diplomat. "The flowers . . . came from the South. The sole was sent down from New York and the wines were all of rare vintages. . . . The whole table was ablaze with jewels." Yet the guest of honor was unable to enjoy the festivities; scarcely would Mills take his seat before he would be called to the telephone. Scarcely would a forkful of fish reach his mouth before he would be called out again. Withdrawals of gold from the banks, he was being told, were accelerating.

Members of the old order were arranging, with a weary air, to vacate their seats to make room for the new. Herbert Feis, an economic advisor to the State Department, received from a colleague a farewell message redolent of exhaustion. "There is a general sense of demoralization and decay in the old crew," it read. "I am restless to have it over and give my seat to a stranger."

Hoover continued to wait for Roosevelt's reply to his letter, complaining of his impotence in the face of his successor's silence. Yet Roosevelt had communicated his position repeatedly to Hoover and the press: the sitting president must act on his own authority right up to March 4, Inauguration Day. Nevertheless, behind-the-scenes contact between the incoming and outgoing administrations was proceeding, even intensifying. On February 21, Roosevelt had named industrialist William H. Woodin as his Treasury secretary. Woodin had promptly gotten in touch with Mills and George Harrison, governor of the Federal Reserve Bank of New York. They brought him up to speed on the quickening crisis. Assisted by Moley, Woodin plunged into work in cooperation with the men of the old regime to find a way out of the emergency.

On March 1, Roosevelt finally delivered a response to Hoover's letter of twelve days before. Hoover could not have been heartened by its casual, even fatalistic, tone. Accompanied by a cover letter blaming its delay on a secretary's error (an explanation Hoover considered transparently insincere), the message rejected Hoover's proposal to extinguish the spreading fire with talk. The situation, Roosevelt wrote, "is so very deep-seated that the fire is bound to spread in spite of anything that is done by way of mere statements."

During the last three days of the Hoover era the atmosphere of calamity rose sharply. A new gold rush was taking place. On March 3 alone, the Federal Reserve Bank of New York lost $200 million in gold and $150 million in currency through wire transfers and exports. The very ground seemed to shake from the impact of banks crumbling to their foundations. Thirty-two states had closed at least some of their banks. The governors of the last two large holdout states, Illinois and New York, were poised to do the same. The nation seemed to be approaching a grand climacteric that would culminate on Inauguration Day either with release, or annihilation.

Hoover made one more attempt to puncture Roosevelt's serene detachment. The occasion was a ceremonial Friday afternoon tea at the White House for the Roosevelts. Before their arrival, Hoover summoned Mills and Eugene Meyer, the governor of the Federal Reserve, and stowed them quietly in an anteroom, ready to spring them on the President-elect once the social formalities were dispensed with. He was sabotaged by Ike Hoover, the White House chief usher, who revealed the ploy to Roosevelt in a whisper. Roosevelt immediately sent for Moley, who was at his hotel trying to steal a catnap from his twin chores of drafting the inauguration address and managing the bank crisis with Woodin.

Moley arrived in time to join a last desultory discussion of emergency options. Meyer pressed for a nationwide closing of the banks; Hoover sought Roosevelt's assurance that he would endorse such a proclamation; Roosevelt again insisted that Hoover had sufficient authority to take action on his own. The meeting ended with a petty incivility by Hoover: understanding that protocol dictated that Hoover return the social call, Roosevelt remarked, "I realize, Mr. President, that you are extremely busy so I will understand completely if you do not return the call." Hoover fixed him in the eye for the first time that afternoon and replied, "Mr. Roosevelt, when you are in Washington as long as I have been, you will learn that the President of the United States calls on nobody."

As the clock ticked toward Inauguration Day, discussions continued in both camps. Shortly before midnight Meyer called Hoover to plead that he declare a bank holiday starting the next morning, when he feared the bank runs would be overwhelming. Hoover petulantly refused, renewing his complaint about Roosevelt's resistance.

"You are the only one with the power to act," Meyer told him. "We are fiddling while Rome burns."

"I can keep on fiddling," Hoover replied. "I have been fiddled at enough and I can do some fiddling myself."

At the Mayflower Hotel, the new administration's temporary headquarters, Roosevelt remained in conference with Moley, Woodin, Glass, Jesse Jones, and other Democratic leaders. Moley left Roosevelt's suite after 1 A.M., heading for his own room. When he stepped off the elevator he ran into Woodin.

"I couldn't even get to the stage of undressing," Woodin told him with an embarrassed grin. "This thing is bad. Will you come over to the Treasury with me? We'll see if we can give those fellows a hand."

In Mills's office they found the secretary in conference with Ballantine, Meyer, and other officials, all red-eyed and haggard. While Roosevelt and Hoover slept that night, separated by a gulf of politics and personal antipathy, their underlings labored as a team. "Everyone forgot political differences," Moley recalled. "Our concern was to save the banking system." The immediate task was to complete the process of shutting down the banking system by getting the last few governors to close their state banks. This was achieved after an exhausted Moley had fallen asleep. At 3 A.M. he was jostled awake by Woodin. Silence had fallen upon the room. Scattered about on chairs and sofas were the nation's preeminent banking and financial regulators, all nearly catatonic with exhaustion.

"It's all right now," Woodin said. "Everything is closed. Let's go."

Inauguration Day would dawn cold and damp. In ten hours, Franklin Roosevelt would take the oath of office, assuming full presidential authority at last over the greatest nation on earth, at that moment a stupefied giant standing face-to-face with insolvency.

PART ONE

THE HUNDRED DAYS

1

"ACTION NOW"

F RANKLIN ROOSEVELT BEGAN Inauguration Day at a 10 A.M. religious service with his family, his cabinet appointees, secretaries, aides, and a few close friends. The location was St. John's Episcopal Church, across Lafayette Park from the White House, chosen because it had no steps to complicate the wheelchair-bound President-elect's entry from the street. Inside, the Reverend Endicott Peabody, rector of Groton, FDR's old school, read from the Protestant Book of Common Prayer and beseeched the Almighty to favor and bless "Thy servant, Franklin, chosen to be President of the United States."

The official party dispersed as soon as the service ended, Roosevelt to the White House for the start of the ritual procession toward the 1 P.M. oath-taking in front of the U.S. Capitol. The wisest among the other attendees had hired cars for the day and promptly drove off. Frances Perkins, the new secretary of labor, found herself standing forlorn on the sidewalk with her daughter, Susanna, and a couple she recognized as Mr. and Mrs. Henry A. Wallace. They introduced themselves to each other, joined forces to hail a passing cab, and tried to figure out how to reach the Capitol entrance reserved for dignitaries.

The members of the new administration drew what encouragement or counsel they could from the faces of the crowds lining the ceremonial routes and assembling before the Capitol. Tugwell remarked on the public's apparent determination to squeeze just a little enjoyment from the festive inaugural parade, "squads and squadrons of marching clubs, fraternal drill teams, silk-hatted and frock-coated Tammany braves, military detachments and uniformed bands," all in such contrast to "the morning's solemnity." Perhaps FDR's decision to proceed with the celebration despite the hard times was the right move after all.

Perkins, who had finally reached her spot on the platform by elbowing her way through the crowds behind Wallace in shoes soaking wet from tramping across the sodden Capitol lawn, could not help being moved by "the terror-stricken look on the faces of the people," many of whom were hearing for the first time the bleak rumors that the last of the banks had closed that morning. "An enormous crowd had come for the inauguration, but they looked frightened, worried, depressed. It was not the kind of gay Democrats that you saw later on. They were just worried to death."

Roosevelt made his way from the White House to the Capitol seated next to Herbert Hoover in an open car. Along the teeming processional route he tried to make conversation with the grim visage to his right, but could elicit no more than the occasional grunt. As he related the tale later to his secretary Grace Tully, he finally decided that the cheering of the throng warranted a more suitable acknowledgment than Hoover's dour scowl. "So I began to wave my own response with my top hat and I kept waving it until I got to the inauguration stand and was sworn in."

After taking the oath of office from Chief Justice Charles Evans Hughes, Roosevelt prepared to deliver his inaugural speech. Hoover did not wait to hear it; at the completion of the oath-taking, the ex-president ceremoniously shook his successor's hand, left the platform, and, trailed by two or three of his cabinet members, continued walking until he reached his car and settled in, at which point it promptly drove off.

"President Hoover, Mr. Chief Justice, my friends," the new president began, then uttered a phrase he had scribbled at the top of his draft just before coming out from the Capitol building to the inaugural stand: "This is a day of national consecration." The addition was so belated that the phrase did not make it into the official text of the speech.

He continued: "First of all let me assert my firm belief that the only thing we have to fear is fear itself . . . nameless, unreasoning, unjustified terror which paralyzes needed efforts to convert retreat into advance."

Roosevelt's flawless delivery, his pausing for dramatic effect before the words "fear itself," invested the phrase with his own confidence and assurance. His critics would later assert that in doing so, Roosevelt was himself taking Hoover's approach to the Depression, reassuring the people that the worst would be over in due course. Yet that is to ignore the context. Hoover's repeated reassurances served a policy of complacency and limited federal action, even inaction; Roosevelt's words heralded "action, and action now," a pledge of direct government employment of the jobless and the construction of projects to exploit national resources, of "definite efforts" to raise the value of farm products, of the prevention of home and farm foreclosures, of the broadening and coordination of relief.

The rest of the speech was a model of concise presidential oratory, not quite 1,900 words requiring not quite twenty minutes to deliver. The text outlined the principles of the coming administration and some of its legislative goals, albeit shrouding them in inspirational flourishes and, here and there, veiled censuring of the departing leadership.

In the most assertive (and to many listeners unnerving) moment of the speech, the new president vowed, if "the national emergency is still critical," to not shrink from asking Congress "for the one remaining instrument to meet the crisis . . . broad executive power to wage a war against the emergency as great as the power that would be given to me if we were in fact invaded by a foreign foe." Roosevelt's admirers and detractors alike would long debate whether those words were a promise or a threat, and in either case whether or when he might deliver on them.

Those rhetorical bookends, the release from fear at the speech's opening and the promise of unstinting effort in its peroration, often obscure other elements of the inaugural address that proclaimed a new era in American politics and policy.

One was the recognition that the economic crisis was the creation of men—"the unscrupulous money changers"—not an artifact of nature. "The rulers of the exchange of mankind's goods," Roosevelt stated, "have failed through their own stubbornness and their own incompetence, have admitted their failures and abdicated. . . . The money changers have fled their high seats in the temple of our civilization."

This insight underpinned Roosevelt's conception of government power as a force to be utilized aggressively. The new administration would not wait passively for recovery, as had the tribunes of "false leadership, [who] have resorted to exhortations, pleading tearfully for restored conditions." The New Deal would act, not plead.

Among the other concepts introduced in the inaugural address were two that would animate the social elements of the New Deal: shared responsibility and the nobility of work. More than any other details of the speech, these reflected the influence of Adolf Berle, who was the most penetrating critic within the Brain Trust of Hoover's infatuation with "individualism" and resistance to regulation, which Hoover had said would lead to industrial "regimentation."

To Berle, Hoover's outlook merely rationalized exploitation of the many by the few, with the tacit acquiescence of government. "Whatever the economic system does permit," he had written Roosevelt during the campaign, "it is not individualism." Warming to the theme he and Means had developed in *The Modern Corporation and Private Property*, he added:

> When nearly seventy per cent of American industry is concentrated in the hands of six hundred corporations; when more than half of the population of the industrial east live or starve, depending on what this group does . . . the individual man or woman has, in cold statistics, less than no chance at all. The President's stricture on "regimentation" . . . is merely ironic; there is regimentation in work, in savings, and even in unemployment and starvation. . . . What Mr. Hoover means by individualism is letting economic units do about what they please.

Berle proposed substituting a "far truer individualism" in which the government acts as a "regulating and unifying agency," so that "individual men and women could survive, have homes, educate their children, and so forth." These points were transformed in the inaugural address into an affirmation of "social values more noble than mere monetary profit."

"The joy and moral stimulation of work no longer must be forgotten in the mad chase of evanescent profits," Roosevelt continued. "These dark days will be worth all they cost us if they teach us that our true destiny is not to be ministered unto but to minister to ourselves and our fellow men."

There could be no more direct break with the "individualism" of Herbert Hoover than through these words.

Roosevelt did nod toward traditional conservative values—for example, in his admonition to state and local officials that they must "act forthwith" on the public's demand for drastic reductions in government costs. He repeated his campaign promise to maintain "an adequate but sound currency," words that might have comforted anti-inflationary conservatives, had not Roosevelt always steadfastly "refused to be drawn into any precise definition of what this meant."

A persistent myth is that Roosevelt wrote the inaugural address in a burst of inspiration over a single evening. Blame for this fabrication belongs to the President himself. A note he signed and attached to a longhand draft now residing at the FDR Library in Hyde Park, New York, designates that draft as the "original manuscript . . . as written at Hyde Park on Monday, February 27th, 1933. I started in about 9.00 P.M. and ended at 1.30 A.M."

In truth, by the reckoning of its principal author, Raymond Moley, the speech's gestation dated as far back as September 22, 1932. That was the tail end of a western campaign trip so triumphant that the candidate allowed himself for the first time the luxury of looking ahead to his administration. For three hours late that night, Roosevelt and Moley laid out the blueprint of an inaugural speech to be delivered the following March: a "mixture of warning and assurance," an "impression of firmness and . . . a strong show of executive leadership" to overrule Congress's inclination to bicker and delay.

Moley worked on his draft on and off for the next five months, searching for the right balance of confidence and humility, of explanation and exhortation, of realism and spirituality. He sampled metaphors for the crisis out of which Roosevelt would be anointed to lead the nation—sickness? failure?—and for the scale of the effort required to prevail. Would mere action do, or even dictatorship? The latter term was by no means as unnerving to American ears in this time of ineffectual leadership as it would become a few years hence. How much should the new president enlist the people in his program of renewal and recovery? How much should he ask for their faith?

Over time Moley moved away from the tropes of sickness and failure, so Hooveresque in their pessimism and self-pity, and toward resolution, rebirth, and restoration. Although he had worked with Roosevelt as closely as any aide for more than a year, what continued to elude him well into February was a way to project the new president's vibrant personality from the podium on the Capitol lawn. Then came February 15. Moley had been ordered south to Miami by Louis Howe, Roosevelt's political majordomo, to bring the President-elect the latest updates on cabinet recruitments. So he was crammed into an overstuffed touring car directly behind Roosevelt's open convertible when one Giuseppe Zangara took aim at the President-elect and, thwarted by the rickety chair he was perched on and the swipe of a bystander's arm, instead wounded Mayor Anton Cermak of Chicago and four other persons.

As his car started to speed off, Roosevelt coolly commanded his driver to stop. He ordered the slumping Cermak bundled into the car and then directed the driver to make for the nearest hospital. (Cermak would die of his wounds nineteen days later.) Moley, like the rest of the official party, was astonished at his boss's unshakable self-possession. "There was nothing—not so much as the twitching of a muscle, the mopping of a brow, or even the hint of a false gaiety—to indicate that it wasn't any other evening in any other place," he observed later. "Roosevelt was simply himself—easy, confident, poised, to all appearances unmoved."

The experience instilled new energy into Moley's draftsmanship. There would be no more toying with images of sickness and despair. "Failure," to the extent it would be evoked at all, would be laid on the shoulders of the stubborn and incompetent leaders of the past, now abdicated and gone. The prevailing images in Moley's newly muscular prose were of action, truth, frankness, and courage.

Roosevelt did not see the draft until February 27, when Moley brought it to Hyde Park in his briefcase. After dinner that evening, Roosevelt began the process of turning Moley's draft into his own by copying it out by hand, working on a folding bridge table before a roaring fire. The two men recrafted the text sentence by sentence, sometimes word by word. Moley had omitted a peroration, a closing appeal to the deity; Roosevelt scribbled out the words, "In this dedication of a Nation we humbly ask the blessing of God. May He guide me in the days to come." Finally Moley got to his feet, took his own copy from the table, and tossed it into the fireplace. He told the President-elect, "It's your speech now."

The next day Roosevelt's handwritten draft went to Howe, the ultimate arbiter of momentous occasions. In his own hand, Howe added three or four opening lines, including perhaps the most resounding phrase of Rooseveltian oratory: "Let me assert my firm belief that the only thing we have to fear is fear itself."

The source of this phrase is lost to history. Samuel Rosenman, FDR's close friend and editor of his papers, believed it must have come from a volume of Henry David Thoreau he had spotted in the presidential suite during the final stages of drafting. The book contained the words, "Nothing is so much to be feared as fear." Moley dismissed that theory, recalling instead that the phrase had appeared in a newspaper advertisement earlier in February, although he was unable later to track down the elusive ad.

Whatever the origin of its most famous expression, the sentiment was scarcely novel or exceptionable. Literary bloodhounds have found precursors as recent as a 1931 speech by U.S. Chamber of Commerce chairman Julius Barnes ("In a condition of this kind, the thing to be feared most is fear itself") and as remote as the aphorisms of the seventeenth-century English philosopher and statesman Francis Bacon ("Nothing is terrible but fear itself").

Yet the greater impression the speech made was of determination to effect change, expressed through plain, potent words such as *vigor, firmness, courage,* and *attack.* "People cried," Perkins would recall. "Tears streamed down the faces of strong men in the audience as they listened to it. It was a revival of faith. He said, 'Come on now, do you believe?' They said, 'Yes, we do.' It made them cry to think that they hadn't believed and that they'd been so near to the brink of the terrible sin of despair."

Roosevelt's speech delighted those who had become frustrated with the inertia of Herbert Hoover's White House. Walter Lippmann, who had expressed his doubts about Roosevelt's character so acerbically a year earlier, had since clambered aboard the bandwagon—even moving somewhat ahead of it, by openly urging the new chief executive to assume "dictatorial" authority. ("The word should frighten no one," he assured his readers on the day of the Detroit collapse. "The man . . . has just received a mandate from the voters.") Following the inauguration he praised Roosevelt as "a man who is fresh in mind and bold in spirit, who has instantly captured the confidence of the people, whose power to act in the emergency will not be questioned." He concluded: "The American people have at last had a lucky break." Disaffection would set in soon enough.

For others, doubts were already surfacing. Rex Tugwell, who expected Roosevelt to seize the opportunity presented by the banking collapse to undertake a radical restructuring of the financial sector, heard his hopes get dashed in the inaugural address. "The money changers have fled their high seats in the temple of our civilization," Roosevelt had said. "We may now restore that temple to the ancient truths." Tugwell asked himself, "What 'ancient truths' were there to be restored to the high seats in the business temple?" Hearing Roosevelt refer to the "sacred trust" violated by selfish banking and business leaders, he thought: "Were banking and business sacred trusts? . . . They were rather occupations intended to make profits . . . by any means within overly permissive rules." The crestfallen Brain Truster steeled himself to witness a new round of political accommodation to entrenched power, as though the Depression had changed nothing.

Some in the audience were immune to the new president's soaring words. The political essayist Edmund Wilson listened in a funereal mood. "Everything is gray today," he wrote. "The people seem dreary, apathetic. . . . The prosperity of America has vanished." The speech itself he condemned as warmed-over Woodrow Wilson: "The old unctuousness, the old pulpit vagueness. . . . The old Wilsonian professions of plain-speaking followed by the old abstractions."

His mood was shared by a thirty-two-year-old government lawyer from Pawtucket, Rhode Island, listening in the crowd. Thomas G. Corcoran had been one of Felix Frankfurter's star students at Harvard Law School. He had clerked for Supreme Court Justice Oliver Wendell Holmes, then, after a brief taste of corporate lawyering in New York, joined the Reconstruction Finance Corporation as legal counsel.

The job had given him a front-row seat at the banking crisis, and a decidedly underwhelming impression of the President-elect. Roosevelt's refusal to join Hoover in a banking rescue left him "angry and dismayed," he recorded later. Convinced that Roosevelt had deliberately let the banks sink to gain political advantage upon his own accession, he judged him "a villainous fool . . . the worst sort of political cad." Standing on the National Mall, stamping his feet to keep warm, and predisposed to disdain the new president, Corcoran heard in Roosevelt's ringing delivery only "an empty collection of platitudes . . . vague, unspecific to a fault." He found it easy to abstain from the crowd's cheers.

Corcoran's own education in the complexities of politics and the intricacies of Franklin Roosevelt's political mind—indeed, Corcoran's intellectual seduction by the man he initially thought a fool and a cad—would begin in only a few weeks. For the moment, he felt deeply discouraged and impatient to share his disappointment with others in his circle. A few days after the inauguration, he joined a small party of family and friends at Holmes's Washington house to celebrate the revered justice's ninety-second birthday. He arrived to find the place vibrating with excitement: the new president had just departed after paying his respects to the old man—a canny maneuver to associate himself with the patriarch of Washington's liberal elite.

In Holmes's presence, Corcoran ventured a few careful criticisms of Roosevelt's vacuous inaugural bromides. The justice fixed him with his stern eye and proceeded to measure the new Roosevelt against the old one. "Theodore was no legal scholar, but he could turn a vivid phrase and vigorously command the people's respect," Holmes said, then unburdened himself of what would become a classic assessment. "This new Roosevelt is just like his cousin: A second class intellect but a first class temperament. And what this country seems to need in a president—right now particularly—is exactly that."

A few hours after leaving the justice, Roosevelt presided over an unusual ceremony in the Oval Room of the White House (not yet sanctified as the "Oval Office"). The occasion was a joint swearing-in of the cabinet, the members of which normally would have been sworn the next day at their individual departments. But Roosevelt had judged it best not to defer the formality by even a single day, Harold Ickes would recall, in recognition of "the veritable slough of despond . . . through which the American people were struggling."

While waiting his turn in the stiffly formal atmosphere (in order of departmental preference, he was seventh in line), Ickes took the measure of his new colleagues. He could recall having met only two before: Secretary of Agriculture Wallace, with whom he had served on a Midwest campaign committee for the Roosevelt ticket, and Perkins, whom he had met at the Sixty-Fifth Street town house on the day Roosevelt offered him his post. "I want the Secretary of Labor to meet the new Secretary of the Interior," Roosevelt had said upon leading Ickes into the library of his home, indicating a prim woman in a print dress. As it happened, these two new acquaintances—one an associate of long standing of the President-elect, the other so new to his circle that Roosevelt had not met him before that day and even mispronounced his name (as "Ikes," not "Ick-iss")—would be the only two cabinet members to serve FDR through his entire twelve-year tenure in office.

The process of recruiting the cabinet had begun months earlier. On January 11, Roosevelt had summoned Moley to Albany to give him the first names, and instructed him to secure their assents. For secretary of state, Roosevelt passed over eminent veterans of the Wilson administration such as former secretary of war Newton D. Baker and Owen D. Young, now chairman of General Electric Company, in favor of Tennessee's humble, lisping, but dignified and high-minded Senator Cordell Hull. Many were skeptical of the choice. To Moley, the appointment of a man unlikely to assert himself in the Cabinet Room—especially the contrast he made with the self-confident and independent Owen Young—signaled that Roosevelt intended to follow Woodrow Wilson's example of acting as "his own foreign minister."

For Treasury, the obvious choice was Carter Glass, Wilson's Treasury secretary and the Senate's undisputed mandarin of banking and financial policy. For attorney general, it was Montana's Senator Thomas J. Walsh, whose judicious chairmanship of the 1932 convention had planed away many obstacles to Roosevelt's nomination.

Agriculture was to go to the Iowan agricultural economist Henry A. Wallace, whose father, Henry C. Wallace, had served Harding and Coolidge in the same post, and whose prescriptions for ending the farm depression tracked Roosevelt's own. For Commerce, FDR vacillated between two Democratic supporters from the business world, William H. Woodin, who ran his family's railcar manufacturing business, and Jesse I. Straus, heir to the Macy's retailing empire. Following tradition, the position of postmaster general was to go to the chairman of Roosevelt's campaign, James A. Farley. For Interior, Roosevelt favored the progressive Republican Hiram Johnson of California—an appointment designed to reward Roosevelt's supporters from that bloc while giving his cabinet a bipartisan flavor.

Nature and the vagaries of human character soon exerted their subversive force. Glass proved to be at once insistent and indecisive. He demanded assurances from Roosevelt that he would not be pursuing an inflationary policy, as well as the authority to appoint Russell Leffingwell, a J. P. Morgan partner, as his undersecretary. Roosevelt rejected both conditions. "We simply cannot go along with Twenty-three," he told Moley, referring to Morgan & Company's address at 23 Wall Street. Glass's anti-inflation condition got no more consideration than it would two weeks later when the same idea reached FDR via Herbert Hoover's letter. "You can say that we are not going to throw ideas out the window simply because they are labeled inflation," Roosevelt told Moley.

Roosevelt and Glass volleyed back and forth over the conditions of his nomination, but both soon wearied of the game. Roosevelt concluded that Glass would be more useful in the Senate, where he could push the administration's banking bills, and where he could articulate his doctrinaire fiscal principles without seeming to speak for the White House. Finally, on February 7, the aged Glass refused the cabinet post, sending Roosevelt a note from his physician expressing the opinion that the cabinet appointment might well prove fatal.

The quest for a Treasury secretary then shifted to Woodin, the sixty-four-year-old head of his family's freight car manufacturing business. Nominally a Republican, Woodin had been an early and generous contributor to the

Roosevelt campaign and possessed many other sterling qualities besides. Short, slender, with amused eyes twinkling over a snow-white toothbrush mustache, Woodin had a shy demeanor but a solid grip on business and finance, as well as sturdy common sense and resolute fair-mindedness. His duty to the family business had forced him to abandon his true love, the study of music, but he often retreated to the piano to relax. Even before Glass's final refusal, Moley had enlisted Louis Howe to press Woodin's name on FDR: in mid-January, while Roosevelt was vacationing at sea on his friend Vincent Astor's yacht, they had jointly sent him a coded message reading, PREFER A WOODEN ROOF TO A GLASS ROOF OVER SWIMMING POOL. LUHOWRAY.

"Call Will Woodin and bring him here tonight," FDR instructed Moley upon receiving Glass's letter. Though frail of health, Woodin promptly accepted and upon receiving the appointment plunged directly into talks with Hoover's Treasury secretary, Ogden Mills. Woodin would remain a steadying and sage influence during the frenetic weeks to come. No one paid him a deeper compliment than the ever-censorious Harold Ickes, who would say years later that Woodin was a man he came to "regret not having met earlier."

Harold Ickes was the beneficiary of one of Roosevelt's impulses. Hiram Johnson turned down his offer of the Interior Department, not with Glass's Hamlet-like indecision but with characteristic finality; he feared that his uncompromising personality would fit poorly in Roosevelt's cabinet. Notwithstanding his admiration for the President-elect, he told his son Archibald: "First, I wouldn't give a tinker's dam [sic] to be in his Cabinet . . . and secondly, I would not give an infinitesimal fraction of a tinker's dam to be Secretary of the Interior. I prize my independence more highly than anything."

Roosevelt turned to Republican Senator Bronson Cutting, a New York socialite who had moved west for his health and established his business and political career in New Mexico. But Cutting turned down the post barely a week before the inauguration.

As it happened, Ickes was then hovering around the Roosevelt inner circle as a potential appointee to an upcoming conference on international debts. He had conceived a desire for the Interior post and prevailed on Johnson and other progressive Republicans to put up his name. His credentials as a progressive Republican were as solid as Hiram Johnson's: he had bolted the party in 1912 to support the Progressive "Bull Moose" ticket of

Theodore Roosevelt, on which Johnson had been the vice presidential candidate, and at the 1932 GOP convention had organized a "dump Hoover" movement, which failed for want of a willing candidate. Ushered into Roosevelt's presence at the Sixty-Fifth Street house for the very first time on the morning of February 22 ostensibly to discuss the debt situation, Ickes was offered the Interior Department job out of the blue. "I liked his jib," Roosevelt explained to Moley. Even Johnson, who was one of Ickes's strongest promoters, was amazed at the mysterious workings of chance. He told his sons:

> If we had not made Ickes part of a little inner group on debts; if he had not gone to New York exactly when he did; if he had not unexpectedly been taken by Moley . . . to the gathering at Roosevelt's house; and if contemporaneously Cutting's refusal had not just been received . . . he would still be waiting disconsolately around hoping for some sort of recognition. . . . I really look to see him make as good a secretary of the Interior as we have ever had.

By many reckonings, Ickes would live up to his expectations.

The very last appointment was that of attorney general, its timing dictated by mischance. Roosevelt had named the seventy-three-year-old Thomas Walsh to the post. On the eve of the inauguration, however, Walsh died of a heart attack on the train carrying him back to Washington from a Cuban honeymoon with his bride of five days. Scurrying for a replacement, Roosevelt settled on Homer Cummings, a Connecticut Democratic leader who had already accepted appointment as governor-general of the Philippines and who agreed to serve in the cabinet on a temporary basis. He would remain there for six years.

Roosevelt's cabinet choices confounded most Washington pundits, devoid as it was of such pillars of establishment Democratic politics as Young, Baker, and Bernard Baruch. Tugwell pronounced it "a quiet, serious group, without prima-donnas"—like most other Democrats, he was yet a stranger to Harold Ickes's prickly moods—"but with a distinct progressive cast."

Walter Lippmann concealed his surprise at the cabinet choices behind a mask of knowing cynicism. Listing the ten most prominent—and unchosen—members of the Democratic Party, he wrote: "No President ever selects such a cabinet." Still voicing enthusiasm for the new administration, he said of the cabinet that "for my own part I am prepared to believe that on the whole Mr. Roosevelt has chosen well. . . . There are men in it who will give the more nervous conservatives the cold shivers. But the Cabinet as a whole should be reassuring to the discontented and disillusioned who are now the great majority." Lippmann identified Ickes, Perkins, and Walsh (still making his way homeward) as the advance guard of the struggle to constrain predatory wealth and "to impose social control and social standards upon corporate property," and their appointments proof of the New Deal's intention to revive the progressive movement after its long eclipse under three Republican presidents. In this he was correct, although the path would be rockier than he or anyone else then predicted.

2

A GOOD CRISIS

MOLEY AND WOODIN did not have the luxury of tarrying after Roosevelt's speech to enjoy the inaugural parade. As soon as they could take their dignified leave, they scurried off together to the Treasury to continue discussions over the banking crisis. In the Treasury secretary's office they found virtually the same weary inhabitants they had left twelve hours earlier—Arthur Ballantine, Ogden Mills, acting comptroller of the currency F. Gloyd Awalt, and their associates; almost the only change in the arrangement was that Woodin took his rightful place behind the secretary's heavy ceremonial desk, and Mills moved to the other side.

The major decisions for the day had already been taken. A few hours after Moley and Woodin had left the Treasury on Saturday morning, they had called on Roosevelt at the Mayflower. While he dressed for the pre-inaugural service at St. John's, they described three actions on which the Treasury conferees had reached consensus before dawn. There should be a proclamation closing all banks pursuant to a statute known as the Trading with the Enemy Act; an order for a special session of Congress to convene before the week was out; and a consultative meeting on Sunday in Washington of eminent bankers from New York, Chicago, Philadelphia, Baltimore, and Richmond. Roosevelt assented to all three. That meant that, hours before bidding his oratorical farewell to the discredited Hoover administration, he had agreed to a plan of action crafted largely by Hoover administration appointees; the New Deal would begin with the program of the old guard. Yet once set aglow by FDR's sunny optimism, the plan and its flawless execution would galvanize the nation in a way that no program launched by Herbert Hoover could have done.

Questions of procedure and legitimacy swirled about the Trading with the Enemy Act. For the better part of a year, Hoover's men had pondered its applicability in a peacetime banking crisis without reaching a consensus. The measure had been enacted in October 1917, six months after America's entry into World War I, to address a novel issue of warfare in the modern age. The traditional forms of trading with the enemy—the smuggling of men and matériel—had been made obsolete by the watertight blockade of German ports by the Allies. It had been replaced by a new form of illicit trade—the transfer of financial credits among banks, especially German bank subsidiaries in Latin America and the Far East, which was crucial to Germany's war effort. The legal limits of American financial relationships in wartime had never been established, so the act was drafted by the Federal Reserve Board to give American bankers a bright line distinguishing legal from illegal transactions in international trade. The act's preoccupation with matters of banking and finance was what made it so valuable a tool in the new peacetime crisis—but what was hotly debated was whether the applicable provisions had survived a partial repeal of the act after the 1918 armistice.

Tugwell was assigned to investigate the issue. The task eventually brought him to the office of Assistant Treasury Secretary Daniel Bell, of whom he inquired whether the President's executive authority to restrict the movement of gold and currency remained intact. Bell smiled, reached into his desk, and pulled out a copy of the act. The passages Tugwell had inquired about were already marked in red.

"So others have been considering this?" Tugwell asked.

"Intensively," Bell replied.

In early 1932, he explained, Hoover and Mills had considered invoking the act to prohibit the transfer of U.S. gold reserves overseas. They consulted with Walter Wyatt, the general counsel to the Federal Reserve Board, who as a law clerk for the board in 1918 had drafted the repeal. Wyatt was confident that the act still could be invoked to outlaw the exportation of gold and the domestic hoarding of U.S. currency. Yet although these trends had accelerated horrifically in the last months of 1932 and into January and February, the Hoover administration quailed at dusting off the Trading with the Enemy Act.

Wyatt further believed that the act gave the President authority to order nationwide bank closures, on the reasoning that restraints on currency and gold transactions were meaningless unless banking activities could be halted, if necessary. But he acknowledged that the point was "debatable." He had drafted a bank-closing proclamation for Hoover and Mills, but advised that any use of it be ratified by Congress as soon as possible, just to be on the safe side.

It was over such congressional ratification that Hoover and Roosevelt had experienced their final impasse. On March 2, a desperate Mills told Woodin that Hoover was willing to impose a bank closure beginning on March 3 if Roosevelt would commit to calling Congress into special session on Monday, March 6, to ratify the proclamation. Still maintaining that Hoover must act on his own authority, Roosevelt refused. The proclamation was set aside, for the moment. But with a few minor revisions it would be promulgated by Roosevelt within hours after his oath-taking. A ratification resolution, also drafted by Wyatt, would be incorporated into the Emergency Banking Act of 1933, the first measure to be enacted by the Hundred Days Congress.

Roosevelt kept under wraps the embarrassing fact that the very first official acts of the New Deal had been drafted in the Hoover White House. He acted as though the Trading with the Enemy Act had been a Brain Trust discovery and its application to the banking crisis a token of his own suppleness on policy matters. At his first cabinet meeting, on Sunday, March 5, he even staged a charade in which he ostentatiously asked the new attorney general, Homer Cummings, to "prepare an opinion" on the act. "Mr. President, I am ready to give my opinion now," Cummings replied. In truth, Cummings's opinion was a mere formality, as the relevance of the act had already been established to Roosevelt's satisfaction.

But in a sense it is proper to give Roosevelt credit, for unlike Hoover he was not timid about testing the act's authority. Hoover had not seriously considered closing down the nation's banks until the very last hours of his presidency; his plan had been to use the act solely to impose limits on withdrawals of currency and gold. By contrast, Roosevelt plainly had resolved even before taking the oath of office to exploit the Trading with the Enemy Act to its utmost. The evidence for this is a strained exchange he had with Senator Glass, who spent the days before the inauguration shuttling between the White House and the Mayflower Hotel carrying proposals and counterproposals for resolving the crisis.

Glass was present in Roosevelt's suite during the President-elect's final phone conversation with Hoover, just before midnight on March 3. Hoover maintained that a nationwide closing was unnecessary, as more than three-quarters of the nation's banks were still technically solvent and therefore capable of meeting their depositors' demands. "I understand, Mr. President," Roosevelt replied. "Senator Glass is here now. He thinks the same way."

After Roosevelt rang off, Glass asked him, "So what are you planning to do?"

"Planning to close them, of course."

Glass's eyes widened. "You will have no authority to do that," he spluttered.

Roosevelt read him the relevant provisions of the act, which empowered the President to limit "the use of coin and currency" under an emergency proclamation.

"President Hoover explored that avenue," Glass replied. "The Attorney General informed him it was highly questionable if the President has any such authority. . . . The likelihood is the act was dead with the signing of the Peace Treaty, if not before."

"My advice is precisely the opposite."

"Then," barked Glass, "you've got some expedient advice."

"Nevertheless," Roosevelt said evenly, "I am going to issue the proclamation."

The following morning, Woodin was able to report to the White House that emergency legislation could be drafted in time for a special session of Congress to begin Thursday, March 9. Mills and Ballantine had already prepared an emergency proclamation based on Wyatt's draft, closing all banks nationwide for four days beginning on Monday, March 6. Woodin and Moley circled back to the Treasury building, where a clutch of prominent bankers summoned by the President's order convened at 10 A.M. in the Federal Reserve's second-floor boardroom. Woodin had hoped to solicit the bankers' suggestions for resolving the emergency, or at least to give them a sense of participation in the planning. In the flesh, however, they proved a weak-kneed bunch, almost entirely bereft of ideas. "A few were so immersed in despair that they saw no way out except nationalizing the banks through some jerry-built contrivance," Moley reported—nationalization being the one step Roosevelt had specifically ruled out. In any event, the die had been

cast by the President. By his order, scarcely a single banking institution in
the United States would be open for business when the sun rose on Monday. (Some people detected Roosevelt's instinct for popular communication
in the proclamation's use of the term *bank holiday*, which actually was based
on British usage. "Herbert Hoover, I am sure, would have used the more
gloomy and technically more appropriate term 'moratorium,'" reflected the
banker James P. Warburg. Yet the proclamation had been drafted largely by
Hoover's people.)

At first, many Americans chose to see the nationwide bank holiday as
a mild inconvenience, an occasion for gentle amusement at the high and
mighty as they tried to manage life short of cash—just as so many people were already doing. "Fay Wray flaunted a lot of dollar bills yesterday
around the studio and got herself hated," the *Los Angeles Times* reported of
the contract player soon to become world-famous as *King Kong*'s ingenue,
"—until her co-workers found it was just stage money!" Pasadena's luxurious Huntington Hotel printed a thousand dollars in proprietary scrip and
persuaded local merchants to accept it in lieu of currency from its patrons,
who included wintering millionaires and European princes, "any one of
whom has enough resources to buy the hotel and still have some change
left."

In big cities and rural hamlets alike, legal tender yielded to barter or
credit. A Wisconsin wrestler agreed to perform for a can of tomatoes and
a peck of potatoes. The *New York Daily News,* which was sponsoring the
Golden Gloves semifinals in Madison Square Garden, accepted any object
worth the equivalent of the 50-cent admission fee, collecting hot dogs,
hats, shoes, overcoats, steaks, jigsaw puzzles, and copies of the New Testament. Major department stores placed newspaper ads inviting their regular
customers to utilize their existing accounts. "We are prepared to extend
without stint the same credit facilities that they have always enjoyed in the
past," assured Bergdorf Goodman, Bonwit Teller, Saks & Company, and
other members of the "Uptown Retail Guild" of Manhattan.

The thrill of shared adversity quickly faded. For Detroiters, now entering
their fourth bankless week, the joke had long since worn thin. The city was
on the verge of paralysis. Retailers had stopped offering credit or accepting
checks against later payment, even from their most dependable customers; consequently business was down by 70 percent. Restaurant counters
accustomed to serving twenty-five at a time for lunch were down to three;
movie theaters that played to a thousand patrons were running shows for

fifty. The occasional city laborer, unable to convert his municipal scrip to cash, fainted on the job from hunger. Detroit's municipal tuberculosis sanatoriums, housing two thousand patients, had only enough food in their storerooms to last four more days. Doctors were buying supplies out of their own pockets—if they had any cash to spend.

The rest of the country soon learned what Detroit already knew. In Boston, it was estimated that the average resident was carrying only $18.23 in pocket money when the banks closed. Small merchants unable to make change had to turn away patrons with only large bills to pay for cigarettes. With theater receipts dwindling, Hollywood film studios dependent on incoming cash to cover their weekly payrolls of $1.3 million began to shut down, throwing out of work the seventy-five thousand laborers who toiled behind the scenes so their stars could sparkle on-screen. Food prices rose as farmers, unable to finance shipments or to secure cash payments, withheld vegetables and livestock from market. Businesses that had already begun to suffer from the sporadic state bank closings of late February and early March foresaw dire prospects ahead. The president of the Iowa-based Sheaffer Pen Company wrote Moley, an old friend: "There must be adequate relief legislation immediately. It would seem that it could not wait for a week or ten days. . . . The country would be at a standstill."

Woodin acted promptly to lift the most inconvenient and unnecessary currency restrictions, issuing proclamations on March 6 allowing banks to make change (as long as no gold was paid out), give customers access to their safe-deposit boxes, and cash government-issued checks. The next day he added permission for banks to pay out funds needed for food, medicine, payrolls, or to alleviate "distress"—but the banks would be responsible for preventing hoarding, as evidenced by any "unnecessary" withdrawal of currency. How they were to divine the intentions of their depositors was not clear, although some banks announced that in cases of suspiciously large withdrawal requests they might require affidavits of nonhoarding from the customer. In practice, the public policed itself and the issue arose only rarely.

Moley and Woodin spent all day Monday cloistered at the Treasury, familiarizing themselves with the plans developed in advance by Mills and Ballantine for resolving the emergency. The Hoover holdovers' idea was to reopen the banks in stages—the healthiest banks immediately, followed by those that required assistance from the RFC or Federal Reserve. Those that could not safely open at all, mostly state banks, were to be placed in the hands of conservators for orderly liquidation. The plan was sound enough to be imported almost wholesale into the Roosevelt program, although the designations of the banks and the reopening schedule would be tweaked to provide for an even geographical (and politically palatable) distribution of opened banks in the first days after the lifting of the holiday.

Woodin and Moley left the Treasury building late Monday night for a respite from two uninterrupted days of conferring with febrile bankers and Treasury officials. "I'll be damned if I go back into those meetings until I get my head cleared," the secretary told Moley. Together they scribbled a general agenda for ending the emergency. The basic requirement was for "swift and staccato action," Woodin observed, reverting in his fatigue to musical terminology. The goal was public confidence, which required conventional, not controversial, measures. A maximum number of banks should be opened quickly and en masse, to signal that the system as a whole remained sound. There should be an explicit gesture by Roosevelt and Congress toward governmental economy, and a direct public appeal for confidence by the President himself. "There was magic, we knew, in that calm voice," Moley observed.

Only one question remained, but it was in many ways the most pressing: how to replenish the reopened banks' vaults with currency, which had been severely depleted by months of hoarding. The shortage was more than an inconvenience. Banks permitted to reopen without enough currency to meet depositors' demands might be compelled to raise cash by liquidating assets, which would continue to undermine the crippled banking system and constrain credit.

Providing a serviceable medium of exchange was also the key to restoring public confidence in the financial system, which was being sapped by the proliferation of informal scrip issued by employers, retailers, even newspaper advertisers. The scrip movement had gained a powerful head of steam in the first days of the emergency. Its leading advocates were New York City bankers, who believed that a scrip system could be put in place sooner than any plan contrived at the federal level and requiring congressional authority; it is probable that they also relished the opportunity to extricate themselves from another measure of federal regulation, that is, currency rules. At Wall Street's behest, the New York legislature voted on the very first day of the bank holiday to permit the issuance of scrip backed by the assets of the big New York City banks. The Treasury Department, bobbing atop the wave, contemplated reviving the blue-tinted Aldrich-Vreeland banknotes authorized by Congress following the Panic of 1907, in the pre–Federal Reserve era.

Across the country, crudely stamped coins and scraps of colored paper were rewriting the very definition of money. ("All you need is a fountain pen and a prescription blank," the homespun humorist Will Rogers observed in his daily newspaper dispatch. "That's what we been looking for years, a substitute for money.") The *Chicago Tribune* paid its employees with "dollars" embossed with a portrait of (the Republican) Theodore Roosevelt. General Fireproofing Company of Youngstown, Ohio, covered its workforce's wages with certificates in $1 and $5 denominations, inscribed as promissory notes on the company's bank deposits, payable in six months.

The phenomenon unnerved economists. If scrip drove official currency, issued and tracked by the Federal Reserve, out of the marketplace, the result might be uncontrollable inflation. Nor were there any legal or financial standards for scrip. Some was backed by sound bank assets, some by deposits frozen on bank ledgers for the moment, some by promises and hope, some merely by fraud. No merchant who was asked to accept any such notes as payment for goods or services could know their real value. At the Federal Reserve Board, Chairman Eugene Meyer condemned the Treasury's dalliance with the idea of government scrip as largely an instrument for backdoor inflation—"a phony lot of words thrown together and called a plan."

The juggernaut had to be derailed. The solution came on Tuesday morning, when Moley came down to breakfast to discover Woodin in an elated and resolute mood. "I've got it!" Woodin exclaimed. "After you left, I played my guitar a little while and then read a little while and then played some more and read some more. . . . And, by gum, if I didn't hit upon the answer!" He slammed the table with his fist. "We don't need scrip. The Reserve Act lets us print all the currency we'll need. It won't frighten people. It won't look like stage money. It'll be money that looks like money."

Quietly, the order went out for the printing of $200 million in new Federal Reserve notes, available for injection into the banking system as emergency currency. What neither Woodin nor Moley could know at the time was that the magic of Roosevelt's voice would be so compelling that the emergency notes would not be needed.

Although the outlines and even many details of Roosevelt's response to the banking crisis had been crafted by Hoover appointees, his approach, as the economist Herbert G. Stein later observed, was "more direct and more drastic" than his predecessor's. Unlike Hoover, who had tried "to demonstrate the advantage of keeping money in the country, [Roosevelt] closed the doors and windows so the money couldn't get out." The Emergency Banking Act would achieve this and more. It suspended the convertibility of dollars into gold for U.S. citizens, a right that has never been restored, and temporarily forbade the export of gold. It also ratified the bank closures and established standards for their reopening, and authorized a broad expansion of the Federal Reserve's lending capability to member banks, eliminating the need for scrip. As Stein observed, these were the first deliberate steps toward the New Deal's goal of liberating domestic monetary policy from international entanglements. The steps that followed would shake the global financial system to its foundations.

On the eve of Congress's March 9 return for its special session, Roosevelt ended another Washington tradition: the glum formality of the presidential press conference. FDR hoped to establish the same friendly give-and-take of the press events he had hosted in Albany—"very delightful family conferences" was how he described them—perhaps because he knew that his personal amiability would be more effective at managing the press than Hoover's condescension.

FDR's first press conference set the pattern of genial banter interspersed with serious newsmaking that would prevail for the next dozen years. "I am told that what I am about to do will become impossible, but I am going to try it," he began. Henceforth there would no requirement that questions be submitted in advance or in writing. He wished it understood that he would never answer hypotheticals—"if" questions, as he put it. While most of his words would be for publication, the exceptions would fall into two categories: "background information," which could be used "on your own authority and responsibility" but was not to be attributed to the White House, and "off the record" information, which was not to be published at all or communicated to anyone outside the room, not even to the reporters' editors.

Roosevelt made clear to the reporters that the bill to be considered by Congress the next day would be provisional, as there was no chance of perfecting permanent banking legislation on such short notice. Asked whether that meant he would "keep hold of this banking situation until permanent legislation is enacted," he replied "yes"—off the record. He continued to dodge questions about whether the country would remain on the gold standard and about his definition of "sound money," as he had during the campaign and in the inaugural address. He observed (again off the record): "You cannot define the thing too closely. . . . What you are coming to now really is a managed currency. . . . It may expand one week and it may contract another week. . . . I don't want to define 'sound' now."

"Can we use that part?" a reporter asked.

"No, I think not."

Finally, he expressed his continued opposition to any guarantee of bank deposits. "You guarantee bad banks as well as good banks," he said. "The minute the Government starts to do that the Government runs into a probable loss." That, too, was off the record.

While the nation struggled through its government-imposed currency drought, the high-level conferences continued their work on emergency legislation inside the walls of the Treasury building. The daunting task of melding dusty old legislative proposals, new suggestions from bureaucrats and bankers, and pet provisions from influential congressmen into a comprehensive bill was dumped on Walter Wyatt. Wyatt cached himself in Woodin's third-floor office, seeking refuge from the incessant bickering consuming the Fed Board and Fed Chairman Eugene Meyer in their lair one floor below.

Time was growing short. Wyatt began working at 11:30 on Tuesday night, knowing he had to produce a final bill by Wednesday morning if it was to be approved by the White House before presentation to the special session the following day. Somehow he kept his focus despite being constantly interrupted by individual Fed governors and others pressing their pet concerns. The first draft came out of his typewriter early Wednesday morning. There ensued several hours of nitpicking and lengthy debates over two issues—a guarantee of bank deposits, and whether to require the Reconstruction Finance Corporation to infuse banks with capital by purchasing preferred shares from them. Both ideas would become so successful in implementation that their most obdurate opponents—Franklin Roosevelt on deposit insurance, and the RFC's Jesse Jones on preferred stock—would later claim their parentage. But that would take time.

The concept of deposit insurance dated back more than one hundred years. A version had been instituted in New York in 1829, and in other states during subsequent bank panics. But at the national level the idea was always contentious: big-city banks believed it would render them finan-cially responsible for the failures of little country banks, while advocates of branch banking (a feature of big banks) contended that it would perpetuate a banking system made up of a multitude of small and weak "unit" banks by giving them a reputation for soundness they did not deserve. It is not surprising that the issue tended to divide supporters and opponents along the line separating countryside from city.

What was clear in the first week of March was that the debate could not be resolved in the heat of a crisis, especially with the President firmly in opposition. The issue was put off to a later day. Still, the Emergency Banking Act would provide an implicit guarantee of depositors against loss by providing for every reopened bank to receive sufficient Federal Reserve banknotes to cover withdrawals. As this would protect any bank from hav-ing to liquidate assets to raise cash, the prospect was drastically reduced that a bank could be forced to close again, at least in the near term. On March 12, in his first Fireside Chat, Roosevelt would supplement that de facto guarantee with a moral one, by promising Americans that every bank permitted to reopen would be "sound."

Jones's objection to a mandate for the RFC to purchase preferred shares was that it deprived him of the ability to tie the size of the agency's capital infusion to the quality of a bank's assets, as was the case when the RFC made a loan against a bank's collateral. Any bank, no matter how impaired, could theoretically float a preferred issue; if the RFC was mandated to buy the issue, so much the better for the bank and the worse for the buyer (and the taxpayers). Jones was partially mollified by amending the provision to allow but not require the RFC to purchase such shares. What finally brought him around to wholehearted support was that preferred stock pur-chases proved extremely effective in shoring up weak but worthy banks while giving him a potent voice in their management. By the end of 1935, RFC-owned preferred stock would amount to nearly 40 percent of total bank common stock in the United States, a token of Jones's enthusiasm as a bank investor.

The emergency banking bill submitted to Congress had four key ele-ments. Title I ratified the bank holiday proclamation and explicitly gave the President authority to regulate all banking functions—in effect, dic-tatorial power over the entire U.S. banking sector—for the duration of the emergency. Title II gave the comptroller of the currency the power to appoint a conservator to take over any bank too impaired to reopen. Title

III allowed banks to issue preferred shares and the RFC, with the approval of the President and at the "request" of the Treasury, to buy them. Finally, Title IV provided for the issuance of Federal Reserve banknotes.

The passage of the act on March 9 has long been held up as a model of swift action by the U.S. Congress, a headlong sprint of legislative deliberation that began at 12:30 that Thursday afternoon with the delivery of Roosevelt's message calling for immediate action, proceeded to approval by unanimous consent in the House of Representatives at 4:05, and ended with the bill's passage by the Senate at 7:23 p.m.

Yet the day was not devoid of outbursts of dramatic oratory, especially in the upper chamber. There the most vehement critic of the legislation emerged in the person of Huey Long, the progressive Democratic "Kingfish" of Louisiana who had taken his seat in the Senate the year before. Long's colleagues had grown accustomed to his charisma and bombast— and to the penetrating intelligence that underlay his theatrical public persona. Now he positioned himself as the scourge of the big-city banks that had brought the financial system to its knees and the defender of the country bankers they had sucked into the whirlpool.

The injustice, he declared, was that the big banks were to be protected by the indulgence of the Federal Reserve while thousands of little state-chartered banks were to be closed—extinguishing the savings of working men and women. His proposed solution was to allow any bank to become a member of the Federal Reserve, thus acquiring the mantle of respectability and the shelter of practically unlimited federal capital.

Long placed the issue in stark populist terms: "I am talking about . . . the bootblacks, the farmers, and widows who have money in these little State banks. . . . You are proposing to take every dime they have away from them, and when Friday morning comes it will be a hanging day for that kind of people."

But Carter Glass was immune to Huey Long's bluster. As the congressional father of the Federal Reserve and Senate manager of the emergency bill, Glass saw in the Kingfish's proposal to dump the country banks into the Federal Reserve system a formula for the contamination, as if with mixed blood, of the one thing that could preserve the economy, a purified central banking system. Crisply he put the debate back in its tracks.

"'Little banks'?" he sneered. "Little corner grocerymen who run banks, who get together $10,000 or $15,000, as it may be, and then invite the deposits of their community, and at the very first gust of disaster topple over and ruin their depositors! What we need in this country are real banks and real bankers . . . yet we have people all over the country from one end to the other calling themselves 'bankers,' and all they know is how to shave notes at an excessive rate of interest. They are not bankers."

The debate limped to a close. Less than three hours after it took up the bill, the Senate voted. Passage was by 73 to 7. Long voted "aye." One hour and fourteen minutes after the vote, at 8:37 P.M., President Roosevelt signed the bill into law. It was the first measure of the New Deal, and the first of the congressional session that would last through one hundred breakneck days.

The completeness of Congress's capitulation to the President's wishes gave pause even to some of Roosevelt's most ardent admirers. One was Felix Frankfurter, no stranger to the doctrine of swift and decisive action but in this case an advocate of more deeply considered policy making. He expressed his concern to Walter Lippmann, but the latter remained an advocate of prompt, even headstrong, action.

"Do you really think," he replied to Frankfurter, "that I should have urged Congress to consider carefully and attempt to understand thoroughly the provisions of the banking bill before passing it, or was it right to call upon Congress to take the thing on faith, suspending debate? . . . I faced that choice honestly in my own mind, and I am prepared to risk the potential dangers which you point out for the sake of averting the much more actual dangers which were right upon us."

After enactment of the banking measure, the next challenge was to instill public confidence that the financial system had been pulled from the brink and was under repair. The key here, as Moley understood, was Franklin Roosevelt. The device was to be a radio address on Sunday, March 12, the night before the banks started to reopen, the first of Roosevelt's renowned Fireside Chats.

With the success of the New Deal's opening initiative hanging on the address, Roosevelt and his advisors took exceptional care with the text. That much is clear; what remains murky is who contributed to the drafting and how. The weight of the evidence suggests that the first draft was prepared by Charles Michelson, a public relations man for the Democratic National Committee who had been seconded to the White House. Michelson was known for his talent for penning slashing rhetorical attacks on Republicans as well as for direct, accessible oratory. He had been serving as a communications consultant for the crisis team at the Treasury Department, where he vexed Arthur Ballantine by declaring that he would not approve any state-ment for public dissemination that he could not personally comprehend. Since he also informed them that he was an economic illiterate, this set a standard for straightforward vernacular in the group's communiqués.

Michelson's draft has been lost, but it undoubtedly hewed to the same principle. He carried it over to the White House, where it was handed to Ballantine, who judged it egregiously ill-informed. Ballantine rewrote it and discarded Michelson's copy. But he went too far in the opposite direc-tion, weighting down the text with a disquisition on the banking crisis in painfully technical language.

It was up to Roosevelt to find the middle ground. The process of balanc-ing Michelson's colloquialisms and Ballantine's learned technicalities took him through Sunday afternoon. That evening he read his version to an audience composed of Louis Howe, Will Woodin, and Gloyd Awalt. The latter introduced the only discordant note in the discussion by question-ing the promise in Roosevelt's text to reopen only "sound banks." Politics and haste being what they were, he explained, some of the reopened banks might not be so sound. Roosevelt thought for a moment, then "stated in no uncertain terms that that was what we were going to do, 'open only sound banks.'"

At 9:50 P.M. Roosevelt was brought in his wheelchair into the Oval Room, which featured a real (but empty) fireplace and was cluttered for the occasion with broadcasting equipment manned by technicians from three radio networks along with folding chairs for the friends, family, and advisors present to witness the speech in person. There was a moment of confusion—the triple-spaced reading manuscript had disappeared. Roo-sevelt took hold of one of the single-spaced copies mimeographed for the press, put out his cigarette, and at 10 P.M. sharp began a historic address to a radio audience of sixty million.

"My friends," he said with an inflection of intimacy that came to define the New Deal for an entire generation, "I want to talk for a few minutes with the people of the United States about banking—with the compara-tively few who understand the mechanics of banking but more particularly with the overwhelming majority who use banks for the making of deposits and the drawing of checks."

He proceeded on to a concise description of the crisis dating back to late February while refraining, for the moment, from pointing the finger of blame. "Because of undermined confidence on the part of the public," he said, "there was a general rush by a large portion of our population to turn bank deposits into currency or gold—a rush so great that the soundest banks could not get enough currency to meet the demand."

He covered the bank holiday and the speedy passage of the Emergency Banking Act, pointedly including the Republicans in his praise for Congress's "devotion to public welfare." Then he looked ahead to the next few days and the staged bank reopenings, starting with sound banks in the twelve Federal Reserve cities on Monday, followed by sound banks in clearinghouse cities on Tuesday and banks in smaller cities on Wednesday and thereafter.

The centerpiece of the address was an appeal to the public to place its trust in any bank the government had allowed to reopen and to resist hoarding, indeed to return withdrawn money to the bank.

> It is possible that when the banks resume a very few people who have not recovered from their fear may again begin withdrawals. Let me make it clear that the banks will take care of all needs—and it is my belief that hoarding during the past week has become an exceedingly unfashionable pastime. It needs no prophet to tell you that when the people find that they can get their money—that they can get it when they want it for all legitimate purposes—the phantom of fear will soon be laid. People will again be glad to have their money where it will be safely taken care of and where they can use it conveniently at any time. I can assure you that it is safer to keep your money in a reopened bank than under the mattress.

Roosevelt wrapped up the speech by blaming the crisis on a "comparative few" bad apples—bankers who "had shown themselves either incompetent or dishonest in their handling of the people's funds." This was not a casual accusation but an important piece of the recovery plan. To restore confidence, it was essential to impute the crisis to a discrete group of miscreants, rather than to fundamental flaws in the system. Only then could Roosevelt make a credible claim that this was a crisis within government's capacity to solve, and enlist the public in the solution. "It was the Government's job to straighten out this situation and do it as quickly as possible—and the job is being performed," he said. "We have provided the machinery to restore our financial system; it is up to you to support and make it work. . . . Together we cannot fail."

As measured by the immediate public response, the first Fireside Chat was a spectacular success. On the surface, FDR's reassuring words and appeal for public confidence had a Hooverian tone; unlike Hoover, his reassurances were not based on the expectation that the traditional cycle of recession and recovery would naturally bring forth prosperity, but rather on the "swift and staccato action" (in Woodin's resonant phrase) of a new administration.

When banks in Federal Reserve cities reopened on Monday morning, they were again confronted with lines of depositors clamoring for entry— this time to return gold and hoarded currency to their accounts, not to drain them. By the end of March, $1.2 billion in currency, half of it in gold and gold certificates, had been returned to the banking system. The worst fears aired inside the Treasury building during the dismal days of early March proved unfounded; of the $200 million in new Federal Reserve notes authorized to supplant scrip, only a token amount was ever released. Doubts about the U.S. government's reputation for creditworthiness—a concern that had Treasury officials and private bankers in a state of near panic during the holiday—were laid to rest on March 15, when a huge $800 million issue of Treasury certificates was brought to market and 100 percent oversubscribed (albeit at interest rates of up to 4¼ percent, the highest paid by the government since the war). The flow of gold back into the system was so great that a federal antihoarding proclamation, which was initially regarded as an indispensable tool for ending the emergency, was not issued until April 5. At that point it was no more than pro forma; the amount of gold and gold certificates still sequestered outside the Treasury and Federal Reserve banks was $760 million, the smallest amount since 1923.

With perhaps pardonable effusiveness, James Farley, Roosevelt's presidential campaign chairman and now postmaster general, observed of the March 12 Fireside Chat that "no other talk in history ever called forth such a wave of spontaneous enthusiasm and co-operation."

More disinterested observers also came to positive, if more measured, conclusions. Walter Lippmann had written on March 7: "There are good crises and there are bad crises. Every crisis . . . is either a disaster or an opportunity. A bad crisis is one in which no one has the power to make good use of the opportunity and therefore it ends in disaster. A good crisis is one in which the power and the will to seize the opportunity are in being. Out of such a crisis come solutions. The present crisis is a good crisis."

After the Fireside Chat, Lippmann advised his readers that the resolution of the emergency did full justice to its promise.

> The great achievement of the past ten days has been the revival of the people's confidence in themselves and in their institutions. They believe that they have a leader whom they can follow. They believe they have a government which can act. They believe again that with human intelligence, a resolute will, and a national discipline the measures that have to be taken can be devised and executed. . . . This change of spirit is of incalculable importance.

As the swift and successful resolution of the bank holiday filled the American people with confidence, so did it fire up the New Dealers. The reaction of depositors "exceeded our most optimistic expectations," Moley recalled. Farley labeled it a "miracle."

The experience charged the New Deal with a vigor that would last well into the next year, encouraging the administration to press audacious solutions to crises in the farm and industrial economies, in social conditions, and in government finance. Roosevelt's popularity among the voters and his ability to assemble bipartisan majorities in Congress to support the New Deal would last beyond the next presidential election in 1936, or until he finally began to take his powers of persuasion for granted. Though Roosevelt described the bank holiday and the Emergency Banking Act in his Fireside Chat as "nothing complex, or radical," they were certainly novel and unorthodox in comparison to his predecessor's approach. That they were also successful gave the New Dealers the confidence to march ahead in the same spirit. That was the positive aspect of the matter; what was not so positive was that the improvisational character of the resolution would become a feature of many future New Deal initiatives. "Bold, persistent experimentation," as the Oglethorpe University speech had put it, had worked this time, brilliantly. That did not mean it would work every time.

Roosevelt's unwillingness to cooperate with Hoover in the waning days of the old administration, and the stunning success of the bank holiday in the opening days of the New Deal, has led to persistent conjecture that as President-elect he deliberately let the banking system collapse, the better to secure a personal triumph by pulling the nation's economy back from the brink.

The grounds for such speculation are equivocal, to say the least. Its chief exponent was Hoover, who cited two items of evidence in concluding that Roosevelt had deliberately fomented an emergency. One was a statement Tugwell made in an unguarded moment during a late-February lunch with James H. Rand, chief executive of Remington Rand, Inc., to the effect that the New Dealers were (in Rand's paraphrase) "fully aware of the bank situation and that it would undoubtedly collapse in a few days, which would place the responsibility in the lap of President Hoover." Rand promptly shared this statement with an apoplectic Hoover, who wrote back that Tugwell "breathes with infamous politics devoid of every atom of patriotism."

The second is a statement Moley made to Hoover many years after the fact, relating that when Roosevelt received Hoover's handwritten letter on February 18, "he either did not realize how serious the situation was or . . . he preferred to have conditions deteriorate and gain for himself the entire credit for the rescue operation."

On even casual inspection neither statement supports Hoover's conclusion. Tugwell never made any secret of his conviction that the banking collapse presented a rare opportunity for a radical restructuring of the financial sector, including nationalization of the banks. Possibly for that reason, he had been deliberately excluded from any discussion of banking policy in the months before the inauguration, and played no role whatsoever in the high-level activities aimed at resolving the crisis. In fact, Tugwell deeply resented his exclusion and Roosevelt's reliance instead on a resolutely conservative group of advisors in the crisis, chiefly Woodin, Ballantine, and Mills. At best, Tugwell was expressing wishful thinking to Rand; Tugwell later asserted in his own defense that he merely had been trying to nettle the industrialist, a goal he certainly achieved.

Nor does Moley's statement, made at a time when he had become deeply disaffected with the New Deal, establish that Roosevelt deliberately intended to sink the banks. The closest Moley comes to that is to observe that Roosevelt's actions prior to Inauguration Day "would conform to any such motive on his part." Importantly, neither of Moley's two books about his experiences in the White House, published in 1939 and 1966, attributes any such intention to Roosevelt.

Two salient truths about Roosevelt's approach to the bank crisis should not be overlooked. First, he always maintained explicitly that Hoover was fully empowered to take any action deemed necessary without his participation, and indeed urged Hoover to utilize all the tools he had at hand;

after all, the Trading with the Enemy Act, from which Roosevelt drew his own authority after his inauguration, first had been identified as relevant by Hoover's own advisors.

Second, Hoover himself set terms for cooperation that Roosevelt could not conceivably have accepted, including an explicit rejection of inflation as a policy. To do that, Roosevelt would have had to repudiate in advance a policy he was planning to implement, or announce it at a time when he was powerless to implement it. This might well have created more turmoil in the financial markets, not less.

The charge that Roosevelt deliberately provoked the emergency paints him as a boundlessly irresponsible and cynical political leader, a characterization that is not supported by the record. Furthermore, it requires the assumption that the successful outcome of the bank holiday was preordained. It was not. No one could have known ahead of time how the public would respond to the new president's approach, much less that depositors would exhibit so much confidence that more currency and gold would return to the banks than had left them in the weeks before the holiday. Poisoned by bitterness, Hoover interpreted the bank holiday's success as evidence that it should never have happened at all. But Hoover was writing twenty years after the event, when the outcome was settled; Roosevelt had been required to act in the moment, when the future was obscured by clouds and fog.

Notwithstanding the general enthusiasm produced by the Fireside Chat, many citizens were made uneasy by the dramatic turn of events in Washington. Americans of a conservative fiscal bent questioned FDR's circumlocutions about sound currency and gold. Just what did he mean when he said "the confidence of the people" was "more important than currency, more important than gold"? Nor did the bank reopenings proceed without a hitch. Decisions about which banks to reopen and when forced Treasury and Federal Reserve officials to make very chancy judgments about individual institutions. Awalt's doubts that every opened bank would be unquestionably "sound" were well founded. The reopenings had to be spread fairly across the country so no region or community would be left underbanked. Nor was the process immune from political pressures, personal conflicts, and the persistent ambiguity of exactly what constituted a "solvent" bank, given the mismatch of capital, deposits, and assets common to all banks.

The most difficult case presented to the bank regulators implicated all these issues. It involved Bank of America, a majestic California institution with $600 million in deposits and 410 branches in the state. If Bank of America failed to open on Monday morning, March 13, public confidence on the West Coast would be profoundly shaken. The shock was likely to reverberate across the nation and possibly place recovery again in doubt. Yet the bank's principal regulator, John U. Calkins, governor of the Federal Reserve Bank of San Francisco, was refusing to certify its soundness. Since it was plain that the Federal Reserve would have to support the ailing Bank of America with heavy infusions of capital for some time to come, it would be almost impossible to reopen the institution as long as Calkins stood his ground.

By the time Roosevelt stubbed out his cigarette in the Oval Room to begin his Fireside Chat, Treasury and Federal Reserve officials had been arguing over the bank for three days under the watchful eyes of California's two U.S. senators, Hiram Johnson and William G. McAdoo, who spent much of the time perched in the anteroom of Will Woodin's Treasury office. They would keep at it for many hours more.

Calkins was relying on an examination his staff had completed in July 1932, when it found that "a continuation of existent economic conditions and the present management will place this bank in jeopardy." He maintained that things had not improved, a judgment that infuriated the bank's founder and chairman, A. P. Giannini.

Giannini maintained that Calkins was hardly a disinterested figure. He was friendly with a group of executives who had been defeated by Giannini in a bitter proxy fight for control of the bank early in 1932; Giannini in return had agitated with Roosevelt for Calkins's removal.

The personal element, along with Awalt's judgment that the bank was not insolvent, persuaded Woodin that it should reopen on Monday. After midnight passed in Washington without a sign of agreement from San Francisco, Woodin ushered all onlookers out of his office and got Calkins on the phone. After an hour of tense conversation, Woodin finally laid a blunt question on the line: "Are you willing to take the responsibility for keeping this bank closed?"

Confronted point-blank with this intimidating burden, Calkins hedged.

"Well, then," Woodin stated, "the bank will open."

3

A RIVER OUT OF EDEN

ROOSEVELT HAD INTENDED to discharge the special session after enactment of the Emergency Banking Act, but Congress's complaisant mood changed his mind. Contributing to the President's determination to keep the lawmakers at their desks was the knowledge that the next item on his agenda was already prepared for introduction. This was the Economy Act, which aimed to make real the rhetorical commitment to government thrift that Roosevelt had voiced in Pittsburgh during the campaign.

The Economy Act was the work of Lewis Douglas, the conservative Democratic congressman from Arizona whom Roosevelt had appointed budget director. The offspring of a wealthy Arizona landowning family, polished by an elite East Coast education (Amherst College), Douglas was a handsome and charming figure, exceptionally popular among his Capitol Hill colleagues. Inside the White House, however, the social engineers of the Brain Trust and the ambitious turf warriors in the cabinet viewed him with mistrust. Even moderates thought him an economic throwback—"a Democrat of the old school," Moley labeled him, "as rigorously dedicated to orthodox fiscal policies as was Grover Cleveland."

To zealous progressives like Tugwell he was a threat. Tugwell's first impression upon meeting Douglas in Hyde Park a few weeks after the election had been of a likable man with a ready intelligence he "wondered at in a congressman." Within days, the familiarity bred of lengthy conversation had soured him on the Arizonan. "I was struck with the almost vindictive way he spoke of bureaucrats" and with Douglas's single-minded devotion to cost cutting, even at the expense of efficiency, Tugwell recalled. Roosevelt dismissed his concerns. "I think we must have a shakeup. . . . It may result in real economy," he told Tugwell. "Douglas will be helpful."

Douglas had driven a stern bargain in his talks with Roosevelt over the budget post, extracting a pledge from the President-elect to honor his campaign commitment for a 25 percent cut in government spending. This was especially important, Douglas lectured Roosevelt, as "the credit of the United States would be, at least, temporarily impaired" by the banking crisis. Only rigid adherence to economy would revive that confidence, Douglas maintained. "To all these things and others FDR gave his unqualified consent," he recalled. Douglas further displayed a marked tendency toward self-martyrdom. "I recollect saying to [Roosevelt] . . . that by accepting the position of Director of the Budget, I was bringing my own political career to an end, because I had no illusions about the effect it would have upon my future in political life."

Roosevelt and his White House circle failed to appreciate the apocalyptic fervor Douglas would bring to the economy drive. "It is conceivable that civilization itself is hanging in the balance," Douglas wrote his father in January. Still, in his fundamental desire for restraint he was by no means out of sync with the President-elect. Roosevelt was fully invested in the notion that federal cutbacks were a key to restoring the government's credit and credibility; his character possessed a strong element of "Dutch thrift," Moley observed, manifested in his "noticeably economical" tenure as governor of New York.

Yet Roosevelt also recognized that political realities would make economizing at the federal level anything but simple. Rising unemployment mandated spending on relief, and the slack in consumer demand created by the stagnation of the private sector had to be compensated for by government programs such as public works. While Roosevelt believed sincerely in government thrift and a balanced budget, those principles would remain at war with imperatives for fiscal action during the first years of the New Deal—in fact, except for a brief, unhappy period in 1937, the principle of economy would always lose the contest. During the first phase of the New Deal, Douglas's entreaties to balance the budget regardless of the political fallout had Roosevelt's ear, at least in theory; but they would presently yield to Harry Hopkins's famous formulation of administration policy: "We will spend and spend."

For the moment, however, *economy* was officially the watchword. Douglas endowed his cost-cutting measure with the resonant title "A Bill to Maintain the Credit of the United States Government," and drafted with the bill a suitably stern message for the President to send to Congress. Moley labored all day Thursday, March 9—while Congress was debating and passing the banking bill—to give the presidential message a Rooseveltian tone leavening admonition with optimism. But the result, sent to Capitol Hill the next day, still was freighted with Douglas's somber worldview. Observing that the accumulated federal deficit would shortly reach $5 billion, the message warned:

> With the utmost seriousness I point out to the Congress the profound effect of this fact upon our national economy. It has contributed to the recent collapse of our banking structure. It has accentuated the stagnation of the economic life of our people. It has added to the ranks of the unemployed. . . . Upon the unimpaired credit of the United States Government rest the safety of deposits, the security of insurance policies, the activity of industrial enterprises, the value of our agriculture products and the availability of employment. . . . It, therefore, becomes our first concern to make secure the foundation. National recovery depends on it.
>
> Too often in recent history liberal governments have been wrecked on rocks of loose fiscal policy. We must avoid this danger.

This passage would strike a later generation of economists oriented toward a countercyclical fiscal policy of deficit spending as being technically incorrect and rife with non sequiturs. To Lewis Douglas it sounded exactly right, especially with its closing sentence assuring Congress that if it were to act immediately, "there is reasonable prospect that within a year the income of the Government will be sufficient to cover the expenditures of the Government." In other words, there would be stringency and pain for a year. But after that—the sunshine of a balanced budget.

The Economy Act gave the President broad discretion to cut government salaries and veterans' benefits—something politicians had long considered sure vote losers. But Congress held to its resolve to stand with Roosevelt. The bill passed both houses by overwhelming margins and was signed into law on March 20, the second legislative measure of the Hundred Days. Roosevelt promptly imposed wage cuts of 15 percent across the

board for federal employees, including members of Congress, and authorized sharp reductions in veterans' benefits—too sharp, as it turned out, for
complaints soon flooded into Capitol Hill offices about overenthusiastic
budget cutters in the Veterans Administration slashing compensation for
disabled vets, who were supposed to receive special consideration. The veterans' lobby mobilized opposition to the government economies, which in
any event quickly lost their luster in Washington. In March 1934, Congress
would vote to restore veterans' allowances, federal salaries, and its own pay
to pre–Economy Act levels. Roosevelt duly vetoed the measure and was
duly overridden, a rebuff that produced an about-face in FDR's approach
to government economies. "It entirely changed the President's attitude,"
Senate Majority Leader James F. Byrnes later reflected. "He immediately
became the leader of those who were advocating liberal spending."

Roosevelt's acquiescence to "liberal spending" should be seen more accurately as the consequence of policies he established during the Hundred
Days, especially his determination to assist the jobless with government
relief and his creation, toward the end of the 1933 special session, of a
multibillion-dollar public works program. That those measures were totally
inconsistent with an economy drive mandating government layoffs and pay
cuts was not lost on the President's aides. "If unemployment was created
at the same time it was being relieved the paradox was obvious," Tugwell
observed. To resolve the policy conflict in favor of spending, not thrift,
Roosevelt needed to be brought to an understanding that "expenditures by
anyone tended to create a demand for goods, and that this created employment." Roosevelt's acceptance of this proto-Keynesian notion developed
slowly but inexorably through the early years of the New Deal—at a time
when the name of John Maynard Keynes and his theories about the role of
deficit-financed fiscal stimulus in combating economic slumps were not yet
widely known in the United States.

Roosevelt's intellectual journey was bound to create a rift with his adamantly conservative budget director. Initially the President was entranced
by Douglas's suave self-assurance and his evident intelligence, even brilliance. Scarcely a month after taking office Roosevelt had praised Douglas
effusively to Colonel Edward M. House, his venerable mentor from his days
in the Wilson White House, as "the greatest 'find' of the administration."
But Washington progressives never warmed to the dashing Lewis Douglas.
Hiram Johnson would denounce him for having a "heart of stone." Tugwell condemned him for shortsightedness, not least because Douglas took

particular glee in hacking away at scientific research programs such as those dear to Tugwell in his new home, the Department of Agriculture. (Tugwell and Wallace were largely successful in sparing the USDA's research budget from the meat-ax.)

Douglas's prediction that he would never again hold elective office after serving in the Roosevelt White House proved accurate. His compensation would be a brilliant career in business and academia, built in no small part upon his sedulous pursuit of thrift and economy. Departing the Roosevelt administration in August 1934, he left behind an acrid reputation as a sort of Hooverite in Democratic clothing: "He represented discredited policies without apology; he hated the New Deal and affiliated happily with the most reactionary Republicans while he was working most intimately with the President," Tugwell observed. "Yet of all those who began their service with the President in March of 1933, Lewis had the most notable career; he was given the most honorific posts, even the Ambassadorship to the Court of St. James's [under Truman, from 1947 to 1950]; he was regarded as the most favored party member. And in 1952 he turned up, after having accepted all these blessings, in the Republican camp, supporting Eisenhower. There is a lesson there somewhere."

While the White House political team occupied itself with the banking crisis and the Economy Act, the members of the new cabinet were left to settle into their new posts on their own. For those with Washington experience the process amounted merely to swapping one routine for another. For others it was like stepping into Wonderland.

Frances Perkins felt disoriented enough in her role as the nation's first female cabinet secretary. Her first encounter with the Department of Labor resembled a scene out of Gothic noir, with a hearty dose of black comedy thrown in. Arising in her Washington hotel room on the first Monday of the New Deal, she realized that she had no idea where the Labor Department building was located, much less what protocol governed her formal assumption of duties. Along with her personal secretary Frances Jurkowitz, a fearsome duenna known as Miss Jay to all those who had had business with Perkins in Albany, she waited for a call from the department.

Finally, as the clock ticked past 10:30, she picked up the phone, commenting to Miss Jay a bit uncertainly, "I am the Secretary of Labor, and I have not only a right but a duty to take possession of the premises." Overruling a string of uncooperative voices on the line, she finally got through to William Nuckles Doak, the outgoing labor secretary. "Suppose I come in half an hour," she told him.

There was a long pause, then he replied: "I guess that'll be all right."

The department filled an ancient converted apartment building not far from the White House. Its interior was dark and foreboding, its shadowy nooks occupied by silent, hulking men whom Perkins mentally labeled "cigar in the corner of the mouth type[s]," many of them conducting inscrutable, muttered conversations on the telephone. Stale ashtrays and spittoons were everywhere, along with wastebaskets surrounded by mounds of misaimed and crumpled papers.

Introduced at last to Doak, a taciturn former trainman from Virginia, she prodded him to summon his staff for introductions. To break the uneasy silence while they waited for the assistant secretaries to be summoned, Perkins asked him to name a few important labor issues of the moment. "The immigration business," he replied after some thought. "That's awful serious."

The assistants filed in one by one, many of them plainly strangers to Doak. So they began to introduce themselves, giving their names and the topics they were in charge of. To Perkins's astonishment, seven in a row introduced themselves with the words, "I'm in charge of immigration." She breathed a sigh of relief when the parade came to an end. One man was left. He said simply, "My name is Harry Hull."

"What's your title?" Perkins asked.

"I'm chief of the immigration service."

That day Perkins evicted Doak by tactfully informing him that he should go to lunch and that she would have his personal effects packed up while he was out. Finally free of her predecessor, she opened the drawer of his desk, from which an immense black creature sprang out at her. It was Perkins's first startling encounter with the southern cockroach, a very large cousin of the small brown northeastern variety with which she was familiar. The building was alive with the giant insects. "For heaven's sake," she told Miss Jay, "see if there's any roach paste in Washington. We'll have to do this job ourselves." Not wanting to spend the taxpayers' money on a thorough paint job in a depression, Perkins and Miss Jay spruced up the building themselves with soap and insecticide.

There was more to clean up than the department's physical quarters. As her first step toward reorganizing the shadowy and hidebound agency, Perkins disbanded a unit that had been identified by a federal investigative commission in 1931 as a hive of corruption. This was the Section 24 squad, named after a provision of immigration law giving the labor secretary the authority to deport undesirable aliens. Section 24's seventy-one undercover dicks reported to Murray Garsson, a sinister figure whose criminal record barred him from entering New York City on pain of arrest, and through Garsson directly to Doak. The squad had evolved into an instrument for employers to use to harass labor organizers and for its members to shake down foreign-born laborers for cash.

The night after she disbanded the unit, Perkins arrived alone at the Labor Department for some after-dinner work. She heard suspicious noises coming from Section 24's office.

"Who's up there?" she asked the elevator man.

"Mr. Garsson and all them fellows," he replied. "They said they was working late."

She threw open the office door, surprising Garsson and his henchmen in the act of rifling the files. Garsson stammered out an explanation that they were just culling "personal belongings and our personal correspondence."

"These files surely can't be personal," Perkins replied. "They look like official files." As the elderly elevator guard nervously watched her back, she commanded the men to depart the building at once, leaving behind all the papers. The atmosphere was electric. Garsson's hulking minions drew themselves up, as if to stand their ground. "I had to be quite definite and hold myself in check," Perkins recalled. "I couldn't be excited, or disturbed, or raise my voice. . . . I just felt that this was the time when you don't show the slightest concern, alarm, or anything."

Finally the men filed out. Perkins summoned a second guard to watch the door for the night and ordered all the locks on the building changed the next day.

As the carrier of social progressivist ideals in the White House, Perkins would be excoriated by critics across the political spectrum: by conservatives resentful of her championing national unemployment insurance and collective bargaining rights for union members, and even more harshly by liberals who blamed her for Roosevelt's willingness to compromise principle in order to get his core programs enacted. The *Nation,* the most liberal mainstream publication in the land, delivered a most thorough bill of particulars in 1935: "Her middle-class mind," it ruled, "accounts for her almost pathological abhorrence of publicity, her fear of conflict, the dreadful chicanery of the 'social security' program she helped to engineer, and her untiring ability to rationalize and excuse the ever-increasing number of betrayals that her White House hero has meted out to labor." In contrast to her modern image as the most humane of Roosevelt's cabinet members, she was not thought of warmly by her contemporaries, partially because she shunned the emerging practice of publicity building in Washington. "I was brought up in the tradition that you don't tell the press anything," she would recall. When reporters at her first press conference ventured to ask personal questions of the five-foot-five labor secretary, she snapped, "Is that important?" They learned to stop asking. She never got used to the formal appellation of "Madam Secretary" as it appeared in print, much less its jocose offspring "Ma Perkins" and "Frances the Perk"—"I just felt a little embarrassed for my fellow countrymen that there were such dumb and ignorant and discourteous people abroad in the land."

Yet Social Security, which she did indeed engineer, would be the New Deal's single most important program, and its most enduring.

In the second week of the Hundred Days Congress, Roosevelt kicked up the pace of legislation. The multiple emergencies left over from twelve years of Republican rule and a torpid four-month interregnum could no longer wait for action.

He started with Prohibition. A month before the inauguration, Congress had voted to repeal the Eighteenth Amendment—repeal standing as perhaps the lone achievement of the lame-duck session of the winter of 1933. The Twenty-first Amendment, carrying repeal, would require months to lumber through the thirty-six state ratifying conventions assembled for the purpose. But Congress was empowered to modify Prohibition's enabling legislation, the Volstead Act, by legalizing beverages with less than 3.2 percent alcoholic content, which was not considered intoxicating. The President was not inclined to dally. Legend has it that a few hours before delivering his first Fireside Chat, he concluded dinner with several close aides with the words, "I think now would be a good time for a beer."

As soon as the radio address on the bank holiday ended he scribbled out a seventy-two-word message to Congress, calling for legalization of wine and 3.2 beer as a device to raise tax revenue for the government. The message reached Capitol Hill before noon the next day and was passed by both houses three days later. For many Americans, this strike against the "drys," who had held sway over national politics for fourteen years, was as remarkable an achievement as the rescue of the banking system. It was only the start.

The next venture, the Civilian Conservation Corps (CCC), virtually sprang from Roosevelt's own psyche. On the morning of March 14—as the banks were opening for only the second day—he startled Moley by sharing an idea that, he said, he had fully formulated only the night before. This was to put platoons of young unemployed men to work in the forests and national parks. The idea reflected Roosevelt's professed love of the countryside and cultivation, and doubtlessly was conceived to raise him to Theodore Roosevelt's stature as a conservationist. Franklin would go TR one better by deploying an army in the wild. "Look here!" he told Moley. "I think I'll go ahead with this, the way I did on beer."

This unnerved the dour Moley, who considered Roosevelt's message on beer, undertaken seemingly on impulse and without a moment's consultation with informed advisors, hair-raisingly precipitous. Imagining the complexities involved in sending hundreds of thousands of young boys into the wilderness armed with nothing but shovels, Moley tried to stall Roosevelt by urging him to consult with Perkins, Wallace, Ickes, and Secretary of War George Dern, whose cabinet departments would have to be involved in any effort to recruit workers for regimented labor in the hinterland. He offered to draft the memo outlining the proposal. Roosevelt consented, but instructed him to get it done without delay.

The memo and a skeleton bill went out to the four secretaries that very afternoon. The next day they returned a joint response proposing a wider relief program, encompassing not only a Civilian Conservation Corps, but a public works program and grants-in-aid to states and municipalities for relief. Yet no one missed the signs that the CCC was the provision closest to the President's heart and the repository of his most grandiose aspirations. "His enthusiasm for this project, which was really all his own, led him to some exaggeration of what could be accomplished," Perkins reflected. "He saw it big. He thought any man or boy would rejoice to leave the city and work in the woods."

The cabinet members hastened to complete an outline of the conservation program in time to meet the President's deadline for its submission to Congress within a week. To Roosevelt, the thought was the thing; the details he was content to leave to his aides. "And there were some difficult details," Perkins recalled: how many recruits there should be, where they should come from, how much they should be paid (labor leaders objected to unskilled workers being paid below union scale), how the camps were to be built and kept safe. Adding to the program's complexity was its novelty. This was to be the first interdisciplinary agency of the New Deal, and the mutual sensitivities of four cabinet departments would have to be carefully oiled over.

Ultimately the decision was made to launch the program with up to a quarter-million recruits selected from relief rolls in cities and rural communities. Pay was set at one dollar a day plus lodging and food—low for wages but high in comparison to conventional relief payments—with up to twenty-five dollars of every month's wages to be paid directly to the laborer's family at home. The Agriculture Department's Forest Service would plot out the work assignments in consultation with relevant branches of the Interior Department; the Labor Department would handle recruitment; and the U.S. Army would handle the logistics of transporting, clothing, and moving the men.

The table was therefore set for Roosevelt's message to Congress on March 21. In deference to the cabinet, he paid lip service to a public works program, an expensive venture about which he was deeply skeptical. What he requested immediately was a Civilian Conservation Corps, to be used for "simple work, . . . confining itself to forestry, the prevention of soil erosion, flood control and similar projects." Assuming an evangelical tone, he observed that "more important . . . than the material gains will be the moral and spiritual value of such work. . . . We can take a vast army of these unemployed out to healthful surroundings." The greatest dividend, he observed, was the elimination of the threat posed by enforced idleness to the "spiritual and moral stability" of the nation.

There were misgivings among special interests. American Federation of Labor President William Green told a joint House-Senate committee that the measure smacked "of fascism, of Hitlerism, of a form of sovietism." Yet such sentiments seemed mere cavils when judged against the wave of public gratitude for this first jobs program of the New Deal. Congress debated and passed the Civilian Conservation Corps in eight days.

By early April the CCC was open for business. The first registrant was nineteen-year-old Fiore Rizzo of New York, who arrived on April 7 at an army recruiting station in downtown Manhattan in a cab with three friends. They could muster only 50 cents among them to pay the taxi driver's 65-cent fare, so an army captain chipped in the rest.

Rizzo belonged to a family of thirteen whose father had not worked in three years. Inside the recruiting depot he signed a chit allowing the government to pay twenty-five dollars of his monthly wage to his family, submitted to a very cursory physical exam, raised his hand to swear an oath, and was directed to a bus bound for an army post in Westchester County. There he was issued two sets of work shirts, trousers, underwear, socks, shoes, and blankets, mostly in army olive drab, and given two weeks of conditioning. His ultimate destination would be a wooded camp somewhere in the Deep South.

Among New Deal programs, the CCC would inspire almost universal affection, even more so than Social Security. To the end of their lives its "boys" would recall with palpable fondness the experience of physical labor in the outdoors, shared with youngsters very much like themselves yet very different: country boys and city boys, teenagers and young adults, many of them separated from their families for the first time and certainly living farther from home than they ever could have imagined. The average enrollee signed up at age eighteen and a half, stayed for nine months (six months was the minimum tour, two years the maximum), and gained up to thirty pounds during his term, thanks to the three meals a day served up by the army quartermasters as fuel for eight hours of daily labor. For many boys this was more abundant fare than they had ever seen, a full stomach being as novel an experience as the indoor plumbing and electricity of the CCC barracks.

The program ramped up quickly. By July there were 1,300 camps housing nearly 275,000 enrollees, already working vigorously on projects that would rank among the most notable legacies of the New Deal: before CCC ended with the coming of war mobilization in 1942, it would build 125,000 miles of road, 46,854 bridges, more than 300,000 dams to check erosion, plant 3 billion trees, and string 89,000 miles of telephone wire.

A more important achievement may have been the corps' knitting together of a generation of young Americans into a patriotic fabric that would be ready, less than ten years hence, for war. The camps instilled in many of these young men the concept of an American identity, an indefinable quality common to boys from rural Tennessee and teeming Canarsie. No doubt the camaraderie was fostered by shared resentment of the camps' martial regimen, the rising with the bugler's call, the mandate to keep their bunks and footlockers in order, the heeding of senior officers without discussion. The army, too, found the experience valuable. As War Secretary Dern confided to Perkins a year into the program, his officer corps had had to learn "to govern men by leadership, explanation, and diplomacy rather than discipline. That knowledge is priceless."

Franklin Roosevelt never tired of visiting CCC camps every time he ventured out to the countryside, often dragging along Ickes or Harry Hopkins for a ride up remote trails for lunch with the boys in the open air. The President was invariably in cheery humor during these excursions, and the army brass in attendance typically fell all over themselves to demonstrate how they were strengthening the youth of America in body and mind. During one such visit a commanding general regaled the President and Ickes with details of the education in trigonometry, English, and even French that the enrollees were receiving in his charge. "There won't be none of these boys leave these camps illiterate," he assured them.

The CCC would serve as a model for national service programs of a later era, such as the Peace Corps, AmeriCorps, and Vista. Like the Tennessee Valley Authority, it would work a lasting change in the American landscape and the American people. "There was pride in the work," one former boy still recalled sixty years later. "We built something, and I knew I helped. . . . It was something you could take pride in, and there wasn't a lot of pride available in those days."

Meanwhile, the emergencies mounted, leaving little breathing room for considered planning or policy making. Once CCC was enacted to meet the instant need for short-term unemployment relief, the New Dealers turned their attention to the equally urgent crisis in the housing market.

Some 250,000 American families had lost their homes in 1932; the following year, foreclosures stepped up to the ferocious pace of a thousand a day. In Philadelphia the journalist Lorena A. Hickok, embarking on a coast-to-coast reporting tour of the Depression for relief boss Harry Hopkins, discovered that unemployment among tenants and homeowners was driving 1,300 properties to sheriff's sales every month, accelerating the deterioration of the inner city. Abandoned houses attracted squatters, who further reduced the properties' condition to the point where "no one who could raise a cent to pay rent would ever live in them." Hickok met an Italian landlord who owned two homes sheltering five families besides his own, "all of whom were on relief and none of whom had paid any rent for many months. Since his rents were his sole income, and that was wiped out, he had applied for relief, but had been turned down." The caseworker, it turned out, resented him for sharing his tenants' relief food.

The Depression exposed a fundamental weakness in the nation's housing market and mortgage system. Like the overheated housing market of modern times, that of the 1920s was based on the assumption that land and home values would steadily rise, effortlessly building up the homeowner's equity. But the standard mortgage was a short-term loan—typically three to five years—in which payments covered only interest. Lenders and borrowers assumed that the loan would be automatically rolled over at the end of each term. The process theoretically could continue forever.

This unexpectedly fragile arrangement collapsed under the pressure of rapidly rising unemployment. The homeowners' failure to build equity left them without a cushion when their household resources dried up, and the mortgages' short terms allowed them to be promptly foreclosed. The effect on the banks holding the mortgages was as devastating as it was on the homeowners: as the income stream dried up, they were forced to dispose of their real estate at fire-sale prices, depressing the market. Homeowners ceased making payments on properties in deeply discounted neighborhoods even as lenders ceased making new loans or renewing the old ones. Buyers remained on the sidelines, waiting for a stabilization in prices that seemed to recede further into the future with every passing month. The typical home, worth $5,000 in 1926, was worth one-third less, or $3,300, in 1932. Values continued to decline into the new year, bringing the middle-class family face-to-face with the ravages of the Depression for the first time.

The Hoover administration had tried to address the crisis by establishing a system of federal home loan banks to provide credit support for mortgage-lending banks and savings institutions. But the remedy was timid and incomplete, in Hoover's fashion. The home loan banks were empowered chiefly to shore up the strongest lenders, not revive those already in crisis; it was a classic case of delivering the medicine mostly to patients who could show they had no need of it. And in terms of direct aid to tottering homeowners, the home loan bank system was an empty shell: in the first two years of the system's existence, it received forty-one thousand applications from individual borrowers for direct loans. Three were approved.

On April 13, Roosevelt sent to Capitol Hill an aggressive solution to the crisis in the form of "a declaration of national policy" that home ownership needed to be preserved "as a guarantee of social and economic stability." His solution was the Home Owners' Loan Corporation, or HOLC. Operating as an arm of Jesse Jones's Reconstruction Finance Corporation,

HOLC was capitalized with $200 million in congressional funding and authorized to raise another $2 billion in the bond market. Its purpose was to take under- or nonperforming mortgages off the banks' books and convert them to fifteen-year self-amortizing mortgages carrying an interest rate no higher than 5 percent. The plan was aimed firmly at the middle class: no loans were to be made on properties valued at more than $20,000. (That sum would be the equivalent of about $340,000 eighty years later.) No mortgage could be issued for more than 80 percent of a property's appraised value or for more than $16,000.

HOLC dramatically restructured the home mortgage market in the United States. The short-term, permanently renewing loan that kept the borrower at the mercy of his lender was relegated to history's dustbin, supplanted by long-term loans providing borrowers with a concrete path toward free-and-clear home ownership. Lenders benefited, too, acquiring stability of assets absent under the old system. The bill reached the President's desk for signature on June 13, three days before the end of the Hundred Days Congress.

In contrast to the home loan banks, HOLC injected itself deeply into the home ownership market. In its two years of active lending (through June 1935), the agency refinanced more than one million loans worth a total of $3.1 billion, approving about two-thirds of all applications. By the time it ceased active lending, HOLC held the mortgages of fully one-fifth of the nonfarm owner-occupied homes in the nation. It would foreclose on fewer than 200,000 properties. Despite Congress's expression of concern in 1933 that the government might lose $1 billion on the scheme, when the corporation closed its books in 1948 it was in the black, showing a profit of $11 million.

Through HOLC, the New Deal transformed home ownership. Yet the venture would serve as another signpost of the New Deal's poor record of follow-through on its nimble solutions to the immediate crises of the Hundred Days. For the creation of the Home Owners' Loan Corporation represented not only the first effort by the Roosevelt administration to address the housing crisis, but virtually the last. And its failure to build on the glittering success of HOLC would bear dire consequences a few short years hence.

The New Deal's growing momentum encouraged progressives to push for programs scorned during twelve years of Republican rule. One of these men was Republican senator George Norris of Nebraska, whose long-deferred dream was to secure for public benefit the hydroelectricity generated by an underutilized wartime dam built in Muscle Shoals, Alabama, at the western end of the Tennessee River Valley. The river basin stretched from Virginia to Mississippi, encompassing 640,000 square miles of frequently flooded territory—the poorest section of the poorest region in the country.

Norris's Muscle Shoals bill had passed Congress twice, only to be vetoed by Presidents Coolidge and Hoover, both foes of public power—ironically in the case of Hoover, namesake of the Colorado River dam that would become the largest publicly owned hydroelectric plant in the country. But Roosevelt, like Norris, saw public power as an indispensable counterweight to the profiteering of the power trust, that centralized web of holding companies dictating the pace of agricultural and industrial development in communities large and small and from coast to coast by virtue of their ability to decide where to run their transmission lines and how much to charge. As New York governor, Roosevelt had jousted with the power trust over his plans for the public development of hydroelectric power on the lower Great Lakes and the St. Lawrence River, especially after he determined that private utilities were charging the average New York family as much as six times the monthly rate paid by residents of the neighboring Canadian province of Ontario, which operated its own public power system.

As President-elect, Roosevelt summoned Norris to Warm Springs to map out a plan for Muscle Shoals. On his return to Washington, Norris was asked by reporters, "Is he really with you?" Dazzled by the grandeur of Franklin Roosevelt's vision, the seventy-one-year-old campaigner allowed his melancholia to lift for the first time in a dozen years: "He is more than with me, because he plans to go even farther than I did."

For reporters, Roosevelt outlined a program of public development that evoked his distinguished cousin's 1907 dream of developing the West by harnessing the Colorado—a plan nearing fruition in 1933 with the impending completion of Hoover Dam. The Tennessee Valley project, Franklin Roosevelt assured his audience, would be "probably the widest experiment ever conducted by a government." It would include reforestation of the barren hillsides and construction of flood control reservoirs across the watershed, the generation of up to three million horsepower of electricity at Muscle Shoals and much more at dozens of other dams to be built, the dredging of a ship canal from one end of the valley to the other, and jobs for two hundred thousand men. "We have been going at these projects piecemeal ever since the days of TR," Roosevelt said. "I believe it is now time to tie up all these various developments into one great comprehensive plan."

On April 10, Roosevelt asked Congress to create the Tennessee Valley Authority, decrying "the continued idleness of a great national investment." (Muscle Shoals's Wilson Dam and its two associated nitrate plants, built between 1918 and 1924, had cost the government $88 million.) The project Roosevelt had first laid out in Warm Springs was to operate under the guidance and planning of "a corporation clothed with the power of Government but possessed of the flexibility and initiative of a private enterprise." TVA would be only a start, Roosevelt said. If it succeeds "we can march on, step by step, in a like development of other great natural territorial units within our borders."

The TVA Act was delivered for Roosevelt's signature by the Hundred Days Congress on May 18, passed overwhelmingly despite some grumbling that it regimented development like "one of the soviet dreams," in the words of a congressman from Massachusetts. Decades later, critics of the TVA still would be insinuating that its creation "snuffed out a growing—and potentially successful—effort to light up the South" by private utilities. To the destitute residents of the Tennessee Valley, no such effort was visible. Of the region's nearly three million residents, fewer than three hundred thousand were served by electricity. In parts of the valley, only one farm out of a hundred had power. The per capita income of $163 was less than half the national average. Industrial development was stagnant, and city and countryside alike were charged profiteering rates on a take-it-or-leave-it basis by private companies that had divided up the region into service areas, each one a monopoly. The state regulatory bodies appointed to oversee the fairness of utility rates and the effectiveness of service were uniformly outgunned and easily outmaneuvered by regulated companies operating on a national scale.

The power trust, then the best-financed and most powerful industry in the country, was not inclined to take lying down the threat to its franchise from a huge public generating program. The utilities had been fighting public power since the Twenties and had developed an impressive arsenal of weapons. These included bribery of public officials, the creation of public "citizens' committees" as fronts to oppose state and municipal public power legislation, the distribution of school textbooks that played up the role of the utilities in building America, even the acquisition of small-town newspapers to secure favorable editorial positions.

The utilities' tactics had been exposed in hearings by the Federal Trade Commission in the late 1920s—in time to thwart the industry's campaign against the government's Boulder Canyon Project (the future Hoover Dam). But they were dusted off for the war against TVA. "Widow-and-orphan" letters—many of them instigated or even drafted by the utility companies—poured into the White House and congressional offices, attesting to the threat to family sustenance if the utilities' dividends were cut. The president of one leading regional holding company, the Commonwealth & Southern, proclaimed at a congressional hearing that if the bill were to pass, "$400,000,000 worth of securities will eventually be destroyed." That executive's name was Wendell Willkie.

At forty-one, the Indiana-born Willkie was the youngest head of a major utility company in the country and in many ways the most publicly appealing. The Commonwealth & Southern was a utility holding company on a grand scale, controlling thirteen subsidiaries from Michigan south to Florida, including companies in every Tennessee Valley state except Kentucky and Virginia; but it was widely viewed as the best of a bad lot, not given to plundering shareholders and customers on quite the scale of such public villains as Chicago's Samuel Insull.

Willkie was a Democrat and a moderate, by some standards even a liberal. He had voted for Al Smith in 1928 and—though he had initially backed Newton D. Baker for the Democratic nomination for President—for Franklin Roosevelt in 1932. He had made a name for himself as a skilled courtroom litigator at the Akron, Ohio, law firm where he apprenticed, which happened to have as its leading clients several Ohio utilities that would eventually become swept up into the gravitational field of the newly formed Commonwealth & Southern. He moved to New York just before the 1929 crash to become legal advisor to the new holding company, and in 1932 was named its president. In that role he became the power trust's point man in its battle against the TVA.

Willkie never lost his midwestern twang or his Hoosier bearing, which was represented by his slightly rumpled appearance and an untamable black forelock. But under the surface lay a core of hard-edged New York determination. The package would provoke ridicule from his political adversaries during the TVA fight and later, when he became Roosevelt's GOP challenger in the presidential election of 1940. "A professional country boy" was the *New Republic*'s description of Willkie in 1938. A nastier gibe came, characteristically, from Harold Ickes, who called Willkie "the barefoot boy from Wall Street"; a more measured assessment came from Raymond Moley, an old friend, who described Willkie's assets as his "singular charm, his breathless energy and his abounding faith in himself."

After failing to derail the TVA bill in Congress, Willkie and the power trust shifted their campaign to the Tennessee Valley itself. Mindful of a TVA policy against duplicating existing private utility lines, the power companies strung networks of "spite lines" bisecting TVA rights of way or blocking access to homes or factories. In some communities the TVA's prospective new customers, irked at finding utility linemen on their property after years of neglect, ejected them at gunpoint.

The power trust's main strategy was to try to intimidate the fledgling TVA into becoming merely a supplier of electricity to the big utilities in the valley, a scheme that would leave the utilities' monopolies in place and shrink the TVA's role to a fraction of what was envisioned by Roosevelt and Norris. This strategy played out in a series of meetings between Willkie and David E. Lilienthal, who projected the mild exterior of a public affairs attorney that was as deceptive as Willkie's Hoosier bluffness. Illinois-born and, like Willkie, Indiana-raised, Lilienthal had been appointed one of the TVA's three original directors by Roosevelt. A protégé of Felix Frankfurter's at Harvard Law School, he had made his reputation as a campaigner against utility profiteering while serving as a commissioner of the Wisconsin Public Service Commission; but he also earned the enmity of the power trust, which connived to deny him reappointment when his initial term on the commission ended in 1933.

On the TVA board he joined Arthur E. Morgan, the president of Ohio's Antioch College, a dam engineer and a man with a pronounced utopian streak, who had been named chairman, and Harcourt Morgan (no relation), an agricultural expert who was president of the University of Tennessee. Their first task was to work out the TVA's relationship with the incumbent utilities of the Tennessee Valley. Arthur Morgan, who had been in office for weeks before the appointment of his fellow commissioners, had conducted the first meetings with the power trust. Morgan was inclined by personality to see things the utilities' way, and was thus inclined to cut generous deals with them on power marketing. Soon after the first board meeting, however, Lilienthal and Harcourt Morgan constrained the chairman's authority by voting to divide the board's responsibilities in three according to their personal interests: Arthur Morgan was to concern himself with the social development of the valley, Harcourt Morgan with agriculture, and

Lilienthal with electrical development. Arthur Morgan resented this assault on what he saw as his broad portfolio as chairman, but he was outvoted two to one. The seed of a violent and lasting conflict within the board was planted.

Lilienthal scheduled his first meeting with Willkie in early October amid the faded elegance of Washington's Cosmos Club, which he judged to be neutral ground. "We were two exceedingly cagey fellows who met at lunch that noon . . . [for] very definite fencing," he would recall. Willkie began by thrusting at Lilienthal a proposal for the Commonwealth & Southern to buy all the power TVA generated at Wilson Dam on a ten-year contract for $500,000 a year. The authority should jump at the offer, Willkie insisted, because TVA's $50 million congressional appropriation likely was the last federal assistance it would ever get. The public was sure to start objecting to excessive government spending any time now, Willkie explained; at that point the TVA would be stuck without resources, without prospects, and without customers.

Such was Lilienthal's introduction to the blustering side of Wendell Willkie. The most potent weapon in the executive's arsenal, Lilienthal soon learned, was the veiled threat, repeated frequently, that Lilienthal should play ball now if he wanted to preserve any chance of obtaining a lucrative private sector job after his inevitable departure from government service. Lilienthal reflected: "This was so crude that I always made it a point to . . . pretend he was talking about somebody else." In any event Lilienthal understood that turning over its electricity to Willkie would throttle TVA at birth. He rejected the overture flat.

A few weeks after Lilienthal's initial meeting with Willkie, the city of Tupelo, Mississippi, became the first municipality to sign a power contract with the TVA. The deal occasioned a civic celebration marked by a parade down Main Street and put an ace in Lilienthal's hand. At their next meeting, Lilienthal informed Willkie that if the Commonwealth & Southern denied TVA the use of its power lines to deliver electricity to Tupelo at a reasonable price, it would build its own grid, an ultimatum Willkie greeted with "a good deal of bellowing and acting." But the tide was turning: TVA was on its way to becoming a competitive counterweight to the power trust. Before the end of the year, utility commissioners in Georgia and Alabama exploited the threat of obtaining alternative power from the TVA to extract rate cuts of up to a third from their private power companies; utilities serving Memphis and Chattanooga slashed their rates voluntarily; and the people of Knoxville, Tennessee, overwhelmingly approved a $3.2 million bond issue to construct power lines connecting with the TVA at the city limits.

Across the Southeast, rates fell so sharply that residents and businesses started thinking up new ways to use electricity—a situation that had been unimaginable only a couple of years earlier, when electrical power was viewed as a luxury to be used sparingly. New electric appliances appeared in homes—refrigerators, washing machines, water heaters—due in part to a TVA program subsidizing their purchase. Ownership of electric appliances tripled overall. "The old fear of the electric meter began to disappear," *Harper's Monthly* reported. "People became conscious of living in a modern electrified world." By 1935 power rates were 30 percent below the national average across the region, which became home to the seven utilities with the highest average power use in the country. All were subsidiaries of the Commonwealth & Southern. Willkie had warned Lilienthal in 1933 that TVA would never find a ready market for its power; by 1936, the demand for electricity from Willkie's company was so great that the Commonwealth & Southern could not meet it without purchasing excess generation from the TVA. Late that year, the progressive Congressman Maury Maverick of Texas pronounced TVA "an outstanding success of the administration." The agency's "national implications are colossal, stupendous, mighty, great. . . . The TVA is not an 'experiment.' It is a part of American life; it is here; it will stay."

The truth, however, was somewhat more complicated. TVA certainly served as Roosevelt's "yardstick" against which to measure the power trust's rates, but how broadly the comparison could be pushed was open to question. The TVA was authorized to build multipurpose dams to serve the federal government's multitudinous purposes—not merely power generation, but flood control, irrigation supply, and river navigation. These services conveniently subsidized each other. Private utilities, by contrast, were constrained to build for power generation alone. Moreover, despite how much the Tennessee Valley's superb hydroelectric potential was a boon to its government exploiters, it was matched in precious few other regions of the country (one being the lower Colorado River, site of Boulder, or Hoover, Dam). As for the retail end of the power business, TVA electricity typically was distributed to customers by nonprofit municipal agencies enjoying a tax exemption, another factor skewing price comparisons in the authority's favor.

As it happens, Willkie's own utility had devised a program to lower rates in early 1933, but had not managed to roll it out before the TVA took the stage. By early 1934 the new rate plan had been widely implemented across Commonwealth & Southern's southeastern service districts, which allowed Willkie to maintain that the company's own rate policy had produced its remarkable growth, and that the TVA had been irrelevant. This theme was soon picked up by the business lobby, which came to depict the TVA as not a paragon of beneficial government planning but rather a hindrance to the natural functioning of competition and free enterprise. Left to itself, the argument went, the free market eventually would have produced lower rates without government interference. This view reduced the TVA at best to an agency suited for the exploitation of topographies that lent themselves to multiple uses, such as public waterways with hydroelectric potential, but perhaps not for other places or other climes. The same debate would arise, time and time again, over New Deal initiatives in many other economic spheres and other parts of the country. Yet the TVA would stand alone. After completing its first dam, named for George Norris, in 1936, it would build or acquire twenty-eight more, complete a 650-mile shipping channel along the Tennessee River, and eventually move into coal, natural gas, nuclear, and solar power generation. The entire Tennessee Valley, transformed by this vast program, would be the grandest tangible legacy of the New Deal.

4

WALL STREET IN THE DOCK

LYA GRAF WAS a thirty-two-year-old, twenty-one-inch-tall performer with the Ringling Bros. and Barnum & Bailey Circus, which lately had pitched its tents in Washington. On June 1 she arrived on Capitol Hill in a blue satin dress, a red woven straw cap framing her pixie's face, and in the company of Charles Leef, a circus press agent with a nose for opportunity.

By the end of the day a photograph of J. P. Morgan, Jr., with the beguiling midget Lya Graf seated on his lap would be transmitted around the world, destined to become the most enduring image produced by the U.S. Senate investigation of Wall Street launched that spring.

Leef had escorted Graf to a Senate lobby teeming with reporters and news photographers gathered to witness Morgan's testimony. During the desultory wait for the proceedings to get under way he led Lya into the hearing room. "Gangway!" he cried. "The smallest lady in the world wants to meet the richest man in the world!"

Jack Morgan, ever courteous and perhaps a tad absentminded at the age of sixty-five, instinctively stood to shake Graf's hand. Then he took his seat, and Leef plunked the performer on his lap.

"I have a grandson bigger than you," Morgan stammered as flashbulbs popped.

"But I'm older," she replied.

"Lya, take off your hat," Leef suggested.

"No, don't take it off," interjected Morgan. "It's pretty."

In the end, the encounter profited neither participant. Lya Graf, unable to shed the mortification of having become a player in a national joke, returned to her native Germany in 1935 and, with tragic timing, resumed her real name, Lia Schwarz. The Nazis arrested her as a "useless person" in 1937 and in 1941 sent her to Auschwitz, where she died in the gas chamber.

Jack Morgan, meanwhile, proved incapable of exploiting the episode to soften his public image as a proud, somewhat detached plutocrat. In private, he groused repeatedly about the very idea that, as the scion of Wall Street's most distinguished clan, he should be hauled before a tribunal and grilled by someone with "the manner and the manners of a prosecuting attorney who is trying to convict a horse thief."

The interrogator in question was Ferdinand Pecora, fifty-one, the immigrant son of a Sicilian cobbler. Pecora had launched his career in public service with a Tammany patronage job in the New York district attorney's office. There he quickly emerged as the office's most dogged prosecutor, the scourge of bucket shop racketeers and political grafters. In 1932 he was hired as chief counsel to the Senate Banking Committee by its new Democratic chairman, the patrician Duncan U. Fletcher of Florida, who felt overmatched by the challenge of investigating Wall Street on his own. Under the previous Republican majority, the committee's investigation of the 1929 crash had drifted aimlessly. The resumption of hearings in the new year and Fletcher's appointment of the "kinky-haired, olive-skinned, jut-jawed lawyer from Manhattan," in *Time*'s supercilious phrasing, endowed it with an electric charge.

The appearance of Morgan and his partners was the star turn of the hearings in early 1933, but they were Act Two. In the opening act, which unfolded in the two weeks prior to Roosevelt's inauguration, Pecora eviscerated Charles E. "Sunshine Charley" Mitchell, the chairman of National City Bank (the historical forebear of Citigroup, the fortunes of which would ebb in a much later economic downturn), for a nationwide audience. Mitchell's bank had pioneered the move from commercial banking—taking deposits and making loans—into investment banking and brokerage. National City was duly transformed into "a gigantic monument to Mr. Mitchell's super-salesmanship, his limitless energy, and driving genius," Pecora later observed.

That was a rare charitable judgment from Pecora about a man he placed in the dock for eight days. Through the testimony he elicited from Mitchell and his associates, Pecora succeeded in casting the nation's largest bank as an impeccably groomed racketeering enterprise. He showed how they dressed up crooked and incompetent enterprises to appear gilt-edged. For example, they marketed a $16,500,000 bond issue for Brazil's Minas Gerais state by vouching for its "prudent and careful administration," despite possessing in their files a letter from the bank's own agent remarking on the "complete ignorance, carelessness, and negligence" of the state's leadership. Pecora documented how the bank pressured small investors into risky ventures, loaded them down with stock loans in the overheated markets of the Roaring Twenties, and left them penniless when the tide ran out.

Most spectacularly, he cornered Mitchell into admitting that he had avoided paying income tax in 1929 by contriving a $2,800,000 loss on National City stock by selling it to "a friend . . . a person of some means," from whom he bought it back in 1932 at the same price. The buyer, it transpired, was Mitchell's wife. Mitchell relinquished his post at National City a few days after this disclosure, and was indicted later in the year for tax evasion. (He was acquitted of the criminal charges but was forced to pay a million-dollar civil judgment to the government.)

After a three-month hiatus to allow the Hundred Days Congress to deal with the new administration's legislative workload, Pecora was back behind the committee table on Tuesday, May 23, with Jack Morgan in the dock. At first Morgan received rather more solicitous treatment than Mitchell, as befit the descendant of a storied family whose business, unlike that of the swashbuckling commercial banker who preceded him, was conducted in such dignified privacy that his firm's door at 23 Wall Street bore only an inconspicuous nameplate.

It was about to be brought into the light, however. "Until last Tuesday," Arthur Krock would observe in the *New York Times,* "Mr. Morgan was a legend."

Despite being hammered by Pecora, Morgan never shed his air of noblesse oblige, remaining always "courteous to a degree and co-operative in his attitude," the prosecutor later acknowledged. "His was the attitude of a man who, far from having any guilty secrets to hide, manifested a pride in his firm and its works which was obvious and deeply genuine."

Sitting next to his august counsel, John W. Davis, a former Democratic candidate for president, Morgan in his opening statement maintained "without hesitation" that he considered private banking "a national asset and not a national danger." The professional banker's stock in trade was "the confidence of the people in his character and credit . . . not financial credit, but that which comes from the respect and esteem of the community."

Pecora proceeded to dismantle that respect and esteem. The reality was that J. P. Morgan & Company did not merely follow the directives of its private clientele, but functioned as an instrument to concentrate wealth and power. Yet by holding itself out as a private concern, it was able to remain exempt from public supervision and regulation.

"But you are serving the public?" Chairman Fletcher inquired of Morgan.

"We are serving only our own clients who are our clients by their own choice," came the reply.

"But you do not turn a man down," Fletcher persisted. "I suppose if I went there . . . and had $10,000 I wanted to leave with the bank, you would take it in, wouldn't you?"

"No; we should not. . . . Not unless you came in with some introduction, Senator."

The web of influence spun by the partners and their "friends" was large: the firm's twenty partners held among them 167 directorships in eighty-nine corporations with assets totaling $20 billion—"incomparably the greatest reach of power in private hands in our entire history," Pecora stated.

Morgan maintained that power through outright gifts to men and families of influence, Pecora demonstrated. The mechanism was the "preferred lists," rosters of favored clients and friends who were offered shares in Morgan-financed companies at prices well below the public market. The public disclosure of these names caused no end of embarrassment for the beneficiaries, who included grandees of both political parties, ex-president Coolidge, Charles Lindbergh (whose father-in-law, Dwight Morrow, was a Morgan partner), and even Senator William Gibbs McAdoo of California, who was a member of the very committee sitting in Morgan's judgment. McAdoo hastily explained that he was not a client of the firm but a personal friend of Morgan partner Russell C. Leffingwell, and that his three preferred investments taken together had produced a net loss of $2,565.

The Morgan partners scrambled to deny that they had expected any quid pro quo, financial, political, or otherwise, from anyone on the lists in return for the near guarantee of profits.

"You did not give them this price so that they would reciprocate and keep on good terms?" Senator James Couzens asked skeptically.

"No; really," replied Morgan partner George Whitney.

"I never heard of anybody quite so altruistic in my life before," Couzens said.

The most discomfited individual named was Treasury Secretary William H. Woodin, who was shown to have taken the firm up on its offer of one thousand shares of Alleghany Corporation for $20 each in February 1929, when their price on the open market exceeded $35. "There are no strings tied to this stock," a partner observed in his letter to Woodin, "so you can sell it whenever you wish. . . . We just want you to know that we were thinking of you. . . ."

Woodin felt sufficiently mortified to place before the President and cabinet—"the members of the family," he called them—the question of whether he should resign. The matter took up a full hour of discussion on May 26, two days after his name emerged in Pecora's hearing room. The strongest voice for resignation was that of Vice President John Nance Garner, who said his concern was that the public would believe that the House of Morgan was dominating the current administration as it had dominated its predecessors.

Roosevelt seemed unperturbed, observing that what looked unethical today had been routine in business in 1929. Ickes seconded that point, adding that at the time of Woodin's purchase he had never served a day in public life and never expected to; so there could have been no question of Woodin's having been offered the gift by Morgan as a bribe or inducement.

That was not true of other names on the preferred list. Ickes pointed the finger at Norman H. Davis, a wealthy and well-traveled Democratic figure who was at that very moment representing the White House at a disarmament conference in Geneva. Ickes noted that Davis had served in public life and expected to continue doing so when he accepted the House of Morgan's gratuity. This made Davis a "distinct liability" to the administration, Ickes rumbled on, the more so because he was openly arguing for closer relations with Europe, a policy that would put money in the pockets of Morgan and his fellows on Wall Street.

The connection, indeed, was not lost on the sizable isolationist bloc in Congress, whose leader, Hiram Johnson, complained that Davis was maneuvering in Geneva to saddle the United States with a moral obligation to enter a European war. Johnson observed the day after Pecora released Davis's name: "The pity of it is that [the decision] has been made by the House of Morgan."

Woodin and Davis both survived the scandal. But the Morgan firm's reputation for probity was shattered, not merely by its dispensing of favors but by the even more explosive disclosure that its partners had effectively avoided paying income tax for 1930, 1931, and 1932. They achieved this feat largely by applying investment losses in earlier years to later income, but the maneuver was facilitated by indulgent examiners at Treasury's Internal Revenue Bureau. As Pecora established, the bureau spent one single day examining the partnership return of J. P. Morgan & Company and its subsidiary, Drexel & Company of Philadelphia, for the year 1930. On another occasion, the return of a Morgan client was accepted without any questions when it was learned that it had been prepared by Morgan & Company. "It has been our experience that any schedule made by that office is correct," the examiner noted.

Pecora's dogged examination of Morgan brought him into conflict with the committee's most important expert on banking affairs, Senator Carter Glass of Virginia. Glass, curiously, established himself as a personal champion of Jack Morgan, asking whether Pecora's questions were designed to help "in enacting legislation or . . . are just in the form for a court inquiry?"

The conflict between senator and investigator soon overshadowed the confrontation between investigator and witness. Glass portrayed himself as protecting the dignity of the Senate and the fairness of its inquiry, no matter how lofty or low its target: "I do not intend to see any injustice done to the house of Morgan or any other house, whether it be of large consequence or of little consequence or of no consequence," he declared. "I am not afraid to do J. P. Morgan & Co. justice, and if they have done anything they ought not to have done I am not afraid to legislate accordingly."

When a particularly pungent remark from Glass provoked Pecora to threaten to resign—"The compensation of $255 a month which I am receiving for these services certainly is no incentive to me to render these services," he said—the gallery erupted with prolonged applause and cheers of support.

"Oh, yes; that is what it is all about," Glass fumed. "We are having a circus, and the only things lacking now are peanuts and colored lemonade." (More applause.)

And in the fertile mind of a Ringling Bros. publicity man, a seed was planted. When the hearing reconvened a few days later, Lya Graf would be on hand.

The revelations from the Pecora hearings propelled the passage of two Hundred Days measures tightening regulation of the financial industry. These were the Securities Act of 1933, enacted May 27, and the Glass-Steagall Act regulating the banking industry, enacted just before Congress adjourned on June 16.

Roosevelt proposed a federal statute regulating the sales of securities and based on the principle of disclosure with a message to Congress on March 29. The goal was to replace the patchwork of state "blue-sky" laws that protected investors from unscrupulous stock promoters. (The old coinage was commonly attributed to a Kansas state legislator bemoaning the sales in his state of shares backed by "nothing but the blue skies.") "This proposal adds to the ancient rule of *caveat emptor* ["let the buyer beware"] the further doctrine 'let the seller also beware,'" Roosevelt stated. "It puts the burden of telling the whole truth on the seller." It emphatically would not guarantee that any new issue would be financially sound, much less profitable, he said.

Bringing the stock market under federal oversight had been an important plank in the Democrats' 1932 platform and was placed high on the agenda of the New Deal. The inspiration was the carnage of the 1929 crash as well as the tales of financial piracy emanating from Pecora's hearing room.

Roosevelt had asked Commerce Secretary Daniel Roper to start the drafting effort. Roper delegated the task to Huston Thompson, a former Federal Trade Commission chairman with a traditional progressive's mistrust of big business. In mid-March Thompson produced a bill imposing stringent disclosure rules on sellers even of previously issued shares. He awarded authority to the FTC to enforce disclosure, even allowing the commission to retroactively revoke a securities registration if it concluded there had been material falsehoods in its prospectus or the underlying business was "unsound." Aggrieved investors were empowered to sue any corporate officer or director for violating the rules.

Roosevelt declared himself pleased with the product; he especially appreciated the broader regulatory role for the FTC, an agency he was determined to wean from its reactionary, probusiness past. Other progressives hailed the draft's heightened civil and criminal liability for officers and directors. William O. Douglas, then teaching at Yale Law School, dis-

missed conservatives' cries that the measure would lead to wholesale res-
ignations by corporate board members. The prospect that lazy or crooked
directors would be culled from the boardroom was "highly commendable,"
he declared. "The fact of the matter is that too many directorships have
become social badges or advantageous trading posts."

FDR sent the draft to Congress on March 29, accompanied by his message proclaiming the new principle of *"caveat vendor."* Yet once it reached
Capitol Hill the bill's flaws quickly became evident. Thompson was an
energetic regulator but an incompetent legislative draftsman, his measure
"a hopeless and unintelligible confection," in Moley's words.

Those portions that were comprehensible were widely abominated
by business leaders, bankers, stock traders, and members of Congress. A
prominent critic objected that Thompson's registration structure, in which
registration became effective immediately but could be revoked by the FTC
if problems surfaced later, "operated only to lock the barn door after the
horse had been stolen," presenting a threat "so dire and so unpredictable"
to sellers that it might drive investment bankers out of the business. That
might please the masses, but it would create an undesirable bottleneck in
the capital-raising process. The bill was simultaneously too inflexible and
too vague, specifying a laundry list of disclosure violations that could warrant revocation or subject corporate officers to civil and criminal penalties,
but leaving most of those violations unnervingly ill-defined. After a week
of hearings, Sam Rayburn of Texas, the chairman of the House Committee
on Interstate and Foreign Commerce, informed the White House on April
5 that the bill was doomed unless it could be completely rewritten.

The very next day, Moley sent up an emergency flare to the only person
he knew capable of rescuing the legislation. The man of the hour was Felix
Frankfurter.

Frankfurter's position as one of Franklin Roosevelt's preeminent advisors
was no less unassailable for being controversial. The controversy stemmed
in part from his role in the celebrated Sacco-Vanzetti case, the murder
trial of two Boston anarchists. Frankfurter had led the unsuccessful campaign for a retrial before the men were executed in August 1927. Although
the campaign would encourage some critics to identify him as a fellow-
traveling radical, Frankfurter's goal had not been to endorse the defendants'
political leanings, but to overturn a trial he saw as a blot on Massachusetts

jurisprudence—a trial in which, as he wrote in the *Atlantic*, "the District Attorney invoked against [the defendants] a riot of political passion and patriotic sentiment; and the trial judge connived at—one had almost written, cooperated in—the process."

The Vienna-born Frankfurter had reached Harvard Law School in 1902 via City College of New York, which was then tuition-free. After receiving his degree he spent two months in a Wall Street law firm, then moved to the U.S. attorney's office in Manhattan under Henry L. Stimson, who was later to become secretary of war for Presidents Taft and Franklin Roosevelt and secretary of state for Herbert Hoover. The experience gave Frankfurter a lifelong taste for public service and brought him under the sway of Supreme Court Justice Oliver Wendell Holmes and the future Justice Louis D. Brandeis, who became his friends and mentors. In 1918, when he served as chairman of the government's War Labor Policies Board, he grew close to the Navy Department's young delegate to the board, Franklin Roosevelt.

With Brandeis's help Frankfurter was granted a faculty appointment at Harvard Law School in 1919, and there he remained, notwithstanding frequent trips to Washington to advise presidents, until FDR placed him on the Supreme Court in 1939.

Frankfurter dominated the intellectual life of the law school; only the brightest students were accepted into his favor, which provided them with more than the opportunity to bask in his fellowship and intellectual glow. There was the Frankfurter employment service, his ability to exploit a circle of friends, former students, and admirers in New York and Washington to secure his best students positions of profit and power. They were known as Frankfurter's "happy hot dogs," and by the score they filled the ranks of presidential administrations from Taft forward. Frankfurter was, a *New Yorker* writer reflected, "an Influence, a prodigious and pervasive one, working upon men and situations in every part of the country."

Not everyone in the New Deal trenches appreciated Frankfurter's seemingly unlimited sway. Exasperated by his interference on the drafting of one important bill, Adolf Berle—himself no diffident kibitzer—griped to Roosevelt that "[t]ypically, F.F. comes in at the last minute with many ideas . . . none of which could be got into legislative shape in less than a year . . . ; but will take no responsibility for getting anything done. . . . Which explains why, in his long and interesting career his opposition has been brilliant, but his ideas have never been brought to fruition." Berle signed his note, "Yours truly, in a mean state of mind, with considerable admiration of F.F.'s public career and an intense personal desire to see him shot."

Frankfurter arrived in Washington the morning after Moley's emergency phone call. With him were two of his happy hot dogs, Benjamin V. Cohen and James M. Landis. A third, Thomas G. Corcoran, was already in the capital, having been placed by Frankfurter's recommendation in the legal counsel's office of the Reconstruction Finance Corporation during the Hoover administration. The three were strangers to one another when Frankfurter summoned them to his side. Singly and as a group, their influence on the New Deal would be incalculable.

Of the three, the thirty-nine-year-old Cohen was the oldest and boasted the most varied professional résumé. He had spent two years in Europe after the Great War as an attorney for the Zionist movement, then returned home to work as a banking and securities attorney during the Twenties boom (and as an investor and trader, to be nearly bankrupted in the crash). Meanwhile he accepted the occasional assignment from Frankfurter, including the drafting of a minimum wage bill for New York state in 1923 and a railroad reorganization bill in 1932.

Landis, Cohen's junior by five years and two days, was a boy wonder on the Harvard Law faculty. After spending a year clerking for Brandeis at the Supreme Court, he had been appointed the school's first professor of legislation. Unlike Cohen and Corcoran, his background was almost entirely academic, but he was a first-rate legislative technician with a superhuman capacity for work.

The outlier of the trio was Corcoran, thirty-three, a native of Pawtucket, Rhode Island, whose leprechaun's visage and predilection for playing Irish tunes on the accordion during social occasions could not mask his cracker-jack legal mind. He had clerked for the revered Justice Holmes, then spent five years in a prominent Wall Street law firm, until Eugene Meyer of the RFC appealed to Frankfurter for help finding a general counsel. Corcoran arrived, as it were, in the next post.

Landis had been near at hand, his office just down the corridor from Frankfurter's in the law school's Langdell Hall, when Moley had called. It was a Thursday, Landis remembered, and his next classes were scheduled for the following Monday, but Frankfurter told him the job could be finished over the weekend. Landis would not return to full-time service at the law school for five years.

After disembarking from the night train in Washington, Landis had his first opportunity to meet Cohen, with whom he would spend weeks in a legislative pressure cooker, drafting an important statute under the glaring eyes of powerful lawmakers and influential Wall Street lawyers. "I was told he was a most brilliant man, knowledgeable in the field of securities, and that he possessed a gentle personality. My information was correct," Landis wrote years later, glossing delicately over the intense personal conflicts that arose between him and Cohen during the drafting process. He could afford to be more candid about the pairing of Cohen and Corcoran, one of the most lasting and important professional relationships in New Deal Washington: "It was a strange team—Corcoran ebullient, moving easily with the new forces in the administration; Cohen reserved and almost shy; but both brilliant and indefatigable workers."

Sam Rayburn's mandate, Corcoran later recounted, was that they "write a good bill and write it fast." Landis and Cohen holed up in a suite in the Carlton Hotel, a block from the White House, emerging only for meals. Corcoran would join the other two bachelors after every day's work at the RFC and throw himself on the bed for all-night drafting sessions. "I memorized the designs on the ceilings and drank so much sugar in my coffee I came away weighing 245 pounds," he recalled. The suite directly above them was occupied by Pecora's witness J. P. Morgan, whom they regularly encountered on the elevator and who could not have known that his anonymous traveling companions were plotting to remake his profession dramatically.

Landis and Cohen, who took the lead in redrafting Huston Thompson's bill, followed Frankfurter's suggestion that they base their work on the English Companies Act of 1929, the most recent version of an antifraud statute dating back to the South Sea Bubble of the eighteenth century. True to Frankfurter's forecast, they had a workable, if hasty, version completed by late Saturday night, structured for reasons of diplomatic draftsmanship as a package of "perfecting amendments" to Thompson's bill.

The new draft retained the FTC as its regulatory instrument. But it made one essential change in the regulatory scheme: rather than give the agency authority to revoke share registration retroactively in cases of inadequate disclosure, it imposed a waiting period of thirty days between a new issue's registration and the start of trading. In the view of the authors this concept had several virtues. It would eliminate the kind of high-pressure sales campaigns that enticed unwary investors into making snap purchases; it would give the FTC a much stronger weapon against dishonest issuers—the threat to keep the shares entirely off the market; and it would give dealers and underwriters some assurance that once permission was granted for a stock issue to trade, it could not be rescinded.

Landis, Cohen, and Corcoran also improved Thompson's liability scheme, at once tightening and broadening his proposal. They limited stock issuers' liability to civil and criminal claims to cases in which the issuers made knowing omissions or misstatements of material facts. But they imposed responsibility not only on a corporation's directors and top executives, but also on accountants, lawyers, appraisers, and other professionals whose contributions were material to the disclosure statement. They made no secret of the fact that their goal was to raise the "ethical and professional standards of the accounting profession" and foster the creation of a body of generally accepted financial reporting standards. Indeed, the raising of standards in corporate accounting and law through this new regulatory regime would become one of the most important legacies of the New Deal.

Their work was so effective that Rayburn was able to call a committee meeting for Monday, three days after the Harvard team's arrival, forcing Landis to put off his classes for another day. That morning the draftsmen breakfasted with Thompson, who listened with conspicuous skepticism to their assurances that they had merely appended a few "perfecting" amendments to his bill. Later that morning Frankfurter led them into the committee room and proceeded, in a "brilliant performance," to explicate the new bill for the congressmen. The session yielded more work for Cohen and Landis, who were now asked to create a final version. Landis believed his return home would be postponed by only a few more days. The delay stretched into two months, in part because of a severe personality conflict between the equally high-strung and intellectually self-confident Landis and Cohen.

After four rewrites, the bill was finally ready to be presented to Rayburn's committee, when Wall Street threw up one last obstacle by insisting that a select group of securities lawyers be given an opportunity to pick it apart before the subcommittee. This session took place on a Saturday morning, with Rayburn presiding and Cohen and Landis in attendance. Heading the Wall Street delegation was John Foster Dulles, whose aristocratic mien could not obscure the fact that he had not bothered to read the bill. Nevertheless, he declared that the measure would "utterly destroy the securities business and the country with it," a statement of such surpassing fatuousness that an exasperated Rayburn brought the meeting quickly to a close. He instructed Landis and Cohen to incorporate a few minor technical amendments offered by the Wall Street delegation and placed the bill on the fast track to passage.

The measure sailed through the lower house on May 5 with "virtually no dissent," Cohen reported to Landis. "When it was all over, Rayburn remarked that he did not know whether the bill passed so readily because it was damned good or so damned incomprehensible."

There remained several weeks of legislative maneuvering. The Senate passed the Thompson bill, the author of which was no longer under any illusion that Frankfurter's team had merely "perfected" it. ("The brain trust crowd has ruined my bill," he grumbled to the White House.) The differences were ironed out in a joint conference committee masterfully controlled by Rayburn, creating a final version passed easily by both houses and signed into law on May 27.

The Securities Act of 1933 shared the flaws of several other Hundred Days measures. It was hastily drawn and imperfect, a "jerry-built" contrivance designed as much to fulfill Roosevelt's political commitments as to fill glaring regulatory gaps. It imposed enormous regulatory responsibilities on an agency utterly unprepared to shoulder them, and avoided some of the most pressing issues in the field, such as regulation of securities exchanges. Though its passage had been greased by Pecora's revelations, it was poorly designed to address the more flagrant frauds he had unearthed. William O. Douglas might have been pleased that it would drive inept directors out of the boardroom, but he was also frustrated that many of the "horrible examples of the last decade" would have no trouble meeting its technical requirements: "The oil well scheme, the gold mine venture, the holding company set-up, or the investment trust, in fact, any enterprise which is just beginning or whose activities, assets, and relations are simple, has no difficulty in registration. . . . [G]o through the Senate hearing in the Pecora investigation and observe how slightly the Act would have touched those exhibits in our Hall of Horrors."

On the other hand the measure established the bedrock principles that officers and directors of stock-issuing corporations owe full disclosure to the investment community, and that oversight of this obligation is prop-

erly the province of the federal government. Roosevelt managed to achieve
this by pushing for the act before Wall Street could mobilize itself for effective opposition. Nor did he demand more than he thought the financial
community would accept without a fight. "It is conservative rather than
extreme," Adolf Berle observed a few days after the bill signing. "The protection it gives is rather minimum than maximum." Its criminal sanctions
were unique in federal law, he noted, but for that reason they were likely
to be used only rarely, and therefore play a smaller role in keeping issuers
honest than the civil penalties the act imposed.

"The main problem," Berle acknowledged, "is still to be tackled." By
this he meant the manipulation of securities after their initial offering, by
traders, self-interested corporate executives, and jobbers of every description. The battle to close those barn doors lay a year in the future, by which
time those whose interests were threatened would be much better prepared
for the fight.

The Glass-Steagall Act had a more distinguished pedigree, and a more
painstaking gestation, than the Securities Act. Carter Glass and Henry
Steagall had drafted a similar measure for the lame-duck session of early
1933, only to be forced to shelve it because of the President-elect's lack of
interest in mustering congressional Democrats for passage.

The Pecora disclosures gave the bill new life. Among the chief evils the
investigation had uncovered was the extent to which commercial banks
had frittered away credit on "hasty and ill-judged speculation in stocks
and bonds," many of which they had engineered for their own profit and
at the expense of their customers and depositors. Glass-Steagall addressed
this through the expedient of requiring commercial banks to divest their
investment banking arms.

This provision evoked squeals of outrage from the bankers, though it
was not the bill's most controversial. That distinction went to the creation
of deposit insurance.

Roosevelt had connived at the death of deposit insurance during the
interregnum, when his signals of opposition to a measure passed by the
House guaranteed its tabling in the Senate. But the dream had not died,
especially among politicians from rural states, who saw it as a means to
protect their single-branch banks from encroachment by money-center
behemoths. The day before the inauguration, a delegation headed by Vice
President–elect John Nance "Jack" Garner bearded Roosevelt in his suite at

the Mayflower. Their hope was that the thunder of banks crashing all about them would finally bring Roosevelt over to their side.

He remained adamant. "It won't work, Jack. The weak banks will pull down the strong," he said, repeating the favorite argument of the New York banking establishment.

"They are all about down now anyway, the weak and the strong," Garner replied. "You will have to come to a deposit guarantee eventually, Cap'n."

As Glass's omnibus banking reform act made its way through the special session, the small bankers favoring deposit insurance kept up the pressure. Their hand was immeasurably strengthened by Pecora's exposure of big-city bankers like Charley Mitchell as rapacious frauds. On May 27, Republican senator Arthur Vandenberg of Michigan took to the floor to read out the *Philadelphia Record*'s editorial gloss on the fresh "preferred list" disclosures. The newspaper warned of "an America without small banks, an America whose credit would be controlled by a few men pulling the strings from New York—the sort of men who weave a net of influence by letting important people in on 'favors.'"

The solution, Vandenberg and his fellows maintained, was to strengthen the position of small banks by guaranteeing their deposits. Only a week earlier, Garner had conspired with Vandenberg to get the latter's deposit insurance amendment into the Glass-Steagall bill. During a lull in the Senate's impeachment trial of federal judge Harold Louderback of San Francisco for bribery (he would be acquitted of all charges), the Vice President had sidled over to the Republican side of the chamber. "Where's that deposit-insurance amendment of yours?" he asked.

"It's never been out of my pocket," Vandenberg replied.

"Well, I am going to suspend this court in a few minutes and recognize Carter Glass," Garner said. "I want you to get on your feet and get your amendment out of your pocket, and I think we can get it in the bill. . . . I don't think he will fight your amendment too hard."

Vandenberg's proposal, which was overwhelmingly approved, was one of the more modest versions of deposit insurance to reach the floor. It limited coverage to $2,500 per depositor beginning January 1, 1934 (raised to $5,000 on July 1), to be paid by premiums from covered banks, which would have to submit to regulatory inspections by a new Federal Deposit Insurance Corporation. But its impact was earthshaking. Bank failures did not entirely disappear, but they became a rarity, rather than a cyclical occurrence. In 1933 there were four thousand bank failures in the United

States; in 1934, following the enactment of deposit insurance, sixty-one—of which only nine were insured banks. This occurred not because the health of the banking sector had improved drastically or because a new regulatory agency came on the scene, but because depositors now had confidence that their money was safe even if their bank failed, which prevented the metastasizing runs that had helped cripple banks across the nation in early 1933. The new system, the economists Milton Friedman and Anna Schwartz would write, "succeeded in achieving what had been a major objective of banking reform for at least a century, namely, the prevention of banking panics."

Glass-Steagall was not fundamentally a New Deal bill, but another product of an essentially conservative legislative approach that happened to address an immediate demand—for medicine to cure the self-destructive habits of a hitherto unregulated industry. It was an improvisation, like so much else in the Hundred Days. But it would work.

5

AGONY ON THE LAND

ONE DAY IN late May of 1933 a farm wife named Ida Gadbois took pen to paper. "On the 22nd day of this month my 80 acre farm four miles from Sioux City on the paved highway was forclosed," she wrote from Jefferson, South Dakota. "We have thirteen reasons to save our home we have thirteen children the oldest is fifteen, we surely belong on the farm with this size family, for we sure would starve in the city. . . . The party who forclosed is a rich man and wants this farm. In the name of the Almighty and the whole family please help us if possible."

Mrs. Gadbois's letter was addressed not to Franklin Roosevelt but to Milo Reno, a lion-maned orator who had spent years organizing farmers' "strikes"—localized blockades of city-bound shipments of food and livestock—with the goal of raising the prices of farm commodities to a level that at least matched the cost of production. Letters like hers had been pouring into Reno's office as well as into the White House and the Department of Agriculture, for the economic agony afflicting the nation's farm families had become unsupportable. Unlike the downturn in the industrial sector, the agricultural depression was not an artifact of the 1929 crash; on the farm, the Great Depression was then well into its second *decade*.

The roots of the farm crisis resembled those of the stock market crash only superficially: overproduction, loose credit, speculation, and what a later generation would term "irrational exuberance." But its fundamental triggers dated back to the collapse of agricultural production in Europe during the Great War, and the ramping up of American production after 1914 to take up the slack. "In Europe seventy million men had been withdrawn from productive labor to kill and destroy," observed agricultural journalist Russell Lord. The breadbasket lands of central Europe had been trampled under the boots of troops on the move or scarified by the trenches of armies in stagnant equilibrium. The allies required 600 million bushels of U.S. wheat a year, a demand that America's wartime food czar, Herbert Hoover, fulfilled by guaranteeing farmers high prices. To provide protein for the stricken allies, Hoover had achieved a dramatic scaling up in production of hogs, which mature much faster than cows, by promising hog producers a healthy profit on a cost-plus basis. The boom fed on itself: land prices soared to $500 an acre, a price that could be rationalized only by continued unbridled production. During the war, higher production dependably begat higher profits. In 1917, Iowa crops returned 10–15 percent on the value of the land, as much as five times the prewar yield.

The land mania in the heartland redoubled, drowning out the few cautionary voices. Henry Wallace, the future agriculture secretary, warned in his family's venerable journal *Wallace's Farmer* that declining land values after the war "will ruin thousands of young farmers who have tried to buy high-priced land with a small payment down." He further predicted that once the natural balance of land values, farmhand wages, and food prices in the cities reasserted itself, the harvest would be depression, unemployment, and "misery to nearly all classes."

For the first few weeks after the armistice on November 11, 1918, demand for foodstuffs to feed a devastated and starving Europe continued to rise. Then, abruptly, conditions changed. Shortly after New Year's Day, Great Britain, France, and Italy canceled their American pork orders, leaving nearly 400 million pounds of meat, much of it already on the high seas, bereft of a market. Hoover kept the cancellations secret for fear of provoking a panic, so hog production disastrously continued at nearly three times the prewar rate. But the evaporation of demand presaged that prices would fall by as much as a third. In August 1920, the land and commodity markets duly cracked.

By March 1921, when Henry C. Wallace, the future New Dealer's father, took office as Warren Harding's agriculture secretary, the farm depression was in full cry. Total farm income had peaked at $17 billion in 1919; in 1920 it had fallen by nearly a third, to $12 billion. That was twice the farm sector's prewar income, but not nearly enough to support land and production costs that had soared into the stratosphere. Sharpening the farmers' agony was the sensation of having plummeted from a prosperous height. During the war boom American farmers became accustomed to well-kept homes and household luxuries; but over the next decade the farmhouses fell into disrepair and the luxuries were put aside. Vanished, too, was the farmer's cherished independence, for the farmer who lost his land to fore-closure became a tenant, tilling what was once his own in indenture to an absent landlord. In Mrs. Gadbois's home state of South Dakota, the population had included 40,000 farm owners and 36,000 tenants in 1920. By 1933, the proportions had reversed, for 10,000 former owners were now miserably sharecropping.

Adding to the crisis, the cost of equipment, fuel, and other industrial supplies remained obstinately high. The purchasing power of the farm dollar fell to 78 percent of its level before the war, that halcyon period now viewed as an era when commodity and industrial prices were in equilibrium—or "parity," to use the preferred term. Throughout the Hoover years, parity receded to a distant memory. When Franklin Roosevelt took the oath of office in March 1933, agriculture seemed to have plunged into an abyss from which there was little hope of rescue.

The farm vote had been indispensable to Roosevelt's victory in the 1932 election. The collapse of parity had been a powerful weapon in his campaign against Hoover, who, as FDR reminded farm voters, had been "the dominant factor in our governmental economic policies" for a decade. Even before the Democratic convention Roosevelt was insisting that the restoration of parity was not only necessary to rescue the farmer from destitution but also to rehabilitate the market for industrial goods, declaring in his famous "forgotten man" speech of April 7, 1932, that without the restoration of "purchasing power to the farming half of the country . . . the wheels of railroads and factories will not turn." On the campaign stump he returned to the issue again and again, notably in his farm policy speech in Topeka, Kansas, in September, when he observed that "the things that our farmers buy today cost nine percent more than they did before the World War in 1914 [and] the things they sell bring them 43 percent less." This was not news, of course, to his audience.

Through the Twenties the farm lobby's preferred solution to stubbornly low commodity prices was for the federal government to buy up farm surpluses at a high fixed price and dump them overseas at whatever price the market would tolerate, leaving the American taxpayer to eat, so to speak, the difference. This idea became known as McNary-Haugenism, after the sponsors of a series of bills to authorize the policy, Senator Charles McNary of Oregon and Representative Gilbert Haugen of Iowa. McNary-Haugenism engendered an almost religious fervor across the farm belt but was predictably unpopular in the cities, where it seemed to guarantee only high prices at the grocer's and butcher's. The first McNary-Haugen bill was rejected by both houses of Congress in 1926. A successor passed in 1927, only to be vetoed by Calvin Coolidge. Coolidge dismissed the principle as "government price fixing . . . an economic folly" in an extraordinary ten-thousand-word veto message that would have destroyed his reputation for taciturnity had it not been widely understood to have been written for him by his commerce secretary, Herbert Hoover. Congress passed yet a third version in 1928; Coolidge vetoed it, too. Once Hoover reached the White House the McNary-Haugen movement gave up the ghost in Washington, but its specter still stalked the farm belt.

The farm crisis confronting Tugwell and Wallace when they took office after the inauguration was not only deep, but dizzyingly complex. The problem was not merely the loss of parity between farm incomes and the cost of industrial goods, but a welter of agricultural economic models that were all dysfunctional, but in different ways. The economic model of corn differed from wheat, feed crops from livestock, dairy cows from hogs, the Midwest from the South. The most complex system, and the one most resistant to reform, involved cotton. The plantation economy was based on the remorseless exploitation of the Negro sharecropper, who was kept in destitute thrall to his landlord by the latter's ownership of the tenant's land, mule, and plow, his stranglehold on capital, and his claim to one-third to one-fourth of the sharecropper's production. As a pair of economists traveling the dusty byways of Texas and Oklahoma reported during the summer of the Hundred Days,

> on each fifteen- or twenty-acre patch stood a board cabin, containing one room and a kitchen, unpainted and unchained against the winter frosts. In these cropper cabins live families of five or more; the average is seven. Working in the cotton patch at the doorstep could be seen the whole family, from six to sixty. Their clothing was a patchwork of old scraps sewn together. Bare feet were the rule, relieved occasionally by rude sandals made of bits of burlap bagging. An old straw sombrero topped the costume.

The likelihood that even dramatic improvements in farm income might trickle down to these people was minuscule.

Every farm interest had lobbyists ensconced in Washington, bolstered by the tender mercies of their regional congressmen. The most formidable figure in this group was George N. Peek. Like Hugh Johnson, the granite-jawed Illinoisan had been an acolyte of Bernard Baruch at the War Industries Board. After the armistice he became president of Baruch's Moline Plow Company, where he hired Johnson as his general counsel. The company soon failed due to the collapse of its agricultural customers' access to the capital needed to buy farm implements—a vivid illustration of the parity crisis. But Peek's view of the possible remedies began and ended with the McNary-Haugen approach of cultivating surpluses and dumping them overseas. Indeed, he had drafted the original McNary-Haugen bill and served as its most assiduous promoter in Congress. He was a hard-boiled conservative who had been provoked by the GOP's nomination of Hoover, whom he labeled "the arch-enemy of a square deal for American agriculture," to swing his allegiance to the Democrats and Al Smith in 1928 and transfer his support to Roosevelt in 1932.

Not one to underestimate his own importance, Peek believed he was destined to be named Roosevelt's agriculture secretary. Given the New Dealers' mistrust of Baruch, that was an impossible dream. Still, Peek's command of agricultural issues guaranteed him some perch in the new administration, from which he was sure to be an irritant to whoever got the secretaryship. "For Peek the world was a sharp black-&-white drawing," observed a wartime colleague who summed up his personality as "impetuous, impatient, impulsive, explosive, restless, driving." It would be especially unfortunate that the new agriculture secretary was Henry Wallace and his assistant would be Rex Tugwell, for Peek regarded both of them with undisguised condescension.

Another agricultural clique was led by Henry Morgenthau, Jr., the son of a public-spirited businessman and a gentleman farmer in Dutchess County, New York, where he was a close neighbor of Franklin Roosevelt. Morgenthau fancied himself a farm expert and harbored, like Peek, the dream of appointment as secretary of agriculture. His intellectual mentor was George Frederick Warren, a professor of farm economics at Cornell, whose pet theory was that the key to resolving the farm crisis was to reduce the gold value of the dollar—which he preached would raise prices and restore parity. But although it had been clear from the earliest deliberations over cabinet choices that Morgenthau was never under serious consideration as secretary, Roosevelt was loath to snub a family friend openly. He therefore granted Morgenthau an informal brief as his representative in Wallace's and Tugwell's consultations with farm leaders, in which capacity he tended largely to get in their way. The experience, indeed, left Tugwell with an enduring disdain for Morgenthau, who he thought "cultivated Franklin [Roosevelt] assiduously" to obtain assignments for which he was unqualified. As Morgenthau "was not an original thinker," Tugwell added, his mind became "monopolized" by Warren's theory to the exclusion of all other ideas. The Warren plan was not taken seriously as a foundation of farm policy by Tugwell or Wallace. Before long, however, it would wreak its peculiar mischief on New Deal monetary policy.

Henry Wallace, who would be tasked with charting a way out of the crisis, was an exasperating figure even for admirers such as Tugwell. Wallace's braininess, which his enemies so easily caricatured, was the quality that Tugwell, his university-bred factotum, found particularly appealing. "He carried pictures of statistical tables in his mind; he thought in exact quantities; and his mind moved outward to the enlarged consequences of small facts and occurrences with ease and rapidity"—the very qualities one should seek in a policy maker, Tugwell believed. Yet Tugwell could not help but feel frustrated at Wallace's diffidence. "Wallace did not yet feel or act like a cabinet member," he recorded. "He took shyly to his large office and sat uneasily sideways at the big desk in the center. He looked at first as though he had just strayed in from somewhere and wanted nothing so much as to find a way out. . . . I had little enough sophistication about proper official behavior, but Wallace was quite hopeless." This diffidence would not last; before the Roosevelt administration ended Henry Wallace would emerge as one of its most ambitious and politically sophisticated members and, for four years, its vice president.

Wallace's talent was for incisively analyzing farm conditions. Having sounded the alarm about overproduction in the early Twenties, he perceived that this habit still lay at the root of the commodity price depression. As a remedy he advocated forcible reductions in farm output. That this made him an unpopular figure in many agricultural districts did not lead him to change his views. "It so happens that sincere idealists, *laissez faire* economists, and certain business groups interested in volume unite in urging unbridled production," he lectured the audience at the 1934 convention of the National Grange. "Resolutely they refuse to admit that surpluses, by wrecking prices, can destroy farmers without contributing one iota to feeding and clothing the needy."

Wallace and Tugwell understood that whatever solution was to be applied to the farm crisis, it must be applied without delay. They pleaded with Roosevelt to submit a farm relief bill before the special congressional session of 1933 adjourned. There were several considerations behind their appeal: First was the submissive Congress's inclination to grant Roosevelt virtually anything he asked. Second was the possibility of enacting dramatic farm reform without excessive debate while the nation's attention remained focused on the banking emergency. Finally, time was of the essence, for every new planting season was another lost opportunity—"We can't legislate next June for a crop that was planted in April," Wallace observed.

Their strategy was to finesse the riotous competition among proposed solutions by bundling them all together in an omnibus bill and empowering the secretary of agriculture to choose among them as he wished. There would be provisions for the marketing of surpluses overseas as well as a protective tariff to mollify Peek and the McNary-Haugenites; direct price subsidies, as demanded by a camp pressing for government assistance (funded by a processor tax that would weigh, unfortunately, on the strapped urban consumer); and even hints of dollar devaluation to create general inflation, one of the most popular nostrums in the farm belt.

But to those who knew Wallace's and Tugwell's minds, the keystone was plainly a provision known as "domestic allotment." In its purest form, this entailed paying farmers to take land out of production. It was the brainchild of Milburn L. Wilson, a wheat expert at Montana State College who had been flogging the concept in Washington since the winter of 1931. Wilson had piqued the curiosity of Hoover's Federal Farm Board, but the notion of paying farmers to go fallow was as yet so alien that the board's interest quickly waned. Wilson had the ear of Henry Wallace, however, who brought the concept to Tugwell's attention during the 1932 campaign.

To Tugwell its virtues were instantly evident. For one thing, domestic allotment would attack the surpluses at their source, the habit of overproduction left over from the war years. It had none of the drawbacks of McNary-Haugenism, which was based on what Wallace and Tugwell viewed as a string of dangerous fantasies: that foreign countries would accept dumped commodities without retaliating with tariffs, that their own production would not naturally recover under postwar conditions, and that uncontrolled production would not eventually result in a global collapse of prices.

Finally, allotment would work hand in hand with the institution of national land planning, a goal that had absorbed Tugwell ever since he took a six-week tour of the Soviet Union in 1927 with a group of American trade unionists. There he had become fascinated by Soviet efforts to improve the almost medieval conditions of the Russian peasantry by establishing production quotas and consolidating fragmented landholdings. Although Tugwell was skeptical that the Soviets could easily modernize peasant culture, he believed that political and economic conditions in the United States might be better suited to centralized agricultural planning. American farmers were unburdened by the crushing backwardness of Russia and blessed with superior access to technology and scientific research. After hearing Tugwell expatiate on the subject, Roosevelt agreed to incorporate the concept of land planning in his acceptance speech at the 1932 convention. Tugwell accordingly provided Ray Moley, the chief speechwriter, with a passage in which Roosevelt could allude vaguely to "such planning of [farmers'] production as would reduce the surpluses and make it unnecessary . . . to depend on dumping those surpluses abroad."

The idea was more explicitly developed for Roosevelt's Topeka speech. Moley estimated that at least twenty-five advisors collaborated on this all-important outline of New Deal farm policy, but its centerpiece on domestic allotment came from M. L. Wilson, Henry Wallace, and Tugwell. "I favor a definite policy looking toward the planned use of the land," Roosevelt said in the address. Any such planning would be voluntary, he assured his listeners, but it would involve generous subsidies for fallowed land so that farmers would have powerful economic incentives to participate.

Soon after the election, Wallace and Tugwell started drafting a farm relief bill with domestic allotment at center. During the long postelection interregnum, however, opposition to the policy had begun to jell—not only from Peek's McNary-Haugenite lobby, but from Morgenthau's circle, which was skeptical of any plan that involved reducing production while want still afflicted the nation.

These two pockets of resistance notwithstanding, Wallace and Tugwell achieved consensus over their omnibus bill by summoning fifty farm organization leaders to Washington on March 9 for a two-day conference. This was a canny move, for it gave the squabbling leaders the impression of having participated directly in the creation of policy and committed them to support whatever legislation emerged. The meeting must have been inde-scribably tedious—Tugwell remarked that the entire first day was wasted as "each leader felt compelled to make a speech for home consumption." But before adjourning, the group issued a "unanimous" communiqué endors-ing an omnibus bill allowing the secretary of agriculture to control produc-tion, market surplus commodities at home or abroad, levy taxes either at the farm or the processing plant to fund the price support system, and, as a catchall, exercise "all powers necessary to the successful carrying out of the purpose to be achieved."

The bill, Russell Lord observed, was "fantastically elastic," legalizing "almost anything anybody could think up." But the Peek camp knew that they had been routed, for it was evident that domestic allotment would be the farm policy of choice in the New Deal. Reading FDR's acceptance speech at the convention in July, Hugh Johnson had been convinced that Roosevelt could be turned into a McNary-Haugenite. "We will get what we want," he had wired Peek. "Hold all fire." But once the farm relief bill was introduced in Congress, Johnson had a different view: "The farm bill breaks my heart," he wrote to Moley. But he offered to help set up its administrative machinery the moment it became law.

That moment was tragically long in coming.

The true owners of economic power in the farm sector were the middle-men—"packers, millers, shippers, converters, brokers," in Tugwell's formu-lation. They had been caught short by the speed with which Wallace and Tugwell had rallied the farmers' lobbyists around what was to be known as the Agricultural Adjustment Act and by the alacrity with which the House of Representatives passed the measure on March 22, six days after its introduction and virtually without debate. The Senate, which was more responsive to the wishes of the economic establishment, gave the processors time to regroup by dawdling over the measure for fifty days.

For a time it looked as if the farm bill would perish from the delay. The farm belt, quiescent since the inauguration, again grew restive at the lack of action. Reports reached Washington of a surge in armed confrontations at farms and courtrooms over foreclosure attempts. The most spectacular eruption came April 27 in Le Mars, Iowa, when a crowd of six hundred farmers stormed the courtroom of District Judge Charles C. Bradley, who had flatly refused to sign a pledge to reject all foreclosure applications. When the sixty-year-old judge defied the crowd by ordering them to take

off their hats and put out their cigarettes—"This is my court!" he barked—
he was dragged from the bench, beaten, threatened with lynching, and ultimately abandoned at the side of a road, stripped to the skin and begrimed
with axle grease. "That's not his courtroom," explained a local spokesman
for Milo Reno's Farmers' Holiday Association. "We farmers paid for it with
our tax money and it was as much ours as his." The next day, martial law
was declared in Le Mars and five adjacent Iowa counties.

Reno meanwhile was threatening to call a nationwide farm strike for
May 13. The call seemed destined to be widely heeded; letters were pouring
into his Des Moines headquarters bristling with the desperation of disenfranchised and dispossessed farmers. Reno's threat goaded the Senate into
action. The chamber passed the AAA on May 12, after adding an amendment sponsored by Senator Elmer Thomas of Oklahoma authorizing the
President to inflate the dollar by coining silver, printing money (creating
a devalued class of currency known as "greenbacks"), deliberately devaluing the dollar by reducing its gold content, or, in an analog to the catchall
provision of the AAA itself, undertaking any inflationary method he chose.

The measure almost foundered on Roosevelt's staunch opposition to
Thomas's original amendment, which placed virtually no limits on possible
inflation. But the President relented when it was rewritten with specific
limitations on his authority. The House and Senate spent a few more days
ironing out their technical differences in conference, and Roosevelt signed
the bill on May 22.

In many ways the Agricultural Adjustment Act was a typical product
of the Hundred Days Congress. It was a hodgepodge passed in the heat
of emergency, inadequately debated, taken mostly on faith, and in its delegation of authority to the executive branch broad beyond measure. Its
constitutionality was questionable but not deeply examined by the drafters
or lawmakers. It expressed no particular theory of government beyond the
necessity of action and experimentation. It was a work in progress from
introduction to passage and well into implementation; although Wallace
and Tugwell had a relief plan in their own minds, divining their intentions
from the bill's text was next to impossible. It could be all things to all men,
a quality that the New Deal of the Hundred Days regarded as a virtue,
and it provoked suspicions about its true nature that Congress consciously
repressed in the name of getting something, anything, done. As Tugwell
observed while the bill was still awaiting a final vote, "For real radicals . . .
it is not enough; for conservatives it is too much; for Jefferson Democrats it

is a new control which they distrust. For the economic philosophy which it represents there are no defenders at all. Nevertheless, in spite of everything, it will probably become law." And it bought time, which was one of the governing impulses of the Hundred Days.

Like many other New Deal bills, the AAA was a sort of treasure chest. One of its less-remarked provisions allowed for the refinancing of hundreds of thousands of farm mortgages.

The government's refinancing efforts had been hopelessly fragmented, with pieces of the whole nested inside five separate agencies. Roosevelt had assigned the task of untangling the program to Morgenthau, partially as a means of relieving Wallace and Tugwell of his unwanted presence. Morgenthau proved an able and effective farm credit administrator, moving promptly to consolidate government farm credit operations under his own authority. Empowered by Title II of the Agricultural Adjustment Act, he would reduce the interest rate on 400,000 mortgages held by federal land banks to 4.5 percent from 5.5 percent, saving the mortgagees some $55 million over the next five years. Then, following the lead of HOLC, he assumed $2 billon in farm mortgages held by banks, insurance companies, and other private institutions in exchange for government-guaranteed bonds. The condition was that the principal on the mortgages had to be slashed to no more than twice the current appraised value of the property. The exchange thus brought mortgages issued during the speculative euphoria of the war years into a rational relationship with Depression values. Interest on the new government-backed loans was also reduced to 4.5 percent from an average of 6 percent, another factor in providing short-term relief to farmers across the Midwest and South and shoring up the condition of banks in the farm belt.

The launch of what became known as "Triple-A" was accompanied by two major blunders, one self-inflicted by Roosevelt and Wallace, the other a consequence of the long delay in AAA's enactment. The first was naming George Peek as director of the new Agricultural Adjustment Administration. In Wallace's view, the appointment carried the twin virtues of mollifying the outspoken Peek and keeping him consumed with work, and therefore out of his hair. Roosevelt viewed the appointment as a sop to Bernard Baruch, Peek's patron. The theory was that Baruch could hardly complain about having no formal role in the administration as long as one of his protégés occupied the hub of agricultural reform. Not long afterward, Roosevelt would double down on this strategy by appointing Hugh Johnson, another Baruch protégé, to head the National Recovery Administration, which fulfilled a function analogous to the AAA's in the industrial sector.

Yet one could scarcely imagine a more disastrous choice than Peek to lead the AAA. For one thing, he was unalterably opposed to crop reduction through domestic allotment. Peek would claim in his memoirs that the preeminence of crop reduction as a reform policy took him by surprise, saying of the act: "I did not have the slightest idea that in its administration it would become principally an instrument to regiment the farmer through acreage control. I had not the slightest idea that it would not be used for the purposes which through the years we had discussed—to open our foreign markets, to sell our surpluses, to improve distribution at home." This is both naïve and tendentious: the primacy of domestic allotment over McNary-Haugenism in the AAA had been thrashed out in public for weeks prior to the act's passage, and nothing in the measure suggested that the "regimentation" of the farmer was its goal.

The hidebound fifty-nine-year-old Peek also found himself constitutionally out of step with the ambitious young men pouring into the capital to join the New Deal. They irritated him with their intellectual arrogance and unnerved him with what sounded suspiciously like radical ideas. "A plague of young lawyers settled on Washington," he remarked. "They floated airily into offices, took desks, asked for papers and found no end of things to be busy about. . . . In the legal division were formed the plans which eventually turned the AAA from a device to aid the farmers into a device to introduce the collectivist system of agriculture into this country."

AAA rapidly became what Russell Lord recognized as "a house divided against itself." The internal conflict was more than one between cosmopolitan city lawyers and seasoned farm agents; it involved totally incompatible visions of farm reform. AAA general counsel Jerome N. Frank, an ally of Wallace and Tugwell, and his fellow citified attorneys saw the AAA at least partially as a consumer-protection agency charged with balancing the demand in the farm belt for parity—that is, higher commodity prices—against the cost of food for the urban consumer, who militated for lower commodity prices. They further believed that they should advance the reform of labor practices on the farm; they hoped to eradicate such vices as child labor in the fields and the abuse of sharecroppers and tenant farmers, whether white or Negro.

By contrast, Peek's administrators tended to be industrialists at heart. They viewed the farm economy through the eyes of landlords and processors, not the tenanting tillers of the soil. With these middlemen they had long since reached a modus vivendi "to get a penny or more for farmers, while the big commercial operators got dollars," Lord observed. In his less diplomatic moments, Wallace was given to referring to Peek's men as "plutocrats masquerading in overalls."

The hallways and offices of the Agriculture Department bristled with tension. Peek set the tone by displaying contempt for the starry-eyed outsiders at every opportunity and deriding them as "a departmental cabal" of utopian socialists bent on destroying the American way of life. He was convinced they met secretly at night to talk "social revolution" and plot the abolishment of capitalism. "They, fanaticlike, believed that their objectives transcended the objectives of ordinary human beings and therefore they could not allow themselves to be hampered by platform pledges, or by the Constitution," he wrote bitterly three years later, looking back on his stint in the AAA. "The tactics pursued were unpleasantly reminiscent of those followed in the setting up of totalitarian governments in Russia, Italy, and Germany."

Such was the atmosphere at the Agricultural Adjustment Administration as it prepared to address its first emergency, which was manifested in two peculiar spectacles that those who lived through the Depression would never forget: the plowing under of cotton, and the slaughter of piglets. They were the consequence of Congress's nearly two-month delay in enacting the AAA.

The measure's passage had come too late to forestall a new planting of cotton and the autumn farrowing of millions of surplus pigs. While there was time for Tugwell's vaunted planning to manage plantings and husbandry for 1934, the only way to reduce production in 1933 was to destroy crops already in the ground and slaughter litters of pigs. The crisis looked so serious that even Peek, averse as he was in principle to reducing production by force, had to acknowledge that harsh measures were warranted for the moment.

The desperation in the cotton lands was palpable. The farm price for cotton, which had peaked at about 35 cents per pound in 1919, had fallen to 6 cents in early 1933, hopelessly beneath the cost of production. That had not dissuaded farmers from planting 10 percent more acres in 1933 than

the year before. Worse (by the perverted standards of the day), they anticipated a bumper crop—the third-best yield per acre ever recorded. "Cursed
by a beneficent Nature," as a newspaperman put it, the cotton planters
braced for a harvest of some 16 million bales. Almost all of this production
was destined to be warehoused along with the existing surplus of 12.5 million bales, which itself exceeded the entire world consumption of American
cotton in each of the preceding three years. There was no way for the U.S.
market to absorb the surplus: cotton goods were durable enough to allow
consumers, who accounted for 60 percent of market demand, to defer new
purchases indefinitely in times of economic want. The other 40 percent
went into industrial goods such as vehicle tires, but demand in those markets also had been sapped by the Depression.

On July 14, Roosevelt signed an order drafted by Wallace allowing the
AAA to pay farmers $120 million to destroy 3.5 million bales, almost a
quarter of the expected crop. On the very day it was issued, Wallace was able
to announce that pledges had already been received from farmers to destroy
the full amount. Money for the bounty was to come from a cotton processing tax of 4.2 cents a pound, levied at the mill and therefore certain to be
passed on to consumers in the form of higher prices. Peek bowed to reality
and toed the administration line, hailing the pledge drive as "the greatest
achievement in the history of American agriculture." The farmer had shown
that he was fully on board with agricultural reform, he proclaimed: "I hope
that those who have accused the farmer of lacking the cooperative impulses
to join in a common cause for the welfare of himself and of his fellowman
will take particular note."

Once the plowing campaign started, however, a wave of buyer's remorse
swept through the cotton belt. Newspapers across the Midwest featured
homely anecdotes illustrating the reluctance of man or beast to eradicate a
mature crop. Pole Mason of Hemphill, Texas, was reported to own a mule
that had been so well trained to walk between the cotton rows without
trampling the crop that it could not now be persuaded to pull the destroying plow over the plants. As a farmer and a politician, Wallace himself was
not immune to the profound distastefulness of his own policy. He found
the sight of living plants being destroyed unutterably painful. Watching
"five tractors drag huge disc plows down rows of boll-laden cotton on a
plantation in the Mississippi delta" (reported the *Arkansas Gazette*), the
secretary became "obviously depressed." The *Gazette* explained charitably:
"Wallace, coming from Iowa, is not a cotton man, but he is a farmer."

His mournfulness was tempered by the knowledge that there had been no alternative. Returning to Washington from his visit to the delta, Wallace reminded the farmers of the harsh realities in a speech. "There are those, of course, who would say to let the weevil at this cotton and trust to luck," he said. "We have been trusting too long to luck. Insects have very small brains. They cannot be counted upon to get us out of troubles of our own making."

Asked if the country might accept the hard medicine more willingly if news photographers and newsreel cameras were barred from the plowed-under fields, he replied that ignoring the reality of overproduction and its consequences would only invite repetition of the same mistakes. "No, we must clear the wreckage before we can build. Rub their noses in the facts."

The plowing under of cotton soon gave way in the public's attention to a more heartrending spectacle. This was the slaughter of more than 6 million piglets and 200,000 pregnant sows, which was to "achieve more notoriety than any other acts of the AAA," Peek observed, accurately.

There could be little question that the forced slaughter of hogs, especially pregnant sows, was the most effective means of ensuring a real shrinkage of hog production in the coming year. But Wallace also understood that it could not be a permanent or recurrent solution—the slaughter was to be a one-time thing. "The real solution must come from the farmers them-selves," he stated during an appearance at the Chicago World's Fair in the summer of 1933. "No fairy wand can be waved over agricultural markets so that they will receive better prices. That thought of the fairy wand stands in the way of progress."

As Peek perceived, the real drawback of the hog slaughter was the dam-age it wreaked on the relief program's image. The spectacle of little piglets being herded to the slaughterhouses of the Midwest bequeathed the agency a reputation for heartlessness it was never to shed entirely. (This was all the more ironic because the plan had been developed by hog and corn producers and processors, not AAA bureaucrats.) Complaints poured into Washington about the suffering of the little pigs at the hands of the AAA. To Wallace, with his farmer's appreciation of the dirty work that went on behind the scenes of the food industry, such sentimentality was absurd. "I suppose it is a marvelous tribute to the humanitarian instincts of the Amer-ican people that they sympathize more with little pigs which are killed than with full-grown hogs," he grumbled impatiently. "Some people may object to killing pigs at any age. Perhaps, they think that farmers should fund a sort of old-folks home for hogs and keep them around indefinitely as barnyard pets."

It was not only among laymen that the crop destruction orders sounded a sour note. By some accounts, half the farmers who signed the government pledges did so only because they were desperate for money. "To the conservative farmer," observed an agricultural correspondent for *Harper's,* "reduction of crops in a world where manifestly people are hungry, if not actually starving, has seemed to be a sacrilege." In coming years, as an elemental drought turned the rich black-earth landscape of the Midwest into the Dust Bowl, it would not be unusual to hear farmers wonder aloud whether their suffering and that of their gaunt, starving cattle might not be God's punishment for their crimes against nature's bounty.

These "were not acts of idealism in any sane society," Wallace wrote later. "They were emergency acts made necessary by the almost insane lack of world statesmanship during the period 1920 to 1932. . . . To have to destroy a growing crop is a shocking commentary on civilization. I would tolerate it only as a cleaning up of wreckage of the old days."

Wallace did take steps to see that the animals' carcasses were put to their highest and best use. Much of the 1.5 billion pounds of pork produced in the slaughterhouses would be given to the unemployed and destitute, he announced, hoping that the step would mollify the public while keeping the meat out of the retail food chain, where it could only depress prices further. As it happened, the piglets whose fate attracted most of the public's hand-wringing were too small for consumption as pork. Their carcasses were converted into inedible by-products such as grease and fertilizer.

Cleaning up the "wreckage of the old days" would take more time and effort than Wallace expected. Since Roosevelt's inauguration, commodity prices had enjoyed a bull market second only to the increase associated with the approach of war in the spring of 1917, based on the assumption that the New Deal would take concrete steps to support farm prices. The rising trend continued for two months before reality reasserted itself. The boom had begun to fade even as cotton farmers were submitting their plow-under commitments and hog farmers were shipping their sows and piglets to the slaughterhouses. From July through September, farmers began to feel caught in an all too familiar vise, as overall farm prices declined by almost 10 percent while prices soared on manufactured goods. The price floor of 10 cents a pound expected for cotton after the plow-under did not hold, in part because nature's bounteous yield on harvested acres overmatched the pace of crop destruction.

Compounding falling prices as a cause of resurgent disaffection in the farm belt was the AAA's failure to deliver promptly on its promises. The plow-under checks for cotton farmers, which had been promised for August, did not begin to arrive until late September. Wheat farmers, who, thanks to the vicissitudes of their planting and harvesting cycles, had escaped the agony of destroying crops in the ground but were promised payments for holding fallow acreage out of production, did not see their checks until November.

The threat of strikes and violence reemerged. Milo Reno, who had moved to the sidelines while euphoria over the coming AAA took root, resurfaced to call a strike in late October. Reno was not above fanning the flames of insurgency by encouraging farmers in their harshest suspicions, as is evident from his reply to a letter he received from Elko, Nevada. The writer maintained that pork processors, who had been expected to pass on to consumers the processing tax imposed to pay for the AAA program, were instead extracting it from the farmers through reduced hog prices.

"I looked up packing house quotations and found a new low price for hogs. Prices down all the way from San Francisco to Chicago," the Nevadan wrote. "Then I realized, under the skillful management of Secretary Wallace, the farmers must pay."

Reno replied, "The whole program of the Brain Trust is in the direction of Russian Communism, German Fascism or Italian Dictatorship. . . . The corn and hog program is . . . surely a bribe in the hopes of quieting the farmer until he could be enslaved."

From the South to the West, pressure returned for "that sovereign remedy for low farm prices: inflation"—more specifically, devaluation of the dollar. "You are becoming very unpopular in the South," a Texas congressman remarked to Roosevelt in late August. He was seconded by House Majority Leader Joseph W. Byrns of Tennessee, who warned by wire, "Situation as to farm prices is critical. I know of nothing that would offer the immediate relief which is needed so badly as a reasonable and controlled expansion of the currency."

Roosevelt hoped to keep his options open. But the clamor for action was becoming irresistible. On October 22, in his fourth Fireside Chat, he struggled to persuade listeners in the farm belt that their condition had improved dramatically through rising prices since his inauguration—though not, he acknowledged, dramatically enough. "I am not satisfied either with the amount or the extent of the rise . . . and it is definitely a part of our policy to increase the rise and to extend it," he said. "If we cannot do this one way we will do it another. Do it, we will."

PART TWO

THE
NEW DEAL
RISING

6

THE GENERAL

E HAD BEGUN crafting his pugnacious legend at the age of four, when his voice could be heard flinging a truculent retort at the teasing neighborhood kids in rural Kansas: "Everybody in the world's a rink-stink but Hughie Johnson and he's all right."

Nearly a half century later he was still at it, sounding the Hughie-against-the-world theme, now as lord of the domain known as NRA—the National Recovery Administration, which he had helped create during the Hundred Days. With the irrepressible General Hugh S. Johnson at its helm, the NRA would burst upon the world like a cannon shell.

Johnson was a shouter, a table pounder, a West Point man with a conspicuous gift for expression of a variety that had not been heard in the mainstream of American politics within living memory. One day after taking command of the NRA he concisely described for the press the daunting scale of the task before him—nothing less than the economic restoration of American industry—and his determination to sacrifice his life in the attempt. "It will be red fire at first and dead cats afterward," he said. "This is just like mounting the guillotine on the infinitesimal gamble that the ax won't work."

Unabashedly he labeled the enemies of recovery "chiselers," "cheats," and "slackers." In September 1933, before ten thousand spectators in New York's Madison Square Garden, he would defend his program against the "prophets of disaster . . . gorged with paper profits." He warned of the "sly and furtive undercut, the sneer, the sarcasm" uttered by the very men "associated with the policies and practices that led this country to the precipice of 1929 and that as we all now know have dragged us through four years [of] as grievous trouble as ever plagued a people."

Though it came early in the New Deal, that speech marked the absolute apogee of NRA, a moment when the General could summon thousands of marchers into the streets to praise his program and force industrialists whose companies he denounced to come groveling to Washington to plead for his approval. Only one dared to openly thwart him: Henry Ford, who groveled to nobody, and whose resistance provoked the General to threaten the industrialist with "a sock right on the nose."

The General brought his theatrics to towns and cities coast to coast, here jawboning recalcitrant chief executives, there settling an outbreak of labor unrest with cajolery and threats. On July 17, a mere month into NRA's life, he unveiled his publicity masterstroke: a nationwide campaign to goad enterprises large and small into staffing up with workers guaranteed a minimum wage. Compliant employers were entitled to display the NRA's insignia on their products and in their shop windows—a stylized depiction of a Native American thunderbird in dark blue, thunderbolts clutched in one talon and a machine cog in the other, over the legend, "We Do Our Part." Should a Blue Eagle establishment be discovered chiseling workers, the General warned, "that blue hawk comes down."

For millions of Americans the NRA was the New Deal incarnate, General Johnson's heavy-lidded, jowly glower the very face of recovery. In 1933, the first year of the New Deal, *Time* named him its Man of the Year, sandwiching him between Franklin Roosevelt in 1932 and Roosevelt again in 1934. In '33, the magazine asserted, General Hugh S. Johnson "burst like a flaming meteorite on the country."

Time forecast that his talk of "chiselers" and "crackdown" and the image of the blue eagle would still be remembered come the millennium year of 2000. Yet while the world today still honors Ickes, Hopkins, and Perkins as iconic figures of the New Deal, it has all but forgotten Hugh Johnson, who for a time outshone them all. In retrospect, his eclipse seems preordained, for any star that shines so brightly holds within its own fire the seed of its own extinction.

Hugh Johnson was born on the plains in 1882 to a lawyer-turned-farmer-turned-Oklahoma homesteader and his culturally inclined wife, who bequeathed her son his lifelong devotion to classical literature and opera.

In 1898 his father, by then a Democratic Party committeeman in the Oklahoma Territory, secured him a place in the U.S. Military Academy.

The pattern of Johnson's West Point career would not have surprised those who knew him in later life. He was intelligent, but disinclined to apply himself to the mandated course of study; sociable, but disdainful of such well-born fellow cadets as Douglas MacArthur and Ulysses S. Grant III, who put on airs or wore their ambitions on their sleeves. He was "a very bad cadet," he acknowledged, yet tenacious: in the harshly Darwinian process that really counted at West Point, by which his class was pared down from 134 cadets when he entered to 94 when he graduated, he survived.

Johnson's military career was uneventful, largely comprising patrol assignments in pacified zones such as the western frontier of the United States and in the Philippines. Still, by 1917, when the United States entered the European war, he had acquired a reputation as an outstanding organizer of supplies and matériel. He also earned a modest income as a writer of boys' adventure fiction (his first novel, *Williams of West Point,* was a romanticized depiction of his own academy years) and held a law degree from Berkeley. Summoned to Washington, he wrote the military draft law of 1917 and served under Quartermaster General George Goethals, the builder of the Panama Canal. As Goethals's representative on the War Industries Board, which organized American industry for the war effort, he caught the eye of the eminent financier Bernard Baruch, the board's chairman. Baruch became his patron.

After war's end, Johnson joined George Peek, another Baruch protégé, at Moline Plow Company, the farm implement manufacturer struggling through the remorseless postwar agricultural depression. Baruch, meanwhile, was building his reputation as an indispensable advisor to presidents on business and fiscal affairs and burnishing his résumé as a "practical economist"—one who (as distinguished from "academic economists") put his knowledge to work making money.

The legend of Baruch's sagacity was based on his having survived the crash of 1929 unscathed. Yet the truth behind the legend is elusive. He claimed to have sold his stockholdings prior to the crash, and his ostentatious lifestyle did not seem to suffer as the Depression took hold. But his claim to have seen the disaster coming is belied by the steady stream of optimistic pronouncements that issued from his office during the Roaring Twenties, blessing popular speculation in the stock market. And in November 1930 Baruch acknowledged to Senate Democratic Leader Joe Robinson, the conduit of his largesse to Democratic congressional campaigns, that "the drop in my securities has been very severe. . . . I may not be able to help out in many of the directions I have heretofore until the ship floats anew on the incoming tide."

Baruch's role as an eminence of the Democratic Party and its liaison with Wall Street continued to grow during the early Thirties. One of the few prominent financiers to escape popular obloquy after the crash, he could bring the Democratic leaders of Congress scurrying to his Washington hotel suite with a single terse wire. "So much Baruch money has been spread around—as campaign contributions and otherwise—that it never does to criticize him publicly," Tugwell confided to his diary. Nevertheless, he added, Roosevelt "does not trust him."

One reason was obvious: Baruch had backed the "stop Roosevelt" movement at the 1932 convention. Moreover, his views on business and economics were decidedly out of step with the Brain Trust. A few weeks after the convention, Adolf Berle analyzed one of Baruch's position papers, reporting to Roosevelt that it hewed close to the mind-set of the Democratic Party's Wall Street wing:

> B.M.B. [Baruch] wants to permit free play to business, which in practice means freedom to six or eight hundred large corporations and banks to fight out among themselves the ultimate mastery of the situation. He believes individuals must suffer for and rectify their own mistakes. Unfortunately, the result reached is that the "forgotten men" suffer for the mistakes of the industrial leaders, who come off relatively unhurt.

Consequently, the great sage and advisor to presidents found himself during the campaign on the outside looking in. Yet it was not easy to shoulder Baruch too far from the center of power. His wealth still spoke loudly; several times he communicated his approval of Berle's campaign speechwriting by awarding Berle a "retainer"—a consulting contract with his financial firms. Fretting that one such award might render the Brain Trust "tainted with outside influence," Berle requested Roosevelt's approval before accepting. Roosevelt replied that he could see "no reason in the world" to turn it down. He cheerfully wrote Berle: "More power to your arm!"

A more important factor keeping Baruch within the candidate's orbit was the expanding campaign role of his protégé Hugh Johnson. Customarily it was Baruch's prestige that opened the door to power for his underlings—indeed, it was he who had introduced Johnson to Ray Moley the day after FDR's nomination. But now the process ran in reverse, with the Brain Trust tolerating Baruch for the sake of his onetime assistant.

Johnson's energy and his flair for razor-sharp phrasemaking endeared him to Roosevelt from their first encounter. Johnson had been escorted to Albany to meet the candidate by Moley. That evening the General performed a dramatic reading of an indictment of the Hoover administration he had drafted as a campaign document. His declamatory roar, which would soon become famous coast to coast, resounded through the governor's mansion, periodically punctuated by applause and Roosevelt's delighted laughter. When the performance was over, Roosevelt called Moley to his side. "It's great stuff," he said. "Water it down 70 percent and make it into a speech."

The peak of Johnson's campaign influence came with his drafting of Roosevelt's October 29 Pittsburgh speech, which stands apart from all other Roosevelt oratory for its edge and pungency. The tone of the attack on Hoover's economic policies was pure Johnson, although its economic viewpoint owed much to Bernard Baruch. The speech assailed Hoover's spending as "reckless and extravagant," his tariffs as "monstrous," his overall policy "a dangerous evil." It concluded with a pledge to cut federal spending by 25 percent, that regrettably specific promise Rex Tugwell would condemn as "unforgivable folly."

Johnson's unflagging energy kept him in the Roosevelt entourage even when Moley and the other Brain Trusters bristled at his refusal (or inability) to perform as a team player. The General's voice was always louder than the others', his stride more forceful, his ideas more sharply expressed. The initial suspicions that he was a mole for Bernard Baruch yielded to the evidence that Hugh Johnson could not function as a subordinate to anyone for very long. Baruch soon was thoroughly eclipsed by his protégé. "It is not easy to specify what [Baruch] contributed to the New Deal," Moley reflected. "Hugh Johnson supplied the color and drama that so vitally contributed to re-employment. . . . But Baruch's hovering presence in those early days led to nothing specific."

The Brain Trust had not initially placed industrial reform very high on its postinaugural recovery agenda. This was not to minimize the issue's importance, but to acknowledge its crushing complexity. Few issues attracted so many conflicting proposals. Henry I. Harriman, president of the U.S. Chamber of Commerce, pressed for relaxing the antitrust laws so corporations could take joint action on wages and production; by contrast, Felix Frankfurter and Supreme Court Justice Louis D. Brandeis advocated increasing antitrust enforcement to prevent monopolists from sapping the public's purchasing power. Franciers such as James Warburg proposed making government loans available to private enterprise to revive manufacturing; others preferred confining such assistance to government guarantees against losses. Within the cabinet strong pressure for a public works program came from Frances Perkins and Jim Farley; equally strong opposition came from Lewis Douglas, FDR's skinflint budget director, who cared less about the positive effect of federal construction spending on unemployment than about its negative effect on the federal deficit.

Then Congress forced the issue onto the front burner by resurrecting a bill drafted by Senator Hugo Black, a progressive Democrat from Alabama, mandating a thirty-hour workweek nationwide, no exceptions. After the Senate passed Black's bill overwhelmingly on April 6, it gathered a stupendous head of steam for passage in the House.

At the White House the measure caused consternation. Roosevelt, Moley, and Perkins recognized that its inflexibility would stifle, not stimulate, the economy—"a completely wooden and rigid idea," in Perkins's words. Black based his measure on the notion that limiting the hours every laborer worked would force employers to spread the work around to more employees, curing economic stagnation. He had calculated the number of potential wage earners in the country and divided it into the number of man-hours he figured were needed to attain "normal" production. The calculation yielded thirty hours as the workweek that would put the entire nation back on the payroll. "It's as easy as that," he told Perkins, who watched nonplussed one day as he traced out the pertinent formulas with pencil on scraps of paper. She replied that unless a minimum wage mandate were attached to the plan, this would merely result in a reduction of individual workers' pay nationwide. That eventuality had not figured into his formula, Black acknowledged; nor had the recognition that some jobs could not be effectively sliced up into thirty-hour weeks or five- or six-hour days, nor that while some industries had a surplus of qualified laborers who could be employed in a thirty-hour scheme, others had shortages that simply could not be filled at the snap of a finger.

Roosevelt sent his labor secretary to Capitol Hill to head off the bill's passage in the House, without disavowing the administration's commitment to reemployment and industrial recovery. Privately contemptuous of the measure as an imagined "panacea that would solve the whole problem of unemployment" at a stroke, in public Perkins followed the instructions of the sage politician in the Oval Office. Appearing at her first full-dress congressional hearing, with First Lady Eleanor Roosevelt peering down from the gallery, Perkins coolly undermined the bill by supporting it in principle while insisting on the addition of a minimum wage provision. This was enough to stall the measure, but it could not be held back for long. The White House knew the only solution was to put up an alternative plan for industrial recovery.

Perkins soon discovered that several efforts were already under way to draft an industrial plan and that they were proceeding sometimes at cross-purposes, sometimes in parallel. FDR did not seem to be aware of any of them. Some were in the executive branch and some on Capitol Hill, but all aimed in one way or another to place a floor under wages and eliminate cutthroat industrial competition, which was thought to be damagingly deflationary. Assistant Commerce Secretary John Dickinson was drafting one measure that would eradicate child labor and sweatshops but allow competitors to collude in setting maximum work hours and minimum wages. Separately, Senator Robert F. Wagner of New York was developing a plan to suspend the antitrust laws in return for a minimum wage and a guarantee of the right of collective bargaining.

Then there was General Johnson. Crossing the lobby of Washington's Carlton Hotel one day in late April, he and Baruch had run into Moley, who was despairing of ever crafting a policy out of the jumble of proposals accumulating in his files. Baruch promptly offered to loan Johnson to the White House to help with the task. Moley put Johnson together with Rex Tugwell to prepare a draft. Within a few days, Johnson would claim—and there is no reason to doubt him—that he had the gist of the National Industrial Recovery Act laid out on a sheet and a half of legal foolscap. It was *echt* Johnson: a nationwide regimentation of industry as if for war, providing for shorter hours, the suspension of antitrust regulation, and wage and price controls, all to be executed in "an extraordinarily short space of time." His goal was to put four million men to work in a mere three months.

Armed with Roosevelt's personal directive to reconcile all these projects and, more important from her point of view, bring them all under the authority of the White House, Perkins confronted the drafting teams one by one and directed them to iron out their differences. She was most impressed by the effort of Tugwell and Johnson, who were sequestered with a few lawyers in a room crammed beneath the sloping mansard roof of the old State Department building. When she showed up, Tugwell and Johnson "were anything but pleased to see me," she recalled. She was the only cabinet officer who had breached their wall of secrecy, and although she could tell that their plan had merit, she was shocked at how far they had proceeded without Roosevelt's knowledge or authority.

This was Perkins's first encounter with Hugh Johnson, and it left a lasting memory. She watched him stomp around the hot, cramped room like a caged animal, throw himself into a chair and fidget like a restless child, then stretch himself over the table, impatient at the lawyers' debate over whether the Supreme Court would find their bill constitutional. He barked at the staff: "You don't seem to realize that people in this country are starving! You don't seem to realize that industry has gone to pot. . . . You don't seem to realize that these things are important and that this law stuff doesn't matter. . . . We've got to *do* this." In the months to come, his blustery admonitions to act *now* would energize, and ultimately exhaust, the nation.

Perkins, appalled and fascinated by the spectacle of General Hugh Johnson in full cry, recognized the signs of a fundamentally insecure personality. She would eventually become his most sympathetic sounding board in the White House. Immediately after that introductory meeting she began working on him in a distinctly maternal way. With his family living in New York, he was lonely in Washington, where his dictatorial manner threw up a social wall around him. Perkins would have him up to the house she shared in Georgetown with the socialite Mary Harriman Rumsey and exercise on him her powers of Brahmin good sense to try to focus his extraordinary energy toward results, not merely bluster. (He returned the favor by announcing one time: "Frances Perkins is the best man in the cabinet.") Johnson's drive, she recognized, was what was needed to propel an industrial recovery plan through the cabinet and Congress. She persuaded him that his concept of placing industry on a hyperorganized fast track would fit perfectly with the public works plan she championed. ("Public works is all right but it ain't enough," he had told her before coming around to her viewpoint. "We'll all be dead before the public works program begins to employ people.") And she forced him to collaborate with the other drafting teams—if for no other reason than that the goodwill of Wagner, the only elected official in any of the groups, would be needed to move the measure through Congress. That meant accepting the progressive New York senator's demand that the bill award labor a minimum wage and the right of collective bargaining.

After that, the National Industrial Recovery Act took shape rapidly, though it lost the conciseness of Johnson's original conception. "Alas for the page-and-a-half bill!" he later lamented. "It was now as long as the moral law." The final bill was built around the concept of "codes." These were agreements establishing wage rates, prices, hours of production, and other principles for every industry. At first they were to be negotiated among the participating companies themselves and implemented following public hearings. But if an industry proved unable to fashion a suitable code, one could be imposed by the President in a procedure called "licensing." To clear a legal path for the collusion implicit in the process, enforcement of the antitrust laws was to be suspended for two years. The draft also included a landmark provision, known as Section 7(a), guaranteeing employees the right of collective bargaining through representatives of their choosing and outlawing "yellow-dog" contracts, in which a worker had to agree not to join a union as a condition of employment. Oversight of the entire program was to be vested in the National Recovery Administration, or NRA, in the executive branch. All that was Title I. A public works program worth $3.3 billion was Title II.

Johnson would describe the underlying principle of the National Industrial Recovery Act, or NIRA, as "*balance*—balance of supply to demand, balance of prices at fair exchange parity throughout the whole economic structure, and balance of benefits among great economic areas." On first glance, however, it was hard to discern how the benefits and compromises of the act could be made to fall evenly on everyone's shoulders. Business would get an enormously valuable antitrust exemption, but it was far from certain that labor's new rights and protections would be enough to counterbalance management's prerogatives, especially given the embryonic condition of labor organizing in major industries such as mining and steel. Who would look out for consumers squeezed in the vise of price-fixing and wage controls? And who would hold the greatest sway—employers, employees, or consumers—with the government bureaucrats who were to supervise the entire vast undertaking?

The public works program was the most curious component of the bill. Roosevelt was a reluctant adherent to "pump-priming" theory, which held that in an economic slump government should compensate with deficit spending for a fall-off in private investment and employment. He was especially skeptical of the virtues of "indirect" spending—that is, stimulating the economy by spending money on programs like construction rather than on direct relief. As late as 1935, Ickes was still grumbling that "no one has been able to mention indirect employment to the President for a long time. He simply has no patience with the thought."

The $3.3 billion appropriation ended up in the bill, Moley suggested, as a compromise figure between the $5 billion public works program being pushed by Perkins and Tugwell, and $900 million, which Roosevelt explained was the maximum value of the "useful" projects Herbert Hoover had been able to find to absorb government spending. Indeed, when Perkins produced a list of $5 billion in proposed projects during a White House discussion in April (the source was a national association of contractors and architects), a skeptical Roosevelt turned to the list for New York state. Evidently drawing from his knowledge of practical needs and possibilities in his home state, "he proceeded to rip that list to pieces," Ickes reported.

As submitted to Congress on May 17, the National Industrial Recovery Act was a spectacularly illiberal piece of legislation to be proposed by an ostensibly progressive administration. Treating competition as the enemy of economic growth, its explicit goal was to supplant the natural forces of free enterprise with "a great cooperative movement throughout all industry . . . to prevent unfair competition and disastrous overproduction," in the words of the President's message to Congress accompanying the bill. Roosevelt did acknowledge that the antitrust laws provided a necessary bulwark against "the old evils of unfair competition." During their suspension, consequently, it would be necessary to "provide a rigorous [government] licensing power to meet rare cases of non-cooperation and abuse." But he suggested that the abuses were on the margin, and that most businesses would cooperate to achieve "wide reemployment, to shorten the working week, to pay a decent wage for the shorter week."

The NIRA illustrates how in its haste to address immediate exigencies, the administration was prepared to look back to the nostrums of an earlier age, rather than creating a genuinely new model of business conduct and government regulation. The effort was driven as much by the instant need to derail the Black bill than by any novel or imaginative economic analysis—even though new ideas were at hand in the work of such Brain Trusters as Adolf Berle and Rex Tugwell. The idea that competition was inherently inimical to growth harked back to the industrial regimentation of the Great War, when the War Industries Board—not coincidentally, the industrial training camp of Hugh Johnson—attempted to foster "enlightened business leadership through trade associations." The notion was one shared by Franklin Roosevelt and Herbert Hoover, who had collaborated in 1922 in founding the American Construction Council to cartelize the construction industry. It was also one of the respectable economic ideas held by "men of established reputation," to recall the words of John Kenneth Galbraith, who accurately observed that to the extent Roosevelt accepted them, his views were not much different from Hoover's.

The idea that business would respond to the NIRA in a spirit of cooperation was one of the dreams infecting the New Deal in its earliest months, when Roosevelt's broad-based electoral victory and the Hundred Days Congress's agreeability made it seem that every economic constituency in the country could be trusted to pull together in pursuit of common goals. The New Dealers perhaps may be forgiven for overlooking a natural truth about the suppression of competition: it invariably benefits incumbent competitors, and bigger competitors more than smaller ones, by raising barriers to new entrants. By this mechanism it also eliminates a counterweight to high fixed prices and the exploitation of labor. This natural phenomenon might be defeated by a regulatory regime that works perfectly to control prices and monitor working conditions, but those were never going to be simple tasks, and in practice turned out to be impossible ones. The Hundred Days would be a period of improvised responses to crises across the economic landscape, with the result that many initiatives launched in those fourteen weeks would require revisions and reconsiderations later on; the NIRA was one so flawed that it could not be repaired.

While threading through Congress, the bill met with considerable opposition from progressives: Huey Long condemned the measure for handing unlimited power to a President who he maintained could not be trusted to protect the people from monopoly. "Every fault of socialism is found in this bill, without one of its virtues," he thundered. "It is a combination of every evil that can possibly be imagined, worse than anything proposed under the soviet."

Meanwhile, Roosevelt struggled with the question of who should direct the program. In General Johnson's mind, at least, there was no doubt: it was his baby. Even before the first congressional vote was recorded he started assembling his team, appointing on his own authority associates to help operate the NRA and managers for the public works program. During social evenings at Mary Rumsey's country home he regaled Perkins with his vision for industrial regimentation.

Then, a few days before the NIRA's final passage, Bernard Baruch showed up at the Rumsey house. Perkins assumed this was a social call, but as she served the financier a tumbler of ginger ale, he startled her with a question.

"Tell me, is there anything at all to the rumor that the President is going to appoint Hugh as the head of this thing?"

"I guess that's going to happen," she replied cautiously.

"You'd better interpose," Baruch said. "Hugh isn't fit to be head of that."

The agitated Baruch proceeded to delineate his former assistant's faults. "He's not fit to be the head of anything where he has to carry heavy responsibility. He just can't do it. Hugh's always got to have somebody to keep him in order."

Baruch concluded: "You must intervene with the President. You must go tell the President this."

Perkins was dismayed not only by Baruch's attack on Johnson but by his insistence that, because he himself was then on poor terms with the President, she must be the one to deliver the message to Roosevelt. (The issue driving a wedge between Baruch and FDR, she learned later, was the government's plan to call in all privately held gold. This was a sensitive matter for Baruch, the largest single owner of bullion in the country.)

Roosevelt was just as dumbfounded when Perkins delivered Baruch's message. "That's astonishing," he said. "We got Hugh from Baruch."

Neither realized that Baruch was alluding chiefly to Johnson's drinking, which had not surfaced as a problem during the long months of the campaign or during the drafting of the NIRA. But Baruch's remarks underscored other misgivings about Johnson already percolating through the administration. During a cabinet meeting on June 6, Roosevelt had been irritated to learn of Johnson's efforts to line up staff for the NRA, none of whom had been cleared in advance with the White House. When the discussion reached the issue of which cabinet department should oversee the NRA, it became evident that none of the secretaries of the most suitable agencies—Labor, Agriculture, Interior, or Commerce—relished having to manage the voluble General. Perkins proposed assigning him to a committee representing all four. This drew the ridicule of Interior Secretary Ickes, who already had wearied of Johnson's dictatorial style. "If he can't work under one secretary," he snapped, "how will he be able to work for four?"

Roosevelt settled the issue with another last-minute improvisation. He required Johnson as NRA administrator to report to a committee comprising the four secretaries, plus Attorney General Homer Cummings and the head of the Federal Trade Commission. Then, on the very day Congress passed the bill and hours before he was scheduled to sign it, he clipped Johnson's wings further by removing the public works program from NRA's control.

In the Cabinet Room, this produced a scene of almost Shakespearean pathos. Summoned to receive his appointment and still unaware that the program was to be cleft in two, Johnson delivered what Perkins recalled as "a pleasant little speech of thanks and promised to devote his life to the great project."

Then the blow fell. In his most amiable tone of voice, FDR informed him that the cabinet had all agreed that to ask any man to administer both Title I and Title II would be "an inhuman burden." Therefore, Title II would be administered by Harold Ickes.

Johnson's smile vanished. As the President explained the new arrangement, the General's face grew a deeper purple. Then, in a "strange, low voice," he began to murmur, "I don't see why. I don't see why." Roosevelt adjourned the meeting and beckoned to Perkins.

"Stick with Hugh," he said. "Don't let him explode."

Perkins ushered Johnson out a side door to evade the press—she feared Johnson might make news with a public blowup—and bundled him into her car. "He's ruined me," Johnson muttered. "I've got to get out." Over the next two hours, as they drove the streets of the capital, she managed to calm him down—though she almost lost the battle when she informed him that even on Title I he would be reporting to a cabinet committee. The only saving grace was that Perkins would be a member. He pleaded abjectly: "You'll stand by me and save me from those harpies, won't you?"

That evening, Roosevelt signed the National Industrial Recovery Act into law, calling it "the most important and far-reaching legislation ever enacted by the American Congress." It was the last measure passed and the last to be signed, on June 16, the hundredth day of the first congressional session of the New Deal.

Hugh Johnson's NRA would provide the leading public demonstration of how the frenzied, crisis-driven legislating of the Hundred Days would translate into action. The General and his rapidly expanding staff created an impression of irrepressible, high-voltage activity. At first they worked out of two anterooms to Ray Moley's State Department office, but they quickly overwhelmed the space. "Visitors waiting for interviews had to sit in rows around the walls of the same room in which important and sometimes confidential conferences were taking place," Johnson reported. "It was Bedlam and all thinking and writing had to be done at night." He demanded more room, only to be relocated to the Commerce Department building erected by Herbert Hoover. This space Johnson cordially detested, describing his quarters as a row of bays and alcoves resembling "the pay toilet in the Union station."

Johnson launched himself into the job with explosive fervor. He crossed the country, stopping to harangue, cajole, and intimidate groups of business leaders everywhere he touched down, hammering at them to draft codes setting maximum hours, minimum wages, and standards of industrial cooperation to supplant their ruinous habits of competition. Speed was of the essence, he lectured them, his goal being to have most of the country under a code regime within two months. Yet he refused to wield the one effective weapon the law gave him to force compliance upon refractory businessmen, the "licensing" provision allowing the President to impose a code on any industry by fiat; to use that power, Johnson believed, would invite a constitutional challenge, which he feared the NRA would lose. So he relied on weapons he thought he could deploy more effectively anyway: the force of his personality and the threat of public censure.

Meanwhile he fought a relentless rearguard battle against efforts to impose bureaucratic limits on the NRA. These included the oversight board of cabinet members and other high-level administrators—the body that Ickes had predicted would be ineffective at keeping Johnson on a short leash. He proved to be right; the so-called Special Industrial Recovery Board would in time morph into a series of supervisory boards that had nothing in common except their inability to impose administrative order on the General's domain. In addition to the special board, the White House appointed three "advisory boards," comprising business leaders (the Industrial Advisory Board), labor leaders and Labor Department officials (the Labor Advisory Board), and public-spirited economists and good-government advocates (the Consumer Advisory Board), the latter of which had been demanded by Perkins on the expectation that in the code-drafting give-and-take between labor and industry, the consumer's interest would be served last, if at all. Johnson ignored them all equally.

For all his kinetic activity, after more than a month Johnson could point only to a single completed code. This was the cotton textile code, which would exemplify the NRA's tendency to extract modest, even trifling, concessions from major industries while bestowing generous gifts on management.

The textile industry was one of the nation's largest—employing more workers in 1933 than steel—and surely among its most abusive. Earnings of five and six dollars a week were standard, as were workweeks of fifty or fifty-five hours and night work by women. The industry was the largest employer of child labor. Its mills dominated rural communities where workers and their families lived in nearly unimaginable destitution. Reported Martha Gellhorn, the writer and novelist (and future bride of Ernest Hemingway) in a letter to Harry Hopkins: "The young girls . . . are really in awful shape. I have watched them in some mills where the naked eye can tell that the work load is inhuman. They have no rest for eight hours; in one mill they told me they couldn't get time to cross the room to the drinking fountain for water. . . . As for their homes: I have seen a village where the latrines drain nicely down a gully to a well from which they get their drinking water. . . . [T]he houses are shot with holes, windows broken, no sewerage; rats. The rent for these houses is twice as high as that of the fine mill houses."

As written, the textile code provided for a forty-hour week, raised the minimum wage to at least ten dollars per week (with some regional variation permitted), and outlawed the employment of children under sixteen. This achievement was one about which Johnson was still pounding his chest years later. He described the moment during the public hearing on the code when the mill owners' spokesman accepted the rule: "There was a moment's silence in that over-crowded audience, and then a thunderous burst of applause. The Textile Code had done in a few minutes what neither law nor constitutional amendment had been able to do in forty years." Roosevelt, in signing the code into existence early in July, repeated the claim: "Child labor in this industry is here abolished. After years of fruitless effort and discussion, this ancient atrocity went out in a day."

Yet paradise was by no means at hand. The mill owners had pulled a neat sleight-of-hand trick. The truth was that child labor had been fading for years in the industry, where wages were so low that an adult could be employed for the same price as a child, and was more productive. ("There is, in fact, practically no child labor today," the owners' spokesman had assured Johnson—obviously an exaggeration, but accurate enough as a signal of the low esteem in which children were held as mill hands.)

In return for what appeared to be a millennial concession, the owners had obtained provisions that would allow them to continue to impoverish their employees with impunity. The new minimum wage became effectively the maximum, and in any event was commonly flouted, for the supervision of code compliance was vested in a committee controlled by the owners. The workweek was shortened but productivity demands raised to even more inhumane levels, a process known as the "stretch-out." And an all-purpose escape clause had been inserted in the wage and hour provisions exempting "learners," which enabled owners simply to fire employees en masse and rehire them in the new category. The lone textile union with any sizable membership, the United Textile Workers of America, had been frozen out of the compliance process, with Johnson's connivance.

The textile code did, however, break the code-drafting logjam. NRA staff and the advisory committees were soon overwhelmed with hundreds of code proposals, all requiring an analysis of conditions in their industries, definitions of terms, the establishment of oversight authorities. The hastily approved codes in major industries followed a pattern: they favored the largest companies in the field by granting them control of the boards and freezing competitive conditions—new plant construction was often barred, as was the reopening of shuttered plants, raising the entry bar for potential new rivals. Johnson cavalierly held that Section 7(a) could be served by the establishment of a "company union," a noxious institution that allowed management to award itself the right of collective bargaining for its own employees.

With the NRA's workload becoming overwhelming, the General opted for a shortcut. This was a campaign for a nationwide blanket code, labeled the President's Reemployment Agreement, fixing the maximum workweek of thirty-five hours for blue collar workers and forty for white-collar employees and a minimum wage of 40 cents an hour or $12 to $15 weekly salaries for white-collar jobs.

The "Blue Eagle" program was a public pressure campaign. Johnson explained its genesis by quoting a 1921 speech by his mentor Bernard

Baruch, who had recalled how the "mobilization of public opinion" kept businesses in compliance with the regulations of the War Industries Board in 1917: "The insignia of government approval on doorways, letterheads, and invoices will become a necessity in business."

Johnson augmented Baruch's principles with his personal brand of ballyhoo, an admixture of patriotic exhortation, religious revivalism, and public shaming. He launched the drive with a massive publicity blast, sending wires on July 21 to the chambers of commerce of every city of more than ten thousand population. "It is an inspiring thing to be a part of a great national movement to restore economic security to our people," they read, "and I appeal to you to marshal all the forces of your community in one united effort to get rid of unemployment." Before the day was out he claimed that thousands of telegrams and phone calls had poured into the NRA, with "not a sour message in the whole lot."

NRA speakers swarmed across the country, with Johnson the star of the traveling carnival. Before an audience of twenty-six thousand in St. Louis—and many thousands more listening on radio—he issued a warning to those chiselers who would "prong pennies in violation of a spontaneous confidence of his government and his neighbors. . . . What should be done with such a man? As happened to Danny Deever, NRA will have to remove from him his badge of public faith and business honor. . . . It is a sentence of economic death. It will never happen. The threat of it transcends any puny public provision in this law." (The literary reference, a hallmark of Johnson's oratory, was to the subject of a Rudyard Kipling poem whose regimental fellows were required to witness his public execution for murder as an exemplary lesson.)

Not everyone was enchanted by Johnson's mass movement. Harold Ickes, constitutionally skeptical of the General's personality—he "ran through official life in Washington like a Model T Ford with a missing cylinder," he would write—groused about having been forced at a movie theater to sit through a film clip featuring "a most disgusting exhibition put on by a low-class comedian as NRA propaganda" before the main show began. (The unnamed comedian was Jimmy Durante.)

"It would hardly appeal to the lowest order of human intelligence," Ickes recorded in his diary, "and I am wondering if this sort of thing is being put on extensively. If it is, it will do the NRA more harm than good." Frances Perkins, overhearing Ickes complain, volunteered that she had heard that "movie audiences in New York City were booing NRA propaganda."

Perkins's anecdote notwithstanding, the public seemed to be eating up the ballyhoo. The Blue Eagle glowered from shop windows everywhere. Two former University of Pennsylvania football teammates partnered to buy the National Football League's bankrupt Frankford, Pennsylvania, Yellow Jackets, moved the team to Philadelphia, and renamed it, in honor of the NRA insignia, the Eagles.

Nowhere was the excitement greater than in New York, which shed its veneer of jaded sophistication for a climactic burst of hype on September 12 and 13. This began with Johnson's stemwinding speech at Madison Square Garden, followed the next day by a Blue Eagle parade up Fifth Avenue from Washington Square to Bryant Park, requiring nine hours and thirty-seven minutes to complete—"the greatest march in New York City's history," officials declared—before a crowd estimated at a million and a half.

Yet no volume of hullaballoo could obscure the troubling rattle of NRA's unfulfilled promise. General Johnson's harangues made employers no more willing to award workers higher pay, much less collective bargaining rights, than they had been in the past: roughly seven hundred strikes by frustrated workers erupted in July and August following enactment of the NIRA and the launch of Johnson's Blue Eagle campaign, compared with forty in the same period a year earlier.

Perkins came face-to-face with the intransigence of the coal and steel industries in late July, during a visit to the coal country of western Pennsylvania. In Homestead, a community whose history of management-labor violence dated to the 1890s, local officials plainly beholden to the mine operators barred her from continuing a meeting with workers in the town hall because it had been infiltrated by "undesirable Reds." They then forbade her to continue the encounter on the sidewalk, or in a public park across the street. She was stymied until she spotted a U.S. flag fluttering in the distance over the post office, which as a federal building stood outside the local burgesses' jurisdiction. There she finished the meeting, ending it "with handshaking and expressions of rejoicing that the New Deal wasn't afraid of the steel trust." But the steel companies would still be resisting New Deal–backed labor organizers as late as 1939.

Business leaders soon learned the limits of Johnson's bluster. The flag carrier was Henry Ford, who proved to be as obstinate in the face of government regimentation in June and July as he had been in February. Ford adamantly refused to sign the automobile manufacturers code negotiated by the rest of the industry, although the wages and working hours in his plants were actually in compliance with its terms. He especially objected to language in the code promoting collective bargaining, and was unmoved by the threat of being denied the Blue Eagle. "Hell, that Roosevelt buzzard," he snapped to an assistant. "I wouldn't put it on the car."

Ford continued his refusal to sign the code even though that meant that his company was forbidden to bid on government procurement contracts for nearly a year, or until the U.S. comptroller general ruled that Ford's technical compliance with the code provisions was good enough. Perhaps most irksome to Johnson, Ford's consumer sales appeared to be unaffected by the absence of the Blue Eagle—in 1934 the firm increased its market share to 28.8 percent of new cars and trucks from 21.5 percent the previous year.

Average Americans soon realized that they had failed to gain material improvement in their economic life from the NRA. The *New Republic* observed as the Blue Eagle campaign was peaking that the mandated minimum wages of $12 to $15 were so low that "only in the worst sweated industries have there been large numbers of workers who were receiving less," meaning that many employers had secured the right to display General Johnson's thunderbird without raising the wage of a single worker. "No one need be greatly surprised if it finally proves that the Blue Eagle did not carry much prosperity under its wing." To Johnson's claim that the NRA had put two million people back to work, AFL president William Green responded that that left 11 million still unemployed. The increase in purchasing power enjoyed by farmers and employed workers in the first half of 1933 was drained away by an even larger increase in retail prices later in the summer. Actual per capita earnings of those employed in manufacturing, statistics showed, declined in July and August.

It was plain by the fall that regimentation of industry and wage and hour controls were not doing the job Roosevelt demanded. More was needed. In October, he decided to try something very new.

7

THE GOLD STANDARD
ON THE BOOZE

A T 9 A.M. on Wednesday, October 25, 1933, Jesse Jones and Henry Morgenthau were ushered into President Roosevelt's bedroom on the second floor of the White House. The President was propped up in bed, surrounded by newspapers, mail, and government reports, the detritus of his early-morning routine, and about to tuck into his breakfast of soft-boiled eggs. The tables at either side of the bedstead were littered with cigarettes, detective novels in a stack, pads, pencils, and telephones.

The three men were preparing to launch what was possibly the strangest financial episode in U.S. history.

After a few minutes of small talk, Roosevelt issued an order for Jones's RFC, acting as the federal government's proxy, to buy gold at the price the three men agreed on, $31.36 an ounce. As this was fully $2.35 over the old dollar parity price of $29.01, with one stroke they had devalued the U.S. dollar by 8.1 percent.

That day the farm commodity markets, apparently responding to the new value of the dollar, rose steadily—exactly as Roosevelt and his two accomplices expected. They congratulated themselves on having manually injected a small measure of inflation into the economy by taking aim at the unyielding relationship between the dollar and gold. As Jones later wrote,

Roosevelt had "begun to haul in the anchor to which the dollar had been tied for thirty-four years."

Roosevelt could only hope that his dollar-devaluation scheme would work in the long term; if it did, it would solve a problem that had been tormenting him since the campaign: how to raise farm prices without setting inflation on a rampage throughout the economy. That question was closely tied to that of "sound money"—whether America should remain on the gold standard—an issue Roosevelt had nimbly evaded all year.

Roosevelt had promised the nation "bold, persistent experimentation" in the Oglethorpe University speech, and the program he implemented that morning was his boldest experiment yet. It was the brainchild of an obscure academic from Cornell University named George Frederick Warren, who had spent years developing a theory of the "commodity dollar." Having observed that commodity prices and the price of gold tended to rise and fall together, Warren concluded that therefore one could move the price of commodities by manipulating the price of gold.

Traditional economists, including many on Roosevelt's staff, thought this conclusion ridiculous. Yes, gold and commodities tended to move together, they acknowledged, but it was the latter that drove the former. To think the relationship applied in the opposite direction was akin to observing a horse pulling a plow on a rope and concluding that by pushing on the plow, one could move the horse.

But orthodox economists had had their chance, and the country was still mired in depression. Roosevelt was enthralled by the superficial logic of Warren's theory, dressed up as it was by reams of bewildering graphs and charts. He was about to give Warren his moment in the sun.

Warren was fifty-nine and head of the department of agricultural economics and farm management at Cornell when Franklin Roosevelt took office. The first member of Roosevelt's inner circle to come under his sway had been Henry Morgenthau, who as a gentleman farmer had consulted regularly with Warren in the 1920s. Morgenthau would occasionally bring his Dutchess County neighbor, Eleanor Roosevelt, to a Warren lecture at Cornell, and it was through her good offices and Morgenthau's that the commodity dollar theory soon reached FDR.

Warren, who owned a five-hundred-acre farm not far from the Cornell campus and scorned textbook theory, projected the air of a no-nonsense intellectual with his boots in the soil. Balding and moon-faced, with a stern expression that bespoke academic depth, he enhanced his oracular image after Roosevelt brought him to Washington in the summer of 1933 by shunning all publicity. Ensconced mysteriously in an office deep within Commerce Department headquarters, he gave no interviews, left the phone unanswered, and answered knocks on the door with a barked "Not in!"

The New Dealers regarded Warren with wary condescension—"Cornell's currency magician," was Moley's dismissive label—condescending because orthodox economists and bankers considered his theory risible, wary because of its unmistakable grip on the President's imagination. They feared that in his determination to use any means to drive up prices on the farm, Roosevelt might reinforce his reputation for headstrong experimentation. Moley would later judge that the early-morning ritual of setting the price of gold by guesswork "gravely marred his image as a responsible statesman." Roosevelt's gold scheme would solidify the notion on Wall Street that the man in the White House was not to be trusted. In the coming years this notion would yield him a sea of troubles.

During the early days of the administration, Warren's influence was diluted by others on the White House economic team. The most experienced among them in matters of banking and finance was James Paul Warburg, an unusual figure within the New Deal in that he was a Wall Street banker who was accepted by Roosevelt and Moley as a well-informed and objective advisor. Then again Warburg was an unusual figure in the banking industry—a sort of financial centaur, half Wall Street scion and half suave boulevardier. His well-pedigreed parents were the prominent banker Paul M. Warburg and the former Nina Loeb, daughter of the founder of the investment firm Kuhn, Loeb & Company. But he was also the husband of the Broadway composer Kay Swift, for whose hit songs "Can't We Be Friends?" and "Fine and Dandy" he had written the lyrics under the pseudonym Paul James.

Warburg met Roosevelt for the first time in mid-February. Moley, who had been trying to recruit the banker to work out an agenda for an international economic conference scheduled for London in June, arranged for him to visit the Roosevelt town house on East Sixty-Fifth Street. On the appointed day, Warburg found himself cooling his heels in a cramped drawing room with ten or a dozen candidates for administration appointments. (Among them was Ickes, the future interior secretary, as yet a stranger to Roosevelt.) The President-elect was wheeled in, giving Warburg his first sight of FDR's "massive shoulders surmounted by his remarkably fine head, the gay smile with which he greeted his guests, and the somewhat incongruous, old-fashioned pince-nez eyeglasses that seemed to sit a little uncertainly on his nose."

Introduced to Warburg, Roosevelt greeted him with the words: "Ray Moley tells me that you're the white sheep of Wall Street." Warburg replied that it was his father, if anyone, who deserved "this flattering distinction," and cautioned that a white sheep does not invariably beget white lambs. Roosevelt chuckled. "I didn't know you were a farmer like me," he said. Warburg was invited to join the Treasury Department as an undersecretary for banking and currency issues. Preferring to work as an informal advisor, he turned the offer down. In any case, it would not be long before he would show that his coloration was better adapted to Wall Street than to the New Deal after all.

On international finance, FDR's chief advisor was William C. Bullitt, another hybrid personality. The offspring of one of Philadelphia's most aristocratic old families, Bullitt had lived in Europe as a newspaper correspondent and diplomat, and had been married briefly to Louise Bryant, the widow of the American radical John Reed. (The marriage broke up in 1930 because of Bryant's alcoholism and, reputedly, her lesbian affair with a British artist.) His membership in the White House inner circle ranked as a comeback, for he had been drummed out of the last Democratic administration for publicly advocating American recognition of the Bolshevik regime in 1919 and testifying before the Senate in opposition to the Treaty of Versailles. Under Roosevelt his star would resume its rise: in November he would be named the first U.S. ambassador to the newly recognized Soviet Union.

Then there was Lewis Douglas, who was struggling to maintain his footing as a conservative against the strong liberal, even radical, winds blowing through the New Deal. There had been precious few victories for Douglas since the Economy Act and not a few humiliations. He told Warburg he was "very depressed" by the AAA's subsidies and production cuts and unnerved by the constant murmurs within the administration about the desirability of inflation. Nevertheless, Roosevelt valued Douglas as a conservative counterweight to the liberals in the White House and a signal to congressional conservatives that the New Deal accommodated a wide range of opinion. This was enough to offset Roosevelt's irritation at Douglas's habit of expressing his differences with New Deal policies in the form of written memoranda: "Lew seems to be trying to establish a record," he griped to Moley.

This economic team faced the challenge of managing for economic growth against buffeting from two sources: an international financial community looking ahead to the London conference; and domestic politicians, especially those representing farmers, seeking inflationary policies. A major issue for both interest groups was the fate of the paradigm of domestic and international finance for the previous half century, the gold standard.

The concept of pegging the value of circulating money to a given quantity of gold, thus benchmarking the conversion of one currency to another, originated in eighteenth-century Great Britain. But the commitment by Britain, France, and Germany, and later the United States, to position gold as the pillar of the international trading system dates back only to the 1880s. The ability of a holder of paper currency issued by any gold-standard government to exchange it for gold coin or bullion at a fixed rate established the relative values of the currencies of all gold-standard countries. This also applied on the government level, where balance-of-payment accounts were settled simply by shipping or earmarking gold from one government's reserve to another's.

The gold standard soon congealed from a concept into an ideology, one that continued to exercise a fetishistic power on national leaders and central bankers through the 1920s. When the balance of payments among trading countries went out of whack, policy makers instinctively moved first to protect the gold standard—that is, to preserve the fixed rate of exchange among their currencies. They did so by resorting to deflation rather than devaluation as the preferred remedy to current account imbalances. In practice, that meant they preferred reducing wages and laying off workers to altering exchange rates.

The gold standard consequently came to be viewed by the working and agrarian classes as an instrument of their own subjugation, designed to preserve the wealth of bankers at their expense. Inflation, as long as it was reasonably controlled, allowed the farmer to pay his debts with ever-cheaper dollars; but it sapped the value of these debts to the banker. Deflation, the remedy for threats to the gold standard, might spell wage cuts and lost jobs to the industrial worker, but it resulted in higher investment values for bondholders. The gold standard protected the banker and the bondholder, but it impoverished the farmer and the laborer.

These inequities animated the movement for "bimetallism" in the United States—the backing of U.S. currency with silver along with gold—which it was assumed would slacken the grip of the gold standard and allow more latitude for inflationary monetary policy. The movement culminated with the 1896 Democratic presidential campaign of William Jennings Bryan whose speech favoring the free coinage of silver at the Democratic convention that year closed with the famous peroration: "Having behind us the commercial interests and the laboring interests and all the toiling masses, we shall answer their demands for a gold standard by saying to them, you shall not press down upon the brow of labor this crown of thorns. You shall not crucify mankind upon a cross of gold."

But in that election the moneyed interests of the East prevailed over the South and the West, hotbeds of bimetallism. Bryan and his cause were defeated. In the United States, as in the rest of the industrial world, the standard of exchange remained gold.

The onset of World War I, which shattered the trade relationships of Europe and necessitated highly inflationary deficit spending by the hostile parties, profoundly rattled the old system. When the war ended, Britain, France, Germany, and the United States attempted to reestablish the gold standard as it had existed before 1914. But the world had unalterably changed. War debts and the victors' demands for reparations from Germany created a stubborn disequilibrium among the major industrial nations, some of which required inflationary and others deflationary policies.

Labor and socialist parties emerged from the war with unprecedented authority to speak for the working class in Europe and the United States. Moreover, the economic balance of power had begun to shift toward the United States, whose war loans had made it the principal creditor of Britain and France. As Bryan's presidential campaigns had shown, the gold standard was treated as a legitimate subject of political debate in the States, unlike Europe. Additionally, postwar deflation landed savagely on the backs of American farmers. Before the war they had been a strong bloc in opposition to the gold standard; after the war their opposition was implacable.

The gold standard, which had been a convenient tool to peg the currencies of trading partners to one another, now became a drag on postwar recovery. Perversely, the gold mentality asserted itself even more strongly as the European and American economies shuddered after 1929. Britain stayed the course until economic imperatives forced it to abandon the gold standard in 1931. To President Hoover, this shifted the moral responsibility for saving the gold standard from London to Washington. He was determined to meet the challenge. But the customary defensive methodology—raising interest rates to maintain the dollar's gold parity—depressed economic activity domestically and promoted American deflation. As Henry Morgenthau, by then Treasury secretary, analyzed the situation retrospectively in 1935: "Europeans knew that we could not maintain our currency at the old gold level without a further ruinous deflation of our prices, trade, and industrial activity." Yet, he added, Hoover stubbornly insisted on defending the gold standard, "evidently under the impression that it was a proud achievement, when it was obviously economic suicide."

The harvest was a deepening of the Depression, more unemployment, the proliferation of Hoovervilles. Despite Hoover's efforts, American banks suffered more frequent runs as depositors, unconvinced that the federal government could stave off devaluing the dollar for long, clamored to get their hands on gold. Hoover's Treasury secretary, Ogden Mills, also a well-to-do Dutchess County neighbor of Roosevelt's, was still insisting in 1935 that "it was not the maintenance of the gold standard that caused the banking panic of 1933 . . . ; it was the definite and growing fear that the new administration meant to do what they ultimately did—that is, abandon the gold standard." This was a classic example of avoiding the fundamental issue, for the phenomenon truly at work was the recognition by wise investors and the man on the street alike that the gold standard was untenable in the world of the Thirties, and that the traditional stratagems for preserving it only worsened the economic slump.

These were the realities governing policy making in the new administration. Yet the possible remedies were still subject to debate and doubt. Roosevelt had carefully avoided telegraphing his intentions during the campaign. Even during the banking holiday, his decision to outlaw personal holdings of gold and its transfer overseas—wholly consistent with a deliberate attack on the gold standard—was camouflaged as a transitory element of the emergency program. ("Gold merely cannot be obtained for several days," Woodin explained to reporters.) But domestic pressure was unrelenting for an inflationary devaluation of the dollar. Among the forces clamoring for inflation was the grandly named Committee for the Nation, which had been organized by a group of industrialists and retailers including James H. Rand, president of Remington Rand, who had been made so apoplectic by Rexford Tugwell's casual remark about banking policy after the election; Lessing J. Rosenwald, the chairman of Sears, Roebuck; and

Frank Gannett, the publisher of a chain of conservative newspapers head-quartered in Rochester, New York. The committee became an early and enthusiastic sponsor of Warren's gold-manipulation nostrum.

In the heartland there were farm agitators like Milo Reno of the Farm-ers' Holiday Association, and rabble-rousers like the Reverend Charles E. Coughlin of Detroit, who was just beginning his sojourn in the national spotlight by staging a series of mass rallies in favor of the free coinage of silver (in which he was later shown to have been actively speculating). In Congress the inflation lobby was based in the mining states and the farm belt, with the veteran Democratic senator Burton Wheeler of Montana carrying the flag for the former and Oklahoma's Senator Elmer Thomas the latter.

By the second week of April, a mere month after the end of the bank holiday, Washington and Wall Street were abuzz with rumors that FDR had secretly decided in favor of inflation. Lew Douglas, beside himself with dismay, telephoned Warburg late one night to share his concern that devaluation would unleash inflation and lead to "social disorder."

Warburg shared Douglas's gloom, if only because he found the President immune to arguments that inflation without supplementary government stimulus would be economically disastrous. "In vain I argued that raising prices would do no good unless wages and incomes could be induced to rise in proportion"; otherwise the higher prices would merely increase the cost of living for the already-strapped consuming class. Warburg tried to convince Roosevelt that the great mass of Americans—"every bank deposi-tor, every owner of a life insurance policy, every wage-earner and every pensioner"—was in some sense a creditor, and therefore likely to be hurt, not helped, by inflation. "It was a losing battle," Warburg lamented.

The pressure for inflation intensified as the administration's farm emergency bill neared a vote in Congress. Senator Wheeler informed the White House that he would submit an amendment providing for the unlimited coinage of silver at the traditional ratio to gold of 16 to 1, a cherished goal of the farm and mining lobbies for half a century. One night he harangued Moley and Woodin on the subject for the better part of three hours, provoking Woodin, the composer manqué, to tap out on his piano an impromptu tune he called "Lullaby in Silver," the better "to get this silver talk off my mind before I go to bed," he told Moley.

Thomas, for his part, had prepared an amendment giving the President almost unlimited power to inflate the dollar, whether by printing green-backs (currency with no formal backing in gold), devaluing the dollar against gold to whatever level the administration wished, or coining silver at whatever ratio the President desired—a measure, in other words, autho-rizing the President to unleash inflation without limitation. In notifying the White House of his amendment, Thomas pleaded the poverty of the farmer: "At the present prices farmers must produce one quart of wheat . . . to secure one cent," he stated. "He must produce three-quarters of a quart of shelled corn to receive half a cent, and must produce enough cotton, ginned, to fill an average-size pillow to equal the sum of five cents."

Reflecting the conviction of speculators that a pro-inflation consensus was developing in Congress, the dollar plunged in mid-April. The specula-tors were correct: on April 17, Wheeler's measure—favoring silver manipu-lations—came up for a vote in the Senate. Roosevelt had to twist the arms of ten otherwise pro-inflation senators to abstain or vote no to keep the amendment from passing. The next test was due in two days, with a vote on the Thomas amendment. Faced with the certainty that this measure would pass, Roosevelt decided to join the inflationists and manage their movement from within. On the morning of April 18 he informed Moley and Woodin that he would support the Thomas amendment, provided it was redrafted with some minor changes designed to limit the scale of pos-sible devaluation.

Roosevelt's capitulation to the pro-inflation forces reflected, at least par-tially, Warren's influence. But the President's other economic advisors were not likely to take the news in good humor. That evening they were sched-uled to convene at the White House to prepare for talks with British Prime Minister Ramsay MacDonald, who was already on the high seas bound for Washington and completely unaware of the changed conditions that would greet him when he disembarked.

The President was in a mischievous mood when his advisors arrived, as though making a decision on the Thomas amendment had liberated him from a great burden. As they filed in—Warburg, Douglas, Bullitt, Herbert Feis (a Hoover holdover as economic counselor to the State Department), Woodin, Secretary of State Cordell Hull, and Senate Foreign Relations Committee Chairman Key Pittman of the silver mining state of Nevada—he greeted them by saying, "Congratulate me. We are off the gold standard."

With that, Moley recalled, "hell broke loose."

Only Woodin, Pittman, and Moley had known in advance of the President's decision. The others were thunderstruck. Each reacted in his particular way. "Moley was . . . delighted by this dramatic move of the President and rather amused at my discomfiture," Warburg later recollected. "Bullitt thought this was a wonderful show—and great stuff. Hull never opened his trap. . . . Feis looked as though he was going to throw up."

Douglas, Warburg, and Feis were so horrified by the Thomas amendment—"a thoroughly vicious bill," in Douglas's estimation—that they lost their composure, scolding Roosevelt "as though he were a perverse and particularly backward schoolboy," Moley recollected. They kept up their harangue for two hours, stepping on each other's arguments until Roosevelt finally shut down the discussion. If he did not accede to the Thomas amendment, he explained equably, the next inflation measure out of Congress might well be mandatory instead of permissive. In any event, since Thomas was amenable to scaling back the authority granted in his original amendment, they had "nothing to worry about."

When the meeting broke up close to midnight, the skeptics remained unconvinced. Moley dropped off Pittman at his home and returned to his suite at the Carlton Hotel, where he found Douglas and Warburg still chewing over the calamitous news they had heard at the White House. As they left in the wee hours, Douglas turned back to Moley. "Well, this is the end of Western civilization," he said.

For hours Douglas and Warburg walked the streets of Washington together in shared sepulchral gloom. They fetched up back at the Carlton at 5 A.M., awakening Bullitt in his suite. Bullitt did not share his visitors' mood. Hearing Douglas repeat his judgment that civilization's apocalypse was upon them, he burst out laughing. He had heard the same statement on many occasions and in many contexts, and it was always overwrought. "It always makes me laugh," he said cheerfully.

As finally enacted as part of the AAA on May 12, the Thomas amendment gave the President unprecedented powers over monetary policy, but also placed hard constraints on his latitude of action. The measure capped the printing of greenbacks at $3 billion and prohibited their issuance unless the Federal Reserve had first refused to expand the money supply by the same amount. The dollar could not be devalued by more than 50 percent. Warburg, who had redrafted the amendment with Douglas's assistance, congratulated himself for "bringing an insane proposal back within the realms of sanity." Douglas, who had contemplated resigning, stepped back from the brink, concluding that Roosevelt was unlikely, in the end, to use the new powers granted him. "I am sure that I must stay on until a real overt act has been committed," he wrote his father back in Arizona.

That day would not be long in coming.

The White House advisors swung from the crisis of the Thomas amendment into the frenzied planning for the London Economic Conference without taking a breath. A slew of preconference foreign missions descended on Washington. The British delegates, who had been in the mid-Atlantic at the moment Roosevelt took the United States off gold, were first to arrive, followed by the French, the Canadians, the Argentines, the Italians, the Germans, and the Chinese. Hull, Moley, Feis, Bullitt, and Warburg were kept in constant shuttling motion.

As the consultations proceeded, the advisors were increasingly gripped by a sensation of futility. For one thing, although the goal of the conference ostensibly was to seek a formula for stabilizing exchange rates among the industrialized countries, Roosevelt's own views on that issue "veered and waffled," Feis recalled. Did Roosevelt believe stabilization was a possibility in the near future? Was he willing to commit to a multilateral fund, and if so, to what extent? Meanwhile, the rise of Adolph Hitler and the National Socialists, who had consolidated their power in German elections only a few weeks earlier, had muddled politics and economic policy in Europe virtually beyond rescue; matters were not improved when Hitler's finance minister, Hjalmar Schacht, tried transparently to deceive his American hosts about the regime's financial plans, earning him a mortifying rebuke from Roosevelt and Hull.

The naming of the American delegation did not instill confidence in the likelihood of a successful meeting. It was a motley group, capriciously selected. Hull was at its head, as befit the secretary of state, but his vice chair was former Ohio governor James M. Cox, chosen for no reason anyone knew other than in recognition of his role as the head of the 1920 Democratic presidential ticket, on which Franklin Roosevelt had been the vice presidential candidate. Filling out the mission were Pittman, who would succumb embarrassingly often to his weakness for drink during his time in London; Republican senator Couzens (sitting in for Hiram Johnson, who had declined the appointment); a Tennessee congressman with no affinity for finance; and a Texas businessman being repaid with a foreign junket for his contributions to the Democratic Party. Feis, Warburg, and Bullitt were the mission's chief advisors, with a support staff of forty. The strings were to be pulled by Roosevelt and Moley from Washington, 3,600 miles away.

Roosevelt seemed content to send off the mission without detailed instructions. On the night before their departure for England, the members sat with the President for a "desultory discussion . . . blurred over by foggy generality," Moley recalled. "Many of those present thought they knew the President's mind. They didn't. . . . A very inchoate die, a very shadowy die, had been cast."

In London the conference proceeded in an atmosphere of contention and confusion. Warburg became drawn into increasingly serious talks with the British and French aimed at a mutual stabilization of the dollar, pound, and franc. When news of these negotiations finally reached Washington, a sharp message emanated from the White House rejecting any such arrangement. At that point Roosevelt decided to dispatch Moley to London to provide on-the-spot guidance, an act almost certain to confuse the mission further by making it seem as if Hull had been replaced as its leader.

Upon his arrival, Moley did his best to reassure Hull that he was still in charge, but nevertheless got swept up himself into the stabilization talks with the British and French that Warburg had begun. Over the next few days he and his British and French counterparts worked out an innocuous declaration committing their governments to restoration of the gold standard eventually, but each on its own timeline. "The most fanatical inflationist could not have objected to this statement," Moley reported later.

He transmitted the declaration late one night to Roosevelt, who was sailing off the coast of Maine. He did not expect a reply for many hours. He would not get one for three days. And when it came, it was devastating. On Monday morning, July 3, Roosevelt dispatched a message from the radio room of the U.S.S. *Indianapolis* that would become famous as "the bombshell." It began:

> I would regard it as a catastrophe amounting to a world tragedy if the great conference of nations, called to bring about a more real and permanent financial stability and a greater prosperity to the masses of all nations should . . . allow itself to be diverted by the proposal of a purely artificial and temporary experiment affecting the monetary exchange of a few nations only.

From his first scathing words, Roosevelt seemed to be responding to a nonexistent proposal, for there was then no concrete stabilization plan on the table. Yet he continued in an even harsher tone. "I do not relish the thought that insistence on such action should be made an excuse for the continuance of the basic economic errors that underlie so much of the present world-wide depression," he wrote. He objected that "old fetishes of so-called international bankers are being replaced by efforts to plan national currencies" that would not meet the "need of modern civilization." The reestablishment of gold and silver as a currency reserve base, he concluded, would have to wait until "the world works out concerted policies . . . to produce balanced budgets and living within their means."

What provoked Roosevelt to torpedo the conference with such uncompromising language? Some delegates believed that, through a communications mix-up, Roosevelt was responding to an outdated message, not the communiqué Moley had sent. When Moley learned that Roosevelt had been sailing in the company of Henry Morgenthau, he concluded that the President's pen had been guided by Professor Warren, who would have little sympathy for even a theoretical return to the gold standard.

Yet despite its rhetorical excesses, the message made several salient points. The conference truly had been diverted from long-term issues toward the immediate question of currency rates. Discussions about a return to the gold standard certainly were premature. But to the crestfallen Europeans, the wire's belligerent, even paranoid, tone spelled the end of the conference and the discrediting of leading politicians in the major European capitals. British Prime Minister Ramsay MacDonald summoned Moley to 10 Downing Street to tell him, "Roosevelt cannot imagine what he has done to me."

Whatever its genesis, Roosevelt's bombshell marked a major divide in international economic relations. The Europeans had expected to use the conference to reinstate multilateral monetary and fiscal policy making. Roosevelt's message made clear that the United States was not yet willing to participate, and that when it did join, it would not do so on terms that tied together the U.S. dollar and foreign currencies anywhere near as tightly as had been the case before the crash. Implicit in the President's words was the signal that U.S. recovery would be fueled by controlled inflation to relieve the pressure of accumulated debt on farmers, businesses, and homeowners and to restore parity between the farm belt, where prices were expected to rise faster than elsewhere in the economy, and industry. Roosevelt was saying that since an international gold standard prevented any one country from creating inflation by manipulating its currency in relation to its trading partners', the gold standard would have to go.

To the Europeans, what gave the bombshell message its explosive force was the impression that it represented a sharp reversal from the U.S. position at the conference up to then. Actually, it represented the first explicit statement of the New Deal's approach to international economic policy after weeks, even months, of dithering—even up to the point of Moley's mission to London, which he had undertaken still without a clear idea of what Roosevelt expected him to achieve. After the bombshell, there was no more doubt. At least for the foreseeable future, the United States would deal with its economic problems strictly on its own.

Moley was the first of the refugees from the London delegation to visit Roosevelt upon his return. He found the President exhilarated, a mood that jarred violently with his own. He felt ill-used and embarrassed. To this Roosevelt seemed oblivious.

"Hello there," he greeted Moley cheerily on July 14. "Have you seen the papers for the days you were gone? My statement certainly got a grand press over there!" He brushed aside Moley's halting efforts to discuss the issue of the London declaration. Later that day a clue to the degree to which domestic considerations had entered into the management of international policy came from Louis Howe, who said of the bombshell message repudiating the stabilization: "Franklin hasn't done anything so popular since the bank crisis." For the first time since the election, Moley contemplated resigning; he decided to wait only long enough for his departure not to be seen as a consequence of the London fiasco.

Ten days later, Warburg came to the White House for an informal office lunch. Determined to confront Roosevelt with the folly of his ways, he promptly placed the President on the defensive. To FDR's plea that the bombshell had been greeted favorably in the American press, Warburg replied that it had been addressed not to the American voters but the nations of the world. "He takes the whole currency question very lightly," Warburg observed in his diary.

He was about to find out how lightly. Roosevelt informed Warburg that he wanted him to sit down with Professor Warren and an acolyte in his quest for the commodity dollar, James Harvey Rogers of Yale, men the banker privately dismissed as "these two newest prophets of the New Deal."

But harboring a glimmer of hope that he might yet exercise a stabilizing influence in the White House, he agreed.

The meeting took place the next day at the Harvard Club in New York. Warburg was already familiar with Warren's theory, having read a package of the professor's papers sent by the Committee for the Nation while he was steaming home from London. Although he had concluded in advance that the theorist's program was "almost ridiculous," in person he could not avoid being impressed by Warren's "complete sincerity" and by his earnest, unassuming personality—"convinced, but not dogmatic or bumptious, as were so many others of the New Deal economists."

More surprisingly, he found that there was not nearly as much difference in their views as he supposed. All three men were agreed that an international accord to stabilize the dollar was essential to eliminate the uncertainty roiling the credit and financial markets, though they differed over the optimum price of the dollar in relation to sterling or gold. While Warren seemed to harbor an almost religious fealty to his commodity dollar theory, he did acknowledge to Warburg that it "contained many practical pitfalls." He seemed amenable to a compromise Warburg proposed, calling for international currencies to be revalued against gold from time to time if "it appears that there really is a gold shortage, and that prices are depressed by such a gold shortage."

But as Warburg would soon learn, Warren was not as flexible as he thought. A few weeks later Warren, Rogers, and Warburg had another encounter, this time at Hyde Park in the presence of Roosevelt and under the eye of the President's mother, still very much the grande dame and in Warburg's estimation "a somewhat frightening old lady." When the three men assembled to talk business, Warburg found Warren as adamant as ever. More disturbingly, he found the President enthralled with Warren's "alluringly simple idea" that all one had to do to drive up the price of commodities was to drive up the price of gold, and transfixed by the cabalistic curves and scrawls that the professor traced over huge rolls of tissue paper to "explain" his theory.

Before they broke up, Roosevelt asked Warren and Rogers to take an unofficial trip to England and France, where they were to "mingle with the hoi-polloi" and discern what the reaction in Europe might be to changes in the dollar's relationship with gold. Warburg would stay home and convene a high-level study group.

As the three visitors rode to the Hyde Park train station in a taxi, Warren turned to Warburg and said ruefully, "Well, I guess you ruined my plan."

"On the contrary," Warburg replied. "You have won. Wait and see."

More than the President's enchantment by Warren's charts and graphs secured the latter's victory. There was also the unruliness of the currency and commodity markets during that summer and fall. Farm prices had risen sharply in May, after passage of the AAA with the Thomas amendment attached. But the boom evaporated in July, when the dollar began to rise and commodity and securities markets slumped. General Johnson's success at pushing industrial prices higher via the NRA only layered more gloom on the farm belt, as the purchasing power of the farm dollar inexorably shriveled. By the end of August, all the gain that farm prices had recorded in relation to industrial prices had disappeared.

Inflationists at the Committee for the Nation, in Congress, and in the farm belt were stirring; Milo Reno was again threatening a farm strike. Through September, Warburg's study group, which included Woodin, Douglas, and Undersecretary of the Treasury Dean Acheson, presented Roosevelt with numerous carefully reasoned papers. Their common theme was that currency manipulation was doomed to fail and only the removal of doubt about the dollar's stability could spur the needed increase in overall business activity.

The President was unmoved. On September he met again with Warburg in the Oval Room, telling the banker: "If we don't keep the price of wheat and cotton moving up, I shall have marching farmers." When Warburg again tried to argue the point, Roosevelt snapped, "Well, what would you do to raise prices?" Warburg had to concede that he had no panacea in mind. He could only repeat that the removal of uncertainty about the dollar would promote confidence and recovery . . . but that nothing would happen overnight. If Roosevelt wanted to help the farmers in the short term, the proper way to do so was with loans or subsidies, not debasement of the currency. The President listened coldly. Warburg left the Roosevelt White House that day, never to be invited back.

Roosevelt's determination to tinker with the price of gold brought him deeply into conflict with officials at the Treasury and in the attorney general's office, where there were grave doubts that the President had the authority to order the direct buying and selling of gold. On the other side was

Morgenthau, who advised him that Farm Credit Administration lawyers disagreed. They proposed empowering the Reconstruction Finance Corporation to handle the gold transactions, an idea that had the enthusiastic approval of Jesse Jones, the autocratic RFC chair, whose support was essential.

Now, with Jones's assent to the gold scheme in his pocket, Roosevelt proceeded to outflank his last opponents. At a stormy White House meeting on October 19, Treasury's Dean Acheson stood virtually alone in his insistence that government purchases of gold, whether done by the Treasury or the RFC, flouted the law.

"I say it is legal," Roosevelt said, ending the conversation. Acheson's next stop was the RFC, where he addressed the board. His face a grim crimson, he repeated his opposition to the plan, but said: "The President has ordered me to do it. I will carry out his orders."

Roosevelt now put his plan in motion. His first step was to explain it to the country via a Fireside Chat, his fourth, on October 22. Moley had been summoned back to the White House to assist with its drafting. It had been six weeks since he submitted his resignation, a period he spent attempting to purchase the *Washington Post* out of bankruptcy with backing from friends in the Harriman family. (He lost out to the financier Eugene Meyer, who had been Jones's predecessor as chairman of the RFC and whose daughter, Katharine Graham, later would lead the paper to distinction; Moley went on to launch a weekly current affairs magazine named *Today*, which soon became absorbed into the nascent *Newsweek*.)

Moley, who often had expressed his profound skepticism about the plan to FDR, approached his new assignment purely as a technician. Under the eye of Warren, who "fluttered over the creation much as he might have watched a hatching experiment in the poultry laboratory at Cornell," he translated the professor's thesis into lucid English for delivery in the President's soothing tones on the coming Sunday night. "My conscience was clear," Moley reflected, concluding that inasmuch as the scheme was unlikely to work it could do the country no harm. "I was right," he observed later. "It didn't work, and it didn't hurt anything—except Warren."

Moley contributed the most important line of the radio speech: "This is a policy, and not an expedient. It is not to be used merely to offset a temporary fall in prices." Thus Roosevelt communicated his utmost seriousness of purpose, which he tried to reinforce by placing the government's buying and selling of gold in the context of "sound money," employing that shibboleth to suggest that his goal was economic stability, not unrestrained inflation. "A sound currency will accompany a rise in the American commodity price level," he said.

At first the markets responded with surprising equanimity to an announcement that, for all its directness, left open to "pure conjecture" exactly what "possible currency experiments" Roosevelt had in mind, as the *New York Times* observed. While he listened to the radio speech at the home of a friend in Chicago, Warburg, who had known well enough what was coming, could not help but feel a sinking sensation of futility, akin to what he had felt on April 18 (the night of the Thomas amendment meeting), and July 3 (when the bombshell message had spooled off the telex machine in London). But "the inflationists roared their delight," he observed, bidding up commodity prices across the board.

Had the denizens of Wall Street understood just how arbitrarily Roosevelt and his two accomplices would be setting the price of gold and the value of the dollar, they would have been less composed. Roosevelt looked forward to the launch of gold buying with almost childlike glee. "I have had the shackles on my hands for months now," he told Morgenthau, "and I feel for the first time as though I had thrown them off." The first day's price of $31.36 had been suggested by Jones, who judged it just large enough to persuade the markets of Roosevelt's resolve, but low enough to discomfit speculators who had been rumor-mongering about a price of $36 or even $40. Indeed, the international markets seemed to react with relief to the comparatively modest hike.

From that point on, however, the only guiding principles were that gold should be pushed inexorably higher, but at wildly varying daily margins— "sufficiently erratic to confuse speculators, sufficiently high to affect world gold and commodity prices," Morgenthau, who was shortly to be named Treasury secretary, confided to his diary. Nor was there to be any hint about what the final price would be, the better to keep international traders off balance. Roosevelt reveled in the caprice at his fingertips: he began one day vacillating between 18 and 22 cents, then took one look at Morgenthau, who seemed to be carrying the weight of the world especially heavily that morning, and chose 21 cents. "It's a lucky number," he explained. The jape failed to relieve Morgenthau's gloom. He wrote in his diary: "If anybody ever knew how we really set the gold price through a combination of lucky numbers, etc., I think they would be frightened."

Yet the resulting confusion worked both ways. The market had no idea what to expect from day to day—and the White House had no idea why commodity prices were not responding as anticipated and failed to hold their gains after the first day. No clear pattern emerged. On the second day, Roosevelt, Morgenthau, and Jones put up the price by another 18 cents, but commodity prices dropped. ("Administration advisers indicated that they were not surprised, however," the *New York Times* assured readers.) On the third day the hike was 22 cents, and commodities rose.

Once put into practice, Warren's theory came apart with stunning rapidity. Within days of its implementation, it became clear that the markets were arbitraging the differing dollar prices of gold in the United States and abroad, which diluted the domestic effect of the gold-buying spree. ("There were now two dollars," Warburg observed, not without satisfaction. "A Warren dollar and a foreign exchange dollar.")

Warren's solution was for the government to buy gold not only domestically but on the international market, in an attempt to eliminate the international differential in gold prices. Roosevelt concurred. This new phase elicited shocked fulminations from the French and British, to Roosevelt's amusement. Informed by telephone of Bank of England governor Montagu Norman's spluttering reaction—"The whole world will be put into bankruptcy!" he exclaimed—Roosevelt caught Morgenthau's eyes. Summoning an image of the dapper, vandyked Norman, whom Roosevelt privately called "old pink whiskers," in a frothing rage, the two of them burst out laughing.

Around that time Roosevelt pushed Acheson out, having concluded that he had been leaking to the press damaging inside dope about the dollar deliberations. Although it later emerged that the leaker was Douglas, Acheson had made no secret of his continuing discontent with policy. This provoked Roosevelt to convene a meeting of his financial advisers, Acheson included, to inform them once and for all that "the buying of gold is an administration policy."

"We are all in the same boat," he declared, his eye gliding over the faces of the men in the room. "If anyone does not like the boat, he can get out of it." The President added that he was not referring to anyone in particular, though Morgenthau, for one, thought Acheson looked "very miserable and very sick through the whole thing." Two weeks later, Roosevelt accepted Acheson's resignation, leaving the path open for him to name Morgenthau to replace the dying Will Woodin as Treasury secretary. It was not an appointment that presaged an independent-minded Treasury Department in the New Deal. "Those who knew Morgenthau well interpreted this to mean that the President would now be his own Secretary of the Treasury," reflected Warburg.

Opposition to the gold-buying scheme built swiftly, especially among the industrial elite. In late November, the U.S. Chamber of Commerce called for a return to the gold standard. Around the same time, Al Smith, shedding the mantle of loyal supporter of the Democratic administration, threw in his lot with big business, declaring, "I am for gold dollars as against baloney dollars," and taking a shot at the Brain Trust—"the inexperienced young college professors who hold no responsible public office but are perfectly ready to turn 130,000,000 Americans into guinea pigs for experimentation." It was Smith's first public step on a road that would lead him clear out of the Democratic Party mainstream.

None of this might have posed much of a problem for Roosevelt had the dollar program worked as he expected; but farm prices were rising only modestly, when they rose at all, in relation to the price of gold. "It's funny how sometimes they seem to go against all the rules," a crestfallen Roosevelt blurted one day. The confusion had spread worldwide, provoking John Maynard Keynes to complain to the President by open letter that "the recent gyrations of the dollar" looked to him "like a gold standard on the booze."

With evidence mounting that the Warren scheme was a chimera, Roosevelt began to lose his taste for manipulation. With Jones and Morgenthau he set the gold price at $34.01 on December 1 and left it unchanged until December 16, when he raised it 5 cents. There it stayed until the program ended January 17. Two days earlier, Roosevelt had asked Congress for the authority to fix the value of the dollar permanently at no more than 60 percent of its former weight in gold, to transfer to the Treasury the ownership of all monetary gold in the United States, and to fund a $2 billion "stabilization" fund from the $2.8 billion profit the government would book from the revaluation of gold. The Gold Reserve Act became law on January 30, and the very next day Roosevelt reinstalled the United States on the gold standard, setting the dollar at 59.06 percent of its former weight, which had been fixed in 1900. The new price of gold was $35.00 exactly. There it would stand until 1971, when the gold standard was shattered again, this time for the long haul, by Richard Nixon.

Roosevelt's experiment was over. The frenzy of October and November quickly receded in people's memories; the stock market began rising again and business showed signs of reviving in the industrial heartland. Farm prices had actually fallen in November and December, but the agricultural rabble-rousing fomented by Milo Reno and his ilk had not amounted to much in the end. Professor Warren returned to Cornell, his theory thoroughly discredited. A new issue gripped the nation: the end of Prohibition, which had been repealed in the November elections, effective December 5. As the financial journalist John Brooks would put it, "the gold standard went off the booze just as the country went back on it."

As Moley had expected, the gold scheme did no permanent damage to the U.S. economy. In political terms, however, its impact would be lasting. From the banking crisis and through the Hundred Days, Wall Street and big business had given the New Deal their cooperation, even to the extent of muting their distaste for the Securities Act in June and acceding to the blustering of General Johnson. Now they were confronted with evidence that the man in the White House just might be the madman of their nightmares, not to be trusted with anything so precious as the health of the financial system, much less with regulation of their business practices. They had given him a long lead, and he had responded by taking them on a harrowing ride, only to end up at a place to which he could have taken a much shorter and simpler route.

The gold scheme was not Roosevelt's worst miscalculation in office, but for the business community it was the first. From then on, they would respond to every New Deal venture with a fight. There would be many fights in the years to come.

8

HARRY AND HAROLD

ARRY HOPKINS TOOK office in Washington after seventy-nine of Franklin Roosevelt's first hundred days had already passed. He seemed determined to make up for lost time. In the first two hours after moving into the ramshackle offices in the RFC building ceded to him as federal relief administrator, he spent more than $5 million, the first trickle of what was about to become a torrent of assistance to the destitute and unemployed in the largest organized relief program in U.S. history.

It was May 22. Ten days earlier Congress had created the Federal Emergency Relief Administration, and eight days after that Roosevelt had named Hopkins as its chief, extracting him from the directorship of New York state's Temporary Emergency Relief Administration following a brief tug-of-war with New York governor Herbert Lehman. (YOU HAVE THE ENTIRE COUNTRY FROM WHICH TO MAKE CHOICE, Lehman had wired his predecessor in protest.)

There was justice in the appointment, for FERA was very much Hopkins's brainchild. Ever since the election he had been attempting by letter and phone call to turn Roosevelt's attention to a plan to distribute grants-in-aid to the states for unemployment relief, which was overstretching state and local budgets nationwide. Like hundreds of other audience seekers he had been blocked by Marvin H. McIntyre, the President's appointment secretary, a former political reporter who "didn't know the sheep from the goats" among the "do-gooder" class (by Frances Perkins's assessment) and therefore barred the door to them all.

From his perch in New York, Hopkins had contemplated with anguish the spreading contagion of joblessness and poverty. In Pennsylvania, one of the few states compiling reliable statistics, more than 1.5 million workers were unemployed on Inauguration Day, an increase of 28 percent from the previous July. In 1932, Governor Gifford Pinchot had asked the federal government for an emergency grant of $45 million, a sum sufficient to keep the poor on subsistence provisions for only six months. Federal officials gave Pennsylvania $11.3 million. Other states in similar predicaments received similar treatment: Illinois asked for $10 million in July 1932 for its 1,150,000 unemployed and received $3 million, then sought another $23 million in emergency funding and received $6 million more.

The tide of destitution washed over every state line. In one county in Arkansas, a state that had experienced flood in 1927, drought in 1930, and bank failures in 1930, 1931, and 1933, a local banker reported to his congressman that "1,500 families are without shoes or clothing and they have not a dollar in money." In southeast Kansas, where the mines had been shut for three years, local relief agencies had done their best to stave off riots and hunger. But now every county in the region was bankrupt, their relief coffers empty.

Although Hopkins had been appointed to his New York position by Roosevelt, the two were not on familiar terms. But Hopkins was close to his former Albany colleague Frances Perkins, and a few days after the inauguration he sought her out in Washington. Perkins had scarcely come to grips with her responsibilities toward the unemployed. "There were on my desk over two thousand plans for federal action to cover unemployment and as many more on the President's," she recalled. But she made time for Hopkins, suggesting they meet at the Women's University Club, where she was staying.

The club was jammed to the rafters with socialites and supplicants, so Perkins and Hopkins took refuge in a hollow under the main staircase. There, crouched under the low overhang, Hopkins outlined his plan in such compelling detail that Perkins was moved to bully McIntyre into securing him an immediate audience with the President. The result of that encounter was a bill, introduced in the Senate by three pillars of progressive politics—Edward P. Costigan of Colorado, Robert La Follette, Jr., of Wisconsin, and Robert F. Wagner of New York—appropriating $500 million for grants to the states. Half was to be paid on the basis of one federal dollar to every three raised by a state from all other public sources. The other $250 million was to be made available for disbursement at the state and local levels at the discretion of the as-yet-unnamed federal relief administrator, chiefly to states that had tapped out all other sources of relief money and were unable even to raise their 75 percent shares for the main program.

Within a day of his installation as FERA administrator, Hopkins had made grants to Colorado, Illinois, Iowa, Michigan, Mississippi, Ohio, and Texas. An unknown figure in American politics on Inauguration Day, by the end of the year he would be the most identifiable New Dealer of all, with the possible exception of the irrepressible Hugh Johnson and the certain exception of the President himself. Hopkins's rise to such prominence, and beyond, was almost entirely the doing of Franklin Roosevelt.

The *New Yorker* described Harry Hopkins as looking like "an animated piece of Shredded Wheat"; the artist Peggy Bacon in the *New Republic* saw him as a figure with "drab coloring and an air of dismal youth. Pale urban-American type, emanating an aura of chilly cynicism and defeatist irony like a moony, melancholy newsboy." His appearance resulted from a lifetime of chronic illness, beginning with a bout of typhoid before the age of ten, followed by persistent stomach problems through adulthood and culminating in the stomach cancer that killed him in 1946 at the age of fifty-five. Still, the great newsman Ernie Pyle saw frank empathy, not illness or world-weariness, in Hopkins's bearing: "You, Mr. Hopkins, I liked you because you look like common people. . . . You sit there so easy swinging back and forth in your swivel chair, in your blue suit and blue shirt, and your neck is sort of skinny, like poor people's necks, and you act honest, too."

Harry Lloyd Hopkins was born on August 17, 1890, in Sioux City, Iowa, where his father was a harness maker—a lowly trade that Hopkins never ceased mentioning. ("Can't you ever stop boasting about your humble origin?" a friend once pleaded.) In 1901 the family relocated to Grinnell, Iowa, where David Hopkins became known for his salty and shiftless manner and Anna Pickett Hopkins for her churchliness, temperance, and industry. It would not be a stretch to conclude that Harry, the fourth of their five children, inherited his sporting blood and cutting wit from his father and his missionary drive from his mother. Hopkins entered Grinnell College with the class of 1912. As he was preparing to graduate, a professor steered him into a settlement house job in New York, work that exposed him to poverty at a level of degradation and squalor he had never encountered in his midwestern upbringing. He made himself an expert analyst of the problems of the poor and sick and a first-class organizer of relief programs, and in 1931 was invited by Jesse I. Straus, the president of Macy's department store and Governor Franklin Roosevelt's appointee as chairman of the state's Temporary Emergency Relief Administration, to become the agency's executive director. When Straus stepped down a year later, he recommended that young Hopkins succeed him as chairman. Governor Roosevelt took his advice. A year after that, President Roosevelt would be inviting Harry Hopkins to Washington.

Hopkins's experience in social work and charity organizing gave him a fresh perspective on the principles of unemployment relief, which up to then had been dictated by big business and community charities. He dismissed the business viewpoint as what we might today call the "trickle-down" theory—"the old Hamiltonian theory that so long as the top of the financial structure were taken care of with credit and subsidy, the foundation of our society, the millions of the population, would receive bounteous prosperity as it percolated to them from the profits above."

Equally contemptible, in his view, was the mind-set of local relief agencies, which held that "the applicant was in some way morally deficient . . . [and] must be made to feel his pauperism. . . . Every help which was given him was to be given in a way to intensify his sense of shame." Chief among these indignities was the "means test," in which the applicant was forced to document his poverty and submit to an investigation of his personal habits, his family life, and his child-rearing practices by a censorious relief agent. Hopkins was determined to staff local relief offices with people who might understand that "the predicament of the worker without a job is an economic predicament not of his own making."

He aimed to revise the distribution of relief to minimize degradation and allow recipients the broadest latitude in spending their allotments. He discouraged traditional institutions such as central food commissaries, which had the virtue of being relatively inexpensive to operate but forced recipients to travel out of their neighborhoods to obtain aid and diverted business from established retailers, including grocers who might have been carrying jobless workers and their families on credit for months or years and deserved to be able to keep them as customers. An especially degrading practice was the issuance of grocery slips, which could be redeemed at any grocer but were subject to a long list of forbidden merchandise—no razors or tobacco, for example. It was not unusual for retailers to conspire with their customers to subvert this system by returning a small portion of the chit in cash, which then could be used to purchase a haircut or an ounce or two of pipe tobacco.

Hopkins preferred to distribute aid in cash: "It is a matter of opinion whether more damage is done to the human spirit by a lack of vitamins or complete surrender of choice," he observed. Over time he shifted most of the government relief funds under his jurisdiction to cash grants, trusting that the wastage would be minimal and more than compensated for by the recipients' gain in dignity.

Hopkins also disliked flying blind. One obstacle to creating an effective national relief program was that information about local conditions was invariably funneled into Washington from local relief officials whose views were muddled by limited vantage points, prejudices against the poor, and the influence of locally powerful interests. As a counterweight, Hopkins established his own network of field observers. The most prominent and effective among them was Lorena A. Hickok, a former newspaper reporter from Wisconsin and an intimate friend of Eleanor Roosevelt, whose reports constitute a peerless chronicle of life in the Depression, delivered by an expert observer with her feet firmly on the ground. Hickok's very first dispatches to Hopkins, from rural Pennsylvania in the late summer of 1933, covered recipients' discontent with merchants who exploited the grocery slip system to short-weight and overcharge the clientele. Even many relief administrators disdained the system, she reported. "'These people aren't children,' you hear over and over again. 'They're honest, self-respecting citizens who, through no fault of their own, are temporarily on relief. The vast majority of them have always managed their own affairs, can be trusted with cash—however little they're going to get to live on— and should be.'"

Hickok identified another important flaw in the relief program: the corruption of patronage. "From the township to Harrisburg, the state is honeycombed with politicians all fighting for the privilege of distributing patronage. . . . One of our staff in Fayette county told me that 75 percent of the men employed on state highways, under the public works program, got their jobs through political influence, and that it was practically impossible for a man on the relief rolls to get one of those jobs." Hickok's reports, brimming with details Hopkins never would have learned from local officials complicit in the system, underscored how difficult it would be to professionalize the delivery of relief to twenty million Americans.

Hopkins's insights might have remained mere theory had he not shown a distinct talent for bureaucratic infighting and a streak of principled obstinacy that old friends attributed to his mother's genes. Next to the President himself, Hopkins possessed the most complicated personality in the Roosevelt White House. In many respects he was a mirror image of Harold Ickes, who would be his most determined adversary in the quest for Roosevelt's attention. Ickes projected the upright, pugnacious mien of the battle-hardened warrior-progressive, his florid expression always on the verge of eruption; Hopkins was sallow and gaunt, his slouching posture perfectly suited to the tatty and careworn offices where he felt most comfortable doing business.

The roots of their conflict lay in their personalities—Hopkins given to confident self-righteousness, Ickes to paranoia—and in their irreconcilably low opinions of each other's skills as relief organizers. To Ickes, Hopkins was a spendthrift whose program amounted to "thousands of inconsequential make-believe projects in all parts of the country." Hopkins disdained Ickes's taste for projects of monumental permanence in which most of the spending went for materials, not men. To him, the desperate need across the country was for wages; getting money to the unemployed and needy was the principal goal of relief—indeed, it was almost the only goal. As he told an audience of relief staffers in Los Angeles in 1936: "When this thing is all over and I am out of the Government the things I am going to regret are the things I have failed to do for the unemployed."

They were both among Roosevelt's most loyal aides: Ickes would be one of the only two cabinet members (with Frances Perkins) who would serve FDR from the inauguration to the President's death in 1945; Hopkins would become personally so close to the President that he would be invited to move into the White House in 1940, where he and his third wife occupied a second-floor suite that included the room in which Abraham Lincoln had signed the Emancipation Proclamation. When war broke out in Europe, Hopkins was sent as Roosevelt's personal emissary to the beleaguered government of Winston Churchill, his recognized intimacy with the First Family taken as a strong (if somewhat misleading) signal that Roosevelt intended to stand fast with the British people.

They were both creatures of paradox. Popularly dubbed "Honest Harold" for his determination that not a single taxpayer dollar stray into corrupt pockets, Ickes pursued a secret love affair with an office assistant that always seemed one misstep short from bursting into public view (but never did during his White House service); Hopkins devoted his career to the relief of destitution, yet displayed a taste for horse playing and habituated the stylish nightspots of Manhattan. Ickes played the game of inside politics remorselessly, assisted by a pair of personal investigators who were not above spying on his fellow cabinet members; but Hopkins, so easily misjudged as a soft-shelled social worker, bested him more often than not in their long war for primacy as almsgivers of the New Deal. In their direct dealings with Franklin Roosevelt they chose diametrically different approaches. Ickes would react to real and perceived slights at Roosevelt's hand by issuing frequent threats to resign, which forced the President to talk him back into the fold with honeyed reassurances. Hopkins never threatened to quit; his response to a distasteful presidential dictum was to comply without cavil, and await patiently the opportunity to reverse it.

The two had very different gifts for invective—Ickes a master of the rapier thrust, Hopkins given to the impolitic wisecrack. The latter was "addicted to the naked insult," his biographer Robert E. Sherwood recalled. He could be especially biting in response to attacks on his relief programs as sentimental coddlers of the undeserved: "I have a real quarrel with people who say such things while seated at a comfortable dinner table drinking cocktails," he declared, adding sensationally in a radio speech in 1935 that "they sit in pompous conclaves . . . and bring forth such ideas as giving the needy unemployed a ham sandwich and letting it go at that." Hugh Johnson, a connoisseur of political invective, wrote in the column he turned out for the Scripps Howard newspapers after his departure from the NRA that Hopkins had "a mind like a razor, a tongue like a skinning knife, a temper like a Tartar and a sufficient vocabulary of parlor profanity . . . to make a mule skinner jealous."

Years later, Ickes would concede defeat in his long battle with Hopkins, attributing it to the emotional bond Hopkins had developed with both Franklin and Eleanor Roosevelt: "While in a contest with Harry I might win the President's mind, his heart would remain with Harry." Hopkins once sardonically described to Ickes his method of keeping his foothold in the President's circle: "Cultivate the President's family—Mrs. Roosevelt, the President's mother . . . and Missy LeHand [the President's personal secretary]. You will not have to pay attention to anyone else. I haven't, and see where I have landed."

FERA was only Hopkins's first effort to expand and professionalize federal relief. As the summer of 1933 turned to fall and it became evident that the needy would become more numerous and more desperate in the coming winter, he appealed to Roosevelt for a new program. This would involve not handouts, but work, and on a massive scale: he estimated that four million unemployed Americans would need jobs on the federal payroll.

Hopkins distinguished the new program from "work relief," in which the work was merely an instrument to invest a small measure of dignity in a process still requiring social workers to subject applicants to a means test. The work relief recipient "feels himself to be something of a public ward, with small freedom of choice," he observed.

That would not be true of the new program, soon christened the Civil Works Administration. CWA was to involve real work, at a government pay scale. The social worker would be dropped from the process—unlike recipients of FERA funds, applicants for CWA work would not have to be on local relief rolls; unemployment would be sufficient qualification. Moreover, in contrast to work relief, in which the work project was viewed predominantly as a "labor-absorber," CWA and its much more ambitious successor, the Works Progress Administration, or WPA, were to invest in projects important enough that they might well be built by their local communities even if there were no workers in need of jobs. Hopkins would proudly repeat the remark of one WPA worker's wife: "We aren't on relief anymore, my husband's working for the government."

What characterized CWA more than anything else was its urgency. Hopkins presented Roosevelt with the proposal for the wintertime work program early in November and encouraged the President to cost it out for himself: four million workers at an average of $100 for the season, or $400 million. Roosevelt decreed that the sum should come out of the $3.3 billion in public works money appropriated under Title II of NIRA and still waiting to pass through Ickes's fine sieve.

As head of the Public Works Administration, Ickes still was being painstaking to a fault. He subjected every proposal, large or not so large, to a rigorous examination that often reduced state and local officials—and their Washington representatives—to apoplexy. Every demand from a politician for faster action provoked him to dig in his heels deeper. On October 28, just as Hopkins was formulating his CWA proposal for FDR, Ickes fended off a delegation of thirty congressmen "who proceeded to bedevil me for post offices," as he groused to his diary. "I told them that we had a special committee making a study of this situation with a view to seeing whether many of these post offices could not be built at such reduced figures as would justify us in going ahead with them," a demonstration of governmental economy they could not have found endearing. Later the same day Ickes turned away a delegation from Utah headed by his cabinet colleague George Dern, the secretary of war (and a former governor of that state), who arrived "to nag again about some reclamation projects for their state. . . . They seem to be proceeding on the theory that they can just wear down our resistance and get what they want"—a sure sign that they failed to understand the psychology of Harold Ickes.

Ickes tried to establish a clear "line of demarcation" between PWA projects and more modest undertakings appropriate for the CWA. The arrangement he reached with Hopkins was that CWA would focus purely on "projects of a minor character"—that is, no sewers or waterworks, bridges or large buildings. Yet it proved almost impossible to keep CWA from poaching PWA projects, especially those delayed by Ickes's financial caution. "Harry Hopkins could always get money," Ickes was still marveling many years later, after Hopkins's death. He "would bear down upon the White House, and the next thing that I would know, an order would be issued impounding all PWA funds that had not yet been allotted or expended." Ickes tried to project tolerant amusement at Hopkins's maneuvering, but in truth his suspicious nature was activated: "It was something more than mere coincidence that there were always workers available for one of Harry's projects, even if there were not for mine."

While Ickes pinched every penny, Hopkins continued to shovel out every dime as fast as it came in. Hopkins disbursed more than $800 million in the first three and a half months of CWA's existence, including much of a $950 million appropriation he obtained from Congress to supplement the initial grant of $400 million. Among the CWA projects under way by early 1934, as compiled by *Time:* "4,464 Indians to repair their own houses on Indian Reservations; 1,104 to excavate prehistoric Indian mounds for the Smithsonian Institution; 211 men to pull up seaside and swamp morning-glories, hosts of the sweet-potato weevil; 198 men to remove debris from Alaskan rivers so salmon can swim up and spawn; . . . a group to wash Manhattan's civic statues; unemployed colored girls to keep house for destitute families."

Before it was shut down in the spring of 1934, CWA built or improved a quarter million miles of road. Cavalierly crossing Ickes's line of demarcation, the CWA workforce put 40,000 schools into shape by installing water and sanitary systems, repairing defective wiring, fixing rickety desks, painting "walls blackened with dirt." More than 12 million feet of sewer pipe were laid, 150,000 privies built to combat typhoid and dysentery in rural communities, 200 swimming pools and 3,700 playgrounds constructed along with community athletic fields, bathhouses, campgrounds, trails, and even the occasional artificial lake. At its peak CWA employed more than 4 million Americans, providing sustenance for 20 million family members.

The record of the CWA and the WPA reflected Hopkins's role as perhaps the least cynical or defeatist member of FDR's inner circle. Few approached their jobs with as much conviction that their work was indispensable to the citizens or even to national security; few defended their programs with as much determination. He was brusquely unapologetic when the press and conservatives in Congress attacked his programs, especially the WPA, for the apparent triviality of some of the projects to put the unemployed— whether blue-collar or white-collar—to work.

A New York City alderman's 1935 investigation of relief projects added the word *boondoggle*, derived from a midwestern regionalism signifying small-scale handicrafts, to the political lexicon as a synonym for wasteful spending—with a WPA-funded study of historic safety pins in New York advanced as the gold standard in boondoggling.

Hopkins was having none of it. At a press conference following a City Hall hearing he stood his ground. A reporter asked: "Have you contemplated making an investigation?"

"Why should I?" he replied truculently, issuing a ringing reproach to those who ridiculed efforts to preserve the dignity of the poor by providing them with work, not handouts:

> They are damn good projects—excellent projects. . . . Dumb people criticize something they do not understand, and that is what is going on up there—God damn it! Here are a lot of people broke and we are putting them to work making researches of one kind or another, running big recreational projects where the whole material costs 3%, and practically all the money goes for relief. As soon as you begin doing anything for white collar people, there is a certain group of people who begin to throw bricks. I have no apologies to make. As a matter of fact, we have not done enough. . . . We have projects up there to make Jewish dictionaries. There are rabbis who are broke and on the

relief rolls. One hundred and fifty projects up there deal with pure science. What of it? I think those things are good in life. . . . You can make fun of anything; that is easy to do.

To the impatient Hopkins, the results were what were important: the distribution of relief to the largest number of Americans at the lowest possible administrative cost and with the smallest component of indignity. Reports from the field validated his instincts. "Today was the first CWA pay day in the state of Iowa," Hickok wrote him from Des Moines on November 25. "Something over 5,000 men, who went to work with picks and shovels and wheelbarrows last Monday morning, lined up and got paid—MONEY. . . . They took it with wide grins and made bee-lines for the grocery stores, NOT to shove a grocery order across the counter, but to go where they pleased and buy what they pleased, with cash. . . . I wonder if you have any idea of what CWA is doing for the morale of these people and the communities."

Despite those positive results, pressure to shut down the CWA as quickly as possible came from conservatives taking their cue from the Republican National Committee, which issued a broadside titled "CWA Scandals" and warning of the "gross waste of public funds" and "downright corruption." Yet when Roosevelt did shut down the CWA in 1934 he was capitulating not to Republicans but to Lewis Douglas, who was warning that the agency was on its way to busting the federal budget and creating a permanent underclass of government wards. The President, always wary of programs that resembled the "dole," ordered Hopkins to close CWA as soon as the killing winter of 1934 had passed. "Nobody is going to starve during the warm weather," he said. Hopkins obediently transferred the agency's remaining funds to FERA. CWA faded away, unlamented even by good-government progressives. Walter Lippmann, damning the program with the faintest praise, listed its virtues thus: "It started quickly and provided immediate employment. It did much genuinely useful work even though examples can be cited where it did useless work. Finally, and this is very important, it was possible to discontinue . . . at short notice."

But the end of CWA was merely the prelude to the creation of the greatest relief program of all. In February 1935, Roosevelt, still preening at having led the Democrats to a resounding midterm victory in the 1934 election, sent Congress a proposal for a $4.9 billion work relief program. The plan generated immediate controversy, not so much because of its scale, but because it was to be administered entirely from within the White House—through procedures that Roosevelt for the moment kept secret, as he did his choice for administrator. Roosevelt divulged only a set of fundamental principles, drafted by Hopkins to resemble those of the late CWA. Among them: the work projects "should be useful," labor-intensive rather than materials-oriented, and short-term and capable of being launched on short notice.

The enactment of the new relief bill in April touched off the most ferocious battle yet between Ickes and Hopkins, the two most obvious candidates to head the program. Ickes entered the lists in his customary passive-aggressive fashion, declaring that he should like nothing better than to be entirely free of responsibility for public works and relief: "I want someone else appointed because I am really beginning to feel the weight of the burdens that I have been carrying," he wrote. "My nerves are all shot and I am sleeping badly."

In fact he continued to guard his PWA allotments and projects jealously, especially after Roosevelt attempted to settle the administrative issue with one of his characteristic non-solution solutions: Hopkins would administer small, labor-intensive projects through the new WPA; Ickes would retain jurisdiction over large, permanent projects, and any question about whether a given project belonged in one or the other basket was to be resolved by a third bureaucrat, Frank Walker, who was installed as head of something called the Division of Applications and Information.

It became plain almost immediately that this arrangement could never resolve the Ickes-Hopkins quarrel. The dividing line between WPA and PWA projects was supposed to be $25,000, but that was easily breached. A series of bureaucratic disputes arose, including one involving a sewer system for the city of Atlanta that was broken up into dozens of individual contracts so WPA could rationalize taking on the job. Ickes grew increasingly convinced that Hopkins had designs on his PWA portfolio. His paranoia increased markedly in August, after Roosevelt insensitively punctured his self-esteem by issuing an executive order requiring that every public works project be submitted to an executive-branch committee for approval. ICKES IS SHORN OF PWA POWER, read the *Washington Star*'s headline that afternoon, a "perfectly justified interpretation" in Ickes's own view. The episode launched him on a now-familiar round of sulking and threats of resignation, if more vehement than the norm. After a heated call with Roosevelt, Ickes reported to his diary: "I never thought I would talk to a

President of the United States the way I talked to President Roosevelt last night. I think I made it pretty clear that I wasn't going to stand for much more of the same kind of medicine."

Roosevelt managed to talk him down by promising to issue a formal statement that Ickes's authority had not changed. But the bad blood between Ickes and Hopkins continued. Near the end of September, Roosevelt tried to bring the two to terms by inviting them both on a long West Coast trip that would culminate in a cruise through the Panama Canal. The political highlight of the trip was to be a personal triumph for Ickes—Roosevelt's dedication of the great Boulder Dam on the Colorado River, which had been launched by Herbert Hoover but completed under the supervision of Ickes's Interior Department. Once the traveling party reached the coast and boarded the navy cruiser *Houston,* Roosevelt tried to reconcile his contentious aides through badinage. In the ship's newspaper appeared one day an item obviously penned by the President:

The feud between Hopkins and Ickes was given a decent burial today. With flags at half mast . . . the President officiated at the solemn ceremony which we trust will take these two babies off the front page for all time. . . . Hopkins expressed regret at the unkind things Ickes had said about him and Ickes on his part promised to make it stronger—only more so—as soon as he could get a stenographer who would take it down hot. The President gave them a hearty slap on the back—pushing them both into the sea. "Full steam ahead," the President ordered.

It is doubtful that anything as modest as these presidential pleasantries could have quelled the feud, and indeed Roosevelt failed in the attempt. The conflict intensified during 1936, causing him no end of discomfort in a presidential election year. The verbal crossfire was sharpening, at least partially because political pundits looking beyond Roosevelt's near-certain reelection in 1936 were mentioning both Hopkins and Ickes as candidates for the Democratic nomination in 1940.

Of greater concern to the President's campaign advisors was the tendency of both to become lightning rods for political criticism. In this category Hopkins was the more troublesome. His salty bluntness and intimacy with the presidential household gave his attackers a convenient target, as did the seemingly ever-expanding empire of WPA. When Congress took up a new $1.5 billion appropriation for the WPA in 1936, GOP Senator Lester Dickinson of Iowa, Hopkins's home state, warned: "If Congress passes this bill giving Hopkins this huge amount, we will be raising an American Caesar in our midst. . . . He has his eye on the Presidency." The *Chicago Tribune,* perhaps the most obdurate foe of the Roosevelt administration in the American press, called Hopkins "a bull-headed man whose high place in the New Deal was won by his ability to waste more money in quicker time on more absurd undertakings than any other mischievous wit in Washington could think of." Yet if Hopkins received most of the abuse in the press, it was Ickes who suffered the torment of feeling vanquished in the battle inside the White House. His competitive blood had cooled ever so slightly after the *Houston* cruise, especially when rumors arose (incorrectly, as it happened) that Hopkins might be preparing to leave the administration. By December he was back on the boil, fired in part by a presidential search for several hundred million dollars to keep WPA in business through the end of June 1936. Unwilling to see public works funds "go down the Hopkins rat hole," he informed Roosevelt that the Public Works Administration's entire allocation already had been committed, which forced the President to back off—for the moment. "Harry Hopkins will need all the loose change that the President can scrape together," Ickes observed to his diary.

The most serious flare-up occurred a few months later. The debate over the new $1.5 billion appropriation occasioned another rash of attacks on the WPA, which was accused of mismanagement, inefficiency, and outright corruption—in contrast to the Public Works Administration, which consistently won praise as a careful steward of taxpayer funds. In recognition of that accomplishment, and to safeguard PWA projects in their home districts, a sizable clique in Congress favored earmarking $400 million of the appropriation for the PWA. Roosevelt told reporters he was adamantly opposed to any such earmarking, even for $200 million. "If you take any of the billion and a half," he said, "you decrease the number of people you can give relief to by that amount."

To Ickes, this was a direct endorsement of the Hopkins relief policy at his expense: Roosevelt "made it perfectly clear that he was prepared to help Harry Hopkins carry out the desire that he has had at heart for the last two years to scuttle PWA and salvage from it whatever he can for the benefit of his own administration." This was a wild overinterpretation of a fleeting exchange at the press briefing, but it placed Ickes in high dudgeon. After allowing his anger to build for two days, he finally secured a meeting with Roosevelt, when he informed the President that "it didn't seem to me to be the part of political wisdom . . . to repudiate one of the best things he had ever done" (that is, establish the PWA), even in the midst of a reelection campaign he was certain to win. Roosevelt assured Ickes that he had the utmost admiration for his work with the PWA, but at a cabinet meeting a week later came another slight. With Ickes scheduled to testify shortly on Capitol Hill about the $1.5 billion appropriation, Roosevelt forbade him to criticize WPA at the upcoming hearing—and specified that talking up the achievements of the PWA would count as criticism of WPA. "It was as clear as day that the President was spanking me hard before the entire Cabinet and I resented that," Ickes reflected.

Ickes dictated a letter of resignation the next morning. He differed "fundamentally" with Roosevelt's (that is, Hopkins's) approach to work relief, he wrote, and regarded the President's recent statements as having "repudiated PWA and indicated a lack of confidence in me as Administrator." He delivered the letter directly to Missy LeHand, and only minutes later received a summons to lunch with the President that day. When he walked through Roosevelt's office door at 1 P.M., "the President looked at me with an expression of mock reproach and then, without saying a word, he handed to me a memorandum in his own handwriting."

"Dear Harold," the letter read, "P.W.A. is not 'repudiated.' . . . I have not indicated lack of confidence . . . I have *full* confidence in you. . . . You are needed, to carry on a big common task. . . . Resignation *not* accepted!"

Ickes, a soft target as always for Roosevelt's insidious charm, was overwhelmed. "I read this communication and was quite touched by its undoubted generosity and its evident sincerity of tone. . . . I must say the President took everything in the best possible spirit."

It may have been impossible for Roosevelt to resolve the tension between Ickes and Hopkins because at a basic level there was no tension: the New Deal required both a construction program of large-scale public works and a work relief program emphasizing spending on labor with a short-term horizon. Each of these programs had its ideal champion—the penny-pinching Ickes, determined that every dollar he spent would serve posterity; the feverish Hopkins, determined to spend every dollar for the alleviation of suffering in the here and now. It is doubtful that either could have succeeded as head of the other's program or as czar of all public construction and work relief.

Roosevelt tried to bring Ickes and Hopkins into mutual harmony because he disliked bickering; but with his all-embracing conception of government he had no trouble reconciling both men's programs as equally valid elements of the New Deal.

The one program Ickes would have been happy to cede to Hopkins was the Division of Subsistence Homesteads, the flagship of which was a model farming community in the hills of West Virginia known as Arthurdale. The problem with Arthurdale and its sister communities was not that they were remote backwaters of the New Deal of no interest to anybody; the problem was that they were the personal projects of a very attentive First Lady.

The subsistence homesteads grew out of a tradition in American social planning dating back to the late nineteenth century, when the industrialization of America had given rise to pathologies such as vagrancy, alcoholism, and prostitution in urban settings where the extended family, church, and community, those mainstays of rural society, were overmatched. The solution proposed by reformers was to return people to the land. Franklin Roosevelt, gentleman farmer, was susceptible to such nostrums. He arranged to insert in the National Industrial Recovery Act a $25 million appropriation to endow twenty-five thousand urban families with farms, and assigned the program to Ickes.

At the suggestion of Lorena Hickok, meanwhile, Mrs. Roosevelt had been touring the soft-coal regions of Appalachia. There she encountered the consequences of decades of exploitation of land and humanity by the mining industry: abject destitution left behind by closed mines in a despoiled landscape. "There were men in that area who had been on relief for from three to five years and who had almost forgotten what it was like to have a job at which they could work for more than one or two days a week," the First Lady reported. She enlisted Louis Howe to purchase for the government the disused agricultural estate of the Arthur family outside the hamlet of Reedsville, and to see that the first subsistence community went up on that site.

Ickes found the program a burden almost from its inception. He was shocked by the cost of housing and equipping the families, which had been budgeted at $2,000 to $3,000 each but had soared above $10,000, and irritated at race-based recruiting that kept the communities lily-white. Worse, he was unable to enlist the President in his efforts to shut the program down or quash the First Lady's desire to meddle in every detail. "This is the only phase of my administration I feel apologetic for," he told the President. Roosevelt replied airily, "My Missus, unlike most women, hasn't any sense about money at all."

The original date set for Arthurdale's launch was Thanksgiving 1933. Owing to such blunders as Howe's ordering prefabricated houses that did not fit their foundations, the deadline kept slipping. The families finally began arriving in mid-June and promptly came under the eye of newspaper and magazine writers seeking evidence of governmental profligacy. The *Saturday Evening Post* criticized the comparative comfort of the families' homes, and revealed that rhododendrons had been hauled sixty miles to beautify the town although rhododendrons were native to the region.

But the fundamental problem was that the community planners were government bureaucrats and social workers with little or no experience in farming, construction engineering, or community building. A plan to endow each of the first fifty families with a milk cow foundered when it was discovered that few had ever milked a cow before. The social workers' scheme for educating the Arthurdale children along progressive lines set forth by the education reformer John Dewey did not sit well with the practical-minded residents, who objected that the pupils were not being taught mathematics or grammar.

The planners' ambitions for industrial development also foundered on reality. A shirt factory, poultry farm, grist mill, tractor plant, and tourist inn all failed for want of business. Unemployment in Arthurdale did not fall until after 1941, when wartime demand forced a reopening of the mines.

Arthurdale eventually comprised 165 homes on plots of two to five acres, plus six school buildings. The First Lady remained a devoted patron, joining the square dances in the school gymnasium during her frequent visits. At no other community of Arthurdale's size was the high school commencement address delivered by the President of the United States (in 1938).

But by the 1940s the government became determined to turn Arthurdale into a private, self-sustaining community. Starting in 1942, its homes were offered to the residents for as little as $750 each, at a huge loss to the government. In 1946, with the last of the homes and the factory buildings sold, the government closed the books on what one historian called "one of the most embarrassing experiments in its history."

This judgment is surely too harsh. Arthurdale was overly ambitious and ill-planned, but it was a serious effort to relieve the suffering of a region that the country long had regarded with contempt and neglect. Eleanor Roosevelt would reflect later that its critics were for the most part "men who had never seen for themselves the plight of the miners or what we were trying to do for them." She regarded the expenditures at Arthurdale as a worthwhile investment in human capital: "I have always felt that many human beings who might have cost us thousands of dollars in tuberculosis sanitariums, insane asylums, and jails were restored to usefulness and given confidence in themselves. Later when during the last war I met boys from that area, I could not help thinking that a great many of them were able to serve their country only because of the things that had been done to help their parents through the depression period."

9

SO MANY SINNERS

NSIDE THE WHITE HOUSE, Supreme Court Justice Louis Brandeis wielded enormous influence. He was known by the fond nickname "Isaiah" and regularly sought out for counsel. Among New Dealers such as Tommy Corcoran and Ben Cohen, the justice's Monday afternoon teas—where tea was copious and other refreshments sparse—were a byword. There he would question the guests closely about their work and their agencies, dispense the wisdom of his years on issues large and small, and bask in the energy of the social upheaval emanating from the White House. "There is much noble thinking and high endeavor," he informed a cousin.

Brandeis mistrusted corporate power in America and believed in the rigorous regulation of business. On Wall Street it was commonly assumed that the justice's well-known antipathy to big corporations lurked behind the Glass-Steagall Act, which had mandated the separation of investment from commercial banking.

"I have little doubt that he inspired it, or even drafted it," Russell C. Leffingwell of Morgan & Company, which shortly would be compelled by the act to cleave itself into pieces, wrote to his partner Thomas W. Lamont just after New Year's Day 1934. "The Jews do not forget. They are relentless. . . . I think you underestimate the forces we are antagonizing. . . . I believe that we are confronted with the profound politico-economic philosophy, matured in the wood for twenty years, of the finest brain and the most powerful personality in the Democratic party, who happens to be a Justice of the Supreme Court."

Yet Leffingwell and other outsiders misinterpreted Brandeis's role in the New Deal. His contribution was not direct, but philosophical. The food on which his acolytes Corcoran and Cohen supped in his presence was his broad social liberalism and his skepticism about the concentration of economic power; but although the younger men were devoted in theory to strict regulation of the stock exchange and the banking industry, they also were evolving into canny legislative technicians, their aim being to craft bills that could be passed by a politically heterogeneous Congress and be accepted at some fundamental level by the business community. They were no more inclined to upend the established economic order than their ultimate patron, Franklin Roosevelt, and they spent almost as much time defending their legislative drafts from the criticism that they did not go far enough as from the charge that they went too far. Through them, Brandeis's principles met political reality—and Old Isaiah was not always happy with the results.

The first fruit of the Corcoran/Cohen partnership, the Securities Act of 1933, was a quintessential product of the Hundred Days: hastily written, jerry-rigged, too narrow, and incomplete. To hustle the bill through the special session that summer, Roosevelt had put it on a diet, setting aside for a later day that keystone of securities regulation, government oversight of the stock exchange.

Wall Street knew that it could not stave off for long an attempt by Roosevelt to complete the job, but it was determined to take every step possible to emasculate any subsequent regulatory measure. As early as April 1933, Richard Whitney, the imperious president of the New York Stock Exchange, had traveled to Washington for a personal visit with the President. He carried with him the advice of Roland Redmond, the exchange's chief counsel, to propose a sweeping program of self-regulation by the exchange in hopes of preempting regulation by the government—at least until the administration could "see if the reforms are effective."

Whitney's proposal fell on the ears of a thoroughly skeptical FDR. The President had spent his life rubbing shoulders with people like Richard Whitney, and he knew that their primary goal—perhaps their only goal—was to preserve their personal prerogatives, if need be at the expense of the community and the nation. Months later, following the bruising battle over what became the Securities Exchange Act of 1934, he would deliver his distilled judgment to Adolf Berle: "As you and I know," he wrote, "the fundamental trouble with this whole Stock Exchange crowd is their complete lack of elementary education. I do not mean lack of college diplomas, etc., but just inability to understand the country or the public or their obligation to their fellow men. Perhaps you can help them to acquire a kindergarten knowledge of those subjects."

After Whitney's visit, Wall Street launched a blistering attack on the 1933 act, a sort of dry run for the greater effort to derail a second bill. The industry's main themes were that the Securities Act had proved unworkable in practice and that its penalties were too harsh for officers and directors who violated the disclosure rules even unwittingly. The measure injected so many uncertainties into the issuing and trading of stocks that the capital markets had ground to a standstill, hampering economic recovery. The situation could be remedied, it was said, by the adoption of only a few minor amendments, obligingly drafted by Wall Street lawyers.

Few knowledgeable observers were fooled. "The real hope and purpose of these helpful friends in wanting to open up the Act for amendment is . . . to destroy its effectiveness completely," observed Bernard Flexner, a New York corporate lawyer who happened to be an old colleague of Benjamin Cohen's from the Zionist movement. Determined not to cede the initiative on Capitol Hill to Wall Street's well-funded professional lobbyists, Roosevelt had launched a drafting effort in September under assistant commerce secretary John Dickinson, who assembled a group virtually guaranteed to lack a majority for anything: the reformers James Landis and Adolf Berle, Wall Street lawyer Arthur Dean, and Henry Richardson, a Washington lobbyist for the banking industry.

Even before the panel convened for its first meeting, it was obvious that its work would come under fierce attack from the left and the right. "Anyone in favor of reopening the Act is supposed to have sold out to the bankers," Berle lamented in a memo for Roosevelt. "From the opposite point of view, those defending the act in its integrity are supposed to have a narrow-minded partisanship of their own drafting." Berle chose the middle ground: "The theory that the Securities Act absolutely must not be touched without disloyalty to the New Deal strikes me as unduly emotional. . . . The act can be, and should be, improved."

As the gunfire from both sides intensified, Berle outlined the areas needing improvement. These fell into three categories. First, of course, came reform of the stock exchange, which Berle derided as "primarily a gambling institution." He advocated strict constraints on brokerage firms and traders to prevent their speculating against their own customers, a severe temptation given their superior knowledge gained by proximity to the trading floor. Trading practices aimed purely at manipulation and devoid of economic purpose should be heavily regulated or eradicated. These included wash sales (back-and-forth trading within a small group designed solely to simulate public interest in a stock), short selling, and pool operations. Berle considered the consequence of inaction in that category so dire he set it off in capital letters in his outline: "WILL THE NEXT PERIOD OF PROSPERITY BE WRECKED BY ANOTHER ERA OF GAMBLING AND POOL MANIPULATORS? It is up to Congress."

The second area was credit: like many other critics, Berle blamed overly liberal margin rules for the infusion of cheap capital that had sent the stock market on a tear throughout the 1920s and set it up for the catastrophe of 1929. "My thought is that margin trading ought not to be permitted," he wrote. Because he was doubtful it could be entirely banned, he would settle for strict limitations on margin accounts.

The third area, one especially close to Berle's heart as coauthor of *The Modern Corporation and Private Property*, involved federal incorporation law. Companies issuing stock to the public should be required to publish annual balance sheets and quarterly income reports, along with monthly reports of stock transactions by officers and directors of the corporation and holders of a threshold percentage of shares—Berle's suggestion was 10 percent. These reports should comply with rules of accounting and standards of intelligibility established by law.

Berle sought to impose a higher duty of professionalism on corporate managements and their advisors, especially lawyers and accountants. This was an imperfectly realized goal of the original act in 1933. Indeed, as concerned as he was about exchange abuses, Berle regarded "the exchanges [as] primarily a symptom, rather than a cause" of the corrupt practices unearthed by the Pecora inquiry. "Gambling, as gambling, we shall never eradicate by any process of law. . . . The main issue consists in having (a) Honest shares, (b) In the hands of a reasonably effective management . . . which is prohibited from using the corporation either as a spring-board device towards power or as a means of securing inside information on gambling transactions."

There remained the question of which agency should be endowed with the unprecedented authority implicit in Berle's outline. Henry Richardson, the Washington lobbyist on Dickinson's committee, envisioned a seven-member Stock Exchange Commission, but he proposed to give it little real authority over the exchanges' internal rules and to award the largest bloc of its seats to exchange members and representatives of business. The idea of creating an independent body to oversee the exchanges would survive from Richardson's draft, but not its details.

While the Dickinson committee was struggling to begin its work, the New York Stock Exchange's position on government regulation was hardening. An important inflection point came one day in October. Richard Whitney had reluctantly agreed to receive two emissaries from Ferdinand Pecora, who wanted to collect information on exchange operations by having Whitney circulate a questionnaire to the exchange membership. One of the emissaries was John T. Flynn, a vituperative financial muckraker from the *New Republic* who was momentarily freelancing on Pecora's staff. At the sight of Flynn, Whitney flushed a deep purple, shot up from behind his vast desk, and stalked out of his office, leaving exchange attorney Roland Redmond to make pregnant small talk with the two nonplussed visitors until Whitney had sufficiently cooled down to return. When he did, he cut the meeting short.

"You gentlemen are making a great mistake," he said. "The exchange is a perfect institution."

Three days later he informed Pecora that the exchange would not be distributing the questionnaire. "We thought we would get the cooperation of the Exchange," Pecora complained theatrically in open committee session. "The net result seems to be zero."

At that time Dick Whitney's name carried, as a *New Yorker* writer put it, "a touch of magic." The magic originated in an act still spoken of with the reverence applied to the gestes of the heroes of legend, the act that saved the New York Stock Exchange.

It was the morning of October 24, 1929, "Black Thursday," when the bottom had fallen out of the stock market. A small party of prominent bankers had slipped through the unmarked door and gathered inside 23 Wall Street, headquarters of the House of Morgan, to contrive a way to quell the panic raging on the exchange floor. Presently they agreed on a plan to counter what Thomas Lamont described to financial reporters, with studied complacency, as "a little distress selling on the Stock Exchange." The bankers would commit $20 million to support share prices. Their agent would be Morgan's chief trader and the exchange's vice president, Richard Whitney.

At 1:30 P.M., Whitney appeared on the floor, making a beeline for Post No. 2, where shares in United States Steel were traded. He seemed the pure embodiment of the exchange's self-image at that moment: six feet tall, an athletic 210 pounds, impeccably groomed, Groton and Harvard in his blood and the tanned glow of the racing paddock and the outdoors on his skin. "A knightly gentleman who knows the ideals of the Stock Exchange," as one financier described him, he was about to enter the lists. Reaching the post, he bellowed: "I bid two hundred and five for twenty-five thousand Steel!"

The effect was electrifying. Steel, which had fallen to 190, instantaneously began moving higher, making Whitney's overbid—a $5 million order at fifteen points above the market—profitable within minutes. (Steel would close that day at 206½.) From U.S. Steel he shuttled to the other blue-chip posts on the floor, calling out one enormous purchase after another, each at the price of the last sale, until all the bankers' $20 million had been spent.

The next day's newspapers breathlessly recorded the feat: *Richard Whitney halts stock panic—Morgan broker buys 25,000 Steel at 205—Heroic action rallies market.*

Never mind that the crash shortly resumed, reaching its catastrophic climax four days later, on "Black Tuesday," October 29; the patrician Whitney's name was henceforth inscribed in history. He became the face of the New York Stock Exchange and its public voice, his every word hung upon by the newspapers as those of an oracle, his every joke recorded. When the presidency of the exchange came up for election in 1930, his victory was preordained. Throughout the dark days to come, Whitney's unflappable presence and the remembered courage of that famous bid on Black Thursday calmed the floor, as much as it could be calmed. The newspapers never failed to admire how he "sauntered nonchalantly across the floor half an hour before closing time, and left the room with a debonair smile."

So it was only to be expected that when this latest challenge to the traditions and independence of the New York Stock Exchange needed to be turned away, Richard Whitney would take command.

What no one knew—not his adversaries in Washington, not even his closest colleagues on Wall Street—was that at the moment Whitney took up arms to lead the New York Stock Exchange in defense of its life, he was already two years deep into one of the most flagrant cases of fraud and embezzlement Wall Street had ever seen. When it was finally exposed, the disclosure would destroy his career and take the clubby independence of his beloved exchange with it.

But that would be years in the future. As 1933 shaded into 1934, Richard Whitney was girding for war.

To the surprise of almost no one, the Dickinson committee failed to produce a usable draft of an exchange bill. But that was not the only reform effort taking place in Washington. Landis, Corcoran, and Cohen had been bridling at the business community's campaign to pick apart their 1933 act—"The bankers try by hook and by crook to bring [our] securities Act into disrepute," Cohen complained to a friend that September. In December they got the chance to strike back, when Pecora asked them to produce a revised bill in time for the new session of Congress in January.

Landis soon dropped out of the drafting, leaving the effort to Cohen and Corcoran, working for the first time on their own as a team of two and functioning as something of a skunk works; Roosevelt himself did not keep tabs on their work, but their progress was monitored at a distance by Ray Moley. The old Brain Truster had officially resigned from the White House staff in September but maintained an informal advisory brief that included helping FDR with the drafts of *On Our Way,* a compilation of his New Deal speeches due out in book form later in the year.

Cohen and Corcoran worked nearly day and night, rewriting the bill thirteen times to incorporate suggestions from Landis and John Flynn, who was still attached to Pecora's staff. It was ready by February 9, when Roosevelt sent a message to Congress proposing to restrict "unnecessary, unwise, and destructive speculation" on U.S. stock exchanges. The Cohen/Corcoran draft was introduced by House Majority Leader Sam Rayburn and Senate Banking Committee Chairman Duncan Fletcher the next day.

The stringency of the Rayburn-Fletcher bill stunned Whitney and his Wall Street cronies. In its constraints on credit for stock trading, restrictions on the activities of exchange members on the floor, and requirements for trading disclosures by corporate officers and for financial disclosures by listed companies, the measure was revolutionary. It reflected an economic and financial philosophy new to the federal government and one that went well beyond the principles underlying the 1933 act: the idea that the affairs of stock-issuing corporations were matters of public interest and, for the protection of the public economy, should be conducted in the open. It was nothing less than Adolf Berle's road map transformed into rigorous legislative language, with Brandeis's mistrust of corporate power underlying the whole.

Now it would have to be defended against an onslaught of lobbyists and propaganda. From Britain, where he was taking a sabbatical at Oxford University, Felix Frankfurter wired Roosevelt with unstinting praise for the bill's draftsmanship and a warning of the exchanges' likely strategy. "Their game, plainly enough, is like . . . that of the utilities . . . namely, to have the 'right' kind of regulatory body . . . devoid of the necessary courage and resourcefulness for making the legislation effective."

Washington was in the grip of a record deep freeze when Tom Corcoran arrived at the Capitol on Monday morning, February 26, expecting to explain the complicated forty-nine-page measure to Fletcher's committee at a private session. Instead he got the shock of his life: his solo performance would take place not behind closed doors, but at a full-dress public hearing in a packed auditorium. Moreover, as a sop to Wall Street, Fletcher had granted the New York Stock Exchange's Roland Redmond the extraordinary privilege of cross-examining the witness during his testimony. Adding to the pressure, Whitney would be looking on from the audience, awaiting his turn to speak. Corcoran's lasting reputation as a man preternaturally quick on his feet would be made over the next two days.

The young lawyer took his place behind the witness table and led the committee members painstakingly through every provision: restrictions on exchange floor brokers, margin limitations, the need for the regulatory commission to have "very large powers"—the alternative, he warned, "would be like advising that one put a baby into a cage with a tiger to regulate the tiger." He had been speaking for nearly an hour when Redmond interposed his first question. The immediate issue was the bill's limitations on margin loans. From the exchange's viewpoint margin lending was a boon, but the bill drafters regarded it as an economic peril. The discussion soon devolved into a lengthy and barbed debate between Corcoran and Redmond, the latter arguing that the measure constituted a moralist's attack on the very principle of stock trading, whether on borrowed funds or not.

"This bill really carries out the social principles of the persons who drafted it," Redmond charged.

Retorted Corcoran, "There is no social philosophy behind this bill. . . .

This is not at all a moral proposal for abolishing stock trading. This is the result of the economic judgment of the community."

Yet the bill indeed was freighted with a certain amount of moral principle, Corcoran revealed, perhaps unwittingly, near the end of his second day under the lights.

"It is your theory, at least," asked Senator Thomas P. Gore of Oklahoma, "that most of the evils that proceed from dealing in stocks, and so forth, result from machinations and sinister activities on the part of the stock exchange as such, or from brokers and outsiders and officers and directors who are manipulating their own stock? Who is the chief sinner in this scheme?"

"It is hard to tell who is the chief sinner, sir," Corcoran replied. "There are so many sinners."

Richard Whitney followed Corcoran to the stand and made an inferior impression. This was partially the result of his transparent dissembling. The previous year, under pressure from Pecora, Whitney had launched an internal investigation of allegedly manipulative trading of "hot" stocks on the exchange, exemplified by liquor-related shares enjoying a speculative frenzy based on the impending repeal of Prohibition. Now his report was read into the record by Pecora. For the most part, Whitney had vouchsafed, "there were no material deliberate improprieties in connection with transactions in these securities," no evidence of "wash sales or of other activities which might have stimulated improperly the activity of these stocks."

Pecora demolished this assertion with evidence drawn from the exchange's own records of trading in American Commercial Alcohol. The evidence showed that four company executives had exploited the good offices of Bernard "Sell 'Em Ben" Smith, a notorious stock jobber, to covertly trade 24,000 shares of their company in a series of wash sales that drove its price from less than 20 in May 1933 all the way up to 89⅞ on July 21, when they sold. The price then collapsed to 32. Grilled by Pecora, Whitney stuck to his position that the trading "was not an unfair influencing of the market." After all, he explained lamely, "all stocks came down in July."

Whitney's final tack before the committee was to offer a compromise between strict federal regulation and unsupervised self-regulation, almost as an act of noblesse oblige. "I do feel that there is a middle course here, granting sufficient, or something, to both sides," he told the members, all graciousness and charm. His concern, he said, was that Congress might later regret having enacted, in the heat of the moment, a law with a disastrous effect on the financial markets. He proposed the appointment of an "authority" with the power to enact regulations, but not subject to detailed mandates from Congress—in other words, one that could be controlled sub rosa by the exchange. "If an authority is to be set up, allow it to be flexible and mobile, and do not have it inflexible, so that if disaster does come, as we predict, it can not be changed without another act of Congress." Even the committee's Republicans could see the flaws in a part-time, quasi-official regulatory body whose members were drawn from the regulated industry. "I am afraid," observed Senator Robert D. Carey, Republican of Wyoming, "your commission would be rather slow in moving."

Back in New York after his maladroit defense of the indefensible in Washington, Whitney plotted out a program to build on business leaders' paranoia about government interference. He reached out to corporate executives to explain all the ways the stock exchange bill would bring their comfortably insular world to an end. In a circular addressed to the presidents of all listed corporations, Whitney warned of the "unlimited character" of the authority over corporate reports that the bill granted to the Federal Trade Commission. "These powers are so extensive that the Federal Trade Commission might dominate and actually control the management of each listed corporation," he wrote. Even the provisions aimed specifically at the exchanges would affect listed companies "by destroying the market for their securities."

Attentive corporate executives did not need Whitney's overheated rhetoric to tell them that the measure would revolutionize business management. Their freedom to peg their stock prices where they wished through wash sales and pool arrangements would disappear, as would their latitude in preparing income statements and balance sheets. These would henceforth have to be issued on a regular schedule and in format dictated by a government agency, and be accurate on pain of criminal prosecution. The lawyers and accountants who had formerly done their bidding would themselves operate under legal constraints and strict professional standards. The responsibilities the law imposed on these advisors would also give them the power to say no—no to stock schemes, no to watered books, no to the multitude of underhanded tricks they had once condoned as a matter of course. The law would implicitly invest accountants and lawyers with new powers in the boardroom, a revolution not relished by the officers and directors who were accustomed to ruling their firms as undisputed dictators.

Congress and the White House were inundated with letters and wires from executives infuriated that regulation of the exchanges had spilled over into regulation of corporate affairs. Milton Dammann, president of the American Safety Razor Corporation, wired to House Majority Leader Sam Rayburn:

> CONVINCED FEATURES OF STOCK EXCHANGE BILL REQUIRING
> REPORTS CONFIDENTIAL NATURE AND OTHER LIMITATIONS ON
> CORPORATE ACTIVITY IF ENACTED INTO LAW WILL DEFINITELY
> RETARD BUSINESS RECOVERY NOW SO WELL ADVANCED STOP
> BEG OF YOU ELIMINATE THESE FEATURES STOP

As Will Rogers wrote, "Those old Wall Street boys are putting up an awful fight to keep the government from putting a cop on their corner."

The relentless exchange campaign could not help but influence the malleable minds on Capitol Hill. The stentorian Sam Rayburn sounded the retreat, returning the bill to Cohen and Corcoran for redrafting in consultation with the Treasury Department, the Federal Reserve, and New York brokerage firms. The effort infuriated Pecora's hard-liners, such as Flynn, who complained that "the chief fruit of these labors was to take out of the bill itself almost all of its teeth." Flynn directed scathing scorn at Roosevelt, whom he blamed for not lifting a finger to save the original draft. He predicted that the President's silence would earn him no appreciation from Wall Street. "The Exchange will turn upon Roosevelt with fury, I have no doubt. They should remember him with gratitude."

He was correct. Wall Street was no happier with the new measure submitted on March 22 than it had been with the original draft—possibly unhappier, since the brokers felt that most of their suggested "improvements" had been ditched. In the final tally, the measure was only mildly diluted, and in some respects not diluted at all. The most notable change was to take regulatory authority away from the FTC and vest it in a new independent body with members appointed to fixed terms by the President, with Senate consent. (James Landis, on the strength of his several months' service as a federal trade commissioner, had cautioned Corcoran and Cohen that his agency would not be up to the task of policing the vast securities business.) Wall Street won some flexibility for this new commission in developing regulations but lost its battle for permanent seats on the body. The restrictions on manipulation schemes and the disclosure requirements for corporations and their officers stayed in, largely unaltered.

Whitney once again appealed directly to Roosevelt, requesting an urgent meeting days before a new round of congressional hearings opened. Enactment of the revised bill "would be a disaster," he wrote the President, identifying as its "immediate and necessary effect . . . a renewed deflation of security prices and a dislocation of business which will unquestionably interfere with your program for recovery." Roosevelt deflected Whitney's alarm with equanimity, instructing his appointments secretary, Marvin McIntyre, to brush him off. "Tell him I should like to see him, but have a definite rule that I cannot see anybody on pending legislation while the bills are in committee." Whitney returned home to New York, where he began to put it out that the bill had been drafted "by a bunch of Jews out to get Morgan."

At that point the attack on the measure veered into absurdity.

The perpetrator of what would reign as the outstanding comic interlude of that legislative season was James H. Rand, the president of Remington Rand Corporation. On March 23, Rand stood before the House Interstate Commerce Committee to make an extraordinary charge.

This was the same James Rand whose nose Tugwell had tweaked in February 1933 by intimating that President-elect Roosevelt was prepared to let the banks collapse and saddle Hoover with the blame. Rand was no credulous buffoon, however. He was a charter member and chairman of the Committee for the Nation, that group of conservative businessmen organized in 1932 to militate for inflationary policy and an end to the gold standard. The committee had backed Roosevelt while he was executing Professor Warren's gold manipulation scheme, but the 1933 Securities Act and the proposed new bill cut sharply against its grain. By early 1934 Rand and his group had shifted over into bitter opposition to the Roosevelt White House on all matters large and small.

Rand's ostensible purpose in testifying before the House committee was to deliver a broadside against the exchange bill, based on what he described as its subversive pedigree. The bill had been drafted by "a group of radical lawyers" subject to "mysterious backstage influences," he said—a veiled reference to Felix Frankfurter. "It carries us much further toward a regimented state. . . . We are being pushed along the road from democracy to communism."

As proof that the impetus lay very close to the White House, Rand uncorked his bombshell. This was a statement by one William A. Wirt, the schools superintendent of Gary, Indiana, an "unusually well-informed and internationally known leader in education . . . and a financier."

Read into the record by Rand, Wirt's statement described a dinner meeting he claimed to have had the previous summer with several "brain trusters."

"I was told that they believed that by thwarting our then evident recovery they would be able to prolong the country's destitution until they had demonstrated to the American people that the government must operate industry and commerce," Wirt stated. When he inquired how President Roosevelt was to be kept in the dark about their scheme, they said they "could make the President believe that he is making decisions for himself." Roosevelt would be kept in office "until we are ready to supplant him with a Stalin. We all think that Mr. Roosevelt is only the Kerensky of this revolution."

Wirt's sensational claim played on the front pages of newspapers coast to coast and led to his being summoned to testify before a congressional committee. The anticipation of his appearance, in which he vowed to identify the subversive New Dealers by name, grew to a fever pitch. Conservatives believed that their most dire suspicions of the New Deal were about to be confirmed. Their speculation as to Wirt's dinner companions fell most heavily on Tugwell, whose ultraliberalism had been public ever since his 1927 visit to the Soviet Union, but not on him alone. Prefiguring the smear technique of the postwar period, Republican Congressman Hamilton Fish of New York issued a list of sixteen "radicals or socialists" in government "who have been affiliated with the American Civil Liberties Union . . . a subversive organization." They included Jerome Frank of the AAA, Donald Richberg of the NRA, James Landis of the FTC, and Clarence Darrow. Yet as Tugwell observed glumly in private, "My name, as usual, headed the list."

When the big moment came, however, Wirt had no big names to reveal, just a few low-level bureaucrats with whom he had had dinner the year before. When those he named testified, they belittled Wirt, saying he had done most of the talking at the dinner. Wirt, like his patrons at the Committee for the Nation, turned out to be a pro-inflation crank. "He started off on the devaluation of the dollar," one dinner guest related, "and when he stopped it was somewhere around 11 o'clock in the evening."

"Thus, flatter than a crepe Suzette, fell the Red Scare of 1934," concluded *Time*.

Yet the affair could not be so easily dismissed. Wirt may have been shrunk during the course of his appearance from heroic truth-teller to fidgety, perspiring bore, but he helped his sponsors at the Committee for the Nation achieve their goal, which was to sow the seeds of doubt about the New Deal in receptive minds among the citizenry. Although even the Republican caucus in Congress quickly abandoned the hapless Wirt, others remained convinced that there were nuggets of truth buried within his discredited tale.

As a diversionary ideological outburst, the Wirt episode failed to derail the exchange control bill, which steamed through in its final version to overwhelming approval in both houses of Congress. The measure was signed by Roosevelt on June 6, with Rayburn, Fletcher, and Ferdinand Pecora at his side.

The financial community agonized over the constraints it would face under the new bill, although the staunchest critics of Wall Street found it a wan shadow of the original. "That first bill . . . on the whole would have dealt a real blow to a serious social and economic evil," grumbled John T. Flynn, who mourned its failure to flatly outlaw margin trading and other manipulative practices. The final version amounted merely "to a collection of regulations to govern the game of speculation as between the speculators, with the United States sitting as umpire. The deeper and more important economic evils of the game were left untouched."

Speculation next turned to whom Roosevelt would nominate as the inaugural members of the new Securities and Exchange Commission. It was commonly assumed that the five names would be closely balanced between Democrats and Republicans (with the former, naturally, in the majority) and that to mollify the bankers at least one member would have respectable Wall Street ties.

The President assigned the task of creating a short list to Raymond Moley, whose initial list included James Landis; Ben Cohen; Robert Healy, a Vermont judge who had investigated the utilities industry for the FTC; and George Mathews, a progressive Republican from Wisconsin. From Wall Street he considered the broker Paul Shields, an adversary of Richard Whitney among exchange members; and Gordon Wasson, a financier who had become close to Cohen and Corcoran during the bill's drafting.

It was the name at the top of Moley's list that would deliver the biggest shock. "The best bet for Chairman because of executive ability, knowledge of habits and customs to be regulated and ability to moderate different points of view on Commission," Moley wrote Roosevelt, was Joseph P. Kennedy. What he did not say in his memo was that Kennedy was so well versed in the "habits and customs" of Wall Street because he was one of the most notorious operators in the business.

But he did not have to. Kennedy's brilliance as a financial manipulator and pool operator was well known to Roosevelt and to his entire inner circle. Indeed it was the source of the conspicuous uneasiness with which many in the New Deal regarded Kennedy, even though he was one of the Democratic Party's most reliable financial backers and a stalwart supporter of progressive causes.

The son of Irish Catholic immigrants, Kennedy had made his fortune—indeed, several fortunes—in the faintly disreputable corners of the investment world occupied by those excluded from the aristocratic businesses of their "betters." The House of Morgan had the luxury of serving only clients it selected for itself; people like Kennedy drifted into low-status businesses like liquor and the movies. In the process, he developed an enviable network of friends and familiars spanning the political spectrum—from William Randolph Hearst to Bernard Baruch and Democratic doyen Owen D. Young, the founder of Radio Corporation of America (RCA) and chairman of General Electric. By 1930 Kennedy had identified the up-and-coming governor of New York, Franklin Roosevelt, as a potential future candidate for president. Moley met Kennedy for the first time shortly before the 1932 convention, when Roosevelt introduced the Brain Truster to a stranger Moley recalled simply as "a ruddy-faced, vigorous, and highly colorful talker."

At the convention, by Kennedy's own account, he was the man who brought Hearst around to FDR's candidacy, an important step in securing the nomination. He also helped cover the party's unpaid bills, possibly to the tune of more than fifty thousand dollars. During the campaign he helped the candidate make contact with such figures as Bank of America's A. P. Giannini and film stars and magnates from Hollywood. To those who inquired about his own political ambitions Kennedy replied that he had none—"There is no public office that would interest me," he told the *Boston Globe*, expanding on his disavowal in his 1936 campaign encomium to FDR titled *I'm for Roosevelt*. "I have no political ambitions for myself or for my children," he wrote, an irony left to be savored by later generations of Americans.

Kennedy expected—quite properly, in Moley's view—to be rewarded with a prominent appointment in the administration. Yet he was left to cool his heels in the New Deal's anteroom while countless important posts, and not a few ceremonial positions such as U.S. treasurer, went to others. What Moley failed to understand at the time was that the obstacle to Kennedy's appointment was Louis Howe. This chief political advisor in the Roosevelt White House nurtured a venomous loathing for Kennedy, whom he considered nothing but a dishonest Wall Street operator. Although he may have been motivated partially by jealousy over the personal friendship between the investor and the President-elect, Howe also feared that a public association with Kennedy would yield FDR only embarrassment and political grief.

Kennedy was well aware of Howe's antipathy—"Howe . . . looked at me as if he were looking at the devil himself," he recalled of a chance encounter at the White House in 1934—and accurately surmised that Howe was to blame for the absence of a job offer. Whatever its cause, Kennedy's feeling of neglect came near to producing a lasting rift between him and Roosevelt. Moley got a sense of the depth of Kennedy's frustration during a three-day sojourn at the latter's Palm Beach home just before the inauguration. "There I heard plenty of Kennedy's excoriation of Roosevelt, of his criticisms of the President-elect, who, according to Kennedy, had no program—and what ideas he had were unworthy of note." Kennedy lashed out at the Democratic Party itself, informing the progressive Democratic senator Burton Wheeler of Montana that he was considering suing the Democratic National Committee for the return of his campaign loan.

It is doubtful that he ever seriously considered instigating such an action, which would have caused a permanent breach with the party. Instead he continued trying to worm his way into the New Deal, at one point offering financial help to support Moley's lifestyle in Washington. (Moley prudently declined.) More successful were his efforts to open the doors to business opportunities for FDR's eldest son, James, then a twenty-five-year-old insurance agent. Still the openings in the administration came and passed. Before the inauguration, Kennedy had openly let it be known that Treasury secretary was the position he truly coveted; the job went to Will Woodin. When deteriorating health forced Woodin to retire in January 1934, Kennedy's heart quickened at the thought that opportunity had finally come knocking. But the appointment went to FDR's Dutchess County neighbor Henry Morgenthau, Jr., a second rebuff that left Kennedy even more "keenly disappointed" than the first, as his wife, Rose, recounted.

The creation of the Securities and Exchange Commission finally presented Roosevelt with an ideal opening for Kennedy. The appointment would be audacious and unexpected, the sort of bombshell FDR always enjoyed detonating, while presenting his anxious supporter with a much-delayed reward. There was no question that Kennedy was well qualified for the job, as Moley perceived, for he combined in his Manichaean personality the skills and percipience of an experienced pool operator with a streak of Roman Catholic moralism and a powerful sense of social responsibility.

Louis Howe's failing health had sapped him of much of his influence in the White House, but there were still other obstacles to consider before announcing the appointment. That it would infuriate progressives was signaled by the reaction of Roy Howard, the publisher and co-owner of the Scripps Howard newspaper chain, who informed Moley that his newspapers would attack the appointment as "a slap in the face to [Roosevelt's] most loyal and effective supporters." Kennedy himself cautioned FDR to brace himself for a firestorm of criticism. "I told him that I had been involved in Wall Street, and, over a business career of twenty-five years, had done plenty of things that people could find fault with," he recalled. "He listened to my speech which lasted fifteen minutes and then put out his hand and said, 'If you are happy, it is perfectly satisfactory to me.'"

But Kennedy was not entirely happy. He threatened to turn down the job if it involved anything less than the SEC chairmanship, a designation that was not, in fact, within the President's purview. Under the act, the commissioners were to designate the chairman from among themselves; as it happened, two other prospective appointees, Pecora and Landis, also indicated they craved the chairmanship. Roosevelt overcame this potential disagreement with a bout of strong-arming, informing Landis, Pecora, and the other nominees, Healy and Mathews, in writing that he expected them to vote for Kennedy.

The announcement generated approving noises from a well-nourished Kennedy claque in the press. Arthur Krock, the Washington bureau chief of the *New York Times*—who had spent many a holiday at Kennedy's Virginia estate, Marwood—published a fulsome panegyric to Kennedy's "amazing success," noting in passing that he "has operated occasionally in stocks and securities," and "participated with highly respectable partners in an alcohol pool during the boom times and made a moderate amount out of it."

But as everyone from Roy Howard to Kennedy himself had predicted, the announcement provoked indignation among progressives. John T. Flynn of the *New Republic* delivered the most disillusioned broadside under the headline "The Jackals of Finance." That alcohol pool glossed over by Krock, he observed, was one of the most "squalid" pools that "Pecora dragged into the light." The scandalized Flynn remarked that he had always expected Roosevelt to appoint a commission chairman acceptable to Wall Street "in obedience to his well known policy of carrying water on both shoulders." But "I did not in my wildest dreams imagine he would appoint a speculator as chairman of that body.

"I say it isn't true," he wrote. "It is impossible. It could not happen."

No one understood better than Kennedy his equivocal position as a Wall Street speculator now responsible for eradicating some of the practices with which he had made his fortune. Straddling the worlds of finance and progressive politics, he was also sensitive to the need to deliver a firm yet reassuring message to the securities industry about the new commission's approach to business. Accordingly he labored long hours with Corcoran and Cohen drafting his maiden speech as chairman—"I lost eight pounds on this one and plenty of sleep," he confided to a Wall Street friend. The speech was delivered to a nationwide radio audience at 2:30 P.M. on July 25, and was so anxiously anticipated on Wall Street that "it was facetiously suggested," the *New York Times* reported, "that the Exchange should either suspend operations for fifteen minutes between 2:30 and 2:45 . . . or provide a loud-speaker to broadcast the talk to members on the floor."

Kennedy sought to strike just the right balance. "There is no belief, at least none in the minds of the Securities and Exchange Commission, that business is to be viewed with suspicion; that it must be harassed and annoyed and pushed around. . . . We of the SEC do not regard ourselves as coroners sitting on the corpse of financial enterprise. . . . There is to be no vindictiveness. . . . There are no grudges to satisfy, no venom which needs victims." The centerpiece of the address was the explicit recognition that "financial enterprises need profit to keep them going. There is not the slightest thought of eliminating or restricting proper profits."

Along with the carrot came the stick. Kennedy warned, "The old things business did—the old practices it followed—are, some of them, no longer the right ones. . . . The Commission will make war without quarter on any who sell securities by fraud or misrepresentation."

Joseph P. Kennedy would remain at the commission for just over a year, but it was an indispensable year. He would establish the SEC as a bulwark against sharp practice but not a guarantor of success for any investor, large or small. He created a philosophical foundation for the commission upon which his immediate successors as chairman—first Landis, then William O. Douglas—would erect a technical and legal framework that would endure for decades. When he resigned in September 1935, even John T. Flynn had to eat his harsh words of fifteen months before. "It is but fair to him to say that he disappointed the expectations of his critics," Flynn wrote, this time under the headline "Hail and Farewell to Mr. Kennedy." "He was, I firmly believe, the most useful member of the Commission."

The Securities Exchange Act was the most important product thus far of the most glittering intellectual collaboration of the New Deal. "Tommy Corcoran and Ben Cohen, taken together, made the brightest man I ever saw," remarked Sam Rayburn.

It was also the last major act they were able to craft in relative anonymity. They had become the outstanding legislative draftsmen of the Roosevelt administration. Now they were about to become something else: targets.

10

THE LITTLE RED HOUSE

I T WAS AN OCTAGONAL five-story, red brick structure in Italianate style
at 3238 R Street, Georgetown, overlooking the passing traffic from
atop a gentle hill, with a white portico out front and a cobblestone
drive at the side. Tom Corcoran had been looking for a house to rent so
Ben Cohen might be encouraged to give up his exhausting weekly com-
mute from New York City and settle in to the full-time business of drafting
legislation.

What enthralled Corcoran on his first visit in June 1933 was the building's enormous living room, featuring a cathedral ceiling, ornate gilded
mirrors, and a rosewood grand piano—the latter speaking especially elo-
quently to his musician's soul. The house was expensive and in need of
refurbishment, but it was big enough to lure Cohen permanently back
from New York. It would not keep its commodious atmosphere for long;
Corcoran would soon fill it up with so many acquaintances, protégés, and
employees, sometimes six or eight at a time—his "little chicks," he called
them—that he and Cohen eventually had to take a separate apartment on
K Street, a couple of miles away, so they might work through the night
in peace.

This house, built by one Alfred Scott in 1858, when Georgetown was a
swampy suburb of Washington, D.C., was draped with a modest mantle
of local lore: during the Civil War it had been the residence of Ulysses S.
Grant, so for a time it had been known as the Scott-Grant House. But its
more famous appellation was the creation of Republican congressman Fred

A. Britten, a florid ex-boxer from Chicago. Britten took the floor April 20, at the height of the Wirt comedy, on what was identified by the *New York Times* as "an oratorical field day afforded to members of the house by a slack calendar," to denounce the drafters of the stock exchange bill. "Every night of the week, from ten to eighteen young men of communistic minds meet, so-called young students," he declared. "They call them Frankfurter's hot dogs." And they were all residents, furthermore, of "a little red house down in Georgetown, where are held the meetings which promote the communistic legislation we all talk about in the cloakrooms."

Britten's sally delighted both sides of the aisle. For Republicans, the "little red house" effectively fixed in the public mind an image of the drafters of New Deal bills as socialists and communists; for Democrats, it conveniently evoked a Republican scandal of relatively recent vintage, the "little green house" on K Street where the Harding administration's "Ohio Gang" had hatched the Teapot Dome affair and other corrupt plots.

Reached by reporters at his RFC office the afternoon of Britten's outburst, Corcoran tried amiably to defuse the controversy—"We live there, but I work here," he told a man from the *Washington Post.* "I haven't been home in many nights." A few days later a reporter from the *Washington Daily News* managed to gain entry to the little red house. Corcoran welcomed him with a cheery shout: "Come in but park your bomb at the door." Inside, the reporter discovered "a group of well-tailored, well-behaving young men harmonizing" around the piano. He was invited to join in on second bass—alas, not on "The International," but on "Git Along Little Dogies."

Yet there was a grain of truth in Britten's febrile attack. Corcoran's protestations notwithstanding, a great deal of New Deal history would be made in the little red house, during interminable phone calls or all-night sessions of law-drafting, speechwriting, or strategizing. The products included Joseph P. Kennedy's inaugural speech as chairman of the Securities and Exchange Commission, drafted by Corcoran in spurts of rapid-fire patter, and edited on the spot, page by page, by Ben Cohen.

Britten's words were significant in another way. Corcoran and Cohen, to their deep disadvantage, were being summoned out of the shadows.

The rise of Tom Corcoran and Ben Cohen as presidential advisors coincided with the New Deal's transition from an impromptu series of experiments to a program based on calculated principles. During 1934, many of

Roosevelt's original advisors had receded or withdrawn from the front lines, and a new group filled the vacuum. The new group comprised, in general, persons of very different character and background from the old. The New Deal could not help but become transformed in the process.

Possibly because the previous Democratic administration was a dozen years in the past when Franklin Roosevelt took office, a large contingent of the original Brain Trusters and cabinet members arrived in Washington with little or no practical experience of political administration at the national level. Moley, Tugwell, and Berle were dyed-in-the-wool academics. Perkins and Cummings had held only state-level offices; Ickes, Wallace, Woodin, and those two acolytes of Bernard Baruch's, George Peek and Hugh Johnson, not even that.

That is not to say they were political or ideological naïfs. The settlement house movement animated the social reformism of Frances Perkins, Harry Hopkins, and Adolf Berle. Ickes's involvement with the progressive movement predated the 1912 presidential campaign of Theodore Roosevelt on the Progressive (Bull Moose) ticket. *The Modern Corporation and Private Property,* published by Berle and Gardiner Means in 1932, provided a scholarly foundation for the New Dealers' aversion to concentrated corporate power and for their skepticism that the financial markets could be self-regulating.

There were common threads in the viewpoints of the first generation of New Dealers, but also many differences and contradictions. That Tugwell's outlook could coexist with Hugh Johnson's in a single administration is a testament to the equable personality and opportunistic management style of Franklin Roosevelt, who bemused his associates by gliding over even the most glaring contradictions in policy as a skater glides over the ice.

Roosevelt could do so because for him, ideological purity did not rank very high as a political virtue. He was determined to address the immediate crisis with whatever tools came to hand. Even those aides who had extracted from FDR an explicit commitment to a program as a condition of their service, such as Frances Perkins, knew they would have to wait until the emergency was past to collect on his promise.

The improvisatory character of the early New Deal was evident to its participants. "When Roosevelt came to Washington in 1933 he did not have what could be called a systematic economic program and he certainly had not spelled one out in his campaign," the economist Leon Keyserling, a contributor to drafts of the NIRA, the National Labor Relations (Wagner)

Act, and the Social Security Act, wrote in a critique of historians' attempts to identify a consistent economic worldview in the early New Deal. The New Deal initiatives of 1933 and early 1934, Keyserling observed, were "highly experimental, improvised and inconsistent," the NIRA in particular the result of "a series of haphazard accidents."

Raymond Moley put it more colorfully: "To look upon these policies as the result of a unified plan was to believe that the accumulation of stuffed snakes, baseball pictures, school flags, old tennis shoes, carpenter's tools, geometry books, and chemistry sets in a boy's bedroom could have been put there by an interior decorator."

As the glue holding these disparate pieces together, the personality of Franklin Delano Roosevelt dominates the memoirs and diaries of his friends, family members, Brain Trusters, and cabinet secretaries. FDR's warmth and joviality come to life in these remembrances, as do his suppleness of mind, his innate fiscal conservativeness, his equanimity in the face of horrific crisis—and his mysterious ability to meld diametrically opposed ideas into a single policy. Yet somehow the man himself remains elusive, the source of his particular magic obscure. Roosevelt left no memoir of his own, but on the evidence of the words he did leave for posterity—personal letters and brief annotations for the collections of speeches and official papers edited by Sam Rosenman—any autobiographical effort certainly would have been at once shallow, formal, and evasive.

Roosevelt's grip on the popular imagination began with his first campaign for the presidency and steadily intensified through his term in office. Within a year of his inauguration the flow of mail in the White House had easily outstripped that of any of his predecessors, exceeding by January 1934 the volume that Hoover had received during his entire four-year term and requiring the expansion of the White House mailroom from three or four clerks to twenty-five.

Possibly because of the serene oratorical voice of his radio addresses, Americans instinctively sought Roosevelt's personal intercession in large matters and small. (He was careful not to overdo the familiarity; the Fireside Chats may have seemed to his fellow Americans to be a nearly weekly event, but in fact he delivered an average of fewer than three a year during his presidency.) "Dear Frank," began a letter from a farm wife in the Midwest asking his advice on an excruciatingly personal dilemma: "Our neighbor, Pete Smith, loaned us $25 on our team. He says he'll take the mules unless he can come to see me when my husband is away. How can I save the mules?"

The members of Roosevelt's inner circle all remark on his predilection for informality, the absence of snobbery in his personal relationships, and his great personal dignity, contradictory as these qualities may sometimes have been. "He called people easily and naturally by their first names or by nicknames, but those about him called him Mr. President, even when fishing or playing poker," recalled Robert H. Jackson, who served FDR as an assistant attorney general and was later appointed by him to the Supreme Court. "No person of taste or discernment would take liberties with him, and the few who attempted it were easily put in their places."

The closest of his aides included Louis McHenry Howe, the disheveled former newspaperman who served him as political advisor with unexampled devotion until his death in April 1936, and Missy LeHand, who had served him as personal secretary since 1920 and became, in Rosenman's words, "the one indispensable person around the Executive Mansion [in Albany] and later around the White House." Until she was invalided by a stroke in 1941, LeHand managed the White House social calendar, occasionally contributed her considerable instincts to policy questions, and exercised indisputable authority over the President's time and disposition. "If she thought he was getting pretty tired or stale in his work, without consulting him, she would arrange a poker game," Rosenman recalled. "He wouldn't know anything about it until 6 o'clock that night. She would come in to him with a list and say, 'These people are coming for dinner tonight—they're going to play poker with you.' Had she asked him, he would have said, 'No, I have too much to do.'"

Roosevelt's informality extended to his preference for doing business with a tiny cadre of trusted advisors—at various points Ickes, Morgenthau, Hugh Johnson, or Harry Hopkins. He frequently created new rubrics for them to operate within—a National Economic Council, a Committee on Economic Security, an Allotment Advisory Committee (this last an entirely bizarre body of which Ickes was chairman and Roosevelt a member, so that when it convened in the Cabinet Room the President of the United States sat to one side of the table while his self-conscious secretary of the interior occupied the President's chair). The apparent formality of these committees was deceptive, for even as the superstructure of White House committees, agencies, and administrations expanded, Roosevelt continued to indulge his preference for face-to-face policy making, reaching momentous decisions in conference with Ickes or Hopkins alone in his office. Nor was there ever any question about who made the final decision. "I can't imagine any other President who felt freer to take or leave advice as much as Roosevelt," recalled Rosenman. "Roosevelt, even with respect to Hopkins and Howe, never followed advice . . . slavishly."

Roosevelt's managerial methods deprived the cabinet of much of its formal importance. It was a rare cabinet meeting that did not leave Harold Ickes feeling bored and impatient, especially if his efforts to have a private word with the President afterward were thwarted by a monopolizing colleague (often the insistent Frances Perkins). Roosevelt, who detested ceremony, made every effort to lighten the atmosphere in the Cabinet Room, customarily opening the agenda with a few minutes of badinage. "Sometimes the President would raise questions," recalled Jackson, who frequently accompanied his boss, Attorney General Homer Cummings, to the meetings. "Perhaps he had read in the newspaper a criticism of some department. . . . He would remind the Cabinet members of the complaints he was getting on this or that subject. Sometimes matters were brought before the Cabinet as a matter of protection to the member, who felt that they were likely to break out into the press and wanted his Cabinet colleagues to be forewarned as to what the facts were."

And sometimes the meetings were consumed by intramural conflicts. Often these involved Ickes, whose prickliness frequently put him at odds with one or another of his colleagues. The most notable incident involved Morgenthau, for whose intellect and character Ickes had little respect. In the midst of a cabinet meeting in early 1935 they blew up at each other over rumors that Ickes had launched a secret investigation of Morgenthau's department. The immediate issue was a construction contract for a Manhattan post office building in which both the Public Works Administration funds and Treasury were involved. Huey Long, who had gotten wind that the contract might have gone to a politically connected builder, demanded a public airing of the deal in the hopes of embarrassing the White House. At that point Morgenthau discovered that an Interior Department employee named Louis Glavis had been nosing around the matter.

Glavis was a unique figure in Washington. Ickes employed him as his personal sleuth purportedly to ferret out corruption in the Interior Department; but the secretary was not above training him on his enemies, real and imagined, around the White House. Glavis's personality fit the job: he was constitutionally suspicious of mankind and "rather more zealous than reliable," in the words of Morgenthau's loyal biographer, John Morton Blum. Even Ickes was sometimes hard-pressed to keep him on a short leash, confiding to Roosevelt scarcely a month before the Cabinet Room eruption that he had been "trying to hold Glavis down as much as possible because . . . he was somewhat of a man-eater."

At the February 15 cabinet meeting, an agitated Morgenthau confronted Ickes, who denied knowing anything of Glavis's investigation. Unable to make himself heard over the two secretaries' exchange of indignant accusations, Roosevelt scribbled a note and held it up to Morgenthau: "You must not talk in such a tone of voice to another Cabinet officer." When that failed to quell the disturbance, the President pounded on the table for silence. "I cannot have Cabinet members disagreeing," he said, ordering an end to the argument. Ickes and Morgenthau stayed in the room, silently glowering at each other until the meeting adjourned. That night Roosevelt privately mollified these deeply loyal retainers with phone calls agreeing with each that the other was in the wrong. "I told the President that Morgenthau was young and he agreed with me," Ickes recollected. "It was very clear that the President thought that Morgenthau was the aggressor." Morgenthau recorded in his diary his own words to Roosevelt: "The trouble with Ickes is that he likes to step on everybody else's toes but if anybody tries to defend himself he cannot take it."

"That is absolutely right," the President replied.

By 1935, many of the original New Dealers were gone. Hugh Johnson had flared out like a Roman candle, and George Peek had succumbed to his inability to see eye to eye with Wallace and Tugwell. Moley had become burned out by the intensity of his responsibilities in the early New Deal, increasingly disaffected by Roosevelt's policies, and preoccupied with his work on the newsmagazine that would eventually become *Newsweek*. (He did maintain an informal brief as advisor and speechwriter well into 1936—close enough to FDR to be personally upbraided by the President for the antiadministration tone of his magazine columns.) Tugwell had been marginalized by political attacks on his leftist politics, and after 1935 devoted his time to the Resettlement Administration, a new agency dealing with rural recovery. Berle drifted into the business world.

The one notable constant among Roosevelt's closest advisors was Felix

Frankfurter. Indeed, his influence increased as his protégés, Ben Cohen and Tom Corcoran, gained in stature. So did that of Louis Brandeis, imbued with his populist preoccupation with the evils of big business.

Corcoran and Cohen brought to the New Deal a refined variety of Brandeis's philosophy, along with a gift for the mechanics of government that many original New Dealers had lacked. In some ways their commitment to ideological orthodoxy was stronger than that of their predecessors, but it was balanced by their commitment to producing a legislative program that would endure. Corcoran would write: "Many early New Deal bills were overturned by the Supreme Court, but not a single one that Ben and I wrote. We developed a method that was practical and political by intention. . . . With a rough draft in hand, I made the rounds of the Capitol to gather the reactions of sympathetic Congressmen and of legislators likely to oppose the measure. As I reported differing views back to Ben, he rewrote and rewrote, honing the language. . . . Given my copious legwork, we prepared astonishingly complex bills that a sometimes slender majority of Congressmen would vote into law. And given Ben's extraordinarily precise and tireless pen, they were laws that withstood judicial review."

Corcoran perhaps is being too harsh on the laws that were overturned, and too smug about those that survived; many factors were at play in the tumultuous relations among the Court and the other two branches of government in those years, and it would have taken but tiny shifts of happenstance to bequeath history a very different narrative. But he is correct in observing that one hallmark of the evolution in the New Deal from 1933 to 1935 is the increasing precision of its legislative program.

Many historians have strived to identify a bright line distinguishing "the first New Deal" from the "second New Deal." It is perhaps more useful to observe that the New Deal, like any presidential program, underwent a natural evolution. "Political and economic conditions in 1933 were such as to call for effort to unite everybody," Keyserling observed. "When the New Dealers found to their surprise that no program could unite everybody and that those who in some ways had benefited most were turning to bite the hand that fed them, they shifted from the political strategy of unity to the political strategy of division."

The continuing debate over where to place the bright line suggests there may be no bright line. Populists and progressives dominated in the White House when the New Deal produced the NIRA, which implemented such nonprogressive goals of the business community as the suspension of antitrust laws and wage and price controls effectively dictated by the biggest companies in every industry. In 1935 and after, when business became convinced that the country was in the hands of radicals and communists determined to bring down the capitalist structure, the people writing the bills were trying as hard as they could to find a relatively conservative middle ground, so that the bills could get passed and remain in effect.

That condition itself would evolve. The team of Corcoran and Cohen would be at the center of that change, too.

The relationship between Corcoran and Cohen was the keystone of life in the little red house. Of its denizens, Cohen was the only man Corcoran could not manipulate (and would not try to), the only one whose intellect he invariably trusted, the only one he regarded as indispensable to his own professional survival. Corcoran, writing wistfully late in life of all the close associates with whom he had broken at one point or another—Brandeis and Frankfurter among them—observed, "I never broke with Ben Cohen." Ray Moley, who in 1933 and early 1934 was serving as the pair's liaison with the White House and with a president they had not yet met, detected "a kind of worshipfulness" in the extroverted Corcoran's attitude toward the retiring Cohen, as well as a curious paternalism—the solicitude of a man of the world toward his solitary, bookish older brother. "Those who interpreted their association as that of 'front' man and scholar missed its inner reality," Moley observed. "It was a combination of a man who loved life, gloried in manipulating people, and of a man who feared life, despised compromise with reality."

The house's other habitués were manifestly Corcoran's brood, often with little in common with each other except their accomplished records at law school and their fealty to the leader—not Franklin Roosevelt, that is, but Tom Corcoran. In the earliest days his group comprised Frank Watson and Merritt Willits III, who had roomed together at Harvard Law School and now held down jobs at the RFC; Richard Gugenhime, a lawyer and scion of a distinguished San Francisco family; and Charles Stuart Guthrie, a Bull Moose Progressive Republican who still worshipped Theodore Roosevelt yet managed to find sufficient similarities between TR and his cousin Franklin to pledge loyalty to the New Deal. From his former colleagues at the Wall Street law firm Cotton & Franklin, Corcoran recruited Richard Quay, a Rhodes scholar and grandson of a Republican senator from Pennsylvania, and Edward Burling, Jr., who would eventually join the Washington firm of Covington & Burling, where his father was a name partner.

Financially speaking, the R Street household operated haphazardly. Frank Watson, who kept the books, would estimate monthly costs with the other residents and assess everyone his share. In practice this was a pointless exercise, for costs constantly careened out of control: some nights Corcoran would arrive with three or four guests in tow, all requiring to be fed; on other nights a lavish spread laid out by the cook would go untouched because no one had warned her that everyone would be out for the evening. Winter months almost always busted the budget because the cranky furnace burned coal with abandon. In some months the telephone bills approached a prodigious six hundred dollars, all on business calls but never billed to the employer, for the federal government had no system in place for the reimbursement of such outside expenses. There were frequent calls from Felix Frankfurter in Cambridge or, in late 1933 and through 1934, from his sabbatical in England; and he always called collect. Corcoran and Cohen would attest that they never knew exactly what they paid in rent; in any event, the shortfalls in the household books almost always came out of their pockets, for their salaries of $7,000 a year were by far the highest in the house, dwarfing the $2,400 touched by the youngest novice members.

As the undisputed paterfamilias, Corcoran not only deployed the men on their professional assignments, but planned their social lives, which might encompass a weekend golf outing to Virginia or a canoe trip down the Potomac. Corcoran frowned on family entanglements, for he viewed wives and children as little more than sources of imposition on his chicks' attention and their devotion to work. "The men that work for Corcoran know no hours," reported the *Saturday Evening Post*. "He won't have anybody about him who grumbles at being kept up till three or four a.m. On that account Tommy developed an aversion to husbands. The benedicts want to see their wives. . . . He regards it as a calamity to the public service when one of his hitherto trustworthy young lieutenants gets married." In negotiations with a congressional adversary, he would wield his staff's bachelorhood as a weapon, scheduling nighttime negotiation parleys "to spoil the evenings of the array of husbands on the other side." Fortified by a torrent of heavily sugared coffee, he would deliberately extend the discussions into the small hours, "in the hope of breaking the morale of the homeloving burghers on the other side."

Free evenings at the little red house were often given over to hilarity and song, with Corcoran at the grand piano. One Saturday night an RFC lawyer named Alfred Hobson showed up with a second baby grand described variously as having arrived either in a hired van or "on the shoulders of four strong men." That evening there were piano duets into the late hours until "Hobby" departed with the piano; whether it was returned to its home by van or by manpower is unrecorded.

Corcoran had no compunctions about deploying his men outside the agencies that were their nominal employers. "Tom would see a job that needed to be done and he'd get one of us and say, 'How'd you like to try this?'" recalled Watson. "If things didn't work out well, we'd be back with him again." The source of his authority to do so was murky at first, but the more he made his men available to perform legislative jobs for cabinet secretaries and congressional leaders, the less it was questioned. Eventually Corcoran could command the ultimate authority in Washington by picking up the phone and barking: "This is Tom Corcoran, calling from the White House," though he had no official quarters in the executive mansion and as often as not was placing the call from a friend's office or from home. Metaphorically speaking, however, his claim was correct, for by then he was doing the personal bidding of Franklin Roosevelt.

Corcoran was thrilled with his rising prominence in the New Deal, especially his acceptance into Roosevelt's personal circle. This appears to have taken place in early 1934, when the President, having heard stories of Corcoran's facility on the piano and accordion, invited him to the White House for an informal musicale. Around then Roosevelt bestowed on him the nickname "Tommy the Cork," which would stick to him for the rest of his life and, like those of Rosenman ("Sammy the Rose") and Morgenthau ("Henry the Morgue"), formalized Corcoran's admission into the official club of White House courtiers.

Corcoran's ascent was not viewed with unalloyed cheer by people close to him, not to speak of those who found themselves on the other side of the bargaining table. Cohen, for one, preferred working anonymously, and although his reputation soared in the White House along with his partner's, his presence was much rarer. Among the most irked was Felix Frankfurter. The Harvard professor had always guarded his access to Roosevelt jealously and found the experience of being upstaged by his own protégés almost intolerable, especially while he was impotently isolated in England. In May

1934 he wrote a condescending and resentful personal letter to Corcoran and Cohen—but plainly directed chiefly at Corcoran—upbraiding them for their presumptuousness:

> What darling children you must be to have wormed your way not only into the heart but even into the mind and will of the President of the United States. . . . While I know it's usually bad for little children, whether they are piano players or draftsmen, to get too much public attention when they are very, very young, I know that you're such hard-headed little youngsters that there isn't the slightest danger of all this public acclaim of your juvenile games and performances either spoiling you or making life as it gets duller when you grow up seem too dull.

Frankfurter was then fifty-two, Cohen forty, Corcoran thirty-three. Irked at his tone, the protégés replied in the same vein: "Much has gone over the dam since you went away and affairs have proceeded pretty far toward concrete forks in the road," they wrote. "You'll need, we should think, considerable detailed knowledge of what has gone on just to listen understandingly."

Frankfurter's concern that Corcoran and Cohen were flying too close to the sun was not entirely misplaced. Late in life, Corcoran penned a candid (but never published) self-assessment on this score: "As Ben and my reputations grew, we were perceived as having much more influence in inner circles than was actually the case," he wrote. "But we didn't gainsay the rumors because Bunyanesque tales of our previous accomplishments helped us get things done."

He seldom displayed such an introspective streak to his contemporaries. "The great mistake of Tommy's career was that of becoming a lobbyist," the magazine writer Alva Johnston would observe. "He should never have been sent out armed with threats and promises in order to line up votes for New Deal bills. He is partly to blame, because he has an exaggerated opinion of his merits as a practical politician."

Corcoran's limitations were tied up with his increasing devotion to Roosevelt, to the principles of a New Deal that he was himself helping to conceive, and to his own advancement. The longer he served as Roosevelt's envoy, errand boy, and fixer, the less toleration he showed for ideological deviation by his fellow New Dealers, Democratic members of Congress, or even party eminences much his senior. His intolerance for doctrinal deviation would permanently sour his relations even with Brandeis, with whom he broke after Brandeis helped torpedo Roosevelt's scheme to pack the Supreme Court in 1937.

Perhaps the most telling breach was the one between him and Frankfurter. This occurred in 1940, after Roosevelt had elevated Frankfurter to the Supreme Court to succeed Benjamin Cardozo. Hankering for appointment as solicitor general, Corcoran brought Frankfurter a letter of recommendation to sign. Frankfurter refused. He considered the solicitor general's job "a priestly task . . . but he felt Tom viewed the Solicitor General's position as just another post from which he could operate politically," recalled Frankfurter's law clerk Edward F. Prichard, Jr. Moreover, Corcoran had become a political liability, having antagonized scores of lawmakers on Capitol Hill with his strong-arming tactics on behalf of the White House. The rumor bandied among the justices' clerks was that the last encounter between mentor and protégé ended with Corcoran barking at Frankfurter, "I put you on the Court; now produce!" Frankfurter never confirmed the anecdote, but he and Corcoran never spoke again.

The most painful breach came with Roosevelt himself, after Corcoran discovered the boundaries of the king's solicitude for the feelings of even his most loyal courtiers. This happened early in 1940, when Tommy announced that he was to marry Peggy Dowd, the efficient and lovely secretary at the little red house. Both Frankfurter and Roosevelt advised him against marriage to the daughter of a Washington, D.C., mailman—"You can do better," the President suggested quietly, in one of the rare displays of snobbery any of his aides witnessed. Yet Corcoran persisted, pulling strings with Missy LeHand to secure for himself and his bride an audience with Roosevelt for his blessing. Peggy bought a new dress and a new hat. They reported to the White House at the appointed time and were shown into the upstairs sitting room. One hour passed, and a second, and then the door opened and Harry Hopkins appeared, mumbling something about "the President's regrets . . . unexpected business has arisen. . . ." Peggy was crushed and Tommy mortified. "I felt a chink open in the armor of my iron loyalty to my President," he would recall. "Our personal relationship could never be the same, and I could not be as comfortable as I'd been as his bachelor at arms." The experience only reinforced the value of Corcoran's one indisputably solid professional relationship, the one with Ben

Cohen. For after the marriage Ben continued to live with the Corcorans until 1941, when their child, Margaret, was born.

Still, in the President's service the rise of Corcoran and Cohen was steady. Each success added to their reputation, yet also to Corcoran's arrogance. The pinnacle of their work as behind-the-scenes legislative magicians came in mid-1935, with the battle over the highly technical and supremely contentious Public Utility Holding Company Act.

Roosevelt expected the Holding Company Act to crown his campaign for public power. The desire to bring cheap electricity to rural America had driven his support of the TVA Act and his efforts to create the Rural Electrification Administration, which would come into existence in mid-1935. Later in the year he would make a pilgrimage to the Colorado River to personally dedicate Boulder Dam (subsequently Hoover Dam). The majestic public works project had been launched by his predecessor and been assailed by FDR during the 1932 campaign as a symbol of excessive federal spending. But Roosevelt now intended to appropriate the edifice for the New Deal as a monument to public power.

While several industry lawsuits against the TVA were still making their way through the federal courts, headed inevitably for the Supreme Court, Roosevelt laid the foundations for his ultimate attack on the power trust. In July he established a special committee to develop a plan for the cooperation of "both public and private" power generators in making electricity "more broadly available at cheaper rates to industry, to domestic and, particularly, to agricultural consumers." The real object of the panel, known formally as the National Power Policy Committee, was to draft legislation to bring the utility holding companies to heel. Its membership, drawn from federal agencies closely concerned with the law and policy of electrification, was reliably oriented to public generation: it included David Lilienthal from the TVA; Elwood Mead, director of the U.S. Bureau of Reclamation, which was building Boulder Dam; Robert Healy, late of the Federal Trade Commission and now a member of the Securities and Exchange Commission; and as chair Harold Ickes, who had made his name as a progressive activist in his native Chicago by crusading against the electric utility baron Samuel Insull, whom he had fought, as *Time* magazine observed, "bravely but utterly without result for 25 years." (After Insull's death in 1938 of a heart attack in a Paris subway station, Ickes confessed: "I always had a sneaking liking for him, as I have found myself having for so many people of whom I have not been able to approve as citizens.") At its second meeting the committee appointed Ben Cohen to the all-important post of legal counsel.

Roosevelt was convinced that defeating the power trust required the destruction of the holding company structure. Holding companies, defined as entities that controlled other companies through ownership of the latter's shares but did not produce anything themselves, were common enough throughout the business world. But nowhere more than in the utility industry was the form as well developed or, arguably, abused. Many experts viewed it as the crux of the problem of misdirected investment that resulted in overpriced electricity, the dearth of power lines serving vast rural regions of the country, and the enrichment of a few well-placed profiteers.

Roosevelt expounded on these views frequently. In late November, at a meeting in Warm Springs, he told the power committee (according to Lilienthal's recollection) that "you can't regulate holding companies so the only thing that can be done is to eliminate them entirely . . . that a holding company which exists for the control of operating companies was against the public interest, and since it couldn't be regulated, should be abolished." During a cabinet meeting a few weeks later, he cut off Commerce Secretary Daniel Roper in the middle of a sanctimonious speech about business's eagerness to cooperate with the administration, interjecting that he was "tired of eighty men controlling the destinies of one hundred and twenty million people," referring to the small cadre of unelected plutocrats who held corporate power in the country. He added that in his opinion "the only way to curb this control was to do away with holding companies."

As it happened, Ben Cohen was already formulating a bill to put utility holding companies on a short leash. While his committee members traveled to Warm Springs to see the President, he stayed behind in Washington to finish a draft. Cohen's view was that while the holding company form had been shamelessly abused, in principle it did offer certain efficiencies in utility management. The remedy embodied in his draft was to attack the abuses, not the concept. He proposed tightening the regulation of utility holding companies by the Securities and Exchange Commission and mandating the restructuring of those that were overly complex or could not show they advanced the cause of efficiency and economy. But he warned that so much capital was tied up in already established holding companies that breaking them all up—as Roosevelt preferred—was impractical.

Cohen's approach underscored the distinction between his economic philosophy and that of Brandeis, whose influence in the White House remained potent. The Brandeis view was that holding companies exemplified the overgrown institutions that created operational inefficiencies while concentrating wealth and power at the expense of democracy. If bigness was bad, in the Brandeisian view, there could be nothing worse than a holding company projecting its power across great swaths of the country, largely immune from commercial competition or regulation at the local or state level. To Cohen this was an extreme and impractical view. Holding companies were often abusive, but they were not inherently exempt from regulation, and that, not abolition, was what he proposed to implement.

But while Cohen was mapping out a nuanced regulatory approach, refining his draft bill with input from Corcoran, Healy, and James Landis, Roosevelt's stance toward the utilities was hardening. One indication of his views, albeit perhaps a subconscious one, was a widely remarked slip of the tongue in the delivery of his State of the Union address on January 4, 1935, in which he pledged "the abolition of the evil of holding companies." This was a departure from the official text, which referred to "the abolition of the evil features of holding companies." Although he assured reporters that the slip was his own, in the fullness of time his spoken words proved to better define White House policy than the written text. Certainly they were more in tune with public opinion, which had been shaped by decades of profiteering and other chicanery by the Insull trust and other utility conglomerations.

Relations between the White House and the power industry cooled further when Roosevelt met with a delegation of utility executives, with Lilienthal in attendance, in the Oval Room a few weeks after his annual address. Among the visitors was Wendell Willkie, who was about to begin the march to national prominence that would make him the Republican candidate for president in 1940. Willkie had the reputation of a reasonable, intelligent, even somewhat public-spirited utility executive. Lilienthal, who had spent hours negotiating with him on behalf of the TVA, knew he also had a short fuse. As Roosevelt genially but firmly turned away his visitors' entreaties to soften the coming bill, Lilienthal kept his eye on Willkie, who he could see "getting hotter and hotter." Finally Willkie took his glasses out of the breast pocket of his coat, and wielding them as a pointer, leaned over and jabbed them in the President's direction.

"If you will give us a Federal incorporation law, we can get rid of holding companies," Willkie said, with a bluntness that instantly chilled the atmosphere in the room. "He didn't preface it by 'Mr. President,'" Lilienthal observed, "and he didn't say it with the courtesy that you would accord if you were addressing the vice president of a bank, much less the President of the United States." The other executives in the room "recoiled as if Willkie had suddenly produced a gun and started shooting." Things went downhill from there, "with the President jutting his chin out and becoming less and less conciliatory as Willkie continued to bark and point his glasses."

Willkie said finally, "Do I understand then that any further efforts to avoid the breaking up of utility holding companies are futile?"

"It is futile," the President answered coldly.

A few days later, Roosevelt convened a White House meeting to iron out the differences among three regulatory approaches. On the table, in addition to Cohen's draft, were proposals from Sam Rayburn's House Interstate Commerce Committee and from the Treasury Department. The latter two differed from Cohen's regulation-oriented approach in that they proposed to bring holding companies to heel through hostile taxation—harsh enough in the Treasury's version to render holding companies effectively extinct.

It was unclear that Congress would accept such an extreme measure, however. Corcoran and Cohen, backed up by Frankfurter and Moley, spoke up forcibly for the moderate approach; Roosevelt objected that it would not send a strong enough message to the power trust. At length Cohen and Corcoran "agreed to sharpen their pencils," Moley reported. Cohen looked ahead without enthusiasm to writing a bill based on principles he opposed. "Tom and I will be branded as dangerous radicals again," he wrote a friend, "although we are in fact about the only real conservatives in Washington."

Following orders, they drafted a provision allowing the SEC to compel the dissolution of any holding company that reached beyond a discrete geographical region and could not demonstrate an economic raison d'être for its existence. This provision, which became Section 11 of the bill, was known as the "death penalty."

With the incorporation of Section 11, the bill fulfilled Roosevelt's specifications for a screaming shot across the power trust's bow. It is not likely that the President, much less Cohen and Corcoran, truly expected the provision to survive intact the process of congressional give-and-take. Moley regarded it as something to be bargained away in return for other gains.

Yet as the battle progressed and the death penalty became the main point of contention, the White House position would stiffen. Moley viewed this trend as a distasteful sign of the mutual reinforcement of ideological doctrine by Roosevelt and his acolytes: "The President, Corcoran, and Cohen managed to sell themselves all they originally asked for," he observed disapprovingly.

As the bill was being prepared for introduction, it seemed to have the wind at its back. The Federal Trade Commission had just wrapped up an investigation of the power trust it had launched back in 1928, when the utilities were shown to have fought the Boulder Dam project with a campaign of bribery and misrepresentation. On January 27 the commission released its final report, couched in language sharper than anyone had been accustomed to hear from a regulatory body saddled with such a long reputation for submissiveness as the FTC's.

"The use of words such as fraud, deceit, misrepresentation, dishonesty, breach of trust and oppression are the only suitable terms to apply . . . on many practices which have taken sums beyond calculation from the rate-paying and investing public," the report stated. As for whether the proper remedy was to eradicate all holding companies or merely "super-holding companies," which held the stock of conventional holding companies, the commission left that up to Congress.

Less than two weeks later, the Public Utility Holding Company Act was introduced by Rayburn and Burton Wheeler, chair of the Senate Interstate Commerce Commission. To no one's surprise, it provoked an immediate furor in the business community, which mobilized behind Willkie's leadership. In due course there were more utility lobbyists swarming over Capitol Hill than congressmen. Unabashed by the FTC's exposure of their dishonesty, they revived the tactics they had deployed against public power and the Boulder Dam project in 1928 and the TVA in 1933, including fabricated mass mailings to congressmen, purportedly from constituents. Taking a page from Wall Street's battle plan against the Securities Exchange Act of 1934, they predicted economic apocalypse: The bill's passage would "paralyze the nation," utility executives projected, and lead to "nationalization of the industry," among other baleful results.

At this point, curiously, the bill's chief instigator, President Roosevelt, absented himself from the debate. Rayburn, who had been unable to muster a committee majority for the administration bill, was promoting an alternative that Wheeler opposed, removing Section 11 and exempting the big holding companies from many other provisions. Press rumors to the effect that the administration was prepared to compromise on the death penalty went unchallenged by the White House. At a party at Joseph Kennedy's Maryland mansion in early June, Wheeler was approached quietly by a succession of Senate colleagues, all voicing the same message: the White House wanted him to back off the death penalty. "You're putting the President on the spot," he was told by James F. Byrnes of South Carolina.

"But this is the *President's* bill," Wheeler replied.

"I've talked to the President and had him talked out of it," Byrnes said, "but he said he was standing behind Burt Wheeler."

"He isn't standing behind me," Wheeler said. "I'm standing behind him."

In these mixed messages, Wheeler detected Roosevelt's familiar habit of mollifying contentious interest groups by telling everyone what they wanted to hear. Early the next morning, he drove to the White House to confront Roosevelt in person. He found the President in bed, propped up by pillows, a cigarette holder jutting from his mouth and dropping ashes on the bedspread. Stating, "I'm tired of being buttonholed by Senators," he presented Roosevelt with two options. If Roosevelt wanted him to back down, he would remove Section 11 from the bill. But if Roosevelt was determined to stand pat on the death penalty, Wheeler demanded that he make a public statement of support.

As always, Roosevelt was reluctant to back himself into a corner. Instead of agreeing to a public declaration, he scrawled a note on a scrap of paper. "You can show this to the boys," he said, handing it to Wheeler.

In early June amid an intense floor debate on an amendment to strike the death penalty, Senator William Dieterich of Illinois rose to claim that the amendment had Roosevelt's support. Wheeler drew the President's note from his coat pocket and read it aloud: "Dear Burt . . . any amendment which goes to the heart of major objectives of Sec. 11 would go to the heart of the bill itself and is wholly contrary to the recommendations of myself. Sincerely, Franklin D. Roosevelt." The death penalty survived by a one-vote margin.

But the Senate vote set up a bitter fight with the House. Corcoran now came into his own as a presidential lobbyist, not entirely to his own advantage. Moley was appalled at the latitude afforded Corcoran to bully important lawmakers. Corcoran's "lobbying proclivities . . . had been given the open throttle," Moley discovered. Most disturbing to the veteran Brain

Truster was Corcoran's doctrinal rigidity. Moley had become accustomed to the style of Dan Roper and Jesse Jones, who did their lobbying in tuxedos at elegant parties and were realists intent on advancing the ball as close as possible to the goal line, ideology be damned. He perceived that in Corcoran's view, however, "they were compromisers . . . , and this was a truceless war."

Corcoran's scorched-earth tactics would presage the great miscalculations of the Court-packing scheme two years hence. All Moley could see now, however, was that Corcoran and Cohen "were in and out of the White House, day after day, night after night, reporting the progress of their campaign to 'put the heat on.'. . . Between them they generated enough indignation over the opposition to the bill to become the victims of their own strategy. The fight became a fight for all or nothing." The death penalty evolved from bargaining chip into "gospel, which it was treason, if not sacrilege, to question."

The ruthlessness of Corcoran's lobbying broke into the open in the dog days of July, when Representative Ralph Owen Brewster, Republican of Maine, rose in the House to oppose the death penalty and, in the process, leveled a sensational charge. While the bill was being debated, he said, "Thomas G. Corcoran, Esq., co-author with Benjamin V. Cohen, Esq., of the bill, came to me in the lobby of the Capitol and stated to me with what he termed 'brutal frankness' that, if I should vote against the death penalty . . . he would find it necessary to stop construction on the Passamaquoddy dam in my district." The dam, known as the "Quoddy," was a $36 million PWA project designed to generate electricity from the ebb and flow of the coastal tides.

Brewster's words produced an instant uproar. The charge seemed to validate widespread resentment about Corcoran's roughhouse tactics. Corcoran, who denied making such a threat, had to explain himself both to the President and to the public—in a tense congressional hearing at which he produced a witness to dispute Brewster's version of their encounter.

Corcoran was vindicated, but his victory proved to be a Pyrrhic one, for he could not dispel the acrid residue of his bare-knuckled lobbying methods. For a brief moment Tommy Corcoran had operated in the open, even successfully defending his tactics before a committee of the House and the national press; but it was not a picture many people inside and out of the White House particularly relished seeing again. Arthur Krock of the *New York Times,* who tolerantly described Corcoran's confrontation with Brewster as an "indiscretion," nevertheless warned that charges such as Brewster's "help to arouse the country's distrust, and to convince those already convinced that rough stuff and the New Deal are synonymous. . . . Mr. Corcoran—if he said anything to Mr. Brewster about the 'Quoddy— would have done better to have said nothing at all."

Corcoran never forgot that lesson—he "drilled his little chicks to 'keep their heads down,'" Alva Johnston wrote later, "to work in secret, to avoid publicity like smallpox." But for Corcoran it was too late, and sadly, his reputation as a political roughhouser rubbed off on Cohen, who had played no part in the Brewster affair. Before then, both were mentioned occasionally for high public posts in the Roosevelt administration—Cohen's name appearing on the President's short list of initial appointees to the Securities and Exchange Commission, Corcoran being led to believe that he might be named solicitor general. But not afterward.

Yet that did not stop them from moving closer to the center of power in the Roosevelt administration. Corcoran retreated to the shadows, but he became much more a trusted advisor to the President, and a key member of his speechwriting staff for the 1936 campaign. This enterprise, like their others, was a joint effort, with Corcoran sometimes present on the campaign train and Cohen always staying home in Washington, and always making his indispensable contribution. As a team, too, they would be sucked together into the debacle of the Court-packing plan of 1937.

The death penalty in its most uncompromising guise was bargained away in the final rounds of compromise between Senate and House. Yet what remained in the bill was stringent enough. It allowed the SEC to permit a holding company to continue if breaking it up would result in "the loss of substantial economies," if the constituent units were located in one state or adjoining states, or if the holding company were not too large to interfere with efficient operation or localized management. The new arrangement had been crafted by none other than Felix Frankfurter, now back from England and anxious to regain his foothold in the administration.

FDR is sworn in by Chief Justice Charles Evans Hughes, March 4, 1933. Hughes would deliver the oath of office to Roosevelt at two more inaugurations, each freighted with tension from the battle between Court and President over the Constitutionality of the New Deal. Behind the new president are his eldest son, James, and the departing President Herbert Hoover.

Crestfallen and isolated in defeat, a lame duck Herbert Hoover stops at the construction site of his namesake dam on the Colorado River, en route from his California home back to a crisis-beset Washington days after the 1932 election. Soon after assuming office, the Roosevelt Administration would strike Hoover's name from the dam, which would not be permanently rechristened Hoover Dam until 1947.

2

A publicity man's stunt produces an unforgettable image from Ferdinand Pecora's Senate hearings on Wall Street misdeeds, June 1, 1933: J.P. "Jack" Morgan, Jr., holds the Ringling Bros. performer Lya Graf on his lap, complimenting her on her hat. Morgan's air of dignity would be forever punctured by the episode. Unable to bear her notoriety, the Jewish Graf would return to her native Germany and perish at Auschwitz.

The "boys" of the Civilian Conservation Corps' camp at Big Meadows, Virginia, hail their patron, FDR. Roosevelt never tired of visiting camps of the CCC, the first relief program of the New Deal and one of its most successful.

The brash and obstreperous NRA chieftain General Hugh S. Johnson, tended to by his omnipresent assistant Frances "Robbie" Robinson. Oblivious to the public impression made by his working relationship with Robinson, Johnson valued her knowledge of agency minutiae, instructing inquiring reporters to "ask the little skirt."

6   7

TVA Director David Lilienthal (*left*) tangled with utility executive Wendell L. Willkie (*right*)—destined to become the GOP's presidential candidate in 1940—over the agency's access to customers in its earliest days. Willkie's leverage over the fledgling TVA evaporated in 1934 when the agency contracted to provide municipal power to Tupelo, Mississippi, a pioneering deal that prompted a celebratory civic parade (*below*).

Social conscience of the New Deal, Frances Perkins stepped from a proper New England background into the formerly all-male bastion of the Cabinet as secretary of labor. She and Interior Secretary Harold Ickes would be the only Cabinet members to serve FDR through his entire twelve-year term in office.

9

Henry Morgenthau, Jr., (here with Secretary of Agriculture Henry Wallace and Mrs. Wallace) parlayed his status as a Roosevelt family friend into the position of treasury secretary, from which he promoted George Warren's unorthodox economic theory and pressed for a balanced budget.

Curmudgeon and fixer: Harold L. Ickes (*left*), progressive Republican and loyal New Dealer, shares a moment with Thomas G. "Tommy the Cork" Corcoran, FDR's ace legislative draftsman in partnership with Benjamin Cohen.

Colleagues and rivals, Harry Hopkins and Ickes squabbled over control of billions of dollars in work-relief funds, prompting FDR to invite them both on a 1935 trip to dedicate Boulder Dam and sail in the Pacific in hopes of settling their disagreement. The strategy failed.

13

General Hugh Johnson and Interior Secretary Harold Ickes share a light moment in 1933. Ickes was among the cabinet members most critical of Johnson's management of the NRA, labeling its ballyhoo "disgusting." But Johnson, by then out of government, praised Ickes' antimonopoly speeches in 1938.

Lewis Douglas, former Arizona congressman appointed budget director and hailed by FDR as "the find of the Administration," later broke bitterly with the New Deal over its deficit spending.

14

15

Before the fall: Sen. Burton Wheeler of Montana (*left*) chats with New York Stock Exchange President Richard Whitney during hearings on the 1934 Securities Exchange Act. Whitney's reputation as leader of the exchange's campaign against government regulation would be forgotten when he was convicted and jailed in 1937 for having engaged in fraud and embezzlement on a spectacular scale for years.

16

The Kingfish: Louisiana senator Huey Long helped tip the 1932 Democratic convention in FDR's favor but became one of the New Deal's harshest critics. Long's emergence as a national figure with presidential aspirations ended with his assassination in 1935.

17

Gentle champion of the elderly, Dr. Francis Everett Townsend (*left*) launched a nationwide movement for old-age pensions that prefigured Social Security. Here he greets Rep. William Lemke of North Dakota, briefly the presidential candidate in 1936 of Rev. Charles Coughlin's Union Party.

18

Iconic symbol of Depression-era desperation, California migrant worker and mother of seven Florence Owens Thompson, 32, captured in 1936 by photographer Dorothea Lange on assignment for Rex Tugwell's Resettlement Administration.

America Builds: Managed by Ickes with an iron hand, the Public Works Administration provided work for thousands on projects of lasting value such as New York's Triborough Bridge.

On the Columbia River in Washington State, the Grand Coulee Dam project launched in 1933 provided up to nine years of employment for men like these lining up on payday.

21

Federal Theatre Director Hallie Flanagan, flanked here by playwright Virgil Geddes and WPA chief Harry Hopkins, endowed the program with her vision for a people's theater that would unite the country.

22

Theater wunderkind Orson Welles achieved nationwide renown and helped launch the Federal Theatre with works including Christopher Marlowe's *Doctor Faustus*, but would leave the government's employ over claims of censorship of his 1937 production of the politically provocative musical play *The Cradle Will Rock*.

Welles's Voodoo *Macbeth*, produced for the Federal Theatre's Negro unit and set in Haiti with Jack Carter in the title role, created a sensation that spread from Harlem to the rest of New York.

The Supreme Court transformed: The Hughes Court majority that began dismantling the New Deal in 1935 and provoked FDR to his ill-fated Court-packing scheme included the conservative "Four Horsemen," Pierce Butler, James McReynolds, George Sutherland, and Willis Van Devanter, typically joined by Owen Roberts and Chief Justice Charles Evans Hughes. Seated in this 1932 group portrait (*left to right*): Louis Brandeis, Van Devanter, Hughes, McReynolds, Sutherland. Standing (*left to right*): Roberts, Butler, Harlan Fiske Stone, Benjamin Cardozo.

By 1940, Roosevelt had remade the Court to his liking through the natural progression of deaths and retirements, creating an enduring liberal majority. Seated (*left to right*): Roberts, McReynolds, Hughes, Stone, Hugo L. Black. Standing (*left to right*): William O. Douglas, Stanley Reed, Felix Frankfurter, Frank Murphy.

6

Relief on the farm: Aunt Nellie Pettway, descendant of slaves, in Gee's Bend, Alabama, an isolated former plantation rescued from destitution by Rexford Tugwell's short-lived Resettlement Administration, one of the few New Deal projects to adequately assist black citizens.

27

Al Smith, former Democratic presidential candidate and the progressive "Happy Warrior" of New York politics, casts his lot with Roosevelt opponents by delivering a savagely anti–New Deal keynote speech at the Liberty League's 1937 white tie fete.

28

Marian Anderson (*center, in dark coat*), barred from the DAR's whites-only Washington auditorium because of her race, sings "America" on Easter Sunday 1939 to a vast crowd before the Lincoln Memorial.

29

FDR

11

PIED PIPERS

ECONOMIC AND POLITICAL currents made 1934 a watershed
year in American labor history. Nearly 1,900 major work stoppages occurred involving nearly 1.5 million workers, both figures
standing as a record for the era. Industrial strife swept the country from
San Francisco on the West Coast to Toledo, Milwaukee, and Minneapolis
in the heartland and into the textile belts of New England and the deep
South.

These disruptions could hardly be ignored in Washington, not least
because the upheavals on the factory floor coincided with convulsions
in society at large. The country was growing anxious and impatient. The
events of that year gave rise to a new generation of radical labor leaders
and thrust a new breed of social activists onto the national stage—figures
who were not so much radical as utopian, but for all that perhaps the more
effective at mobilizing popular sentiment.

They would emerge with two very different styles. The Midwest and
South produced a truculent populism closely identified with two masters
of radio oratory, the Reverend Charles E. Coughlin and Huey Long. In
California emerged a milder, more idealistic movement whose figureheads
were a pair of elderly prophets, Upton Sinclair and Dr. Francis Everett
Townsend. The seeds they planted would be harvested in 1935 with the
creation of the quintessential Rooseveltian program, Social Security. The
New Deal was about to come of age.

The most important factors in labor's emergence as a national force were

213

the appearance of signs that the economy was finally on the mend and a growing conviction that the promises made to workers by the NRA—the right to a minimum living wage and to collective bargaining—were empty ones. On the factory floor, the reaction would be seismic.

It was perhaps unsurprising that the most violent eruption would take place in Toledo, Ohio, a city of 290,000 so dependent on the auto industry it was sometimes described as a junior Detroit. Toledo was the home of Electric Auto-Lite, the nation's leading independent auto parts maker, which also provided the community with a local industrial villain in the person of Clement O. Miniger, the company's founder and the owner as well of the Ohio Bond & Security Bank. That institution had failed spectacularly in 1931, wiping out the savings of thousands of Toledo residents. Despite the crash Miniger remained the richest man in town, a builder of ostentatious industrial monuments, a community philanthropist, and a ferocious enemy of organized labor.

Months of conflict between Auto-Lite and the American Federation of Labor came to a head in April 1934, when Miniger reneged on a prior agreement to open contract negotiations. When the factory local launched a walkout on April 12, Auto-Lite issued a call for strikebreakers and resolved to stay open.

A new organization now joined the conflict: the American Workers Party. The AWP was led by A. J. Muste, a radical activist, socialist, and pacifist whose career in political agitation would stretch from the Lawrence, Massachusetts, textile strike of 1919 to the antiwar movement of the Vietnam era. Muste pursued the novel strategy of organizing not only the Auto-Lite employees but unemployed local workers, who were formed into the "Lucas County Unemployed League."

It did not take long for the establishment to grasp the significance of this approach, which was designed to deprive employers of a ready supply of strikebreakers. Roy Howard wired Louis Howe, "It is nothing new to see organized unemployed appear on the streets, fight police, and raise hell in general. . . . At Toledo they appeared on the picket lines to help striking employees win a strike, tho [sic] you would expect their interest would lie the other way—that is, in going in and getting the jobs the other men had laid down."

By May 23, in the fifth week of the strike, as many as six thousand demonstrators thronged the factory premises, effectively besieging the handful of strikebreakers the company had managed to enlist. Sheriff's deputies took up positions on the factory roof and rained tear gas canisters on the crowd below. Skirmishing continued for seven hours, the crowd firing back with rocks and bricks and engaging in "hand-to-hand fighting" with company guards. The battle of Toledo had begun.

That night seven hundred members of the Ohio National Guard entered the city. By afternoon the guardsmen and rioters were engaged in a full-scale crossfire of tear gas and stench bombs from the guard's side and bricks, stones, and unexpended gas canisters from the rioters. As the crowd forced the outnumbered guardsmen back against the factory gates, they were ordered to fix bayonets and fire over the rioters' heads. When that failed to disperse their attackers, they lowered their guns and fired directly into the crowd, prefiguring another tragic confrontation between Ohio guardsmen and unarmed citizens some three decades later. Two civilians were slain and at least fifteen others injured.

The violence set the stage for an eventual settlement under the leadership of Charles P. Taft, who as the son of a former Republican president personified the Ohio establishment. Over the following two weeks Taft mediated an agreement calling for recognition of the AFL-affiliated International Brotherhood of Electrical Workers, direct negotiations in accordance with the principles of Section 7(a) of the NIRA, and a 5 percent wage increase. The agreement undercut Auto-Lite's detested company union, but as it specifically rejected the "tactics" of communists, it also undercut Muste's American Workers Party.

If the Toledo riots were "a test case in the battle for industrial democracy," as the *New Republic* judged, then organized labor won the battle, if superficially. Disturbingly, the system of supervised federal arbitration established by the NIRA under Section 7(a) plainly had won neither the respect of management nor the confidence of the workers; neither side had been willing to submit the dispute to a federal tribunal. Toledo also revealed the disaffection lurking not far beneath the surface of the working class, where any spark could ignite it into violence. "The sorry American scene in Toledo," the *New Republic* concluded, "finds its setting in broken promises of the New Deal."

A few months later, another such scene unfolded at the edge of the continent. What became known as the San Francisco general strike had its roots in an inhumane portside practice known as the "shape-up." Every morning, longshoremen thronged the ferry terminal at the foot of Market Street seeking work "like a bunch of sheep," in the words of the insurgent labor leader Harry Bridges. Thousands more reported than were needed, which gave the employers' foremen autocratic power over the ill-paid workforce.

The year 1934 promised to be a turning point in the balance of power on the San Francisco docks. The enactment of NIRA and its Section 7(a) hinted at the possibility of forming a union and establishing a union hiring hall to distribute jobs fairly, replacing the shape-up. Talks had proceeded sporadically among the employers, the International Longshoremen's Association local, and unionists led by the charismatic Bridges, a pugnacious Australian immigrant. When they broke down in an impasse in May, the ILA struck ports all along the West Coast, effectively shutting down commerce from Seattle to San Diego.

San Francisco was the epicenter of the strike. Shippers there tried to break the walkout by hiring their own trucks to move freight in and out of the port; in retaliation the longshoremen enlisted an ever-lengthening roster of local unions—teamsters, ferrymen, and cable car engineers among them—to call sympathetic walkouts. After strikers and police escorting the shippers' trucks engaged in a daylong melee that took the lives of two workers, more than one hundred San Francisco unions voted to participate in a general strike starting Monday, July 16.

The scale of the walkout created an atmosphere of palpable panic in the editorial suites of California's major newspapers, a fanatically Red-baiting group that included Hearst publications in San Francisco and Los Angeles and the *Los Angeles Times,* which was owned by California's preeminent conservative businessman, Harry Chandler. The latter saw the situation on the Bay not as a "general strike" but "an insurrection, a Communist-inspired revolt against organized government." The newspaper advocated putting down the revolt "with any force that may be necessary."

The editorialists' hysteria soon reached Washington. President Roosevelt had departed for a fishing trip off the coast of Costa Rica, leaving Secretary of State Cordell Hull in functional command of the government. On the second day of the walkout, Hull telephoned Labor Secretary Perkins from the office of Attorney General Homer Cummings, where he and Cummings were holed up, stoking each other's anxieties.

"We think it's very serious," Hull said of the San Francisco strike. "I am, after all, Acting President, and I think we should take some very severe and drastic steps immediately." Perkins already had reached Labor Department officials in San Francisco, who assured her that the city was peaceful and

the strike was likely to blow over in due course. But she despaired of com-
municating calm to her querulous colleagues over a phone line. Hasten-
ing to Cummings's office, she found them consulting ancient law books,
looking to establish the scope of their authority in the face of an incipient
government overthrow. Neither one, she reflected, had ever been "nearer to
a strike than you can get by reading the newspaper over the breakfast table,"
and she struggled to convince them that San Francisco was far from facing
an utter breakdown of civil order.

Their ears were closed to her appeals. "I think the federal troops should
be sent in there to break this up," Hull told her.

Perkins tried to keep the quaver out of her voice. "How would they
break it up, Mr. Secretary?"

"By military means."

"You mean force men to get on the bakery wagons, force them to drive
them?"

"Yes, or drive them themselves, with armed guards, so that if any group
of bakery wagon drivers attempts to stop them, they can be . . ."

"Shot at?" Perkins asked.

"Yes, shot at."

"Wouldn't that be rather a serious situation?"

"It's a very serious situation to have local government break down."

Perkins finally persuaded them to send a message to Roosevelt and wait
for him to reply. To her relief, the President responded by empowering her
to establish an arbitration procedure for the strike and limiting Hull's and
Cummings's authority to ensuring that food supplies got through to the
city.

But Perkins's troubles were not over. That Monday, Hugh Johnson had
flown into San Francisco to receive an award from his alma mater, the
University of California. He found the temptation to involve himself in
the strike irresistible, declaring upon landing that "anything so affecting
the entire Pacific Coast must be dealt with as a national problem. . . . This
strike must stop."

The General was only warming up. He would write later of being physically shocked by the situation in San Francisco: "The economic life of the
city was being strangled. . . . A foreign enemy could scarcely threaten more
than that." These words show only that Johnson had succumbed to his own
imagination. The city was in fact calm, unionized milk and bakery drivers
had been given dispensation to continue deliveries, and the strike was fray-

ing of its own accord in only its second full day. Nevertheless, at the award ceremony in Berkeley the next afternoon, Johnson put his foot down.

"I think that labor is inherently entitled to bargain collectively through representatives of its own choosing," he declared. "But there is another and a worse side to this story. You are living out here under the stress of a general strike. . . . It is a threat to the community. It is a menace to government. It is civil war."

In Johnson's version of history, "the general strike was broken" by his talk. In fact, he had allowed himself to be made a tool of the employers, who exploited his words in an attempt to paint the unions as instigators of the strike. It was left to Perkins to undo Johnson's damage by insisting that the dispute be permitted to follow its natural course, which resulted several months later in a federal labor board awarding control of waterfront hiring halls to the unions and establishing shorter hours and improved overtime pay. For the first time in memory—Johnson's activities notwithstanding—the federal government had refused to take the employers' side in a major labor dispute.

"Hugh thinks strikes are for settling," Perkins once observed of Johnson. Her point was that Johnson viewed strikes as aberrations designed to interfere with the smooth regimentation of commerce and industry that was his goal as administrator of the NRA—the labor counterpart to the "chiseling" engaged in by industrialists who violated the principles of the Blue Eagle. "Johnson thought that the Department of Labor ought to 'rule' labor. . . . There was no such power in the office of the Secretary of Labor, nor should there be." Johnson's interference did nothing to change the course of the general strike. But it would cost him Perkins's support in the looming battle to save his own career.

The Canadian-born Reverend Coughlin was a parish priest at a wood-frame, shingled church in suburban Detroit in 1926 when he had the brainstorm of broadcasting his Sunday sermons over a local radio station. Out of this came an uncannily perfect melding of medium, voice, and subject. The voice was a theatrical, baritone brogue, and the subject, the plundering of the middle class by Herbert Hoover and his henchmen, who included the banker J. P. Morgan and Treasury Secretary Andrew Mellon.

A half dozen years later Coughlin was speaking through sixteen stations of the Columbia Broadcasting System and enjoying nationwide fame. One sermon identifying Morgan, Mellon, Ogden Mills, and Federal Reserve chairman Eugene Meyer as the Four Horsemen of the Apocalypse brought him six hundred thousand letters. That, too, was a foundation stone for greater fame. By 1933 it would be said that Father Coughlin, the Radio Priest of Royal Oak, Michigan, received more mail than anyone in the United States—more than twenty thousand letters a day, often enclosing money orders averaging $5 or $6 each. Much of the money went toward the construction of a new shrine dedicated to the parish's patron saint, the nineteenth-century nun Thérèse de Lisieux, known as the "Little Flower," who had been canonized in 1925. This project supplanted the original frame-and-shingle church with a stone edifice designed by a prominent New York architect and featuring a nine-story tower bearing the carved image of Christ on the cross.

Through the election of 1932 and the preinauguration interregnum, Coughlin's rhetoric corresponded reasonably well, if not entirely comfortably, with the New Deal platform. Coughlin excoriated Wall Street, the "money powers," and "international bankers," and invoked the "cross of gold" in proclaiming the virtues of inflation to his immense radio audience, while Roosevelt indicted "the unscrupulous money changers" in his inauguration address and plotted to take the country off the gold standard. Whether it was because they had an inkling of the acrid future path of Coughlin's oratory or the kernel of anti-Semitism in his rants against internationalism and the League of Nations, or were merely made uneasy by his immoderate entrepreneurial ambition, Roosevelt's aides understood that it might not be wise to embrace the mercurial Coughlin too closely. Coughlin had come to consider himself as much a public figure and tribune of the people as the President of the United States; he could not be casually manipulated, much less ordered about, by Franklin Roosevelt. Moreover, he was not the promoter of a specific program so much as the spokesman for generalized alienation and resentment, aimed at a broad spectrum of targets. He denounced capitalist bankers for their profits and communist agitators for their disdain of profit; upheld the right of unions to collective bargaining, but vilified union leaders for taking dues from their members' pay envelopes. He was a supporter of the New Deal's agenda but opposed many of its individual initiatives: in September 1933 he had informed the White House that he had no use either for the NRA, which he predicted would be "a colossal failure," or for the crop reductions and pig slaughters of the AAA—"foolish proposals aimed at starving us into prosperity."

The administration walked a tightrope with Coughlin, striving to keep the Radio Priest ideologically on the reservation but at arm's length from their policy councils. A proposal by fifty-nine congressmen and six U.S. senators (including Huey Long) to name Coughlin as an economic advisor to the delegation to the June 1933 London Economic Conference received no reply from the White House, but Coughlin's lobbying for petty administrative posts for his protégés often was honored. As late as 1935, Roosevelt, at the urging of Joseph P. Kennedy, received Coughlin at Hyde Park. The priest took that opportunity to present the President with what he said was evidence that several New Dealers were communists, which Roosevelt accepted with ostentatious interest and quietly ignored. By then Roosevelt had concluded that the priest's public influence owed more to his novelty on the public stage than to the allure of his message, and that the allure would fade in time. He wrote his friend Ray Stannard Baker, the biographer of Woodrow Wilson: "People tire of seeing the same name day after day in the important headlines of the papers, and the same voice night after night over the radio."

In mid-1934, Coughlin was nearing the high-water mark of his public standing. Journalists visiting the Shrine of the Little Flower in Royal Oak reported on the unceasing "click of typewriters, mimeographs and addressograph machines," the army of 145 stenographers at work around the clock, file cabinets bearing the names and addresses of two million adherents, mountains of mail sacks arriving every day. "Father Coughlin is a going concern," reported the *New Republic* in May. A month earlier, Coughlin had turned decisively against Roosevelt by announcing the launch of the National Union for Social Justice, quite conceivably the framework for a third political party. Critics ridiculed the sixteen points of its platform as unexceptionably pious platitudes—calls for "liberty of conscience," "a just and living annual wage," "fair profit for the farmer"—yoked to murkily populist proposals such as the nationalization of oil and natural gas, regulation of industry (albeit not regimentation à la NRA), and, of course, inflationary fiscal and monetary policy.

Coughlin's launch of the National Union would not have rattled the White House's serenity much had it occurred in isolation. But as it roughly coincided with the birth of a new phase in the career of Huey Long, it seemed to signal a dangerous new stage of populist reaction to the New Deal, one that traditional progressives found deeply unnerving.

Over a nationwide radio hookup on February 23, Long had announced the founding of the nationwide "Share Our Wealth Society" behind the slogan "Every Man a King." The society's platform held that any family's wealth should be capped at $5 million and income at $1 million a year, both figures about three hundred times that of the average family. These ceilings were to be achieved through federal taxation, with the revenue thus raised to be spent on providing every family in the country with a nest egg, or "homestead," of five thousand dollars—"enough for a home, an automobile, a radio, and the ordinary conveniences," Long declared. Every family would be guaranteed an annual income of at least two thousand dollars, every aged person a pension of thirty dollars a month, every qualified student a college education, every veteran a bonus.

Long claimed to have drawn up the program in a single night with pencil and yellow pad. In truth its principles were a distillation of goals he had articulated since arriving in the U.S. Senate two years earlier, now energized by an impatience born of witnessing the calculated give-and-take of politics in Roosevelt's capital. Weary of hearing endless excuses for allowing the bankers and financiers their plunder, weary of being outvoted by the northeastern urban bloc, weary of being told that it would take time for recovery to reach the common people even as the nation's great fortunes resumed their growth and corporate profits surged—and openly devoted to his own political ambitions—Long chose not to worry very much about the mechanism for achieving his goals. Like any experienced politician he understood the visceral appeal of a platform stated succinctly and based on figures even the simplest voter could grasp effortlessly. To Democratic Party leaders, Share Our Wealth sounded like the opening trumpet blast of Huey Long's 1936 presidential campaign.

The cavils of economists and sober political pundits carried no weight against the promises of Share Our Wealth. The *New Republic* sent Long a tendentious questionnaire—"If you limited wealth to $5,000,000 a person, could enough be taken from those above this amount to give everyone a minimum of $5,000? . . . Upon what statistics or economic studies do you base your conclusions?" Not receiving a reply, the weekly concluded that "Senator Long's economics are those of a naïve utopian."

Long was unmoved by such criticism, or by the accusation that he had deliberately put forth an unworkable plan as an easy path to winning votes. "My enemies believe I'm faking," he said. "Let them think it . . . All the time that they fight me, they fight upon a mistaken basis." To another questioner—one to whom he chose to reply—he described his approach to criticism as "Never explain, my boy, never explain! . . . First you must come into power—*POWER*—and then you do things."

Share Our Wealth clubs sprung up across the country under the leadership of an outspoken minister from Shreveport named Gerald L. K. Smith, whom Long had placed in charge of his movement. Smith's talent for exhorting the dispossessed and disenfranchised made him an ideal choice to carry Long's gospel to a rural audience, promising them "not a little old sow-belly black-eyed pea job but a real spending money, beefsteak and gravy, Chevrolet, Ford in the garage, new suit, Thomas Jefferson, Jesus Christ, red, white, and blue job for every man." By the end of its first month the Share Our Wealth campaign claimed more than 200,000 members, by the end of the year 3 million, by late 1935 more than 4.5 million.

The similarities between the trajectories of Long and Coughlin were hard to overlook. In January 1935 they both campaigned against a treaty affiliating the United States with the World Court. Vehement opposition to such foreign entanglements long had been identified with Republican progressives such as California's Hiram Johnson, but the treaty debate revived an isolationism latent in the countryside. Coughlin took up the issue as a personal cause. His radio discourses attacking the largely symbolic treaty produced telegrams to Washington from his listeners in such volume that they had to be carted into the offices of startled congressmen by wheelbarrow. On the Senate floor Long led the opposition: "We are being rushed pell-mell to get into this World Court so that Señor Ab Jap . . . can pass upon our controversies," he declared (ethnic sensitivities having no standing in his vernacular).

To be sure, even before the outbursts by Coughlin and Long, voter sentiment on the treaty had turned negative. Vice President Garner believed that if put to a vote of the people, the treaty would be defeated two to one. Ickes mused: "I have been surprised all along that the President should make this such an issue as he has made it." But the White House still expected the treaty to squeak through to the required two-thirds Senate ratification by a margin of one or two votes. Instead it fell short by seven—"a decisive defeat of the Administration," in Ickes's judgment.

The World Court campaign energized gossip about a possible Long-Coughlin alliance, though to what end was not clear. To those who knew them well, their similarity began and ended with their mastery of oratory. Their political platforms were hopelessly incompatible, even assuming that either one—Long's liquidation of large fortunes, Coughlin's unleashing of inflation—could be made to work in economic terms. In any drive for personal power their personalities were bound to clash, and by the general reckoning in Washington, in any face-to-face conflict Long would roll over Coughlin like a tank. Of the two, Long was by far the more adept political practitioner. He regarded Coughlin as merely an instrument to be played, and not one that would be effective for long, at that. "Coughlin is just a political Kate Smith on the air," he said privately, echoing FDR. "They'll get tired of him."

While his aides eyed the relationship between the two orators uneasily, Roosevelt dismissed it as part of the predictable jockeying of aspirants for nomination in 1936, fomented by the GOP. "All of these Republican elements are flirting with Huey Long and probably financing him," he speculated to Colonel House. "A third Progressive Republican ticket and a fourth 'Share the Wealth' ticket they believe would crush us." For the moment, he was content to watch the jockeying play out.

Watchful waiting, however, was not Hugh Johnson's style. On March 4, the second anniversary of Roosevelt's inauguration, the deposed chief of the NRA leveled a thunderous cannonade at the two men he identified as the Pied Pipers of "the emotional fringe." The occasion was a banquet thrown for Johnson by *Redbook* magazine to mark the publication of his memoir, *The Blue Eagle from Egg to Earth.* No one was sure whether the speech was a plant by the administration, as was rumored—but denied by both the White House and Johnson, who called himself "a gratuitous volunteer"— or whether it merely reflected Johnson's own desperation to thrust himself back onto the public stage. But as a nationally broadcast speech by a figure known for his outspokenness, it attracted bountiful attention.

Johnson charged Long and Coughlin with exploiting the pain of the Depression for self-aggrandizement: "I think we are dealing with a couple of Catalines and that it is high time for somebody to say so," he declared— the gravity of the charge muted only by the obscurity of the reference to Catiline, a Roman senator who conspired to seize power by overthrowing the Roman Republic.

The rest of his speech was more accessible. "Hitler couldn't hold a candle to Huey in the art of the old Barnum ballyhoo," Johnson stated—"A new sucker every second! . . . Added to that there comes burring over the air the dripping brogue of the Irish-Canadian priest . . . musical, blatant bunk from the very rostrum of religion—it goes straight home to simple souls weary in distress and defrauded in delay." He concluded, "Between the team of Huey and the priest, we have the whole bag of crazy or crafty tricks possessed by any Mad Mullah. . . . And if you don't believe they are dangerous you just haven't thought much about it or you don't know the temper of this country in this continued moment of distress."

Johnson's blast served to reinstate him on the nation's front pages. If his intention was to quell Long and Coughlin, however, he failed. He merely provided them with a further platform to promote themselves.

Long was first into the lists, delivering a response from the Senate floor the next morning. Possibly the only figure in public life whose talent for vituperation matched the General's, Long took the opportunity to hang Wall Street around Johnson's neck—and Roosevelt's—in the guise of the General's patron, Bernard Baruch. Baruch, he said, "is the man who was running the country. . . . We thought we were swapping from Hoover to Roosevelt, and we were swapping from Baruch to Baruch."

Two days later, he cadged a coast-to-coast broadcast slot from the National Broadcasting Company on the principle of equal time. This time, Long disposed of Johnson in four brief paragraphs (labeling him "one of those satellites loaned by Wall Street to run the government"). He proceeded to use the rest of his forty-five allotted minutes soberly, humbly, and without a touch of buffoonery to depict his Share Our Wealth plan to an audience of 25 million listeners as a reasonable alternative to the New Deal. General Johnson's cannon had backfired, concluded the *New York Times*. Instead of taking the Kingfish down, the newspaper declared, he "probably transformed Huey Long from a clown into a real political menace."

A few days later came Coughlin's turn to respond to Johnson on an NBC hookup. "While you were content to vomit your venom upon my person and against my character," he lectured the General, "the American public is fully cognizant that not once did you dare attack the truths which I speak." Compared to Long's expert retort, even the Radio Priest's sonorous words lacked punch. But the donnybrook seemed to establish the bounds of progressive debate—Coughlin and Long on the radical left and Roosevelt to their right. Nothing had yet happened to change Roosevelt's view that with the next presidential election yet twenty months away, the purpose served was entertainment, not serious politics. "The diversion by the trinity of Long, Coughlin, and Johnson was long overdue," he wrote to House, "and it is vastly better to have this free side-show presented to the public at this time than later on when the main performance starts."

No one was ever to learn how a Long-Coughlin alliance would play out in a presidential election year. On September 8, 1935, only days after signing a contract to write a book titled "My First Days in the White House," Long was making his way through a corridor in the Baton Rouge statehouse when a figure stepped out from behind a pillar and shot him in the abdomen. Long staggered a few feet and crumpled to the ground. His rattled bodyguards fired three dozen shells into the assassin's prostrate corpse. "What did he want to shoot me for?" the Kingfish moaned while waiting for an ambulance. Told the assailant had been identified as Dr. Carl Weiss, the son-in-law of a state judge Long had been trying to unseat, Long replied, "I don't know him." Thirty hours later the Kingfish was dead, aged forty-two. Witnesses said his last words were "God, don't let me die. I have so much to do."

After Long's death, Coughlin's attacks on Roosevelt and the New Deal grew increasingly febrile. By mid-1936 the priest, who had once supported the President with the slogan "Roosevelt or ruin," was proclaiming "Roosevelt *and* ruin." The Democratic Party platform of 1936 would be "discredited before it is published," he declared a week before the convention. After all, the 1932 platform "was plowed under like the cotton, slaughtered like the pigs. . . . The veracity of future pledges must be judged by the echoings of the golden voice of a lost leader."

But Coughlin's turn against the President backfired. Coughlin may have had a radio audience numbered in the millions, but Franklin Roosevelt still commanded Americans' hearts and their votes, as he demonstrated with his landslide victory in November, sweeping in with himself enhanced majorities in both houses of Congress. Increasingly, Coughlin's prodigious mail sacks included missives warning him to lay off Roosevelt: "You could talk for the rest of your life and you could never turn me against our president," a follower wrote in October 1936.

Instead Coughlin's worldview turned more apocalyptic than ever, aimed at a narrowing audience of the most disaffected and alienated—not only those the New Deal had failed to help, but those who could not imagine ever being helped. Now the enemy was the New Deal itself: "You people living on WPA envelopes filled partly from the money confiscated . . . from those who are working," Coughlin's sepulchral brogue declared from the radio speakers across America. "How long can that last? . . . There's an accounting to be held, an accounting that will make the Depression of 1929 seem as a prosperity when it breaks upon you. . . . One step backwards, one step towards dictatorship . . ."

The final stage of Coughlin's journey in the limelight would be rank anti-Semitism, as though he were determined to pursue that quest for novelty cited by Franklin Roosevelt or to stave off the public boredom forecast by Huey Long. He expressed sympathy for Hitler's occupation policies in Paris, described Bolshevism as a Jewish phenomenon, published the notorious anti-Semitic forgery "The Protocols of the Elders of Zion" in his magazine, *Social Justice*. When war came, this behavior was seen as conflicting with the national interest. The U.S. Post Office barred *Social Justice* from the mails and the Justice Department launched an investigation into whether Coughlin was giving aid and comfort to the enemy and whether, as a naturalized citizen, he ought to be deported back to Canada. Detroit's Archbishop Edward Mooney, appointed in 1937, had nowhere near the tolerance for Coughlin's ministry of his predecessor, Bishop Michael Gallagher. In 1942 Mooney forced Coughlin off the air. The Radio Priest would live out his years in pastoral obscurity until his death in 1979, aged eighty-eight.

For all that Long and Coughlin functioned as nationwide progressive noise machines, the true seedbed of radical political movements was California. There, possibly due to the contrast between the salubrious weather and the dismal economic climate, "swarms of self-appointed 'saviors' poured out of every pecan grove, each with a large pink pill for the cure of every social and economic ill." So observed the journalist George Creel, who would play an important role in the bizarre political drama to come. The state would produce a pair of unusual "saviors"—one a socialist author of worldwide repute, the other a humble physician who had relocated from North Dakota to Long Beach, there to be rudely consigned to the ranks of the unemployed.

Upton Sinclair and Dr. Francis Everett Townsend possessed a superficial resemblance—gaunt and white-haired, they shared an air of the antique (though Townsend was a decade older than the fifty-six-year-old author). Each projected an unmistakably messianic sincerity. Their political platforms shared a superficial resemblance, too: both involved a radical redistribution of wealth in the name of economic recovery.

The Baltimore-born Sinclair had published his precocious masterwork, *The Jungle,* in 1906 at the age of twenty-six. Based on seven weeks' research inside the Chicago meatpacking industry, the bestselling exposé made his reputation and his fortune. Over the succeeding decades he turned out a string of politically charged novels on such topics as abuses by the coal and oil industries and the Sacco and Vanzetti case, along with militant tracts on religion, the newspaper industry, finance, and education. He founded an unsuccessful utopian community in New Jersey and joined the Socialist Party. In the Twenties he moved to Southern California, and after two unsuccessful campaigns for the state legislature on the Socialist ticket retired from electoral politics. But in August 1933 an elderly Democratic committeeman from Santa Monica urged him to run for governor as a Democrat. "This old gentleman would not be put off," Sinclair recollected.

Certainly the committeeman's appeal was timely. The Golden State had sent Republicans to the governor's mansion for thirty-seven years straight, but had joined the Roosevelt landslide in 1932. Prospects looked good for partisan change in Sacramento in the 1934 statewide election. The public blamed the state's ineffectual GOP leadership for the persistent slump afflicting its industrial and farm sectors, where annual income had been cut in half since 1929. The colorless Republican governor, Frank Merriam, was thoroughly detested for maintaining a sales tax that overburdened the middle class while vetoing an income tax, thereby leaving the upper classes in full possession of their wealth. But decades on the sidelines had left the Democrats rent by irreconcilable factionalism. They were in desperate need of a leader who could unite the party's perpetually squabbling northern and southern blocs behind him.

Sinclair stepped into the vacuum. Within weeks of the committeeman's overture he had mapped out a radical economic platform. The plan, which he called EPIC, for "End Poverty in California," appeared as a booklet styled after the utopian writer Edward Bellamy's *Looking Backward 2000–1887*. Sinclair's contribution to this visionary genre was titled *I, Governor of California and How I Ended Poverty—A True Story of the Future*.

Like all utopian nostrums, EPIC relied on deceptively simple logic. Its theme was that California's economic stagnation was rooted in the failure to put its abundant industrial assets to use. Sinclair proposed to create a triumvirate of public agencies to acquire idle land, purchase idle factories, and issue scrip to pay workers to produce goods in those plants. The hated sales tax would be replaced by a progressive income tax and a steeply raked estate tax to limit accumulated and inherited wealth; the property tax would be abolished on homes and farms assessed at less than three thousand dollars (or about fifty thousand dollars in 2011); and elderly, disabled, and needy residents would be guaranteed a state pension of fifty dollars a month.

"No political program was ever more free from doubt," George Creel wrote later, citing a Sinclair pledge from *I, Governor:* "I say positively and without qualification we can end poverty in California . . . and it won't take more than one or two of my four years." But Sinclair's program was innocent of basic economics, not to say basic mathematics. His new taxes could not come close to replacing the revenues lost by the sales tax he intended to repeal, and because of the peculiarities of property assessment in California, his property tax exemptions would strip the state's fifty-eight counties of almost every cent of their income. The pension plan would cost $300 million a year, no small change in a state already burdened by a $30 million deficit.

Yet the promise of employment, tax cuts, pensions, and hope sounded its siren's call. *I, Governor* sold two hundred thousand copies, and eight hundred "Sinclair Clubs" sprouted across the state to seduce undecided voters with rodeos, picnics, and barbecues. Sinclair was a novelty on the California political scene, untainted by corruption and immeasurably assisted in his rise by the Democratic establishment's preoccupation with internecine intrigue. The party leaders "continued merrily whetting knives and oiling guns" while EPIC built up a head of steam, reported the veteran California journalist Carey McWilliams, who listed among Sinclair's heterogeneous supporters "socially-minded clergymen, quack astronomers, single taxers, mind readers, members of the powerful Utopian Society, leaders of the unemployed co-operatives, a few Santa Barbara dowagers . . . miscellaneous political has-beens." Adding to his appeal, Sinclair was unique among the Democrats in speaking directly to the disaffected and dispossessed middle class. These voters, like those other more marginal groups, "gravitated to Sinclair by default," McWilliams observed.

Underscoring the Democrats' disarray, Sinclair was opposed in the primary by seven challengers. The man given the best chance to dislodge the author as front-runner was George Creel. A magazine writer and unpaid northern California organizer for Hugh Johnson's NRA, Creel left off hectoring the editor of *Collier's* for paying assignments long enough to accept the call of the party leadership. The thinking was that his New Deal credentials would enable him to secure the endorsement of the Roosevelt White House, which it was assumed would be enough to bury the Sinclair campaign.

Things did not work out that way. The White House, reluctant to get involved in state-level politics, took a hands-off posture and waited, not without uneasiness, for events to take their course. On primary day Sinclair trounced all his Democratic opponents by fifty thousand votes. As he had also outpolled Governor Merriam, the leading candidate on the Republican side, he now looked to be the presumptive victor in the November election. He had become someone the White House could not afford to take lightly.

Harry Hopkins greeted Sinclair's victory with characteristic ebullience: "I think it's great stuff," he remarked. "He's on our side. A Socialist? Of course not! He's a Democrat. A good Democrat." Jim Farley, the President's political advisor, issued a pro forma statement recognizing Sinclair as the official Democratic nominee. But after Sinclair sent a telegram formally requesting a meeting with the President, the White House was left at a loss about how to deal with the party's new California flag bearer. The matter was finessed by granting his request with the proviso that no politics would be discussed during the meeting, a condition Sinclair immediately accepted. "I appreciated Roosevelt's position fully," he recalled, acknowledging judiciously that "the nomination of an ex-Socialist put him very much 'on the spot.'"

The meeting took place on September 5 at Hyde Park, in the presence of Hopkins and Tugwell. The latter recorded his surprise to discover the author of *The Jungle* to be "a pale and pleasant gentleman of 56 with a kind mien and a soft voice." He added: "The revolutionary in him was not of the fanatic strain. . . . It appeared that the New Deal was pretty much the fulfillment of his hopes. He wanted the Presidential blessing and was happy to be regarded as respectable after a lifetime of being more or less an outcast."

Sinclair, for his part, was thoroughly disarmed by FDR's charm. "I found that he had read my book and knew the EPIC plan," he wrote later—implausibly, to say the least. He claimed that Roosevelt had promised to give a speech within the next few weeks promoting the idea of "production for use," which was then an economic catchphrase with vaguely socialist connotations. "If you do that, Mr. President, it will elect me," Sinclair replied, according to his own recollection of the meeting.

But Roosevelt never gave such a speech, and it might be said that the meeting at Hyde Park marked the apogee of Sinclair's political career. His primary victory unleashed a ferocious backlash. Establishment Democrats began repudiating the nominee almost as soon as the primary results were certified; an anti-Sinclair "League of Loyal Democrats" was established, chaired by William Jennings Bryan, Jr., the Great Commoner's son. An especially damaging blow was landed by Creel, who announced that he could not support Sinclair and his "unsound, unworkable, and un-American" plan. What made Creel's attack so harmful was that it came within days of a visit to the White House, making it seem as if Roosevelt himself had bailed out on EPIC.

The concerted opposition of Democrats and Republicans took its toll on Sinclair's standing with the voters. Sinclair himself provided much of the ammunition; few men in history have run for high political office after having produced so much damaging material to use against them. Sinclair's enemies assiduously mined his books and pamphlets for radical statements, with a particularly rich lode excavated from a 1918 tract titled *The Profits of Religion,* in which Sinclair ridiculed the Episcopal, Roman Catholic, Mormon, and Christian Science churches as havens for quacks and liars.

California's movie industry, which despite its self-image as a people's art was headed by some of the state's most reactionary businessmen, produced newsreels depicting tramps and hobos surging over the state line to partake of EPIC's generous pensions, with much of the "documentation" drawn from feature films then in production. The daily newspapers lampooned Sinclair mercilessly. In editorial cartoons he was drawn as an eyelash-batting Southern belle, a starry-eyed goblin, Don Quixote tilting at a windmill, a shipwrecked sailor going down for the third time, and a starving baby bird (the cheeps coming from his beak labeled "Empty Promises in California")—and never without his trademark pince-nez. His enemies distributed a purported EPIC campaign flyer depicting him gazing admiringly at the Communists' hammer-and-sickle banner. It was signed by the "Young People's Communist League . . . Vladimir Kosloff, secretary." Neither the league nor its secretary existed in reality.

To this last calumny Sinclair took particular exception. "Having been a Socialist for thirty-two years," he wrote, "I really thought I was safe from being called a Communist." The real Communists, meanwhile, denounced EPIC as "the most reactionary plan ever put forward."

Increasingly frantic efforts by the Democrats failed to persuade Sinclair to drop out of the race in favor of a compromise candidate, the progressive Republican Raymond Haight, lest the party's internal split hand a victory to Merriam. Knowing a good thing when he saw it, Merriam moved toward the center in a bald appeal for Democratic votes. On election day he easily beat Sinclair, with Haight running a distant third. Sinclair returned home to write his campaign memoir, which he mordantly titled *I, Candidate for*

Governor: And How I Got Licked. By the time it appeared, the banner of radical economics had already been snatched up by a new figure: Dr. Francis Everett Townsend, who would acquire even greater, and more unlikely, eminence as a national political figure.

The foundation myth of the Townsend movement was that the doctor, unemployed at the age of sixty-six, glanced out his Long Beach bathroom window while shaving one morning in 1933 and spotted three "haggard, very old women" in an alley, rooting in garbage cans for food even though a fully stocked grocery stood a block away. The doctor dropped his razor and let loose a tirade of profanity, bringing his wife scurrying to his side.

"Doctor, you mustn't shout like that! All the neighbors will hear you!" she cried.

"I want all the neighbors to hear me!" he bellowed in reply. "I want God Almighty to hear me! I'm going to shout till the whole country hears!"

The story has the ring of a public relations concoction, or at least an embellishment of the truth by Townsend's business partner, a slick real estate man named Robert E. Clements. It seems to have gained currency in 1936, several years after the founding of the Townsend movement, and does not appear in the doctor's interviews in 1935 or, indeed, in the ghost-written biography he published in 1943.

The Townsend movement's origin can be more precisely traced back to a letter he wrote to his local newspaper, the *Long Beach Press-Telegram,* which printed it on September 30, 1933. Put simply, his idea was to coax workers sixty and older into retirement by granting them a rich government pension, financed from a broad-based sales tax.

> It is estimated that the population of the age of 60 and above in the United States is somewhere between nine and twelve millions [*he wrote*]. I suggest that the national government retire all who reach that age on a monthly pension of $200 a month or more, on condition that they spend the money as they get it . . . [t]hereby assuring a healthy and brisk state of business, comparable to that we enjoyed during war times.

The idea caught fire. In short order there were Townsend newsletters, Townsend flyers, Townsend clubs all over the country claiming membership of more than five million and adherents numbering twenty million more. While the specific figures were subject to dispute, it is certainly true that the Townsend movement became the first true mass lobby for old-age security in the nation's history and the number one grassroots movement in the country, outstripping both Huey Long's Share Our Wealth movement and Father Coughlin's National Union for Social Justice. In the election of 1934 several new members of Congress won election on the Townsend platform. "On Capitol Hill in Washington," *Harper's Monthly* reported, "the politicians are amazed and terrified by it." When Townsend died in 1960 at the age of ninety-three, some four hundred Townsend clubs still dotted the landscape. His plan may have been impractical but its legacy was great, for it set the stage for Social Security.

Townsend's personal sincerity, like Upton Sinclair's, was never in doubt. In person he was mild and tolerant, professing a desire merely to succor his fellow pensioners and get the country moving again. He abjured elective office; in public appearances he seemed ill at ease, innocent of the charismatic evangelism Long and Coughlin carried onstage as though bestowed on them by Nature. Instead he played the role of "gentle general of a growing army," as the *New York Times* described him.

He had been born in 1867 in an Illinois farmhouse, a genuine log cabin located in an agricultural community infused with the duty of Christian churchgoing and the principle of self-sufficiency. At the age of twenty he had moved to California, where he found work driving teams, then circled back to the midwestern prairie and a series of jobs mucking out mines, teaching school, and selling cookstoves. He began his medical studies in Omaha at the age of thirty-one, the oldest student in the first medical school class of the University of Nebraska. After graduation he migrated to the Black Hills of South Dakota, where for nearly twenty years he practiced medicine among pioneer families very much like his own, with a brief break for service on the home front during the Great War.

In 1919, his health broken by an attack of peritonitis, he decamped for the mild climate of Long Beach, where oil had recently been struck beneath a low mound-shaped outcropping known as Signal Hill. "It was a time of amazing prosperity," Townsend recalled. The city of Long Beach collected millions of dollars in oil royalties to spend on magnificent civic amenities, parks and promenades and the public health clinic that provided Townsend with his weekly pay envelope. On the debit side, the beach where he had taken a daily swim with his son became permanently fouled by the bilgewater left behind by the tankers that came to haul away Long Beach's oil—

"If you went into the water with a filthy body, you came out with a filthier one." Townsend's duties at the city clinic exposed him to abject destitution, a side of urban life he had never witnessed before. After the 1929 crash, he came face-to-face every day with the "soul-wracking" cases of "men and women suddenly reduced to absolute begging penury from comparative affluence. They were lost—gamely and hopelessly groping for something to cling to, some tangible enemy against whom they might prove their courage by a valiant fight for themselves and their dear ones." But there was no one to fight. The banks that had held their savings and the brokerages their stocks and bonds were all defunct.

Worst were the homes where unemployed men and women had taken in their fathers and mothers. "The aged were in the way of the young," Townsend observed. In one of these homes, he discovered one day that the aged gentleman he had been treating on his rounds had just taken his own life. "Not because he wanted to die, but because he knew himself a burden upon those he loved. He killed himself so his grandchildren might have more to eat."

The shadow of joblessness presently fell on the Townsend home. The public health service that employed him was dissolved, another victim of the Depression. He was too old to start over, too weary to succeed in the world of commerce. His answer to his predicament and that of millions of other aged Americans like him, indeed for the nation as a whole, was the Townsend Plan.

As was the case with Sinclair's EPIC and Long's Share Our Wealth, the program Townsend laid out in that newspaper letter on September 30 bore an arresting simplicity. Recipients of the monthly two-hundred-dollar pensions would have to give up all employment, making room in the workforce for younger, hardier individuals. The mandate that they spend the money within thirty days guaranteed a high "velocity" and therefore potent economic impact for the handout, a favorite concept of the doctor's. Financing the program was also simplicity itself: a 2 percent sales tax (later refined into a tax levied on every economic transaction). "The easiest tax in the world to collect," Townsend argued, "for all would realize that the tax was a provision for their own future, as well as the assurance of good business now."

Although the plan bore superficial similarities to the period's other popular grassroots panaceas, it was perhaps made more palatable by lacking the class-warfare aura of Huey Long's Share Our Wealth (not to mention the latter's transparent political motivation), the anticapitalist, isolationist, and eventual anti-Semitic politics of Reverend Coughlin, or the socialist coloration of Upton Sinclair's EPIC. As for its intellectual roots, these became the topic of considerable debate. Some thought an essay by the advertising man Bruce Barton in a 1931 issue of *Vanity Fair* had been Townsend's inspiration, though there was no evidence that Townsend ever had been a reader of the publication. Barton had proposed pensioning all citizens at the age of forty-five, paying them a stipend matching half their earnings for the previous five years to improve business and provide employment for the young—"almost precisely the theory of the Townsend plan," *Harper's* observed. But Barton's essay, titled "How to Fix Everything," was intended as satire, and Townsend's plan was remorselessly serious. In any case, proposals to pension off large swaths of the populace to advantage younger workers were by no means uncommon then or later: a similar proposal had emerged from the state of Washington in 1934, and another, to pay the elderly thirty dollars every Thursday, known as the "ham 'n' eggs plan," would surface in California in 1938, only to be narrowly rejected in a statewide referendum.

Others found the origins of Townsendism in the simple verities of the doctor's native region: "His plan has a long Midwestern lineage," wrote the *New Republic's* Bruce Bliven.

> In its belief in financial magic it goes back to the days of Greenbackism, the Populists and Sockless Jerry Simpson [a populist Kansas congressman of the 1890s]. Midwestern, also, is the evangelical fervor with which the plan is promulgated. The prairie has bred many a self-anointed Messiah, all alike in their fundamental characteristics; the burning zeal, the simplicity of economic argument, the automatic assumption that every opponent is a limb of Satan who . . . has sold out to "the interests."

Bliven's reckoning of the movement's character may have been overwrought, but his skepticism about its economics was well placed. Simple as it was to articulate, the Townsend Plan was even simpler to debunk. It amounted to a gross transfer of wealth to the elderly at the rate of $2,400 a year per recipient—more than $24 million a year going to 9 percent of the country (based on a conservative estimate of 10 million recipients) at a time when the total income of all Americans came to only $40 million.

The money needing to be raised would come to more than twice the total of federal, state, and local taxes already levied from coast to coast.

New Deal officials would struggle for words to explain the plan's folly to members of Congress unnerved by its popularity. "It seemed to me to be in the realm of fancy rather than in the realm of practical statesmanship," related Frances Perkins. Walter Lippmann, straining to understand Townsend's thought process, learned from correspondence with the physician that Townsend had "read somewhere that in 1929 'the United States did $1,208,000,000,000 of business.'" In other words, he had mistaken the sum of all transactions in the United States for the actual volume of business. A mere 2 percent of that $1.2 trillion, Townsend reasoned, would pay the pension bill.

"Apparently, he believes if a farmer sells a bushel of wheat for $1 to the miller, who sells it for $2 to the baker, who sells it for $3 to the ultimate consumer, there is a fund of $6 subject to tax," Lippmann wrote, observing that a levy on such a scale would bring the entire economy to a screeching halt. "I knew the scheme was fantastic. But in reading about it, it was difficult to find the particular delusion which had possessed Dr. Townsend. Now that difficulty is cleared up."

Another difficulty was the challenge of spending $2,400 annually per person—$4,800 for a couple—at a time when national income per capita was less than $500 a year and a new Ford sedan could be had for about $600. Townsend's supporters issued proposed budgets for the expenditure of the windfall, which included $150 a month for buying and operating a car, $20 to $30 a month for fuel (when gasoline cost less than 20 cents a gallon and the average car delivered up to twenty miles per gallon), and $75 a month for the wages of a chauffeur. "In other words," cracked Abraham Epstein, the nation's preeminent authority on old-age pensions, "all the old people in California and North Carolina and Michigan and everywhere else are going to hire a chauffeur. . . . The whole idea seems to be that if you just run a car to the ground quick enough and use up enough gas you get prosperity."

Of course, the backers of the Townsend Plan and the millions of Townsend club members had no more interest in the mathematical or actuarial details of the program than most churchgoers did in the practical plausibility of biblical miracles. The program drew its strength from its adherents' honest faith in its principles, never mind that their faith was stoked by "clever organizers and skilled promoters, playing on the heart-strings of millions of elderly citizens." As 1934 drew to a close with the Townsend movement scarcely one year old, it seemed to many in Washington, in the words of the *New Republic,* that "whatever the exaggerations of its publicity . . . it will score to the extent of giving an immense impetus to some form of national legislation on old-age pensions." And so it would.

12

THE CORNERSTONE

T HE SUBJECT OF OLD-AGE pensions was already on the President's mind.

Roosevelt's commitment to a comprehensive social insurance program was the handiwork of Frances Perkins, who had demanded that he make it part of the New Deal before she accepted appointment as labor secretary. Once Roosevelt took office, she subordinated her quest for the program to the urgency of recovery; through the New Deal's first year and well into 1934 she patiently stood aside while Hugh Johnson's NRA consumed all Washington's political attention, like a giant planet sucking up stray asteroids.

Perkins spent that time laying the political groundwork for her pet program. With funding from the Rockefeller Foundation, she sent social insurance experts from Great Britain on tours of chambers of commerce and Rotary clubs to allay business leaders' concerns about the "practicability of unemployment and old-age insurance." She worked conscientiously to keep the issue before the cabinet: "I made a point of bringing it up, at the least, at every second meeting. Gradually the other cabinet members became sincerely and honestly interested," she recalled. This may be a bit of self-delusion—she overlooked how her relentless politicking for the President's attention irritated her cabinet colleagues. "I continue to be astonished at Miss Perkins' lack of sense of proportion," Ickes confided peevishly to his diary on one occasion. "Yesterday I noticed that the Vice President and one or two members of the Cabinet looked distinctly bored and amused while she pursued her subject into the smallest and most obscure corners. . . . I could see that the President was simply not listening to her at all."

What was hard for the administration to overlook was how the elderly population's destitution gave substance to Dr. Townsend's grassroots pension movement. Technically speaking, the Depression may have run its course by the end of 1933, but conditions at ground level remained beyond dismal. A profound pall lay over the countryside, and millions of Americans were still picking their way through the economic wreckage. Unemployment had peaked at more than 25 percent of the industrial workforce in 1932, but among nonfarm workers it was closer to 38 percent and as high as 54 percent among men over age sixty-five looking for work. The latter group constituted a burgeoning segment of the population, for the proportion of Americans older than sixty had doubled in the first three decades of the twentieth century. They were the least able to find gainful employment and the most harshly dispossessed by the banking collapse, which deprived many of them of their life savings at a point in life when they no longer had the time or energy to start over. Their poverty was shocking: a New York survey in 1929 and one in Connecticut in 1932 both found that among residents over sixty-five, nearly half had incomes of less than three hundred dollars a year. Their economic spiral was exemplified by the written appeal of a Texas widow to President Roosevelt on behalf of her aged mother: "She is helpless, suffering from Sugar Diabetes, which has affected her mind. She has to be cared for in the same manner as an infant. She is out of funds completely. Her son whom she used to keep house for is in a hospital in Waco, Texas—no compensation for either himself or her. . . . I appeal to you to place your dear mother in my dear mother's place—With no money and no place to go unless it be to the poor house."

The provision of relief for the unemployed and the aged traditionally had been left to the states. But the states' resources had been drained off as surely as those of the working Americans who had trusted to the banks. Of the twenty-nine states with old-age pension programs in 1934, at least four had run out of funds to pay benefits; the average monthly pension payment among the others was $14.34.

The plain truth of these conditions helped Perkins achieve her goal. Responding to her urgings, and with the recovery beginning to look more sure, FDR raised the subject of a comprehensive program of social insurance during a speech on June 8, 1934, marking the adjournment of the Seventy-third Congress. It was time, he said, to offer working Americans "security against the hazards and vicissitudes of life."

Roosevelt's goal was not merely to protect citizens against acts of God, but to preserve social stability: "Fear and worry based on unknown danger contribute to social unrest and economic demoralization. If, as our Constitution tells us, our Federal Government was established among other things, 'to promote the general welfare,' it is our plain duty to provide for that security upon which welfare depends." This statement of the government's responsibility for social conditions, ranging far beyond a role in protecting Americans from the immediate emergency or helping them maintain or acquire decent housing, marked as expansive a view of federal reach as any president had ever articulated.

Three weeks later, in a Fireside Chat on June 28, Roosevelt repeated his call for "sound and adequate protection against the vicissitudes of modern life." The next day he announced the formation of a Committee on Economic Security, chaired by Perkins and composed of Treasury Secretary Morgenthau, Agriculture Secretary Wallace, Attorney General Cummings, and relief administrator Hopkins. The panel was to formulate a program for unemployment insurance, health insurance, and old-age insurance in six months, or by December 1. (The deadline was later extended to mid-January.)

All America was swept up in Roosevelt's vision. The speech "fell like a bombshell on the country," wrote Abraham Epstein. "The most ardent advocates of social insurance in America were bewildered by its boldness and political audacity. . . . Governors made it their campaign issues. Congressmen spoke for it. Candidates for state legislatures made it a plank in their platforms. Even candidates for city councils and sheriff's offices felt compelled to declare themselves in favor of social security."

In its enthusiasm, the public overlooked Roosevelt's vagueness about the program's scale and timing: "Next winter we may well undertake the great task of furthering the security of the citizen and his family through social insurance," was the closest he came to a concrete promise. Observing that Roosevelt appointed to the Committee on Economic Security "five of his busiest Cabinet members, already driven to distraction by the many tasks of the New Deal program," Epstein speculated that Roosevelt was determined not to enact the program in the near term. There was a grain of truth in this. Roosevelt's statements had a strong political flavor, and in politics timing is everything. The politics of the summer of 1934 were dominated by the coming midterm elections and by the President's need to mollify progressives on his left without antagonizing economic conservatives on his right.

"Very delicate balances were involved," Tugwell would recall. Indeed, the progressive bloc was already restless. Senator Wagner of New York, who had authored the prolabor Section 7(a) of the NIRA, had responded to its negligent enforcement by General Johnson by introducing a new bill creating an independent board to oversee labor organizing and investigate employer misconduct. (This would become the National Labor Relations Act of 1935.) Voters were also displaying doubts about the efficacy of Johnson's NRA and its sister "alphabet" agencies in promoting recovery. Huey Long and the Townsendites were busily exploiting the simmering discontent. "Social security," Tugwell judged, "was the broadly appealing issue which, in spite of disappointments with NRA, AAA, and PWA, carried conviction that Franklin would keep trying until he found the means for ensuring permanent well-being for the people of the United States."

Roosevelt's deadline requiring that the committee report before the end of the year but *not* before the election enabled him to navigate neatly through the political maelstrom of 1934. "Here was a chance to have a big issue, namely, the security of the men, women, and children of America . . . without having to defend the details" in an election campaign, recollected Thomas H. Eliot, who would become the principal draftsman of the Social Security Act. "All he had to say was, 'Well, the Committee is studying that.'"

The stratagem seemed to work: at the midterm elections, the voters gave Roosevelt's party the largest congressional majority in its history.

Despite its tight deadline, the committee got off to a slow start. The first problem was assembling a technical staff, for which Congress in its haste to adjourn that July had failed to appropriate a budget. Perkins overcame that obstacle by cadging $145,000 from Hopkins's Federal Emergency Relief Administration, on the premise that the money would be serving relief purposes because "plenty of statisticians, plenty of college professors, plenty of people who knew how to dig for facts and so forth . . . were unemployed," she recalled.

Many other experts in the various disciplines of social policy— unemployment, retirement, health care—were effectively donated by the educational institutions that employed them by being granted paid sabbaticals to come to Washington. For staff director, Perkins engaged Edwin E. Witte of the University of Wisconsin, a distinguished economist and, more to the point, an experienced smoother of ruffled academic feathers. "Witte was just perfect," Perkins recollected. "He was accustomed to dealing with irate and excited scholars who didn't want to be disputed about things they knew, or thought they knew."

Indeed, the chief drawback of employing the nation's leading social policy academics was that most of them held settled ideas about how to implement the long-sought program. Not all would be pleased to see their ideas merged with those of their professional rivals and homogenized by Witte's hand into a single omnibus plan. The committee succeeded in avoiding total discord on its old-age subcommittee only by excluding from the panel Abraham Epstein, who may have been the preeminent American expert in the field but also was known for his uncompromising, suspicious, acerbic, and occasionally irrational personality. Ultimately this tactic backfired, for after the committee's program was released, Epstein surfaced as its most vociferous and influential critic.

Among the committee's most important challenges was finding a way to inoculate a federal social program from constitutional attack. Its vulnerability arose chiefly from the necessity of imposing federal mandates on the states. The federal-state relationship was always a sensitive issue, and one on which many initiatives from Washington had foundered in the past.

The committee's members and drafting staff were justifiably anxious about the potential reaction of the Supreme Court. The Court had not yet embarked on its campaign of active hostility to the New Deal, in the course of which it would overturn eight major statutes from early 1935 through late 1936. But the obstinacy of the Court's conservative bloc was no secret. "Every knowledgeable New Deal lawyer thought he could count the votes of the justices," Eliot recalled: "Brandeis, Cardozo, and Stone to sustain most New Deal laws, the 'battalion of death,' McReynolds, Butler, Van Devanter, and Sutherland, to call them unconstitutional, and Roberts and Chief Justice Hughes *probably* siding with the McReynolds foursome."

A potential solution to this threat came from within the Court itself, when Brandeis and fellow Justice Harlan Stone separately tipped the New Dealers to virtually identical solutions. The first clue was offered by Brandeis via his daughter, Elizabeth, and her husband, Paul A. Raushenbush, who were both economists at the University of Wisconsin and intimately involved in the drafting and enactment of their home state's pioneering unemployment insurance program.

As the couple explained to Brandeis during a Washington visit at Christmas 1933, the Wisconsin legislature had been deferring the program for fear that its costs would undermine local businesses' competitiveness with out-of-state rivals. The only way to level the playing field was through a federal program—but that introduced the constitutional question.

For Brandeis, the dilemma evoked the Court's 1927 ruling in *Florida v. Mellon.* The issue then was inheritance taxes. Florida had been luring rich taxpayers south by advertising its lack of an inheritance tax, a key source of revenue for states in the populous Northeast. Those states prevailed on Congress to enact a federal estate tax against which state taxes could be deducted, thereby eliminating Florida's competitive advantage at a stroke. Florida sued to overturn the federal law and lost, as the Court ruled that Congress's power to levy taxes was virtually absolute.

Brandeis was confident that the same principle could be applied to unemployment insurance—let the federal government impose a nationwide payroll tax on employers, with the proviso that the employers' contributions to state unemployment funds could be deducted from their federal bill. Brandeis was properly wary of having a hand in legislation he might be asked to rule on from the bench, but he was even more determined to encourage the states to remain laboratories of progressive policy, if necessary with the financial assistance of the federal government. He authorized Elizabeth to quietly communicate his insight to the committee, which she did shortly after New Year's Day at a dinner with Senator Wagner, who incorporated the idea in a sample unemployment bill he introduced in 1934.

A few months later Justice Stone primed Perkins with a similar hint. The occasion was an afternoon tea at the Stones'—one of the numerous social obligations the prim secretary shouldered less out of pleasure than raw obligation—"In Washington you don't go to parties just because you want to go; you go because you have to," she remarked later.

During the visit the justice took Perkins aside for a private chat. "How are you getting on?" he asked. She lamented that the Economic Security Committee was having trouble figuring out how to avoid infringing on state prerogatives. Stone glanced around to make sure no one would overhear a Supreme Court justice giving legal advice to a cabinet member. "The taxing power, my dear, the taxing power," he said in a low tone. "You can do anything under the taxing power."

"I didn't question him any further," she reported later. "I went back to my committee and I never told them how I got my great information. As far as they knew, I went out into the wilderness and had a vision." That two of the Court's liberal pillars helped build the foundation for Social Security's survival under judicial review remained a secret for years.

A more troubling obstacle for the drafters than the constitutional issue was the President's wavering support for old-age insurance. Roosevelt had never made a secret of his distaste for any program resembling a "dole," defined as the wholesale transfer of wealth from the earning class to the needy via general taxation (the relief programs administered by Hopkins excepted, as emergency legislation). His misgivings made financing of the old-age program an especially delicate issue for Perkins, as some proportion of the needy elderly would have to be supported by government grants, at least in the near term.

As governor of New York, Roosevelt had implemented one of the most generous state pension plans in the nation, but his presidential statements on social insurance failed to clarify his position on a national old-age program. His talk of security against the "vicissitudes of modern life" could be seen as consistent with an old-age program or, alternatively, with a scheme limited to unemployment insurance, which addressed what was surely the most immediate crisis facing millions of families. Adding to the confusion was Roosevelt's tendency to retreat into ambiguity when pressed to take a stand on controversial policy questions.

The President's position on old-age pensions was still indistinct in November, when Perkins convened the National Conference on Economic Security at Washington's Mayflower Hotel. The event brought together two hundred experts for a series of roundtables and panel discussions and an exchange of learned papers. It had been billed as a milestone in the development of a social insurance program. Instead it turned into a fiasco.

The high point was to be an address by the President on November 14. That afternoon Harry Hopkins had pumped the delegates up to a high pitch of excitement, proclaiming that "now is the hour" for "a bold stroke" for social security. "I cannot see why we should wait until Kingdom Come to give security to the workers of America," he declared.

So the audience was primed for a ringing endorsement from Roosevelt along the same lines. The first words of his address seemed to match their expectations: after assuring them that unemployment insurance would be in the bill he would submit to Congress in the coming year, he observed that "old age is the most certain, and for many people the most tragic of hazards. There is no tragedy in growing old, but there is tragedy in growing old without means of support."

Then he pulled the rug out. "I do not know whether this is the time for any Federal legislation on old-age security," he stated. Without identifying Townsend or Long by name, he indicated that their activities had diminished, not improved, the prospects for pension legislation. "Organizations promoting fantastic schemes have aroused hopes which cannot possibly be fulfilled," he warned, before concluding his remarks with the ominously ambiguous pledge, "I hope that in time we may be able to provide security for the aged. . . ."

Roosevelt's address sparked a furor reminiscent of his "bombshell" to the London Economic Conference. The next morning, the *New York Times* reported that FDR had "chopped the entire social security program down to one subject for early enactment—unemployment insurance." Social insurance advocates moved to head off the President's apparent retreat by making sure the press understood the consequences of his words. "It's the kiss of death," Barbara Armstrong, a strong-willed pension expert from Berkeley who served on the Economic Security Committee's old-age task force, complained to a *Baltimore Sun* reporter.

Blame for the President's backtracking fell unfairly upon Witte, who had drafted much of the President's speech—but not the offending line, which the President had interpolated on his own without forewarning. Faced with an embarrassing revolt, FDR changed course once again, but left it to Perkins to explain away his misstep. At his directive, the next morning she called a press conference—perhaps her least favorite form of public appearance—to issue assurances that Roosevelt had not meant what his audience heard. Indeed, she said, she was surprised and annoyed at the "interpretation" placed on his words. She promised that her committee would make "real recommendations" for old-age insurance and maintained bravely that those who had heard the speech in person at the White House had greeted it in "a state of exaltation."

But skepticism about Roosevelt's intentions persisted. In the *New York Times,* Arthur Krock called the brouhaha a "first-class political enigma" and suggested it be labeled "The Mystery of the President's Speech, or Does the English Language Mean Anything?". Goaded by Perkins, who warned that the expectations stirred up by movements like Townsend's would not be easily quelled, Roosevelt finally issued an explicit "clarification" on November 22, to the effect that he had hedged about an old-age scheme merely to cover the possibility that any such plan might encounter a "hitch" in Congress. He promised to make old-age security part of his bill without fail.

The conference having adjourned, the committee and its fractious advisory panels returned to the challenge of assembling a bill out of their findings on unemployment and old-age pensions. In some respects, the question of unemployment insurance was the simpler. Numerous state programs already existed, typically granting laid-off workers some portion of their prior weekly wages for a limited period, say three or four months. The two prevailing models were known as the Wisconsin and Ohio plans; their chief difference was that the former required each employer to establish its own insurance fund, while the latter created a single statewide fund financed from payroll taxes. These were typically levied at the rate of 1 percent of paychecks from covered workers and 3 percent from their employers.

Insurance experts generally favored the Ohio plan, in part because a single publicly supervised pool was easier to administer than a multitude of funds controlled by individual employers. But neither model was beloved by business, largely because both involved a "merit rating" system that required firms with histories of frequent layoffs to pay higher premiums.

Even though the committee had only two models to choose from, it still had to confront numerous complexities. Among these was the question of whether to create a truly national system, as Witte and Agriculture Secretary Wallace favored, or merely to funnel federal subsidies to the states and allow them to craft their own programs. Perkins was skeptical that a purely federal program could win the approval of Congress. Protracted debate in the House and Senate over such issues as how to implement merit ratings or whether to require contributions from workers, she feared, could "easily kill the bill."

The shadow of review by the Supreme Court still loomed over a federal system. The suggestions by Brandeis and Stone to exploit the government's taxing power did not ensure that a Court majority would find that the Constitution gave Congress any authority to distribute money in furtherance of social purposes. Attorney General Homer Cummings, Perkins recalled, had warned that this was "a doubtful constitutional point and that we should be extremely careful." The proponents of a combined federal-state scheme argued, consequently, that the surest way to protect the program from Court nullification was to limit the federal government's role to the provision of financial assistance to states implementing their own unemployment programs in their own way.

The committee's tug-of-war over these questions intensified as its deadline neared for reporting to the White House. Finally, Perkins issued an ultimatum. On December 22 at 8 P.M. sharp the committee would convene at her home, where the telephone was to be disconnected and the doors barred until the form of an unemployment program was settled. "We sat until two in the morning, and at the end we agreed, reluctantly and with mental reservations . . . to recommend a federal-state system." With minor adjustments, the recommendation became Title IX of the Social Security Act.

Old-age pensions presented the committee with an entirely different set of challenges. In this case, there was a surfeit of models to choose from. The concept of government pensions had a decades-long history: the first state pension had been enacted by Arizona in 1914 (though it was promptly overturned in state court). Three states enacted pension programs in 1923, eight more by 1929, and sixteen others by 1933.

Unfortunately, there was little consistency in their approaches. Some programs were voluntary, typically left to the option of county government; others were mandatory statewide. Eleven states set the pension age at 65, one at 68, the rest at 70. Most states set the maximum stipend at $15 a month, some at $30; New York and Massachusetts alone set no limit.

Every state imposed a means test requiring documentation that a candidate had not only reached pension age but lacked the resources for life's necessities. Social insurance experts acknowledged that a means test was inevitable in any system not funded at least partially by contributions from enrollees. But that underscored the urgency of creating a national safety net: "A contributory system of old age insurance not only may be justified on theoretical grounds," Epstein had written in 1933, "but will become inevitable as . . . more and more aged persons become unable to earn their own living. The adoption of such a plan cannot be long delayed."

Counterbalancing the complexity of the issues in old-age coverage was the expertise of the committee's old-age task force, which was chaired by Berkeley's Barbara Armstrong and J. Douglas Brown of Princeton University. Following their lead, the committee agreed that the pension program should be compulsory, contributory (by employer and employee alike), and federal in scope. But several other issues remained. The choices the committee made in addressing these would dictate the course of Social Security for generations.

One question was whether benefits should be paid on a sliding scale related to earnings, like unemployment insurance, or at a flat rate. In this case the committee preferred to link benefits to lifetime earnings on the grounds that a flat rate, though simpler to administer, would require a larger redistribution of wealth and therefore might be seen as favoring unskilled workers at the expense of the skilled. "The easiest way would be to pay the same amount to everyone," Perkins acknowledged. "But that is contrary to the typical American attitude that a man who works hard, becomes highly skilled, and earns high wages 'deserves' more than one who had not become a skilled worker."

A thornier problem was what to do about the near retired, those aged between 45 and 65 in 1935. They no longer had enough years of work ahead of them to fund adequate pensions from their annual contributions. Yet to pay them only what they would be due from their own contributions plus interest would mock the very principle of social insurance. With a contribution of 1 percent of pay per year, the savings of a worker who earned an average monthly wage of $50 and paid in for five years before retiring at 65 would fund an annuity of 24 cents per month; even after ten years that monthly stipend would grow to only 78 cents. As Witte later explained the dilemma for the House Ways and Means Committee, the magic of compound interest would eventually increase the value of workers' contributions to substantial levels, but it would take decades to work. The contributions would "not count much in the first years."

Roosevelt himself recognized this outcome as untenable. "Congress can't stand the pressure of the Townsend plan unless we have a real old-age insurance system," he told Perkins. "Nor can I face the country without . . . a solid plan which will give some assurance to old people of systematic assistance upon retirement." But pumping up pensions for the retired and near retired meant that the program would not be self-sustaining at its inception, as he insisted it must be; instead it would require a substantial subsidy from the federal budget. When Perkins informed him that the committee proposed to fund decent pensions for older workers by borrowing from the contributions of the young, he complained: "This is the same old dole under a different name." Learning that her solution would build up a deficit in the old-age program over its first forty years, to be covered by a lump-sum government contribution when the obligation came due, he was shocked by the prospect. "It is almost dishonest to build up an accumulated deficit for the Congress of the United States to meet in 1980," he rumbled.

Yet, he acknowledged reluctantly, "We have to have it." Perkins in her memoirs charitably excuses the President's self-contradiction on this score as "one of the minor conflicts of logic and feeling which so often beset him but kept him flexible and moving in a practical direction."

To resolve this particular "minor conflict," the committee contrived a hybrid financing scheme through which the program's initial funding source, a payroll tax of 1 percent of earnings split fifty-fifty between workers and their employers starting in 1937, would gradually rise over time to a combined 5 percent in 1956. Monthly benefits would start in 1942, with a set minimum paid to older workers without regard to their contributions. By the committee's final calculations, the money borrowed to fund the older workers' pensions would have to be reimbursed by federal appropriation sometime in the mid-1960s, after which the program would pay for itself.

Epstein, like many other experts, found the resulting scheme utterly illogical, impractical, and unfair. It yoked an unduly small federal subsidy to a highly regressive payroll tax, overburdening poorer workers. This arrangement ignored the bitter lesson learned by Germany, which had pioneered social insurance in the 1880s under Otto von Bismarck—that social insurance is best paid for out of the national wealth, not from the earnings of the poorest members of society. The reason is that as unemployment increases and economic activity slows, the lowering of living standards for workers forced to carry the entire cost of social insurance as both wage earners and consumers becomes intolerable. In Germany this imbalance helped lead to Hitler's accession to the chancellorship, a few weeks before Franklin Roosevelt's presidential inauguration. "Blood cannot be squeezed from turnips," Epstein warned. "German workers were slowly but surely driven to desperation. The crying injustices added fuel to Hitler's fires. The finale has been indelibly written in tears and blood since January 1933."

Epstein delivered this verdict directly to Armstrong and Brown during the November National Conference, the only occasion on which official Washington solicited his views on the gestating Social Security program. His warning, however, was trumped by the demands of American politics, which favored a contributory scheme; he would not be invited to participate in the committee's deliberations again, and would presently emerge as the Social Security bill's most uncompromising critic.

After extending the Committee on Economic Security's deadline by six weeks by executive order, Roosevelt applied the whip. In his State of the Union message on January 4 he again raised the issue of "security against the major hazards of life," advised Congress that "the time has come for action by the national Government," and promised to send formal recommendations to Capitol Hill "in a few days."

These words provoked pure consternation on the committee, which had still not settled on the legislative details of its program. But FDR's goading worked; in mid-January Perkins and Harry Hopkins brought a draft report to the White House and spent an evening with Roosevelt going over the details. They departed with what they thought was his final approval of every provision, and instructed Witte and Eliot to wrap up the committee report and the bill.

But there was one more hiccup. On January 15, after all the committee members had signed off on the report and two days before Roosevelt was to reveal it to the world, Henry Morgenthau chanced upon a White House press release stating that "contributions from general revenues" would be required to shore up the contribution fund in 1965. Perhaps flustered at seeing that representation in print, he suddenly rebelled. Demanding a special meeting of the committee, he declared that for the government to subsidize what was ostensibly a contributory insurance system was a fraud on the taxpayer—never mind that he and the rest of the committee had discussed and approved this exact scheme only days before. As Eliot recalled the scene:

> Wallace rolled his eyes and looked at the ceiling. Harry Hopkins and Mr. Holtzoff [Alexander Holtzoff, Attorney General Cummings's delegate to the committee] stared, open-mouthed. Miss Perkins, her voice rising, said, "But Henry! But *Henry!*" Morgenthau interrupted her by slamming his hand down on the table and shouting, "This is Henry Morgenthau Jr. speaking and these are his opinions!"

Morgenthau carried his objections directly to the President in the Oval Office, and got his way. Before the day was out, instructions came from the White House to double the initial payroll tax for the old-age program to 1 percent each from employer and employee to build up a reserve of nearly $50 billion by 1980, the idea being to relieve the Treasury of its future obligation.

The President's abrupt about-face perplexed many on the committee staff, though not Perkins, an experienced observer of the Rooseveltian temper. In reply to Tom Eliot's question about how FDR could have been made to change his mind after making a commitment in person to her and Hopkins, she sighed, "Oh, I can guess. Right after breakfast Henry's sure to appear in the president's bedroom, insisting on this change. The president tells him to go away. He comes back to the White House at noon and tells his story again. And then about four o'clock, when the president's getting tired, he puts his head in the door *again,* and the president says, 'Oh, all right, Henry, all right!'"

The President's last-minute capitulation would assuage Morgenthau's feelings but open a new wound on Capitol Hill. There, congressional conservatives were openly hostile to building up a government pension reserve of any significant size, which would be the effect of Morgenthau's demand. Republican senator Arthur Vandenberg of Michigan erupted in apoplexy upon learning that the reserve would reach $47 billion—nearly three times the outstanding federal debt of the time. He asked Arthur Altmeyer, a staff member of the Committee on Economic Security who was helping to shepherd the measure through the Senate, "What in heaven's name are you going to do with $47 billion?"

"You could invest it in U.S. Steel and some of the large corporations," suggested Altmeyer, who would shortly be named the first Social Security commissioner.

Vandenberg threw up his hands in horror. "That would be socialism!" he exclaimed.

Congress kept Social Security out of the stock market by mandating that the program invest its spare cash exclusively in U.S. Treasury securities. In 1939 the lawmakers expanded Social Security enrollment and raised benefits, partially to sop up some of the trust fund and brake its growth. The 1939 amendments increased employee and survivor benefits, added supplementary stipends for aged spouses and dependent children, and reduced the payroll tax by canceling the increase of 1 percent scheduled to go into effect in 1940. Congress knew when it made these changes that the program consequently would require contributions from general taxes by the 1980s, precisely the outcome that Morgenthau had been determined to avoid. The program would not be self-sufficient, as many conservatives and indeed Roosevelt himself had hoped; on the other hand, it would no longer risk "socialism" by creating a huge government reserve.

In pestering Roosevelt for a rise in the payroll tax in 1935, Morgenthau had played on the President's innate distaste for the dole. The more the program relied on contributions from enrollees rather than general tax revenues, the more it suited the President. Yet the resulting shift in the program's financing toward the payroll tax has fostered confusion over the drafters' intentions for decades. The drafters agreed with Epstein and other social insurance experts that while the beneficiaries should contribute to the program and employers should be taxed as well, the program's entire weight should not rest on their shoulders. The committee "assumed that before long, others . . . would also contribute—in other words, that both payroll taxes [paid by employers] and income taxes would supplement the employee's contributions," Eliot informed Congress in the 1970s, during a debate on a plan to shore up the system's reserves from general government revenue. "All, that is, agreed, except the Secretary of the Treasury, Henry Morgenthau."

The program's near-total dependence on enrollee contributions has been both a blessing and a curse. (Economists consider the employers' payments to be employee contributions under another guise, on the theory that if the employer tax were not levied the money would flow to the workers as wages instead.) Although the contributory element makes the program's financing regressive—that is, wealthier Americans pay a smaller portion of their income than lower-paid workers to support a program of broad social utility—it has also helped protect it from political attack by giving its enrollees what appears to be a concrete stake in its survival.

Roosevelt recognized the shortcomings and the virtues of this arrangement. Interviewed in 1941 by Luther Gulick, an expert on public administration conducting a survey for the Treasury Department, FDR called the contributory tax "politics all the way through." "We put those pay roll contributions there so as to give the contributors a legal, moral, and political right to collect their pensions and their unemployment benefits. With those taxes in there, no damn politician can ever scrap my social security program. Those taxes aren't a matter of economics, they're straight politics." Roosevelt may well have been trying to place the best light on a political necessity by claiming to have carefully weighed the virtues of the payroll tax; he was, after all, speaking six years after the program's enactment.

But the contributory tax has also fostered a fundamental misconception about Social Security, by encouraging generations of Americans to view the program as something akin to an investment fund, as if every worker's ultimate benefits should be the product of his or her lifetime payments plus interest. Social Security, of course, is nothing of the kind: it is a social insurance program—a safety net—designed to provide a subsistence floor for aged and disabled workers, indexed to inflation and payable to the end of life, as well as assistance to their dependents. The drafters understood that some beneficiaries would receive a meager return on their contributions and others would receive many multiples of their lifetime payroll taxes. This meant that the system might prove in the end to be fairer to some beneficiaries than others; what makes it fair overall is that no individual can know ahead of time whether he or she will die before collecting a cent, or live to a ripe old age and collect benefits for decades; "the hazards and vicissitudes of life" are, by definition, capricious.

When the sixty-three-page Economic Security Act arrived on Capitol Hill on January 17, 1935, it won no plaudits for elegance of draftsmanship. The lawmakers were confused by what appeared to be a hybrid of unemployment insurance and old-age pensions and by the murky distinction between government funding of some old-age grants (for those already retired or near retirement age) and the contributory system applicable to younger workers. The very term *social security* was unfamiliar to most senators and congressmen, having been only recently popularized by Epstein.

Newspapers attacked the measure as "a hodgepodge, an ill-drafted legislative monstrosity," Eliot recalled. This was a fair criticism, in the sense that provisions for the program's various components were strewn haphazardly through the text, with related provisions sometimes separated from each other by thousands of words of boilerplate. Yet there was method in the monstrosity: the drafters' goal was to immunize the program from wholesale nullification by a hostile Supreme Court. In crafting the funding mechanism for pensions, for example, "we separated the tax title and the benefits title—one was title II of the bill and the other was title VIII," recalled Eliot. "Nobody was being fooled by this. The idea was to give Justices, who might want some kind of an out, a legal peg to hang their hats on." In other words, the justices would be able to overturn a provision they might dislike, such as the payroll tax, without invalidating the basic principle of federally funded old-age assistance.

The task of explaining the bill to Congress fell chiefly to Edwin Witte. The Wisconsin professor's skill at quelling faculty quarrels would be tested to the utmost by the challenge of pacifying lawmakers disgruntled by the measure's complexity. He took the witness table on Monday, January 21, to begin two full days of testimony before the House Ways and Means Committee. Most of the ensuing discussion would concern the plight of the aged, for old-age security had been driven to the forefront of Congress's collective mind by the rise of the messianic Townsend movement.

Witte opened with a stark accounting of the economic crisis facing the aged. In 1935 there were more than 7 million Americans over 65 years of age, including more than 4 million over 70. Their numbers were rapidly rising in absolute terms and as a proportion of the population—in 1930, those over 65 comprised 5.4 percent of all Americans—and would continue to do so at least for another half century. By 1970, the United States would have 15 million people over 65, and by 1980 more than 18 million. "By that time," Witte said, "we will have approximately one-eighth of the population [that is, 12.5 percent] in the age group 65 or over." (Witte's forecast underestimated the growth of the elderly population and overestimated their share of the total forty-five years hence: by 1980 there would be 25.5 million residents 65 and over, comprising 11.3 percent of the U.S. population.)

This presented the nation with an immense responsibility. "The cost of supporting the old people is necessarily very great, whether met by themselves or by someone else," Witte said. "This bill contemplates that where old people do not have means to support themselves and no children able to support them, they shall be supported by the public in a decent and humane manner." Whether the aged were supported by their children or by society, the economic price would have to be paid, for the money expended by families in support of their elders was money unavailable for the new generation's support, or for investment and growth. "Whether you enact pension laws or not, that cost is there. The growing number of old people will have to be supported by the generation then living, and whether you do it in the form of pensions or in some other way, there is no way of escaping that cost."

This sobering message delivered, Witte walked the committee through its options. The easiest task was dealing with those just embarking upon their working lives. The committee had settled on a contributory program similar to those in Great Britain and France, in which the bulk of the cost was shouldered by the workers and their employers, with only a residual cost devolving to the government. Dealing with those already at or past the customary retirement threshold of 65 was only slightly more complicated. Plainly they were past the point where they could contribute more to their own support; the extent to which the government would help them was "a question of social policy" more than economics, Witte advised. The cost of grants-in-aid for this population was actuarially computable, as was the size of the group: in 1935 there were about 200,000 elderly in public alms-houses, another 700,000 receiving federal emergency relief, and 180,000 receiving pensions from their states, which were spending about $31 million a year.

The Economic Security Committee had proposed that the federal government provide the states with half the cost of this group's pensions, up to $15 a month per pensioner. Because the government would require in return that all state programs be made mandatory and would set minimum stipends and a retirement age of 65 (half the states set a minimum age of 70), and because the federal role would no doubt spur more states to enact their own programs, the committee estimated that $50 million would be required in the first year and $125 million a year thereafter. Those were large sums, but Witte reminded the members that the scale of the crisis was also exceptional. "We have to contemplate that this depression has created a tremendous havoc with people's savings," he said. "The situation that we are facing in the immediate future certainly is a great deal worse because of the depression that we have been in."

Finally, Witte addressed the thorny issue of those who had passed middle age but were not yet retired, many of whom had seen their life savings destroyed in the Depression. The administration proposed to give anyone who reached 65 after participating in the contributory system for at least five years an annuity equal to 15 percent of the wages from which they had contributed—"a slight gratuity from the Government," Witte said.

The rationale, of course, was to avoid paying insultingly meager pensions, based only on their contributions, to workers already nearing the end of their careers. "This bill does not contemplate only an earned pension to people that are past middle age," Witte said. "It does not propose to pay people 24 cents a month."

Toward the end of Witte's first day on the stand, the committee members demonstrated how much they had been unnerved by the Townsend movement by asking him to outline its flaws. Witte here had to walk a fine line, exploiting the lawmakers' terror of the Townsendites to ensure they enacted an old-age program, but explicating the Townsend plan's flaws clearly enough to dissuade them from overdoing things.

"We considered the Townsend plan," he said carefully. "It is not within our economic system. I think it is probably not within the structure of any governmental or economic system that is conceivable, but certainly not this economic system that we now have." The amount of money required to be raised, he explained, "is more than twice the total of Federal, State, and local taxes combined—to be paid to 9 percent of the population of the country."

Asked by the Illinois Democrat Chester Thompson whether the committee had recognized that a worker unemployed at the age of 45 would most likely never find steady work again, Witte warned against government pensions for such young workers. "If you construct your economic system on the assumption that everybody over 45 shall be pensioned, you cannot finance it. You will get a Townsend plan, then."

After a few days of grilling, Witte yielded the witness table to Perkins, who focused on the need for government grants to succor those already nearing retirement. "You could make a perfectly self-supporting system without any aid whatever from Government sources if you are willing to say that you will postpone the payment of benefits for 30 years or 35 years," she observed, "but most of us want to see something done about those who are now old or middle aged and approaching this crisis of insecurity in their lives before them." She warned that leaving these millions of Americans to struggle without adequate purchasing power would merely prolong the Depression.

But Perkins was not the cabinet member who left the deepest impression upon the committee. That was Henry Morgenthau, who seized his moment in the spotlight to undo some of what the Committee on Economic Security had achieved.

Morgenthau bore his painstakingly tailored mantle as the administration's sober fiscal guardian to the hearing room on February 5. Perkins was in the audience, steeled to dislike what she was about to hear, yet still unprepared for what occurred.

The Treasury secretary warned that in launching an old-age program, even one based on worker contributions, the government would be "undertaking very heavy responsibilities extending from year to year into the indefinite future," with billions of dollars to be paid out annually. He then introduced his proposal to double the initial payroll tax so the program could be "launched and maintained on a sound financial basis." Cannily, he stated that on the new payroll tax schedule, "those of us who have worked on this bill are in complete accord"—gliding over his last-minute end run to the White House.

Then, suddenly, he introduced another new concept. Much as he desired "personally" to provide universal old-age coverage across the country, regrettably he had concluded that doing so would present an insuperable administrative burden for the Internal Revenue Service, which was charged with collecting the payroll tax. The measure before Congress proposed covering "every employee in the United States, other than those of governmental agencies or railways who earns less than $251 a month. That means that every transient or casual laborer is included, that every domestic servant is covered, and that the large and shifting class of agricultural workers is covered." Even without them, he said, the task of the Treasury in administering the contributory tax collections would be extremely formidable. With them, it would be impossible. "I am simply pointing out the administrative difficulty of collecting the tax from those classes," he said.

Perkins listened to Morgenthau's unctuous testimony in dismay. The principle of universal coverage had been thoroughly aired in the Committee on Economic Security and won unanimous approval; it had been expressed as a bedrock principle by Roosevelt himself: "There is no reason why everybody in the United States should not be covered," he had told Perkins. "I see no reason why every child, from the day he is born, shouldn't be a member of the social security system. . . . Everybody ought to be in on it—the farmer and his wife and his family . . . from the cradle to the grave."

Yet now Morgenthau single-handedly exploded this basic principle—stripping away protection for the most insecure members of the workforce on the flimsy reasoning that it would be difficult to collect their contributions. "One could concede that it would be difficult for the Treasury to collect these taxes," Perkins reflected. "But the whole administration of the act was going to be difficult."

With a sinking heart, she witnessed congressmen grasping at the opportunity to whittle down the cost of her social insurance program by snatching away coverage for those at the very bottom of the economic pyramid. "There was nothing for me to do but accept," she wrote later. "There were enough people afraid of the deflationary effect of this large money collection, enough people afraid of too large a system, and enough people confused about the desirability of social legislation by the Federal Government, to make it a foregone conclusion that if the Secretary of the Treasury recommended limitation, limitation there would be."

It would be fifteen years before Congress would begin returning the excluded workers to the system. Domestic workers would be covered in 1950, under President Truman. Four years later, under Dwight Eisenhower, Congress would enact the largest single expansion of Social Security coverage by adding to the rolls more than ten million workers, including farm employees and hotel workers. By then, plainly, Social Security had become a bipartisan cause and a permanent feature of the nation's economic landscape.

The Senate Finance Committee's consideration of the economic security bill overlapped by several days the hearing before the Ways and Means Committee, forcing the administration witnesses to shuttle back and forth between the two ends of the Capitol. There Perkins found the deepest skepticism to come not from Republicans, but from conservative southerners of the President's own party—and from none more so than Thomas P. Gore, the blind Oklahoman whose political career dated back to his state's 1907 admission to the union. Gore was nominally a populist, but a curious one. In the words of his grandson, the writer Gore Vidal, "he was a genuine populist; but he did not like people very much"; and he liked the idea of government assistance even less.

Her colloquy with Gore would leave a lasting impression on Perkins, who set it down in detail in her 1946 memoir, *The Roosevelt I Knew:*

> Old Senator Gore raised a sarcastic objection. "Isn't this Socialism?" he asked me.
> My reply was, "Oh, no."
> Then, smiling, leaning forward and talking to me as though I were a child, he said, "Isn't this a teeny-weeny bit of Socialism?"

Perkins must have misremembered the event, or at the very least distilled it in her mind down to a sort of metaphorical truth. The exchange, which long has been a cherished anecdote of the birth of Social Security, appears nowhere in the hearing record.

Perkins's recollection does, however, capture Gore's opinion of the legislation with reasonable fidelity. To him the bill represented the redistribution of wealth pure and simple, making it an uncomfortably close cousin to the Share Our Wealth program trumpeted by Huey Long.

"I know the theory of private property used to be—I do not say it is now—that the man who earned the dollar honestly has a better right to it than anyone else," Gore badgered Perkins. "What I am trying to get at now is whether this legislation is not out of line with that once established principle. . . . Has a citizen no guarantee under our constitutional system, that that thing cannot be done? Isn't this plan, and the Long plan, in effect to take private property for public use?"

"Isn't that a question for the Supreme Court to decide?" interjected Senator James Couzens of Michigan, a Republican and the richest man in Congress, throwing Perkins a lifeline.

"It is not for me to decide," Perkins assented, with palpable relief.

The congressional hearings were followed by weeks of redrafting in committee executive sessions, overseen by Witte and Thomas Eliot. The program, the title of which had been changed from "Economic Security" to "Social Security" by the Ways and Means Committee, was passed in the House on April 19 by a vote of 372–33, with 81 of the 102 Republicans joining the Democratic majority.

Two months later, on June 19, it reached the Senate floor. All eyes in the chamber turned expectantly to Huey Long, who had made no secret of his discontent with the bill's meager pension schedule. Would the bill be blocked by a burst of Longian oratory?

But the Kingfish was spent. Only a few days earlier he had staged a heroic filibuster to preserve a pet provision in a bill proposed to replace the NRA, which had been overturned by the Supreme Court. For fifteen and a half hours he had held the floor, speaking late into the night, sometimes addressing galleries filled with onlookers in evening wear who had opted for Long's floor show over those of Washington's nightclubs.

Returning for the Social Security debate, he looked pale as he introduced several amendments designed to keep control of the program in federal hands, lest it fall victim to the penuriousness of poor states and the discriminatory instincts of southern politicians. They all were defeated, and Long joined his Democratic colleagues in passing the bill overwhelmingly, 77–6. The lone Democratic vote against the measure came from A. Harry

Moore, a political timeserver from New Jersey, who explained: "It will take the romance out of old age."

On August 14, FDR signed the measure on which he had equivocated so much over the previous year. That afternoon, meeting with the press off the record, he promised he would "say a few kind words" at the signing ceremony. In the event he did more. Flanked by a dozen luminaries, with Perkins standing over his right shoulder, his political instincts showing brightly, he placed the bill at the center of the New Deal.

> We can never insure one hundred percent of the population against one hundred percent of the hazards and vicissitudes of life, but we have tried to frame a law which will give some measure of protection to the average citizen and to his family against the loss of a job and against poverty-ridden old age. This law, too, represents a cornerstone in a structure which is being built but is by no means complete. . . . If the Senate and the House of Representatives in this long and arduous session had done nothing more than pass this Bill, the session would be regarded as historic for all time.

There would be naysayers, as is inevitable for any program of this scale and complexity. The myriad compromises made necessary by the political process weakened both the old-age and unemployment programs beyond repair, they said; as much as it represented an advance in social policy over American traditions, the bill still left the nation far behind many European countries in its solicitude for the unfortunate and the aged.

In testimony before a congressional committee early in the year, Abraham Epstein had praised the measure as "perhaps the most outstanding case of social legislation or any form of legislation that has ever been before Congress." In the fullness of time he revised his opinion, calling it a "slovenly program" that would stifle economic growth, unduly burden the working class, and most likely fail constitutional muster before the Supreme Court.

"The 'New Deal' Social Security program is not only inherently menacing," he wrote; "it may actually stifle the growing movement for social insurance and turn us from the road of social legislation by shattering the hopes of a distressed people."

The decades would prove these judgments wrong. Social Security passed the scrutiny of the Court, won the admiration of political leaders on both sides of the aisle, and remained the bedrock of an ever-expanding program of social welfare through the decades. Far from Epstein's "menace," it remained Roosevelt's cornerstone, to this day the single most successful government program in American history, the succor of generations of American families beset by the vicissitudes of injury, penury, and age.

13

BLACK MONDAY

B Y THE END OF 1933, scarcely more than six months after the
National Recovery Administration had burst upon the country
with monumental éclat, the agency had disappointed almost all
its constituencies. Consumers, workers, and business owners—all but the
biggest manufacturers in the biggest industries—had become deeply disaffected with the Blue Eagle.

Industrialists had quickly come to see the fulminating, desk-pounding
General Johnson as a paper tiger. To get their way in code negotiations,
they needed only to wait for his bluster to fade or for his habitual antipathy
to organized labor to assert itself. The *New Yorker* retailed the story of one
executive who announced his intention to return to his business after days
of fruitless inveighing by Johnson at the conference table.

Johnson leaped to his feet. "I *command* you to stay," he thundered.

"I'm sorry, General," the businessman replied evenly, "but you can't
command me."

Industries capable of meeting Johnson's truculence with matching
stubbornness were often able to co-opt him into supporting their interests against the unions. That was the strategy followed by the coal industry, which refused to sign a code incorporating collective bargaining,
as required by Section 7(a), while Johnson spent months histrionically
cursing them in public. Johnson's characteristic effort to inject himself
into a situation he did not understand and could not control needlessly
prolonged the negotiations. At the opening of a crucial meeting between

the coal operators and John L. Lewis's United Mine Workers at which both sides appeared poised to reach an agreement, Johnson announced that he would "clarify" Section 7(a), prompting the employers to shut down the talks on the expectation that he was about to qualify or even suspend the collective bargaining rule. The talks only resumed after President Roosevelt interceded, demanding that they continue seven days a week and around the clock until a settlement was reached. The landmark contract conceded to the mine operators an eight-hour day and forty-hour week (the union had sought six-hour workdays and thirty-six-hour weeks); but the union achieved a dues checkoff, the end of the monopoly of the company store and of the payment of wages in scrip, and the outlawing of child labor. Johnson only reinforced his reputation as no friend of labor. In this case as in several others, the job of neutralizing the General's blundering interference fell to Roosevelt.

Johnson's credibility had begun to ebb almost before the last marching band passed before the reviewing stand at the great New York City Blue Eagle parade of September 1933. No organization could maintain for long the hyperthyroidal pitch he had set for the NRA, especially given the widening gulf between his words of principle and his policies in action. As popular discontent with Johnson was gathering, the *New Republic* described his "technique" thus: "Speak loudly for one side in order to convince people you are fair. But act promptly and decisively on the other side, when action counts. . . . No one has been more eloquent than he on the necessity for safeguarding consumers' interests and preventing monopolistic practices under the codes; no one more active in squelching and ignoring consumers' representatives, in letting trade associations and institutes get away with murder. . . . [U]nder the General's administration the economic life of the country has been handed over to organized business, with scarcely a check on behalf of employees or the public interest."

Johnson was inclined to view such critiques as orchestrated attacks by political opportunists and aggrieved business interests. "Pretty early in this story two or three young politicians discovered the Little Fellow," he wrote in his own career postmortem. "Just what they meant by the Little Fellow they are coy about saying—but it is a juicy political mouthful."

The bill of particulars against Johnson steadily lengthened. By the beginning of 1934 it included such matters as his disregard of the NRA's consumer advisory board and the increasingly frequent appearance of "open-price" provisions in industry codes; these mandated the public dissemination of price changes, a practice that facilitated price-fixing. NRA hearings in early January revealed that the agency had never studied the potential monopolistic effect of open pricing, thus enabling large manufacturing firms to take advantage of the government's ignorance to trample smaller rivals.

Johnson's personal behavior contributed to disaffection with him inside and outside the White House. Stories about his resorting to multiday alcoholic benders to escape the pressures of office circulated freely in Washington, as did rumors about his relationship with his pert "girl Friday," a twenty-six-year-old former secretary at Democratic headquarters in New York named Frances Robinson.

Robinson—"Robbie," as she was known—was unmarried, a devout Catholic, preternaturally efficient, and fiercely loyal to Johnson. She had joined the NRA shortly after its inception, succeeding two female and two male candidates who each had lasted only a few days in the superheated crucible of Johnson's office. Robbie was made of sterner stuff despite her five-foot, hundred-pound frame, and within weeks of her arrival she had established herself as the second-most formidable figure at NRA headquarters, after only the General himself.

Robbie's control of access to Johnson evoked intense resentment from those she kept at bay. Chief among them was the NRA's second-in-command, Donald Richberg, whom Johnson came to suspect of intriguing against him. Richberg soon took to lurking outside his boss's office, waiting for Robbie to become distracted with another visitor so he could slip in for a private conversation, locking the office from the inside and leaving her to bang angrily on the door for entry until Johnson himself relented and let her in.

But others valued Robinson's ability to keep the General's excesses in check. The country owed Robinson "a real debt," Perkins later observed of the "ruthless" Robbie, "because without her Johnson would have been a total flop a great deal earlier." Perkins estimated that Robinson herself "made about half the decisions that the General was supposed to have made," because often he was too inebriated to make them himself. But Robbie's constant presence at Johnson's side at public events while his shy and unassuming wife, Helen, kept to herself in Virginia fueled gossip that she served as more than his secretary. The whispering was further encouraged by Johnson's innocence about how the relationship between a government official and his female assistant might play in public. Robbie's command of NRA information and statistics was so complete that Johnson, at a loss to answer a reporter's question, would reply indelicately, "Ask the little skirt." Toward the end of 1933, when the NRA's payroll was publicly released, it was discovered that Johnson's "stenographer" was earning a salary of $6,800, making her the fourth-highest-paid employee in his agency. Confronted by reporters' insinuations that this hinted at services not in her formal job description, Johnson barked, "I think that was one below the belt," inspiring a new round of public snickering.

The NRA staff was among Washington's most skilled in the emerging art of public relations, but Johnson's obliviousness often threatened to undo their efforts at burnishing the NRA's reputation for effectiveness and dynamism. In the run-up to New York's Blue Eagle parade, its organizers warned the White House that the event would be ruined if Robinson appeared on the reviewing stand next to Johnson, as she was wont to do. A panicky call went out from Roosevelt's office to Frances Perkins. "What am I going to do?" Roosevelt asked her. "They don't want her to go over there."

As a woman constantly struggling with male insensitivities in Washington, Perkins felt a certain kinship with Robbie. She had already counseled the young woman not to be photographed with Johnson. But now Roosevelt assigned her personally to keep Robbie off the General's plane to New York. "You're a woman," Roosevelt told her. "You'll know how to say it to her."

Perkins sped out to the airport and contrived to summon Robinson from the plane moments before its departure. "You know I'm a friend of yours, don't you, Miss Robinson?" she said.

"Yes, you are," Robbie replied. "You're the only friend I've got."

"Somebody has told the President that there will be a rumpus in New York if you go," Perkins told her. "I know it's dirty gossip and I know it's horrid, but I'm a woman and know the position you're in." She understood that the salacious gossip arose "[b]ecause you're a woman doing the same thing that a good man secretary would do." Still, she advised Robinson to find a pretext to delay her departure, and not to tell Johnson the truth.

"Oh, I couldn't tell the General this," Robbie agreed. "He'd hit the ceiling."

Johnson could not ignore the proliferating demands in Congress for investigations into price-fixing and other favoritism built into NRA codes, especially as they emanated from the progressive wing of both parties, pillars of

Roosevelt's New Deal coalition. In January 1934, he headed off a Senate investigation spearheaded by the progressive Republican Gerald Nye of North Dakota only by agreeing to the appointment of an independent inquiry commission. Asked to suggest a chairman, Johnson, in what he later called a "moment of total aberration," nominated the eminent trial lawyer Clarence Darrow, declaring that he had "always admired [Darrow's] consistent intransigence and his barnyard philosophy."

This sentiment evaporated almost as soon as Darrow convened his inquiry and revealed that he brought to the task the presumption that NRA was engaged in fostering monopoly and was stunting, not promoting, recovery. Johnson later groused: "Bloody Old Jeffries at the Assizes never conducted any hearings to equal those for cavalier disposal of cases. . . . It was a Cave of Adullam to which every man who had a grievance, real or fancied, could come to the wailing wall and have his complaint avidly encouraged and promptly underwritten without the slightest inquiry into its merits." (Johnson's characteristically erudite allusions were to the notorious "hanging judge" George Jeffreys of seventeenth-century England and to David's fortified refuge from King Saul in the Book of Samuel.)

Meanwhile Johnson convened his own public stock-taking, scheduling what he called a "Field Day of Criticism" for February 27. The event would stretch on for four full days.

Two thousand people packed the auditorium of the Department of Commerce on day one to air their grievances to Johnson and his deputies. The open-price provisions came in for particular denunciation: E. J. Condon of Sears, Roebuck & Company produced data showing that while goods subject to codes with price regulations or no codes at all had fallen in price since 1929, those subject to open-price codes had risen by 21 percent—a sharper rise even than increases seen under codes explicitly allowing price-fixing. Over the same period, agricultural prices had fallen by nearly half. The widening gulf between farm and industrial prices presented a stark illustration of how the General's habit of condoning price-fixing in the industrial sector had driven the agricultural economy further into depression.

NRA price-fixing was impoverishing state governments and their taxpayers, volunteered Mary E. O'Connor, a purchasing officer for New York state. She revealed that New York had been forced to freeze $10 million in purchase orders because bids from ostensibly competing companies protected by codes came in at identical prices. The state would not resume purchasing, she told the Field Day audience, "so long as NRA codes are being used as a cloak to disguise illegal, unethical, and unfair combinations in restraint of trade."

The most resonant criticism was delivered by Cornelia Pinchot, the wife of Pennsylvania's progressive Republican governor, Gifford Pinchot. Mrs. Pinchot was a former suffragette famous for her flaming red hair and fiery personality. She related how local officeholders beholden to steel and coal companies in her state had physically ejected her from public venues when she attempted to educate workers about their rights under Section 7(a). She denounced Johnson for failing to take action against the steel magnate Ernest T. Weir and the railcar manufacturer Edward G. Budd—the first had flouted the law by allowing elections at his three steel plants only for company unions, and the second had defied an NRA order to settle a strike by allowing a union election. Neither company lost its Blue Eagle, though that punishment was routinely meted out to small merchants snared for minor infractions of the reemployment code.

"Until men like Mr. Weir and Mr. Budd are made to obey the law," Pinchot declared, "I see no sense in taking the Blue Eagle away from a little beauty shop or a small restaurant. The failure of the NRA to deal promptly with Weir and Budd was taken as a signal by the lesser fry that they could chisel on the labor section of the act. . . . I wonder if General Johnson ever stays up nights and sees the faces of the people who are jobless and without resources, who went ahead and organized as allowed by the law and who lost their jobs . . . and nothing issues but a silence so dramatic it almost has the power of shaking their faith in the United States Government."

Johnson responded to the four days of critical testimony with a pro forma pledge to reorganize the code-setting process and revise the most abusive agreements. But there was more flak in the offing. In late May the Darrow committee released its report (following a months-long effort by Johnson to suppress the document). Darrow declared that "there is no hope for the small business man or for complete recovery in America in enforced restriction upon production for the purpose of maintaining higher prices." But he tipped his hand ideologically by observing that "the choice is between monopoly sustained by the government, which is clearly the trend in the NRA, and a planned economy, which demands socialized ownership and control."

Remarks like that gave Johnson and Don Richberg convenient grounds to dismiss the Darrow board's report, Richberg denouncing its chairman as "a noted Socialist, who advocates complete government control of business." Johnson, for his part, wrote in a letter addressed to FDR but designed for public dissemination: "A more superficial, intemperate and inaccurate document than the report I have never seen."

As General Johnson's hour upon the New Deal's stage neared its end, he served increasingly as the principal agent of his own destruction. As early as the autumn of 1933, Johnson's bouts of excessive drinking required Frances Robinson occasionally to escort him personally to Washington's Walter Reed Hospital for treatment. By the following spring the General's affliction was no longer a secret at the White House. "Don't you think something's got to be done about Johnson?" Roosevelt's appointments secretary, the dour Marvin McIntyre, inquired of Perkins. "It's all over town." What was yet unclear was how much the President knew—and neither McIntyre nor Perkins had the courage to ask him.

A sequence of events in the summer and fall of 1934 ensured Johnson's departure from the administration. The General had typically been a high-functioning alcoholic, able to perform his duties adequately even when associates detected the strong scent of liquor on his breath. But his behavior became distinctly more erratic as the attacks on the NRA intensified. He would negotiate a code one day, disappear for a week, and, upon reappearing, evince no recollection of his previous action. In early summer, New York's Senator Robert Wagner, the leading champion of labor rights on Capitol Hill, was eager to introduce a bill giving teeth to the rights enumerated under the NIRA's Section 7(a). His goal was to establish a national labor relations board to oversee union elections and safeguard the collective bargaining process. Johnson, who viewed his agency as a permanent addition to the Washington landscape and, absurdly, as one into which the departments of labor and commerce could eventually be absorbed, demanded that the board be part of the NRA, a concept that Wagner, backed by Frances Perkins, vehemently opposed: he was determined to invest the board with rigorous standards as an objective arbiter, which meant creating it as an independent agency of the executive branch.

Avoiding a public spat with NRA on this central issue was essential if the bill were to succeed in Congress. Yet as the deadline loomed for its introduction in the current session, an increasingly frantic Wagner was unable to tie Johnson down for a meeting, much less an agreement in principle.

As Perkins recalled, she and Wagner were about to get "our most serious dose of [Johnson's] total incapacity to understand what was going on and therefore his total incapacity to agree to anything."

Perkins had arranged for Richberg to escort Johnson to her office one day at ten in the morning. This was early enough, she hoped, to secure the General's attention before he could start drinking. Wagner would be present to meet him, and two hours would be set aside without interruption for the resolution of every issue pertinent to the bill. Perkins carefully coached Wagner, who was himself prone to temperamental outbursts, in the care and handling of General Johnson. "We were all sweetness and light," she would recall. To her dismay, the moment Johnson walked through the door the odor of liquor permeated the room.

Yet for the better part of an hour, the General kept a grip on himself. If not exactly amenable to all Wagner's suggestions, he remained at least engaged. Then Perkins noticed his expression acquiring "a glassy, way-off look. I knew then he wasn't listening. He wasn't focusing. He wasn't paying attention." She could not imagine he had had enough to drink that morning to account for his condition; what she did not know was that he had been drinking all the previous night and had never gotten to sleep. Abruptly, the General leaped to his feet, announced he had "duties" to attend to, and delegated Richberg to deal with the remaining issues on his own authority, promising to accept any agreement he reached.

The ever-vigilant Robbie hustled Johnson to Walter Reed, where he remained out of touch for several days. Wagner and Perkins finally gained admittance to his room to show him the completed bill, due to be introduced that day. Upon discovering that Richberg had agreed to leave the national labor board outside the NRA's jurisdiction, he exploded. "I never agreed to anything!" he howled. "What are you trying to put over on me?" Up to then, Wagner had tolerated Johnson's moods and behavior as an acceptable price to pay for his conspicuous energy and organizational skills. That was no longer true. "He's not fit to do business, Frances," Wagner told Perkins as they drove away from the hospital. Wagner's cherished bill would not pass Congress that year; but it would become law in 1935, after Hugh Johnson was out of office.

Perkins was Johnson's next supporter to fall away. The wedge was his inclination to inject himself into situations that were sufficiently fraught with uncertainty even without him—this time into the general strike in San Francisco.

The most important relationship Johnson destroyed was with Donald Richberg, the number two man in the NRA. Richberg was a former railroad lawyer from Chicago whose skill at organizing a large bureaucracy and ability to hack through legalistic brambles in the service of the NRA's goals made him an invaluable aide to Johnson. The two men maintained a largely cordial friendship through the first year of the agency's existence. But as drink and the pressure of work and politics stoked Johnson's paranoia, he began to see Richberg as an invidious foe, undermining him from within. This was not an entirely irrational view. Richberg had better access than Johnson to President Roosevelt, who had asked him to help rein in the General's more outlandish instincts. Moreover, toward the end of 1933, Richberg had come to the conclusion that disorderliness at NRA headquarters allowed powerful business interests to manipulate the agency for their own ends. NRA was in desperate need of reorganization. Richberg undertook that task on his own, for he knew better than anyone else that the biggest obstacle to getting it done was General Johnson.

By early 1934, Richberg had become convinced that the only way to set NRA back on course was to halt further code making and use the resulting breathing space to reorganize its bureaucracy, for under Johnson's command the agency's responsibilities had constantly expanded, overwhelming its staff. "The diagnosis made by a physician of the illness of a very fat woman seemed to apply to the NRA," Richberg reflected later. " 'Madam, you must either eat less, digest more, or bust.'" On the evening before the Field Day of Criticism he made this point in a national radio broadcast, stating that the NRA's "formative period is drawing to a close" and that what was needed now was "the rededication of a very young and immature department of Government to a great task which is just unfolding." One can imagine the General's eyes narrowing at this implicit critique of his management of an agency to which he felt he had given life, as though molding it with his own hands from primordial clay.

Relations between Johnson and Richberg continued to deteriorate. In May, after a diplomatic lunch at the Canadian embassy, Richberg sat on a park bench on the National Mall with David Lilienthal and unburdened himself for two straight hours about the difficulties of life with the General. Richberg plainly struggled with mixed feelings of affection for his colorful superior and exasperation at the General's administrative incompetence. "The recent troubles of NRA he attributes to the fact that Johnson has worn himself out, to the point where he doesn't want to work," Lilienthal confided to his journal, "and yet the whole thing is built up so that only he can decide. . . . Apparently Don takes the bit in his teeth frequently to straighten things out . . . but Johnson is extremely sensitive to criticism."

By then President Roosevelt had come around to the idea that Johnson must go. But FDR's habitual reluctance to confront a difficult decision, especially a personnel change, kept delaying the sentence of execution. He flailed about desperately for a way to edge Johnson out gently. Roosevelt's first idea was to appeal to Bernard Baruch to take Johnson back. Baruch, approached by Perkins, flatly refused. Instead he suggested she make inquiries with the industrialist Walter Chrysler, who also knew Johnson personally. But Chrysler quailed at the idea: "I can't manage him," he told Perkins, who came away startled and dismayed that two of the country's richest business leaders, ostensibly friends of both Hugh Johnson's and Franklin Roosevelt's, would refuse to help the administration by extricating the damaged Johnson from an untenable situation.

Roosevelt's next idea was to ease the general out by sending him to Europe to survey the economic recovery there. Perkins endorsed the scheme, which she thought would spare the psychologically fragile Johnson public humiliation. Roosevelt promptly summoned Johnson to the White House to deliver the order. That night the President telephoned Perkins to say the interview had gone well. "You must have been very diplomatic," she told him.

They both had misjudged their man. The next day Johnson turned the offer down, prompting a second summons to the White House. After a ninety-minute private meeting—remarkably long for Roosevelt—Johnson emerged from the executive office and met with the press. To the reporters who swarmed about him outside the office, he related that the President had assured him, "I need you and the country needs you." He added, "I guess my feet are nailed to the floor for the present. I am not going to resign now."

Perkins was en route to a friend's house in Upstate New York for a week's vacation when Johnson's statement hit the newspapers, startling Roosevelt, who was under the certain impression he had extracted a promise from Johnson to step aside. By the time Perkins arrived at her destination, the White House had been calling frantically for hours. Placed in contact with McIntyre, she was ordered back to Washington to meet with Roosevelt at 10 A.M. the next day. "What does he want me for?" she asked McIntyre. "Haven't you seen the morning papers?" he snapped. "Figure it out."

When she reported to the White House the next morning after a full day in transit, she discovered Richberg also in attendance. Admitted to the President's office, they found FDR seated grimly behind his desk, mentally bracing himself for battle. Roosevelt's habit was to establish an unruffled atmosphere for every meeting, no matter how fraught the topic, with pleasantries and casual banter. There was to be none of that now. Perkins tried to lighten the mood with a sarcastic joke. Roosevelt did not crack a smile. Then the General arrived, "looking very red in the face and very puffy." Plainly he had been drinking heavily.

"Sit down," Roosevelt commanded. "General Johnson, I think we've been misunderstanding each other," he said brusquely. Perkins and Richberg kept their eyes fixed on the floor. "I have asked you, General Johnson, to go on a mission to Europe. . . . If you don't wish to go to Europe, I think you should resign at once. Frankly you have become a problem. I can't discuss it much further, but I think you should resign immediately."

Johnson tottered to his feet. "Very well, Mr. President. I'm a good soldier. I'll do what I'm asked to do by my Commander in Chief."

McIntyre ushered Johnson out of the building by a back way. Perkins and Richberg stayed behind. Roosevelt looked as if he had come through a fiery ordeal. "I knew I had to have witnesses," he told them. "Gee, that was awful. Thanks for coming."

Bizarrely, that was not the end of it. Johnson obligingly drafted a letter of resignation and dispatched it to the White House before midnight. A reply came back promptly from FDR—within an hour, by the General's recollection. Roosevelt's constitutional aversion to ending a relationship on harsh terms again asserted itself, and he again offered Johnson the olive branch of an overseas commission: "Forget that [resignation] letter and come and talk with me Friday morning early." At that meeting Roosevelt again tried to persuade Johnson to give up the reins of NRA willingly; the pretext this time was that the General would be devoting himself to "reorganization" of the agency, not day-to-day operations. From then on, NRA was to be placed in the hands of Richberg and his deputies, reporting directly to Roosevelt; but the deferment of a formal transfer of power provided Johnson with one more opportunity for mischief. His antipathy toward organized labor surfaced again in mid-September, and finally sealed his downfall.

The issue this time was a nationwide strike called for Labor Day weekend by the United Textile Workers. The immense cotton textile industry had been the first to enact an NRA code, but Code No. 1 was shot through with loopholes and enforcement vested in a committee so firmly under the control of the mill owners that conditions for workers had not improved one iota. The writer Martha Gellhorn, touring the mill districts of North Carolina for the Federal Emergency Relief Administration, wrote to Harry Hopkins: "Gaston County is my idea of a place to go to acquire melancholia." Disease, filth, ignorance, and illiteracy were the common afflictions of the populace. Gellhorn found "syphilis uncured and unchecked; spread by ignorant people who have no conception of the disease, and no special interest in getting cured. . . . The private doctors do what they can which isn't much. And all are appalled by what the future holds for these people, who are absolutely unequipped for life." Mill workers earned less than government relief workers yet lived in fear for losing their meager livelihoods. Whether the strike would improve their lot or simply make it even worse was an open question. But the workers "are apt to strike even though they realize they can only lose."

The strike shut down mills in ten states, with more than 375,000 workers participating. As had become the dismal custom, accusations of communist agitation were sounded by governors and national guardsmen deployed. Inevitably, dozens of tense confrontations between strikers and police or soldiers ensued, several breaking into violence.

In some respects the walkout was doomed from the beginning, for the mill owners' warehouses were filled with finished goods, enabling them to wait out the strikers for weeks if necessary. Roosevelt tried to resolve the situation by appointing a board of inquiry under the chairmanship of granite-featured New Hampshire governor John G. Winant, a progressive Republican. But the challenge of fashioning a workable compromise in a situation where the employers plainly held the upper hand proved too daunting even for the resolute Winant.

It was while Winant was grappling with his dilemma that Johnson weighed in, with a speech at New York's Carnegie Hall on September 14. The event originally had been organized as a discussion of the NRA's record and prospects for its reorganization. Johnson, taking the floor with a radio audience listening in, launched an outrageously intemperate attack on the United Textile Workers, accusing its leadership of reneging on a deal he had brokered to end a strike threat the previous June.

"The present strike is an absolute violation of that understanding," he declared. "I must say here, with all the solemnity which should characterize such an announcement, that if such agreements of organized labor are worth no more than this one, than that institution is not . . . a responsible instrumentality." He charged the union's leadership with plotting to "unleash the forces of riot and rebellion"; to the union's further fury he held up as an exemplary agent of compromise George Sloan, the mill owners' negotiator, who in fact had worked assiduously but covertly to undermine the June agreement. "When I think of George Sloan my heart weeps," Johnson said. "It is a pity that he now has to take the rap in the dissension between labor and management."

Johnson's speech only reinforced the NRA's reputation as a tool of management. (In the event, the textile strike would end in a rattling defeat for the union.) But buried in the address was an even greater blunder. This was a casual reference to Justice Brandeis, with whom Johnson said he had been "in constant touch" while planning a reorganization of the NRA in advance of its coming legislative reauthorization. "He thinks NRA is too big, and I agree with him," Johnson said.

Johnson may have been attempting to mollify his progressive critics by invoking the name of Brandeis, a towering progressive figure. But his remark placed Brandeis in a profoundly difficult position by suggesting that the justice had engaged blatantly in political activity—worse, that he had involved himself with an agency that was almost certain to come before the Court during the forthcoming term. New Dealers were panicked by the thought that Johnson's statement might lead to recusal on NRA cases by Brandeis, who was counted by the White House as a dependably friendly vote on New Deal matters. Indeed, the conservative press hammered away at Brandeis's purported indiscretion, with the *Chicago Tribune* predictably labeling the justice's role "as truly revolutionary as any project in the program of the New Deal." Other conservative papers called for Brandeis's withdrawal from all NRA cases.

Brandeis remained silent in public, but privately pronounced himself mystified by Johnson's remarks. His contact with Johnson had amounted to a single face-to-face meeting and three telephone calls, all dealing with the NRA in the most general terms. From the beginning, he told intimates, he had informed Johnson that he was against the NRA "experiment" in any form—contradicting Johnson's suggestion that he had provided counsel on how to make it legally palatable. Brandeis considered recusal, polling each of his colleagues personally on the question; all told him they thought the step unwarranted.

Brandeis warned Roosevelt that Johnson would continue to embarrass the administration unless he was reeled in. But he turned away Roosevelt's offer to force Johnson to apologize publicly for his indiscretion, mostly out of concern that the unstable general might commit a new act of folly in trying to paper over the last. Confident that if all the players would only remain silent, the incident would presently fade from public view, Brandeis told Felix Frankfurter that it was best "regarded as a casualty, like that of being run into by a drunken autoist, or shot by a lunatic."

For Roosevelt there was no question of ignoring the matter. Johnson's critics inside the administration had pounced on the speech, Richberg counseling Marvin McIntyre: "Insanity in public performances, added to insanity in private relations, is pretty dangerous." Richberg's salvo was unnecessary, for Roosevelt already had had his fill; reports now were reaching him daily of Johnson's drinking and public indiscretions, including an episode in which an inebriated Johnson supposedly committed a "disgraceful and slightly obscene" act in a public place—the prim Perkins, in alluding to the incident years later, kept its details carefully under wraps.

On September 24, Johnson tendered the formal resignation Roosevelt had been awaiting for weeks. This time it was quickly and decisively accepted. The fifteen months Johnson had been administrator of the NRA had felt more like ten years, Perkins reflected, thinking of the General's remorseless pace, the fire and tumult of his regime, triumphs like the Blue Eagle drive and abject disasters like the textile speech. Johnson had contributed a propulsive spirit to the New Deal in its very first months, and it was perhaps to be expected that he would burn himself to a cinder before the finish.

By the time of Johnson's resignation, the guiding principle of the NRA had become largely discredited. The regimentation of industry into cartels mocked progressive ideals and failed to achieve recovery in practice. Under Hugh Johnson, the NRA politicized labor-management conflicts in a way that disconcerted industrialists and disenfranchised workers—precisely the opposite of the outcome the agency's creators had sought. The program might not have worked regardless of who stood at its head; but with the charismatic Johnson in charge it became a charismatic movement, destined to fray as his personality frayed, and to collapse with his removal.

The residual glow of Hugh Johnson's NRA would remain long after he was gone, exerting a negative influence on New Deal industrial policy. The principles of restricted competition and the suppression of antitrust enforcement persisted as New Deal nostrums longer than they should have, in part because the memory of Hugh Johnson was so hard to eradicate.

In a Fireside Chat on September 30, a few days after Johnson's resignation, Roosevelt obliquely bid farewell to the General. After paying an obligatory compliment to the "able and energetic leadership of General Johnson," he made it clear that he intended to continue the NRA experiment in a new guise informed by the lessons learned during the previous fifteen months. He acknowledged doubts about whether the minimum wage worked as intended for the lowest-paid laborers or whether the code process merely served big employers in the big cities at the expense of small enterprises and rural communities: "There may be a serious question as to the wisdom of many of those devices to control production, or to prevent destructive price-cutting . . . or whether their effect may have been to prevent that volume of production which would make possible lower prices and increased employment," he said. He also paid heed to public discontent with the wave of industrial strikes that had washed over the country in recent months and "the inevitable losses to employers and employees and to the general public through such conflicts." But he observed that "the extent and severity of labor disputes during this period has been far less than in any previous, comparable period."

This last assertion was a flagrant falsehood. The truth was that by any measure labor discord in the United States was at its highest tide in more than a decade. As a monthly average, man-days lost to strikes had doubled in July 1933 and nearly quadrupled in August over the equivalent figures for the first six months of that year, and the number of work stoppages for all of 1933 was higher than in any year since 1921. The four major strikes of 1934—the San Francisco waterfront strike, the Auto-Lite walkout in Toledo, a Teamsters strike in Minneapolis, and the nationwide textile strike—were watersheds for the labor movement. In 1934 the American worker had turned strike-happy. A twenty-eight-year-old playwright named Clifford Odets turned the foment of that year into a one-act play about working-class taxi drivers called *Waiting for Lefty,* bringing the curtain down on a line that reverberated coast to coast: *"Strike, strike, strike!!!"*

General Johnson left one more legacy. When he departed the White House that September day, a lawsuit over the fate of a number of scrawny chickens in Brooklyn was on its way to the Supreme Court. At the heart of the case lay the constitutionality of the National Recovery Administration itself.

The poultry business occupied a scrofulous corner of the commercial world, "an unsavory, sordid business, frightened by racketeers and ruled by monopolies," in the words of a prominent social reformer. The chicken that would vanquish the Blue Eagle, he observed, was "no chanticleer."

On the surface, the live chicken trade seemed to be immune from interstate regulation, a strictly local business centered in New York and Brooklyn and chiefly serving a clientele of kosher Jews. This was a misimpression. The "marketmen" in their linen aprons in the New York Central Railroad's receiving yard on Manhattan's West Side set prices across the eastern United States as effectively as the traders of the Chicago futures pits dictated the price of corn and wheat in the Midwest. Nor was this a secret to prosecutors or judges; as recently as February 1934, the U.S. Supreme Court had affirmed the conviction of several live poultry dealers in New York and Jersey City for conspiring in restraint of interstate trade.

State and municipal authorities in New York had been trying to clean up the poultry business for twenty years, without success. Upon the advent of the NRA they leaped at the opportunity to bring federal oversight to the marketplace. The drafters of the NRA's live chicken code tried to address the most conspicuous abuses—price-fixing, short-weighting, the counterfeiting of the seals that signified kosher slaughtering, and the sale of diseased chickens to unwitting customers. The chicken code mandated health inspections, the filing of detailed sales and price reports to combat collusion, and the enforcement of "straight killing," a principle that required large customers to be sold whole coops or half coops rather than allowing them to select individual birds from inventory. Straight killing was designed to prevent unscrupulous dealers from reserving the best birds for favored clients and deceiving all others about the quality of their goods.

The four Schechter brothers who operated the A. L. A. Schechter Poultry Corp. were the largest poultry dealers in Brooklyn. They were the first merchants to be charged with felony violations of the poultry code—sixty counts, later reduced to thirty-three, of which they were found guilty at trial on nineteen. Their convictions on seventeen of the counts, which exposed the brothers to jail terms of more than a month each, had been upheld by a federal appeals court in New York City. But the court invalidated two counts on the grounds that the poultry code's imposition of a minimum wage and maximum hours for slaughterhouse workers—the basis of those changes—improperly extended the federal government's authority over interstate commerce into activities within a single state. The defendants and the government were equally determined to bring an appeal to the Supreme Court.

The wisdom of testing the NRA's constitutionality via the Schechter case had been the subject of urgent debate at the agency and the White House. General Johnson had always been fretful about the NRA's ability to withstand any judicial scrutiny; for that reason he had avoided implementing the licensing provisions of the act, which allowed the President to impose a code on any recalcitrant industry, the legality of which provisions Johnson considered especially doubtful.

Donald Richberg, who had become NRA administrator after Johnson's departure, was more determined than his predecessor to obtain a constitutional ruling from the Supreme Court. He perceived that doubts about the legal viability of the agency were eroding agency morale, and he believed that Congress would not take up the reauthorization of the agency, which had to be completed by mid-1935, until the Court had spoken.

Richberg also differed with Johnson over the Schechter appeal. Johnson had scorned it as the "sick chicken" case, a nickname that stuck for good. But Richberg considered it a promising test case. There did not seem to be any question that the Supreme Court would treat the poultry business as one involving interstate commerce, for in its decision the year before it had acknowledged that "live poultry for sale and consumption in the New York metropolitan area continuously moves in great volume from points in distant states." Richberg was anxious to obtain the Court's endorsement of the NRA's jurisdiction over unfair business practices, which stood at the heart of the Schechter convictions. The sick chicken case would establish the validity of the NRA "right across the board," he announced.

This was not the view of Roosevelt's chief legal kibitzer, Felix Frankfurter, who issued a warning via Tommy Corcoran that the time was not ripe to bring any NRA case to a Supreme Court loaded with doctrinaire conservatives. Even in more propitious times, he felt, *Schechter* would be the wrong case to carry into battle. Frankfurter flatly predicted "the Court would rule against the government if this case came before it," Corcoran recorded. Frankfurter did not explain his reasoning, prompting Corcoran to assume that he had been in touch with Brandeis and that the latter had communicated his own doubts.

Frankfurter's misgivings prompted Corcoran to send a frantic wire to Roosevelt, then fishing on the high seas aboard Vincent Astor's yacht *Nourmahal*:

> FF SUGGESTS MOST IMPOLITIC AND DANGEROUS TO YIELD TO
> ANTAGONISTIC PRESS CLAMOR NOW BECAUSE FUNDAMENTAL
> SITUATION ON COURT NOT CHANGED. FURTHER SUGGESTS
> YOU WIRE CUMMINGS NOT TO TAKE HASTY ACTION AND HOLD
> SITUATION ON NRA APPEALS IN ABEYANCE UNTIL YOU RETURN.

The message reached Roosevelt just before Attorney General Homer Cummings was scheduled to announce that the government was bringing the Schechter case to the Court. Roosevelt duly wired Cummings to hold off, but the attorney general filed the appeal anyway and declared it to the world. Cummings later pleaded that FDR's wire had not arrived until after the announcement, but Corcoran privately speculated that he merely desired to show his disdain for the interfering Frankfurter: "I know he resented FF being 'super attorney general.'" In any event, the case's presentation to the Court was out of the administration's hands: even if the government did not appeal, the Schechters were sure to do so (although one brother later remarked that he would have opted for the jail term if he knew their legal bill for the appeal would come to a steep sixty thousand dollars). The sick chicken case was argued on May 2 and 3 and decided before the end of the month.

The atmosphere was electric and the Court's chamber in the U.S. Capitol packed as the justices filed in for the reading of decisions on Monday, May 27.

It was not only the importance of the leading case on the calendar that brought a throng to the Capitol that day; it was the chance to divine the overall mind-set of the Court in advance of a wave of New Deal cases headed for its docket. Despite the presence of a solid bloc of four conservative justices, the signals delivered by the entire Court thus far had been equivocal.

The confused picture arose from two decisions earlier in 1935. The first involved the so-called gold clause. To stem the outflow of gold and protect the U.S. dollar during the banking emergency, Roosevelt had repudiated a clause in government bonds allowing owners to redeem them for gold. The financial world was "on the verge of nervous prostration" waiting to see whether the Court would uphold that action, then–SEC Chairman Joseph P. Kennedy recounted. The administration was poised to take drastic steps to counter an adverse ruling on decision day, February 14: Kennedy would order the temporary closure of all U.S. stock exchanges to guard against financial chaos, and Roosevelt would nullify the ruling by executive order on grounds that it imperiled "the economic and political security of this nation." But the Court majority found that, although the repudiation was indeed unconstitutional, the plaintiffs had no standing to sue to overturn it. With this expedient decision allowing the repudiation to stand, the majority averted a constitutional crisis but infuriated the conservative bloc. As Justice James Clark McReynolds grumbled in an extemporaneous dissent from the bench, "Shame and humiliation are upon us now."

The second decision, on May 6, overturned the Railroad Retirement Act of 1934, which had established a pension fund for railroad workers. The ruling, in which Justice Owen Roberts joined the conservatives, raised doubts over whether the federal government had any authority to implement social welfare legislation. Whether Roberts had now joined a permanent conservative majority was among the questions to which many people hoped for answers on that Monday in late May.

Notwithstanding the intense interest in the May 27 calendar, the momentous Supreme Court session opened soporifically, with the reading by Justice Pierce Butler of a minor insurance law decision. Only then came the three 9–0 decisions in which the Court systematically dismantled the edifice of law and practice erected by the New Deal and changed the course of the Roosevelt administration. The date would become known by progressives as "Black Monday."

In the first case, *Humphrey's Executor v. U.S.*, Justice George Sutherland overturned, with unseemly relish, Roosevelt's ouster of William E. Humphrey from the Federal Trade Commission. Humphrey's reactionary views had hobbled an agency the President desired to endow with an aggressive regulatory portfolio. A Coolidge appointee who had belittled the FTC as "a publicity bureau to spread socialistic propaganda," Humphrey battled Roosevelt's removal order in court right up to his death in February 1934. That the plaintiff was now a corpse mattered little to the law. Humphrey's cause passed to the executor of his estate, who continued the lawsuit to recover the salary due Humphrey from the date of his purportedly illegal dismissal.

At the White House, the case had been regarded as an easy victory; the new solicitor general, Stanley Reed, had chosen it for his first argument before the Court for that reason, as unwritten tradition held that every new solicitor general should win his first case. The government's position was that Roosevelt's action was consistent with the principle laid down in 1926 by Chief Justice William Howard Taft, an ex-president, in *Myers v. United States*—that the President's removal power over executive officers was absolute. *Myers* had been decided 6–3, with the majority including four justices who would still be on the Court in 1935: Sutherland, Butler, Willis Van Devanter, and Harlan Stone.

On May 27 those four voted with their five brethren to overturn their own nine-year-old precedent. Worse, Sutherland in his majority opinion seemed determined to deliver a personal humiliation to Roosevelt by suggesting that the President had deliberately set upon an illegal course by ousting Humphrey, when the truth was that the Court had chosen to perform its own unexpected volte-face. Years later, Roosevelt's associates would look back to *Humphrey,* even more than to the judicial rebukes that would follow on that dark day, to explain the bitterness of the President's attack on the Supreme Court in 1937. "It may very well have been that case," Tugwell wrote, which magnified an effort at judicial reform into an "attempt to humiliate the Court in turn."

After the *Humphrey* ruling it was Brandeis's turn to read a decision invalidating the 1934 Frazier-Lemke Farm Bankruptcy Act, which changed bankruptcy law to allow a farm debtor to buy back his foreclosed farm and make new arrangements to pay his mortgage. This unanimous opinion held that the law's extension to preexisting mortgages, not simply new ones, rendered it unconstitutional.

Then Chief Justice Charles Evans Hughes read off the docket number of the Schechter case. Leaning forward, he declared that he would read the decision himself. Witnesses would never forget the "unusual vehemence" of his voice, or the way he rocked back and forth in his tall chair, his hand occasionally drifting up to stroke his full white beard. As the import of his words sank in, Donald Richberg, who had personally argued the case before the Court three weeks earlier, paled and buried his head in his hands.

The destruction of the NRA was complete and uncompromising. Rather than follow the judicial custom of deciding cases on the narrowest grounds, the Court cast a wide net, posing three questions broadly applicable to the entire New Deal: Did the extraordinary economic crisis warrant extraordinary government powers? (This had been the central point of Richberg's oral argument.) Did Congress properly delegate authority to the President?

Did the NRA comply with the Commerce Clause of the Constitution by exercising its authority only on interstate commerce?

Hughes answered all three in the negative. "Extraordinary conditions may call for extraordinary remedies," he acknowledged. But "extraordinary conditions do not create or enlarge constitutional power."

On the second question, he stated, "Congress is not permitted to abdicate or transfer to others the essential legislative functions with which it is . . . vested." The "sweeping delegation" Congress granted the President through the NIRA was "beyond precedent," Hughes said. "It supplies no standards for any trade, industry or activity. . . . Instead of prescribing rules of conduct, it authorizes the making of codes," granting the President power that is "virtually unfettered."

Regarding the interstate commerce claim, "much is made of the fact that almost all the poultry coming to New York is sent there from other States." But "the mere fact that there may be a constant flow of commodities into a State does not mean that the flow continues after the property has arrived. . . . The poultry had come to a permanent rest within the State." If the Commerce Clause could be interpreted to cover any transaction with even a tangential effect on interstate commerce, he cautioned, "the federal authority would embrace practically all the activities of the people." This was a remarkably pinched definition of "interstate commerce," one with which justices Cardozo and Stone specifically differed in a separate concurring opinion. But their objection on this one point was not enough to prompt them to dissent from the whole.

Once Hughes finished speaking, Black Monday was over. To the New Dealers, the Court's rulings were not merely blows struck at a couple of legislative initiatives undertaken to address an economic crisis; they amounted to a warning that the ambitions and scale of the New Deal would be weighed in the future against old, outdated traditions of governmental circumspection. Yet in making that point, the Court upended the tradition of judicial circumspection.

Few commentators were as disturbed and perplexed by the Court's apparent overreaching in *Schechter* as Felix Frankfurter. Having doubted the wisdom of bringing the case in the first place, he now objected that the Court not only had failed to confine its ruling to the poultry code and others that might resemble it even superficially, but "it did so in language seemingly applicable, especially in the political and emotional context of the times, to many other and widely different types of legislation." Seldom had the tenet that the Court should "never . . . anticipate a question of constitutional law in advance of the necessity of deciding it" been so thoroughly flouted. The code process at the heart of the *Schechter* case was scheduled to expire twenty days after the decision, Frankfurter observed; there were no constitutional issues at hand except those that might be implicated in *future* acts of the legislature, which the Court was required by tradition to ignore until they were properly brought before it. There could be no question that this Court aimed to warn Congress and the President away from acts yet to come.

Indeed, Frankfurter's friend Louis Brandeis wished to make that very point crystal clear. The Court chamber had not yet emptied when a page picked out Tom Corcoran from among the spectators and handed him a summons to meet Brandeis in the robing room. Corcoran was too crest-fallen over the string of unanimous decisions to fully appreciate the rare honor of being invited into the justices' inner sanctum. But the majesty of the place struck him the moment he entered. Brandeis "appeared like a condor—a tall, long-limbed creature with a fleshless beak of a nose and glaring eyes." The justice, who had raised his arms aloft so a retainer could remove his gown, then became transformed before Corcoran's eyes into an avenging angel. "You go back and tell your President," Brandeis said without preliminaries, "that this Court has told him it is not going to permit the centralization of power which his advisors are imposing on this country. He is overcentralizing this country with his planning and you are to tell him so because I have told you so. . . . Send back to the states all those bright young men you have brought to Washington. It's in the states where they are needed and it's in the government of the states where they belong."

It was Brandeis's old distaste for bigness—in government no less than in industry—summoned back into the open by his concern that the government had gone out of control. And it was a sign that, though the New Deal-ers had fretted that General Johnson's indiscretion might force Brandeis to recuse himself from the coming decisions, they were deeply mistaken about his opinion of much of what they had done.

Roosevelt was perhaps the most surprised of all. "What about Old Isa-iah?" he asked when news of the judicial rout reached him at the White House.

"With the majority," he was told.

"Where was Cardozo? Where was Stone?"

"They too were with the majority," the bleak reply came back, like news of a cataclysmic battlefield defeat.

In the political universe, conservative delight at Roosevelt's humiliation met progressive despair at the blow to the New Deal agenda and concern about what Black Monday portended for the checks and balances at the heart of the federal system. Hiram Johnson grappled with both sentiments simultaneously: "It was a terrible wallop, and it is made worse by the fact that a lot of the men around the President are as gleeful as the standpat Republicans," he wrote his elder son. "Every rat seems to have come out of his hole and is making faces at the White House. None of them would have dared up to this time to have more than snarled a little in the dark."

Johnson expressed both the distaste felt in Washington for General Johnson's hoopla and the progressives' horror at the emergence of an adamantine conservative bloc on the Court. "What a commentary upon our intelligence . . . when we must be driven into a policy by signs and symbols . . . and with tattooing the eagle on our anatomy," he wrote. "And how stranger still is it that a modern, progressive, sensible, presumably intelligent government, rests in its final analysis for the determination of social questions and the policies to be pursued for humanity upon the veto power of nine old men."

Roosevelt kept his counsel for four days, weighing advice that included leaving the NRA to die, erecting a wall of protective statutes to constrain the Court's incursions into legislative and executive prerogatives, or trimming the Court's wings by constitutional amendment. Then, on May 31, he summoned reporters to the White House for an extraordinary press conference.

Press secretary Steve Early arrived at the family quarters to escort Roosevelt to the Oval Room for the 11 A.M. event. While the President dressed, Early related that he had driven to work that morning with his brother-in-law, George Holmes, the Washington bureau chief of Hearst's International News Service. They had pondered what motivated the Court to issue the *Schechter* decision. "George says that those boys up there think that this is still the horse-and-buggy age," Early observed. Roosevelt said nothing in reply, just signaled that it was time for him to meet the press.

There could have been no question about the topic of the day; the reporters gathered in the Oval Room could see a copy of the *Schechter* decision, well thumbed and heavily marked up, on the President's desk.

One of them fed Roosevelt the opening line: "Do you care to comment any on the NRA?"

"If you insist," FDR replied.

Roosevelt spent the next two hours delivering a dramatic reading of the Court's opinion, almost paragraph by paragraph, and in some places line by line, interpolating his own commentary. When he got to Hughes's stringent interpretation of the interstate commerce clause, he summoned the words of Steve Early's brother-in-law. "The country was in the horse-and-buggy age when that clause was written," he said. "There wasn't much interstate commerce at all—probably 80 or 90 percent of the human beings in the thirteen original States were completely self-supporting."

By overlooking how even seemingly local transactions in the modern world impacted commerce across the country directly or indirectly, Roosevelt said, the Court's antiquated position threw responsibility for dealing with economic issues of national import back on the states, which were manifestly ill-equipped to meet them. "The big issue is this: Does this decision mean that the United States Government has no control over any national economic problem?

"That is why I say it is one of the most important decisions ever rendered in this country," he concluded. Then he repeated, lest no one mistake his point: "We have been relegated to the horse-and-buggy definition of interstate commerce."

The reporters, like Roosevelt, recognized an attention-grabbing phrase when they heard one. "Can we use the direct quotation on that horse-and-buggy stage?" one asked.

"I think so," the President replied.

The phrase instantly became one of Roosevelt's most memorable quotes, exciting agreement and condemnation in equal measure across the political spectrum. Lost in the furor was the fact that the President had nimbly dodged the question of what he intended to do about the Court. "I am going to tell you very, very little on that," he had remarked. "Let the bigger things sink in for the next four or five days." When the reporters asked again whether he might propose a constitutional amendment to address the decision, he chuckled.

"We haven't got to that yet," he said.

14

FEDERAL ONE

THE QUESTION Harry Hopkins posed to Hallie Flanagan one day in July 1934 was typically direct. "Can you spend money?" he asked. Flanagan answered him with a quip: the inability to spend money had never been among her faults.

They were aboard a train passing from Chicago toward the midwestern prairie. Flanagan had known Hopkins for a quarter century, since they were classmates at Grinnell College in Iowa. A few weeks earlier, he had appointed her to head the Federal Theatre Project, one of four arts programs he was launching as part of the new Works Progress Administration, the largest work relief program in history.

His question had been deadly serious. "It's not easy," he explained, speaking from bitter experience. "It takes a lot of nerve to put your signature down on a piece of paper when it means that the government of the United States is going to pay out a million dollars to the unemployed in Chicago. . . . You can't care very much what people are going to say because when you're handling other people's money whatever you do is always wrong. If you try to hold down wages, you'll be accused of union-busting and of grinding down the poor; if you pay a decent wage, you'll be competing with private industry and pampering a lot of no-accounts; if you scrimp on production costs, they'll say your shows are lousy and if you spend enough to get a good show on, they'll say you're wasting the taxpayers' money. *Don't forget that whatever happens you'll be wrong.*"

He did not at that moment identify the problem that would truly require all of Hallie Flanagan's nerve and that of her fellow supervisors of what would soon become known as Federal Project No. 1, or "Federal One"—encompassing the Federal Art Project, Federal Writers' Project, and Federal Music Project along with her theater program. The problem was that government funding of intellectual endeavors was qualitatively very different from paying people to perform physical labor. A man wielding a shovel or driving a bulldozer, whether for the meanest of sewer lines or the grandest edifice, was creating a legacy that any taxpayer or politician could comprehend. The cast of a play, painter of a mural, composer of a score, or writer of prose was involved in work that often achieved its effect by challenging the audience's perceptions or subverting its expectations. Somewhere, sometime, somebody was likely to be confused or offended. That somebody might well occupy a position commanding attention and power.

Could the arts administrators withstand the pressure? Hopkins addressed the question during a dinner at the University of Iowa the evening after his conversation with Flanagan: "I am asked whether a theater subsidized by the government can be kept free of censorship, and I say, yes, it is going to be kept free from censorship. What we want is a free, adult, uncensored theater."

Federal One deserves special attention in comparison to the WPA's conventional projects—its highways, airports, fish hatcheries, stadiums, and parks—because as an effort to extend federal assistance to unrecognized artists, writers, and performers it was unique in American history. There had been government art programs before, notably a Treasury Department effort to place works of art in public buildings, but these typically involved established artists whose works were selected by professional juries. Federal One would employ not only established artists and talented novices, but also the worker ants of the cultural world—technicians, journeymen, craftspersons. The historian and critic Bernard DeVoto, looking back on the Federal Writers' Project in 1942, observed "without any shadow of derogation" that "most of the people employed by the Project have never been, even in the humblest sense, genuine writers. . . . It has been, in fact, a project for research workers." Something similar could be said about each of the other three components of Federal One. They were work relief programs, not cultural endowments. But they left a mark on American culture nonetheless.

The four arts programs together consumed a minuscule portion of the WPA budget: when Congress appropriated the initial $1.4 billion for the agency in January 1935, it set aside $27 million, less than 2 percent, for the arts. By 1943, when the WPA closed its books having spent a total of $13 billion, Federal One accounted for roughly the same ratio, or slightly more than $250 million. Its employment rolls never exceeded a few tens of thousands, out of total WPA employment that peaked at more than 3.3 million workers (in November 1938).

WPA auditors struggled to find a way to account for the output of Federal One. The progress of an airport construction project could be measured in cubic yards of concrete poured, but judging the quality or utility of a musical performance, public mural, or entry in a guidebook was purely subjective. The agency's final report, published in 1946, tabulated miles of highways paved, libraries and schools erected, golf holes built. But of dramatic performances delivered, books printed and read, hours of oral histories recorded by aged former slaves, there appear no official figures in the WPA's accounting.

Flanagan, however, ferreted out some statistics for her 1940 memoir, *Arena*. She reported that the Federal Theatre spent $46.2 million during its brief four-year life span, 90 percent of it on wages. Its 30,400,000 audience members paid an average of 6 cents a seat in admission (many performances were free). The unit's expenditures during its life came to about two-thirds of a percent of the WPA's spending, and its average employment of 10,000 men and women came to about four-tenths of a percent of the WPA payroll.

For many Americans, Federal One *was* the WPA. They thought of their WPA airports and state capitols in terms of the murals and statues by Federal Art Project painters and sculptors that graced their terminals and rotundas. Millions of Americans were exposed to classical music for the first time by the traveling orchestras funded by the Federal Music Project. The prodigious series of state guidebooks turned out by the Federal Writers' Project showed its value in 1940, when Congress conditioned the program's survival on its finding local sponsors to put up 25 percent of its expenses; every one of the forty-eight states advanced its share. And Hallie Flanagan's achievement in creating a vital national theater would resonate for decades through the vigor of the Negro voice in American drama, which she nurtured, as well as the platform she provided—not entirely to her agency's advantage—for a wunderkind named Orson Welles.

The arts programs, however, became a lightning rod for attacks on Hopkins, Roosevelt, and the WPA—zealous conservatives used Federal One as a proxy for the entire New Deal. But that was only one manifestation of the political establishment's uneasiness with the concept of paying workers to create culture rather than to assemble bricks and mortar. Local politicians treated Federal One as a dumping ground for the halt and the lame—not everyone could hoist a shovel, the theory went, but anyone could scribble on paper or daub paint. To some, the corollary was that almost the only people employed in Federal One *were* the halt and the lame. Such was the opinion of Colonel Francis C. Harrington, the army engineer who succeeded Hopkins as WPA administrator in 1938, after the latter joined the cabinet as secretary of commerce. Asked at a Senate hearing whether the workers of Federal One could be absorbed elsewhere by the WPA if Congress killed the arts programs, Harrington replied: "Many of these people are not physically fit for manual labor."

Colonel Harrington's disdain for Federal One was not unusual among WPA bureaucrats. Most had been engaged for their skills in managing construction, which was, after all, the point of more than 90 percent of the agency's spending. Typical was Lieutenant Colonel Brehon Somervell, who as regional WPA director in New York City wielded direct authority over the arts programs. The Arkansan West Pointer had compiled a brilliant record as a logistician with the Army Corps of Engineers. The WPA stationed him in New York in 1936 after Congress killed his previous WPA project, a ship canal designed to bisect Florida from the Atlantic to the Gulf of Mexico. On paper his new assignment seemed a wise move, given that the massive WPA effort in New York would include the largest agency project of all, the municipal airfield that would become LaGuardia Airport. But the cultural projects were a closed book to Somervell, a cocksure philistine of a familiar type. "He was not only of the school of critics who felt that 'his little Mary could do as well' as, shall we say, a distinguished painter like Ben Shahn or Stuart Davis, but, in addition, he had a profound conviction that to create 'pictures' was not 'work,'" recalled Audrey McMahon, the Federal Art Project director in New York. At one point he commanded that every writer under his jurisdiction turn in a minimum of three hundred words a day. The project supervisors accepted the mandate graciously, without informing Somervell that their writers had already produced eight million words for a guidebook to New York City. The unit's production crisis was a surfeit, not shortage, of verbiage.

Even some distinguished intellectuals considered the idea of a federally sponsored arts program foolhardy, as the interface between art and politics had been a danger zone through history. W. H. Auden called Federal One

> one of the noblest and most absurd undertakings ever attempted by any state. Noblest because no other state has ever cared whether its artists as a group lived or died. . . . Yet absurd, because a state can only function bureaucratically and impersonally—it has to assume that every member of a class is equivalent or comparable to every other member—but every artist, good or bad, is a member of a class of one.

Still, expanding work relief beyond the conventional confines of blue-collar labor had long been a goal of Harry Hopkins. Barring white-collar workers from relief had never made sense to him. It was true enough that the physical labor of the unemployed carried "almost immeasurable benefits" for the public; but the "less tangible ones made by our professional and service workers" might prove even greater. Yet the idea of work relief devoted to the work of the mind, not the body, was a difficult concept to put over to Congress or the taxpayer. Upon his first meeting with Flanagan over the theater job, Hopkins had exclaimed in mock frustration, "I don't know why I still hang on to the idea that unemployed actors get just as hungry as anyone else."

For every skeptic like Auden, however, there was a champion like Gutzon Borglum, the sculptor whose Mount Rushmore project was still under way when he wrote Hopkins via the latter's assistant, Aubrey Williams: "Civilization contains all that is precious in what we think we are. . . . You are not after masterpieces, and you should not be discouraged if you have many failures; the real success will be in the interest, the human interest, which you will awaken; and what that does to the Nation's mind."

Franklin Roosevelt did not specifically call for projects to assist artists and performers when he announced his new work relief program in a Fireside Chat on April 28, 1935. But they were implicit within the "fundamental principles" he set down for what would become the WPA, among them that "the projects should be useful . . . [and] of a nature that a considerable proportion of the money spent will go into wages." The concept had been quietly written into the relief act passed on April 8 via a provision authorizing "a nation-wide program for useful employment of artists, musicians, actors, entertainers, writers . . . and others in these cultural fields." Roosevelt created the WPA by executive order on May 6, and the four components of Federal One were announced to the public in early August.

The four arts directors all faced the same fundamental administrative conflict, which was that their ambitions to produce quality art could not always be reconciled with the program's goal of providing work relief to unemployed Americans who happened to have worked in the cultural milieu. Recognizing that cultural programs required a certain amount of elite input, Hopkins agreed to a modest dispensation from the rule that all the WPA's beneficiaries must be eligible for relief—that is, certified as destitute by WPA bureaucrats empowered to verify their income and family status. (At Congress's insistence, the means test had crept back into Hopkins's relief programs.) The arts programs were permitted to hire up to 25 percent of their staffs from outside the relief rolls, and these "non-relief" personnel often accounted for the projects' professional core. When the Art Project's administrator, Holger Cahill, received a roster of its employees divided into relief and nonrelief categories—the latter comprising skilled professionals—he exclaimed, "Thank God for that 25 percent." But it was a fragile arrangement; over time, as budget pressures forced funding cuts in Federal One, the permissible level of nonrelief staff was reduced in steps from 25 percent to 5 percent.

Unsurprisingly, given the subjectivity of the creative process, the four components of Federal One mirrored their administrators' personalities. The most culturally conservative was the Federal Music Project, whose chief, Nikolai Sokoloff, was a Kiev-born violinist and founding conductor of the Cleveland Symphony, steeped in the mainstream of the European classical and romantic tradition.

American popular musical taste tended toward jazz, traditionals, gospel, the parlor songs of Stephen Foster, and the marches of John Philip Sousa. But to Sokoloff, music's gods were Mozart, Beethoven, and Brahms, and he saw it as his duty to bring them to the widest audience that federal largesse could provide. He believed that the American public ignored the great Western masters simply out of unfamiliarity, a flaw he was determined to correct.

The Thirties were a time of unexampled creativity in American music. The phenomena driving this trend were the advent of radio in the 1920s and the rise of jazz as a popular genre, leavened by an influx of classical and avant-garde musicians fleeing the European crisis that would bring Hitler to power. To those hoping to advance the cause of an American music that incorporated all these influences, Sokoloff seemed miscast for the role of shepherd. He disdained swing, the principal vocabulary of popular big band music: "I like to dance when I am dancing but to compare it with music, why it is like comparing the funny papers to the work of a painter," he told a Seattle newspaper. Contemporary composers seeking to pursue their craft on the government's dime consequently gravitated to the more welcoming arms of Flanagan's Federal Theatre, which Virgil Thomson, one of those refugees, described as "the most vigorous new art movement in the whole West."

Still, if one viewed the Federal Music Project's goal as the bringing of fine culture to the masses, it is impossible to overlook Sokoloff's achievement. At the time of the project's founding, the United States had eleven recognized symphony orchestras; Sokoloff provided funding for thirty-four more. Opera, that most refined of musical forms, was introduced to a mass audience with a free production of Mascagni's *Cavalleria Rusticana* performed in San Diego by a Federal Music Project orchestra, a fifty-member FMP chorus, and singers in costumes sewn by WPA-employed seamstresses; the Boston opera used FMP funding to open its doors to the populace at 83 cents per ticket. This was opera not for Ward McAllister's Four Hundred, but "for the Four Million," crowed a WPA publicity man. "The sign warning, 'Drivers, chauffeurs, footmen not allowed to stand in the vestibule' might just as well have been draped, for the drivers, chauffeurs, and footmen were occupying the seats of the master and the madame."

The most intellectually inclusive unit of Federal One was the Federal Art Project, again as a reflection of its administrator's personality. Holger Cahill, born Sveinn Kristjan Bjarnarson in 1887 to an Icelandic farm family, had emigrated with his parents to Canada around the turn of the century. In his youth he tried out a series of wildly variegated careers: cattle driver in Nebraska, coalman on a Pacific freighter, insurance salesman, short-order cook, newspaper reporter and editor, and publicity agent. During the Twenties he fell among the painters of Manhattan's artistic bohemia, soon to emerge as an expert on American folk art and a penetrating analyst of the modern art movement. He had spent a year as acting director of the Rockefeller family's Museum of Modern Art and completed two books on American art and modern art when he was named head of Federal One's art program. He would prove to be an ideal program chief, "warm, enthusiastic, careful, and understanding," judged the veteran cultural administrator Olin Dows, with "a sensitive eye for quality."

The job would require every ounce of Cahill's judgment and diplomacy. Visual artists were not as generally associated with leftist sentiments as writers and theater folk, but the inescapably public nature of their murals and sculptures meant that any controversy they did arouse was more likely to be detonated in public than quietly hushed up. Memories were still fresh in New York of the 1933 dispute between the left-wing Mexican artist Diego Rivera and the Rockefeller family. Young Nelson Rockefeller, hoping to establish himself as a patron of the fine arts, had commissioned Rivera to paint an immense mural for the lobby of Rockefeller Center, only to discover that depicted among the throngs peopling the sixty-three-foot work *Man at the Crossroads* was the Bolshevik leader Lenin. After Rivera refused to paint over the image he was barred from the building and the mural was jackhammered off the wall.

Holger Cahill's catholic tastes established the Federal Art Project as a refuge for talented artists from "the pressure of cliques, the insistence of dealers, the noise of publicity," as the abstract artist Rosalind Bengelsdorf Browne recalled. Many artists credited him for giving them the freedom to discover their own personal styles—the diametric opposite of Sokoloff's constricted focus on European masters of the eighteenth and nineteenth centuries. "How many of us and the other artists of the people might have been discouraged or derailed in their creative calling if the Project did not exist," pondered the Russian-born painter Joseph Solman. "A five to eight year span, which is the period most of us worked in, cannot be underestimated in the development of artists fresh from their initial encounters with galleries."

Of the four arts units, Cahill's project probably made the most lasting impression on the public' memory, thanks in part to the 2,566 murals and 17,744 sculptures FAP artists placed in public spaces across the country. There were murals in the town hall of Danvers, Massachusetts, the New York Public Library, the rotunda of the Utah State Capitol in Salt Lake, and San Francisco's Coit Tower; the fifteen-foot *Smoke Signal* cement sculpture in Lincoln, Nebraska's Pioneer Park; the Muses of music, dance, and drama erected in granite at the gates to the Hollywood Bowl (by George Stanley, also the sculptor of the Oscar statuette). But the project's most important legacy may be a scholarly endeavor—the Index of American Design (now part of the collection of the National Gallery of Art), a heroic effort to preserve the nation's heritage of craftsmanship through eighteen thousand watercolor renderings of such folk objects as dolls, furniture, pottery, textiles, toys, cigar store figures, and clothing.

The Writers' Project was headed by an appropriately rumpled former editorial writer for the then liberal *New York Post* named Henry Alsberg, who had been working for Hopkins as an editor of relief agency newsletters. He was judged "an anarchistic sort of a fellow incapable of administration but one with a great deal of creative talent," which made him sound to Hopkins like someone who might keep the Writers' Project output elevated above mediocrity without pressing its obstreperous staff too hard.

Alsberg wrestled with the question of how to define *writer,* a term that could embrace doggerel poets, advertising copywriters, and newspaper scribes, as well as novelists of transcendent craftsmanship. Since the number of available nonfiction and technical writers vastly outstripped writers of real refinement, he decided to unify his motley staff by focusing them on a single overarching project. The result would be the WPA Guides, a monumental collection of 152 state, local, and city guidebooks amounting to what the critic Lewis Mumford called "the first attempt, on a comprehensive scale, to make the country itself worthily known to Americans." This "biggest literary job ever undertaken" (in *Time*'s words) would stand as an antidote to Americans' tendency to "whizz over the surface of their country, picking up such information as they can get from signboards, gasoline station attendants, road maps, Chamber of Commerce handouts."

The guides were uneven in merit—indeed, their prose quality often varied from page to page, depending on whether an entry was produced by a committee or an individual writer, or by an inspired writer or a hack. Some local administrators faced the dilemma of identifying enough qualified writers to meet their staff quota. In Minnesota, Mabel S. Ulrich, a physician and author of a book on sexual hygiene, was installed as head of the Writers' Project and instructed to hire 250 writers in ten days. "Was it possible . . . that we could have that many mute inglorious authors" in a state that was still 50 percent agrarian? she wondered. "It didn't seem likely." In state relief files she found the cards of a few ex–newspaper writers, added a few teacher's college graduates and advertising writers, and began interviewing. "There were preachers, lawyers, executives, and editors mostly of country papers. . . . There was a graduate from the University of Edinburgh and a Ph.D. from Munich . . . a colored woman physician, and a writer of vaudeville skits. . . . All had 'written a little.' " She filled out her staff largely by defining *writer* very broadly.

In New York City, the problem was an abundance of qualified—even overqualified—writers and a dearth of what they considered suitable projects. The Polish immigrant novelist Anzia Yezierska was assigned to count the trees in Central Park for the New York guide. Poet Harry Roskolenko earned twenty-three dollars a week to produce "a maritime history of New York, a labor history, and a skiing guide," all based entirely on research at the New York Public Library's main branch on Forty-Second Street. When not so occupied he hung out at a Third Avenue cafeteria with a glittering group of relief recipients that included Richard Wright, John Cheever, Lionel Abel, and Philip Rahv. They all shouldered assignments "out of a weekly grab-bag," but some handled them in better cheer than others. A young unemployed newspaperman with literary aspirations wandered disconsolately about the Bronx, copying down street names for a planned street map of the borough.

> Exhausted by the deadening of his spiritual side [Roskolenko recalled], the abject wandering poet came to his supervisor orating, "If you don't take me off that mundane project, I'm going to commit suicide! I, who have dedicated my whole life to poetry, prefer death to a new street map of the Bronx!" His sole published work, then, was one small poem—an ode to a goat in the Bronx Zoo.

The supervisors were not entirely philistine. Toward the end of the project they decided to launch a "creative section," and allowed several writers to shed their more utilitarian assignments and stay home to write. Granted the WPA's forbearance, Wright used the time and its wages to complete his masterpiece, *Native Son.* Nor was he the only one; Auden, a friend of Yezierska, observed years later that "it is easy . . . for the artists to sneer at [the WPA] for its bureaucracy, but the fact remains that, thanks to it, a number of young artists of talent were enabled, at a very critical time in their lives, to get started on their creative careers."

Given Hallie Flanagan's background, it was almost preordained that the Federal Theatre Project would become the most inventive and popular unit of Federal One. Born Hallie Ferguson in South Dakota in 1890, she had settled with her family in Grinnell, Iowa, and earned a degree from the college and then a teaching position in theater before moving to George Pierce Baker's pioneering playwriting program at Harvard in 1923. Three years later she received the first Guggenheim Foundation grant ever awarded to a woman, for a survey tour of European theater. The tour ultimately brought her to the Soviet Union, where she discovered a flourishing vernacular theater helping to mold a new society. She returned to the United States and a position as director of the Vassar College Experimental Theatre, where in 1931 she cowrote and produced a milepost of Thirties drama. This was the documentary play *Can You Hear Their Voices,* which depicted the struggles of southern dirt farmers to survive drought in the face of congressional indifference—"searing, biting, smashing propaganda," as the playwright Emmet Lavery described it for the *New York Times.*

Flanagan was determined to use the Federal Theatre to test what she had learned abroad about developing a people's theater. Conferring with Elmer Rice, the expressionist playwright she persuaded to become the project's New York coordinator, she hit upon staging a series of "living newspapers." These were to be inexpensive, bare-bones productions—"just living actors, light, music, movement"—based upon the most attention-grabbing headlines of the moment, transferring the immediacy of the newspaper in a straphanger's hand directly to the stage.

The idea appealed to Rice, who had melded surrealism and stark realism into uncompromising portrayals of contemporary life for his stage successes *The Adding Machine* (1923) and the Pulitzer Prize–winning *Street Scene* (1929). Rice had not been an easy man to snare—he insisted on reporting solely to Flanagan so he would be insulated from any political second-guessing from Washington. His was a brittle personality, and at the first sign of interference from above it was bound to shatter.

Flanagan launched her program with a speech to the project's regional directors on October 5, 1935. The venue was WPA headquarters—Washington's Evalyn McLean mansion, where agency employees surrounded by priceless furnishings clattered away on typewriters and kept phone lines humming. Taking her cue from the ornate European accoutrements, Flanagan argued forcibly that the time had come for an indigenous and vernacular art, its value measured not by its market value but its enrichment of the communal soul. "Behind us, hidden by a discreet panel, there is a carved wood serving table, imported from Italy, which cost

$25,000. . . . The hideousness of the chandeliers in the great ballroom, the busts and statues in the court, the gold faucet on the gigantic bathtubs, are only equaled by their excessive cost." She called for an end to an "American culture in which the value of a work of art [is] measured in terms of its cost and the distance from which it was imported . . . the conception of art as a commodity to be purchased by the rich, possessed by the rich, and shared on occasional Wednesday evenings with the populace."

Americans would no longer be satisfied viewing great art at a distance or being fobbed off by the third-rate, she declared. They had been educated by the cinema and radio to recognize quality, and the fresh start afforded the theater by its share of the WPA budget could provide it. She left her listeners with an exhortation from Hopkins ringing in their ears: "We were to bend our energies toward creating theater units which would be so vital to community needs that they would continue to function after our funds are withdrawn." Theater could change society, she told them, relating that not many years before she had seen "the faces of Stalin, Litvinov, Lunacharsky, Petrov and other leaders" reflected from the walls of the Hall of Mirrors of the czars' Peterhof Palace as they discussed how a proletarian theater "could serve in educating the people and in enriching their lives." No one could say Hallie Flanagan lacked dramatic flair.

The first production mounted by the Federal Theatre in New York was its most elementary: a circus, staged at a Brooklyn armory arena in October 1935—the production inherited from Hopkins's FERA program and thus ready for launch with a ringmaster, clowns, acrobats, and a few animal acts, though no elephants, Flanagan explained in the playbill, because "none were on relief."

Production already was gearing up for the inaugural Living Newspaper. The most compelling subject at hand was Mussolini's invasion of Ethiopia, which had begun in the first days of October. Battles between the Italian army and troops loyal to Ethiopian Emperor Haile Selassie raged well into the new year. That kept the conflict boiling on the front pages, although Rice and Flanagan had another reason for making the war their first subject: a troupe of African musicians stranded in New York after an unsuccessful tour had fortuitously become wards of the Federal Theatre. "Now they were to beat drums, sing, and shout in the courtyard of Haile Selassie," Flanagan decreed.

Then a producer made a blunder that almost ended the Living Newspaper before it could be born. With the idea of assembling the script from the actual words of the participants in the conflict, he sought permission from Washington to quote from a speech by FDR. The White House, alerted to the intention of a government program to depict heads of state in a way that might suggest the United States was taking an official position on their words or deeds, promptly disallowed the "impersonation of a ruler or cabinet officer" onstage without advance approval of the State Department. Plainly, *Ethiopia* could not proceed as planned.

Rice threatened to resign (not for the first time in his brief tenure), despite Flanagan's argument that the government policy was not so unreasonable under the circumstances. This time his resignation was accepted with alacrity by Hopkins's deputy, Jacob Baker. Rice issued a statement charging the government with censorship and with playing a "shabby game of partisan politics at the expense of freedom and the principles of democracy" and departed, quite likely inspiring a few sighs of relief in New York at the removal of his obstreperous personality. The Federal Theatre acquired the first glimmer of a reputation, however unfair, for radicalism.

Taken as a whole, the hallmark of the Federal Theatre was not radicalism but diversity. On its stages, experimentation rubbed shoulders with the comfortably familiar, the avant-garde with the stolidly traditional, the frivolous with the somber. Within a few weeks of Rice's resignation, the program staged productions of the English medieval morality play *Everyman*, T. S. Eliot's *Murder in the Cathedral*, and the Yiddish folk drama *The Idle Inn*. The lineup for that March included, finally, the first Living Newspaper, *Triple-A Plowed Under*, which dealt pointedly and by no means timidly with the farm crisis, taking as its dramatic climax the nullification of the AAA by the Supreme Court that January. The New York theater critics reacted to the presentation with some surprise, considering that it was "obviously loaded with a charge of controversial dynamite," in the words of the anonymous reviewer for the *New York Times*. The simple and economical staging, dictated by Flanagan, set the pattern for future Living Newspapers dealing with the power industry, labor conflicts, social diseases, and unemployment.

Flanagan's most audacious project was the simultaneous premiere on October 27, 1936, of twenty-one productions of a play based on Sinclair Lewis's 1935 antifascist novel *It Can't Happen Here*, which tells the story of a homegrown dictator, based transparently on Huey Long. The origin of the idea to open the play on the same night in seventeen states (Louisiana was dropped from the schedule in sensitivity over Long's assassination) is murky, but it was instantly embraced by Flanagan. The weeks leading up to opening night were frenetic, with Lewis and a coauthor rushing to complete the dramatization despite no longer being on speaking terms while troupes in large cities and small struggled with the unfinished playscript. The press pondered the ramifications of coast-to-coast openings exactly one week before the 1936 presidential election. "Some people thought the play was designed to re-elect Mr. Roosevelt," Flanagan recalled; "others thought it was planned in order to defeat him. Some thought it proved Federal Theatre was communistic; others that it was New Deal; others that it was subconsciously fascist." Some detected irony in the fact that Lewis's work had been spurned by every studio in a Hollywood notoriously leery of provoking the government, only to be tackled by a government agency operating with taxpayer funds.

Flanagan felt energized by the thought of a single play given individualized spin in twenty-one separate locations at once, truly unifying the Federal Theatre in its diversity. In Seattle the drama was handled by the city's Negro Theatre unit; in Birmingham, Alabama, it was staged as a political convention, with bunting on the set and a brass band stationed in the boxes; in New York there was a Spanish-language production and another in Yiddish. On opening night there were critical kudos for almost every production except New York's English-language staging, which critics panned as insufficiently electrifying. Flanagan calculated that *It Can't Happen Here* in all its multifarious guises ultimately played for the equivalent of 260 weeks, or five years.

Hallie Flanagan's inclusive conception of national theater encouraged the formation of numerous ethnic and foreign-language units under her program's umbrella. The most important of these, the Negro Theatre Project in New York, would bring together for their first extended collaboration two men who would become the provocateurs of the program's worst crisis, John Houseman and Orson Welles.

To lead the Negro Theatre, Flanagan originally paired the distinguished black actress Rose McClendon with Houseman, a thirty-three-year-old theatrical producer and director with numerous artistic successes on his résumé. Houseman, born Jacques Haussmann in Bucharest, Romania, would later recall with mixed relief and amazement how in the haste and confusion of the project's founding he had managed to be placed on the federal payroll without anyone discovering that he was living in the United States illegally and under a false name.

Houseman and McClendon (who soon stepped down because of poor health) struggled to navigate the shoals of political and artistic contention within the Harlem community, where the project was headquartered. They scorned the custom of restaging Broadway hits with black casts as "undesirable, if not downright offensive," as would be the revival of such "Negro" successes written by whites as Eugene O'Neill's *The Emperor Jones* and DuBose Heyward's *Porgy*, which recently had been reconfigured by George Gershwin into *Porgy and Bess.*

Houseman suggested organizing the Negro Theatre partially along the lines of his 1934 staging of the Virgil Thomson/Gertrude Stein opera *Four Saints in Three Acts,* which featured an all-black cast selected for their artistic abilities alone in a work devoid of specifically Negro themes. He proposed the formation of two separate but interrelated companies: one presenting plays written, directed, and played by Negroes for Negro audiences; the other staging classic works interpreted by black performers, without the condescension of an overtly "Negro" spin. He demanded that the professionalism of both units be of the highest order.

But his next step instantly undermined the purity of his conception. He placed the classical troupe in the hands of Orson Welles, who promptly conceived a *Macbeth* to be set on the island of Haiti, the witches reconceived as voodoo priestesses. The production would be one of the most spectacular successes in the Federal Theatre's short history, with a propulsive effect on the careers of its two white impresarios.

The working relationship between Houseman and the twenty-year-old Welles was yet in its infancy, encompassing a single theater production that had run for three performances in 1935. Four decades later Houseman would still remember his first backstage meeting with Welles after the latter's bravura performance on Broadway as Tybalt in *Romeo and Juliet*—his first sight of the actor without the false noses and heavy makeup he favored onstage. "I could see his features now, finally: the pale pudding face with the violent black eyes, the button nose with the wen to one side of it and the deep runnel meeting the well-shaped mouth over the astonishingly small teeth . . . and the voice that made people turn at the neighboring tables—startled not so much by its loudness as by its surprising vibration." The summons to Harlem, of course, was not to Welles the actor but Welles the theatrical prodigy.

While Welles rehearsed the company of what was presently labeled the "Voodoo *Macbeth*," Houseman sought out a property to distinguish the indigenous side of the Negro Theatre Project from what was bound to be a provocative launch of its classical unit. His choice was *Walk Together Chillun!*, a pastoral oratorio by Frank Wilson, a prominent black actor who had created the character of Porgy in Heyward's stage play. The play was, in Houseman's judgment, "an awkward hodgepodge of theatrical clichés . . . that could offend absolutely no one." It got the nod for "tactical reasons," and thanks to the cancellation of *Ethiopia,* opened on February 6 as the WPA's first production in New York City, running for several weeks to moderate houses.

Macbeth opened on April 14, at once a landmark theatrical production and a community event. Flanagan recorded a jumble of impressions from inside and outside Harlem's Lafayette Theatre, the project's home stage: "Flash of ten thousand people clogging the streets, following the scarlet and gold bands of the Negro Elks, marking with flying banners bearing the strange device: *Macbeth by Wm. Shakespeare*—flash of police holding back the crowds, of newsreel men grinding their cameras. . . . Inside, African drums beat, Lady Macbeth walked on the edge of a jungle throbbing with sinister life. . . . Macbeth, pierced by a bullet, took his terrific headlong plunge from the balustrade." *Macbeth* played uptown all summer, then moved to Broadway for two months more—very much Hallie Flanagan's ideal of classical art transformed into vernacular theater.

Following *Macbeth*'s success, Houseman and Welles were both itching to move on from Harlem. Flanagan listened receptively to Houseman's proposal to create a classical theater program downtown for the Federal Theatre. In the fall of 1936, she gave him the green light. He and Welles mapped out an ambitious program for what was designated WPA Project #891. The first production would be a knockabout farce based on a French trifle titled *The Italian Straw Hat*—rechristened *Horse Eats Hat* for Federal Theatre audiences—to be followed by Christopher Marlowe's *Tragical History of Doctor Faustus. Horse Eats Hat* proved a popular confection, bright and broad; *Doctor Faustus* a triumph of artistic interpretation and technical stagecraft under Welles's rapidly maturing hand. The latter would run to full houses for four months at the project's midtown home, the nine-hundred-seat Maxine Elliott Theatre. Among its eighty thousand paying customers was Harry Hopkins, who inconspicuously took a seat one night in the back of the hall, where he was recognized by an observant manager.

Houseman escorted him backstage after the curtain to meet Welles, who was lying half conscious on a sofa, still gasping in a clammy sweat from the rigors of the title character's climactic descent into hell. Hopkins asked only one question: were they having a good time on the Federal Theatre? "We told him we were," Houseman recalled.

The fun was about to end.

Political storm clouds were gathering nationwide, some of them lowering on Federal One's horizon. A new wave of labor unrest had arrived in late 1936, including a rash of sit-down strikes in the auto industry. The sit-down was a novel weapon that employers found especially obnoxious: instead of picketing on the streets outside a factory, workers downed tools and commandeered the production floor, hampering the deployment of strikebreakers. The week that *Doctor Faustus* opened, sit-down strikes shuttered seven major auto plants and an organizing drive began in the steel industry. In that atmosphere, Welles proposed as Project 891's next production an opera about a steel strike written by a gifted but openly Marxist composer named Marc Blitzstein. The opera was titled *The Cradle Will Rock,* and it would make theatrical history by failing to open.

Marcus Samuel Blitzstein had been born in 1905 into a middle-class family of modest leftist leanings in Philadelphia, where he won local fame as a child prodigy on the piano. In 1926 he moved to Paris to study with the renowned conductor and teacher Nadia Boulanger. There he married Eva Goldbeck, a ferociously Marxist literary critic who would be his last heterosexual partner. Through her, Blitzstein was introduced to Bertolt Brecht and other members of Berlin's cultural avant-garde. Blitzstein's output had been sparse but accomplished, including a short opera based on the case of Sacco and Vanzetti (*The Condemned*). One day in 1935, he played a song titled "Nickel Under the Foot" for Brecht. The bitter plaint of a young woman forced to sell herself sexually to ward off starvation, the song prompted Brecht to suggest, "Why don't you write a piece about all forms of prostitution—the press, the church, the courts, the arts, the whole system?" The remark planted the seed for *The Cradle Will Rock.*

Blitzstein started writing *Cradle* in late 1936 in an attempt to dispel his grief after Eva's death, from an implacable case of psychotic anorexia. Once started, he carried the project through "at white heat," finishing a full-length, ten-scene comic opera in five weeks. The work employed a highly varied musical palette, ranging from college chants and snatches of classical symphony to jazz and sophisticated modernism, to tell the story of Steeltown, U.S.A., on the eve of an industrial strike. The town's whores, workingmen, cops, industrialists, and society matrons connive against one another in the setting of a night court, where a group of town leaders marching against the unionization of the steel mill have been hauled before a judge after their mistaken arrest as union agitators. All Brecht's "prostitutes" are represented: crass reporters, crooked judges, a sanctimonious preacher, artists truckling to their patroness. Blitzstein's libretto is satirical and rock-hard, with a huge cast of twenty-nine characters.

Back in New York, Blitzstein licensed the work to the Actors' Repertory Company, a leftist group that had recently staged Irwin Shaw's antiwar play *Bury the Dead*. The company announced *Cradle* for its 1936–37 season and secured a commitment to direct from Orson Welles. But the winter of 1936 was a hard season for independent troupes, and the Actors' Repertory Company went out of business. Welles and Houseman jumped at the chance to transfer *Cradle* to Project 891, summoning Hallie Flanagan to a private performance at the apartment Houseman shared with Virgil Thomson. Flanagan found herself swept up by Blitzstein's "hard hypnotic drive" as he played, sang, and acted his show. "It took no wizardry to see that this was not a play set to music, nor music illustrated by actors, but music + play equalling something new and better than either," she recalled. "This was in its percussive as well as its verbal beat Steel Town U.S.A: street corner, mission, lawn of Mr. Mister [the mill owner], drugstore, hotel lobby . . . America, 1937."

Flanagan agreed to a staging of *Cradle,* which she thought would fit comfortably within Project 891's tight budget. Houseman would produce, Welles would direct, "and I didn't see why they needed any scenery." She failed to reckon with Welles's grandiose conceptualization, which would involve towering illuminated sets on sliding platforms. By the time the production's exploding costs became an issue, she would be embroiled in a greater crisis, for WPA's enabling legislation would be coming up in May for renewal in Congress, which was of a mood to cut its budget by a third.

Yet even at the start she expressed a few misgivings about the piece's political content. "She's crazy about it," Blitzstein wrote to his parents following the audition, "and is also terrified about it for the Project. So she'll take no responsibility, but is having us—I, John Houseman, and Orson Welles—fly down to Washington to show the work to Harry Hopkins. . . . I've apparently turned out a firebrand that nobody wants to touch." Houseman suspected that Flanagan, fully alive to *Cradle*'s provocative, prolabor theme, opted to go full speed ahead on the curious theory that with the arts programs already coming under political pressure "there was no safety in prudence and no virtue in caution." This viewpoint may have occurred to him only in hindsight; no independent evidence exists that Washington was then any more concerned with the political content of *The Cradle Will Rock* than it had been with any other Federal Theatre production, perhaps excepting *Ethiopia*. The House Un-American Activities Committee of Representative Martin Dies, which would mount a concerted political assault on Federal One with the work of the Federal Theatre as its Exhibit A, would not even exist for another year.

In Chicago, the location of the biggest mill of Republic Steel Corporation, the nation's third-largest steelmaker, a battle between picketers and police took place on Memorial Day 1937. It would go down in labor history for its sheer violence. "They charged like a bunch of demons," one worker would recall of the moment of attack by the Chicago police. "No one had a chance in the world." Ten picketers were killed by gunfire, seven of them shot in the back. The melee broke the momentum of the steelworkers' organizing campaign against the independent steel companies known collectively as Little Steel (to distinguish them from United States Steel, which was "Big Steel"). Worse from the union's standpoint, the Roosevelt administration refused to take a direct role in mediating the conflict. The workers would not prevail for another seventeen months, or until the National Labor Relations Board concluded a marathon investigation of the Republic Steel strike by ordering the reinstatement of seven thousand workers with back pay. Meanwhile, the Memorial Day riot heightened anxieties within the Federal Theatre Project over *The Cradle Will Rock*. "Mrs. F is getting scared all over again," Blitzstein wrote a friend on June 2. "I suspect *The Cradle* will be suppressed before it opens." WPA headquarters in Washington dispatched an envoy to view the production. To the relief of Flanagan and Blitzstein, he "pronounced it magnificent."

Yet the atmosphere continued to darken. All of Federal One was ordered on June 10 to institute nationwide budget cuts; a 30 percent cut in New York meant the dismissal of 1,701 staff workers. A harsher blow for the arts programs came on June 12: because of the budget crisis, no new play, musical performance, or art gallery would be permitted to open until July 1 at the earliest. Flanagan, Blitzstein, Houseman, and Welles leaped to the conclusion that their show was the order's real target. "This was obviously censorship in a different guise," Flanagan commented. *Cradle* was scheduled to open for previews, for which fourteen thousand tickets had been sold, in four days.

Yet the truth was that under normal circumstances postponing the production would not have been difficult or even, for a Welles play, unusual. "Orson and I were not noted for our punctuality," Houseman conceded. *Macbeth* had been postponed five times, *Horse Eats Hat* twice, *Doctor Faustus* thrice—and *Cradle* already once. Indeed, *Cradle's* company had persistent problems dealing with Welles's monumental stage machinery and coordinating with an entirely new feature of a Welles production, a twenty-eight-piece orchestra.

Although it is unclear whether Welles and Houseman genuinely believed that the postponement order was a pretext for killing *The Cradle Will Rock*, certainly they were fully alive to the dramatic possibilities of flouting the WPA in plain view of the New York press. On June 15 they telephoned around to friends and VIPs in the city, issuing invitations to that evening's final dress rehearsal—intimating that this might be the only chance to see *The Cradle Will Rock* onstage. The hastily assembled audience, which included such theater notables as George S. Kaufman and Moss Hart, was treated to a decidedly ragged performance in which the actors struggled to be heard over the blaring orchestra. The stunt got a rise out of the WPA, but perhaps not the one the impresarios anticipated: the very next morning, uninformed guards were stationed at the theater, blocking all entryways except one opening into a ladies' powder room in the basement. Welles, Blitzstein, Houseman, and a few others huddled there to plot their next move.

Welles would later maintain that he had been prepared to accept the postponement—until the guards appeared: "I wasn't sure that we weren't wrecking the Federal Theatre by what we were doing. But I thought if you padlock a theater, the argument is closed. . . . The padlock was an insult. That's what unified everybody." Houseman would add a more considered, and perhaps more candid, recollection: he and Welles understood that their days with the Federal Theatre were numbered, largely because they had achieved all they thought possible under the government's aegis. "We had served it well and had, in the process, made reputations such as we could not possibly have achieved elsewhere. Having nothing further to gain, we might as well make our departure as explosive and dramatic as possible."

After a frantic search, they identified a theater to which they could move the production, available for the rent of one hundred dollars for the night. At that point, the producers of this frankly prolabor play came close to being confounded by a union obstacle, for Actors Equity decreed that as *Cradle* remained the property of the Federal Theatre, Equity members were forbidden to appear in it onstage in any other venue. More hours in conference followed, yielding a makeshift solution: cast members would not appear onstage, but seat themselves in the audience. When their cues came, they would rise to their feet, speaking or singing their parts "as U.S. citizens," Houseman explained. Many in the company fretted that this act of defiance might cost them their desperately needed WPA stipends of twenty-eight dollars a week. How many of the company would follow their producers into the theatrical and economic unknown would be a mystery until the curtain rose.

At 6 P.M., Houseman and Welles left the Maxine Elliott to lead the cast and crew and an army of ticketholders by bus, taxi, subway, and on foot twenty blocks uptown to the Venice Theatre on Fifty-Ninth Street, where *The Cradle Will Rock* was to be performed at 9 P.M. Inside the dusty, underused Venice, a spotlight was clamped to a balcony rail and trained on the stage, from which Blitzstein would play his score on an upright piano. At the appointed hour, Houseman and Welles strode out onstage together. Houseman delivered a few brief remarks to the effect that the company was engaged in an act of artistic, not political, defiance. He turned the floor over to Welles, whose sonorous voice described the production the audience might have seen if not for "the Cossacks of the WPA"—evoking sympathetic jeers from the audience. Then he set the scene and described the characters.

From behind the curtain, Blitzstein, seated at his piano in shirtsleeves and suspenders, heard "an enormous buzz of talk in the theater." The curtain rose. He looked out at a hall jammed to the rafters, its side aisles lined with newsreel cameramen and photographers. Not knowing how many of the actors had chosen to follow Welles uptown, he placed his fingers on the keyboard, "ready to do the whole show myself." He sounded the opening chords and began voicing the first words of the opening number, the plaint of the struggling prostitute Moll—"*For two days out of seven / two dollar bills I'm given. . . .* "—when he suddenly heard his words echoed by Olive Stanton, the actress playing Moll, a thin girl in a green dress and dyed red hair rising to her feet in a front box, presently sought out and lit by the lone spotlight in the house.

"If Olive Stanton had not risen on cue in the box, I doubt if the rest of us would have had the courage to stand up and carry on," a cast member recalled. But she did, launching a theatrical legend. With its spare storyline and uncompromising message, *The Cradle Will Rock* might have been overwhelmed by Welles's extravagant staging and full orchestra. In the Venice Theatre, with the characters seated among the spectators awaiting their cues, accompanied solely by Blitzstein's percussive piano, the immediacy of the setting and the immediacy of the work merged in nearly perfect harmony.

Welles made one final effort to open *Cradle* under WPA auspices, flying to Washington the morning after the triumphant performance at the Venice. His intention was to plead personally with Hopkins to lift the ban. Hopkins, perhaps wisely, dodged the hyperactive director, fobbing him off on an underling named David Niles and Federal One administrator Ellen Woodward. They tried to pacify Welles with the observation that the production had not been canceled, merely postponed, adding that *Cradle* was hardly the only show facing the same predicament. "We get letters in not from New York alone but all over the country," a harassed Niles told him. Welles replied that if the postponement were not rescinded, he might open *Cradle* with private backing. Niles called his bluff: "In that case we would no longer be interested in it as a property." In other words, Welles would have to comply with the postponement, or give up on a WPA *Cradle* altogether.

Welles returned to New York, where he and Houseman, taking advantage of a moment of supreme serendipity, announced that the play would continue its run at the Venice, with the actors continuing to sing their parts from the seats with piano accompaniment from the stage. "There has always been the question of how to produce a labor show so the audience can be brought to feel that it is a part of the performance," Houseman explained. "This technique seems to solve the problem."

Cradle ran for two weeks. Their high-profile gunfight with the WPA helped launch Houseman and Welles on their brilliant careers. From the wreckage of the WPA *Cradle* rose their Mercury Theatre, soon to create sensations of its own with a radio broadcast of *War of the Worlds* and the film *Citizen Kane*. Hallie Flanagan would later express a certain bemusement, if not resentment, at what might be regarded as their exploitation of the Federal Theatre. "Probably it was worth a case of censorship," she wrote, "to launch a group of our most brilliant directors and actors with a play for which the cast and rehearsal time had been provided, as well as an audience and a springboard for publicity."

Changing fiscal and political attitudes in Washington toward the arts programs made all the Federal One directors uneasy. The music project's director, Nikolai Sokoloff, chose as a survival strategy the introduction of a hyperpatriotic approach to programming. Local FMP orchestras made sure to include a rendition of "The Battle Hymn of the Republic" along with the great masters; acceptably mainstream American composers like Sousa and Foster showed up more frequently on the playbills. Flanagan took no such steps. Around the time that *Cradle* was driven uptown to the Venice, WPA bureaucrats closed down the *Federal Theatre Magazine,* which had evolved from a mimeographed leaflet into a repository of solid dramatic criticism. There was talk in Congress of communist influence among its editors and of Marxist references in its articles. "Literary allusions are dangerous things in Washington," Flanagan concluded. The *Federal Theatre Magazine*'s "economic, racial, and social point of view, in line with administration and WPA policies in 1935, was considered inimical in 1937." Flanagan recognized the complaints about the journal and the furor over *The Cradle Will Rock* as harbingers of what was in store for the Federal Theatre. Things would soon get worse.

15

THE MOST FORGOTTEN MAN

I N MAY 1935, Howard University and a coalition of Negro advocacy
groups staged a three-day conference to assess the New Deal's impact
on black Americans. The attendees' judgment was somber. The black
community's hopes that Franklin Roosevelt would be the man to deliver on
the nation's promise to all Americans were being dashed.

Two years after Roosevelt's inauguration, Negro workers still bore three
to four times their share of unemployment and received much less than
their share of relief. The black community had been marginalized within
the spheres of influence of both the NRA and AAA; unemployed black
workers faced stringent quotas on New Deal work relief programs, and
those who obtained jobs were shortchanged in wages by New Deal pay
policies; black families consistently were barred from New Deal residential
communities. Although the federal government had projected itself into
many areas of responsibility formerly left to state and local authorities,
racial justice was not among them. The conference reported: "As far as the
Negro is concerned, New Deal social planning generally has availed him
little either because of its underlying philosophy, or because its administration has been delegated to local officials who reflect the unenlightened
mores of their respective communities."

The policies of the Hoover administration had all but ended six decades
of black loyalty to the Republican Party dating back to Lincoln and Reconstruction—the mirror image of the "Solid South" of white voter loyalty to
the Democrats. "The indictment which Americans of Negro descent have

against Herbert Hoover is long, and to my mind, unanswerable," W. E. B. Du Bois had written in his monthly magazine, *The Crisis,* immediately prior to the 1932 election. Du Bois's indictment encompassed Hoover's inaction in the face of attacks on Negro voting rights in the South; his appointment of William Doak, the head of a militantly whites-only union (the Brotherhood of Railroad Trainmen), as secretary of labor; and his failure to support an antilynching law in Congress although fifty-seven Negroes had been lynched during his term. There was also a long string of casual racial slights: the Hoover White House had sent black Gold Star mothers on separate ships with inferior accommodations to visit their fallen sons' graves in Europe and made fewer appointments of Negroes to top administrative posts than "any President since Andrew Johnson." Hoover, Du Bois wrote, "adopted into the program of the 'Lily-Whites,' and sought to disenfranchise Negroes in the councils of the Republican Party."

The heart of Du Bois's brief, however, was Hoover's failure to address the Depression. The crisis struck with particular force at the black community, which barely had a foothold on even the lowest rung of the economic ladder. In 1930 most American blacks lived in the South. Although almost two-thirds worked in the agricultural sector, fewer than one in five owned their own land. The rest were sharecroppers or day laborers; as a group they earned the lowest income of any workers in the United States. They were ruthlessly misused by their landlords, denied capital or credit, and deprived of decent machinery, electricity, or irrigation water. Less than 1 percent of all farm owners in the South had an income of $1,500 or more in 1932, and less than 8 percent earned $500. Black sharecroppers and tenants could not hope to touch even a fraction of those sums. The Negro farmer, observed an agricultural expert of the Thirties, was "hedged about by the encircling factors of history, geography, occupation, race, and class." In the industrial sector the picture was every bit as grim: black workers tended to belong to the unskilled class and were therefore condemned to be the lowest-paid workers, the most dispensable, and the most vulnerable to mechanization.

The Depression destroyed their precarious foothold on subsistence in both sectors. Black sharecroppers were displaced by poor whites dispossessed from their own farms or fleeing poverty in the cities. Blacks who migrated north were barred from many jobs in industry, even as the stepped-up pace of mechanization accelerated the contraction of job listings. Black workers were the last to be hired and the first to be fired, often to make room for downwardly-mobile white laborers. As industrial workers of all grades moved down the employment ladder, black workers were forced off the ladder entirely—thrown out of even modest jobs. A department store in Newark, New Jersey, avoided laying off sales clerks by reducing some of them to elevator operators, displacing blacks from the only job classification that had been open to them. At the height of the Depression, the nation's overall unemployment rate was estimated to be 25 percent. Among black workers it was more than 50 percent—as high as 75 percent in some cities.

Yet the Negro community was slow to transfer its allegiance to the Democratic Party. In the 1932 election, black voters in the industrialized cities of the North and Midwest gave Herbert Hoover a majority, in some places as large as 82 percent. But black leaders were shifting toward support of Franklin Roosevelt. In the vanguard was Robert L. Vann, the influential publisher of the *Pittsburgh Courier,* a black newspaper with 70,000 subscribers. Vann had been approached during the presidential campaign by the Pittsburgh oilman Michael Benedum, a Democratic financier who believed that Pennsylvania's 181,000 registered black voters might be crucial to swinging his state to the Democratic column. He asked Vann point-blank: "What have the Negroes ever got by voting the Republican ticket?"

The answer was nothing, Vann preached to a standing-room crowd in a Cleveland church one Sunday. "I see in the offing a horde of black men and women throwing off the yoke of partisanship practiced for over half a century," he declared. "I see millions of Negroes turning the pictures of Abraham Lincoln to the wall. This year I see Negroes voting a Democratic ticket."

Yet the Roosevelt campaign did little to make the transition compelling. Issues of race or racial justice had no place in the Democratic platform and no part in the candidate's speeches. (Civil rights received a single paragraph in the GOP platform, which declared that the party "stands pledged to maintain equal opportunity and rights for Negro citizens.") A questionnaire prepared by the National Association for the Advancement of Colored People seeking the candidates' views on racial issues, including disenfranchisement, discrimination in the civil service and on federal construction projects, and segregation in the armed forces, went unanswered by Roosevelt and Hoover alike. Benedum's insight aside, the Negro vote was judged unimportant in the North and, justifiably, almost nonexistent in the South, where local poll regulations disenfranchised all but a paltry few thousand black voters. The paragon of racial sensitivity in the Roosevelt family circle was Eleanor Roosevelt, whose antidiscrimination activities would not always be greatly appreciated by her husband; in any case, during the 1932 campaign her influence regarding the issue plainly was negligible.

Despite all that, black Americans were swept up like so many others in the optimism that greeted Roosevelt's inauguration. In the early days of the New Deal, they had reason to believe that their concerns might at last be addressed from the White House. One positive sign was the appointment of Harold Ickes, a former president of the NAACP's Chicago chapter, as interior secretary. Soon after taking office, Ickes created the post of special advisor on Negro matters in his department, although the process of making the appointment underscored the political delicacy of race relations for the New Deal: to appease southern Democrats, he awarded the job to Clark Foreman, an outstanding civil rights advocate from Georgia, but a white man.

Foreman was fully alive to the absurdity of his appointment. "As I understand this job, the main thing that I would be supposed to do is get jobs for Negros," he recalled telling Ickes. "Well, one job that a Negro could certainly handle would be the one that I am taking, so it would seem that it would be much better for you to appoint a Negro than me."

"That may be true," Ickes replied, "but I don't know any Negro that I would give the job to, and if you don't take it I'll give it to another white man."

Foreman accepted the job, but insisted on appointing a black assistant. This was Robert C. Weaver, a Harvard-educated economist then teaching at a small North Carolina college. Weaver would eventually become the first black member of a presidential cabinet—but that would not happen until 1966, under Lyndon Johnson, when he was named secretary of the new Department of Housing and Urban Development.

Ickes also inserted a clause barring discrimination on racial or ethnic grounds in the standard contract of the Public Works Administration. As one of the cabinet secretaries involved in setting up the Civilian Conservation Corps, he surely played a role in imposing on the CCC's recruitment policy a prohibition against discrimination "on account of race, color, or creed."

One place Ickes failed to have any influence was on the construction site of Hoover Dam (which he renamed Boulder Dam). Although the high-profile project came under his departmental jurisdiction, the construction contract drafted by his predecessors in the Hoover administration gave the private contractors building the dam almost unassailable authority over the labor force. Black employment at the massive project averaged no more than a dozen at any one time, out of a workforce that sometimes exceeded five thousand men. When Ickes objected, reclamation commissioner Elwood Mead, the supervising government official and one of the drafters of the contract, informed him that, regrettably, there was nothing he could do to revise its terms.

Greater disappointments lay in store for the black community. The New Deal's alphabet agencies were all designed to lift up the economic condition of the working man—the "forgotten man," in New Deal parlance—but almost every program served to widen the gulf between white workers and black. The first hint of limitations in the New Deal's approach to delivering relief emerged with the very first New Deal relief program, the CCC.

Soon after recruitment began in April 1933, reports reached Frances Perkins of flagrant discrimination against black youths. In Clarke County, Georgia, about sixty miles northeast of Atlanta, not a single resident had been selected for the CCC although the county was 60 percent black. The same pattern was discovered statewide, provoking a long tussle between program coordinators in Washington and the CCC's local administrators in Georgia. The impasse was resolved only when Washington threatened Georgia's conspicuously racist governor, Eugene Talmadge, with the withdrawal of all CCC funding unless black youths were given a more representative share of CCC slots. That ended the logjam, but not by much: black CCC enrollment in Georgia improved, but never exceeded token levels.

Georgia was merely one battleground. In Florida, Arkansas, and Mississippi, local recruiters resisted selecting black workers and relented only begrudgingly, often after similar threats of the loss of their state allocations. Typically the remedy was modest. In Mississippi, where blacks made up 50 percent of the population, only forty-six young men were recruited into the CCC, accounting for 1.7 percent of its enrollment. Complaints about discrimination flowed into the White House from black sources ranging from the NAACP to families seeking slots. "If war was declared, would they pick all the white boys first and leave the negro boys as the last called for service? This is what they do in the CCC," observed a letter to the CCC. It was signed, "Just a Colored Mother."

The problems did not end with recruitment. No CCC camps were integrated, but all-black camps located near white communities provoked local protests against their mere presence. Nor were such objections limited to the South. One community in the Pocono Mountains of northeastern Pennsylvania petitioned the CCC to cancel the establishment of a black camp nearby on the grounds that local girls "just attaining youth and early womanhood . . . should not be exposed to dangers that are possible, if not indeed, probable" from "unattached Negro males."

The repeated uproars over black recruitment and black camps finally prompted CCC officials to consider ceasing all recruitment of black workers nationwide except to fill vacancies in existing black camps. The plan split the CCC leadership so deeply that the decision was bumped up to the President himself. Roosevelt, caught between saving his pet agency and avoiding racial provocation, especially in the politically crucial South, approved the policy but took pains to keep his intervention secret. Despite its formal prohibition against racial discrimination, the CCC ended up perpetuating that social malady—even augmenting it, for it provided one more path to relief for white families that was closed to blacks. Negro workers did not move into the CCC in increased numbers until late 1941, when the boom in military procurement drew white youths off into war industries, rendering black recruitment necessary to keep the program going. But the CCC shut down less than a year later.

It seemed that virtually every New Deal agency had its loophole to keep the Negro citizen underserved. The NRA perpetrated a cruel joke with its very first approved code, which governed the cotton textile industry. Because black laborers had been shouldered out of skilled classifications in this dominant industry of the deep South, their numbers tended to predominate in the worst-paid positions, as cleaners and members of outside crew gangs. Yet these were the first jobs lost when plants cut back production for economic reasons or to meet quotas in the code. Adding to the black workers' misery, the textile code contained no provisions for minimum hours or minimum wages for these humble jobs. "The group most in need of consideration was put off to the last," observed John P. Davis, a leading Negro activist of that time.

The indignities suffered by black laborers in textile plants and other industries were subtly condoned by the NRA. Some codes pegged wage rates to 1929, providing proportionately larger raises for those who had been paid wages above a given benchmark. This widened the racial wage differential, as blacks' wages typically had been below the benchmark. Even when codes provided for flat percentage increases across the board, black workers fell behind: the hotel code called for a 20 percent increase in all wages, but as Davis reported, that only meant that black bellboys received a 20 percent raise on salaries averaging $15 a month, while white clerks received theirs on salaries of $100 a month.

NRA officials answered complaints about unequal treatment by alluding to the culture and economic structure of the South. "NRA inherited the Negro problem," explained A. Howard Myers, an NRA official addressing the Howard University conference of May 1935. The mistreatment of black laborers in the region stemmed from "very hard, very concrete economic realities and they can't be eliminated from the world merely by a gesture of moral nausea." John P. Davis labeled this response "unpardonable sophistry."

The AAA provided the agricultural counterpoint to the NRA's treatment of black industrial workers. The black agricultural class was the most exploited group in America. The sharecropper or tenant status of 80 percent of black farmworkers guaranteed their nearly permanent subjugation. After every harvest the total crop was divided equally between landlord and farmer, a confiscatory ratio favoring the landlord, who had contributed no labor and often only minimal capital to the effort. The landlord further exploited the farmer through excessive prices for housing and equipment and usurious interest charges on loaned money or materials. The long farm depression gave landlords more incentive to mechanize their farms, which further marginalized the most marginal tenants. When domestic allocation payments began to flow from the AAA to compensate for acreage reductions, these were often appropriated by landlords rather than split equitably with the tenants; but supervision of the disbursements was left in the hands of local white officials, so the inequity was almost impossible to rectify from Washington. Through 1940, as many as two hundred thousand black farmers were driven off their land by the combination of the agricultural depression and the diversion of AAA payments by landlords. The economic path for most of these black workers and their families pointed down the economic scale, toward wage labor or dispossession and homelessness.

The one bright spot for the black community in this sector—and arguably in the entire New Deal—was the creation of the Resettlement Administration in 1935. Resettlement was the brainchild of Rexford Tugwell. As its administrator, Tugwell would run the RA with admirable color-blindness.

Tugwell faced daunting challenges in getting the new agency off the ground. He had conceived the RA to rationalize the New Deal's rural rehabilitation programs, which were scattered throughout the executive branch—some in Agriculture, some in Interior, some reporting directly to the White House. The task was to integrate all these programs while meeting the goals of putting people to work, removing them from substandard land, removing that land from cultivation, and reclaiming land that could be put into production. As Tugwell reflected, the idea "had logic; it was necessary; and the plan of operation seemed feasible." But he and President Roosevelt had not reckoned with the difficulty of operating a new agency without its own dedicated source of funding, for the RA had to rely on the original allotments for the programs it absorbed. Nor were they prepared for the hostility that a relief-and-relocation agency would engender in the agricultural zones. These factors, Tugwell recalled, "encouraged those who viewed all the New Deal 'experiments' with chilly disapproval to regard this one with especial venom."

As long as it continued in operation, the RA (later renamed the Farm Security Administration) pursued its goals energetically. Among its 150 rural projects were 115 all-white, 9 all-Negro, and 26 mixed-race communities. The model Negro project was located at Gee's Bend, a black community twenty miles south of Selma, Alabama, sequestered from its neighbors by an immense horseshoe bend of the Alabama River. Most of the bend's 115 Negro families were descendants of the slaves of an antebellum plantation that had occupied the site. They lived virtually in a world of their own except for the rare occasion when they were subjected to the scrutiny of a visiting writer, photographer, or anthropologist like exhibits in a museum. And they were destitute, victimized first by the collapse of cotton to 5 cents a pound, and then by the probate agents of the white merchant who had warehoused their cotton but died in 1931, leaving no records. The agents seized everything the farmers owned—their crops, livestock, equipment, household goods—except their derelict shacks. The residents survived that winter by picking wild plums and blackberries and killing squirrels by slingshot.

The Red Cross eventually shipped in subsistence supplies, but the community's condition did not improve until the Resettlement Administration arrived in 1936. The government gave the Gee's Bend residents "steers and seeds and some fertilizer, and they made a crop," recalled Will W. Alexander, the former (and first) president of Dillard University in New

Orleans, whom Tugwell had appointed as his right-hand man at Resettlement. "They did so well that the next year we helped them get their mules back. We finally decided to see what would happen if they got the land." In 1937 the agency bought more than ten thousand acres of Gee's Bend plantation land for $122,000, subdivided it into parcels, and turned it over to ninety-seven families on lease-purchase contracts with forty-year terms at 3 percent interest. The Resettlement Administration built barns, smokehouses, wells, and homes—which the oldest residents were still referring to, six decades later, as "Roosevelt houses." By 1940, Gee's Bend had been transformed into a thriving farm community of seven hundred residents.

The Resettlement Administration came closest of all the New Deal programs to achieving an equitable distribution of assistance, providing black tenants and sharecroppers with a share of benefits that closely matched their proportion among all southern farmers. Nonetheless it did operate under limitations imposed by the politics and the social pressures of its time and place. Even the mixed-race communities maintained segregated amenities; and with white residents always in the majority, the black voices were faint indeed. All-black settlements were generally established only after local communities were consulted. This precaution was applied even to the assistance offered to Gee's Bend, where emancipated black families had been living since the Civil War. Sometimes the agency was unwilling or unable to neutralize the indignities visited on black families resulting from their occupancy of the lowest socioeconomic tier of the region. Forty black families living as squatters on an undeveloped parcel acquired by the Interior Department's Division of Subsistence Homesteads—the office that had overseen communities such as Arthurdale before being folded into Tugwell's new agency—were given one week to vacate after Resettlement decided to revive the project in 1937. "The women folks knowed hardly what to do and we just went to cryen' and cryen'," a refugee recorded. The families were relocated onto forty worthless acres, reduced to living in shanties and shacks and hauling water from a distant stream, while white families in new houses supplanted them in their former community, now equipped with a sewage system, streets and sidewalks, and a central water supply.

The resettlement program was fated to be short-lived. As Tugwell reflected, its benefits were aimed at poor rural folk, black and white, a class that "had in it no influential citizens, no campaign contributors, and hardly any voters—almost none in the poll-tax states [that is, the South]."

The Resettlement Administration's ability to give these people a place on the national agenda, he found, was "feeble indeed." Compounding the difficulty was Resettlement's advocacy for land-use policies that drew scorn from entrenched interests across the South and Midwest and in their congressional delegations. In the aftermath of the droughts of 1934–36—the infamous "dust bowl" droughts—the agency strived to take submarginal lands out of production, deeding them to state and local governments for parks and recreational areas. But this conflicted with long-standing policies aimed at keeping people on the land, even land that had proven hopelessly unsuitable for cultivation. The resettlement idea itself, with its subtle hint of coercion, further cut against the conservative grain. "The critics' objection . . . centered in the idea that it limited peoples' freedom," Tugwell commented. "That the freedom involved was limited to the right to be dispossessed and to migrate, or perhaps to sink deeper into misery, seemed not to affect loyalty to principle." By 1937 the renamed Farm Security Administration had acquired so many enemies on both sides of the political aisle that its demise was inevitable. The moment arrived following Roosevelt's disastrous campaign to pack the Supreme Court, in the aftermath of which Congress acquired the upper hand over the White House for the first time since the Hundred Days. The lawmakers honed their axes to chop away at New Deal agencies, and the former Resettlement Administration, Tugwell recorded, "was one of the first to go." With it went the New Deal's most effective program of assistance for the black community.

Negro workers in the industrial zones of the North fared scarcely better than their agricultural brethren. Their foothold on subsistence was even more precarious: 90 percent of those employed were marginalized in unskilled jobs. The few employment surveys made at the time traced their baleful journey: in 1930, blacks constituted as little as 8 percent of the industrial workforce in Detroit and 6 percent in New York, well below their share of the population in those cities. By 1934, those figures had certainly deteriorated, as blacks counted for 14 percent of the employable persons on relief rolls in New York and 23 percent in Detroit. Yet black laborers continued to stream into the industrial North. By 1936, one-fifth of the black families on the relief rolls in the South no longer had employable male workers at home—they had all headed for the cities. "These unemployed, untrained hordes, hungry for work, furnish an added competition to all marginal labor already employed, and increase the insecurity under which Negro workers suffer," observed Urban League executive T. Arnold Hill. Laid-off domestic and "personal service" workers added to the pressure—703,600 former hotel and restaurant hands, laundry workers, barbers, bootblacks, charwomen, and elevator tenders were on urban relief rolls in May 1934, according to a survey by Hopkins's Federal Emergency Relief Administration.

Black families on federal relief rolls were subjected to such indignities as shortchanging on their benefits. The discrimination suffered by sharecroppers in the South is "equaled by the more subtle practices in the distribution of relief in the North," reported the Negro activist Edward Lewis. He acknowledged that the fault was not FERA's, but the local administrators who were assigned by the agency to oversee disbursement and conducted "a sustained movement to keep relief standards for Negroes low and to differentiate on the basis of color." White caseworkers addressed black relief clients by their first names, while white clients received the honorific Mr. and Mrs.—a trivial distinction on the surface, but one that unmistakably served to put black clients in their place as undeserving recipients of charity. In Maryland, the emergency relief commission provided social workers with different sample menus for their white and black clients. "Needless to say the one for Negroes was made up of the cheapest foods," Lewis observed. "Is there any reason why Negroes should be advised to limit themselves to meat loaf and pork chops, while white clients are advised to eat roast beef and lamb chops?" The pernicious influence of local officials was no secret to the recipients themselves, as an anonymous resident of Hattiesburg, Mississippi, informed the President by letter in May 1936: "Mr. Presedent Sir We are starving in Hattiesburg. . . . Mississippi is made her own laws an dont treat her destituted as her Pres. has laid the plans for us to live if the legislators would do as our good Pres. has Said."

As for the New Deal's landmark initiatives on behalf of organized labor, Section 7(a) of the NIRA and the Wagner Act guaranteeing the right of collective bargaining, these also tended to leave the Negro worker on the outside looking in, for the simple reason that the labor unions they protected were seldom less bigoted and discriminatory than society at large, and sometimes more so. In 1930 at least nineteen major unions excluded Negroes from membership, ten segregated them in auxiliary locals, and many others practiced subtler, but still effective, forms of discrimination. That year the NAACP estimated the number of black members of national unions at fewer than 50,000, out of total U.S. union enrollment of 3.4 million. Half of those 50,000 were members of a single union, A. Philip Randolph's all-black Brotherhood of Sleeping Car Porters.

"The most sinister power that the N.R.A. has re-inforced is the American Federation of Labor," thundered W. E. B. Du Bois in the pages of *The Crisis*. "The A.F. of L. has from the beginning of its organization stood up and lied brazenly about its attitude toward Negro labor. . . . They do not wish to organize Negroes. They keep Negroes out of every single organization where they can." To keep the improved job security for union members created by Section 7(a) from disadvantaging the black worker, the NAACP and the Urban League jointly lobbied the White House to incorporate an explicit antidiscrimination clause in the NIRA. This was all the more important because the guarantee for collective bargaining in Section 7(a) was expected to facilitate the creation of closed shops, in which union membership would be a prerequisite for employment. "It is not a 'closed' shop which is in the offing, but a 'white' shop," declared an NAACP director. But the clause was not included.

In the NAACP's view, the Wagner Act, which supplanted Section 7(a) after the Supreme Court invalidated the NIRA, contained a provision even more damaging to black interests. This was a mandate that employers rehire all striking workers after a contract settlement. The sad truth was that one of the most common entryways to industrial work for Negroes was employment as strikebreakers; the NAACP and the Urban League protested that a mandatory rehiring clause without commensurate protection against union discrimination would mean the end of "the one weapon left to the Negro worker whereby he may break the stranglehold that certain organized labor groups have utilized in preventing his complete absorption in the American labor market." Senator Wagner did add a clause to his bill permitting a closed shop only for unions without discriminatory policies. It was removed at the insistence of the AFL, which threatened to kill the entire measure if it stayed in.

Another indignity was delivered by the Social Security Act. The measure's drafters envisioned Social Security as a universal program. But as the bill made its way through Congress its scope was ruthlessly narrowed to exclude domestic workers and agricultural labor—the trades providing work to 65 percent of employed black Americans. Excluding these workers, among whom joblessness averaged 50 percent, from the act's provision of unemployment insurance only underscored its irrelevance to the black community. These workers "have nothing to gain under this act," observed a crestfallen Albion Hartwell, a black expert on social insurance. "It disowns them and denies them any assistance whatsoever."

Given all this, it was unsurprising that T. Arnold Hill could state in 1936 that "the Negro remains the most forgotten man in a program planned to deal new cards to . . . millions of workers." Black labor had sunk to a worse condition than it had occupied at the onset of the Depression, he observed. "A government which is honest in its claims of a New Deal, and which wishes to improve the lot of the forgotten man, should protect those who are the least protected—and there can be no question but that the Negro is the lowest in the industrial scale. . . . The Negro worker has good reason to feel that his government has betrayed him under the New Deal."

Anyone examining the administration's approach to civil rights could not help but be disappointed by its overall silence on the subject. The most glaring example was the fate of an antilynching bill drafted by the NAACP in 1933 and sponsored by two leading progressives in the Senate, Wagner of New York and Edward Costigan of Colorado.

The bill targeted state and local officials who failed to protect citizens or arrest or prosecute violators, or who aided the mob; those guilty of the latter offense would be subject to a life term. Once hearings began on the measure in February 1934, the NAACP stressed the urgent necessity of applying federal pressure on local officials: its president, Walter White, testified that no indictments had been laid in fifteen of the twenty-one lynchings in 1930, and in the other six cases only four of the forty-nine defendants had been convicted. More often than not, coroners' juries ruled that the victims had died "at the hands of parties unknown."

The antilynching bill had broad public approval even in the South, where a Gallup poll recorded 65 percent of respondents in favor, and boasted an impressive roster of prominent supporters: one petition delivered to the White House bore the signatures of nine governors or ex-governors, fifty-eight bishops and other clerics, fifty-four college professors and presidents, and more than one hundred writers, scholars, judges, and other luminaries. The bill was reported to the Senate floor on March 28, 1934. There it would die.

Vehement opposition to the measure centered in the southern delegations, but there was precious little counterbalancing support in the rest of the chamber—or for that matter in the White House, although the toll of lynchings had not ebbed since the Hoover years. (Sixty-three would be reported from 1933 through 1935.)

Roosevelt was never eager to stir the cauldron of race relations. One of the few occasions on which he spoke out on a specific lynching case followed a horrific incident in 1933, when two black men suspected of kidnapping and murdering a department store heir in San Jose, California, were dragged from the county jail and hanged in a downtown park before ten thousand baying onlookers. Afterward the Republican governor, James Rolph, Jr., declared the lynchings "the best lesson California has ever given the country." Roosevelt responded to the spectacle of an American governor standing up for a lynch mob by telling a national radio audience, "We do not excuse those in high places or low who condone lynch law."

But he made only glancing reference to the horrors of racial violence in his 1934 State of the Union address: "Crimes of organized banditry, cold-blooded shooting, lynching and kidnapping have threatened our security. . . . [T]hese violations of law call on the strong arm of Government for their immediate suppression; they call also on the country for an aroused public opinion," he declared. Then he moved on to the repeal of Prohibition and the relief of unemployment. The President and the Senate leadership understood that the southern bloc would not yield on antilynching legislation and was prepared to tie up all Congress's work to have its way.

At a meeting with White arranged by an insistent Eleanor Roosevelt, the President was candid, if condescending, about political reality. "I did not choose the tools with which I must work," he told White while they basked in the spring sun with the First Lady and the President's mother on the south portico of the White House. "But I've got to get legislation passed by Congress to save America. The Southerners by reason of the seniority rule in Congress are chairmen or occupy strategic places on most of the Senate and House committees. If I come out for the anti-lynching bill now, they will block every bill I ask Congress to pass to keep America from collapsing. I just can't take that risk." White did not find the President's expression of powerlessness in the face of truculent racism very convincing.

Wagner reintroduced his bill in 1935, impelled by abject appeals for action like this one from an anonymous Negro resident of Georgia: "Saturday Night Oct 27th thay mobed a Negro man he is Not Dead but looking to Die Any Day i Want you to Do your best to Stop this. . . . i wont Rite my Name fer that it Would be Publish and thay Will Kill me as i A Negro."

But the bill ran up against a filibuster. "We will be here all summer," North Carolina's Josiah Bailey assured Wagner. The measure did not reappear until 1938, when Wagner forced the southern bloc to make good on its threat to hold the Senate hostage. The result was not the dramatic filibuster of Hollywood screenplays but a desultory affair. By general consent the pretense of filibuster was maintained by a technicality that allowed the southerners to conduct their blockade during business hours and go home at night, eliminating the traditional test of physical endurance. The Senate leadership thus made sure that the filibuster of Wagner's antilynching bill would not interfere with regular business, which of course allowed it to continue indefinitely without inconveniencing anyone. But neither could the antilynching measure come to a vote. Wagner twice moved a cloture vote to end the filibuster, but as Roosevelt had refused to designate the bill an administration "must," it could not hope to attract enough support, and the motion failed both times.

Finally Wagner withdrew the bill. It would never become law. Walter White, who had been among the first black leaders to transition away from the Republican Party, communicated his disillusionment with the administration directly to the President, writing after the bill's failure in 1935:

> It is a matter of great disappointment that you as President did not see your way clear to make a public pronouncement . . . giving your open indorsement to the anti-lynching bill and your condemnation of the shameless filibuster led by a wilful group of obstructionists. . . . It is my belief that the utterly shameless filibuster could not have withstood the pressure of public opinion had you spoken out against it.

The NAACP consoled itself with the observation that merely the threat of a federal law seemed to have suppressed the lynching impulse in the South. After 1935, when twenty lynchings were recorded, the average in 1936 through 1941 fell to fewer than six a year. It was as though the publicity attending the association's bill had at last made the barbarous practice socially unacceptable.

Roosevelt was content for the most part to leave public discussions of minority rights to Harold Ickes and the First Lady; the former functioned effectively as an ambassador to Negro organizations, delivering a well-received keynote speech titled "The Negro as Citizen" at the 1936 NAACP convention. Roosevelt could, if necessary, characterize his wife's activities as reflections of her much-remarked independence rather than as expressions of White House policy. Such deniability came in handy as Eleanor became less shy about making public displays of fellowship with minority leaders. In 1938 she created a furor at the founding meeting of the Southern Conference for Human Welfare in rigorously segregated Birmingham, Alabama. The city's police commissioner, Eugene "Bull" Connor (who would become notorious for his racism during Birmingham's desegregation battles in the 1960s), announced he would enforce the municipal segregation law personally by arresting violators on the spot and transporting them to jail in a fleet of Black Marias. These were already parked in a cordon about the meeting hall when the conferees arrived for their opening session. The organizers hewed meticulously to the law, arranging racially separate seating on the main floor and even marking routes for speakers to follow to the podium to make sure that neither black nor white strayed over an invisible segregation line in the auditorium.

Then Mrs. Roosevelt arrived and made her own rules. "She took a folding chair and put it plumb right in the middle of the aisle and said that she would not be segregated," recalled one of the organizers, the white civil rights activist Virginia Foster Durr. "And they were scared to arrest her. After all, she was the wife of the President of the United States, so she got by with it."

Some New Dealers were sensitive to the charge that the administration had not done enough to assist Negroes or other minorities. Speeches by Harold Ickes and the symbolic gestures of Eleanor Roosevelt could not outweigh the institutionalized racism the government condoned in the distribution of federal benefits, much less its failure to help integrate blacks into residential settlements, work programs, and labor unions brought under its increasingly capacious umbrella. The Tennessee Valley Authority might have the ability to raise an entire region out of near-medieval poverty, but black Americans were not permitted to reside next to the white dam workers in the TVA work camp of Norris, Tennessee; Franklin Roosevelt would personally travel to the edge of the Colorado River gorge to dedicate the showpiece public works project then known as Boulder Dam, but its workforce had been almost all white, and none of the handful of Negro laborers was permitted to live within the confines of its government-owned residential camp, Boulder City. Almost every federal settlement, work relief camp, and construction crew that accommodated blacks did so on a racially segregated "Jim Crow" basis.

On the other side of the ledger, the Roosevelt administration had appointed more blacks to high-ranking federal posts than any other; among them were Robert C. Weaver in the Interior Department and the prominent educator Mary McLeod Bethune at the National Youth Administration. The work and residential projects may have been Jim Crow, but in most federal programs there was some work and housing for Negroes—of the rural teachers hired by Harry Hopkins's FERA in thirteen southern states, more than 30 percent were black, and of the sixty Public Works Administration housing developments completed by the end of 1935, black residents occupied twenty-eight.

The most effective argument the New Dealers could make as an appeal to black voter loyalty was that their efforts to raise all Americans out of unemployment and poverty benefited all races. Weaver raised exactly that point in the pages of the Negro journal *Opportunity.* "One is forced to admit that Federal relief has been a godsend to the unemployed," he observed. Yes, it was true that abuses against Negroes in the distribution of relief "undoubtedly existed and do exist. . . . We can admit that we have gained from the relief program and still fight to receive greater and more equitable benefits from it." He added that the racial abuses were, "for the most part, problems of a system and their resistance to reform is as old as the system." But "the New Deal, insofar as it represents an extension of government activity into the economic sphere, is a departure which can do much to reach the Negro citizens."

As the election of 1936 approached, black leaders weighed the achievements of the New Deal against its potential and found it wanting—though not unpromising. Their commitment to the Democrats was distinctly ambivalent, as though they were still fighting off the spell cast by the party of Lincoln. "If the Republican said little of significance on the Negro in their platform the Democrats went them one better by saying nothing," *The Crisis,* now the NAACP's official organ, lamented after the 1936 conventions. The journal was especially disappointed to find lynching go unmentioned in either party's platform: "We must have economic security, we must have education, and free exercise of the ballot, but lynching must go, and the political party which temporizes on lynching must be prepared to have its protestations of good intent accepted by the Negro voter with considerable salt." Unfortunately, both parties had temporized.

On the very eve of the election, the influential Baltimore *Afro-American* pondered the baleful choice presented at the polls by the four candidates running for president—Roosevelt and Alf Landon representing the two major parties, and Earl Browder of the Communist Party and Norman Thomas of the Socialist Party filling out the ballot: "If all four had an equal chance of election the colored people would fare best under Browder, with Thomas, Roosevelt, and Landon falling in that order." But they did not have an equal chance, and the newspaper urged a vote for Roosevelt as an expression of "political opportunism."

Black voters took the opportunity, with 71 percent voting for Roosevelt nationwide. Only 44 percent identified themselves as Democrats, but the bedrock of a Democratic coalition had been established—still an incomplete coalition in 1936, but one destined to endure.

PART THREE

RETURN TO EARTH

16

BACKLASH

I N WASHINGTON, D.C., the most eagerly anticipated political event of January 1936 was not, as one might expect, the State of the Union message to be delivered by a president launching his reelection campaign. It was a gala dinner to be held in the elegant Mayflower Hotel by the American Liberty League, which had been founded by a group of wealthy business leaders and old-guard Democrats from the anti-Roosevelt camp.

The Liberty League's most glittering ornament was Alfred E. Smith, the Democrats' 1928 presidential candidate, Franklin Roosevelt's predecessor as governor of New York, and an increasingly strident critic of the New Deal. The Mayflower banquet on January 25 would mark the apogee of the Liberty League's political credibility and influence. Al Smith's keynote address on that occasion would mark the nadir, even the end, of his political career.

Criticism of the New Deal had been building on the left and the right. Both camps were unhappy with the political accommodations Roosevelt had made over the previous three years. The Left was discontented by his failure to impose dramatic change on the structure of finance and industry. On the Right, the New Deal's regulatory schemes, its proliferation of executive agencies with broad yet ambiguous new powers, and its hostile rhetoric about "money-changers" and wealthy malefactors reinforced suspicions about Franklin Roosevelt dating back to the 1932 campaign. The listless pace of recovery fueled misgivings among the public. The man on the street had yet to see the return of a robust job market, farm prices were still depressed, and economic activity was still heavily dependent on relief programs, the latest of which was the $4.9 billion WPA, launched in 1935.

Big business saw the Roosevelt administration as an unreliable and uncooperative partner in efforts to get the country moving again. True, the New Deal had granted some of industry's most cherished wishes by suspending the antitrust laws via the NRA and instituting an inflationary monetary policy; but what it gave with one hand it took away with the other—new banking laws, securities regulation, a strengthened Federal Trade Commission, and a general reluctance to accept business leaders into White House councils.

The chorus of complaint grated on New Dealers' ears. Passing through Manhattan on his way home to Washington from an Upstate speaking engagement in January 1935, Rex Tugwell got dragooned into "one of the so-called 'Moley dinners,'" a sort of salon maintained by Ray Moley, the former Brain Truster (and still an intimate of the White House). Tugwell found the event tedious and unedifying, notwithstanding the eminence of the guests, who included the presidents of Lehman Brothers, Johns-Manville, General Foods, and Westinghouse Electric. Also present was Wendell Willkie, who was still smarting about the harsh treatment he had received from the TVA's David Lilienthal in negotiations over power sales in the Tennessee Valley.

The businessmen harangued Tugwell about the unfriendliness of the administration, Roosevelt's "cracks at businessmen," and the meagerness of the recovery. Tugwell answered that the conditions they were complaining about were, at heart, conditions of their own making—the administration was merely responding to the mood of the public. "What you are really objecting to," he told them, "is the psychological reaction of the people to the depression which you are really responsible for through the break down of the management of your industry. . . . [W]hen any group charged with leadership in a community finds itself in the position of having no constructive suggestions which have to do with causes of distress and yet has bitter complaints about the attitude of the public toward them, it is in a very serious state." On that disagreeable note, the dinner ended.

Moley's wealthy guests may not have appreciated how good they had it. Taking rhetorical "cracks at businessmen" was one thing, but hitting them in the pocketbook was another—and thus far most of the tax burden of the New Deal had been borne by the middle and working classes.

The reason was that the tax structure had been established by Herbert Hoover's Revenue Act of 1932. The act reduced the share of federal tax revenues derived from corporate and personal income taxes, which fell most heavily on the rich, to 40 percent in 1933 from 56 percent the year before. Taking up the slack were new excise taxes on merchandise and services, including cars and gasoline, radios and phonographs, tickets to movies and other amusements, and long-distance phone calls and telegrams. The tax on tobacco was increased. Typically levied on the manufacturers or service providers and passed through to the customer, these taxes were steeply regressive, taking an ever-larger bite out of disposable income as one moved down the wage scale. A few excise taxes were aimed at upper-income goods such as yachts, jewelry, and furs, but these generated much less revenue than other, more broad-based, levies. The tax on furs, for example, produced less than half the revenue of the tax on cosmetics, a purchase that transcended class barriers.

The 1932 act had scheduled most of these excises for early expiration, but the Roosevelt administration connived at pushing regular extensions through Congress; extending an existing tax was always easier than creating a new one. From 1933 to 1936, annual federal tax revenue more than doubled to $3.9 billion but the share coming from income and corporate taxes continued to fall. And of course a new regressive excise appeared after the repeal of Prohibition in 1933: the alcohol tax, which produced more than a half-billion dollars in revenue, or 13 percent of all federal tax collections, in 1936.

By their incessant grousing about their treatment while they reaped tax benefits and other government coddling, in other words, the business community was playing with fire. In 1935 it would get singed.

Many people inside and outside the White House recognized the phenomenon of businessmen thwarted in their desire to have things their own way—or worse, of having gotten their own way and become resentful at not having gotten more. No one perceived it better than Jesse H. Jones, a hugely successful Democratic businessman from Houston who was a New Deal insider and chairman of the Reconstruction Finance Corporation, the clearinghouse for government bailouts of banks and railroads.

In September 1933, Jones invited himself to the American Bankers Association annual convention. In his keynote speech, he crisply upbraided his audience for refusing offers of government capital to shore up their balance sheets, purely out of their distaste for Roosevelt and the New Deal. "Such tactics are not only unpatriotic but contemptible . . . a menace to society," he thundered. He concluded his talk with the memorable exhortation, "Be smart for once. . . . Go partners with the President in the recovery program without stint."

Jones's speech put an end to the bankers' perverse shunning of low-cost federal assistance, but their peevishness about the government's role in business lived on. Humorist Will Rogers recalled the scene at the U.S. Chamber of Commerce annual dinner in 1933, which he attended as Jones's guest. "The whole constitution, bylaws and secret ritual of that Orchid Club is to 'keep the government out of business,'" Rogers related to the readers of his daily newspaper column. "But here was the joke: They introduced all the big financiers. . . . As each stood up Jesse would write on the back of the menu card just what he had loaned him from the R.F.C. Yet, they said 'keep the government out of business.'" Rogers preserved that menu card for proof, he said.

The American Liberty League traced its origin to an exchange of letters in March 1934 between a retired executive of E. I. du Pont de Nemours & Company (and a member of the du Pont family by marriage) named Robert Ruliph Morgan "Ruly" Carpenter and John J. Raskob, the former Democratic Party chairman, also a du Pont executive. Carpenter was expanding on the ancient plaint about the difficulty of getting good help, especially when government work relief programs offered laborers an alternative to menial work at rock-bottom wages in the private sector.

> Five Negroes on my place in South Carolina refused work this Spring, after I had taken care of them and given them house rent free and work for three years during bad times, saying they had easy jobs with the government. Planters in our vicinity were unable to get enough labor to harvest crops in the Fall, due to CCC employment. A cook on my houseboat at Fort Myers quit because the government was paying him a dollar an hour as a painter when he never knew a thing about painting before.

Raskob should get Roosevelt to explain why he was so determined to destroy the capitalist class, Carpenter wrote: "A man like yourself, a supporter of his . . . could do a lot of good and set many minds at rest by getting the administration to answer these queries."

Raskob pleaded that he was out of politics, but he encouraged Carpenter to muster his friends in opposition to the New Deal. "I know of no one that could better take the lead in trying to induce the du Pont and General Motors groups, followed by other big industries, to definitely organize to protect society from the suffering which it is bound to endure if we allow communistic elements to lead the people to believe that all business men are crooks, not to be trusted, and that no one should be allowed to get rich."

A few months later, the Liberty League was chartered in Washington. Du Pont and General Motors interests dominated its board of directors and its roll of financial backers, with the list of subscribers filled out with conservative industrialists such as Ernest T. Weir of Weirton Steel, Edward F. Hutton of General Foods, and J. Howard Pew of Sun Oil. Four of its six officers were conspicuously Democrats, but not Roosevelt Democrats: Raskob, Al Smith, Irénée du Pont, and Raskob's protégé Jouett Shouse, who had been chairman of the Democratic National Executive Committee until 1932, when Roosevelt's victory banished the old guard from the party leadership.

The league bore a veneer of nonpartisanship, but in reality its membership came from a narrow class united by wealth and fear of its confiscation. The organization announced as its two founding principles: "1. To teach the necessity of respect for the rights of persons and property; 2. To teach the duty of government to encourage and protect individual and group enterprise, to foster 'the right to work, earn, save and acquire property.'"

Franklin Roosevelt's opinion of the league was withering. He described it to reporters a few days after the launch as "an organization that only advocates two or three out of the Ten Commandments." Taking the opportunity to contrast its principles sharply with the New Deal, he continued: "The two particular tenets of this new organization say you shall love God and then forget your neighbor. For people who want to keep themselves free from starvation, keep a roof over their heads, lead decent lives, have proper educational standards, those are the concerns of government besides these two points, and another thing which isn't mentioned . . . is the protection of the life and the liberty of the individual against elements in the community that seek to enrich and advance themselves at the expense of their fellow-citizens."

Roosevelt revealed that Shouse had visited the White House to inform him of the Liberty League's founding.

"Did Mr. Shouse invite you to become a member?" a reporter asked.

"I don't think he did," FDR replied. "Must have been an oversight."

The alliance between Al Smith and the rich reactionaries affiliated with the du Ponts surprised contemporary observers. Smith and Roosevelt had seemed personally close since their days in New York state politics and their careers had been inextricably entwined for twenty years—it had been Roosevelt who bestowed on Smith the nickname "the happy warrior," at the 1924 Democratic convention. Their goals were in many respects identical: an end to child labor, factory reforms, a living wage, farm relief, the repeal of Prohibition.

Some speculated that Smith, misled about the league's true nature, believed it to be a genuine effort to create broad-based support for a middle-of-the-road platform. The evidence for this was a subcommittee report to the league leadership to which Smith contributed, stating, "There appears to be . . . a real chance to secure the support of millions who represent the backbone of the nation . . . a platform which should straddle no issues but which, at the same time, should not hurt its cause by being highly controversial."

Yet this overlooked the complexity of the bond between Smith and Roosevelt. It is easy to mistake the studied sociability of politics for real warmth; in truth, their relationship was an admixture of friendship, competitiveness, and resentment, and the difference in their upbringings—one the unschooled child of the Lower East Side, the other the product of old money and a Groton and Harvard education—created what was in many respects an unbridgeable gulf between them. In political terms, Roosevelt allied with Smith in the 1920s as a way to cozy up to Tammany Hall, the great New York City Democratic machine; Smith saw their alliance as his ticket to the support of Upstate party leaders. Smith maneuvered to secure Roosevelt the nomination to succeed him as governor in 1928, but kept Roosevelt far from the center of his presidential campaign. Roosevelt had bristled at being treated by Raskob and Belle Moskowitz, Smith's indispensable political advisor, as "window dressing" to keep Upstate and Protestant interests in the camp of the downstate Catholic candidate.

After the 1928 election swept Roosevelt into the governor's office and Smith out of politics, the tables were turned. Smith condescendingly held to the traditional view of Roosevelt as a dilettante who could be manipulated by a strong power behind the throne—that is, Al Smith. Like so many others, he would be rudely surprised. Roosevelt rejected Smith's advice to keep Moskowitz and her lieutenant Robert Moses (with whom FDR shared a bitter mutual disdain) on the gubernatorial payroll, which Smith took as a personal slight. Smith's ostentatious proffers of advice to Roosevelt grated on the new governor, who heeded little of it; the warmth that seemed to reign between them in public soon concealed an underlying chill.

Part of the problem was that Smith had no paying job that might keep him out of Roosevelt's hair. That vacuum was finally filled when he was named the president of a company planning to build the world's tallest skyscraper, to be known as the Empire State Building, in Midtown Manhattan. The project was an ostentatious artifact of the Roaring Twenties. Its financial support looked gold-plated, coming from Raskob and the du Ponts. Its steel-frame engineering and art deco design bespoke modernity. But its timing was disastrous: the announcement of its construction was made on August 29, 1929. The stock market crash would arrive two months later, almost to the day.

As the 1932 convention approached and both Smith and Roosevelt jockeyed for the presidential nomination, the former's bitterness toward the latter boiled to the surface. "Do you know, by God, that he has never consulted me about a damn thing since he has been Governor? He has taken bad advice and from sources not friendly to me. He has ignored me!" Smith groused at the end of 1931 to a mutual friend, who promptly relayed the complaint to FDR. This nursing of slights would eventually come to play an important role in Smith's attitude toward the New Deal.

The crash had wiped out Smith's personal investments, many of them in stocks purchased on margin. His increasingly desperate financial straits— the Empire State Building investment proved an embarrassing failure— only drew him closer to his would-be benefactors, Raskob and the du Ponts, until he seemed utterly blind to the realization that the road they were leading him on pointed toward political oblivion.

The American Liberty League was not the only organization formed to protect finance and industry from the supposed depredations of the New Deal, or even the first; James H. Rand's Committee for the Nation had pressed for the suspension of antitrust regulation and for inflationary monetary policy as early as the Hundred Days, before linking up with the hapless Dr. Wirt in early 1934. But the league was certainly the most august such organization and by far the best funded, boasting a budget of nearly a half million dollars in 1935.

Other anti-Roosevelt business groups echoed its axiomatic linkage between the preservation of private property, the glorification of the Constitution's ostensible first principles, and the concept of "liberty." There were the Crusaders, founded to promote the repeal of Prohibition, only to move on, once that goal was achieved, to oppose the Tennessee Valley Authority, the AAA, and Wall Street reform; and the Farmers Independence Council, which trained its fire primarily on the AAA. These shared more than their ideology with the Liberty League. They drew their financing from the du Ponts, Alfred P. Sloan of General Motors, and Pew, Weir, and Hutton—in other words, the same bankrollers as the league. In 1935 these figures' distaste for the New Deal seduced them into an especially noisome investment in the political career of a suspender-snapping southern bigot, Georgia's Democratic governor Eugene Talmadge.

Talmadge was a reactionary who had come to big business's notice by yoking a string of crudely provocative antilabor nostrums—concentration camps for strikers, the deployment of state troopers as strikebreakers—to attacks on the New Deal's banking reforms, the AAA, the TVA, and other targets of the Liberty League. For the national electorate his appeal was always likely to be thin, however. Talmadge's "Grass Roots Convention of Southern Democrats," a shadow Democratic convention staged in Macon in 1936 and funded by Raskob, Pierre du Pont, and Sloan, would serve simultaneously as the high-water mark of his national career and its finale. Talmadge's keynote speech was broadcast to a nationwide radio audience, but his movement could not survive the glare of attention. Press reports revealed that the hall was only half filled, that Talmadge's anticommunist and antisocialist rantings were leavened by racial hatred. Deposited on every seat in the hall was a race-baiting magazine clipping depicting Mrs. Roosevelt and members of the administration in the company of black persons, along with an editorial comparing Andrew Jackson and Roosevelt in terms of their solicitude for the Negro, to Roosevelt's disadvantage. "Andrew Jackson didn't try to ram an anti-lynching bill down the throats of the Southern people," it read. "When Andrew Jackson got to be President he didn't put in Socialists, Communists, and Negroes to tell him how to run these good old United States."

Racism did not invariably drive the opposition to the New Deal after 1934. Its beating heart was economic, more particularly the property-holding class's fear that FDR was covertly plotting a Share Our Wealth program of his own. Although this fear was counterbalanced on the Left by the impression that Roosevelt had gone out of his way to *preserve* the fortunes of the affluent, it was much the stronger sentiment, as the journalist Marquis Childs observed in a 1936 piece for *Harper's* titled "They Hate Roosevelt."

"The phenomenon to which I refer goes far beyond objection to policies or programs," he wrote. "It is a passion, a fury, that is wholly unreasoning . . . a consuming personal hatred of President Roosevelt and, to an almost equal degree, of Mrs. Roosevelt. It permeates, in greater or less degree, the whole upper stratum of American society." Curiously, "the majority of those who rail against the President have to a large extent had their incomes restored and their bank balances replenished since the low point of March, 1933." Yet "the larger the house, the more numerous the servants, the more resplendent the linen and silver, the more scathing is likely to be the indictment of the President." Here was another manifestation of the phenomenon Will Rogers had noticed at that Chamber of Commerce dinner, where the recipients of billions of dollars of lifesaving federal largesse stood up one after another to denounce the government for its involvement in business.

Childs could perhaps be faulted for treating the extreme anti-Roosevelt rhetoric of the extremely rich as emblematic of all criticism of the New Deal. For it was also possible to be disquieted by the sheer ambiguity of Roosevelt's methods, if not his goals. Robert Lee Hale, a lawyer and self-described "Tory" who would later make his reputation as the exponent of a doctrine of property and tort law called legal realism, replied to Childs that the problem with the New Deal was not that the rich feared the confiscation of their wealth, but that no one knew where the line between rich and not-rich would be drawn. The resulting uncertainties, he argued (in a piece for *Harper's* titled "But I, Too, Hate Roosevelt"), "victimize not merely the rich, but all individuals who either live on savings or aspire to obtain security or any kind of economic privilege from any kind of savings." Property rights were not to be lightly dismissed as belonging only to the idle rich, he warned: "I might, in passing, ask for a show of hands on those who can define the distinction between a property right and a human right."

In 1934 and 1935 many people detected an ever-widening gulf between what Roosevelt had promised voters as the Democratic Party's standard-bearer in the 1932 election and what he was giving them as President. Prominent in this camp were such disappointed conservative Democrats as Lewis Douglas, who resigned as budget director in August 1934, and the

Wall Street investment banker James Paul Warburg. The latter had stood fast with FDR during the banking crisis and through the Hundred Days, only to lose faith during the currency manipulation scheme of late 1933. Warburg's manifesto of discontent was published in book form in 1935 as *Hell Bent for Election,* in which he compared and contrasted the fiscally conservative 1932 party platform and the rather more flexible policies promulgated from the Roosevelt White House. Douglas's thoughts were outlined in his own 1935 book, *The Liberal Tradition,* an astringent attack on "the oppressive state" and the evils of central economic planning, larded with sidelong swipes at the Soviet system that were designed to draw an implicit parallel to the New Deal.

Roosevelt struck back at his well-heeled adversaries on June 19, 1935, by proposing a tax package aimed squarely at the wealthy. "Our revenue laws have operated in many ways to the unfair advantage of the few," he said in his accompanying message to Congress. The Revenue Act of 1935 would recognize that "wealth in the modern world does not come merely from individual effort. . . . [T]he people in the mass have inevitably helped to make large fortunes possible." Rather mischievously, FDR quoted Andrew Carnegie, certainly an industrialist hero: "Where wealth accrues honorably, the people are always silent partners."

To supplement the existing estate tax, which was levied on bequests in toto, the measure proposed an inheritance tax aimed at individual legatees. Income tax rates would be raised and made more progressive at the high end—here the President quoted his illustrious Republican cousin Theodore to the effect that "a heavy tax upon a very large fortune is in no way such a tax upon thrift or industry as a like tax would be on a small fortune." And there would be a newly graduated tax on corporate profits, in recognition of the benefits bestowed upon corporations via their government charters.

The package had been cobbled together over several months by Morgenthau and his Treasury aides, but its inspiration was manifestly political. Roosevelt had grown weary of getting hammered on the left from critics like Father Coughlin and Huey Long. In early summer he had attempted to mollify one of his harshest Democratic critics, William Randolph Hearst, by hosting Hearst's chief editor, Edmond Coblentz, in a lavish style rarely seen at the White House short of a state dinner—caviar flown in from Russia, California wines, cordials, highballs—with Ray Moley and Roosevelt's millionaire crony Vincent Astor in attendance. "I am fighting

Communism, Huey Longism, Coughlinism, Townsendism," the President lamented to Coblentz. He outlined Long's Share Our Wealth proposal to confiscate large estates and explained, "To combat this and similar crackpot ideas, it may be necessary to throw to the wolves the forty-six men who are reported to have incomes in excess of one million dollars. This can be accomplished through taxation." One of those forty-six was William Randolph Hearst. Another was Vincent Astor, who remarked sheepishly at dinner that Roosevelt's plan might bankrupt him. "The attitude of the President to this remark," Coblentz reported, "seemed to be, 'Well, that's just too bad.'"

Moley, who drafted the tax message in collaboration with Felix Frankfurter, understood that Roosevelt's intention was to "steal Long's thunder." But he was uncomfortable with the President's evident glee at supplanting Long's Share Our Wealth program with a "soak-the-rich" scheme. Referring to the prickly Mississippian chairman of the Senate Finance Committee, Roosevelt exclaimed to an appalled Moley: "Pat Harrison's going to be so surprised he'll have kittens on the spot."

Moley tried to talk Roosevelt out of what he considered the most extreme elements of the tax plan. Chief among these was a tax on undistributed corporate profits, which Moley contended would encourage big companies to pay out surplus cash to shareholders as dividends, instead of preserving it for working capital in lean times. He managed only to persuade the President to consign the tax to a study committee; it would resurface and get enacted in 1936. Other than that concession, Roosevelt was adamant. "The sense of regaining the whip hand gave him the first buoyant, cheerful moment he had known for weeks," Moley recalled.

Roosevelt was meeting with Ickes in the Oval Room on June 19 when word came from Capitol Hill that the Social Security bill had passed the Senate and that the chamber was now hearing the tax message read. Confiding to Ickes that he thought the message "the best thing he had done as President," he proceeded to deliver a dramatic reading of the text to his appreciative audience of one. At one point—possibly at the passage decrying "the perpetuation of great and undesirable concentration of control in a relatively few individuals"—he glanced up, beaming. "That is for Hearst," he declared.

The Revenue Act of 1935 was the only New Deal measure specifically aimed at the redistribution of wealth. Yet it was a fairly modest effort even in those terms. The Treasury expected it to produce only $250 million in additional revenue, less than 10 percent of all federal income in 1934. Of that, about $45 million would come from the higher personal income tax on the wealthiest taxpayers. This was achieved by raising rates on incomes over $50,000 (the equivalent of $840,000 in buying power in 2010) and adding new brackets for incomes over the then-stratospheric sum of $1 million, on which the rates were raised from the pre-1936 maximum of 63 percent to new levels ranging from 77 percent to 79 percent—but even at those rates the additional revenue contribution of taxpayers in the $1 million–plus stratosphere would come to only about $4 million a year.

Congress rejected Roosevelt's inheritance tax but increased the estate and gift taxes to produce $100 million in new revenue and accepted the new income tax schedule. As it happened, the modest increase in the progressivity of the tax structure achieved by these changes would be swamped by the new, regressive payroll tax instituted in 1936 to fund Social Security. This would take $1 billion a year out of the pockets of workers and their employers, without returning any money in the form of retirement benefits until pension checks started issuing in 1940.

Nevertheless, editorialists around the country condemned the administration for engaging in politically-motivated class warfare. The *New York Herald Tribune* described the Revenue Act as "composed of equal parts of politics and spite"; the *Philadelphia Inquirer* as "a bald political stroke." Arthur Krock in the *New York Times* ridiculed the measure as "neither fish nor fowl, but perhaps a good red herring," pointing out that while it "has a popular sound," it would impose new costs on "only a fraction of one percent of the population." On the West Coast, the *San Francisco Chronicle* detected "the ugly look of a reprisal" in the tax message, and the arch-conservative *Los Angeles Times* concluded that Roosevelt and Long had now made common cause. "The Kingfish must perforce applaud," the newspaper remarked acidly.

By 1936, it looked as though Roosevelt was losing the newspaper pundit class. To be sure, some commentators had never been on his side, among them the *New York Herald Tribune*'s Mark Sullivan, a onetime progressive who had moved steadily rightward, coincident with his becoming a fishing companion of President Herbert Hoover. Sullivan's view of the New Deal had turned frankly apocalyptic in late 1935, when he wrote that "so much of what is being done to America is tragic." After the passage of Social Security he took up the cause of his stenographer, Mabel Shea, asking in a column why she should give up 35 cents out of her $35 monthly paycheck if she chose of her own free will not to save it for her retirement.

Sullivan's attempt to position himself as a friend of the workingperson backfired when *Time* was prompted to ask why Mabel Shea was being paid only $35 a week by a columnist who earned $23,417 a year. He also opened himself to a mischievous tweaking by FDR, who was asked at a press conference about Sullivan's complaint. With Sullivan in the room, Roosevelt interpreted the columnist's piece as having implied that Shea had "absolute freedom, as an American citizen, to starve to death when she got to be sixty-five if she wanted to." For her own part, Shea told interviewers that she was "wholly a New Dealer" and considered Social Security a "good thing." "Pundit's Secretary Becomes National Symbol," reported *Life* magazine.

But Roosevelt was also losing such judicious supporters as Walter Lippmann. Perhaps the preeminent centrist voice in the press, Lippmann by 1936 was experiencing a dire case of buyer's remorse, as he pondered the vast expansion of executive power he had so zealously urged upon Roosevelt during the 1932 campaign and the Hundred Days.

The change seemed to come upon Lippmann suddenly, like an epiphany. Through mid-1935 he continued to counsel energetic action. He told Joseph P. Kennedy that the New Deal's combination of reform and recovery legislation "has made more secure free institutions and private enterprise, and . . . no believer in either has any ground for fear"; rebuked Lewis Douglas for "misleading" overstatements of the per capita levels of tax and debt in the United States as compared to England; and advised Roosevelt to press Congress for votes endorsing New Deal policies to uphold their "moral, political, and psychological" authority.

Scarcely six months later he was expressing nodding agreement with the misgivings of the Democratic old guard. To Newton D. Baker, the stalwart aide to Woodrow Wilson and perennial candidate for the Democratic presidential nomination from 1924 through 1932 who had been railing against the New Deal's "frightful extravagance," Lippmann wrote cautiously in January: "Increasingly, since last spring, I have begun to feel that a situation might develop as a result of a kind of loss of balance where it would be absolutely necessary not to re-elect Mr. Roosevelt." By April, with the election only seven months away, he was actually helping Lewis Douglas draft a declaration of principles for a faction of conservative Democrats aiming to seize the party leadership back from the New Dealers.

As the declaration made plain, Lippmann's concerns coincided with the barrage Roosevelt was fielding from the right—he was creating too large a federal bureaucracy and concentrating too much power in his own hands (the crime, therefore, simultaneously of excessive delegation and excessive centralization), federal spending was out of control, and "soak the rich" taxes would stifle American competitiveness. Lippmann's draft read: "The record shows, . . . we are convinced, that this enormous concentration of power in the hands of appointed officials cannot be exercised wisely. . . . That it can lead only to waste, confusion, bureaucratic rigidity, and the loss of personal liberty."

Making the remarkable assertion that "the New Era [that is, the 1920s policies of Harding, Coolidge, and Hoover] and the New Deal are two streams from the same source," Lippmann's declaration urged a dramatic reduction in the authority of bureaucrats in alphabet agencies such as the AAA and the return of responsibility for jobless relief to the states, with the federal government providing assistance only in conditions of "exceptional need"—thus dismantling the system of federal unemployment insurance that had been so painstakingly worked out by the Committee on Economic Security more than a year before.

Lippmann's journey across the political spectrum would not end at the conservative wing of the Democratic Party. In the 1936 presidential election he would cast his vote for the Republican candidate, Alf Landon.

The Liberty League's Mayflower gala took place against the backdrop of growing political uncertainty for the New Deal. Roosevelt's personal popularity had plunged to 50.5 percent, according to a Gallup poll dated September 1, 1935. The emergency that had inspired the bursts of energy of the Hundred Days and the early successes of the New Deal had faded; Roosevelt's days seemed to be occupied less in dealing with economic crisis than with internecine quarreling among his aides, including the squabble between Ickes and Hopkins over the new $4.9 billion relief program. Conservative Republicans and the business lobby were stepping up their attacks on the New Deal and on Roosevelt personally. During a private conversation with the President on New Year's Eve of 1935, Ickes "bluntly asked him how much further we were going to retreat before standing to face the enemy." FDR assured his pugnacious interior secretary that the State of the Union address, to be delivered three days hence, would be "a fighting message."

"I hope so," Ickes rumbled in reply.

And so it was. Delivered to an evening session of Congress to obtain access to a nationwide radio audience, the speech revisited many of the themes of Roosevelt's inaugural address. This approach had been questioned by the speech's chief draftsman, Ray Moley, who observed that for all the fiery rhetoric there would be no new proposed legislation or objectives. Therefore the speech would merely shore up an already secure liberal voting bloc and further antagonize business without effectively challenging the right wing with a program for the year ahead.

Yet Roosevelt understood this was not the time for a new legislative program; it was time to launch the reelection campaign with a stemwinding campaign speech. After opening with a discussion of the darkening mood in world affairs—still a remote concern for most Americans—he turned to the domestic scene.

> In March, 1933, I appealed to the Congress of the United States and to the people of the United States in a new effort to restore power to those to whom it rightfully belonged. The response to that appeal resulted in the writing of a new chapter in the history of popular government. . . . [O]ur aim was to build upon essentially democratic institutions, seeking all the while the adjustment of burdens, the help of the needy, the protection of the weak, the liberation of the exploited and the genuine protection of the people's property.
>
> To be sure, in so doing, we have invited battle. We have earned the hatred of entrenched greed. . . . [B]ut now . . . they seek the restoration of their selfish power. They offer to lead us back round the same old corner into the same old dreary street. . . . They steal the livery of great national constitutional ideals to serve discredited special interests. . . . The principle that they would instill into government if they succeeded in seizing power is well shown by the principles which many of them have instilled into their own affairs: autocracy toward labor, toward stockholders, toward consumers, toward public sentiment. . . . "By their fruits ye shall know them."

The speech was a bigger hit with the general public than with the commentating class. While the former flooded the White House with complimentary letters and wires, the latter condemned Roosevelt for converting an occasion for statesmanship into a "political diatribe," as even such a steadfast progressive journal as the *Nation* complained.

With the annual address behind them, the New Dealers turned their attention to the looming Liberty League event and the keynote by Smith. "He has been getting a wonderful build-up for this meeting," Ickes fretted obsessively to his diary. "Harry Slattery [a well-connected Ickes assistant at the Public Works Administration] tells me that his information is that it will be the biggest banquet ever held at the Mayflower Hotel. Demands are coming in at such a rate that tables will be placed in the main corridor. . . . Smith is to have up to an hour on a national hookup . . . and every indication is that he is going after the Administration with a savage attack. The whole country will be listening in and the newspapers will give wide publicity to the speech."

Yet the Liberty League's platform had long since lost the advantage of novelty, along with its pretense of speaking out for the common man in quest of "liberty." Its critique of the New Deal had deteriorated into a repetitious litany of big business's grievances, often delivered by self-important capitalists draped in luxury—Shouse warned of "a great distrust of the present administration," before boarding an ocean liner for "several months in France, Switzerland, and England" with Mrs. Shouse; GM's Sloan returned from three weeks' vacation in the south of France to condemn the "shorter hours and pay rises" urged upon his company by the government. "Of course I believe in more leisure for workers," Sloan said upon disembarking from the German liner *Europa*. "But we should get it by reduced costs and increased efficiency, not by government edict. We should earn our leisure."

The Mayflower gala glistened with the same plutocratic sheen. When Smith's moment arrived, he mounted the podium in white tie and tails to declare that he spoke for "the best interests of the great rank and file of the American people in which class I belong." He proceeded to castigate the administration for pitting "class against class," for establishing an autocracy, seizing power from the states, and for confounding every plank of the 1932 Democratic platform (in perhaps an unwitting echo of Warburg's brief in *Hell Bent for Election*).

"Make a test for yourself," Smith said. "Just get the platform of the Democratic party and get the platform of the Socialist party and lay them down on your dining-room table, side by side. . . . After you have done that, make your mind up to pick up the platform that more nearly squares with the record, and you will have your hand on the Socialist platform."

Of the "young brain trusters," he said, "it is all right with me if they want to disguise themselves as Karl Marx or Lenin or any of the rest of that bunch, but I won't stand for allowing them to march under the banner of Jackson or Cleveland." Pausing for a round of applause, he threw down a challenge for the coming party convention in June. "Where does that leave us millions of Democrats? . . . There is only one of two things we can do, we can either take on the mantle of hypocrisy or we can take a walk, and we will probably do the latter."

He concluded with a "solemn warning": "There can be only one capital. Washington or Moscow. There can be only one atmosphere of government, the clear, pure, fresh air of free America, or the foul breath of communistic Russia. There can be only one flag, the Stars and Stripes or the flag of the godless Union of the Soviets."

The intemperance of Smith's words stunned his friends and foes alike. "I just can't understand it," FDR told Frances Perkins. "Practically all the things we've done in the Federal Government are like things Al Smith did as Governor of New York. They're things he would have done if he had been President of the United States. What in the world is the matter?"

As a progressive Republican, Hiram Johnson's judgment was scathing. His antennas, so well tuned to hypocrisy, were set aquiver by the bizarre display of fellowship between the league's wealthy sponsors and the erstwhile happy warrior they had not so long ago held in deepest contempt. "Every rat is out of its hole politically," he wrote his son Hiram Jr.

> The Liberty League, with its setting of millions upon millions, with shirt-front respectability militantly displayed, and with a boy from the side-walks of New York and the East side, in the role of the hero and savior of wealth and entrenched dishonesty, really put on a good show. . . . [I]t was an inspiring sight to see Dave Reed of Pennsylvania, the great Republican regular there, and Jimmy Wadsworth of New York, who represents ultra-conservatism in New York, and Alice Roosevelt Longworth, who leads the army of envy and spite, and the hundreds of others, who, in 1928, tilted their noses and said "Who, the Al Smiths in the White House?"

For the press, Smith's threat to "take a walk" at the June convention was the headline news of the evening. His speech, "in the opinion of Republican leaders at least, will increase greatly the chance of the election of a Republican President," reported the *New York Times,* which found that it heartened "anti–New Deal Democrats" as well.

The New Deal forces wasted little time before striking back. By Monday, two days after the Mayflower event, the White House had unearthed a 1928 speech in which Smith ridiculed the same charge of "socialism" from Hoover that he now leveled against Roosevelt. The document was supplied to Ickes, who was scheduled to make a joint appearance that night with Democratic senator Alben Barkley of Kentucky.

Prompted by Barkley to explain "a certain controversy about what constituted socialism" during the 1928 campaign, Ickes produced the speech from inside his jacket with a flourish and quoted Smith's own words: "The cry of socialism has been patented by the powerful interests that desire to put a damper on progressive legislation. Is that cry of socialism anything new? Not to a man of my experience. I have heard it raised by reactionary elements and the Republican party . . . for over a quarter century."

But the main counterthrust was delivered the next day by Senate Majority Leader Joe Robinson, who had been Smith's vice presidential running mate on the 1928 ticket. Robinson's goals in his own nationwide radio broadcast were to ridicule Smith's new persona and read him out of the mainstream of the Democratic Party. He began by conjuring up the audience of Smith's address, as described by a Washington newspaper: "Jammed elbow to elbow, fluttery bouffant dress to sleek black velvet dress . . . A billion-dollar audience." To this he added his own gloss: "It was the swellest party ever given by the du Ponts."

He reminded his listeners that the same policies Smith attacked in January 1936 had been endorsed by Smith in the 1928 campaign or as a New Deal supporter as recently as 1933.

> Somehow I think there must be two Al Smiths. One is the happy, carefree fellow behind whom we marched and shouted in 1928, proud of his principles. . . . Now we have this other Al Smith, this grim-visaged fellow in the high hat and tails, who warns us that we are going straight to Moscow. . . . The list of directors and officers of the American Liberty League reads like a roll-call of the men who have despoiled the oil, coal, and water-power resources of this country. . . . It was strange to see you in such company, Governor Smith.

Al Smith's sad journey out of the Democratic bosom was not yet complete. Roosevelt avoided making direct attacks on Smith himself. But he did not have to. By early June it was clear that Smith had failed to rally an anti-Roosevelt faction around him; even members of the party's established conservative bloc, men such as Bernard Baruch and Lewis Douglas, declined to offer him open support.

Roosevelt won renomination handily. That fall, Smith endorsed the Republican candidate, Alf Landon, for president. From then until his death in 1944, Al Smith would be a marginal figure in the Democratic Party, bereft of any role in domestic affairs but respected for his outspoken defense of the victims of fascism in Europe, cherished as a living artifact of a period of progressive hope in New York state and across the land, and held up, sometimes, as a symbol of how the lure of wealth and glitter can distance a man from his roots. His onetime Albany protégé, Franklin Roosevelt, beat Landon by a landslide in the 1936 election, a victory on such scale that it, too, would engender powerful lessons about how far a man can stray from his own principles.

17

NINE OLD MEN

THE LANDSLIDE ELECTION victory of November 1936, in which FDR carried all but two states, filled loyal New Dealers with euphoria. There were problems to vanquish, promises to keep, new social ventures to launch—and with a reinvigorated general in command, the battlefield was theirs.

Any detached observer examining the election returns of 1936, Rex Tugwell reflected later, would have seen "a leader completely vindicated, victorious in a free election as few political leaders have ever been. Clearly he possessed the confidence of the American people, clearly they had expressed the wish that he should go forward in the way he had pointed out."

Yet one year later, what would that same observer see? "That leader defeated, his program rejected, and he himself subjected to furious abuse. . . . The interests he had excoriated in the late campaign would be threatening again; agricultural surpluses would be building up with all the sinister implications of former years; unemployment would be returning; and he—the leader—would be calling into extraordinary session during the autumn the Congress he had been unable to manage during the spring and summer."

Franklin Roosevelt would have discovered the tragedy of hubris. The instrument of his self-destruction would be his decision to take on the Supreme Court.

Roosevelt had kept uncharacteristically silent about the Court's overreaching since his "horse-and-buggy" remark after the *Schechter* ruling of 1935.

Over the following two years, Congress carried the ball, entertaining more than one hundred bills to curb the Court, among other things by eliminating the right of judicial review in specific fields, diluting the conservative bloc by adding justices to the bench, and giving lawmakers the power to overturn court rulings by supermajorities. All were introduced amid fiery rhetoric condemning the Court for thwarting the plain intentions of the people. None passed.

Looking ahead to the cases making their way to the Court, New Dealers had reason for more worry. On the docket were lawsuits involving the Securities and Exchange Commission, the AAA, the National Labor Relations Board, and Social Security.

The AAA was the first of these on which the justices were heard. On January 6, 1936, in *U.S. v. Butler*, they overturned the agency's processing tax by a 6–3 vote. It was one of the first decisions to be issued from the Court's new Cass Gilbert–designed building, which had been completed and occupied a few weeks before the start of the justices' October 1935 term—"a magnificent structure," judged the *New Yorker*, "with fine big windows to throw the New Deal out of."

The majority opinion by Justice Owen Roberts struck down the linchpin of the New Deal's agricultural policy. Roberts found that the federal government's ostensibly unlimited power to levy taxes for the general welfare must be constrained here, because the "avowed purpose and operation" of the AAA, to which the processing tax would be applied, was "a step in an unauthorized plan" (by which was meant the "coercion" of farmers to remove acreage from production).

The dissent by Harlan Stone (with Brandeis and Cardozo concurring) picked the majority position apart as an abuse of judicial power based on "groundless speculation" about how the AAA would be administered. Nothing in the record, Stone wrote, suggested that the domestic allotment plan was coercive; quite the contrary, since the farm program offered generous subsidies to cooperating farmers. "Threat of loss, not hope of gain, is the essence of economic coercion," he wrote. To overturn an otherwise legal tax simply because the majority did not like the program it served required "a tortured construction of the Constitution."

By wiping out at a stroke expected allotment checks worth $2 billion in the coming year, the *Butler* decision added farmers to the lengthening roll of Americans whose skepticism about the Court was growing. Yet the justices still showed themselves capable of confounding expectations. On

February 17, 1936, they issued their opinion in *Ashwander v. Tennessee Valley Authority*, which concerned a challenge to the TVA's right to sell its electricity on the open market. The nearly universal assumption among legal experts and business leaders was that the government's case was doomed; on the day of the announcement, utility stocks soared when news tickers reported that Chief Justice Hughes had begun reading out the majority opinion.

Yet the outcome only illustrated that "speculators are just as poor guessers as anybody else," TVA Chairman David Lilienthal observed. For the Court upheld the TVA's position. Lilienthal, who had been tormenting himself for months with worries about how to run his agency if the case went against him, initially found victory hard to absorb. "I had completely resolved myself to a bad decision," he wrote in his diary, "only holding out hope that . . . unlike AAA and NRA we would not be swept completely out to sea, bag and baggage. To have a decision by an undivided court [actually the vote was 8–1] . . . [is] too much to comprehend in such a short time."

The optimism generated by the ruling was short-lived. Within a few weeks the Court would clip the wings of the Securities and Exchange Commission (albeit without nullifying the crucial Exchange Act of 1934) and invalidate the Guffey Coal Act, a sort of NRA for coal companies. Its most shocking decision involved not a federal statute, but New York state's minimum wage act for women. On June 1, in a case known in shorthand as *Tipaldo* after its detestable protagonist, the Court ruled 5–4 (with Hughes, Stone, Brandeis, and Cardozo in the minority) that the states had no power to interfere with contracts reached between employers and their workers—even where, as in this case, the "contract" was between female laundresses and the Brooklyn laundry owner who was flagrantly defrauding them of their legal wages.

No decision in that period was more damaging to the Court's prestige. The uproar over *Tipaldo* crossed partisan boundaries, eliciting condemnation even from Herbert Hoover, who proposed a constitutional amendment to return to the states "the power they thought they already had." In his diary, Harold Ickes castigated the Court for upholding "the sacred right . . . of an immature child or a helpless woman to drive a bargain with a great corporation." He added, not without a certain smug satisfaction, "If this decision does not outrage the moral sense of the country, then nothing will."

Tipaldo momentarily brought Roosevelt out of his self-imposed silence.

At a press conference the next day, he observed that the Court had now defined a "'no-man's-land' where no government can function. . . . A state cannot do it and the Federal Government cannot do it."

"How can you meet that situation?" a reporter inquired.

"I think that is about all there is to say on it," FDR replied levelly.

Over the months of reelection campaigning, that was about all he did say about it. Roosevelt's Republican challenger, Alf Landon of Kansas, had structured his campaign largely as a referendum on Social Security, a program Roosevelt defended with ease. One evening toward the end of the campaign, when it had become clear that victory was near, he was bantering with his speechwriters Stanley High and Sam Rosenman, the latter a close friend since the Albany days.

"You know, boys, I had a lovely thought last night," he said. "I thought what fun it would be if I could now be running against Franklin D. Roosevelt. . . . I certainly would have given him a close race—a darned sight closer than Landon is doing."

"What would you do?" Rosenman inquired.

First, FDR mused, he would repudiate William Randolph Hearst and the du Ponts, those iconic plutocrats backing the Republicans and conservative Democrats. Then he would attack the Democrats' only vulnerability—not the meat of their progressive program, but the sloppiness of its execution. "I would say: 'I am for Social Security, work relief, etc., etc. But the Democrats cannot be entrusted with the administration of these fine ideals.' . . . You know, the more I think about it, the more I think I could lick myself."

Roosevelt's conviction that the voters supported the New Deal's social principles held through election day. His indignation had mounted over a campaign against Social Security staged by big employers, who were stuffing their workers' pay envelopes with alarmist propaganda. For the last major speech of the campaign, at a vast rally in New York's Madison Square Garden on October 31, he instructed his speechwriting team of Rosenman, High, Tom Corcoran, and Ben Cohen to "take off all gloves."

Armed with their words, he funneled all his anger into a stemwinding delivery.

Tonight I call the roll—the roll of honor of those who stood with us in 1932 and still stand with us today. Written on it are the names of millions who never had a chance—men at starvation wages, women in sweatshops, children at looms. . . . Written on it are the names of farmers whose acres yielded only bitterness, business men whose books were portents of disaster, home owners who were faced with eviction, frugal citizens whose savings were insecure.

He threw a subtle challenge at the Supreme Court by calling the roll of New Deal initiatives the justices had thwarted . . . or might be inclined to thwart in the not too distant future. With an eye on the Court's 1937 docket, he said:

Of course we will continue to seek to improve working conditions for the workers of America—to reduce hours over-long, to increase wages that spell starvation, to end the labor of children, to wipe out sweatshops. Of course we will continue every effort to end monopoly in business, to support collective bargaining, to stop unfair competition, to abolish dishonorable trade practices. For all these we have only just begun to fight.

And he threw down the gauntlet at the reactionary forces arrayed behind Landon.

Never before in all our history have these forces been so united against one candidate. . . . They are unanimous in their hate for me—and I welcome their hatred. I should like to have it said of my first administration that in it the forces of selfishness and of lust for power met their match. I should like to have it said of my second administration that in it these forces met their master.

If there was a hint in these words of the hubris that would defeat his own program in the two years to come, it was lost in the clamor of support. At the polls on November 3, Alf Landon carried Maine and Vermont. Roosevelt carried the other forty-six states.

To outside appearances, Roosevelt had put the Court issue behind him. After the election and a round of triumphant appearances in Washington and his Upstate New York home region, he journeyed to South America for a Western Hemisphere peace conference. Upon returning, he put Rosenman, Corcoran, and Donald Richberg to work on his State of the Union address, to be delivered January 6 to a joint session of Congress. Rosenman, sensing that a resolution of the Court issue might be in the wind but with no idea what it might be, asked how the recalcitrant justices should be treated in the text.

"Leave the whole thing very general," Roosevelt told him blandly. "Let's just point up the need and when we get ready we'll submit the solution. I'm not quite ready yet."

Following his directive, the writers peppered the speech with a few oblique references to the New Deal's judicial travails. They had Roosevelt praise the "spirit of cooperation" prevailing between the executive and the legislature, implicitly reproaching the unmentioned third branch. He would pick at the scabs of Court decisions gone by: "The statute of N.R.A. has been outlawed. The problems have not. They are still with us." And he would question the Court's relevance to modern times: "During the past year there has been a growing belief that there is little fault to be found with the Constitution of the United States. . . . Difficulties have grown out of its interpretation; but rightly considered, it can be used as an instrument of progress, and not as a device for the prevention of action." The speech would close with a veiled warning: "It is not to be assumed that there will be prolonged failure to bring legislative and judicial action into closer harmony. Means must be found to adapt our legal forms and our judicial interpretation to the actual present national needs of the largest progressive democracy in the modern world. . . . The process of our democracy must not be imperiled by the denial of essential powers of government."

These interpolated barbs glided over the heads of most listeners. "The President does not speak like a man thinking of new experiments and new crusades," editorialized the *New York Times*. The editor of a respected legal journal concluded that Roosevelt had "made plain that he does not at the present time have in mind any legislation directed at the Court."

Yet those who read and reread the text detected sinister overtones. "It is very plain that he has something definitely in mind," Breckinridge Long, an old friend of FDR's serving as ambassador to Italy, wrote in his diary. "I say it is very plain, but I mean that it is very plain to those who read with a discriminating eye . . . and use as a background his whole history in connection with the Supreme Court."

Of course, he did have something very definitely in mind. He may have told Rosenman that he was "not quite ready yet," but he was close.

FDR's next major public speech would become one of his most famous.

The preliminary draft of the second inaugural address, delivered on January 20, had been prepared by Rosenman, Corcoran, and Richberg, revised to an unusual degree by the President. It was Roosevelt, Rosenman recalled, who contributed the passage beginning with the imagery of "the promised land" ("Shall we pause now and turn our back upon the road that lies ahead? Shall we call this the promised land?") and continuing to a resounding litany of challenges to America's democracy:

"In this nation I see tens of millions of its citizens . . . denied the greater part of what the very lowest standards of today call the necessities of life.

"I see millions of families trying to live on incomes so meager that the pall of family disaster hangs over them day by day. . . .

"I see millions denied education, recreation, and the opportunity to better their lot and the lot of their children. . . ."

On the draft, Rosenman had written his own summation with a final "I see" in pencil. Roosevelt took the draft, leaned back in his swivel armchair, stared intently at the ceiling, and then scribbled in his own hand the words "I see one-third of a nation ill-housed, ill-clad, ill-nourished." He read them aloud with great satisfaction. They were pithy, blunt, and direct, and they pointed seamlessly to his next, uplifting statement: "It is not in despair that I paint you that picture. I paint it for you in hope."

The words rang out on an Inauguration Day soaked by a driving rain. And not only those words: he concluded the address with a paean to the American democratic spirit.

"Overwhelmingly, we of the Republic are men and women of good will; men and women who have more than warm hearts of dedication; men and women who have cool heads and willing hands of practical purpose as well.

"They will insist that every agency of popular government use effective instruments to carry out their will"—from the podium Roosevelt gave particular emphasis to the word *every*, prompting Rosenman to cast a glance at Chief Justice Charles Evans Hughes, who had administered the oath of office and was seated behind the President on the Capitol porch. "There was no doubt that the Chief Justice understood what the President meant," he concluded.

Nor was there any doubt that Roosevelt meant to drive the point home. As he told Rosenman later, he had made a mental reservation when Hughes in reciting the oath called upon the President to "support the Constitution of the United States."

"I felt like saying, 'Yes, but it's the Constitution as *I* understand it, flexible enough to meet any new problem of democracy—not the kind of Constitution your Court has raised up as a barrier to progress and democracy.'"

What he did not reveal to Rosenman on that occasion was that he had been working toward a solution to the Court problem for more than a year—and that he had settled on an approach before Inauguration Day. In a few weeks he would drop his greatest bombshell.

That is not to say that Roosevelt had made any secret of his interest in finding some new approach. He had talked over the matter in private conversations with dozens of friends and associates, often maintaining that the Court's claimed authority to declare congressional acts unconstitutional—"judicial review"—was a "usurpation" of power granted it nowhere in the Constitution. At a cabinet meeting in late December 1935 he outlined a constitutional amendment that might address that issue. It would grant the Court the right of judicial review, but specify that if an overturned statute was repassed by a subsequent Congress—that is, following the biennial election of the full House of Representatives—the law would stand. "By this method there would be in effect a referendum to the country, albeit an indirect one," observed an approving Harold Ickes.

Yet amending the Constitution presented major difficulties, not least of which was the labyrinthine path to ratification. An amendment had to be approved by two-thirds of both houses of Congress and three-fourths of the states. Therefore it could be killed if thirteen governors refused to submit the bill to their legislatures. Under the best circumstances the process could take years, and it could be thwarted by a well-financed opposition; given that the Court's conservative cast pleased the well-heeled denizens of Wall Street and corporate boardrooms, that was a daunting obstacle. In early 1936, Attorney General Cummings, who had become Roosevelt's principal confidant on the matter, cautioned against placing too much hope in an amendment. "No one has yet suggested an amendment that does not either do too much or too little," he wrote, "or which does not raise practical and political questions which it would be better to avoid."

On the other side of the coin, a major problem with legislation to trim the Court's sails was that the Court might declare it unconstitutional. At one point Roosevelt openly mused about provoking a constitutional crisis via an anti-Court statute, letting the public, in effect, choose sides among the branches of government. As Ickes reported the President's "plan," if the Court overruled a bill pertaining to its powers and duties he would go to

Congress and "ask it to instruct him whether he was to follow the mandate of Congress or the mandate of the Court." If the answer was the former, "the President would carry out the will of Congress through the offices of the United States Marshals and ignore the Court."

The flaw in this stratagem was that it was not at all clear that Congress or the people were quite ready to follow him down that road. The Court had attracted much public anger, but perhaps not yet enough. "The President is really hoping that the Supreme Court will continue to make a clean sweep of all New Deal legislation," Ickes discerned, "throwing out the TVA Act, the Securities Act, the Railroad Retirement Act, the Social Security Act, the Guffey Coal Act, and others. He thinks the country is beginning to sense this issue but that enough people have not yet been affected by adverse decisions to make a sufficient feeling."

After the 1936 election, Roosevelt summoned George Creel, who had returned to *Collier's* weekly, where he served as the President's direct conduit to the voters. Roosevelt outlined a proposal to attach a rider to sensitive bills instructing the Court that the law was enacted "pursuant to the Constitutional provision vesting *all* legislative power in the Congress and explicitly authorizing it 'to provide for the general welfare.'"

And if that didn't discourage judicial meddling? " 'Then,' said the President, his face like a fist, 'Congress can *enlarge* the Supreme Court, increasing the number of justices so as to permit the appointment of men in tune with the spirit of the age. And what is there radical about it? The country started out with six justices and has had as many as ten.'"

Creel was certain that Roosevelt's words, which appeared in the December 26, 1936, issue of *Collier's,* would create a furor. "Incredibly enough, not a newspaper in the country caught the significance of the statement," he wrote later, still feeling the pique of a reporter with a major scoop that had gone utterly unnoticed. "When, therefore, he asked Congress some three months later to enlarge the Supreme Court, it came as a bombshell."

Creel's article does indicate that by the end of December, Roosevelt had settled on what became known as the Court-packing scheme. In its ultimate form, which involved supplementing justices who had reached the age of seventy with younger appointees, the plan originated with Edward Corwin, a Princeton law professor who had cobbled it together from suggestions made by progressive friends on law faculties across the country. Among its virtues was that it exploited a power the Constitution left to Congress, for as Roosevelt correctly observed to Creel, the size and composition of the Supreme Court lay entirely within the legislative purview, and legislative precedent dating back to the Judiciary Act of 1789 was abundant.

Attorney General Cummings discovered another virtue in the scheme. He learned that in 1913, Woodrow Wilson's attorney general had recommended offering retirement at full pay to any elderly federal judge below the Supreme Court. To the extent any refused to retire, the President would be required to appoint another judge with seniority over the elder. The attorney general who had come up with that plan for Wilson was James Clark McReynolds, now one of the reactionary Four Horsemen of the Supreme Court. This built-in irony delighted the President.

In its new form, the plan applied to all federal judges. If any failed to retire within six months of reaching age seventy, the President could appoint another judge to that court—up to six additional judges to the Supreme Court.

There was a certain crass logic in attributing the New Deal's problems with the Court to the aging bench; the oldest justice among the conservative Four Horsemen, Willis Van Devanter, had been born during the administration of James Buchanan, an era rendered hopelessly remote from contemporary America not only by the tolling of the years but by the social and political changes wrought by the intervening Civil War. But the argument had a serious shortcoming. The liberal Justice Louis Brandeis, as sensitive a jurist as any to the issues and travails of modern life, was the oldest member of the Nine—*he* had been born during the administration of Franklin Pierce, Buchanan's predecessor. And the argument was not likely to have much appeal for the influential bloc of septuagenarians in Congress, of whom the dean was Senator Carter Glass of Virginia, seventy-nine.

Roosevelt's superb feel for political strategy abandoned him in the preparation of the Court plan. His blunders were many. First, he failed to engage key members of his own staff or Congress in its development. Although Cohen, Corcoran, and others had participated in discussions about the Court over the previous two years, the evidence indicates that none had been intimately involved with drafting the plan after early 1936 other than Homer Cummings and a small group of Justice Department aides—and many of the latter were kept in the dark by being assigned to research compartmentalized aspects of the whole. No congressional leader had any idea of the coming proposal until its unveiling.

This approach denied the leaders of Roosevelt's party in Congress the chance to build up support for the plan in advance and denied Roosevelt the counsel of veteran political minds on Capitol Hill. Congressional Democrats, who had done so much to push the New Deal's programs to passage even when they disagreed with its details, were deprived of that all-important feeling of ownership of a bill that helps maintain cohesion throughout a hard fight.

Roosevelt's greater blunder was to publicly portray the plan as a device to address the Court's age, not its ideology. By draping his initiative with a transparently deceptive rationale, he planted the seeds of its failure.

The President's message to Congress accompanying the bill and its supporting memo by Cummings emphasized the necessity of relieving the federal judiciary of its burden of overwork and inefficiency. Cummings's memo offered mounds of specious data about excessive caseloads exacerbated by the doddering condition of elderly jurists—"aged or infirm judges," in Cummings's infelicitous description. It was as though Roosevelt and Cummings were determined not only to insult the very dignity of the judiciary, but also the intelligence of the American public.

Had Roosevelt stated candidly that his rationale for the Court plan was to drag a recalcitrant bench into the twentieth century in recognition of the unique challenges of contemporary economic conditions, he might well have retained the support of progressives anguished at the Court's menace to the New Deal. Instead he weakened his best argument and put forth one that was much weaker and self-evidently disingenuous. He would abandon this argument at an early stage of the battle, but it would not save the plan.

In the days following his inauguration in 1937, Roosevelt gingerly began taking his closest aides into his confidence.

Rosenman's turn came on January 30, the date of the President's annual "cuff links" birthday reception, reserved for that select group of friends and advisors who had received from FDR a pair of gold cuff links, one engraved with his own initials and the other with the recipient's, for their loyalty and service. When Rosenman arrived at the White House, Missy LeHand steered him away from the main reception hall and upstairs to the Oval Room, where a luncheon table had been set for five. Already seated with the President were Attorney General Cummings, solicitor general Stanley Reed, and Donald Richberg. Rosenman sensed something momentous in the air, but the small talk over lunch did nothing to illuminate the mystery, least of all an anecdote Roosevelt told about a World War I combat ship called the *Santee*. The vessel had been camouflaged to resemble an ordinary merchantman, FDR related. It would meekly submit when ordered to stop on the high seas by a marauding German U-boat—until the enemy vessel came into close range, at which point the *Santee* would drop a false side wall, revealing a rank of guns that would unload on the unfortunate sub. Rosenman could detect no connection at all between the yarn about an old combat ship and "this pleasant, rather aimless luncheon for five."

Finally, Roosevelt unsheathed his own guns. The dishes cleared and the door closed, he began to read aloud a letter from Cummings and the draft of a proposed message to Congress. Rosenman was astonished at the audacity of the Court plan and dumbfounded to discover that everyone else in the room had been apprised of the contents well in advance—and evidently had been discussing the matter with great intensity for days or weeks. He joined in the discussion as best he could, agreeing with the group that the message would have to be rewritten—"pepped up," in Roosevelt's words— if it was to have popular appeal. It turned out that was Rosenman's assignment. "Try to get up another draft," FDR told him as he departed.

According to Tommy Corcoran's recollection, his introduction to a plan that would draw him deeply into the legislative maelstrom was even more belated. Although he and Cohen had participated in discussions of anti-Court tactics after the *Tipaldo* decision, including (Frankfurter's idea) a constitutional amendment to authorize a minimum wage, he was under the impression that the issue had been dropped prior to the Democratic convention in June.

Corcoran would not learn differently until "hours before the President loosed it upon the land," he recalled later. Summoned to the White House on February 5, he was handed a set of papers by Missy LeHand, and instructed to look them over "confidentially."

On top was the message to Congress. "I had to skim it twice to confirm that it said what I feared on first reading," he recalled. Mentally he slashed his way through the thicket of transparent arguments about overloaded dockets, delayed calendars, and the administrative difficulties of the lower federal courts to reach the real agenda. He was stunned by "the implied insult to the memory of Justice Holmes and the actual slap in the face to the living Justice Brandeis. Roosevelt might just as well have called everyone over 70 senile and be done with it." (Things would get worse: in a Fireside Chat a month hence, Roosevelt would observe that come that

June five justices would be older than seventy-five, implicitly including the eighty-year-old Brandeis as an exemplar of the Court's "hardening of the judicial arteries.")

The problem raised by the reference to "aged and infirm judges" in the message to Congress was immediate. Corcoran asked LeHand to let him in to see the President. She hesitated, reminding Corcoran how much Roosevelt disliked argumentation on the eve of battle. But sensing Corcoran's urgency, she relented. Opening the door to the Oval Room, she said, "Five minutes."

Roosevelt was, indeed, disinclined to hear any argument against the plan, but one of Corcoran's points told: for Old Isaiah, the affront was so direct he might take it personally. What if it provoked him to join the behind-the-scenes opposition? Corcoran asked. Worse, what if it started to color his opinions on the upcoming New Deal cases?

The President allowed that the same thought had not escaped him; he had toyed with calling Brandeis himself, but dropped the idea out of fear of getting into an argument with his old friend and mentor. He authorized Corcoran to go to meet Brandeis at the Court, though he instructed him to hail a taxi inconspicuously on the street instead of taking a White House car.

Reaching the Court building, Corcoran talked his way into the robing room by mumbling to the guard that he needed to speak to Brandeis about "a matter of life-or-death importance." ("I didn't actually say that the jurist's nearest living relative had just been run over by a Mack truck," he would recall, "but if the bailiff inferred something of that magnitude, in my haste I failed to disabuse him.") In the robing room the Court was preparing for oral arguments. The justices all recognized Corcoran by sight as one of Roosevelt's men, earning him a scowl from Hughes and a glare from McReynolds as he sought out the startled Brandeis. Corcoran whipped out a copy of the President's message and started to explain to Brandeis in an excited whisper what was about to happen, only to be hushed instantly by a wave of the justice's hand. Brandeis hung back with Corcoran as the rest of the Supreme Court followed the chief justice out to the courtroom. Then Brandeis took the paper and began to read. Meanwhile, Corcoran kept talking: the President had meant to exclude him from the plan, but that would have meant undermining the whole proposal.

At length Brandeis looked up from the page, shook his head, and uttered a few solemn words.

"Tell your President he has made a great mistake," he said. "All he had to do is wait a little while. I'm sorry for him." Then he disappeared through a red velvet curtain to join his colleagues. Flustered and embarrassed, Corcoran missed the chance to ask him what he meant by "wait a little while." He would learn soon with the rest of the country, but then it would be too late.

Corcoran made his own way to the courtroom, where he took a seat in a privileged row reserved for current and former clerks. While he and Brandeis had been having their colloquy, the President's message had gone up to Capitol Hill and the word had gone out. As Corcoran watched, a clerk materialized from behind the red curtain and handed a sheaf of papers to the chief justice. A page passed copies to the justices. An attorney was standing on his feet before the bench, haplessly trying to make his oral presentation to the justices in what might well have been the most momentous case of his career; but Corcoran could see they were not listening. They were scanning the mimeographed documents before them, casting glances at one another, and sitting back with inscrutable expressions on their faces. Roberts and Butler caught each other's eyes, and chuckled softly.

Notwithstanding the aides' disavowals, Washington gossip fingered Corcoran and Cohen as the creators of the Court plan from the start, if for no other reason than they were widely known as FDR's legislative geniuses. Brandeis did not know what to think. The night of his robing-room conference with Corcoran, the jurist, perhaps desperate for some concrete assurance that his two young protégés had not played their rumored role, wrote a letter to his friend Felix Frankfurter. "Whom did F.D. rely on for his Judiciary message and bill?" he asked. "Has he consulted you on any of his matters of late?"

In time the cheering news came from other New Dealers that the plan had been contrived in the attorney general's office, and that Frankfurter's two hot dogs were innocent. Roosevelt also had kept Frankfurter out of the loop, at least partially to inoculate him from the controversy sure to erupt, and partially to avert any premature disclosure to Brandeis. Unable to resist saying *something*, however, he had dropped a single hint to Frankfurter in mid-January.

"Very confidentially," he had written, "I may give you an awful shock in about two weeks."

While Corcoran was on his way to alert Brandeis, Roosevelt was convening a meeting of the cabinet and members of the congressional leadership.

They had been summoned in an air of great mystery to hear what was described simply as "an important announcement." They assembled in the Cabinet Room, chatting among themselves, staring out the windows. None but Cummings, who wore a faintly smug look, was aware of what was in store.

The doors flew open and Roosevelt rolled in, accompanied by his secretaries carrying piles of mimeographed papers. These were planted along the conference table as the President began to speak hastily, explaining that he was due at a press conference in a matter of minutes. His torrent of words rolled over the audience, most of whom may have been too stunned to raise their own voices. For more than a year they had been complaining about the Court, all in agreement that it had stepped over the line of juridical judgment into ideological opposition to the two other branches of government, all eager to consider any method to clip its wings. Yet now that they were confronted with a concrete program, they felt the stirrings of unease.

Ickes glanced at the others. Vice President Garner, he noticed, had said not a word—"the first time I have ever seen him at a cabinet or any other meeting sit entirely silent." William B. Bankhead of Alabama, who had been Speaker of the House for barely six months, wore a "distinctly 'pokerish' face." Senate majority leader Joe Robinson of Arkansas "indicated a mild assent." Hatton Sumners of Texas, who as head of the House Judiciary Committee would have the first crack at the proposal, "said nothing but his pleasure was apparent."

Plainly, Ickes's perception was clouded by his delight at an initiative he considered "fully justified," as he wrote in his diary a few days later. "No one can see into the future, but I suspect that this adroit move . . . will be one of the outstanding things in American history for all time to come. This will be true whether the President wins or loses."

Even before he set down those words, the die was being cast in a very different direction. The guests drove away from the White House in two cars. In one, carrying Garner and an assortment of senators and congressmen, "we were all so stunned we hardly spoke," Garner recalled. The other carried Robinson and Sumners, the latter of whom stewed for two or three blocks before announcing his judgment. "Boys," he said, "here's where I cash in my chips."

By then, the press had assembled in the White House for a most extraordinary news conference. It was 10:55 A.M. "I have a somewhat important matter to take up with you today," Roosevelt began, stressing an absolute embargo on the news until his message was sent to Capitol Hill later that day. Copies would not be handed out until the press filed out of the Oval Room.

Roosevelt proceeded to read Cummings's letter accompanying the bill, followed by his legislative message. Here and there he interpolated a personal remark, often jocular, as when he reached a point in his message where he recalled the old practice of forcing Supreme Court justices to "ride circuit" around the country to hear cases—"Riding Circuit in those days meant riding on horseback. . . . It might be called a pre-horse-and-buggy era," he said, to appreciative laughter.

The entire session lasted some two hours. "And that is all the news," Roosevelt concluded. The reporters were so dazed and exhausted that they mustered only four desultory questions, then departed.

A day later, while the President's message was being read on the Senate floor, Vice President Garner stepped off the rostrum and, passing a group of senators, held his nose with one hand and made a thumbs-down gesture with the other. The Democratic leaders of both houses assured reporters and their members that the bill was certain to pass, but any percipient observer could tell that its support was dangerously thin.

What was notable about the opposition that began to jell in the first few days and weeks was that the deepest skepticism about the Court plan came from progressives in both parties. Ickes was so perplexed by the opposition of Hiram Johnson, a Republican who had run for vice president on Theodore Roosevelt's Bull Moose progressive ticket in 1912, that he found himself speculating about Johnson's ulterior motives: "Perhaps . . . he sees a chance to make one of his spectacular fights on the floor of the Senate and thus go out in a blaze of glory," he wrote of the aging California senator in his diary, adding nervously: "He undoubtedly is in a position to do considerable damage to the President's cause."

Ickes misjudged his old friend. Johnson genuinely feared that Roosevelt's tampering with a "familiar" system endangered the republic. "If he can do it once, he can do it again, and when the country veers around his successor can do it," he wrote his son Hiram Jr. "Down that road lies dictatorship."

The opposition of progressive Democrats was even more damaging to the President's cause. Republicans, no matter their ideological leanings, were a discredited party following the humiliating rout of November, and the conservative Democrats rallying to their side were too few in number to make a difference. Liberal and progressive Democrats, however, were

Roosevelt's natural constituency in Congress, the direct beneficiaries of the New Deal's popularity. They were November's victors, yet they were proving disturbingly obstinate. On the very day of Roosevelt's message, no less a New Deal icon than George Norris of Nebraska—the father of the TVA, the outstanding liberal of the Senate, and the sponsor of a bill requiring a 7–2 vote of the Court to overturn a congressional act—had stated bluntly: "I am not in sympathy with the plan to enlarge the Supreme Court." His objection paralleled Hiram Johnson's: the precedent and the power were too despotic to unleash in a country where the next man to wield them might not be as benevolent as the last.

More dangerous than Norris, because more powerful, was Burton Wheeler of Montana. Roosevelt and Wheeler had a prickly relationship dating back to the currency program of 1933, when the President had torpedoed Wheeler's silver-coinage amendment to the AAA bill. After hearing the Court message Wheeler let the White House know that he was firmly resistant to tampering with the Court. He would presently emerge as the leader of the congressional opposition.

The Republicans detected their first opportunity in four years to get the better of Franklin Roosevelt. Watching Democratic unity in Congress fray over the Court plan, they opted for silence—although their former standard-bearer had to be dragged from the arena kicking and screaming. "This morning ex-President Hoover phoned me from the Waldorf-Astoria in New York, eager to jump into the fray," Arthur Vandenberg of Michigan recorded in his diary the day after Roosevelt's announcement. "Now here is one of the tragedies of life. Hoover is still 'poison.' . . . Borah is prepared to lead this fight," Vandenberg added, referring to William Borah, the veteran progressive Republican from Idaho. "But he insisted that there is no hope if it is trade-marked in advance as a 'Hoover fight' or a 'Republican fight.'"

Hoover was unwilling to be silenced. He let it be known that he was preparing a radio speech as follow-up to a bitter statement he had issued on the very day of the presidential message, condemning the Court plan as an effort at "subordination of the court to the personal power of the Executive." Vandenberg called the ex-president to plead with him to stand down. Hoover responded with an angry blast over the phone from Palo Alto. "Who's trying to muzzle me?" he demanded. He went through with his radio address on February 20, accusing Roosevelt of plotting to create a Court "that will revise the Constitution so it will mean what he wishes it to mean." After that, however, he acceded to his party's wishes, fuming about the Court plan privately at home. The rest of the GOP maintained the required discipline, goading Ickes to grouse to his diary with perfect accuracy: "The Republicans are as meek as skimmed milk. None of them raises his voice. The strategy apparently is to let the Democrats tear each other to pieces and then . . . to move in and enjoy the fruits of victory, if the President is defeated, without suffering any casualties."

Wheeler hoped to launch his attack on the Court plan with a "resounding bang" when Senate hearings on the Court plan convened in mid-March. But he was at a loss for the proper weapon, short of producing a member of the Court to testify in opposition. Overtures in that vein to Chief Justice Hughes seemed briefly to bear fruit; Hughes expressed a willingness to appear if at least one other justice joined him—preferably Brandeis, whose liberal reputation was unassailable. But Brandeis disapproved of a personal appearance by any member of the Court. Instead he proposed that the justices write a joint letter.

On March 20, two days before the start of hearings, the wheels for a formal, yet oblique, response from the Court were quietly set in motion. According to the story handed down over the decades, Justice Brandeis's wife, Alice, upon paying a social call to Wheeler's daughter and her new baby, remarked, "Tell your father I think he is right." Wheeler, taking this as a signal that Brandeis opposed the bill, called the justice, who told him: "You call up the Chief Justice, and he'll give you a letter." The point of the inside story was to create the impression that the initiative came from members of Congress, not the Court. In truth, discussions aimed at securing a letter had been going on for several days among Hughes, Brandeis, and members of Congress.

Hughes placed the document in Wheeler's hands the next day, a Sunday. "I am not interested in who are to be the members of the Court," he told the senator. "I am interested in the Court as an institution. And this proposed bill would destroy the Court as an institution."

At 10:30 the next morning Wheeler took his seat behind the witness table in the ornate Senate Caucus Room. He was secretly armed with a bombshell on a scale that that master of the surprise detonation, Franklin Roosevelt, might himself have appreciated. The room was packed.

Wheeler wasted little time before producing his weapon. He informed the committee that having heard Cummings's words about the punishing workload of the court, "I went to the only source in this country that could know exactly what the facts were and that better than anyone else." Theatrically, he reached into his inside coat pocket. "I have here now a letter by the Chief Justice of the Supreme Court, Mr. Charles Evans Hughes, dated March 21, 1937, written by him and approved by Mr. Justice Brandeis and Mr. Justice Van Devanter. Let us see what these gentlemen say about it."

The room stayed utterly silent as Wheeler read out Hughes's point-by-point demolition of Roosevelt's rationale for packing the Court. "The Supreme Court is fully abreast of its work," Hughes stated. "There is no congestion of cases upon our calendar. This gratifying condition has obtained for several years." There followed several pages of statistics related to caseloads, as well as a learned explication of the constitutional and legislative history underlying the Court's jurisdiction.

The volley hit home. The letter itself became almost a totemic object. "The newsreels photographed it, newspaper reporters clamored for copies, and it was all I could do to keep it from being snatched from my hands when the session was recessed," Wheeler recalled.

But the document also strained relations among the justices. Stone and Cardozo were both offended by the public implication that the letter represented the opinion of the entire Court. Stone wrote Frankfurter to say that he had not seen the letter before its publication, and that he "certainly would not have joined in that part of it which undertakes to suggest what is and what is not constitutional." Cardozo, for his part, quietly let his staff know that he was "as opposed to the Hughes-Brandeis intervention as he was to the plan itself," his clerk Joseph L. Rauh, Jr., recollected.

Hughes's gambit infuriated Roosevelt's aides, none more so than the truculent Ickes, who suggested a "head-on attack" on the chief justice. Brandeis's public association with the letter strained his relations with Roosevelt and provoked a complete break with Corcoran, who complained that Brandeis "did not shoot straight with us" in taking a stand he knew would torpedo an important New Deal initiative. He never saw the justice again.

Progressives strived to find violations of judicial decorum in Hughes's words. The *New Republic,* in an unsigned item later attributed to Thurman Arnold, a Justice Department attorney, accused Hughes of having "[thrown] all judicial discretion to the wind" by explicitly advising that one counterproposal in the air, which would allow some cases to be heard by fewer than the full complement of justices in an enlarged Court, also would be unconstitutional. "Here we have the final step in the usurpation of judicial power," the article argued—"a statement in advance to Congress of the kind of laws which the Court intends to condemn."

Yet those who expressed shock at the notion of members of the Court involving themselves in politics were perhaps protesting overmuch. The definition of judicial propriety was murky; Stone and Brandeis, after all, had given Perkins advice on how to tailor the Social Security bill to survive challenge before the Court of which they were members; Stone, furthermore, was confidentially providing information to newspaper reporters to help them puncture Roosevelt's "overburdened Court" argument. In any event, most of the justices were no strangers to politics. Stone and four others had served in elective or appointed political office before ascending to the Court. Hughes had been a governor of New York and a candidate for president. George Sutherland, one of the conservative Four Horsemen, had served as a U.S. representative and senator.

The reading of the Hughes letter had an explosive effect, but whether it decisively influenced the battle over the Court plan is debatable. Few on Capitol Hill, and almost no one in the White House, thought that it dealt the bill a mortal blow. The political battle lines had already been drawn when Wheeler produced it from his jacket pocket. Moreover, the argument the letter specifically addressed, that the Court was overworked, had been discredited virtually from the moment it had been uttered. It certainly was no longer an important part of the debate in Washington, where the issue long since had been reconfigured as a political battle between the Court and the New Deal. As Ickes observed, "We abandoned this ground some time ago." In a Fireside Chat devoted to the judiciary plan on March 9, Roosevelt had not mentioned the workload of the Supreme Court at all; he no longer depicted his scheme to infuse "new blood into all our Courts" as an effort to ease the burdens of aged and doddering justices but rather as a means of introducing into the judiciary "younger men who have had personal experience and contact with modern facts and circumstances." The original error, Ickes conceded, was Roosevelt's, in having placed his poorest argument in the vanguard and left it exposed to attack. "Shrewdly," he wrote, "Hughes chose to fight his skirmish where we were the weakest."

Hughes's audacious injection of the Court itself into the debate on the Court plan signaled a new phase in his leadership on the bench. Cardozo, who had watched Hughes's performance for five years, considered him a "brilliant and efficient Chief Justice but one without wisdom." For a few months he had been exercising that latter quality privately among the justices. One week after his letter was read aloud in the Senate Caucus Room, his wisdom showed itself in public and affected the plan's fate much more convincingly.

It has often been remarked that the Court's abrupt shift on the constitutionality of the minimum wage could not have been a response to the President's Court-packing plan, for the justices had already conferred and voted on the case titled *West Coast Hotel v. Parrish* on a January Saturday, several days before the plan was unveiled.

Yet there can hardly be any doubt that the Court recognized that its public standing had become equivocal in the wake of *Tipaldo*. Following the decision, Justice Stone wrote to his sister with unusual heat, labeling the Court's 1936 term "in many ways one of the most disastrous in its history. . . . We seem to have tied Uncle Sam up in a hard knot." Then came the 1936 election, with its resounding endorsement of the New Deal and its implicit repudiation of the Court.

Tipaldo had been decided by a 5–4 vote, with Justice Roberts supplying the swing vote to invalidate the law and writing the majority opinion. A few weeks after the election a new minimum wage case had been argued before the Court, this one from Washington state. The legal issues presented by the two cases were almost identical. Elsie Parrish was a chambermaid in an eastern Washington resort hotel, which she contended had cheated her of $216.19 by paying her less than the state minimum wage for nearly two years. Although the minimum wage law had been upheld repeatedly by Washington courts, the state rulings had been trumped by the Supreme Court. The Washington supreme court was not satisfied; when a lawyer for the hotel company asked a state supreme court justice why he upheld Parrish's claim even after the U.S. Supreme Court had spoken, he replied, "Let's let the Supreme Court say it one more time."

What provoked Roberts to reverse his vote on the minimum wage in *Parrish* remains a mystery, but his joining the majority to uphold the Washington law does have the appearance of a lunge for a lifeline. Conceivably, his fellow centrist Hughes may have had something to do with it, perhaps through a subtle suggestion that the Court's prestige, even its survival, hung in the balance.

Hughes assigned himself to write the new opinion. When the moment arrived to read it, he summoned all the majesty of his position and his person: distinguished and courtly, with his painstakingly groomed white beard, he looked the very model of a chief justice, complete with the aura of infallibility. On March 29, the courtroom was packed and bustling, as the old courtroom in the Capitol had been on Black Monday. Hughes had to raise his voice to be heard. Before he was finished, he had reversed not only *Tipaldo* but also consigned to the ash heap fifteen years of Court precedent hostile to the minimum wage. The precedent arose from a 1923 Washington, D.C., employment case known as *Adkins v. Children's Hospital,* in which four of Hughes's present colleagues had voted with the majority, including Sutherland, who wrote the opinion striking down a minimum wage for women. Hughes nevertheless held that "the economic conditions that have supervened, and in the light of which the reasonableness of the exercise of the protective power of the state must be considered, make it not only appropriate, but we think imperative, that . . . the subject should receive fresh consideration." That led him to the conclusion that *Adkins* "was a departure from the true application of the principles governing . . . the relation of employer and employed."

The ground had shifted under the feet of the Four Horsemen. By alluding to "economic conditions," Hughes signaled that this Court, like Congress and the executive branch, now recognized governmental responsibilities and authorities found not in the explicit words of the Constitution, but in its interstices.

The basis for overruling minimum wage laws in the past had been their violation of freedom of contract, Hughes observed.

What is this freedom? The Constitution does not speak of freedom of contract. It speaks of liberty . . . But the liberty safeguarded is liberty in a social organization which requires the protection of law against the evils which menace the health, safety, morals and welfare of the people. . . . The bare cost of living must be met. We may take judicial notice of the unparalleled demands for relief which arose during the recent period of depression and still continue to an alarming extent.

Parrish marked a watershed for the Court, but it was not the only New Deal victory that day; the justices also upheld a farm foreclosure moratorium and an act granting collective bargaining rights to employees of interstate railroads. More victories were to come. In early April the Court upheld the National Labor Relations Act in five separate rulings, all 5–4. Then, in two opinions on May 24, it upheld the cornerstone of the New

Deal, the Social Security Act. The author of both opinions was Cardozo, his arguments detailed and rigorous, his vision of modern America profoundly felt and poetically expressed, on his sixty-seventh birthday:

> The purge of nationwide calamity that began in 1929 has taught us many lessons. Not the least is the solidarity of interests that may once have seemed to be divided. Unemployment spreads from State to State, the hinterland now settled that, in pioneer days gave an avenue of escape. . . . Spreading from State to State, unemployment is an ill not particular, but general, which may be checked, if Congress so determines, by the resources of the Nation. . . . But the ill is all one, or at least not greatly different, whether men are thrown out of work because there is no longer work to do or because the disabilities of age make them incapable of doing it. Rescue becomes necessary irrespective of the cause. The hope behind this statute is to save men and women from the rigors of the poor house, as well as from the haunting fear that such a lot awaits them when journey's end is near.

Against that vision was interposed "a pungent lecture from the bench" by McReynolds, the most hidebound of the Four Horsemen. With a cold smile projecting "no imagination or sympathy . . . just meanness," in the words of newspaper columnist Raymond Clapper, McReynolds denounced the majority opinions as soft-minded. "No volume of words and no citation of irrelevant statistics and no appeal to feelings of humanity can expand the powers granted to Congress," he said. "Neither can we, by attempts to paint a white rose red, view the situation differently from that seen by the fathers of the Constitution." With these rulings, he snarled, "unquestionably our federate plan of government confronts an enlarged peril."

He spoke as the emperor of a shrunken domain. And his four-man minority was destined to become even smaller. Six days earlier Willis Van Devanter had announced his retirement, handing Roosevelt the Court opening he had so desperately craved, the very first of his presidency. It also explained Brandeis's cryptic statement to Corcoran two months earlier that it would have been wiser to "wait a little while"; the seventy-eight-year-old Van Devanter's intention to retire in 1937 had been known to his colleagues, although its actual timing may have resulted from tactful pressure applied by Hughes.

From the day Hughes read out his opinion in *Parrish,* the Supreme

Court never invalidated another New Deal statute—ruling for the government in twenty cases in the 1937 winter term alone. The turnabout was so sudden and complete that New Dealers sounded like travelers lost in an unfamiliar landscape. "I was taken for a ride on a chicken truck in Brooklyn two years ago and dumped out on a deserted highway and left for dead," Hugh Johnson wrote FDR in April, after the Court upheld the NLRB. "It seems this was all a mistake."

The New Deal's enemies thought they knew whom to blame for the phenomenon. "Roosevelt largely accomplished his purpose of destruction of the Supreme Court," Hoover grumbled in his memoirs. He observed that *Parrish*, the NLRB cases, and the Social Security rulings all had been issued "within four months after the attack." A few days after the Social Security rulings, Wendell Willkie suggested to Walter Lippmann that the justices seemed "terrorized" by the Court plan. Lippmann demurred: "I think the decisions this year would have been about what they have been without the Judiciary Bill. I think the President has been hammering on a door that was already open." For the public, the agent of the Court's about-face was identified in a catchphrase that swept the country: it was "the switch in time that saved nine"—Justice Roberts's conversion to membership in the liberal bloc, whether or not he had been guided on his way by Chief Justice Hughes.

The judicial struggle against the New Deal had ended. Yet it was at that very point that Franklin Roosevelt turned the Court-packing proposal into his worst defeat. Having been handed victory, he proceeded to lose the war. In the words of the New Deal loyalist Senator James F. Byrnes of South Carolina (a future Supreme Court justice), Roosevelt had kept running for the train after he had caught it, because he had not caught the train he wanted.

The final act of the Court scheme unfolded as tragedy.

The President seemed oddly less than jubilant about the ringing endorsements of New Deal initiatives issued from the Court that spring. After *Parrish*—not a New Deal case, but a pointer nevertheless toward the Court's new view of social legislation—he was asked by a reporter if he thought "the Supreme Court is curing itself." He replied, "To tell you the honest truth, I haven't even had the time to read the opinions." After the NLRB rulings, he allowed that he had been "chortling all morning" but asked, "Could we in any way tell from these decisions whether the same extension of judicial policy would be extended to things like child labor, for example." Not even the Social Security rulings seemed to persuade him that a revolution had come to pass. "There are a great many things that have occurred in the past that still have not been ruled on," he cautioned the press.

To be fair, Roosevelt had good reasons to be dissatisfied with the new 5–4 split on the Court and with Van Devanter's retirement. The new majority was razor thin; an untimely switch back by Roberts could destroy it in a heartbeat. More troubling, two years earlier the administration had promised the first Supreme Court vacancy to come along to Senate Majority Leader Joe Robinson, for whom a seat on the Court had been a lifelong ambition, and whose yeoman work shepherding New Deal legislation through his House warranted a lavish reward. But the Arkansan Robinson, though a loyal Democrat, was fundamentally a southern conservative—he might be exactly the kind of appointee who confounded the expectations of his president, a breed that had been common throughout Court history.

Roosevelt was in a box. On the day of Van Devanter's retirement announcement, Robinson's colleagues had thronged around him in the Senate chamber, slapping his back and addressing him as "Mr. Justice"; at Roosevelt's regular press conference one reporter needled the President by asking if he intended to "confirm the Senate nomination of Senator Robinson to the Supreme Court." (Roosevelt replied warily that he had thought about the nomination "really, not at all.")

But it would not do to renege on such a widely publicized promise to a powerful Senate leader. The only way to safeguard the majority after a Robinson appointment, it seemed, was to envelop him in a phalanx of four additional new justices. The Court plan was still on. On the plus side of the ledger, Roosevelt's lieutenants told him that the prospects for passage were still good.

Yet with the Van Devanter retirement and the string of positive rulings, the air was quickly draining out of the balloon. Roosevelt's usual emollient method of dealing with recalcitrant Democrats in Congress yielded to rougher tactics. Tom Corcoran underwent the last of his metamorphoses as a New Deal figure, a sequence that had transformed him from backstage legislative draftsman to public advocate for the bills he had created. Now he found himself made into "a political operative, pure and simple." It was not a role that he particularly relished, especially given that the Court plan on which he was spending all his waking hours was beginning to look like "an iceberg that will sink us all."

Moreover, the politicians he was trying to wrangle were becoming distinctly uncooperative. The worst was Vice President Garner, habitually among the shakiest of New Deal supporters inside the administration and never a fan of the Court plan. In mid-May, Corcoran confided to Ickes that Cactus Jack was "off the reservation"—indeed, "almost in open revolt."

Before the next cabinet meeting, on Saturday, May 15, Roosevelt had it out with his vice president in a private session, reminding Garner crisply that he had been reelected president in November by a resounding vote, that many congressmen and senators had ridden back into office on his coattails, and that he did not appreciate men who owed their election to him suddenly discovering "that they are statesmen in their own right." It was as bald a statement of the divine right of the landslide victor as Roosevelt was known to have uttered. When he and Garner entered the Cabinet Room twenty minutes late, Ickes observed, "the Vice President looked as if he had had a thoroughly sound spanking." But the trip to the woodshed did not have a lasting effect; about a month later, Garner announced that he was leaving Washington for his home in Uvalde, Texas. He would not return until late in the session, depriving the White House of a dependable, if reluctant, arm-twister and a presumed vote for its Court plan in the event of a tie in the Senate.

A greater blow was coming. On June 14, the Senate Judiciary Committee majority issued its report on the bill. The vote against the measure had been 10–8. Seven members of the majority came from the President's party, but they produced as unsparing an attack on a presidential bill as had ever emerged from the chamber. The words *devious* and *vicious* leaped from the page, and the conclusion was devastatingly blunt:

> We recommend the rejection of this bill as a needless, futile, and utterly dangerous abandonment of constitutional principle. . . . It is a proposal without precedent and without justification. It would subjugate the courts to the will of Congress and the President and thereby destroy the independence of the judiciary, the only certain shield of individual rights . . . a proposal that violates every sacred tradition of American democracy. . . . It is a measure which should be so emphatically rejected that its parallel will never again be presented to the free representatives of the free people of America.

Roosevelt, queried the next day by the press about this remarkable repudiation by his own party, delivered what was by now his stock response to bad news: "I haven't read it."

He became even more insistent. He still had a potent weapon, his personal charm, and he turned it up to maximum power for one last sally. Joe Robinson had worked out a compromise bill allowing new Court appointments but limiting their timing and number. Roosevelt invited every Democratic congressman and senator to a three-day outing beginning June 24 at the salubrious Jefferson Islands Club on Chesapeake Bay to politick for the arrangement. The event unnerved an opposition fully alive to FDR's skills at persuasion—"I confess I am worried because of the closeness of the vote," Hiram Johnson reported to his son Hiram Jr. Indeed, at the end of the weekend Robinson seemed convinced that the plan had secured a majority.

But the endgame was near. Roosevelt had invested Robinson with full authority to compromise, and for the next two weeks the majority leader worked like a packhorse. His friends on Capitol Hill feared his health would crack under the remorseless pressure, not to say the remorseless weather. Washington was consumed by a heat wave, oppressing the legislators in their sweltering offices to a degree that gave Roosevelt, in the air-conditioned White House, wicked pleasure.

On July 6, when debate opened in the Senate chamber on his compromise plan, Robinson was in full cry, roaring, bellowing, swatting away impertinent questions, his face livid with passion. He held the floor for two hours straight, then suddenly faltered. He turned ashen, looked around in evident confusion, drew a cigar from his pocket, and put a match to it in a shocking affront to Senate protocol. Another question came from the floor. Robinson suddenly realized where he was, shook his head, said, "No more questions today. . . . That's all, good-bye."

The next day he was back, and the day after that. He continued to lead the charge, occasionally retreating to the Senate cloakroom gasping for breath.

On July 14 his maid arrived at his apartment early, prepared his breakfast, and went to wake him. She found him facedown on the floor, dead of a heart attack.

That the fight over the Court bill had killed Joe Robinson seemed plain to almost everyone in politics except the President. Bernard Baruch, already aboard a ship prepared to cast off for Europe, canceled his passage upon hearing the news and called Roosevelt, pleading with him to drop the bill and "not kill any more Senators," in Ickes's words. Roosevelt's rejoinder was that it was not the bill killing senators, but the machinations preventing a vote. Senator Wheeler declared that in pursuing the bill, the President was "fighting God," a statement the ever-loyal Ickes regarded as being "in especially bad taste."

If Roosevelt felt any remorse for his role in Robinson's overwrought final hours he did not show it. Instead he insisted the battle go on, appalling the delegation of senators who came to the White House the next day to plead that he give up. He seemed wholly unaware that in losing his field general he had lost the war, or, worse, that in forbidding retreat from a lost cause he might be writing an end to the New Deal itself.

On July 22, a few days after Robinson's funeral in Arkansas, the Senate returned the last version of the Court-packing bill to committee, and oblivion. On the Senate floor, Hiram Johnson rose to ask the presiding officer to clarify the action just taken.

"The Supreme Court is out of the way?" he asked.

"The Supreme Court is out of the way."

Johnson replied, "Glory be to God!"

The words echoed across Washington, and the country, as the Court plan's epitaph.

"Who lost the Supreme Court 'packing' fight?" Thomas Corcoran would ask rhetorically many years later. "Almost everybody. The Court, which suddenly looked like a political football, lost dignity and prestige. Men in the street lost faith in the idea of an unassailably independent judiciary— the idea that the Law stood above the partisan fray of politics. Congress lost the united leadership of the Grand Coalition. The Administration lost momentum that it would never regain. The President lost the battle and he lost a measure of his immense stature.

"But Roosevelt won the war," Corcoran concluded, referring to the Court's newfound support for his programs. "And as a consequence he then won the totally unexpected prize of an unprecedented third term."

Whether Roosevelt truly won the war, much less rode that victory to his third term, is debatable. What is not debatable was that the colossal blunder of the Court-packing scheme would stand forever as a benchmark of presidential hubris.

18

ROOSEVELT'S RECESSION

T HE DEMISE OF the Court-packing plan briefly dispelled the clouds
over the New Deal. On Friday, July 23, 1937, the day after Hiram
Johnson proclaimed the scheme's end, Harold Ickes visited the
White House for a cabinet meeting and judged the President's mood sun-
nier than a few days earlier, when the scheme's fate was still marginally in
doubt—a "natural" change of mood, Ickes judged: "A certainty, even an
undesirable one, is less disturbing than a desirable uncertainty."

The economy was continuing to improve. Recovery seemed to pick up
steam through the summer, with production rising in major industries.
Department store sales had gained by 11 percent in 1936 over 1935, more
than twice the growth rate of a year earlier. Over the first nine months of
1937, the Federal Reserve's index of industrial production finally exceeded
the mark set in 1929; national income in the same period was running at
an annualized rate that seemed sure to bring it to nearly double that of
1932. The government appeared to be within striking distance of its goal of
restoring the overall economy to the level of 1929—indeed, the torrid pace
of recovery raised concerns about overheating, to the point that Roosevelt
in his March 9 Fireside Chat momentarily digressed from his discussion
of the Court scheme to warn: "Recovery is speeding up to a point where
the dangers of 1929 are again becoming possible, not this week or month
perhaps, but within a year or two." Two days later, Federal Reserve governor Marriner Eccles hand-carried a memo to the White House warning of
"grave danger that the recovery movement will get out of hand . . . excessive

growth in profits and a boom in the stock market will arise, and the cost of living will mount rapidly. If such conditions are permitted to develop, another drastic slump will be inevitable."

With recovery seemingly at hand, Roosevelt paid heed to the penny-pinching urgings of Treasury Secretary Morgenthau. The latter, on FDR's directive, had shed the cares of office by taking a summerlong vacation in Hawaii, relaxing on Molokai and sailing about Pearl Harbor, amid flotillas of Japanese fishing vessels. Looking in at the White House upon his return to Washington in mid-September, he found Roosevelt to be "simply delighted" at his proposals to cut public works expenditures by $20 million, defer another $23 million in construction of post offices, and cut Reconstruction Finance Corporation lending to zero. The President even seemed amenable to proposing a balanced federal budget for fiscal 1938. Beaming at his budget-cutting staff, Morgenthau announced: "You have scraped the barrel clean. Now, what I want to do is take the barrel apart . . . so they can't fill it up again."

Then the economy cracked.

In truth, the recovery of late 1936 and the first part of 1937 had been built upon a foundation of sand. The government had pumped the economy full of billions of dollars of one-time stimulus in 1936, including the payment of $1.7 billion in World War I soldiers' bonuses (mandated by Congress over Roosevelt's veto) and the implementation of the undistributed business profits tax, which fulfilled its goal of coercing corporations to step up dividend distributions to shareholders before the end of the year. These cash inflows produced a sharp pickup of growth across the board, showing up in purchases of consumer goods, autos and other durable goods, industrial equipment, and housing.

But all this activity was transitory. Unemployment remained stuck at more than 5 million persons—a vast improvement over 1932, when the figure was 11.5 million, but at 10 percent of the labor force far from full employment. The spike in economic stimulus from the bonus payments had evaporated entirely by late 1936; and once corporations had paid out their dividends, the industrial sector's cash surplus turned into a capital shortage. Starting on January 1, 1937, a new tax appeared—the Social Security payroll tax of 2 percent, half of it paid by employers, which would remove nearly $1 billion a year from workers' purchasing power without counterbalancing the drain with retirement benefits, which would not begin to be paid until 1940. Three years of government economic pump priming, an unprecedented infusion of cash raised by deficit spending, suddenly reversed. The government had "stopped priming the pump and is instead taking some water out of the spout," observed the *New Republic.* "Under the circumstances a slump is easy to explain," as private enterprise was not taking up the slack with hiring and investing of its own.

Yet the severity of the 1937–38 recession took contemporaries by surprise and still confounds economists. From September 1937 to June 1938, industrial production and payrolls fell by more than a third, profits by 78 percent, and stock prices by more than half.

Blame for the recession typically has been apportioned among several factors. The leading causes cited at the time included the new federal taxes, a tightening of credit policy by the Federal Reserve early in 1937, and a surge of labor militancy and consequent rise in manufacturing costs following passage of the National Labor Relations Act in 1935. These developments occurred against the backdrop of a speculative boom in industrial production through 1936, which created backlogs of inventory that became deadweights on economic growth beginning in 1937 and lasting as long as consumption was suppressed.

An important driver of the speculative boom was political instability in Europe. The prospect of war had sent gold flowing from European accounts into U.S. banks, which pushed the assets back out the door in the form of low-interest loans. Through 1936 and into 1937 the heady inflow of gold provided the capital for heady investment in industrial production in the United States, but since the investing was spurred more by the availability of capital than by a fundamental growth in demand for plants and equipment, the spree was bound to end in a painful morning-after.

Another factor blamed for the recession, especially by business leaders, was industry's lack of confidence in the economic future. The doubts ostensibly were stoked by the New Deal's business bashing, the chief exhibit being Roosevelt's acceptance speech at the 1936 Democratic convention, in which he took aim at "the royalists of the economic order . . . [who] denied that the government could do anything to protect the citizen in his right to work and live," and proclaimed that "our allegiance to American institutions requires the overthrow of this kind of power." Yet Roosevelt's slashing rhetoric against business was hardly novel. The New Deal's anti-business image dated back to the Wall Street regulations of the Hundred Days—and had not braked industrial growth from early 1933 through 1936. In that period industrial production had more than doubled and gross national product had grown spectacularly, at a rate averaging more than 8 percent a year.

None of the negative developments cited could have caused the slump by themselves. But they did come together roughly simultaneously, at a time when the memories of 1929 and the long subsequent decline were still painfully fresh. Yet it is most accurate to say that the recession of 1937–38 was the ultimate reproach to the fundamental timidity of the New Deal's economic stimulation efforts. On the federal, state, and local levels, government pump priming during the Thirties was weaker than in 1929 except in two years, 1931 and 1936. As the prominent economist E. Cary Brown observed, fiscal stimulus was unsuccessful during the Thirties "not because it did not work, but because it was not tried."

Indeed, through 1935, virtually every stimulative program of the New Deal was counterbalanced by a deflationary one. The administration's very first fiscal initiative during the Hundred Days was Lewis Douglas's deflationary Economy Act, which cut government salaries and veterans' benefits sharply. The repeal of Prohibition was expected to be stimulative but was accompanied by new liquor taxes; the inflation-oriented AAA, chockablock with ideas to pump up farm prices, was to be paid for by deflationary processing taxes; the $3 billion public works program of the NIRA's Title II was placed in the hands of Harold Ickes precisely because he could be trusted to disburse the money at a trickle. The New Deal disdained other opportunities for stimulus: for example, after passage of the Home Owners' Loan Corporation Act in 1933, the administration did almost nothing to pump up the all-important residential housing sector. Even the New Deal's explicit expansionary initiatives were flawed. As James Paul Warburg perceived during the gold-manipulation scheme of late 1933, Roosevelt's efforts to drive prices higher in the farm and industrial sectors relied less on organic economic stimulus than on fiat—on manipulative steps that, Warburg counseled Roosevelt, were doomed from the first.

Roosevelt was aware of the fiscal ramifications of the early New Deal, but unsure how to reverse the deflationary trend, especially without increasing the budget deficit. A mere month after his inauguration he wrote to his old mentor Edward M. House: "While things look superficially rosy, I realize well that thus far we have actually given more of deflation than of inflation—the closed banks locked up four billions or more and the economy legislation will take nearly another billion out of Veteran's pay, departmental salaries, etc. It is simply inevitable that we must inflate and though my banker friends may be horrified [here he was undoubtedly thinking of Warburg], I am still seeking an inflation which will not wholly be based on additional government debt."

A cadre of progressive economic officials attempted to fashion a consistently stimulative policy for the New Deal, but they were thwarted by economic policy making that was "lacking in coherence and consistency," in the judgment of Lauchlin Currie, a Harvard economist who joined Eccles at the Federal Reserve. Many other economists would later remark on the haphazard and contradictory character of fiscal policy in the first years of the New Deal; but its temperament did not change until 1938, when the consequences of five years of inattention finally became inescapable, and policy coalesced in favor of stimulus.

This record is sharply at odds with the popular image of the New Deal as a veritable laboratory of Keynesian deficit-driven pump priming. Currie, who helped Eccles draft the Banking Act of 1935 to reform the Federal Reserve, struggled to concoct a deficit-spending program of a size and duration that would secure recovery—one that would be "consistent with the humanitarian drives of New Dealers and yet not too outrageously offend the prejudices of a Morgenthau." His calculations suggested in 1935 that sustainable recovery would require $5 billion to $6 billion in annual federal deficits for another three years. Those figures were much larger than the $3.6 billion deficit in 1934; indeed, deficits on such a scale would not appear in the federal budget until after the war began.

Henry Morgenthau's "prejudice" against deficit spending was by no means the only obstacle to implementing such a policy. "Roosevelt and most members of the Cabinet were either uneasy, unconvinced, or opposed," Currie reflected, in part because of the sheer novelty of Keynesian principles at the time. John Maynard Keynes's argument that government deficit spending should substitute for private investment when the latter disappeared was not widely known in the United States before the mid-1930s, though Keynes had been an established economic thinker in Great Britain since 1919. Currie, who had become acquainted with his work while studying in England, returned home to find that the Keynesian approach had not "made the slightest dent on a set of beliefs so firmly entrenched as to be articles of faith." On the contrary, economic orthodoxy in the United States was built around a devotion to fiscal austerity that Hoover had embraced and FDR himself held dear. Even Marriner Eccles, a leading proponent of deficit-driven government stimulus, appeared to be ignorant of Keynes's formalization of what he had gleaned as a banker in Utah by "naked-eye observation"—that government spending could compensate for the collapse of private-sector investment and employment. Eccles had not read a single page of Keynes when he was first invited to consult with the New Dealers in late 1933. At the close of his career in 1951 he was still claiming never to have read the economist's writings "except in small extracts."

Keynes met Roosevelt during a brief visit to the White House under the auspices of Frances Perkins in 1934, six months after he published an open letter urging the President to focus on recovery and set aside reform for the moment: "It will be through raising high the prestige of your administration by success in short-range Recovery, that you will have the driving force to accomplish long-range Reform," he had written. (It was in this document that Keynes had criticized Roosevelt's gold-buying scheme as "a gold standard on the booze.") Face-to-face, the two men failed to achieve a melding of souls. "I saw your friend Keynes," Roosevelt told Perkins. "He left a whole rigamarole of figures. He must be a mathematician rather than a political economist." Keynes, for his part, told her that he had "supposed the President was more literate, economically speaking."

But their intellectual conflict ran deeper, for Roosevelt refused to see recovery and reform as separate policies. "The attempt to make a distinction between recovery and reform is a narrowly conceived effort to substitute the appearance of reality for reality itself," he told Congress in his State of the Union address in January 1935. "When a man is convalescing from an illness, wisdom dictates not only cure of the symptoms, but also removal of their cause." He might have been addressing his remarks directly to Keynes; certainly he was setting the stage for the forthcoming wave of reforms that encompassed Social Security, the National Labor Relations Act, and the Public Utility Holding Company Act, complete with its "death penalty" clause.

Keynes's theories were still alien to the administration when the new economic crisis erupted in the second half of 1937. Morgenthau was still stepping up pressure on Roosevelt to announce a balanced budget for the 1938–39 fiscal year; on October 5 he counseled the President that preliminary estimates pointed to a $275 million deficit (a figure that would have struck advisors like Currie as too small to sustain recovery). Morgenthau hoped to inject himself into the budgeting process, which was not normally within the portfolio of the Treasury secretary: "It seems to me extremely important that before you obligate yourself to spend anything at all in addition to the commitments already made, you give . . . me an opportunity to go into this situation with you fully," he wrote the President. His chances of achieving this goal, he told Treasury staff with self-deluding optimism, were "two out of three."

The ground was about to shift under Morgenthau's feet. Starting in September, the stock market had suffered a string of "nose dives" (as Ickes called them). Looking for someone to blame, business leaders redoubled their attacks on the administration. On October 14, a broadside fired by Winthrop Aldrich, chairman of the Chase National Bank, landed on the front page of the *New York Times*. Aldrich ascribed the market's weakness entirely to government policies—especially the capital gains, inheritance, and income tax increases of 1935; regulations outlawing insider trading in stocks; and "inquisitorial visits" to trading houses by Securities and Exchange Commission agents ferreting out manipulative schemes. It was the old story of business leaders kicking at governmental oversight, not for the first time and certainly not for the last. To Roosevelt it suggested that the thin markets on Wall Street resulted from a "capitalists' strike" aimed at wringing concessions from the White House for lighter SEC regulation and a clampdown on sit-down strikes and other acts by organized labor—indeed, "a complete reversal of social and economic policy," as he described industry's goals to the cabinet.

More than the stock market crisis contributed to Roosevelt's darkening humor in late 1937. On October 6, Harry Hopkins's wife, Barbara, succumbed to breast cancer; the loss of this appealing habitué of the White House was felt deeply by the President and those in his inner circle who had witnessed the Hopkinses' mutual devotion—"one of the few couples that I have known who were really happy together," recalled Harold Ickes. Having recently lost his estranged wife in an automobile accident, Ickes was sufficiently moved by Hopkins's tragedy to invite him for a stay at his Maryland farm. There the two uncompromising foes spent several companionable days together, until Hopkins departed for the Mayo Clinic, where doctors removed part of his stomach to treat his own cancer.

By late 1937, the prospect of war on a sizable scale loomed in Europe and Asia. On October 21 Roosevelt lunched with the British writer H. G. Wells, who expressed his opinion that war was almost certain to break out in 1940. (FDR, marginally less pessimistic, thought 1941.) On December

12, during the Japanese attack on the Chinese city of Nanjing, Japanese fighters and shore batteries fired on and sank the American gunboat *Panay* a few miles from the beleaguered city, taking three lives in what was soon shown to be a deliberately provocative act. The incident led to talk in the cabinet of embargos and war against Japan—even Ickes, who fashioned himself a pacifist, observed, "Certainly war with Japan is inevitable sooner or later, and if we have to fight her, isn't this the best possible time?" Roosevelt pondered ways of opposing Japanese aggression short of war, perhaps through a trade quarantine in cooperation with Great Britain and France. But all such discussions were confounded by Congress's isolationism, which curiously had been heightened, not quelled, by the *Panay* incident.

That was not the only respect in which Congress was at odds with Roosevelt, who had squandered his landslide 1936 victory through the arrogance of the Court-packing scheme and his indifferent leadership as recession took hold. Inside the Cabinet Room there was still sympathy for the boss. Ickes remarked early in August on Roosevelt's physical sickliness—"he is punch drunk from the punishment he has suffered recently," he commented in his diary.

But after a cross-country trip by rail to take the country's political temperature, Roosevelt returned to Washington seemingly energized by the adoration and affection for him displayed at every stop. He then irked Congress again by calling a special session for November 15. The agenda was to include a wage-and-hours bill the lawmakers had set aside in the regular session, a new farm relief law to supplant the overturned AAA, a reorganization of the executive branch, and the establishment of seven regional land-use agencies known as the "little TVAs." The Congress that convened for the special session was overwhelmingly Democratic: members of the President's party outnumbered Republicans by more than five to one in the Senate and nearly four to one in the House. Yet when the session adjourned five weeks later it had not passed a single administration bill (although it did manage to appropriate $225,000 in mileage expenses for the lawmakers' trips home). It was as though the electoral triumph of a year before had never happened.

Roosevelt complained that he seemed to be the only leader in Washington taking serious measure of the economic crisis, which cast its shadow over everything else. At a cabinet meeting in October he had snapped at Commerce Secretary Daniel Roper for issuing "so many Hooverish statements"—meaning anodyne reassurances that business conditions were fundamentally sound and that no crisis portended for the future. Roper spluttered his excuses, after which Roosevelt privately grumbled to Ickes: "Nobody pays any attention to a statement from the Secretary of Commerce any more. Isn't that a fine state of affairs?"

Morgenthau blundered into the same bed of quicksand a few weeks later. The slump had deepened; the dreaded word *depression* was now being bandied about. Morgenthau, fearing that the deficit-spending lobby was gaining the President's ear, chose to hector him again about balancing the budget and "desterilizing" gold—that is, allowing gold reserves into the money supply as a credit-loosening device—in a late-evening phone call on November 2. Roosevelt reacted sharply, reiterating his view that the business community was deliberately causing the recession to thwart his policy of reform, speaking in a tone "very excited, very dictatorial, and very disagreeable," as the Treasury secretary reported in his diary. Morgenthau gave as good as he got in this conversation with his old friend and Dutchess County neighbor; his wife later admonished him that his own voice had "sounded like the drippings of an icicle."

Morgenthau repeated his views in a letter he delivered to Roosevelt the following afternoon. "You told the newspapers that your first interest was the one-third of the nation who are ill-nourished, ill-clad, ill-housed," he wrote. "I hardly need tell you that the first to feel another depression will be this same one-third. . . . Mr. President what can we do to stop it?"

The next cabinet meeting commenced with a series of grim forecasts from around the table, provoking Roosevelt to mirthless sarcasm: "Of course, I am glad to hear from various members of the Cabinet their sad story of how bad business conditions are." He turned his glare on the hapless Morgenthau. "Last night alongside my bed was the darnedest letter you ever saw from Henry. I am sick and tired of being told by the Cabinet, by Henry and by everybody else for the last two weeks what's the matter with the country and nobody suggests what I should do."

Morgenthau ventured to puncture the ensuing silence. "You must do something to reassure business. What business wants to know is: Are we headed toward state Socialism or are we going to continue on a capitalistic basis?"

Roosevelt lost his patience upon hearing this tired trope again. "You want me to turn on the old record," he said. "I have told them that again and again." Morgenthau, chastened, "looked and acted like a spanked child," observed Ickes, not without satisfaction.

What the meeting presaged was a long stretch of stagnant policy making. The President resisted taking a firm stand either on the balanced budget or pump priming, betraying "a steadily deepening indecision," in Ray Moley's words. Only a few days after the cabinet meeting, Roosevelt approved a speech by Morgenthau to be delivered in New York on November 10, proclaiming that the administration intended to achieve a balanced budget by slashing spending on public highways, public works, unemployment relief, and agriculture. The need for the deficit of the past four years had disappeared with the arrival of recovery, Morgenthau assured his audience in a burst of "Hooverish" oratory. "The emergency that we faced in 1933 no longer exists." From somewhere in the audience came a disbelieving guffaw.

The same disbelief, albeit without the open ridicule, was felt at the Federal Reserve, where Morgenthau's speech fulfilled Marriner Eccles's worst fears. Only two days earlier Eccles had met with Roosevelt in the company of Lauchlin Currie and Leon Henderson, a government economist with impeccable New Deal credentials, to communicate their view that the pullback in government spending had precipitated the new recession and that a resumption of spending was imperative. "There were indications that Roosevelt was impressed by the argument," Eccles recalled.

The contradiction between Morgenthau's speech and Roosevelt's apparent assent to pump priming left the banker wondering ungenerously "whether the New Deal was merely a political slogan or if Roosevelt really knew what the New Deal was." Eventually Eccles concluded that the President accommodated the two contradictory policies "because he was really uncertain where he wanted to move," which was probably closer to the truth.

Morgenthau's speech had scarcely stopped echoing off the gilded walls of the Hotel Astor ballroom when Roosevelt gave the green light to a plan by Corcoran, Cohen, and Ickes to fire another rhetorical shot at big business. The effort was designed in part as an antidote to the President's gloom, which had worried Ickes during a joint trip to Florida for barracuda fishing in early December. The glow from Roosevelt's train trip in the fall had been extinguished by the rebellious special session. "He looked bad and he seemed listless," recalled Ickes, who found himself wondering whether "his trouble was spiritual or physical." Ickes's advice was to resist business's call to reverse reform, or "we will very probably be engulfed in a reactionary wave and all of the benefits of the New Deal will be swept away."

The campaign broke publicly at Christmastime, first with a pair of speeches by Assistant Attorney General Robert H. Jackson, a loyal New Dealer whom Roosevelt would name as attorney general in 1940 and elevate to the Supreme Court in 1941.

Jackson's first speech, delivered over radio on December 26, blamed the recession on "monopolists." These profiteers had "priced themselves into a slump," he said, and were now trying to shift the blame onto government. "When the business goes into a slump, the workmen go home without jobs. When workmen go home without jobs, the grocer, the baker, the clothier and all the rest have lost their customer. When the customer is lost, the merchant cancels his order for goods. And when the cancellation reaches back to big business, where it started, the big business man clamors that government should give him 'confidence.'"

Jackson amplified his attack on December 29 before the American Political Science Association in Philadelphia: "The blunt truth is that today we have in command of big business by and large the same Bourbons who were in command of the defeat of 1929. . . . As the President stated in Chicago during the campaign, the Bourbons now feel strong enough to throw their crutches at the doctor."

The following day Ickes delivered a characteristically pugnacious radio speech cowritten by Corcoran and Cohen. He took aim at the same targets as Jackson: concentrated economic power generally and monopolies specifically—"It is the old struggle between the power of money and the power of the democratic instinct," he said. "In the last few months this irreconcilable conflict . . . has come into the open as never before, has taken on a form and an intensity which makes it clear that it must be fought through to a finish—until plutocracy or democracy—until America's sixty families or America's 120,000,000 people—win." (His allusion was to *America's Sixty Families,* an exposé of the nation's concentrated wealth by the muckraker Ferdinand Lundberg.)

From Ickes's standpoint the speech was a roaring success: "Nothing that I have ever done has been the cause of so much publicity," he crowed. "There has been a great stirring of the animals and this isn't likely to subside for several days." To Ickes's surprise, his talk garnered the admiration of an old adversary. Hugh Johnson, now thundering as a newspaper columnist and radio commentator, had read an advance copy and called Ickes to say he would advise his listeners to tune in to the speech. Yet Ickes worried over whether Roosevelt would carry the fight through to his State of the Union talk on January 3. "I hope that he won't let us down entirely," he wrote in his diary. "The fight in this country today is one between the great mass of the people and wealth." If Roosevelt chose not to make this the central theme of the 1938 midterm elections, he mused, "I don't know what issue we are going to run on."

In the event, Roosevelt in his annual address tried to straddle all the issues before him. He pledged a balanced budget in principle, but not immediately and not at the expense of unemployment relief or national security. He warned about "misuse of the powers of capital" and "selfish suspension of the employment of capital"—the bankers' strike about which he had been complaining—but assured his audience that he was attacking *abuses* of the capitalist system, not all business. "Government can be expected to cooperate in every way with the business of the Nation," he concluded, "provided the component parts of business abandon practices which do not belong to this day and age."

The policy drift continued into February and March, with Roosevelt's advisors all riding their personal hobbyhorses: Eccles and Currie pleading for renewed pump priming and Morgenthau for a balanced budget; Jesse Jones of the RFC pressing for repeal of the corporate surplus profits tax; Ickes, Hopkins, Corcoran, and Cohen for a continuation of the anti-monopoly campaign.

On February 1 Roosevelt received unsolicited and not especially welcome advice on combating the recession from John Maynard Keynes, who described himself in a private letter to the President as "an enthusiastic well-wisher of you and your policies." Keynes analyzed the drivers of the prior recovery chiefly as easy short-term credit, the relief programs for the unemployed, and public works spending. But he observed that the latter had been "greatly curtailed in the past year" and argued that this stifled the recovery's momentum. What was needed was increased investment in housing, public utilities, and transport, but the administration's performance disappointed on all three counts. Housing was "by far the best aid to recovery because of the large and continuing scale of potential demand" and its "wide geographic distribution. . . . I should advise putting most of your eggs in this basket." Yet the administration had done "next to nothing. The handling of the housing problem has been really wicked."

Undoubtedly the most irksome passages in the letter were those dealing with Roosevelt's attacks on big business, which Keynes regarded as counterproductive. He was especially critical of the New Deal's hostility toward private utilities. This was dangerous ground, given that the Holding Company Act was one of Roosevelt's most cherished initiatives. Keynes acknowledged that public ownership of electrical generation was probably the right thing in an ideal world, but he counseled Roosevelt to bow to the reality of private ownership. "What is the object of chasing the utilities around the lot every other week?" he asked tactlessly. "I would make peace on liberal terms." In a broader sense, Keynes wrote, businessmen need "different handling" from politicians: "Easily persuaded to be 'patriots' . . . pathetically responsive to a kind word. You could do anything you liked with them, if you would treat them (even the big ones), not as wolves or tigers, but as domestic animals by nature."

Roosevelt's reaction to Keynes's message has not been recorded, but it would be understandable if he regarded those final words, at least, to be hopelessly naïve. In fact, the administration had been assiduously cozying up to the business community. On January 11, Donald Richberg had escorted into the White House a clutch of the most anti–New Deal business leaders in the country, including the steel magnate Ernest T. Weir and Alfred P. Sloan of General Motors, for a heart-to-heart with the President; Adolf Berle and Rex Tugwell brought another group a few days later. Yet these overtures failed to lessen the business community's animosity. For all the palaver about cooperation and counseling, business valued tax cuts and reduced regulation more than invitations to the White House, and these were not forthcoming.

As the weeks dragged on without direction or decision from the Oval Office on economic policy, members of the inner circle continued to fret about Roosevelt's emotional state. "It looks to me as if all the courage has oozed out of the President," Ickes recorded. "There is no fight and no leadership." Morgenthau, lunching at the White House in mid-March, accused the President of "just treading water . . . to wait to see what happens this spring."

"Absolutely," Roosevelt replied.

He did not have to wait very long. On March 25, the stock market cracked again, some indices touching their lowest points since 1932. U.S. Steel, which had peaked only a year earlier at 126½, closed the day below 45. Roosevelt, who had retreated to Warm Springs, received a string of aides sensing that the time was finally ripe to goad him into action. Hopkins carried a new plea for pump priming from Leon Henderson and a request for new appropriations for the WPA. Separately, Henry Wallace and Jesse Jones showed up with plans for new spending on housing, flood control, and loans to industry.

At last the logjam broke. Roosevelt was "rarin' to go," Wallace informed Morgenthau by telephone from Georgia. Morgenthau, clutching at straws, drafted a memorandum calling instead for a war on waste and inefficiency in government. But he was about to get squelched. On April 10 he handed in his memo at the White House, only to receive from Roosevelt in return a blueprint for stepped-up public works spending; a doubling of loan capacity for the U.S. Housing Authority, which lent to low-income borrowers; and a $500 million construction appropriation for the Federal Housing Administration. There was also a proposal for a transcontinental highway, a pet project for which Roosevelt had been penciling out possible routes for months on scraps of paper.

Morgenthau quailed. "What you have outlined not only frightens me but will frighten the country," he told the President. "How much is it going to cost?"

Roosevelt waved the question away. Morgenthau knew the die was cast. The next morning he called together his aides at the Treasury to vent his discontent. "The way it was put up to me last night just scared me to death—worse than I've been scared—and the thing hasn't been thought through." He blamed Ickes, Hopkins, and Jones. "They have just stampeded him. He was completely stampeded. They stampeded him like cattle."

But they had not needed to stampede the President; reports from the countryside had turned horrific. In Cleveland, one-third of the entire population was reported to be on relief, applying for relief, or working for the WPA. In Dayton, Columbus, and Toledo—the nation's industrial heartland—city relief budgets were tapped out. The same was true in Chicago, which had closed its twenty-three relief bureaus, leaving ninety thousand families without means of support.

Roosevelt was now leading the stampede. On April 14 he delivered to Congress a message asking for a $3.75 billion relief program. That night he took to the airwaves for his first Fireside Chat in five months. It was Holy Week, three days before Easter, he acknowledged, "but what I want to say to you, the people of the country, is of such immediate need and relates so closely to the lives of human beings and the prevention of human suffering that I have felt that there should be no delay."

What followed was the most direct articulation of the New Deal as an economic stimulus program Roosevelt ever delivered. This was appropriate, for the program he outlined was the first explicit recommendation for fiscal stimulus he had ever made. It was, indeed, exactly the sort of stimulus program that later generations would identify as the essence of the New Deal, the sort of program against which the fiscal initiatives of later presidents— Lyndon Johnson's Great Society, Barack Obama's American Recovery and Reinvestment Act—would be measured. Yet for Franklin Roosevelt it was an unprecedentedly audacious and ambitious step.

Roosevelt reminded his listeners how far the country had come from the dark days of 1932. "Your money in the bank is safe; farmers are no longer in deep distress . . . ; dangers of security speculation have been minimized; national income is almost 50 percent higher than it was. . . . And government has an established and accepted responsibility for relief." But he knew that many Americans were still unemployed, or newly unemployed. "I do not propose that the Government shall pretend not to see these things."

He vowed to resist any effort to roll back the reforms of the New Deal—"in our rehabilitation of the banking structure and of agriculture, in our provisions for adequate and cheaper credit for all types of business, in our acceptance of national responsibility for unemployment relief . . . , in our provision for Social Security itself, the electorate of America wants no backward steps taken."

To combat the new slump there would be more money for WPA, more for the Farm Security Administration, the National Youth Administration, and the Civilian Conservation Corps. Some $1.4 billion in gold held by the Treasury would be released—"desterilized," in economic jargon—to help pay these expenses. And as a third step—"You and I cannot afford to equip ourselves with two rounds of ammunition where three rounds are necessary"—there would be an appropriation of $300 million to the U.S. Housing Authority for slum clearance, $1 billion for new public works, $100 million for highway construction, $100 million for flood control, and $25 million for construction and maintenance of federal buildings. It was as though he had examined Morgenthau's November list of programs to cut to balance the budget, and decided to expand every one of them instead.

"It is a big program," Roosevelt conceded. Yes, there would be more federal debt. But getting out of the recession would repay the cost "several times over," for the greatest tax on the economy was time lost to unemployment: "Because of idle men and idle machines this nation lost one hundred billion dollars between 1929 and the spring of 1933, in less than four years." Roosevelt described the recovery program in terms of national security, a theme likely to resonate with listeners becoming increasingly uneasy about the rise of fascism in Europe. "Democracy has disappeared in several other great nations," he stated—"disappeared not because the people of those nations disliked democracy, but because they had grown tired of unemployment and insecurity. . . . Finally, in desperation, they chose to sacrifice liberty in the hope of getting something to eat." He would not let that happen here.

He concluded with a direct appeal to his listeners, exploiting the "magic in that calm voice" that Ray Moley had remarked upon during the banking crisis, six long years before.

I should like to say a personal word to you. I never forget that I live in a house owned by all the American people and that I have been given their trust. I try always to remember that their deepest problems are human. . . . I believe that we have been right in the course we have charted. To abandon our purpose of building a greater, a more stable and a more tolerant America would be to miss the tide and perhaps to miss the port. I propose to sail ahead. . . . For to reach a port, we must sail—sail, not lie at anchor, sail, not drift.

In Congress, which had been so captious in 1937 and had turned down Roosevelt's proposal for a major reorganization of the executive branch only a few weeks earlier, the conversion was complete. Roosevelt's recovery measure was passed before the end of June. The renewed willingness of Congress to follow the President's lead was also manifested by the passage, finally, of the wage-and-hours bill he had been trying to push through for a year. This was nothing like an unalloyed victory for the White House; the bill had been subjected to fierce wrangling between North and South, between industry and labor, and even within the labor movement, with the AFL withdrawing its support for a draft supported by John Lewis's Congress of Industrial Organizations. After a conference committee removed vast categories of workers from its jurisdiction, the bill was finally passed and sealed with Roosevelt's signature on June 25. It established a federal minimum hourly wage of 40 cents and a maximum workweek of forty hours, and outlawed child labor, launching a quiet revolution in federal regulation of the workplace that created a model for future Congresses.

But it was passage of the recovery measure that marked a new phase, arguably the final phase, of the New Deal. The bold fiscal experiment that Eccles, Currie, Hopkins, and Ickes had been urging was finally at hand.

The new spending, along with the monetary expansion produced by Roosevelt's agreement to desterilize the Treasury's gold hoard, marked the bottom of the Roosevelt recession. Robust growth resumed in the third quarter of 1938. The economy recorded a spectacular increase of 49 percent in real gross national product from 1938 to 1942, at which point economic output finally returned to its "normal" level—that is, the point it would have reached had its pre-1929 growth rate continued over the following thirteen years—signifying full recovery from the Great Depression.

How much of the recovery was due to the stimulus of 1938, and how much to the spurt of deficit spending that accompanied the buildup to war, is impossible to determine. Roosevelt, in a Fireside Chat about unemployment on November 14, 1937, had observed that the problem of joblessness had been solved in some countries by launching huge armament programs, "but we Americans do not want to solve it that way." Sadly, global events overwhelmed his pacific intentions. The war cut short the New Deal's fiscal experiment, leaving only the logical conjecture that had deficit spending on a large scale been undertaken from 1933 to 1937, rather than after 1938 and into the 1940s, its economic effect would have been just as gratifying.

It may have been only war that could have forestalled an increasingly conservative Congress from trying to reverse the New Deal's aggressive pump priming. Only a few months after recovery resumed in late 1938, conservative Democratic senator Harry F. Byrd, Sr., of Virginia addressed a taxpayers' group in Boston to call for an end to "nine years of fiscal insanity," the "present orgy of spending." He demanded a balanced budget, a cut in the size of the federal government, a ruthless purging of the relief rolls, and the end of public works projects big and small—"the green belts, the tree belts and other such dispensable activities."

It was one of many signs that the country had grown exasperated with the economic slump, even in the face of renewed upturn. In technical terms the Depression was over, but with labor unrest on the rise, unemployment still disturbingly and perplexingly high, clouds gathering on the distant European horizon, and Roosevelt's air of command fading, the New Deal's power to inspire was on the wane. Perceiving the country's changed mood, aspirants to political power were sniffing the air, sensing new opportunities.

19

PURGATORY

T HE ANTIMONOPOLY CAMPAIGN spearheaded by Jackson and Ickes whet appetites on Capitol Hill for a headline-grabbing investigation of big business. In April 1938 the White House and Congress jointly created the Temporary National Economic Committee, or TNEC, which was conceived as "the most exhaustive analysis of the American economic system and its problems" ever attempted. Over its three-year life span TNEC would take testimony from 552 witnesses, produce 31 volumes of transcripts and exhibits totaling 17,000 pages, and publish 43 monographs by 188 government economists at a cost of $1 million. When it closed up shop in April 1941, its recommendations would be almost completely ignored.

It was not that the corporate concentration of economic power did not exist. This trend, which had been described by Louis Brandeis in *Other People's Money* in 1913 and the Brain Truster Adolf Berle in *The Modern Corporation and Private Property* two decades later, had continued unabated during the ostensibly antibusiness New Deal. TNEC established that 5 percent of all corporations owned 87 percent of all corporate assets and that one-tenth of 1 percent of all corporations accounted for half of all corporate profits. In one bravura exposé, the committee showed how a single firm, the Hartford-Empire Company of Connecticut, controlled the manufacture of 67 percent of all glass containers made in the United States, including 100 percent of milk bottles, despite owning nary a single piece of glassmaking equipment. What it did own was a portfolio of patents covering industrial glassmaking. These had enabled the firm to record $40 million in income in the dozen years prior to 1938.

Yet TNEC never captured the public's imagination. One reason was the plodding personality of its chairman, a beetle-browed senator from Wyoming named Joseph O'Mahoney, who signaled from the start that the inquiry would focus on issues rather than personages. "There will be no midgets," he announced, dashing hopes of an investigational circus like the Pecora hearings of 1933, which had forever dismantled J. P. Morgan Jr.'s façade of public dignity. "O'Mahoney Wants Facts—Not Scalps," the Chamber of Commerce organ *Nation's Business* reassured its anxious readership.

O'Mahoney's complacency might have found its counterweight in the obstreperous WPA economist Leon Henderson, who was appointed TNEC's staff director, or by the six White House New Dealers whom Roosevelt appointed to the panel, among them Thurman Arnold, the Justice Department's aggressive new antitrust chief, and Securities and Exchange Commission chairman William O. Douglas. But all were more involved in their executive jobs and other work demanded by the President, and therefore ineffective at providing the committee with inquisitional verve. As it happened, this may have suited Roosevelt's taste, for by 1938 he was no longer seeking to pick fights with the business establishment; not with the darkening international situation raising the prospect of wartime industrialization.

To Ray Moley, who was now entirely on the outs with Roosevelt and the administration, TNEC looked like another tool to defer hard decisions by interring them in a study commission, just as Roosevelt had created the Committee on Economic Security to defer debate over social insurance until after the 1934 election. The new committee, in Moley's acid judgment, represented "the final expression of Roosevelt's personal indecision about what policy his Administration ought to follow in its relations with business. . . . It merely put off the adoption of a guiding economic philosophy."

Three years after its birth, TNEC would wrap up with the issuance of twenty-one recommendations. These were unexceptionable and self-evident, of the sort destined to be filed and forgotten: there should be slum clearance, more hospitals, more vocational and cultural programs for the underprivileged; more antitrust action, more equitable taxation, centralized government purchasing. But TNEC called for no truly radical changes in corporate structures or government regulation. "The Temporary National Economic Committee . . . avows its faith in free enterprise," the final report assured the nation. "Ours is a positive affirmation."

Wrote *Time:* "With all the ammunition the committee had stored up, a terrific broadside might have been expected. Instead, the committee rolled a rusty BB gun into place, pinged at the nation's economic problems." The committee's reams of economic data and volumes of testimony deserve to be appreciated as fruits of the first government effort to draw a comprehensive baseline picture of the American economy. Yet they would also rapidly be rendered obsolete, as a more cataclysmic change rolled over the nation than even the Depression: global war.

The congressional session of 1937–38 was the unhappiest of the New Deal, contaminated by the animus of the Court fight, riven by sectional controversies, and generally resistant to leadership by a President who, it was felt, should be looking ahead to retirement at the end of his historically allotted two terms. "After the election of 1936 I was told . . . that I should coast along, enjoy an easy Presidency for four years, and not take the Democratic platform too seriously," Roosevelt observed in a 1938 Fireside Chat, after the Court ordeal was over. But that was a formula, he said, for a "small minority . . . in spite of its disastrous leadership in 1929 . . . to resume its control over the Government of the United States." Roosevelt intended instead to pursue an unreservedly liberal agenda.

Other than the huge antirecession spending program of 1938, he would get little he asked for. His one significant nonspending victory, for a wage-and-hours bill nominally endorsed by organized labor, was achieved only after heroic legislative maneuvering to overcome opposition from Republicans and from conservative southern Democrats, many of whom would form the core of the breakaway States' Rights Democratic Party—the "Dixiecrats"—during the 1948 presidential election. The southerners viewed the wage bill as an attempt to destroy the cost advantage of southern manufacturers over northeastern factories by imposing nationwide labor standards. The measure was finally passed only after its standards were set low enough not to disadvantage southern plants for many years.

That modest victory was counterbalanced by a stinging defeat on an executive branch reorganization bill, which seemed destined to sail through to enactment—until the Court fight and other missteps undermined Roosevelt's command. The reorganization measure would have allowed the

President to reshuffle executive bureaus in the name of efficiency. By the time it came up for a vote, however, the atmosphere on Capitol Hill had been poisoned by the Court-packing scheme. Additionally, the *Anschluss* of March 1938, Hitler's forced annexation of Austria to the Nazi Reich, gave Roosevelt's enemies a talking point against the concentration of executive power. Baseless rhetoric about Roosevelt's "dictatorial" inclinations, rarely heard since 1933, reappeared. Frank E. Gannett, a conservative newspaper publisher in Rochester, New York, inveighed against the measure as chairman of the National Committee to Uphold Constitutional Government, a successor in spirit to the Committee for the Nation and the Liberty League. Father Coughlin briefly reemerged into the limelight to claim that the bill would empower Roosevelt to seize all the Catholic parochial schools in the country.

Overwhelmed by a tide of hysteria, the reorganization bill went down to defeat in April 1938. Roosevelt reacted wearily. "Every time I ask for more legislation they raise the cry of 'dictator,'" he complained to his postmaster general and political aide, Jim Farley. The defeated bill had been shot through with so many exemptions that there was not much left to it "except the principle of the thing," he reflected. "I can't understand it. There wasn't a chance for anyone to become a dictator under that bill."

The country spoiled for a vehicle by which to register its discontent with the unsatisfactory recovery, labor unrest, the rumblings of fascists and Reds from abroad (and perhaps from within, too), and a governing cadre perhaps grown too long in the tooth. As often happens, the hour produced the man. The new spokesman for popular petulance was Martin Dies, Jr., a conservative Democratic congressman from a Texas district sprawled along the western shore of the Gulf of Mexico.

Dies was a pudgy, rude man with an unruly blond forelock and seemingly modest career ambitions. After his election to the House in 1930 he made great use of his connection to Vice President Garner, who had served in Congress with his father and who orchestrated Dies Jr.'s appointment to the powerful House Rules Committee. The assignment did not consume much of his energy. "Mr. Dies seemed to have infinite leisure," a congressional observer recounted of his early days in office. Sprawled on the leather couches of the House cloakroom, he contented himself with crafting coarse jokes about his colleagues: "He and his especial friends would arrange elaborate hoaxes for new members. He became a gang leader, very close to a small town bully."

Notwithstanding his indolence, Dies was not unalert to the stirrings of national discontent. After delivering a speech attacking the 1937 sit-down strike at the General Motors factory in Flint, Michigan, he emerged as the leader of the anti–New Deal bloc in the House. He fashioned himself president of the Demagogues Club, the genial veneer of which overlaid a deadly serious commitment by its members never to vote "aye" on a tax bill. The club commanded so much legislative power that Roosevelt, with a show of good-naturedness, allowed himself to be inducted into membership during the Jefferson Islands outing of June 1937, between his arm-twisting sessions for the Court bill.

In May 1938, during a surge of public panic over the activities of Nazi Bundists in the United States, Dies offered a resolution calling for an investigation of purported Nazi summer camps in New York and New Jersey. The probe was approved and Dies named as chairman. Thus was born the notorious House Committee on Un-American Activities.

The House leadership stacked the panel with two other conservative anti–New Deal Democrats and two Republicans and voted a stringent $25,000 budget, sufficient for no more than about a month of superficial investigating. It was assumed that Dies would expose the Nazi camps and return to his customary stupor. He was cleverer than that. He managed to stretch the appropriation indefinitely by the simple expedient of not spending it on actual investigating. Instead he hired volunteers to collect testimony for free, accepting as gospel the words of anyone with a grievance against the New Deal, the American Civil Liberties Union, progressive politicians, or organized labor. "From all over the country, labor-baiting individuals wrote and telegraphed Mr. Dies, asking to appear as witnesses and offering to pay their own carfare," reported an early chronicler of the committee.

The Dies Committee barreled ahead despite starting off with a string of gaffes. One of its first forays into the field took it to Hollywood, always a fertile hunting ground for Red-baiters. There it received testimony that a group of movie stars had sent anniversary congratulations to a Paris newspaper, *Ce Soir*, which supposedly was owned by French communists. The signatories included Shirley Temple, who was then ten years old. Amid the general ridicule Ickes jibed, "They have found dangerous radicals out there, led by little Shirley Temple," and speculated about "a burly Congressman leading a *posse comitatus* in a raid . . . to collect her dolls as evidence."

A few months later Dies permitted several Republican witnesses to vilify Michigan governor Frank Murphy, a New Deal favorite running for reelection, as a communist dupe who had deliberately soft-pedaled his response to the Flint sit-down strike. This attack earned Dies a public rebuke from Roosevelt, who excoriated him for permitting himself "to be used in a flagrantly unfair and un-American attempt to influence an election. . . . Most fair-minded Americans hope that the committee will abandon the practice of merely providing a forum to those which they could not otherwise obtain. . . . The Dies committee made no effort to get at the truth." FDR pointedly defended Murphy's efforts to negotiate an end to the sit-down strike instead of calling in the National Guard, which was the tactic urged by Murphy's critics but which would certainly have led to bloodshed. Due to Murphy's forbearance, Roosevelt observed, "hundreds and even thousands of human lives were saved. That is the American way of doing things." Murphy lost his bid for reelection, but would be appointed attorney general by Roosevelt in 1939 and to the Supreme Court in 1940.

By the time of the Murphy affair the committee's taste for testimony from self-styled investigators and ex-radicals had been on public display for months. Its method had been unveiled on August 20, when Dies announced his intention to "get down to the meat in the coconut, as the saying goes," and introduced a witness named J. B. Matthews. A quintessentially pious reformed sinner, Matthews was prepared to disclose everything he had seen and heard during his years as a committed socialist and to provide a gloss on its significance. He would soon be elevated to director of research for the Dies Committee and its "consulting expert on who is and who is not a good American," the *New Yorker* commented.

At his inaugural appearance, Matthews painted a horrific portrait of an America overrun by card-carrying communists, fellow-travelers, and dupes. Among those he described as a former confederate was the popular newspaper columnist Heywood Broun, who was a founder of the Newspaper Guild, the AFL-affiliated trade union of newspaper writers and editors, and an avowed socialist. Broun, Matthews testified, had once informed him that he was resigning from the Socialist Party "to have greater freedom to work with the Communists." Broun appeared before the committee to rebut Matthews by testifying that he was not a communist and had never been one. He had just got out the words "Before you shut me off, let me say that I think you are wasting your time"—when Dies shut him off.

The committee's appetite for dirt on the Federal Theatre and Federal Writers' Project was voracious. Shortly before its first round of public hearings, committee member J. Parnell Thomas, Republican of New Jersey, revealed that he had been taking secret "informal" testimony about the two programs. He had learned that the Federal Theatre "not only is serving as a branch of the communistic organization but also is one more link in the vast and unparalleled New Deal propaganda machine." Declaring the program "infested with radicals from top to bottom," he demanded that Hallie Flanagan appear before the committee in open session.

Flanagan issued a statement labeling Thomas's charges "obviously absurd" and expressing her willingness to answer them in person. But the WPA, like the entire White House, scorned the Dies Committee as merely a display of congressional clownishness—Ickes, himself a committee target, labeled Dies "the outstanding zany in all our political history." The WPA forbade Flanagan to issue further public statements, but her instincts told her that silence was an unwise tactic. "It was the fashion at that time, in the W.P.A. and out, to laugh at the Dies Committee; but it never seemed funny to me," she reflected. Indeed, lacking a response from the accused, the newspapers simply shoveled Dies's unrebutted charges into print.

The committee's star witness against the theater project was Hazel Huffman, who had been a mailroom clerk in the New York office until 1936, when she was unmasked by the staff as a snitch for the Red-baiting Hearst press. She proved a voluble witness, chain-smoking nervously as she gave freely of her opinions of the program's leaders. Flanagan, she averred, "was known as far back as 1927 for her communistic sympathy, if not membership." The evidence for this was Huffman's dog-eared copy of Flanagan's book on her Guggenheim Fellowship tour, *Shifting Scenes,* of which "147 pages of a total of 280" were devoted to "eulogizing Soviet Russia and the Russian theater." Under Flanagan, Huffman testified, "propaganda plays have been the rule." *Ethiopia* and *The Cradle Will Rock* "were so definitely propaganda that they were not permitted to go on . . . but Mrs. Flanagan herself gave personal, enthusiastic approval to many of these plays at run-throughs and previews."

She concluded, "We consider these plays as part of their communistic activity."

Dies agreed. "I don't see how they could be any more so," he said. "It is almost unbelievable to me that they would use public funds of the taxpayers intended for relief, for the purpose of spreading communism in the United States."

"Yes, sir," Huffman assented. "That is true."

Shortly after Huffman's appearance, the committee adjourned for the traditional congressional campaign season break.

Roosevelt viewed the preparations for the Democratic congressional campaigns of 1938 with a sour disposition. In the Court fight he had been "completely humiliated," as Rosenman observed; the defeat of the reorganization plan and the unexpected resistance to his wage-and-hours bill could scarcely have improved his mood. Roosevelt had always maintained a strict hands-off policy in local elections before, but that was about to change.

There were several explanations for Roosevelt's decision to play an active role in local congressional races around the country, an episode that became known as the "purge." One was the rise of the direct primary as the instrument of candidate selection. In earlier elections where candidates were decided by state nominating conventions or in the proverbial "smoke-filled rooms" of party leaders, the national party leadership could influence the process covertly; no whistle-stop campaign for or against local candidates was necessary, and with very few exceptions sitting presidents maintained a public neutrality. The shift toward primary elections, however, made it not only possible, but even necessary, for a national leader to sway public opinion by making his wishes known openly.

Another factor was the overwhelming dominance of the Democratic Party in many regions of the country. The Republicans' weakness raised the stakes in Democratic primaries in the Northeast and the South; for it was on the party ballots, not in the general election, where the future of the New Deal was to be decided. Roosevelt was fully aware that the Court plan had been defeated not by Republicans but by renegade Democrats, who formed the most potent conservative bloc on Capitol Hill. "The real fight," wrote Raymond Clapper, the veteran Washington observer for the Scripps Howard syndicate, "is taking place inside the Democratic lines."

Roosevelt surely was further motivated by personal pique. During the Court fight, Rosenman noticed, he had acquired "a very, very strong animus" against Democrats who were thwarting this key administration initiative. He had upbraided Vice President Garner at the time for failing to ride herd on lawmakers who Roosevelt felt had coasted to victory on his coat-tails in 1936; he maintained that they had been elected on a "national platform" and had no right to abandon it. Rosenman felt this argument was "only partially true": most voters did not see themselves as electing senators and representatives inextricably bound to the national leader's program. It was widely believed that Tom Corcoran played a role in stirring up Roosevelt's resentment, which would have been consistent with the doctrinaire partisanship Moley had detected in Corcoran's mind-set during the 1935 battle over the Public Utility Holding Company Act; but Roosevelt's bitterness after his loss on the Court plan may not have needed further stoking.

By late 1937, the President's decision to inject himself in several local races was widely rumored and the tea leaves telling of which candidates he might favor in the coming year were being closely studied. After one cross-country trip, he complained to his press secretary, Steve Early, that the reporters were mostly "writing columns on whether I shake hands with Mr. X with my left hand, or looked away when Mr. Y greeted me, or spent forty seconds longer talking with Mr. Z than with his colleague. It would be a lot cheaper if all your newspapers would hire Walter Winchell and save railroad fares."

On June 24, 1938, his intentions broke into the open with a Fireside Chat styled as a postmortem on the congressional session just adjourned. Despite its having been elected on an "uncompromisingly liberal" platform in November, Congress had turned in a wretched record, he observed. He would not be "taking part in Democratic primaries." But he claimed the responsibility of "carrying out the definitely liberal declaration of . . . the 1936 Democratic platform," and the right to speak out "where there may be a clear-cut issue between candidates for a Democratic nomination."

In retrospect, the disastrous outcome of the purge campaign owed much to its sloppy execution. Roosevelt targeted popular senator Walter George of Georgia, but his agents failed to file candidacy papers for a pro–New Deal opponent until fifteen minutes before the deadline; by then most of the state's Democratic newspapers and officeholders had already announced for George. A similar fiasco occurred in Maryland, where the attack on Senator Millard Tydings, who had voted against not only the Court plan but the NRA, AAA, TVA, and Wagner Act, was carried out by a popular congressman who had already announced for reelection to the House and was unable to raise new funds for a primary battle for the Senate.

Another source of confusion was the purge campaign's inconsistency.

"You cannot on paper draw a clear-cut formula to fit the purge list," Clapper observed. Anti–New Deal incumbents who could not be beaten, such as Nevada's Senator Pat McCarran, were given a presidential pass. With the exception of Tydings, most of those on the list were far from unalloyed opponents of the New Deal. Clapper noted that Walter George had a better voting record on New Deal legislation than Senator Robert J. Bulkley of Ohio, "who received the Presidential benediction."

Taken as a referendum on the New Deal, the 1938 midterm election showed public sentiment to have turned equivocal. The Republican Party expanded its tiny minority in the Senate by 6 seats and nearly doubled its House membership to 169 (leaving it still short of a majority). The pain of joblessness made itself felt in the election of several House candidates endorsed by the redoubtable Dr. Townsend and by the near victory of a California ballot initiative to create a pension program awarding every unemployed citizen over fifty a pension of thirty dollars a week—"thirty dollars every Thursday" was the slogan of the backers of this so-called "ham 'n' eggs" plan. Of the candidates targeted for purging by President Roosevelt, only one, a conservative in New York City, lost his seat. On the other side of the ledger, Senator Bulkley, who had won Roosevelt's endorsement, lost his race. Rather than demonstrate Roosevelt's leadership and the continuing support of the electorate for "uncompromisingly liberal politics," the purge turned out to be another humiliating defeat in that demoralizing season.

Dies easily won reelection in his south Texas district, a conservative southern Democrat bobbing along with the Republican tide. In December he reconvened his committee to hear more testimony about Federal One. Hallie Flanagan wrote her husband, Philip Davis, that inside the WPA "they are in the panic they should have been in three months ago." But the agency still refused to allow administrators to speak up for themselves. Instead, on the eve of the hearings the WPA brass informed Flanagan and Writers' Project director Henry Alsberg that they would be represented before the committee by Ellen Woodward, the WPA assistant director.

The Mississippi-born Woodward opened her testimony December 5 with a spirited defense of the agency. Addressing in magnolia-scented tones the charge that the writers' and theater projects harbored communists, she reminded the committee that the relief act of 1938, like its three predecessors dating back to 1935, prohibited discrimination against relief applicants on the basis of "political affiliations." She observed that the Federal Theatre had presented 924 plays in its three years, of which the committee's own witnesses had fingered only 26 as "communist propaganda." That made the charge of communist infiltration an "absurdity." The 152 WPA Guides comprised the "largest and most comprehensive editorial enterprise ever carried out on this continent," with many of its individual volumes sponsored or underwritten by governors, legislators, and leading universities.

But Woodward's appearance soon degenerated into a fiasco. Despite serving as the senior WPA official overseeing Federal One, she was unfamiliar with most of the works and productions that had come under attack by earlier witnesses, and thus unable to provide chapter-and-verse refutations of their charges. Her testimony was frequently interrupted by committee members' questions, some of them openly rude. The conservative Democrat Joe Starnes of Alabama sidetracked her into a discussion of *American Stuff,* an anthology of essays written and published by members of the Federal Writers' Project on their own time. Starnes was fascinated by an article titled "The Ethics of Living Jim Crow," by Richard Wright. This was an autobiographical sketch about "how to live as a Negro" in a white world, punctuated liberally with profanity—"the most filthy thing I have ever seen," Dies interjected.

"Do you find anything rehabilitating in that, I ask you?" Starnes asked Woodward, who had not read the piece.

"No. I do not," she replied unhelpfully. "I think that it is filthy and disgusting."

After a full day at the witness table, the overmatched Woodward arranged permission for Flanagan and Alsberg to testify. Flanagan doubted that she would achieve much. "Could a few hours offset the months in which allegations had gone unanswered, and charges had been magnified by the press?" she asked herself.

Even for such an experienced habitué of the performing world as Flanagan, the hearing room was an intimidating stage, jammed as it was with reporters and cameramen. Flanagan steeled herself by imagining the faces of theater people depending on her to uphold their reputations: "Clowns in the circus . . . telephone girls at the switchboards . . . actors in grubby rehearsal rooms . . . acrobats limbering up their routines . . . costume women busy making cheap stuff look expensive . . . carpenters, prop men, ushers. These were the people on trial that morning."

Dies welcomed her to the witness table with the words, "Just tell us briefly the duties of your position."

"Since August 29, 1935," she replied, "I have been concerned with combating un-American *inactivity.*"

"Inactivity?" Dies asked.

"I refer to the inactivity of professional men and women; people who, at that time when I took office, were on the relief rolls; and it was my job to expand the appropriation . . . for the relief of the unemployed as it related to the field of the theater."

Yet the committee was less interested in the complexities of keeping men and women on relief than in establishing Flanagan's communistic background. Had she not traveled twice to Russia? Yes, she stated, to study its theater. Had communistic propaganda been circulated on the project? She acknowledged that some Living Newspaper productions might indeed be labeled "propaganda"—"One-Third of a Nation" was "definite propaganda . . . for better housing for American citizens. . . . 'Power' was propaganda for a better understanding of the derivation and the scientific meaning of power and for its wide use. . . . 'Injunction Granted' is propaganda for fair labor relations and for fairness to labor in the courts."

To Huffman's assertion that the program "couldn't get any audiences for anything except communistic plays," Flanagan responded that the sponsoring bodies for Federal Theatre performances had included 263 social clubs, 264 welfare and civic organizations, 271 educational organizations, 95 religious bodies, and nearly 200 organizations of other description. "Every religious shade is covered and every political affiliation and every type of educational and civic body," she told the members. "It is the widest and most American base that any theater has ever built upon."

Parnell Thomas grilled her about the complaints of the *New York Times* drama critic Brooks Atkinson and of a New York sixth deputy police commissioner about the children's play *Revolt of the Beavers,* the story of the overthrow by a beaver colony of their oppressive chief, which play they considered Marxist. ("The newest adventure of the WPA theatre ought to improve our diplomatic relations with Soviet Russia," Atkinson sniffed.) "All I could say about it was that the play was for children, and that the children had found it pleasant and entertaining," she countered, artfully repressing her own equivocal opinion about the play, which she had described to her husband, Philip Davis, as "very human and amusing and tragic and very class conscious."

Finally came the exchange that would forever signify the essential philistinism of the committee's crusade against un-American activities. Starnes turned to Flanagan's article "A Theatre Is Born," from the November 1931 issue of *Theatre Arts Monthly,* and read: "The workers' theaters intend to remake a social structure without the help of money—and this ambition alone invests their undertaking with a certain Marlowesque madness."

He raised his eyes from the page. "You are quoting from this Marlowe. Is he a Communist?"

"I was quoting from Christopher Marlowe," she replied.

"Tell us who Marlowe is, so we can get the proper reference, because that is all we want to do."

"Put in the record that he was the greatest dramatist in the period of Shakespeare, immediately preceding Shakespeare."

"Put that in the record," Starnes duly commanded.

Finally, after nearly three hours, Dies moved to hustle her appearance to an end, declaring a lunch recess. "I would like to make a final statement," she protested.

"We will see about it after lunch," Dies replied. Flanagan was never called back.

Her place at the witness table was taken that afternoon by Henry Alsberg, the Writers' Project director, who made a very different impression. The bookish Alsberg chose emollience, not confrontation. He described himself to the committee as a devoted anticommunist, disclosing that in 1925 he had edited a collection of letters by Soviet political prisoners that was considered "the most devastating attack on the tyrannical Russian situation," and that cost him "most of my friends at the time . . . because a lot of the liberals at that time felt there should be nothing said about Russia that was not completely favorable." As a result, he said, he was unable to get his own work published "in any of the liberal journals. . . . I was blacklisted."

Alsberg allowed that he had had his own troubles with communists on the Writers' Project, had given explicit orders that there was to be no subversive activity on the staff, and that he had even objected when he found staff members selling communistic literature outside the project offices in New York. "I said the last time I was up there . . . 'For Christ's sake, cannot they peddle their literature somewhere else except the entrance to the project door?'"

The session ended as a lovefest between Alsberg and Dies. "The chair wants to commend you, Mr. Alsberg, for your frankness . . . and for the attitude you have assumed, rather than to come here in a belligerent way," Dies said, eliciting the reply: "I want to thank the committee for being fair in questioning me, and I am at their disposition at any time to furnish anything they want."

Alsberg's friends gave him the benefit of the doubt by concluding that he had attempted to kill the committee with kindness, without yielding on any point of importance, and certainly not implicating project members in subversive activities. But if he thought his performance would inoculate his project from the Dies Committee's wrath he was mistaken; its treatment of the Writers' Project differed only slightly from that of the Federal Theatre, whose director's bearing before the panel had been one of pure truculence.

The committee report on Federal One thoroughly condemned the Writers' Project for communist influence and took an evidence-free swipe at the Federal Theatre: "We are convinced that a rather large number of the employees . . . are either members of the Communist Party or are sympathetic with the Communist Party." But that did not end the programs' ordeal. There would be more congressional investigations and hours of hearings and congressional debate. The sultry actress Tallulah Bankhead arrived in Washington, perched herself atop a committee table, and hectored her Alabaman father, House Speaker William B. Bankhead, and her uncle, Senator John H. Bankhead II, to save the Federal Theatre. They turned her down. Republican congressman Everett Dirksen of Illinois combed the titles of the project's plays for hints of salaciousness and read them aloud on the House floor: "Lend Me Your Husband," "The Mayor and the Manicurist," "Up In Mabel's Room," "Did Adam Sin?" In early June, the House Appropriations Committee reported out a $1.735 billion relief bill for 1940 (down nearly $1 billion from the 1939 appropriation), appending riders specifically forbidding the use of federal money for theater projects and stipulating that the rest of the Federal One units find state or local sponsorship to supplement their federal subsidies, or else close up. A loyalty oath was to be required of all WPA employees.

When the appropriation bill went to the House floor, Hallie Flanagan confronted Howard Hunter, a Hopkins deputy, in his Washington office. "Who's in charge of the fight to save Federal Theatre?" she demanded.

"There isn't going to be a fight for Federal Theatre," he replied.

The fate of the entire WPA hung too much in the balance for the White

House to go to the mat with Congress over the relatively tiny programs of Federal One. At stake was a relief appropriation of nearly $2 billion, the sustenance of millions of people whose work relief would end on July 1 if the bill did not go through, and further battles looming on the horizon. Flanagan morosely contemplated her program's demise as a sacrificial lamb: "These opponents were out to hang the New Deal. Perhaps a hanging in effigy would do." Roosevelt leveled a discontented blast at Congress for conniving at "discrimination of the worst type," but he signed the relief bill. The same night, the New York unit staged its final performance of its children's play *Pinocchio,* with a rewritten ending. The puppet did not become transformed into a real boy but was laid away in a simple pine box bearing the inscription, "Born December 23, 1938; Killed by Act of Congress, June 30, 1939."

The vote on the relief bill did not mark the end of the New Deal, but in Washington it signified that six years of nearly single-minded dedication to domestic affairs were drawing to a close. The economy was again on the upswing. By the end of 1939 the Federal Reserve's industrial production index would exceed the peak levels reached in mid-1937, before the onset of Roosevelt's recession. Fueled by the demands of war, it would nearly double over the next six years.

Through 1939, the crisis overseas increasingly demanded President Roosevelt's attention. In his State of the Union message that January he candidly prepared the country for "storm signals from across the seas." This meant assuming new responsibilities on the world stage: "There comes a time in the affairs of men when they must prepare to defend, not their homes alone, but the tenets of faith and humanity on which their churches, their governments and their very civilization are founded."

As for domestic policy, the time had come to consolidate gains, not embark on new programs. "We are a wiser and a tougher nation than we were in 1929, or in 1932," Roosevelt said.

The fight to create new tools for government in a modern democracy had been a bitter one, he acknowledged. But the American public were, as a whole, satisfied with the results, even if "some of these tools had to be roughly shaped and still need some machining down. . . . We have now passed the period of internal conflict in the launching of our program of social reform. Our full energies may now be released to invigorate the processes of recovery in order to preserve our reforms."

There would be no new initiatives—but there would be a few novel applications of the old ones.

Roosevelt's implicit pledge not to seek new battlefields was very much the product of necessity. The Seventy-sixth Congress, elected in 1938, was billed as the most independent of the four Congresses of Roosevelt's tenure. It seemed to build on the success the legislative branch had recorded in defeating the President's Court plan and the reorganization scheme. The Republicans were still a minority in the new Congress, but no longer an insignificant one. There would be no more procedural "jamming through" of New Deal bills, but nor would there be wholesale reversals. "Only the extremists talk of turning back," reported the veteran Washington journalist Ernest K. Lindley—he who had drafted FDR's Oglethorpe speech so many years, and an era, before.

Hitler's armies crossed the Polish frontier on September 1, initiating the Second World War. Six weeks later, Roosevelt granted an audience to a Russian-born scientist of his acquaintance carrying a letter that had been jointly drafted by the Hungarian physicist Leo Szilard and Albert Einstein. Bearing Einstein's signature, the letter described in technical terms the most recent research in nuclear fission, and posited that the new science could lead to "extremely powerful bombs of a new type." Roosevelt surely did not grasp the ultimate gravity of Einstein's words, but he understood enough to summon his military aide, General Edwin M. "Pa" Watson. "This requires action," Roosevelt told him.

The period between the defeat of the Court plan and the onset of war saw the tying up of loose ends.

On the Monday before Thanksgiving 1937, William O. Douglas met with an envoy from the New York Stock Exchange. Douglas's goal was to bring the exchange under the thumb of the New Deal once and for all; his guest's plan was to call his bluff.

But Douglas was not bluffing. He had taken office as the Securities and Exchange Commission's third chairman only two months earlier, after nearly two years' service as an SEC commissioner. Raised in poverty in Washington state, Douglas combined a craggy outdoorsmanship with a brilliantly analytical mind that had won him places on the law faculties of Columbia and Yale prior to his appointment to the commission.

The SEC's first chairman, Joseph P. Kennedy, had established the agency as a working partner with Wall Street in professionalizing the financial and corporate sectors. After fifteen months in office he was succeeded by James M. Landis, a brainy acolyte of Felix Frankfurter and a codrafter of the New Deal's two securities acts, who strengthened the legal foundations of the agency's rules and regulations. Landis served as chairman for two years, then relinquished the job to Douglas, whose legacy would be the SEC's reputation for firm, fair, and aggressive enforcement of the rules. Or as Douglas bluntly defined the agency's evolution for the press: "Under Joe the gains made toward protecting the rights of investors through President Roosevelt's legislative program were consolidated. Under Jim we were taught how to get things done. Now we're going to go ahead and get them done."

Since 1934, the agency had been playing cat-and-mouse with the exchange's longtime president, the well-born Richard Whitney, whose uncompromising defense of the institution was a byword on Wall Street. In the view of Douglas and his predecessors at the SEC, the stock exchange had been operated for too long as a private club for the benefit of its members, particularly the floor traders traditionally aligned behind Whitney. For an institution serving as the linchpin of the capital markets and plainly vested with the public interest, this was a hopelessly anachronistic structure. Douglas's line in the sand was that the Big Board must be reorganized as a public institution, with a salaried president and staff reporting not to its members but an independent board; if the exchange resisted, he was prepared to nationalize it, effectively converting it into an arm of the SEC. Whitney was no longer president, but his influence over the exchange was weighty enough for him to place his stamp on its own proposal for reorganization. This document offered a few modest concessions to the government but rejected the very idea of an independent president and management.

On that Monday afternoon, William Harding Jackson, the exchange's lawyer, had come to Washington for one last effort at compromise with Douglas.

"Have you read our proposed statement?" he asked.

"The SEC has read it, and it is not satisfactory," Douglas growled. "The negotiations are off."

"Well, I suppose you'll go ahead with your own program?"

"You're damned right I will," came the blunt reply.

"When you take over the Exchange, I hope you'll remember we've been in business one hundred and fifty years. There may be some things you will like to ask us."

"There *is* one thing I'd like to ask," Douglas said.

"What is it?" Harding said hopefully.

"Where do you keep the paper and pencils?"

Yet it would not come to that. Only a few months later, Richard Whitney's power over the New York Stock Exchange ended forever, as did the last vestiges of the exchange's resistance to the SEC's demands. For Whitney—the hero of Black Thursday 1929, J. P. Morgan's personal broker, a Wall Street figure of unquestioned probity, and the living embodiment of exchange pride—stood exposed as a confidence man and an embezzler.

For years Whitney had been keeping his own failing investments afloat by raiding his clients' accounts and quietly juggling loans from exchange members. Numbered among his victims were his wife, his clients, his exchange colleagues, the New York Yacht Club, of which he was treasurer, and the dependents of deceased exchange members, the benefit fund for whom had been entrusted to his care and remorselessly looted.

In one last desperate attempt to stave off exposure he had approached "Sell 'Em Ben" Smith, a notorious speculator who had survived the 1929 crash by selling short into the plunge, and who despised Whitney and his entire Morgan-connected crowd. Whitney asked Smith for an unsecured $250,000 loan "on my face."

"You're putting a pretty high value on your face," Smith said, and refused to loan Whitney a nickel.

Whitney's firm publicly collapsed on March 8, 1939. Two days later he was indicted by New York's dynamic young district attorney, Thomas E. Dewey, and a week after that expelled from the New York Stock Exchange. He pleaded guilty to the criminal charges, and on April 11, facing justice with the poise of an earl, heard himself sentenced to five to ten years in Sing Sing, where he would distinguish himself as one of the prison yard's baseball nine.

Whitney's true legacy to Wall Street and the New York Stock Exchange revealed itself a few weeks later, when the SEC placed his friends and enablers on the stand in its own investigation. Coming under the dogged questioning of SEC staff attorney Gerhard A. Gesell—later to win fame as a federal judge in cases involving the Pentagon Papers and Watergate, among other landmarks of Washington jurisprudence—was Morgan partner Thomas W. Lamont.

Gesell asked Lamont why he had not raised a public alarm when his partner at the firm, George Whitney, requested a $1 million loan to cover securities his brother Richard had misappropriated.

Sincerely bewildered by the question, Lamont, the upright son of a Methodist minister who had worked his way through Harvard before acquiring the dignified wealth of a Morgan partnership, replied: "Did you expect me, Mr. Gesell, to say to Mr. George Whitney, 'I must trot down to the district attorney's office and denounce your brother forthwith'?"

"You did not conceive that you had any obligations as a citizen . . . or any obligation as a member of the Exchange?"

"Why, no, Mr. Gesell. I did not."

Of Whitney's confession that he had stolen a million dollars of client securities, Gesell asked: "You knew it was illegal and unlawful?"

"Sure, but you used the word stealing," Lamont replied indignantly. "It never occurred to me that Richard Whitney was a thief. . . . I am not a lawyer and I did not consult a lawyer and I moved as my heart dictated."

And so the fraud remained undetected for months more.

Lamont's testimony, with its casual absolution of fraud and embezzlement as gentlemanly offenses best handled as between friends, vividly demonstrated how the New York Stock Exchange's conduct as a private club had confounded the public interest. But he was already speaking as a relic of a bygone age. A month earlier, the exchange's members had voted to place the institution under the management of a paid president and independent professional staff. Its constitution was rewritten to meet every specification demanded by William O. Douglas. Resistance to the amendments had crumbled after the Whitney revelations, and the vote for approval was overwhelming. After five years of battling, the stock exchange was submitting to the jurisdiction of federal regulators and remaking itself, at least nominally, as a servant of the people.

In March 1938, Roosevelt moved to bring the New Deal's antitrust policy full circle by appointing Thurman Arnold as the Justice Department's antitrust chief. The appointment was among the President's most controversial, for Arnold, then a forty-six-year-old law professor at Yale, was known for his caustic attacks on the very concept of antitrust enforcement.

Arnold's reputation was based on *The Folklore of Capitalism*, a bestselling book he had published the year before. In the chapter devoted to antitrust in this characteristically witty dissertation on law and economics, Arnold seemed to imply that antitrust law was a fraud designed to acclimate society to ever-larger business combinations through the pretense that "unfair" or "immoral" ones would be prosecuted out of existence—"part of the struggle of a creed of rugged individualism to adapt itself to what was becoming a highly organized society."

Such a cynical approach to antitrust law seemed to be thoroughly at odds with the antimonopoly campaign then being conducted by Robert Jackson and Harold Ickes, and with the morbid solemnity with which the law was treated by progressives.

Arnold's critics attacked him as a "professional smart aleck." As he reported to his parents in Wyoming, "*The New York Times* and *New York Sun* have urged that I be thoroughly investigated because I am a sarcastic joker not fit for solemn duties." Yet the nominee's humor masked his rigorous legal mind and sober understanding of the issues at stake—"He is often at his most serious when he is funniest," a friend observed in the *New Republic*—and this came through at his confirmation hearings.

The President had become deadly serious about antitrust enforcement, especially after the Supreme Court overturned the NRA in 1935. This was a new tack for the New Deal, which had launched its industrial policy in 1933 by suspending antitrust enforcement under the NRA.

The antitrust division of the Justice Department was then a backwater employing a few dozen lawyers. It would be Arnold's job to revive the division, and the law. "Years of disuse of the Sherman Act," he observed later, "had made violation of the antitrust laws common, even respectable." After winning Senate confirmation, he set out "to convince American businessmen that the Sherman Act represented something more than a pious platitude; second, that its enforcement was an important economic policy."

The record of Arnold's five years in office would stand among the New Deal's most important legacies in the field of business regulation. Before departing for a federal appellate judgeship in 1943, he had brought more than 50 percent of all the proceedings instituted under the Sherman Act in that statute's half century of existence. He nearly quadrupled the antitrust division's budget and quintupled its staff.

Arnold established the consent decree, in which companies agree in civil court to end anticompetitive behavior in order to avoid criminal prosecution, as a primary tool of enforcement. Rather than pursue individual companies for violations of the law, he took aim at whole industries, winning cases that leveled the commercial playing field and eliminated collusive practices in ways that saved consumers hundreds of billions of dollars, and still do so today.

Arnold's first major target was the automobile industry, where the "Big Three" of Ford, General Motors, and Chrysler required dealers to finance car sales through their own captive credit companies and forbid them to steer buyers to outside lenders. After he indicted the Big Three and eighty-three other companies and individuals, the industry capitulated. Arnold then took on Hollywood, whose eight major studios exploited their ownership of nationwide theater chains to freeze out independent exhibitors. That lawsuit led ten years later to the studios' forced divestment of their theaters, a consumer-friendly severing of production from distribution of entertainment content that lasted for more than sixty years.

Arnold broke the American Medical Association's boycott of group health plans—the health maintenance organizations of the day—thereby establishing the principle that professional organizations may not use their market power to discourage alternative methods of delivering health care. Another lawsuit forced the Associated Press to distribute its news reports to its member newspapers' competitors, thus turning the abstract ideal of freedom of the press into a business precept. (This earned him so many denunciations from newspaper editorialists—"an idiot in a powder mill" was the contribution of the *Chicago Tribune*'s owner, Colonel Robert McCormick—that they filled two bound volumes published by the AP, which Arnold later listed "among my most treasured possessions.") And he handed the Temporary National Economic Committee one of its few concrete achievements by prosecuting the Hartford-Empire Company, which TNEC had condemned for monopolizing glass bottle manufacture through its control of patents. Arnold's settlement in that case required Hartford to license its patents to others—affirming the principle that patents are charters granted by the government to encourage the broad dissemination of knowledge for the public good, not to allow unlimited profiteering by commercial gatekeepers.

The administration's reorientation toward deficit spending to combat recession in 1938 created a rift between Roosevelt and the outstanding anti-Keynesian in his cabinet, Henry Morgenthau. Frustrated by a federal deficit heading back above $2 billion after it had been brought below $100 million in 1938 (in part by the collection of the new Social Security payroll tax), Morgenthau argued forcibly that the goal of government policy should be to restore "business confidence." This would reverse the decline of business investment, which he believed had caused the recession. His argument amounted to a brief for cutting the top income tax rates for wealthy individuals and large corporations, which was the program favored by conservative Democrats on the Senate Finance and House Ways and Means committees.

The administration's Keynesians—notably Marriner Eccles, Lauchlin Currie, and Leon Henderson—argued, to the contrary, that the recession had been caused by the curtailment of federal spending. It was they who had the President's ear. Roosevelt further believed that the concessions on tax policy sought by Morgenthau would embolden business leaders to demand a rollback of other initiatives. He was not about to appease them by scrapping the New Deal in pursuit of the nebulous goal of "confidence."

At a meeting in the White House on March 8, 1939, Roosevelt brusquely upbraided Morgenthau for seeking tax policies that would favor big business at the expense of the working class. Morgenthau had informed him that he measured his policy decisions against a placard on his desk reading, "Does it contribute to recovery?" Roosevelt replied that he considered the thought "very stupid," and in crisp tones lectured his Treasury secretary that bowing to the business community would "put a man in as President who . . . would be controlled by a man on horseback, as Mussolini and Hitler are. . . . [T]his simply would mean we would have a fascist President."

Morgenthau continued to agitate on behalf of "business confidence." In early May, Roosevelt authorized him to testify on Capitol Hill in favor of policies encouraging corporate investment, yet forbade the Treasury secretary to endorse or even mention a tax cut. The self-contradictory directive left Morgenthau more disillusioned than ever with a president who seemed to be moving the nation further from fiscal soundness with every passing day. Adding to his dejection, their policy disagreement had poisoned their personal relationship; Roosevelt had always enjoyed teasing his easily flustered Dutchess County neighbor, but of late the barbs had taken on an unaccustomed asperity.

A few days after receiving his marching orders, Morgenthau unburdened himself privately to the Democratic caucus on the Ways and Means Committee. "We have tried spending money," he said. "We are spending more than we have ever spent before and it does not work. . . . I want to see this country prosperous. I want to see people get a job. I want to see people get enough to eat. We have never made good on our promises. . . . There are four million that don't have that much income. We have never done anything for them."

Gingerly he touched on tax policy, but his words seemed to come closer to Roosevelt's views than otherwise: "We have never begun to tax the people in this country the way they should be," he said. "People who have it should pay." He concluded by returning to the central theme of his tenure as secretary, the necessity of balancing the budget. "After eight years of this Administration we have just as much unemployment as when we started. . . . And an enormous debt to boot! We are just sitting here and fiddling and I am just wearing myself out and getting sick. . . . When I have got to become a deficit spender and believe in this compensatory theory"—that is, Keynesian theory—"the President ought to get somebody else to sit in this chair."

These remarks came from a man exhausted from embracing incompatible policies, as was required of those who served the politically supple Franklin Roosevelt. But he was wrong, and not merely in miscalculating the length of the administration as eight years rather than six. The ranks of the unemployed had in fact fallen sharply over those six years, to about 6.8 million men and women in 1938 from 11.5 million at the end of 1932. The unemployment rate would settle at 11.3 percent in 1939, down from more than 22 percent when Roosevelt took office. The working population of the United States, including as many as 3.5 million workers employed on government programs, grew by roughly 20 percent during the New Deal, from 41 million in 1933 to 49 million six years later.

Henry Morgenthau never presided over a balanced budget. Inflated by the cost of war, the federal deficit soared to $54 billion in 1943, from $2.8 billion the year of his outburst to the Ways and Means Democrats. The federal budget did not return to surplus until 1947.

Roosevelt's appointment of Hugo Black to succeed Willis Van Devanter on the Supreme Court was followed, in his second term, by the elevation to the bench of Stanley Reed, Felix Frankfurter, William O. Douglas, and Frank Murphy, and by the appointment of James F. Byrnes, Robert Jackson, and Wiley Rutledge in his third term. The president who had attempted to create a favorable Supreme Court by legislative fiat ended up placing his stamp on the Court by more conventional means, for in the end he appointed more justices than any president other than George Washington. A Roosevelt majority would sit on the Supreme Court well into the 1950s, providing the core of the unanimous 1954 decision in *Brown v. Board of Education of Topeka* and a host of other progressive rulings. The last Roosevelt appointee to retire, William Douglas, stayed on the Court until 1975. Unsure that he wanted the job when the call to the Court came in 1939, Douglas would serve longer than any justice in history.

Despite the efforts of Harold Ickes and Eleanor Roosevelt, the administration's poor record in the field of civil rights would be its most significant shortcoming. Notwithstanding that flaw, there could be no doubt about the New Deal's devotion to the dignity of the average citizen, and the New Dealers' willingness to stand for equality for the common man and woman. This was signaled by one of the final acts of the Roosevelt administration in the New Deal era.

In early 1939, the nationwide concert tour of the outstanding operatic contralto Marian Anderson hit a brick wall in Washington, D.C., where she was scheduled to perform on Easter Sunday, April 9. Anderson was black, and the most suitable auditorium, the 3,700-seat Constitution Hall, was owned by the Daughters of the American Revolution, which maintained a strict policy allowing only white performers to appear on its stage. The DAR refused to waive the rule for Anderson, a nationally known performer who three years earlier had delivered a recital at the White House.

The controversy simmered for weeks before jumping up to a new stage of public notoriety on February 27, when Eleanor Roosevelt disclosed in her syndicated column, My Day, that she had resigned from the DAR. The First Lady's disclosure was oblique—she did not even name the organization but identified it only as one that had "taken action which has been widely talked about in the press." But her letter to DAR national chair Sally Robert was blistering: "You had an opportunity to lead in an enlightened way and it seems to me that your organization has failed."

The stage was set for the New Deal's most moving expression of public solidarity. Within two weeks of Mrs. Roosevelt's resignation, NAACP chairman Walter White had hatched a plan with Anderson's concert impresario, Sol Hurok, to stage the Easter recital on the steps of the Lincoln Memorial. Harold Ickes, who as interior secretary held jurisdiction over the memorial and who was a former officer of the NAACP's Chicago chapter, jumped at the idea. Still, given the sensitivity of the event and the involvement of the First Lady, Ickes thought it advisable to secure Roosevelt's approval before issuing his own. The President was equally enthusiastic. "She can sing from the top of the Washington Monument if she wants to," he told Ickes.

Easter Sunday dawned briskly cold. A sleet storm that struck Washington the previous day had passed, leaving behind scudding clouds but the prospect of clear weather for the free 5 P.M. concert. No one was sure how many people would attend, although Ickes's prediction of a crowd of fifty thousand seemed wildly optimistic.

Ickes had looked forward to the event with undisguised glee. Every newsreel company would have cameras in attendance and a nationwide radio hookup had been arranged. Ickes was perversely gratified that the response of Washington's elite to his invitations had placed a few in a hypocritical light—especially Vice President John Nance Garner of Texas, whose failure to respond to two telegrams inviting him to cosponsor the concert Ickes duly leaked to the Washington gossip columnist Drew Pearson. From among the justices of the Supreme Court, the only attendee was Hugo Black of Alabama, a civil libertarian whose appointment by Roosevelt had been marred, ironically, by the revelation that he once had been a member of the Ku Klux Klan.

Marian Anderson was keeping to herself. Despite her marvelous gifts she was a modest individual, so uncomfortable with the public uproar against the DAR that Hurok had kept her in the dark about his assiduous scheming to show up the organization. The program had been compiled from Anderson's touring repertoire: a Donizetti aria, Schubert's setting of *Ave Maria,* and, following a brief intermission, three spirituals. The half-hour recital would open with a rendition of "America." No member of the listening audience would ever forget it.

Early that afternoon, stepping out onto the makeshift stage with her trusted piano accompanist Kosti Vehanen for a sound check, Anderson had looked out over a deserted venue, the surface of the Reflecting Pool rippling in the stiff wind. Now it was time. Shortly before five, wrapped in a warm mink coat, she was escorted from an anteroom inside the memorial to the stage. Ickes stepped to the microphone to introduce her. "In this great auditorium under the sky, all of us are free," he said, his rough Chicago growl cutting emphatically through the chill. "When God gave us this wonderful outdoors, and the sun, the moon, and the stars, *He* made no distinction of race or creed or color. . . . Genius like justice is blind. For Genius with the tip of her wing has touched this woman. . . . Genius draws no color line." Ickes, a liberal judge of his own oratory, pronounced his four-minute introduction "the best speech I have ever made."

Marian Anderson came out into the open and stopped short, overcome by the sight before her. Some seventy-five thousand people had gathered in the open space, confounding every prediction. "There seemed to be people as far as the eye could see," she recalled. "The crowd stretched in a great semicircle from the Lincoln Memorial around the reflecting pool on to the shaft of the Washington Monument. I had a feeling that a great wave of good will poured out from these people, almost engulfing me."

She glanced at Vehanen, seated at the piano just to her right. His fingers settled on the keys, sounding the introductory chords, and then came her powerful, soaring contralto voice.

> *My country, 'tis of thee,*
> *Sweet land of liberty,*
> *For thee we sing.*

Whether deliberately or by inadvertence, she had subtly altered the last line of the verse: no longer the descriptive phrase "Of thee I sing," it was now an apostrophe to the nation, as though the event itself were offered to bless its quest for racial equality.

> *Land where my fathers died,*
> *Land of our pilgrims' pride,*
> *From every mountainside . . .*

The voice reached over the crowd, out to the future. This concert was the first of the great gatherings to assemble on the Mall, Marian Anderson the first link in a chain of aspiration stretching from the social and political upheaval known as the New Deal to the social and political upheaval known as the civil rights movement. Twenty-four years later, on this very site, Martin Luther King, Jr., would deliver his "I have a dream" speech to an even larger crowd and in the presence of, yes, Marian Anderson. King was at the beginning of his movement to galvanize America to deliver on the promises made by the New Deal, just as Anderson's earlier appearance had aimed to give tangible form to promises that, in the maelstrom of political contention and economic crisis, might sometimes have seemed only abstractions. On the platform before the Lincoln Memorial that Easter Sunday 1939, she shut her eyes and furrowed her brow, as if summoning the strength to bear the weight of hopes and expectations the New Deal had instilled in the American people and, like all human endeavors, fulfilled imperfectly. Then she sang out the final words of the anthem, the sound of hope underlying six years of social, political, and economic transformation in the United States of America:

. . . Let Freedom ring.

DEFINING THE NEW DEAL

D URING THE YEARS of the New Deal, America's government built as it never had before—or has since.

The New Deal physically reshaped the country. To this day, Americans still rely on its works for transportation, electricity, flood control, housing, and community amenities. The output of one agency alone, the Works Progress Administration (renamed the Works Projects Administration in 1939), represents a magnificent bequest to later generations. The WPA produced, among many other projects, 1,000 miles of new and rebuilt airport runways, 651,000 miles of highway, 124,000 bridges, 8,000 parks, and 18,000 playgrounds and athletic fields; some 84,000 miles of drainage pipes, 69,000 highway light standards, and 125,000 public buildings built, rebuilt, or expanded. Among the latter were 41,300 schools.

The transformative power of this effort is immeasurable. The Tennessee Valley in 1933 was a backwoods region of "grim drudgery, and grind," in the words of its savior George Norris: beleaguered by floods, drained of its manpower by the siren call of the cities, the latent wealth of its river and lumber left fallow. The TVA of Norris and Franklin Roosevelt turned it into a land of plenty that called its workers home, put its natural endowments to productive use, and delivered to its residents the promise of a secure American middle-class lifestyle.

The Public Works Administration provided Harold Ickes with a larger construction budget than any American government official ever had received: $3.3 billion, more than twenty times the $150 million the government spent on public construction projects in 1929. Ickes was determined to make the most of it. The impression is accurate that he disbursed the money with the tightfistedness of a man spending from his own pocket; but there is no denying that he thereby ensured that it would create for the nation a greater patrimony.

PWA built or helped build monumental projects from sea to sea. In Washington state, Grand Coulee Dam put eight thousand men to work starting in 1933, and using materials and equipment acquired from forty-six of the forty-eight states. In Southern California, PWA helped repair or replace 536 school buildings damaged or destroyed by the great Long Beach earthquake of March 10, 1933. Most of them, rebuilt to the most exacting seismic standards of the time, are still in use at this writing. In Florida, the exemplary project was the Overseas Highway, 127 miles of causeways and bridges connecting the mainland and Key West, built on the remains of a railroad line destroyed by hurricane in 1935, and transforming the latter island from a dismal outback of dispossessed relief recipients to one of America's premier tourist destinations. In New York was built the greatest project of them all—the Triborough Bridge, tying together three of the city's five boroughs, rescued from insolvency in 1933 by a PWA grant and loan totaling $44 million, and dedicated in 1936 with FDR in attendance despite his loathing for the project's municipal overseer, Robert Moses, whom the President had repeatedly tried to remove from the project. But he swallowed his enmity for Moses long enough to bask in the nationwide publicity marking Triborough's completion.

The Triborough ceremony marked a coming of age for the New Deal's approach to spending for physical infrastructure. At first Roosevelt and his aides had a murky understanding of how to balance the need to put people to work with the goal of efficient and lasting construction. Tugwell had witnessed an especially telling exchange between the President and New York mayor Fiorello LaGuardia about government funding for what would become LaGuardia Airport. "They were happily agreeing that bulldozers and other powered machines should be banned," he related. "There should be only hand tools so that more men would be employed." Finally, Tugwell interjected that if they *really* wished to put the maximum number of men to work, why not restrict them to trowels? The point was driven home that they might indeed employ more men, but they would never be able to finish one airport, much less build any others.

FDR came to understand the political glamor of great public works bet-ter than any president since his estimable fifth cousin Theodore. Whenever possible, he dedicated them in person—even when, as in the case with the structure that would ultimately be known as Hoover Dam, credit for its construction belonged to his Republican predecessors. Skeptical early in his first term about such works' cost and utility, he soon became an enthusiast, demanding more plans and more works—more bridges, more dams, even a highway spanning the American continent from sea to shining sea.

A good portion of Franklin Roosevelt's immortality rests upon the New Deal's physical works; but even more rests upon its reformation of the nation's social and economic structures.

Here we must consider Americans' relationship with what is, after all, *their* government. The New Dealers did not think about government in the limited terms of their predecessors, as an agency of national defense and little else. They did not perceive it as an antagonist of the common man, an enemy of liberty, or an entity interested in its own growth for growth's sake. They understood that it was a powerful force and that its power could be exercised by inaction as well as action, to very different ends. The condition of the American people when the New Dealers assumed office demanded ameliora-tive action, and this they strived to deliver. They did not invariably achieve their goals, but in appraising their performance it is important to acknowl-edge that the crisis they addressed was uniquely cataclysmic in American history, and that suitable precedent for addressing it simply did not exist.

Federal deposit insurance, by eliminating bank runs even in times of economic crisis, cut the number of bank failures from the peak of four thousand in 1933 to sixty-one the next year (including only nine federally insured banks.) Bank failures would not exceed seventy-five in any one year until the savings and loan crisis of the 1980s, and for a three-decade stretch beginning in 1943 never exceeded single figures. The importance of this record for depositor confidence and the safety of the nation's monetary stock is incalculable.

The reforms implemented under the Securities Exchange Act of 1934, which established the Securities and Exchange Commission, profession-alized an industry burdened in the aftermath of 1929 with a reputation for insider transactions and sharp dealing. The transparency of financial reporting for public corporations and brokerages mandated by the act set the foundations for the explosive growth of the U.S. capital markets and corporate economy ever since.

The New Deal instilled in Americans an unshakable faith that their government stands ready to succor them in times of need. Put another way, the New Deal established the concept of economic security as a collective responsibility. As of this writing, Social Security, by any measure the outstanding domestic achievement of the Roosevelt administration, serves 54 million beneficiaries. Over the decades the program has kept many millions of American workers and their families out of poverty. The promise of corporate pensions has largely disappeared from the employment contract and the investment markets have disappointed many workers' expectations of comfortable retirements, but Social Security endures, providing retirees with benefits that grow with inflation and that cannot be outlived. Social Security began as an "awkward and insufficient" program, as Rexford Tugwell would observe; but it was expanded in succeeding decades, under Republican and Democratic presidents alike, in a continuing effort to uphold its original promise. Its 1960s addendum, Medicare, sprang organically from that promise.

In 1939, Congress began restoring to the Social Security system benefits it had removed at Henry Morgenthau's insistence four years earlier. Old-age payments were increased and protection extended to elderly wives and dependent children of beneficiaries and to surviving widows and children of covered workers; a scheduled payroll tax increase was suspended for three years and the date of the first retirement payments moved forward to 1940 from 1942. By mid-1940, some 50 million Americans had been issued Social Security numbers and 42 million were already making contributions toward protection in their old age.

The New Deal effectively ended in 1939, amid doubts about Roosevelt's leadership and under the shadow of war, as a work in progress. To a great extent it is still unfinished.

Bank failures periodically surge because of outbreaks of imprudent management inadequately monitored by federal regulators, as occurred in the savings and loan crisis of the 1980s and the financial crisis of 2008. The business reforms of the Thirties sometimes have proven unequal to the challenge of combating the chicaneries of later ages, and periodically must be updated. The physical infrastructure bequeathed by the Thirties has been allowed in many places to crumble from inattention. The public debate about the proper role of the federal government in Americans' lives is never-ending, as perhaps it should be. Yet because the New Deal's principle of collective security has become ingrained in the American system, efforts to roll back the programs founded under Franklin Roosevelt almost always seem invested with the scent of unreality. Catastrophe snuffed out the economic and governmental structures of the 1920s and the march of modernity buried them.

The shelf of historical works on the New Deal is a long one, a healthy subset of the prodigious literature on Franklin Roosevelt's life, career, and legacy. Nevertheless, the New Deal remains one of the most poorly understood and myth-encrusted periods of our recent past. After more than seventy years of historical analysis, vigorous debate continues over its fundamental aspects. Was it a success or a failure? The plot of a dictator? A socialist bridgehead? A paragon of progressive government or a harbinger of oppressive federal interference in American life? A lifeline to the "forgotten man," or an anchor dragging him beneath the waves?

Some of these questions are perfectly legitimate, some merely tendentious and partisan. But the fact that they can still be asked hints at the complexity of the phenomenon under discussion. For even to the educated twenty-first-century American, the New Deal has appeared to be shrouded in mist. I hope this work has helped to demystify the period.

The New Deal presents a persistent challenge to our memory because so much of it is still with us—not only programs such as Social Security and federal deposit insurance, but physical monuments such as Grand Coulee Dam and LaGuardia Airport. These vestiges of the Thirties have been profoundly altered over the years. Social Security has been expanded to cover spouses, dependents, and the disabled, and supplemented by Medicare; deposit insurance covers far greater sums, even accounting for inflation, than it did at its inception; airports and bridges have been rebuilt, reconfigured, hemmed in by residential neighborhoods, or overwhelmed by traffic.

Yet much more about the New Deal has been forgotten. Many of its remarkable leaders, men and women like Harry Hopkins and Frances Perkins, have remained strong in the national consciousness. But seldom remembered is General Hugh Johnson, who was prominent enough as administrator of the National Recovery Administration and creator of its Blue Eagle to be named *Time*'s 1933 Man of the Year. Thomas Corcoran's long career as a Washington power broker and political fixer overshadowed his earlier work as a master legislative craftsman for Roosevelt, who gave him his famous nickname, "Tommy the Cork." Even less remembered is

Corcoran's devoted friend and New Deal partner, Benjamin V. Cohen, the legal genius responsible for crucial pieces of the Roosevelt program.

Re-creating an accurate and objective picture of the New Deal may be more important today than at any time in the last eight decades. To study the period is to be struck by the parallels between the economic and political conditions of the 1930s and those of the opening years of this century. Among the factors contributing to both the Great Depression and the "great recession" were excessive speculation in housing and financial assets, inadequate regulation of financial institutions, and imprudent behavior by the managements of major banks and investment houses. Corporate wealth was excessively concentrated in a few hands, and the business community wielded what many believed was excessive influence in the White House and the halls of Congress. President Roosevelt had no effective model for fighting the worst economic downturn in his generation's experience. Barack Obama did have a model: the New Deal.

Franklin Roosevelt ran for office on a platform that overlaid the rhetoric of progressive politics upon a distinctly more centrist mind-set. He inherited and extended many of Hoover's policies, including plans for resolving the banking crisis and a tax structure heavily dependent on regressive excise taxes—much as Barack Obama inherited a financial bailout and tax structure crafted under President George W. Bush. Roosevelt and Obama both encountered marked hostility from business leaders riled by their populist rhetoric and regulatory initiatives, especially in the financial arena. Both worked dramatic changes in the federal government's relationship with the American people. Overemotional critics attacked Roosevelt, as they have Obama, as a "socialist" and "tyrant"; yet both presidents appear to have shared a conviction that their task was not to dismantle the American capitalist system, but to save it from its own excesses.

My purpose in writing this book has been to clear away many of the myths, misunderstandings, and prejudices that hamper an objective appraisal of the program. The principal myth, treasured by Franklin Roosevelt's most devoted admirers and severest critics alike, is that he originated the New Deal as a fully conceived political and economic program prior to his election.

Roosevelt occasionally voiced this notion himself, perhaps motivated by pride of ownership. Yet like any president's political program, the New Deal was necessarily a patchwork. Franklin Roosevelt did not conceive, or even favor, some initiatives that are now seen as his most important achievements; and some of his own initiatives rank as the New Deal's outstanding fiascos. As Ray Moley observed in 1939: "That Roosevelt could look back over the vast aggregation of policies adopted between March, 1933, and November, 1936, and see it as the result of a single, predetermined plan was a tribute to his imagination." Instead, Moley explained, the New Deal was the product of "varying circumstances, impulses, beliefs" that often stood in flagrant contradiction with one another.

Another misconception is that the New Deal was based entirely on a progressive paradigm. The truth is that, especially in its early phases, much of it harked back to cherished conservative principles. One of the first bills Roosevelt sent Congress during the Hundred Days was a measure aimed at sharply curtailing federal spending, by no means a progressive ideal; and the emblematic New Deal program of Roosevelt's first year in office was the National Recovery Administration, which promoted an ostensibly business-friendly agenda involving the suspension of antitrust law and official toleration of a wide range of anticompetitive acts. One can hardly imagine a more explicit rejection than the NRA of the progressive precepts of Louis D. Brandeis and Adolf A. Berle, two of FDR's most important advisors, who believed that an illiberal concentration of economic power in fewer and fewer hands had undermined the democratic process and aggravated the extremes of the business cycle.

Those who characterize the New Deal as the product of Franklin Roosevelt's resolute progressivism and unerring foresight must acknowledge that he was unenthusiastic about government old-age pensions, firmly opposed to deposit insurance, and hopeful that the billions of dollars appropriated for projects like airports and bridges would be doled out slowly, stingily—even, if possible, not at all. Conversely, those who view the New Deal as a reflection of Roosevelt's single-minded grasp for imperial power must explain why he rejected legislation giving him unlimited authority to inflate the U.S. economy until it was rewritten with concrete limitations, and why progressives in Congress continually complained that he compromised too readily with big business and with southern and conservative forces. Even the pioneering banking reforms of the early New Deal, the Brain Truster Rexford Tugwell lamented, were the product of "humiliating compromises" with Wall Street.

The outstanding personality trait of the Franklin Roosevelt of the New Deal was, in fact, pragmatism. The trait, as we have seen, did not always sit well with the members of FDR's Brain Trust—the group of university professors and trusted friends who helped him prepare to seek the presidential nomination in 1932. (Most of them disliked the label, originally coined as "the Brains Trust" by a newspaper reporter with disparaging intent.) Like subsequent members of Roosevelt's inner circle, they were disconcerted by his tendency to flit from policy to policy in search of one that would accomplish his goals while mollifying congressional adversaries. The memoirs of Roosevelt's closest associates are brimful of attempts to apologize for his flexibility or explain it away, often unconvincingly, as the sign of a supple and canny political intellect at work.

But the same trait enabled him to turn a multifaceted and internally contentious group of advisors into something resembling a movement. Remarkable was the loyalty he elicited as much from the rock-ribbed conservative Lewis Douglas as from the radical agrarian Rexford Tugwell; from Harold Ickes and Harry Hopkins, one a curmudgeonly miser, the other a spendthrift idealist; from Henry Morgenthau, gentleman farmer, and Frances Perkins, the prim social activist from New England.

Roosevelt tolerated dissension, even on occasion enjoyed fomenting it himself. But after a storm passed, he expected disagreements and harsh words among his aides to be set aside. During the drafting of his acceptance speech for the 1936 Democratic convention, he had it out with Ray Moley, one of the speechwriters, over critical columns Moley had written for his new magazine, *Today*. (One of its financial backers was Roosevelt's close friend Vincent Astor.) The exchange was bitter—"for the first and only time in my life, I saw the President forget himself as a gentleman," Rosenman related. A few days later Moley was surprised to get a call from Roosevelt asking that he continue working on the speech. Moley was still nursing his wounds, but he assented.

In recent years, historical works on the New Deal have fallen into two distinct categories: treatments of discrete events such as the Hundred Days or the Court-packing scheme of 1937; and polemical analyses, often built around the contention that the New Deal exacerbated or even prolonged the Great Depression. These approaches, skillful as some may be in execution, are inadequate as windows onto the New Deal as a whole. For example, the Hundred Days, which attracts new attention with the accession of every new president, is a most unrepresentative period of the New Deal. (Although the term is commonly applied today to the first hundred days of a new administration, originally it referred to the length of the special session of Congress called by Roosevelt, which convened on March 9 and adjourned on June 16, one hundred days later, day 105 of FDR's first term.)

During these hectic weeks the new administration was preoccupied with a succession of emergencies to which it applied solutions that had been concocted by the Hoover administration, or cobbled together from bits and pieces of special-interest nostrums, or rushed to premature or incomplete enactment. It is not too much to say that the administration's energies during much of the following twelve months were occupied in refining or repairing policies and programs introduced during its first three. The catchall Agricultural Adjustment Act of the Hundred Days enabled the more carefully considered farm reforms implemented by Agriculture Secretary Wallace and Rexford Tugwell; many of the hasty infelicities of the Securities Act of 1933 were repaired via the professional draftsmanship of the Securities Exchange Act of 1934. And the Court-packing scheme in its single-minded arrogance was a stark departure from Roosevelt's customary approach to legislation, not representative of the New Deal's character as a whole but rather the defining disaster of the New Deal's unsuccessful final act.

Then there is the contention that the New Deal's aggressive management of the economy hampered economic recovery or even prolonged the Depression by several years. Exhibit A in this brief is the National Recovery Administration, which promoted a European-style cartelization of American industry by suspending antitrust law and allowing companies to collude on wages and prices, production levels, and other forms of competition. Such collusion, critics say, suppressed growth in employment and output.

Yet the NRA's direct influence over American industry lasted scarcely one year. The agency, which was established in June 1933, was declared unconstitutional by the Supreme Court in March 1935 but had run out its string long before that: its militant founder and director, Hugh S. Johnson, had been forced into retirement in September 1934, after months of ineffective leadership.

Critics argue that the conditions established under the NRA, such as lax antitrust enforcement and encouragement of collective bargaining by labor, continued to exert their deadening influence on economic growth through the 1930s. But antitrust enforcement was a backwater of government regulation even in the 1920s; the NRA merely codified what had become unwritten tradition—to cite Thurman Arnold, violation of the antitrust code was "almost respectable" in the business community long before the founding of the NRA in 1933. And wage increases, whether or not associated with union organizing, continued through the 1930s and persisted into 1939, spanning periods both of recession and of powerful economic growth. During the NRA's reign, moreover, the flouting of its anticompetitive rules was common, either through subterfuge or loose drafting of the industry codes governing wages, prices, and production. Industry, of course, had promised to invest in recovery if the shackles represented by price wars and antitrust enforcement could be removed. That promise was not kept. In summary, it is difficult to correlate the rise and fall of the economic cycle in the 1920s and 1930s to policies of the U.S. government related to industrial competition.

The second pillar of New Deal criticism is that the government undertook a misguided proto-Keynesian fiscal stimulus, creating deficits that squeezed private investment and opportunities for profit out of the marketplace, and competing unfairly for available labor and capital. This critique has been voiced frequently in recent years as a reproach to the frankly Keynesian stimulus policies of the Obama administration.

The critique has two major shortcomings. First, the New Deal was not chiefly a fiscal "stimulus" program in the sense we use that term today— that is, an effort to prime the economic pump with tax relief, subsidies for private economic activity, and public works, all financed through large-scale government borrowing. Franklin Roosevelt was a reluctant disciple of pump priming and never a complete convert to the cause. This was a consequence partially of his innate fiscal conservatism, a mind-set that in many respects mirrored Herbert Hoover's, and partially of the sheer novelty of deficit-financed pump priming in the mid-Thirties before the theories of John Maynard Keynes took hold in the United States.

From 1933 through 1937, the federal deficit—the sine qua non of government economic stimulus—averaged less than $3.2 billion a year, or about 4.5 percent of gross domestic product. As the government economist Lauchlin Currie observed in a penetrating analysis in 1935, that was significantly below the $5 billion to $6 billion annual deficit needed to achieve sustainable recovery. But deficits on that scale were not reached until the war years of 1941 and later, when the deficit climbed to as much as $4.5 billion a month.

Indeed, in only one year of the New Deal did federal fiscal policy have a more expansionary effect on employment than it had had in 1929. That was 1936, when the bonus paid to World War I veterans pumped $1.7 billion into the economy—a payment Roosevelt had vetoed (as had Hoover), only to be overruled by Congress. The end of the bonus payments in 1937 contributed to the onset of recession that year. Moreover, the structure of federal taxes—established under Hoover in 1932 and extended repeatedly by Roosevelt—worked to dampen the effect of the few deliberately expansionary programs initiated by the New Deal.

To repeat the justly famous conclusion of economist E. Cary Brown, New Deal fiscal policy was unsuccessful as a recovery device in the 1930s "not because it did not work, but because it was not tried." New Deal fiscal policy turned explicitly expansionary only in 1938, when a surge of federal spending brought the so-called Roosevelt recession promptly to an end.

None of this validates the argument that the New Deal hampered recovery prior to 1938. On the contrary, programs such as work relief and government construction helped to maintain or increase consumer demand. Of even greater moment, according to modern economic analysis, was rapid monetary expansion beginning in 1933. This was fueled initially by an inflow of gold attracted by Roosevelt's devaluation of the dollar, and later by the deteriorating political situation in Europe, which drove gold holdings seeking safety and security from continental banks to the United States. It is fair to note that Roosevelt's devaluation was motivated not by the expectation that it would attract gold from abroad, but rather the misguided notion that it would directly result in higher prices for goods at home. Nevertheless, it had a significant effect on the course of recovery.

During most of the New Deal period the U.S. economy expanded strongly. The Federal Reserve's industrial production index more than doubled from the month of Roosevelt's inauguration through the end of 1936. Real gross national product grew at a blistering pace, averaging 8 percent a year between 1933 and 1937. The unemployment rate fell sharply, from more than 22 percent in 1932 to 9 percent in 1937. The trend toward lower unemployment was broken in 1938 by the "Roosevelt recession," when the rate rose back to about 12.5 percent, but it resumed its steady decline the following year, bottoming out at about 1 to 2 percent during the Second World War. Between 9.5 million and 10 million more Americans were employed in 1937 than in 1932, an increase of 25 percent in the labor force. The stock market, too, responded positively: from Roosevelt's

inauguration to early 1937, the Dow Jones Industrial Average nearly quadrupled, a performance unmatched in any other four-year time span.

With the exception of total employment, none of these measures managed to reach precrash levels before 1941. But given the circumstances of
a cataclysmic worldwide economic collapse, the New Deal's achievement
in superintending recovery should not be underrated. It is plain that both
monetary expansion and Keynesian deficit spending served their functions
during the New Deal, and that more stimulus would have fueled even
stronger peacetime growth prior to the war.

The New Deal's most important accomplishment in the economic sphere
may have been the liberation of American fiscal policy from the shackles of
the past—notably the gold standard. Decoupling the dollar from gold, as
Roosevelt did in the first months of his administration, facilitated expansionary fiscal policy to the benefit of almost every president since.

The Great Depression exposed the economic orthodoxy of the nineteenth century as obsolete for the twentieth. Economic nationalism, the
gold standard, the insularity of the capital markets, and many other tenets
and habits of commerce and industry were revealed as antique supersti-
tions, as unequal to the challenge of fighting economic collapse as the nostrums of medieval doctors were to fighting disease.

The New Deal initiated the development of new economic principles
and new social and political institutions to put them into practice. This
process required improvisation, for the causes of collapse were still being
diagnosed while the first remedies were being applied. But the remedies
could not wait for a final diagnosis: people had to be fed and sheltered and
found employment, the economic system had to be protected from whatever diseases of greed and imprudence had been identified, and the transition toward a governmental structure suited to the new world had to begin.

The New Deal was a work in progress from its beginning to its end,
when it yielded to preparations for war. Its principles and institutions
still are works in progress, the debate over them ongoing. What is surely
beyond debate is that the Great Depression marked an upheaval in American history, and the New Deal a turning point in the relationship between
government and the governed. Its legacy lives on: that shining ideal that
American government should serve the people, all the people, and that
none should be forgotten.

NOTES

CUOHROC   *Columbia University Oral History Research Office Collection*
FDRL   *Franklin D. Roosevelt Library*
LAT   *Los Angeles Times*
LOC   *Library of Congress*
NYT   *New York Times*
PC   *Press Conferences of Franklin D. Roosevelt*
PP   *The Public Papers and Addresses of Franklin D. Roosevelt*
TNR   *The New Republic*

PROLOGUE: THE LONG WINTER

page
1 *Samuel I. Rosenman always claimed*: This version of the drafting of the acceptance speech comes from Rosenman, *Working with Roosevelt*, pp. 66–73.
2 *Moley had written*: See Moley, *After Seven Years*, p. 23n, for a partial transcription of the cover letter.
2 *"A New Deal for America"*: TNR, June 29 and July 6, 13, 27, 1932. The quotation cited appears in Part IV.
3 *Earlier in the day*: Tugwell, *The Democratic Roosevelt*, p. 20.
4 *"It's incredible"*: Ibid., p. 21.
4 *"The economy was seized"*: Tugwell diary, p. 4, MS in Tugwell papers, *FDRL*.
4 *Wilson's intellectual guide*: For the relationship between Wilson and Brandeis see Urofsky, *Louis D. Brandeis*, pp. 337ff.
5 *"forgotten in the political"*: *PP-I*, vol. 1, p. 648.
5 *"forgotten man at the bottom"*: Ibid., p. 625.
5 *"a veritable cancer"*: Ibid., p. 811.
6 *"Well, Felix"*: Smith, *An Uncommon Man*, p. 140.
6 *"class antagonisms"*: Hoover Address, Madison Square Garden, Oct. 31, 1932, on The American Presidency Project at www.presidency.ucsb.edu/ws/ (accessed Jan. 7, 2010).
6 *"He has wrapped"*: Stimson Diary, Nov. 11, 1932, quoted in Schwarz, *Interregnum of Despair*, p. 197.
6 *"He makes excellent speeches"*: TNR, June 1, 1932.
6 *"Mr. Roosevelt is a highly impressionable"*: Lippmann, *Interpretations 1931–1932*, pp. 259–62. (*New York Herald Tribune*, Jan. 8, 1932.)

6   *"hurlyburly"*: Lippmann, "The Peculiar Weakness of Mr. Hoover," *Harper's Magazine*, June 1930.

7   *he made only eight more*: Hoover, *Memoirs*, vol. 3, p. 233.

7   *"abundant hospitality"*: Moley, *The First New Deal*, p. 6.

7   *"autointoxication of the intelligence"*: Moley, *After Seven Years*, p. 11.

7   *"Roosevelt read the two"*: Moley, *After Seven Years*, p. 48. The speech, delivered at Sioux City, Iowa, on Sept. 29, advocated bringing down the "outrageously excessive" tariffs by "international negotiation" and creating a bipartisan Tariff Commission, which had been vetoed by Hoover.

7   *"A practical streak"*: Moley, *The First New Deal*, p. 6.

8   *"all on Mr. Hoover's side"*: Galbraith, "On the Economics of F.D.R.," *Commentary*, Aug. 1956.

8   *"The country needs"*: Commencement speech, Oglethorpe University, given May 22, 1932.

8   *"a kind of watchword"*: Rosenman, *Working with Roosevelt*, p. 66.

9   *"We are now providing"*: PP-I, vol., p. 750ff.

9   *"The air is now surcharged"*: PP-I, vol., p. 807.

9   *"unforgivable folly"*: Schlesinger, *The Crisis of the Old Order*, p. 433.

9   *"a good and convincing explanation"*: Rosenman, *Working with Roosevelt*, p. 87.

10   *"The campaign speeches"*: Eccles, *Beckoning Frontiers*, p. 95.

10   *"Your distant relative"*: White to Theodore Roosevelt, Jr., Feb. 1, 1933, *Selected Letters of William Allen White*, p. 329.

10   *"no one has power"*: Lippmann, *Interpretations: 1933–1935*, p. 1.

10   *"The rest of the world"*: Hoover, *Memoirs*, vol. 3, p. 40.

10   *"With the ominous"*: Ibid., p. 176.

11   *Although fewer banks*: See "Bank Suspensions and Banks Reopened," *Federal Reserve Bulletins*, Feb. 1932–Jan. 1933.

11   *more than $400 million*: Hoover, *Memoirs*, vol. 3, p. 160.

11   *"We were far"*: Jones, *Fifty Billion Dollars*, p. 16.

11   *"radical and collectivist"*: Hoover, *Memoirs*, vol. 3, p. 196.

11   *"rests upon those now vested"*: Moley, *The First New Deal*, p. 24.

12   *"I did not like the ring"*: Hoover, *Memoirs*, vol. 3, p. 179.

12   *"had spent most of their time"*: Stimson Diary, Nov. 22, 1932, cited in Freidel, *Franklin D. Roosevelt: Launching the New Deal*, p. 35.

12   *"President Elect Roosevelt"*: Moley, *The First New Deal*, p. 140.

13   *"My Dear Mr. President-Elect"*: The full text of the letter is in Myers and Newton, *The Hoover Administration: A Documented Narrative*, pp. 338–40.

13   *"The breaking point"*: Moley, *After Seven Years*, p. 140.

13   *2,298 banks failed*: See *Federal Reserve Bulletin*, March 1932, p. 156.

13   *"frantic, rumor-spreading depositors"*: Jones, *Fifty Billion Dollars*, p. 73.

14   *the group would collapse*: Testimony of Alfred P. Leyburn, Hearings, "Stock Exchange Practices," Senate Committee on Banking and Currency (Jan. 5, 1934), p. 4626.

14   *"that normal times"*: Ballantine, "When All the Banks Closed," *Harvard Business Review*, March 1948.

14   *"quite incensed"*: Hearings, "Stock Exchange Practices," (Jan. 12, 1934) p. 4695.

14   *the subsidiary banks were losing*: Testimony of Ernest Kanzler, Hearings, "Stock Exchange Practices," Senate Committee on Banking and Currency (Jan. 5, 1934), pp. 4591–94.

14   *Ford replied*: Ballantine, "When All the Banks Closed," *Harvard Business Review*, March 1948.

15   *"All right then"*: Jones, *Fifty Billion Dollars*, p. 138. Jones quoted a "verbatim" report by Ballantine and Chapin to the RFC. See also Moley, *The First New Deal*, pp. 137–38.

15 *$28 million*: Barnard, *Independent Man*, p. xvi.
15 *"denounce from the housetops"*: *Time*, Aug. 28, 1933. Numerous versions exist of this quote. See, for example, Bingay, *Detroit Is My Own Home Town*, p. 129 ("I will scream from the housetops"); and Leyburn testimony, Hearings, "Stock Exchange Practices," (Jan. 5, 1934), p. 4627 ("shriek from the housetops")—the latter repeated by Leyburn in the presence of Couzens, who did not demur. In any event, Couzens's severe disapproval of such loans was not in doubt.
15 *"For once in his life"*: Jones, *Fifty Billion Dollars*, p. 64.
15 *"Those two old roosters"*: Ibid., p. 61.
15 *offering personally to put up half*: Barnard, *Independent Man*, p. 233.
15 *shuttering 550*: Kennedy, *The Banking Crisis of 1933*, p. 95.
16 *"we shall have a riotous"*: Barnard, *Independent Man*, p. 240.
16 *"unduly long"*: Hoover, *Memoirs*, vol. 3, p. 203.
16 *Although he portrayed himself*: See, for example, ibid., pp. 193–94.
16 *"ill-concealed hostility"*: Willis and Chapman, *The Banking Situation*, p. 86.
16 *"I realize that"*: Myers and Newton, *The Hoover Administration*, p. 341.
17 *one could buy a passbook*: Roth, *The Great Depression: A Diary*, p. 92–93.
17 *Gold and currency were draining*: Ballantine, "When All the Banks Closed," *Harvard Business Review*, March 1948.
17 *ran off the Federal Reserve chart*: See *Federal Reserve Bulletin*, Mar. 1933, p. 135.
18 *"Balance budgets"*: "Investigation of Economic Problems," Senate Committee on Finance, Feb. 13, 1933, p. 18.
18 *"The biggest and finest crop"*: *Time*, Feb. 6, 1933.
18 *"a dinner of the Old World"*: Moffat, *The Moffat Papers*, p. 87.
18 *"There is a general sense"*: Feis, *1933: Characters in Crisis*, p. 87.
19 *Roosevelt finally delivered*: Hoover, curiously, dates the reply as Feb. 23, only six days after his own letter (*Memoirs*, vol. 3, p. 206), hardly a delay long enough to carry the significance Hoover attaches to it. The date of March 1 is documented by Myers and Newton, *The Hoover Administration*, p. 344, and Moley, *The First New Deal*, p. 144.
19 *On March 3 alone*: Francis Gloyd Awalt, "Recollections of the Banking Crisis in 1933," *Business History Review*, Autumn 1969.
19 *Thirty-two states had closed*: See Kennedy, *The Banking Crisis of 1933*, n155–56.
19 *Roosevelt immediately sent for*: Moley, *The First New Deal*, p. 149.
20 *"I realize, Mr. President"*: Tully, *F.D.R., My Boss*, p. 64.
20 *"You are the only one"*: Memo, Walter Wyatt (general counsel, Federal Reserve Board) to Moley, Mar. 16, 1966, quoted in Moley, *The First New Deal*, pp. 147–48.
20 *"Everyone forgot political differences"*: Ibid., p. 152.
21 *face-to-face with insolvency*: See Henry Morgenthau, *NYT*, May 14, 1935.

1: "ACTION NOW"

25 *"Thy servant, Franklin"*: Freidel, *Franklin D. Roosevelt: Launching the New Deal*, p. 198.
25 *"squads and squadrons"*: Tugwell, *Roosevelt's Revolution*, p. 28.
26 *"the terror-stricken look"*: Perkins, *CUOHROC*, Part IV, p. 26.
26 *"So I began"*: Tully, *F.D.R., My Boss*, p. 68.
26 *Hoover did not wait*: Perkins, *CUOHROC*, Part IV, p. 25.
28 *"Whatever the economic system"*: Berle to Roosevelt, Aug. 15, 1932. The entire memo is reprinted in Berle, *Navigating the Rapids*, pp. 57–58.
28 *"refused to be drawn"*: See Stein, *The Fiscal Revolution in America*, p. 41. Stein misquotes the inaugural line as "adequate and sound currency."
29 *Roosevelt and Moley laid out*: Moley, *The First New Deal*, pp. 98–99.

30 *"There was nothing"*: Moley, *After Seven Years*, p. 139.
30 *There would be no more toying*: See Houck, *FDR and Fear Itself*, p. 84.
30 *"Nothing is so much"*: The quotation appears in Thoreau's journal for Sept. 7, 1851.
30 *Moley dismissed that theory*: See Moley, *The First New Deal*, pp. 115–19.
31 *"In a condition of this kind"*: *NYT*, Feb. 9, 1931.
31 *"Nothing is terrible"*: The quotation is from Bacon's *De Augmentus Scientiarum* ("The Advancement of Learning"), Book VI, Chapter III.
31 *"The word should frighten"*: Lippmann, *Interpretations: 1933–1935*, p. 8 (Feb. 14, 1933).
31 *"a man who is fresh"*: Ibid., pp. 17–18 (Mar. 7, 1933).
31 *"What 'ancient truths'"*: Tugwell, *Roosevelt's Revolution*, p. 27.
32 *"Everything is gray"*: Wilson, "Washington: Inaugural Parade," *The American Earthquake*, p. 478.
32 *"angry and dismayed"*: Corcoran, "Rendezvous with Democracy: The Memoirs of Tommy the Cork" (unpub.), Corcoran Papers, Library of Congress.
33 *"the veritable slough"*: Ickes, "My Twelve Years with F.D.R.," Part 2, *Saturday Evening Post*, June 12, 1948.
33 *While waiting his turn*: Ibid.
33 *"his own foreign minister"*: Moley, *The First New Deal*, p. 89.
34 *Agriculture was to go*: Farley, *Behind the Ballots*, p. 203.
34 *"We simply cannot"*: Moley, *The First New Deal*, p. 81.
34 *Glass refused*: For letters between Glass and Roosevelt regarding the Treasury appointment, see Smith and Beasley, *Carter Glass*, pp. 331–33.
35 *No one paid him a deeper*: Ickes, "My Twelve Years with F.D.R.," Part 2, *Saturday Evening Post*, June 12, 1948.
35 *"First, I wouldn't give"*: Johnson to Archibald M. Johnson, Jan. 21, 1933, *Diary Letters, vol. 5*.
36 *"I liked his jib"*: Moley, *The First New Deal*, p. 94.
36 *If we had not made*: Johnson to "My Dear Boys," Feb. 26, 1933, *Diary Letters, vol. 5*.
36 *Walsh died*: *NYT*, March 3, 1933.
36 *"a quiet, serious group"*: Tugwell Diary, Feb. 26, 1933.
36 *"No President ever selects"*: Lippmann, *Interpretations: 1933–1935*, p. 13 (Feb. 28, 1933).

2: A Good Crisis

39 *a novel issue of warfare*: See Quinn, "Note," *Trading with the Enemy Act*, National Bank of Commerce in New York, 1917.
39 *Bell smiled*: Tugwell, *Roosevelt's Revolution*, p. 23.
40 *"Mr. President, I am ready"*: Moley, *After Seven Years*, p. 148.
41 *"So what are you planning to do?"*: The exchange between Glass and Roosevelt is from Smith and Beasley, *Carter Glass*, p. 341, and is generally taken to reflect Glass's verbatim recollections.
41 *"A few were so immersed"*: Moley, *After Seven Years*, p. 167.
42 *"Herbert Hoover, I am sure"*: Warburg, *The Long Road Home*, p. 108.
42 *"Fay Wray flaunted"*: *LAT*, Mar. 5, 1933.
42 *Pasadena's luxurious Huntington Hotel*: *LAT*, Mar. 6, 1933.
42 *accepted any object*: Manchester, *The Glory and the Dream*, p. 78.
42 *"We are prepared"*: Advertisement, *NYT*, Mar. 7, 1933.
42 *Retailers had stopped*: *NYT*, Mar. 6, 1933.
43 *With theater receipts dwindling*: *LAT*, Mar. 7, 1933.
43 *Food prices rose*: *LAT*, Mar. 9, 1933.

43 *"There must be adequate"*: Moley, *The First New Deal*, p. 161.
43 *Woodin acted promptly*: See Regulations 1–14, *Federal Reserve Bulletin*, March 1933, pp. 122–24.
44 *"I'll be damned"*: Moley, *After Seven Years*, p. 151.
44 *"There was magic"*: Moley, *The First New Deal*, p. 172.
44 *At Wall Street's behest*: *NYT*, Mar. 7, 1933.
45 *"All you need"*: *Will Rogers' Daily Telegrams*, No. 2055 (Mar. 6, 1933).
45 *The* Chicago Tribune *paid*: Kennedy, *The Banking Crisis of 1933*, p. 172.
45 *General Fireproofing Company*: Roth, *The Great Depression: A Diary*, p. 100.
45 *"a phony lot of words"*: Meyer, *CUOHROC*, quoted by Kennedy, *The Banking Crisis of 1933*, p. 173.
46 *"more direct and more drastic"*: Stein, *The Fiscal Revolution in America*, p. 40.
47 *Wyatt cached himself*: Wyatt to Ballantine, Aug. 1, 1944, reprinted in Moley, *The First New Deal*, p. 175.
47 *Wyatt began working*: Interview with Wyatt, Feb. 5, 1954; internal memorandum, Federal Reserve Board, at fraser.stlouisfed.org/docs/historical/brookings/16807_04_0036.pdf (accessed Feb. 1, 2010).
48 *As this would protect*: See *NYT*, Mar. 10, 1933.
48 *By the end of 1935*: See Lester Telser, "The Reconstruction Finance Corporation During the New Deal Period." Working paper: Stigler Center for the Study of the Economy and the State, University of Chicago, July 28, 2008.
48 *The emergency banking bill*: The text of the Emergency Banking Act of 1933 can be found at *Federal Reserve Bulletin*, March 1933, pp. 115–18.
49 *"I am talking about"*: *Congressional Record*, Mar. 9, 1933, p. 54.
49 *" 'Little banks?'"*: Ibid., p. 58.
50 *"Do you really think"*: Lippmann to Frankfurter, March 14, 1933, in Lippmann, *Public Philosopher: Selected Letters*, p. 305.
51 *Ballantine rewrote it*: Kiewe, *FDR's First Fireside Chat*, pp. 78–79.
51 *"stated in no uncertain terms"*: Awalt, "Recollections of the Banking Crisis in 1933," *Business History Review*, Autumn 1969.
53 *$1.2 billion in currency*: *Federal Reserve Bulletin*, April 1933, p. 209.
53 *of the $200 million*: Ballantine, "When All the Banks Closed," *Harvard Business Review*, March 1948.
53 *a huge $800 million issue*: Ibid.
53 *the amount of gold*: *Federal Reserve Bulletin*, April 1933, p. 213.
53 *"no other talk"*: Farley, *Behind the Ballots*, p. 210.
53 *"There are good crises"*: Lippmann, *Interpretations: 1933–1935*, p. 18.
54 *The great achievement*: Ibid., p. 35.
55 *"fully aware of the bank situation"*: See Myers and Newton, *The Hoover Administration*, p. 356.
55 *"he either did not realize"*: Hoover, *Memoirs*, vol. 3, p. 215.
57 *He was friendly*: James and James, *Biography of a Bank: The Story of Bank of America*, p. 379. Giannini did not succeed in unseating Calkins, who remained in place until the Federal Reserve system was reorganized in 1935.
57 *"Are you willing"*: Moley, *The First New Deal*, p. 192. Moley and Awalt both dispute the assertion by the Jameses (*Biography of a Bank*, p. 373) that William Randolph Hearst, a Roosevelt supporter and friend of Giannini's, interceded with the White House to open the bank. They say Hearst representatives were not involved, and that Roosevelt had specifically refused to get personally involved in the discussion when his counsel was sought by Woodin. (See Awalt, "Recollections of the Baking Crisis in 1933," *Business History Review*, Autumn 1969.)

3: A RIVER OUT OF EDEN

58 *"a Democrat of the old school"*: Moley, *The First New Deal*, p. 353.
58 *"wondered at in a congressman"*: Tugwell Diary, Dec. 23, 1932, *FDRL*.
58 *"I was struck"*: Tugwell, *In Search of Roosevelt*, p. 216.
59 *"the credit of the United States"*: Douglas to Moley, May 4, 1964, cited in Moley, *The First New Deal*, p. 201.
59 *"It is conceivable"*: Browder and Smith, *Independent: A Biography of Lewis W. Douglas*, p. 80.
59 *"Dutch thrift"*: Moley, *The First New Deal*, p. 201.
59 *"We will spend and spend"*: The full quotation is "We will spend and spend, and tax and tax, and elect and elect": See *NYT*, Nov. 9, 1938. In a letter to the newspaper two weeks later, Hopkins denied having uttered the phrase, but was rebutted by its Washington bureau chief, Arthur Krock. (*NYT*, Nov. 28, 1938.)
60 *Moley labored all day*: Moley, *The First New Deal*, pp. 202–3.
60 *With the utmost seriousness*: "A request to the Congress for authority to effect drastic economies in government," Mar. 10, 1933, *PPA*, vol. 2, pp. 49–50.
61 *"It entirely changed"*: Byrnes, *All in One Lifetime*, cited in Moley, *The First New Deal*, p. 207.
61 *"If unemployment was created"*: Tugwell Diary (undated), FDRL.
61 *"the greatest 'find' of the administration"*: FDR to Col. Edward M. House, Apr. 5, 1933, FDRL.
61 *"heart of stone"*: Freidel, *Franklin D. Roosevelt*, p. 453.
62 *"He represented discredited"*: Tugwell Diary (undated), FDRL.
63 *"cigar in the corner of the mouth"*: Perkins, *CUOHROC*, Part IV, p. 97.
63 *As her first step*: Russell Lord, "Madame Secretary-II," *The New Yorker*, Sept. 9, 1933.
64 *The night after she disbanded*: The following details are based on Perkins, *CUOHROC*, Part IV, pp. 229–33.
64 *"Her middle-class mind"*: Paul W. Ward, "Please Excuse Miss Perkins," *The Nation*, Mar. 27, 1935.
65 *"I was brought up in the tradition"*: Perkins, *CUOHROC*, Part IV, p. 185.
65 *"I just felt a little embarrassed"*: Ibid., p. 190.
65 *"I think now would be a good time"*: Davis, *FDR*, p. 63.
66 *"Look here!"*: Moley, *After Seven Years*, p. 174.
66 *"His enthusiasm for this project"*: Perkins, *The Roosevelt I Knew*, p. 177.
67 *"of fascism, of Hitlerism"*: Schlesinger, *The Coming of the New Deal*, p. 337.
67 *The first registrant*: *Time*, Apr. 17, 1933.
68 *To the end of their lives*: Donald Dale Jackson, "They Were Poor, Hungry, and They Built to Last," *Smithsonian*, September 1994.
68 *125,000 miles of road*: Ibid.
69 *"to govern men"*: Perkins, *The Roosevelt I Knew*, p. 180.
69 *"There won't be none"*: Ibid., p. 80.
69 *"There was pride"*: Jackson, "They Were Poor, Hungry, and They Built to Last."
69 *Some 250,000 American families*: Schlesinger, *The Coming of the New Deal*, p. 297.
69 *"no one who could raise a cent"*: Hickok to Hopkins, Aug. 6, 1933, in *One Third of a Nation*, p. 3.
70 *Lenders and borrowers assumed*: See Harriss, *History and Policies of the Home Owners' Loan Corporation*, p. 7.
70 *The typical home*: Jackson, *Crabgrass Frontier*, p. 193.
70 *Three were approved*: Jackson, *Crabgrass Frontier*, p. 194.
70 *"a declaration of national policy"*: *NYT*, Apr. 14, 1933.
71 *the agency refinanced more than one million*: Harriss, *History and Policies of the HOLC*, p. 29.

71 *Despite Congress's expression*: *Time*, Apr. 22, 1946.
72 *As New York governor*: McCraw, *TVA and the Power Fight*, p. 27.
72 *"Is he really with you?"*: *TNR*, Feb. 15, 1933.
72 *"probably the widest experiment"*: *NYT*, Feb. 3, 1933.
73 *"the continued idleness"*: *PPA*, vol. 2, pp. 122–123.
73 *"one of the soviet"*: Leuchtenburg, *Franklin D. Roosevelt and the New Deal*, p. 55.
73 *"snuffed out a growing"*: See Shlaes, *The Forgotten Man*, p. 8.
73 *Of the region's nearly three million*: Callahan, *TVA and the Power Fight*, p. 27.
74 *"Widow-and-orphan"*: *TNR*, Sept. 2, 1940.
75 *"singular charm"*: Moley, *27 Masters of Politics*, p. 46.
75 *"spite lines"*: *TNR*, Sept. 2, 1940.
76 *"We were two exceedingly"*: Lilienthal, *Journals*, vol. 1, p. 711.
76 *"This was so crude"*: Ibid., p. 712.
76 *Before the end of the year*: *TNR*, Dec. 27, 1933.
77 *"The old fear"*: Nichols, William I., "Teaching Grandmother How to Spin," *Harper's*, July 1936.
77 *"an outstanding success"*: Maury Maverick, "T.V.A. Faces the Future," *TNR*, Nov. 18, 1936.

4: WALL STREET IN THE DOCK

79 *"Gangway!"*: *Time*, Jun. 12, 1933.
79 *"I have a grandson"*: *NYT*, May 26, 1963.
80 *The Nazis arrested her*. Ibid.
80 *"the manner and the manners"*: Leuchtenburg, *Franklin D. Roosevelt and the New Deal*, p. 59.
80 *"kinky-haired, olive-skinned"*: *Time*, June 12, 1933.
80 *"a gigantic monument"*: Pecora, *Wall Street Under Oath*, p. 82.
81 *"prudent and careful administration"*: Hearings, "Stock Exchange Practices," Senate Committee on Banking and Currency, pp. 2155–56 (Feb. 28, 1933). Henceforth "SEP."
81 *contriving a $2,800,000 loss*: Ibid., p. 1812 (Feb. 21, 1933).
81 *"Until last Tuesday"*: *NYT*, May 28, 1933.
81 *"courteous to a degree"*: Pecora, *Wall Street Under Oath*, p. 5.
81 *"a national asset"*: SEP, p. 6 (May 23, 1933).
82 *"But you are serving"*: Ibid., pp. 105–6.
82 *167 directorships*: Ibid., pp. 51–52.
82 *"incomparably the greatest reach"*: Pecora, *Wall Street Under Oath*, p. 36.
82 *McAdoo hastily explained*: SEP, p. 154 (May 25, 1933).
82 *"You did not give them"*: Ibid., p. 172 (May 25, 1933).
83 *"There are no strings"*: Ibid., p. 143 (May 24, 1933).
83 *"the members of the family"*: Ickes, *The Secret Diary*, vol. 1, p. 45 (May 26, 1933).
83 *"distinct liability"*: Ibid., p. 46.
83 *"The pity of it"*: Johnson to Hiram Johnson, Jr., and Archibald Johnson, May 26, 1933, Johnson, *Diary Letters, vol. 5*.
84 *the bureau spent one single day*: SEP, p. 48 (May 23, 1933).
84 *"It has been our experience"*: Ibid.
84 *"in enacting legislation"*: SEP, p. 15 (May 23, 1933).
84 *"I do not intend"*: SEP, p. 344 (May 26, 1933).
85 *"This proposal adds"*: "Recommendation for Federal Supervision of Investment Securities," Mar. 29, 1933, *PP–II*, Vol. 2, p. 93.
86 *"highly commendable"*: *NYT*, April 9, 1933.
86 *"a hopeless and unintelligible confection"*: Moley, *The First New Deal*, p. 312.

86   *"operated only to lock"*: James M. Landis, "The Legislative History of the Securities Act of 1933," *George Washington Law Review*, 1959–1960.

86   *After a week of hearings*: Parrish, *Securities Regulation and the New Deal*, p. 57.

86   *The very next day*: Landis, "The Legislative History of the Securities Act of 1933."

86   *Frankfurter's goal*: Fred Rodell, "Felix Frankfurter, Conservative," *Harper's*, October 1941.

87   *"the District Attorney invoked"*: Felix Frankfurter, "The Case of Sacco and Vanzetti," *The Atlantic*, March 1927.

87   *"an Influence"*: Matthew Josephson, "Jurist-I," *The New Yorker*, Nov. 30, 1940.

87   *"[t]ypically, F. F. comes in"*: Berle to Roosevelt, Jan. 11, 1933, in Berle, *Navigating the Rapids*, p. 83.

88   *Frankfurter arrived in Washington*: See Frankfurter, Diary, May 8, 1933, at http:// www.sechistorical.org/collection/papers/1930 (accessed Mar. 7, 2010).

88   *the thirty-nine-year-old Cohen*: For background on Cohen, see Lasser, *Benjamin V. Cohen*, pp. 25–65.

89   *"I was told"*: Landis, "The Legislative History of the Securities Act of 1933."

89   *"write a good bill"*: Corcoran, "Rendezvous with Democracy," unpublished MS, LOC.

89   *"I memorized the designs"*: Louchheim, Katie, "The Little Red House," *Virginia Quarterly Review*, Winter 1980.

89   *The new draft*: This digest of the draft's provisions is based on Landis, "The Legislative History."

90   *"ethical and professional standards"*: Ibid.

90   *"brilliant performance"*: Ibid.

90   *This session took place*: Landis, "The Legislative History." Curiously, Landis credits Moley with having insisted on the meeting, while Moley (*The First New Deal*, p. 313) states that it was Rayburn who "insisted."

91   *"utterly destroy the securities business"*: Corcoran, "Rendezvous with Democracy."

91   *"virtually no dissent"*: Cohen to Landis, May 5, 1933, SEC historical archives.

91   *"The brain trust crowd"*: Parrish, *Securities Regulation and the New Deal*, p. 65.

91   *"jerry-built"*: The term is Parrish's, ibid., at p. 47.

91   *"horrible examples of the last decade"*: William O. Douglas, "Protecting the Investor," *Yale Review*, March 1934.

92   *"It is conservative"*: Berle, "New Protection for Buyers of Securities," *NYT*, June 4, 1933.

93   *"It won't work, Jack"*: Timmons, *Jesse H. Jones*, p. 184.

93   *"an America without small banks"*: *Congressional Record*, May 27, 1933, p. 4429.

93   *"Where's that deposit-insurance amendment"*: Timmons, *Jesse H. Jones*, pp. 193–95.

94   *"succeeded in achieving"*: Friedman and Schwartz, *A Monetary History of the United States*, p. 440.

5: AGONY ON THE LAND

95   *"On the 22nd day of this month"*: John L. Shover, "Depression Letters from American Farmers," *Agricultural History*, July 1962.

96   *"In Europe seventy million"*: Lord, *The Wallaces of Iowa*, pp. 195–96.

96   *"will ruin thousands"*: Ibid., p. 207.

96   *Total farm income*: Ibid., p. 219.

97   *In Mrs. Gadbois's home state*: Clifton Hicks, "Upheaval in the Corn Belt," *Harper's*, October 1934.

97   *"the dominant factor"*: Speech, "A Restored and Rehabilitated Agriculture," at Topeka, Kansas, Sept. 14, 1932, *PP–I*, p. 693.

97   *"forgotten man" speech*: See ibid., p. 624.

97 *"the things that our farmers buy"*: Ibid.

98 *"government price fixing"*: Calvin Coolidge, veto message, Feb. 25, 1927.

98 *on each fifteen- or twenty-acre patch*: Powell, Webster, and Cutler, "Tightening the Cotton Belt," *Harper's*, Feb. 1934.

99 *"the arch-enemy"*: Peek quoted in *Time*, Nov. 6, 1933.

99 *"For Peek the world"*: Grosvenor B. Clarkson, in *Time*, Nov. 6, 1933.

99 *His intellectual mentor*: Blum, *Roosevelt and Morgenthau*, p. 39.

100 *"cultivated Franklin [Roosevelt] assiduously"*: Tugwell, *The Democratic Roosevelt*, p. 174.

100 *"was not an original thinker"*: Ibid., p. 161.

100 *"He carried pictures"*: Tugwell, *Roosevelt's Revolution*, p. 54.

100 *"Wallace did not yet feel"*: Ibid., p. 53.

100 *"It so happens"*: Wallace, "The Farm Situation," delivered Nov. 20, 1934, *Vital Speeches of the Day*, Dec. 3, 1934.

102 *"I favor a definite policy"*: "A Restored and Rehabilitated Agriculture."

103 *"each leader felt compelled"*: Tugwell, *Roosevelt's Revolution*, pp. 73–74.

103 *"fantastically elastic"*: Lord, *The Wallaces of Iowa*, p. 330.

103 *"We will get"*: Ohl, *Hugh S. Johnson and the New Deal*, p. 93.

103 *"The farm bill breaks my heart"*: Moley, *The First New Deal*, p. 254.

103 *"packers, millers, shippers"*: Tugwell, *Roosevelt's Revolution*, p. 83.

103 *The most spectacular*: NYT, Apr. 28, 1933.

104 *"That's not his courtroom"*: Karl Pretshold, "Do Farmers 'Revolt'?" *North American Review*, July 1933.

104 *"For real radicals"*: Leuchtenburg, *Franklin D. Roosevelt and the New Deal*, pp. 49–50.

105 *Morgenthau proved an able*: Blum, *From the Morgenthau Diaries: Years of Crisis: 1928–1938*, pp. 42–47.

106 *"I did not have the slightest"*: George N. Peek, "In and Out," *Saturday Evening Post*, May 16, 1936.

106 *"A plague of young lawyers"*: Ibid.

106 *"a house divided"*: Lord, *The Wallaces of Iowa*, p. 343.

107 *"plutocrats masquerading"*: Ibid., p. 359.

107 *"They, fanaticlike, believed"*: Peek, "In and Out," *Saturday Evening Post*, May 16, 1936.

107 *The desperation in the cotton lands*: For price and production statistics see Richards, *Cotton and the AAA*, pp. 10–17.

108 *"Cursed by a beneficent"*: NYT, Aug. 27, 1933.

108 *"the greatest achievement"*: NYT, July 15, 1933.

108 *Pole Mason of Hemphill*: *Chicago Tribune*, Aug. 28, 1933.

108 *Watching "five tractors drag"*: Cited in *Chicago Tribune*, Aug. 17, 1933.

109 *"There are those"*: Lord, *The Wallaces of Iowa*, p. 362.

109 *"No, we must clear the wreckage"*: Ibid.

109 *"achieve more notoriety"*: Peek, "In and Out," *Saturday Evening Post*, May 30, 1933.

109 *"The real solution"*: Ibid.

109 *"I suppose it is a marvelous tribute"*: Wallace, *Democracy Reborn*, p. 104, cited in Leuchtenburg, *Franklin D. Roosevelt and the New Deal*, p. 73.

110 *"To the conservative farmer"*: Hicks, "Upheaval in the Corn Belt."

110 *"were not acts of idealism"*: Lord, *The Wallaces of Iowa*, p. 366.

110 *grease and fertilizer*: Peek, "In and Out," *Saturday Evening Post*, May 30, 1933.

110 *From July through September*: See Perkins, "The AAA and the Politics of Agriculture," *Agricultural History*, October 1965.

111 *"I looked up packing house quotations"*: George J. Fox to Reno, Dec. 23, 1933, and

Reno reply, Dec. 30, 1933, in Shover, "Depression Letters from American Farmers," *Agricultural History*, July 1962.

111 *"that sovereign remedy"*: Perkins, "The AAA and the Politics of Agriculture."

6: THE GENERAL

115 *"Everybody in the world's"*: Johnson, *The Blue Eagle from Egg to Earth*, p. 8.

115 *"It will be red fire"*: Johnson, *The Blue Eagle*, p. 208.

115 *"prophets of disaster"*: *NYT*, Sept. 13, 1933.

116 *"a sock"*: "The General-I," *The New Yorker*, Aug. 18, 1934.

116 *he unveiled his publicity masterstroke*: Johnson, pp. 250ff.; *NYT*, July 18, 1933.

116 *"that blue hawk"*: *NYT*, July 22, 1933.

116 *"burst like a flaming"*: *Time*, Jan. 1, 1934.

116 *Hugh Johnson was born*: These details of Johnson's early life are based on Ohl, *Hugh S. Johnson and the New Deal*, pp. 3–17, and Johnson, *The Blue Eagle*, pp. 1–29.

117 *"practical economist"*: Schwarz, *The Speculator*, p. 255.

117 *Yet the truth*: See Grant, *Bernard M. Baruch*, pp. 232–33.

118 *"the drop in my securities"*: Baruch to Robinson, Nov. 10, 1930, quoted in ibid., p. 243.

118 *he could bring the Democratic*: Schwarz, *The Speculator*, p. 257.

118 *"So much Baruch money"*: Tugwell Diary, Feb. 26, 1933.

118 *B. M. B. [Baruch] wants to permit*: Berle to Roosevelt, July 20, 1932, in Berle, *Navigating the Rapids*, p. 51.

118 *Fretting that one such award*: Ibid., p. 74.

119 *"It's great stuff"*: Moley, *27 Masters of Politics*, p. 168.

119 *"reckless and extravagant"*: *PPA*, vol. 1, p. 807.

119 *"It is not easy"*: Moley, *The First New Deal*, p. 387.

120 *Frankfurter and Supreme Court Justice Louis D. Brandeis*: See Bellush, *The Failure of the NRA*, p. 3.

120 *"a completely wooden"*: Perkins, *CUOHROC*, Part IV, p. 441.

120 *"It's as easy"*: Ibid., p. 444.

121 *Privately contemptuous*: Ibid., p. 196.

121 *Appearing at her first*: *NYT*, April 26, 1933.

121 *Within a few days*: Johnson, *The Blue Eagle*, p. 196.

121 *"an extraordinarily short"*: Ibid., p. 197.

122 *"Frances Perkins is the best man"*: Perkins, *The Roosevelt I Knew*, p. 204.

122 *"Public works is all right"*: Perkins, *CUOHROC*, Part V, p. 32.

123 *"Alas for the page-and-a-half"*: Johnson, *The Blue Eagle*, p. 204.

123 *"balance of supply to demand"*: Ibid., p. 169.

124 *"no one has been able"*: Ickes, *The Secret Diary*, p. 438 (Sept. 13, 1935).

124 *The $3.3 billion appropriation*: Moley, *After Seven Years*, p. 173, n8.

124 *"he proceeded to rip"*: Ickes, *The Secret Diary*, p. 28 (Apr. 29, 1933).

125 *"enlightened business leadership"*: Bellush, *The Failure of the NRA*, p. 4.

125 *American Construction Council*: Ibid.

125 *"Every fault of socialism"*: *Congressional Record*, June 7, 1933, p. 5178.

126 *Bernard Baruch showed up*: Perkins, *CUOHROC*, Part V, p. 95.

126 *"That's astonishing"*: Ibid., p. 98.

127 *"If he can't work under one"*: Ickes, *The Secret Diary*, p. 48.

127 *"a pleasant little speech"*: Perkins, *The Roosevelt I Knew*, p. 202.

128 *"Visitors waiting for interviews"*: Johnson, *The Blue Eagle*, p. 368.

128 *He crossed the country*: For an examination of the code-making process in the first months of the NRA, see Bellush, *The Failure of the NRA*, pp. 36ff.

129 *Earnings of five and six dollars a week*: Bernstein, *Turbulent Years*, p. 298.

129 *"The young girls"*: Gellhorn, *The View from the Ground*, pp. 13–17.
129 *"There was a moment's silence"*: Johnson, *The Blue Eagle*, p. 233.
130 *"There is, in fact, practically no child labor"*: Ibid., p. 232.
130 *The new minimum wage*: Bellush, *The Failure of the NRA*, p. 127.
131 *"The insignia of government approval"*: Johnson, *The Blue Eagle*, p. 251.
131 *"It is an inspiring thing"*: *NYT*, July 22, 1933.
131 *"prong pennies in violation"*: Johnson, *The Blue Eagle*, p. 265.
131 *"ran through official life"*: Ickes, "My Twelve Years with F. D. R.," Part 2, *Saturday Evening Post*, June 12, 1948.
131 *"a most disgusting exhibition"*: Ickes, *The Secret Diary*, vol. 1, p. 93 (Sept. 16, 1933).
132 *"the greatest march"*: *NYT*, Sept. 14, 1933.
132 *roughly seven hundred strikes*: Bellush, *The Failure of the NRA*, p. 56.
132 *"undesirable Reds"*: For the encounter at Homestead, Perkins, *The Roosevelt I Knew*, pp. 218–19.
133 *"Hell, that Roosevelt buzzard"*: Sidney Fine, "The Ford Motor Company and the N.R.A.," *Business History Review*, Winter 1958.
133 *"only in the worst sweated industries"*: *TNR*, Aug. 23, 1933.
133 *Actual per capita earnings*: See Bellush, *The Failure of the NRA*, p. 56.

7: THE GOLD STANDARD ON THE BOOZE

135 *"begun to haul in the anchor"*: Jones, *Fifty Billion Dollars*, p. 249.
135 *The first member*: Blum, *From the Morgenthau Diaries, Years of Crisis 1928–1938*, p. 20.
136 *"Not in!"*: John Brooks, "Annals of Finance: Gold Standard on the Booze," *The New Yorker*, Sept. 13, 1969.
136 *"Cornell's currency magician"*: Moley, *The First New Deal*, p. 228
136 *"gravely marred his image"*: Ibid., p. 304.
137 *"massive shoulders"*: Warburg, *The Long Road Home*, p. 107.
137 *"Ray Moley tells me"*: Ibid.
137 *"very depressed"*: Warburg diary, Mar. 23, 1933, *FDRL*, cited in Browder and Smith, *Independent*, p. 90.
138 *"Lew seems to be trying"*: Moley, *27 Masters of Politics*, p. 353.
138 *But the commitment*: For a comprehensive discussion of the rise and fall of the gold standard, see Eichengreen, *Golden Fetters: The Gold Standard and the Great Depression, 1919–1939*.
140 *"Europeans knew that we could not maintain"*: Morgenthau, May 13, 1935; see text in *NYT*, May 14, 1935.
140 *"it was not the maintenance of the gold standard"*: *NYT*, May 15, 1935.
140 *"Gold merely cannot be"*: Eichengreen, *Golden Fetters*, p. 329.
141 *"In vain I argued"*: Warburg, *The Long Road Home*, p. 118.
141 *"Lullaby in Silver"*: Moley, *After Seven Years*, p. 157.
142 *"At the present prices"*: See Feis, *1933: Characters in Crisis*, p. 127.
142 *"Congratulate me"*: See Moley, *After Seven Years*, p. 159. Many of the participants left their own recollections of this seminal meeting; while all differ in certain details, Roosevelt's words, "Congratulate me," are common to almost all of them.
143 *"Moley was . . . delighted"*: Warburg, *CUOHROC*, cited in Feis, *1933: Characters in Crisis*, p. 129.
143 *"a thoroughly vicious bill"*: Douglas to J. S. Douglas (father), April 23, 1933, cited in Freidel, *Franklin D. Roosevelt*, p. 334.
143 *"as though he were a perverse"*: Moley, *After Seven Years*, p. 159.
143 *"Well, this is the end"*: Ibid., p. 160.
143 *he burst out laughing*: Ickes, *The Secret Diary, Vol. 1*, p. 659.

143   *"bringing an insane proposal back"*: Warburg Diary, April 19, 1933, cited in Browder and Smith, *Independent*, p. 93.

144   *"I am sure that I must stay on"*: Ibid.

144   *"veered and waffled"*: Feis, *1933: Characters in Crisis*, p. 144.

145   *"desultory discussion"*: Moley, *After Seven Years*, pp. 218–19.

145   *"The most fanatical inflationist"*: Ibid., p. 247.

147   *"Hello there"*: Ibid., p. 270.

147   *"He takes the whole currency question"*: Warburg, *The Long Road Home*, p. 142.

147   *"these two newest prophets"*: Warburg, *The Money Muddle*, p. 134.

148   *"it appears that there really is"*: Ibid., p. 136.

148   *"alluringly simple idea"*: Ibid., p. 137.

149   *"Well, I guess you ruined"*: Ibid., p. 144.

149   *"If we don't keep"*: Ibid., p. 147.

150   *"fluttered over the creation"*: Moley, *After Seven Years*, p. 282.

151   *"pure conjecture"*: *NYT*, Oct. 29, 1933.

151   *"the inflationists roared"*: Warburg, *The Money Muddle*, p. 149.

151   *"I have had the shackles"*: Blum, *From the Morgenthau Diaries: Years of Crisis: 1928–1938*, p. 68.

151   *a price of $36*: See *NYT*, Oct. 26, 1933.

151   *"sufficiently erratic"*: Blum, *From the Morgenthau Diaries*, p. 69.

151   *"It's a lucky number"*: Ibid., p. 70.

152   *"Administration advisers"*: *NYT*, Oct. 27, 1933.

152   *"There were now two dollars"*: Warburg, *The Long Road Home*, p. 149.

152   *"the buying of gold"*: Blum, *From the Morgenthau Diaries*, p. 72.

153   *"Those who knew Morgenthau well"*: Warburg, *The Long Road Home*, p. 150.

153   *"I am for gold dollars"*: See *NYT*, Nov. 25, 1933.

153   *"It's funny how sometimes"*: Brooks, "Annals of Finance," *The New Yorker*, Sept. 13, 1969.

153   *"a gold standard on the booze"*: J. Maynard Keynes, "An Open Letter to President Roosevelt," *NYT*, Dec. 31, 1933.

154   *"the gold standard went off the booze"*: Brooks, "Annals of Finance."

8: HARRY AND HAROLD

155   YOU HAVE THE ENTIRE COUNTRY: Schlesinger, *The Coming of the New Deal*, p. 265.

155   *"didn't know the sheep from the goats"*: Perkins, *CUOHROC*, Part IV, p. 478.

156   *In Pennsylvania*: Hopkins, *Spending to Save*, p. 91.

156   *"1,500 families are without"*: Ibid., p. 93.

156   *"There were on my desk"*: Perkins, *The Roosevelt I Knew*, p. 184.

157   *"an animated piece of Shredded Wheat"*: *The New Yorker*, Aug. 7, 1943; see also *TNR*, Feb. 13, 1935.

157   *"You, Mr. Hopkins"*: Quoted in Sherwood, *Roosevelt and Hopkins*, p. 61.

157   *"Can't you ever stop"*: Sherwood, *Roosevelt and Hopkins*, p. 14.

158   *"the applicant was in some way"*: Ibid., p. 100.

159   *"These people aren't children"*: Hickok to Hopkins, Aug. 6, 1933, Lowitt and Beasley, eds., *One Third of a Nation* (henceforth *OTN*), p. 4.

159   *"From the township to Harrisburg"*: Hickok to Hopkins, Aug. 7–12, 1933, *OTN*, pp. 8–9.

160   *"thousands of inconsequential"*: Ickes, *The Secret Diary*, vol. 1, p. 378 (June 18, 1935).

160   *"When this thing is all over"*: Sherwood, *Roosevelt and Hopkins*, p. 85.

161   *"addicted to the naked insult"*: Ibid., p. 80.

161   *"I have a real quarrel"*: *The New Yorker*, Aug. 14, 1943.

161 *"While in a contest"*: Ickes, "My Twelve Years with F. D. R.," Part Three, *Saturday Evening Post*, June 19, 1948.

161 *"Cultivate the President's family"*: Ibid.

162 *"feels himself to be something of a public ward"*: Hopkins, *Spending to Save*, p. 114.

162 *"We aren't on relief"*: Ibid.

162 *"who proceeded to bedevil me"*: Ickes, *The Secret Diary*, vol. 1, p. 114 (Oct. 28, 1933).

163 *"projects of a minor character"*: Ibid., p. 119 (Nov. 11, 1933).

163 *"Harry Hopkins could always get money"*: Ickes, "My Twelve Years with F. D. R.," Part Three, *Saturday Evening Post*, June 19, 1948.

163 *Hopkins disbursed*: Sherwood, *Roosevelt and Hopkins*, p. 45.

163 *"4,464 Indians to repair"*: *Time*, Feb. 19, 1934.

164 *"walls blackened with dirt"*: Hopkins, *Spending to Save*, p. 121. The accompanying statistics all come from this work.

164 *They are damn good projects*: Press conference April 4, 1935, in Sherwood, *Roosevelt and Hopkins*, pp. 59–60.

165 *"Today was the first CWA pay day"*: Hickok to Hopkins, Nov. 25, 1933, *OTN*, p. 112.

165 *"Nobody is going to starve"*: Leuchtenburg, *Franklin D. Roosevelt and the New Deal*, p. 122.

165 *"It started quickly"*: Lippmann, *Interpretations*, pp. 230–231 (Dec. 11, 1934).

166 *"I want someone else appointed"*: Ickes, *The Secret Diary*, vol. 1, p. 285 (Feb. 2, 1935).

166 ICKES IS SHORN: Ibid., p. 424 (Aug. 27, 1935).

166 *"I never thought I would talk"*: Ibid.

167 *The feud between Hopkins and Ickes*: Sherwood, *Roosevelt and Hopkins*, pp. 78–79.

168 *"If Congress passes this bill"*: Ibid., p. 81.

168 *"go down the Hopkins rat hole"*: Ickes, *The Secret Diary*, vol. 1, p. 487 (Dec. 16, 1935).

168 *"If you take any"*: *Complete Presidential Press Conferences*, vol. 7, p. 238 (May 5, 1936).

168 *"made it perfectly clear"*: Ickes, *The Secret Diary*, vol. 1, p. 575 (May 9, 1936).

169 *"It was as clear as day"*: Ickes, *The Secret Diary*, vol. 1, p. 589 (May 16, 1936).

169 *"the President looked at me"*: Ickes, *The Secret Diary*, vol. 1, p. 593 (May 16, 1936).

170 *"There were men"*: Roosevelt, *This I Remember*, p. 126.

170 *"This is the only phase"*: Ickes, *The Secret Diary*, vol. 1, p. 219.

171 *"one of the most embarrassing"*: Ibid., p. 255.

172 *"men who had never seen for themselves"*: Roosevelt, *This I Remember*, p. 131.

9: SO MANY SINNERS

173 *"There is much noble thinking"*: Urofsky, *Louis D. Brandeis*, p. 693.

173 *"I have little doubt"*: Chernow, *The House of Morgan*, p. 379.

174 *the advice of Roland Redmond*: Parrish: *Securities Regulation and the New Deal*, pp. 108–9.

175 *"As you and I know"*: FDR to Berle, Aug. 15, 1934, in Berle, *Navigating the Rapids*, pp. 103–4.

175 *"The real hope and purpose"*: Bernard Flexner, "The Fight on the Securities Act," *The Atlantic*, February 1934.

175 *"Anyone in favor of reopening"*: Berle to Roper (for transmission to FDR), Jan. 27, 1934, Berle Papers, *FDRL*.

175 *"primarily a gambling institution"*: Berle, "Memorandum to the Committee on Stock Exchange Regulation," Oct. 24, 1933, Berle Papers, *FDRL*.

176 *Richardson . . . envisioned*: Parrish, *Securities Regulation and the New Deal*, p. 114.

177 *"You gentlemen are making"*: Joseph Alsop, and Robert Kintner, "The Battle of the Market Place," *Saturday Evening Post*, June 11, 1938.

177 *"We thought we would get"*: "Stock Exchange Practices," Hearings, Senate Committee on Banking and Currency, p. 2509 (Oct. 20, 1933).

177 *"a touch of magic"*: Matthew Josephson, "Groton, Harvard, Wall Street," *New Yorker*, April 2, 1932.

177 *"a little distress selling"*: Brooks, *Once in Golconda*, p. 124.

178 *"A knightly gentleman"*: Josephson, "Groton, Harvard, Wall Street."

178 *Richard Whitney halts stock panic*: Ibid.

178 *"sauntered nonchalantly"*: Ibid.

179 *"The bankers try"*: Lasser, *Benjamin V. Cohen*, p. 87.

179 *In December they got*: Parrish, *Securities Regulation*, p. 115.

179 *"unnecessary, unwise, and destructive speculation"*: Message of the President, Feb. 9, 1934.

180 *"Their game, plainly enough"*: Frankfurter to FDR, Feb. 22, 1934, cited in Parrish, *Securities Regulation*, p. 121.

180 *"very large powers"*: "Stock Exchange Practices," Hearings, Senate Committee on Banking and Currency, p. 6467 (Feb. 26, 1934).

180 *"This bill really carries out"*: Ibid., p. 6499 (Feb. 26, 1934).

180 *"There is no social philosophy"*: Ibid., p. 6552 (Feb. 27, 1934).

181 *"there were no material deliberate improprieties"*: Whitney to Committee on Business Conduct, NYSE, Oct. 1, 1933, in Senate, "Stock Exchange Practices," p. 6613 (Feb. 28, 1934).

181 *"was not an unfair influencing"*: Ibid., p. 6617. See also De Bedts, *The New Deal's SEC*, pp. 63–64.

181 *"I do feel"*: "Stock Exchange Practices," Hearings, Senate Committee on Banking and Currency, p. 6734 (Mar. 1, 1934).

182 *"I am afraid"*: Ibid., p. 6736.

182 *"unlimited character"*: Whitney to "the Presidents of All Listed Corporations," Feb. 14, 1934, Berle Papers, FDRL.

183 CONVINCED FEATURES OF STOCK EXCHANGE BILL: Letter, Dammann to Rayburn, April 24, 1934, Library of Congress. Used by permission of Securities and Exchange Commission Historical Society's virtual museum and archive at www.sechistorical .org.

183 *"Those old Wall Street boys"*: *Will Rogers' Daily Telegrams*, Mar. 23, 1934.

183 *"the chief fruit of these labors"*: John T. Flynn, "The Marines Land in Wall Street," *Harper's*, July 1934.

184 *"would be a disaster"*: Letter, Whitney to FDR, April 12, 1934, collection of FDRL.

184 *"Tell him I should like"*: Note, FDR to McIntyre, April 13, 1934, collection of FDRL.

184 *"by a bunch of Jews"*: See Parrish, *Securities Regulation*, p. 130.

184 *"a group of radical lawyers"*: *NYT*, Mar. 24, 1934.

184 *a veiled reference*: See Tugwell diary, April 11, 1934, *FDRL*.

185 *"radicals or socialists"*: *LAT*, Mar. 31, 1934. See also Tugwell diary, April 11, 1934, FDRL.

186 *"That first bill"*: Flynn, "The Marines Land on Wall Street."

187 *"The best bet for Chairman"*: Ibid., p. 518.

187 *"a ruddy-faced, vigorous"*: Moley, *The First New Deal*, p. 379.

187 *"I have no political ambitions"*: Kennedy, *I'm for Roosevelt*, p. 3.

188 *"looked at me as if he were looking at the devil"*: Joseph P. Kennedy, "Memorandum," c. April 1934, in Smith, *Hostage to Fortune: The Letters of Joseph P. Kennedy*, p. 128.

188 *"There I heard plenty"*: Moley, *The First New Deal*, p. 381.

188 *Kennedy lashed out*: Beschloss, *Kennedy and Roosevelt*, p. 79.

189 *"keenly disappointed"*: Kennedy, *Times to Remember*, p. 197.

189 *"a slap in the face"*: Moley, *The First New Deal*, p. 519. See also Beschloss, *Kennedy and Roosevelt*, p. 86.

189 *"I told him that I had been involved"*: Kennedy, "Memorandum," Smith, *Hostage to Fortune*, p. 138.

189 *Kennedy's "amazing success"*: NYT, July 4, 1934.

190 *"The Jackals of Finance"*: TNR, July 18, 1934.

190 *"I lost eight pounds"*: Kennedy to Lucius Pond Ordway, July 26, 1934, in Smith, *Hostage to Fortune*, p. 141.

190 *"it was facetiously suggested"*: NYT, July 25, 1934.

190 *"There is no belief"*: Address of Joseph P. Kennedy, National Press Club, July 25, 1934.

191 *"It is but fair to him"*: TNR, Oct. 9, 1935.

191 *"Tommy Corcoran and Ben Cohen"*: Lasser, *Benjamin V. Cohen*, p. 86.

10: THE LITTLE RED HOUSE

192 *What enthralled Corcoran*: Katie Louchheim, "The Little Red House," *Virginia Quarterly Review Online*, Winter 1980, at www.vqronline.org (accessed May 1, 2010).

192 *he and Cohen eventually had to take*: McKean, *Tommy the Cork*, p. 45.

193 *"an oratorical field day"*: NYT, April 21, 1934.

193 *"We live there"*: *Washington Post*, April 21, 1934.

193 *"Come in but park your bomb"*: Louchheim, "The Little Red House."

193 *The products included*: Ibid.

194 *"When Roosevelt came to Washington"*: Arthur M. Schlesinger, Jr., who received Keyserling's critique in 1958, graciously excerpted it at length in the notes to *The Politics of Upheaval*, pp. 691–3.

195 *"To look upon these policies"*: Moley, *After Seven Years*, pp. 369–70.

195 *exceeding by January 1934*: Henry F. Pringle, "The President-I," *The New Yorker*, June 16, 1934.

195 *"Dear Frank"*: Ibid.

196 *"He called people easily"*: Jackson, *That Man*, p. 15.

196 *"the one indispensable"*: Rosenman OH, FDRL.

196 *Allotment Advisory Committee*: Ickes, *The Secret Diary*, vol. 1, p. 357 (May 3, 1935).

197 *"I can't imagine"*: Rosenman OH, FDRL.

197 *"Sometimes the President would raise"*: Jackson, *That Man*, p. 28.

198 *"rather more zealous"*: Blum, *From the Morgenthau Diaries, Years of Crisis 1928–1938*, p. 89.

198 *"trying to hold Glavis down"*: Ickes, *The Secret Diary*, vol. 1, p. 270 (Jan. 11, 1935).

198 *"I told the President"*: Ibid., p. 297 (Feb. 17, 1935).

198 *"The trouble with Ickes"*: Blum, *From the Morgenthau Diaries*, p. 91.

198 *personally upbraided by the President*: Rosenman, FDRL. Moley often dismissed Rosenman's version of this episode as an exaggeration.

199 *"Political and economic conditions in 1933"*: See Schlesinger, *The Politics of Upheaval*, p. 692.

200 *"I never broke with Ben Cohen"*: Corcoran, "Rendezvous with Democracy," (unpublished memoir), LOC.

200 *"a kind of worshipfulness"*: Moley, *After Seven Years*, p. 285.

201 *"The men that work for Corcoran"*: Ibid.

202 *"on the shoulders"*: Louchheim, "The Little Red House."

202 *"Tom would see a job"*: Watson in Louchheim, *The Making of the New Deal*, p. 108.

202   *"This is Tom Corcoran"*: Joseph L. Rauh, Jr. in Louchheim, *The Making of the New Deal*, p. 110.

202   *What darling children*: Frankfurter to Corcoran and Cohen, May 15, 1934, Corcoran papers, LOC, cited in Lasser, *Benjamin V. Cohen*, p. 98.

203   *"Much has gone over the dam"*: Corcoran and Cohen to Frankfurter, June 18, 1934, Frankfurter papers, LOC, cited in Lasser, ibid., p. 97.

203   *"As Ben and my reputations"*: Corcoran, "Rendezvous with Democracy."

203   *"The great mistake"*: Alva Johnson, "White House Tommy," *Saturday Evening Post*, July 31, 1937.

204   *"a priestly task"*: Prichard in Louchheim, *The Making of the New Deal*, p. 69.

204   *"I put you on the Court"*: Joseph L. Rauh, Jr., in Louchheim, ibid., p. 65.

204   *"You can do better"*: Corcoran, "Rendezvous with Democracy."

205   *Ben continued to live*: Lasser, *Benjamin V. Cohen*, p. 236.

205   *"both public and private"*: Roosevelt, *PPA*, vol. 3, p. 461.

205   *"bravely but utterly"*: *Time*, Sept. 15, 1941.

205   *"I always had a sneaking"*: Ickes, *The Secret Diary*, vol. 2, p. 425 (July 23, 1938).

206   *"you can't regulate holding companies"*: Lilienthal, *Journals: The TVA Years*, p. 45.

206   *"tired of eighty men"*: Ickes, *The Secret Diary*, vol. 1, pp. 244–45.

206   *The remedy embodied in his draft*: See Lasser, *Benjamin V. Cohen*, p. 116.

207   *widely remarked slip of the tongue*: Lasser, *Benjamin V. Cohen*, p. 109.

207   *"getting hotter and hotter"*: Lilienthal, *Journals: The TVA Years*, pp. 46ff.

208   *"Tom and I will be branded"*: Cohen to Jane Harris, Jan. 12, 1935, cited in Lasser, *Benjamin V. Cohen*, p. 119.

208   *Moley regarded it*: Moley, *After Seven Years*, p. 303.

209   *"The use of words"*: See *NYT*, Jan. 28, 1935.

209   *"paralyze the nation"*: Schlesinger, *The Politics of Upheaval*, p. 310.

210   *"You're putting the President on the spot"*: Ibid., p. 196.

210   *Corcoran's "lobbying proclivities"*: Moley, *After Seven Years*, p. 315.

211   *"Thomas G. Corcoran, Esq."*: *Congressional Record*, 74th Cong., 1st Session, p. 10660 (July 2, 1935).

212   *"help to arouse the country's distrust"*: *NYT*, July 3, 1935.

212   *"drilled his little chicks"*: Johnston, "White House Tommy."

11: PIED PIPERS

213   *Nearly 1,900*: The figures are from Bernstein, *Turbulent Years*, p. 217.

214   *"It is nothing new"*: Howard to Howe, July 3, 1934, *FDRL*, cited in Bernstein, ibid., p. 221.

215   *"hand-to-hand fighting"*: *NYT*, May 24, 1934.

215   *"a test case in the battle"*: *TNR*, June 6, 1934.

216   *"like a bunch of sheep"*: Bernstein, *Turbulent Years*, p. 255.

216   *"an insurrection"*: *LAT*, July 17, 1934.

216   *"We think it's very serious"*: Perkins, *CUOHROC*, Part VI, p. 294.

217   *"anything so affecting"*: *LAT*, July 17, 1934.

217   *"The economic life"*: Johnson, *The Blue Eagle*, p. 322.

218   *"I think that labor is inherently entitled"*: Ibid., p. 323.

218   *"Johnson thought"*: Perkins, *The Roosevelt I Knew*, p. 237.

219   *"a colossal failure"*: See James P. Shenton, "The Coughlin Movement and the New Deal," *Political Science Quarterly*, September 1958.

220   *As late as 1935*: Coughlin (interview), *American Heritage*, October 1972.

220   *"People tire of seeing"*: FDR to Ray Sannard Baker, Mar. 20, 1935, *F.D.R., His Personal Letters*, vol. 1, p. 467.

220   *"Father Coughlin is a going concern"*: *TNR*, May 2, 1934.

220 *Over a nationwide radio*: Williams, *Huey Long*, p. 692.

221 *"If you limited"*: *TNR*, Mar. 20, 1935.

221 *"My enemies believe"*: Williams, *Huey Long*, pp. 695–96.

222 *"Never explain, my boy"*: Stolberg, Benjamin, "Dr. Huey and Mr. Long," *The Nation*, Sept. 25, 1935.

222 *"not a little old sow-belly"*: Glen Jeansonne, "Gerald L. K. Smith: From Wisconsin Roots to National Notoriety," *Wisconsin Magazine of History*, Winter 2002–2003.

222 *Coughlin took up the issue*: Shenton, "The Coughlin Movement and the New Deal."

222 *"We are being rushed"*: Leuchtenburg, *Franklin D. Roosevelt and the New Deal*, p. 216.

222 *"I have been surprised all along"*: Ickes, *The Secret Diary*, vol. 1, p. 284 (Jan. 30, 1935).

223 *"Coughlin is just a political"*: Stolberg, "Dr. Huey and Mr. Long," *The Nation*, Sept. 25, 1935.

223 *"All of these Republican"*: FDR to House, Feb. 16, 1935, *F.D.R.: His Personal Letters*, vol. 1, p. 452.

223 *"I think we are dealing"*: Johnson, "The Pied Pipers," delivered Mar. 4, 1935, *Vital Speeches of the Day*, Mar. 11, 1935.

224 *"is the man who was running"*: *Congressional Record*, vol. 79, pp. 2933–34 (Mar. 5, 1935).

224 *"one of those satellites"*: Long, "Our Blundering Government and Its Spokesman—Hugh Johnson," Mar. 7, 1935, *Vital Speeches of the Day*, Mar. 25, 1935.

224 *"probably transformed Huey Long"*: *NYT*, Mar. 10, 1935.

224 *"The diversion by the trinity"*: FDR to House, Mar. 20, 1935, *F.D.R.: His Personal Letters*, vol. 1, p. 468.

225 *Long staggered a few feet*: This account of the assassination is from Williams, *Huey Long*, pp. 865–76.

225 *"was plowed under like the cotton"*: Coughlin discourse, June 19, 1936.

225 *"You could talk"*: Shenton, "The Coughlin Movement and the New Deal."

226 *He expressed sympathy*: Ibid.; See also *TNR*, Nov. 2, 1938.

226 *"swarms of self-appointed 'saviors'"*: Creel, *Rebel at Large*, p. 280.

227 *"This old gentleman"*: Sinclair, *I, Candidate for Governor*, p. 7.

227 *The Golden State had sent*: For the backdrop to Sinclair's candidacy, see Charles E. Larsen, "The Epic Campaign of 1934," *Pacific Historical Review*, May 1958.

227 *The hated sales tax*: Larsen, ibid.

227 *"No political program"*: Creel, *Rebel at Large*, p. 281.

228 *"continued merrily whetting"*: Carey McWilliams, "Upton Sinclair and His E.P.I.C.," *TNR*, Aug. 22, 1934.

228 *"socially-minded clergymen"*: Ibid.

229 *"I think it's great stuff"*: *NYT*, Aug. 30, 1934.

229 *"I appreciated Roosevelt's position"*: Sinclair, *I, Candidate for Governor*, p. 76.

229 *"a pale and pleasant gentleman"*: Tugwell diary (undated), *FDRL*.

229 *"I found that he had read"*: Ibid., p. 84.

230 *"unsound, unworkable, and un-American"*: Creel, *Rebel at Large*, p. 288.

230 *In editorial cartoons*: Sinclair reproduced all these cartoons and the specious flyer in *I, Candidate for Governor*.

230 *"Having been a Socialist"*: Sinclair, *I, Candidate for Governor*, p. 58.

231 *"haggard, very old women"*: Richard L. Neuberger, and Kelley Loe, "The Old People's Campaign," *Harper's Monthly*, March 1936.

231 *It is estimated*: Townsend, *New Horizons*, p. 138.
232 *"gentle general of a growing army"*: *NYT*, Dec. 29, 1935.
232 *"It was a time"*: Townsend, *New Horizons*, p. 125.
233 *"The easiest tax in the world"*: Ibid., p. 139.
234 *"almost precisely the theory"*: Neuberger and Loe, "The Old People's Campaign." See also Schlesinger, *The Politics of Upheaval*, p. 32.
234 *"His plan has a long"*: "The Midwestern Messiah," *TNR*, May 6, 1936.
235 *"It seemed to me"*: Hearings, Economic Security Act, House Committee on Ways and Means, p. 203 (Jan. 23, 1935).
235 *Walter Lippmann, straining to understand*: Lippmann, "Dr. Townsend's Trillions," *LAT*, Jan. 10, 1935.
235 *"all the old people in California"*: Hearings, Economic Security Act, House Committee on Ways and Means, p. 573 (Jan. 29, 1935).
235 *"clever organizers and skilled promoters"*: Neuberger and Loe, "The Old People's Campaign."
236 *"whatever the exaggerations"*: *TNR*, Dec. 19, 1934.

12: The Cornerstone

237 *"practicability of unemployment"*: Perkins, *The Roosevelt I Knew*, p. 279.
237 *"I continue to be astonished"*: Ickes, *The Secret Diary*, vol. 1, p. 407 (Aug. 3, 1935).
238 *Unemployment had peaked*: Scheiber and Shoven, *The Real Deal: The History and Future of Social Security*, p. 21.
238 *"She is helpless"*: See "Letter to President Roosevelt Regarding Old-Age Pensions" at http://www.ssa.gov/history/lettertoFDR.html (accessed May 25, 2010).
238 *Of the twenty-nine states*: Statistics are from Old Age Security Staff Report to Committee on Economic Security, January 1935.
239 *"security against the hazards and vicissitudes"*: "Message to Congress Reviewing the Broad Objectives and Accomplishments of the Administration," June 8, 1934.
239 *"fell like a bombshell"*: Abraham Epstein, " 'Social Security' Under the New Deal," *The Nation*, Sept. 4, 1935.
240 *"Very delicate balances"*: Tugwell, *The Democratic Roosevelt*, p. 337.
240 *"was the broadly appealing issue"*: Ibid.
240 *"Here was a chance"*: Eliot, "The Legal Background of the Social Security Act," speech delivered at Social Security Administration Headquarters, Feb. 3, 1961, at http://www.socialsecurity.gov/history/eliot2.html (accessed May 25, 2010).
240 *"plenty of statisticians"*: Perkins, "The Roots of Social Security," speech delivered Oct. 23, 1962, at www.socialsecurity.gov/history/perkins5.html (accessed May 27, 2010).
241 *"Witte was just perfect"*: Ibid.
241 *Not all would be pleased*: See Witte, *The Development of the Social Security Act*, pp. 36–37.
241 *Abraham Epstein, who may have been the preeminent American expert*: See Epstein, Pierre, *Abraham Epstein: The Forgotten Father of Social Security*, pp. 148–50.
241 *"Every knowledgeable New Deal lawyer"*: Eliot, *Recollections of the New Deal*, p. 95. (Emphasis in the original.) The justices Eliot referred to were Louis D. Brandeis, Benjamin N. Cardozo, Harlan Fiske Stone, James Clark McReynolds, Pierce Butler, Willis Van Devanter, George Sutherland, Owen J. Roberts, and Charles Evans Hughes.
242 *As the couple explained*: Ibid., p. 75.
242 *Florida v. Mellon*: The decision is 273 U.S. 12 (1927).
242 *"In Washington you don't go"*: Perkins, "The Roots of Social Security," speech

delivered Oct. 23, 1962, at http://www.socialsecurity.gov/history/perkins5.html (accessed May 29, 2010).

243 *"now is the hour"*: *NYT*, Nov. 15, 1934.

244 *"old age is the most certain"*: "Address to the Advisory Council of the Committee on Economic Security," Nov. 14, 1934, *PPA*, vol. 3, pp. 452–54.

244 *"chopped the entire social security program"*: *NYT*, Nov. 15, 1934.

244 *"It's the kiss of death"*: Davis, *FDR*, p. 460; see also Arthur Krock, "In Washington," *NYT*, Nov. 20, 1934.

244 *left it to Perkins*: See *NYT*, Nov. 16, 1934.

244 *"first-class political enigma"*: *NYT*, Nov. 20, 1934.

245 *"easily kill the bill"*: Perkins, *The Roosevelt I Knew*, p. 290.

245 *"a doubtful constitutional point"*: Ibid., p. 291.

246 *"We sat until two in the morning"*: Ibid., p. 292.

246 *there was little consistency*: See Abraham Epstein, "The American State Old Age Pension System in Operation," *Annals of the American Academy of Political and Social Science*, November 1933.

246 *"A contributory system of old age insurance"*: Ibid.

246 *Following their lead*: See Davis, *FDR: The New Deal Years*, p. 453.

247 *"The easiest way"*: Perkins, *The Roosevelt I Knew*, p. 292.

247 *"not count much"*: Hearings, Economic Security Act, House Ways and Means Committee, p. 98 (Jan. 21, 1935).

247 *"Congress can't stand the pressure"*: Perkins, *The Roosevelt I Knew*, p. 294.

248 *"Blood cannot be squeezed"*: Abraham Epstein, "Our Social Insecurity Act," *Harper's Monthly*, December 1935.

249 *Perkins and Harry Hopkins brought a draft report*: Eliot, *Recollections of the New Deal*, p. 101.

249 *Wallace rolled his eyes*: Ibid., p. 102.

249 *the initial payroll tax*: See Davis, *FDR: The New Deal Years*, p. 460.

250 *"Oh, I can guess"*: Eliot, *Recollections of the New Deal*, p. 102.

250 *"What in heaven's name"*: Interview with Arthur Altmeyer, Mar. 23, 1966, Special Collections: Oral History Interview, Social Security Administration, at http://www.ssa.gov/history/ajaoral2.html (accessed Dec. 28, 2010).

251 *"assumed that before long"*: Eliot's letter to Rep. James Burke of Massachusetts appears in Eliot, *Recollections of the New Deal*, p. 103.

251 *"politics all the way through"*: Luther Gulick, "Memorandum on Conference with FDR Concerning Social Security Taxation, Summer, 1941," FDRL, copy at www.ssa.gov/history/Gulick.html (accessed Dec. 29, 2010).

252 *The very term* social security: See Edwin E. Witte, "The Development of the Social Security Act," interview Aug. 12, 1955, at www.ssa.gov/history/witte2.html (accessed July 5, 2010).

252 *"a hodgepodge"*: Eliot, *Recollections of the New Deal*, p. 104.

252 *"we separated the tax title"*: Thomas H. Eliot, "The Legal Background of the Social Security Act," speech delivered Feb. 3, 1961, at www.ssa.gov/history/eliot2.html (accessed July 5, 2010).

252 *In 1935 there were more than 7 million*: The statistics come from Hearings, Economic Security Act, House Ways and Means Committee, p. 64 (Jan. 21, 1935).

253 *"The cost of supporting"*: Ibid., p. 83.

253 *"Whether you enact"*: Ibid., p. 88.

254 *"a question of social policy"*: Ibid., p. 103.

254 *"We have to contemplate"*: Ibid., p. 88.

254 *"a slight gratuity"*: Ibid., p. 90.

255 *"We considered the Townsend plan"*: Ibid., p. 110.

255 *"You could make a perfectly self-supporting"*: Ibid., p. 178 (Jan. 22, 1935).

255 *"undertaking very heavy responsibilities"*: Ibid., p. 897 (Feb. 5, 1935).

256 *"There is no reason"*: Perkins, *The Roosevelt I Knew*, pp. 282–83.

256 *"One could concede"*: Ibid., p. 298.

257 *"he was a genuine populist"*: Vidal, *Point to Point Navigation*, p. 19.

257 *Old Senator Gore*: Perkins, *The Roosevelt I Knew*, p. 299.

257 *Perkins must have misremembered*: Perkins's appearance before the committee is recorded at Senate Finance Committee, Hearings, Economic Security Act, pp. 99–140 (Jan. 24–25, 1935). The author could find no source for this oft-cited exchange prior to the publication of Perkins's memoirs in 1946.

258 *"I know the theory"*: Ibid., p. 133.

258 *For fifteen and a half hours*: Williams, *Huey Long*, pp. 832–33.

259 *"It will take the romance"*: *Time*, Aug. 9, 1943.

259 *"perhaps the most outstanding case"*: Senate Finance Committee, Hearings, Economic Security Act, p. 462 (Feb. 6, 1935).

259 *"slovenly program"*: Epstein, "Our Social Insecurity Act," *Harper's Monthly*, December 1935.

13: BLACK MONDAY

261 *"I command you to stay"*: *The New Yorker*, Aug. 25, 1934.

261 *Johnson's characteristic effort to inject himself*: Bernstein, *Turbulent Years*, pp. 43–45.

262 *"Speak loudly for one side"*: *TNR*, Aug. 1, 1934.

262 *"Pretty early in this story"*: Johnson, *The Blue Eagle*, p. 271.

263 *NRA hearings in early January*: Bellush, *The Failure of the NRA*, p. 69.

263 *She had joined the NRA*: See Ohl, *Hugh S. Johnson and the New Deal*, pp. 108–9.

263 *Richberg soon took to lurking*: Ibid., p. 154.

263 *"The country owed Robinson"*: Perkins, *CUOHROC*, Part V, p. 362.

264 *"Ask the little skirt"*: Ohl, *Hugh S. Johnson and the New Deal*, p. 153.

264 *"I think that was one"*: *Time*, Sept. 10, 1934.

264 *"What am I going to do?"*: The crisis over the New York event is recounted in Perkins, *CUOHROC*, Part V, pp. 376–81.

265 *"moment of total aberration"*: Johnson, *The Blue Eagle*, p. 272.

265 *E. J. Condon of Sears*: Bellush, *The Failure of the NRA*, p. 73.

266 *"so long as NRA codes"*: *NYT*, Mar. 1, 1934.

266 *"Until men like Mr. Weir and Mr. Budd"*: Ibid.

266 *"there is no hope"*: *NYT*, May 21, 1934.

266 *"Don't you think"*: Perkins, *CUOHROC*, Part V, p. 503.

267 *"our most serious dose"*: Ibid., p. 507.

268 *"The diagnosis made"*: Richberg, *The Rainbow*, p. 179.

269 *"formative period is drawing"*: Ibid., p. 180.

269 *"The recent troubles of NRA"*: Lilienthal, *The TVA Years*, pp. 41–42.

270 *"I can't manage him"*: Ibid.

270 *"I need you"*: Johnson, *The Blue Eagle*, p. 386.

271 *"Forget that [resignation]"*: Roosevelt to Johnson, Aug. 20, 1934, *F.D.R.: His Personal Letters, vol. 3*, p. 412.

272 *"Gaston County is my idea"*: Gellhorn to Hopkins, Nov. 19, 1934, Hopkins Papers, FDRL.

272 *Roosevelt tried to resolve*: Bernstein, *Turbulent Years*, p. 310.

272 *"The present strike"*: The text of General Johnson's speech is in *NYT*, Sept. 15, 1934.

273 *Sloan, the mill owners' negotiator*: See Bernstein, *Turbulent Years*, p. 304.

273 *the* Chicago Tribune *predictably*: Urofsky, *Louis D. Brandeis*, p. 702.

274 *Brandeis warned Roosevelt*: Ibid.

274 *"regarded as a casualty"*: Ibid., p. 703.

274 *"Insanity in public"*: Ohl, *Hugh S. Johnson and the New Deal*, p. 250.

274 *"disgraceful and slightly obscene"*: Perkins, *CUOHROC*, Part V, p. 547.

275 *As a monthly average*: Bernstein, *Turbulent Years*, p. 172.

276 *"an unsavory, sordid business"*: Weybright, Victor, "Chickens Come Home to Roost," *Survey Graphic*, July 1935.

276 *as recently as February 1934*: The case was *Local 167 v. United States*, 291 U.S. 293; see Richberg, *My Hero*, p. 190.

277 *"right across the board"*: *NYT*, Apr. 5, 1935.

277 *Frankfurter flatly predicted*: Corcoran, "Rendezvous with Democracy."

277 *"FF SUGGESTS"*: Ibid.

278 *"I know he resented"*: Ibid.

278 *a steep sixty thousand dollars*: *NYT*, May 28, 1935.

279 *"on the verge of nervous"*: Joseph P. Kennedy, memorandum, Feb. 18, 1935, in Smith (ed.), *Hostage to Fortune*, pp. 149–50.

279 *imperiled "the economic and political security"*: A draft of this undelivered message can be found in *F.D.R.: His Personal Letters*, vol. 3, pp. 456–60.

279 *"Shame and humiliation"*: See Leuchtenburg, *Franklin D. Roosevelt and the New Deal*, p. 144.

279 *Humphrey's Executor v. U.S.*: 295 U.S. 602.

279 *"a publicity bureau"*: Leuchtenburg, *The Supreme Court Reborn*, p. 54.

280 *"It may very well have been"*: Tugwell, *The Democratic Roosevelt*, p. 392.

280 *Frazier-Lemke Farm Bankruptcy Act*: See Urofsky, *Louis D. Brandeis*, pp. 703–4.

280 *"unusual vehemence"*: *NYT*, May 28, 1935.

280 *The destruction of the NRA*: *A. L. A. Schechter Poultry Corp. v. United States*, 295 U.S. 495.

281 *"it did so in language"*: Felix Frankfurter and Henry M. Hart, Jr., "The Business of the Supreme Court at October Term, 1934," *Harvard Law Review*, Nov. 1935.

282 *"never . . . anticipate a question"*: Ibid., citing Justice Stanley Matthews at 113 U.S. 33, 39 (1885).

282 *"appeared like a condor"*: Corcoran, "Rendezvous with Democracy."

282 *"What about Old Isaiah?"*: Urofsky, *Louis D. Brandeis*, p. 705.

283 *"It was a terrible wallop"*: Hiram Johnson to Hiram Johnson, Jr., June 2, 1935, *Diary Letters*.

283 *"George says that those boys"*: Rosenman, *Working with Roosevelt*, p. 111.

284 *"Do you care to comment"*: The transcript of the press conference is at *PC*, vol. 5, pp. 309–37.

14: FEDERAL ONE

285 *"It's not easy"*: Flanagan, *Arena: The Story of the Federal Theatre*, p. 26.

286 *"I am asked whether"*: Ibid., p. 28.

286 *"most of the people"*: Bernard DeVoto, "The Writers' Project," *Harper's*, January 1942.

287 *Its employment rolls*: Average monthly WPA employment can be found in *Final Report on the WPA Program*, pp. 106–7.

287 *She reported*: Flanagan, *Arena*, pp. 434–36.

287 *every one of the forty-eight states*: *Time*, Aug. 12, 1940.

288 *"Many of these people"*: Mangione, *The Dream and the Deal*, p. 17.

288   *"He was not only of the school"*: Audrey McMahon, "A General View of the WPA Federal Art Project in New York City and State," in O'Connor, ed., *The New Deal Art Projects*, p. 56.

288   *minimum of three hundred words*: Mangione, *The Dream and the Deal*, p. 169.

289   *one of the noblest and most absurd*: "Introduction to Red Ribbon on a White Horse, by Anzia Yezierska," Auden, *The Complete Works: Prose, Vol. III*, p. 181.

289   *"almost immeasurable benefits"*: Hopkins, *Spending to Save*, p. 174.

289   *"I don't know why"*: Flanagan, *Arena*, p. 9. This sentiment by Hopkins is most frequently rendered as, "Hell! They've got to eat just like other people" (referring to all beneficiaries of Federal One), and attributed to Sherwood, *Roosevelt and Hopkins*, where it appears at p. 57. Sherwood cites no authority for the quotation, and the present author can find no earlier citation. Flanagan's version is preferred here because she ties it to a specific date and event.

289   *"Civilization contains all"*: Borglum to Williams, Dec. 20, 1933, cited in Sherwood, *Roosevelt and Hopkins*, pp. 58–59.

289   *"a nation-wide program"*: Emergency Relief Appropriation Act of 1935, P.L. 74-11. See Mangione, *The Dream and the Deal*, p. 39.

290   *"Thank God for that 25 percent"*: O'Connor, ed., *The New Deal Art Projects*, p. 315.

291   *"I like to dance"*: Bindas, *All of This Music Belongs to the Nation*, p. 13.

291   *"the most vigorous new art movement"*: Virgil Thomson, "Why Composers Write How," in *The Virgil Thomson Reader*, p. 131.

291   *Sokoloff provided funding*: Young and Young, *The Great Depression In America: A Cultural Encyclopedia*, p. 166.

291   *performed in San Diego*: Taylor, *American-Made: The Enduring Legacy of the WPA*, p. 286.

291   *"for the Four Million"*: Memo of Harry L. Hewes, project supervisor, Feb. 1, 1937, cited in Ross, *The Rest Is Noise*, p. 278.

292   *"warm, enthusiastic, careful"*: Olin Dows, "The New Deal's Treasury Art Program: A Memoir," in O'Connor, ed., *The New Deal Art Projects*, p. 44.

292   *"the pressure of cliques"*: Rosalin Bengelsdorf Browne, "The American Abstract Artists and the WPA Federal Art Project," in O'Connor, ed., *The New Deal Art Projects*, p. 223.

292   *"How many of us"*: Joseph Solman, ibid., p. 125.

292   *2,566 murals*: For figures on public installations, see *Final Report on the WPA Program*, Table XVI, p. 133.

293   *"an anarchistic sort"*: Mangione, *The Dream and the Deal*, p. 58.

293   *"the first attempt"*: TNR, Oct. 20, 1937.

293   *"biggest literary job"*: Time, Jan. 3, 1938.

293   *"Was it possible . . . that we could have"*: Mabel S. Ulrich, "Salvaging Culture for the WPA," *Harper's Monthly*, May 1939.

294   *The Polish immigrant novelist*: Auden, *The Complete Works: Prose, Vol. III*, p. 182.

294   *Exhausted by the deadening*: Roskolenko, *When I Was Last on Cherry Street*, p. 151.

294   *"it is easy"*: Auden, *Prose, Vol. III*, p. 182.

295   *"searing, biting, smashing"*: NYT, May 10, 1931.

295   *he insisted on reporting*: Rice to Flanagan, Oct. 4, 1935, FDRL.

295   *"Behind us, hidden"*: Typescript of Flanagan talk, entitled "Is This the Time and Place?" FDRL.

296   *"none were on relief"*: Taylor, *American-Made*, p. 252.

296   *"Now they were to beat"*: Flanagan, *Arena*, p. 65.

297   *"impersonation of a ruler"*: Ibid., p. 66.

297   *a "shabby game of partisan politics"*: Ibid., pp. 66–67.

297   *Within a few weeks*: Ibid., p. 69.

297 *"obviously loaded with a charge"*: *NYT*, Mar. 16, 1936.
298 *"Some people thought the play"*: Flanagan, *Arena*, p. 117.
298 *born Jacques Haussmann*: Houseman, *Run-Through*, p. 175.
299 *"I could see his features"*: Ibid., p. 150.
300 *"an awkward hodgepodge"*: Ibid., p. 186.
300 *"Flash of ten thousand people"*: Flanagan, *Arena*, p. 74.
301 *"We told him we were"*: Ibid., p. 241.
301 *"at white heat"*: Blitzstein, "Marc Blitzstein Presents," *NYT*, Apr. 12, 1964.
302 *"It took no wizardry"*: Flanagan, *Arena*, p. 200.
302 *"She's crazy about it"*: See Gordon, *Mark the Music*, p. 138.
303 *"there was no safety"*: Houseman, *Run-Through*, p. 247.
303 *"They charged like a bunch"*: Bernstein, *Turbulent Years*, p. 488.
303 *"Mrs. F is getting scared"*: Gordon, *Mark the Music: The Life and Work of Marc Blitzstein*, p. 140.
303 *"pronounced it magnificent"*: Flanagan, *Arena*, p. 202.
303 *budget cuts*: Ibid.
304 *"Orson and I were not noted"*: Ibid.
304 *and* Cradle *already once*: Leaming, *Orson Welles*, p. 135.
304 *"I wasn't sure that we weren't"*: Ibid.
304 *"We had served it well"*: Houseman, *Run-Through*, p. 258.
305 *"an enormous buzz of talk"*: Blitzstein, "Marc Blitzstein Presents."
306 *"If Olive Stanton had not"*: Houseman, *Run-Through*, p. 259.
306 *"We get letters in"*: Memo, meeting of Orson Welles, David Niles, and Ellen Woodward, June 17, 1937, NARA, cited in Quinn, *Furious Improvisation*, p. 183.
306 *"In that case"*: Houseman, *Run-Through*, p. 255.
306 *"This technique seems"*: *NYT*, June 20, 1937.
307 *"Probably it was worth"*: Flanagan, *Arena*, p. 203.
307 *"Literary allusions are dangerous"*: Ibid., p. 204.

15: THE MOST FORGOTTEN MAN

308 *"As far as the Negro is concerned"*: "Editorial Comment," *Journal of Negro Education*, January 1936.
308 *"The indictment which Americans of Negro descent"*: W. E. B. Du Bois, "Herbert Hoover," *The Crisis*, November 1932.
309 *militantly whites-only*: See David E. Bernstein, "Racism, Railroad Unions, and Labor Regulations," *The Independent Review*, Fall 2000.
309 *In 1930 most American blacks*: Donald Holley, "The Negro in the New Deal Resettlement Program," *Agricultural History*, July 1971.
309 *Less than 1 percent*: See Olive M. Stone, "The Present Position of the Negro Farm Population," *Journal of Negro Education*, January 1936.
309 *"hedged about"*: Ibid.
310 *A department store in Newark*: T. Arnold Hill, "The Plight of the Negro Industrial Worker," *Journal of Negro Education*, January 1936.
310 *Among black workers*: Albion Hartwell, "The Need of Social and Unemployment Insurance for Negroes," *Journal of Negro Education*, January 1936.
310 *In the 1932 election, black voters*: Weiss, *Farewell to the Party of Lincoln*, p. 30.
310 *"What have the Negroes"*: *Time*, Aug. 12, 1935.
310 *"I see in the offing"*: Weiss, *Farewell to the Party of Lincoln*, pp. 14–15.
310 *A questionnaire prepared by the National Association for the Advancement of Colored People*: White, *A Man Called White*, pp. 139–40.
311 *"As I understand"*: Interview with Clark Foreman, Nov. 16, 1974, Southern Oral History Program Collection, University of North Carolina.

311   *One place Ickes failed*: Hiltzik, *Colossus*, p. 315.

312   *In Clarke County, Georgia*: John A. Salmond, "The Civilian Conservation Corps and the Negro," *The Journal of American History*, June 1965.

312   *In Mississippi*: Ibid.

313   *girls "just attaining"*: Ibid.

313   *"The group most in need"*: John P. Davis, "Blue Eagles and Black Workers," *TNR*, Nov. 14, 1934.

314   *"NRA inherited"*: A. Howard Myers, "The Negro Worker Under NRA," *Journal of Negro Education*, January 1936.

314   *"unpardonable sophistry"*: Davis, "Blue Eagles and Black Workers."

314   *When domestic allocation payments began*: Holley, "The Negro in the New Deal Resettlement Program."

315   *"had logic; it was necessary"*: Rexford G. Tugwell, "The Resettlement Idea," *Agricultural History*, October 1959.

315   *"encouraged those who viewed"*: Ibid.

315   *The residents survived*: J. R. Moehringer, "Crossing Over," *LAT*, Aug. 22, 1999.

315   *"steers and seeds"*: Holley, "The Negro in the New Deal Resettlement Program."

316   *"Roosevelt houses"*: Moehringer, "Crossing Over."

316   *The Resettlement Administration came closest*: Holley, "The Negro in the New Deal Resettlement Program."

316   *"The women folks"*: Conkin, *Tomorrow a New World: The New Deal Community Program*, p. 202.

316   *now equipped with*: Ibid., p. 167.

316   *"had in it no influential citizens"*: Tugwell, "The Resettlement Idea."

317   *"The critics' objection"*: Ibid.

317   *90 percent*: See Hill, "The Plight of the Negro Industrial Worker."

317   *"These unemployed, untrained"*: Ibid.

318   *"equaled by the more"*: Edward Lewis, "The Negro on Relief," *Journal of Negro Education*, January 1936.

318   *"Mr President Sir"*: Letter in McElvaine, *Down and Out in the Great Depression*, p. 88.

318   *That year the NAACP*: Raymond Wolters, "Section 7a and the Black Worker," *Labor History*, Summer 1969.

319   *"The most sinister power"*: W. E. B. Du Bois, "The A. F. of L.," *The Crisis*, December 1933.

319   *"It is not a 'closed' shop"*: Wolters, "Section 7a and the Black Worker."

319   *"the one weapon left"*: Ibid.

319   *"have nothing to gain"*: Hartwell, "The Need of Social and Unemployment Insurance for Negroes."

320   *"the Negro remains the most forgotten"*: Hill, "The Plight of the Negro Industrial Worker."

320   *"at the hands of parties"*: Ibid.

320   *Gallup poll*: Ibid.

321   *(Sixty-three would be reported)*: Robert L. Zangrando, "The NAACP and a Federal Antilynching Bill, 1934–1940," *The Journal of Negro History*, April 1965.

321   *"the best lesson"*: *San Francisco Chronicle*, Nov. 23, 2008.

321   *"We do not excuse"*: Roosevelt, "Address Before the Federal Council of Churches of Christ in America," Dec. 6, 1933.

321   *"Crimes of organized banditry"*: Annual Message to Congress, Jan. 3, 1934, *PPA*, vol. 3, pp. 12–13.

321   *"I did not choose the tools"*: White, *A Man Called White*, pp. 169–70.

321   *"Saturday night Oct 27th"*: See Leuchtenburg, *Franklin D. Roosevelt and the New Deal*, p. 186.

322 *The result was not*: O. R. Altman, "Second and Third Sessions of the Seventy-fifth Congress, 1937–38," *The American Political Science Review*, December 1938.

322 *It is a matter of great disappointment*: *The Nation*, June 5, 1935.

322 *After 1935*: Zangrando, "The NAACP."

323 *"She took a folding chair"*: Virginia Foster Durr, Mar. 13–15, 1975, Interview G-0023-2, Southern Oral History Program Collection, University of North Carolina.

324 *"One is forced to admit"*: Robert C. Weaver, "The New Deal and the Negro: A Look at the Facts," *Opportunity*, July 1935.

324 *"If the Republicans said little"*: W. E. B. Du Bois, "The Democrats Speak," *The Crisis*, August 1936.

325 *"If all four had an equal"*: See James A. Harrell, "Negro Leadership in the Election Year 1936," *The Journal of Southern History*, November 1968.

16: BACKLASH

330 *"one of the so-called 'Moley dinners'"*: Tugwell's report of the event is in his diary entry for Jan. 29, 1935, FDRL.

331 *The act reduced*: See Leff, *The Limits of Symbolic Reform: The New Deal and Taxation*, Table 1, p. 12.

331 *"Such tactics are not only"*: *NYT*, Sept. 5, 1933.

331 *Jones's speech put an end*: Jones, *Fifty Billion Dollars*, p. 26.

331 *"The whole constitution"*: *Will Rogers' Daily Telegrams*, #2417, May 2, 1935.

331 *Five Negroes on my place*: See *NYT*, Dec. 21, 1934. The letters were released by the Senate's Nye Committee, which was investigating munitions trading by du Pont and other companies. Carpenter's letter was dated Mar. 16, 1934, and Raskob's reply March 20, 1934.

333 *"I know of no one"*: Ibid.

333 *"To teach the necessity"*: *TNR*, Sept. 5, 1934.

333 *"an organization that only advocates"*: Press conference #137, Aug. 24, 1934, in *Complete Presidential Press Conferences of Franklin D. Roosevelt*, vol. 4, pp. 18–20.

334 *"There appears to be"*: "Report to the Executive Committee of the American Liberty League," Dec. 20, 1934, in Finan, *Alfred E. Smith*, p. 309.

334 *"window dressing"*: Ward, *A First-Class Temperament*, p. 787.

335 *"Do you know, by God"*: Clark Howard to FDR, Dec. 2, 1931, in *F.D.R.: His Personal Letters*, vol. 3, p. 229.

336 *funded by Raskob*: For backing of the "Grass Roots Convention," see Anderson, *The Wild Man from Sugar Creek*, p. 137.

336 *Press reports revealed*: See, for example, *TNR*, Feb. 19, 1936.

337 *"The phenomenon to which I refer"*: Childs, "They Hate Roosevelt," *Harper's Monthly*, May 1936.

337 *"victimize not merely the rich"*: Hale, "But I, Too, Hate Roosevelt," *Harper's Monthly*, August 1936.

338 *"I am fighting Communism"*: Davis, *FDR*, p. 543.

339 *"The attitude of the President"*: Nasaw, *The Chief: The Life of William Randolph Hearst*, p. 512.

339 *"steal Long's thunder"*: Moley, *After Seven Years*, p. 308.

339 *"The sense of regaining"*: Ibid., p. 312.

339 *"That is for Hearst"*: Ickes, *The Secret Diary*, vol. 1, p. 384 (June 19, 1935).

339 *The Treasury expected*: Leff, *The Limits of Symbolic Reform*, p. 93.

340 *"composed of equal parts"*: These editorial citations are from *NYT*, June 21, 1935.

340 *"neither fish nor fowl"*: *NYT*, July 28, 1935.
341 *Sullivan's attempt to position himself*: See *Time*, Nov. 22, 1937.
341 *Roosevelt interpreted the columnist's piece*: Press conference #409, Nov. 9, 1937, *PC*, vol. 10, p. 319.
341 *"Pundit's Secretary"*: *Life*, Nov. 22, 1937.
341 *he continued to counsel*: See Lippmann, *Public Philosopher: Selected Letters*; to Kennedy, p. 335 (May 22, 1935); to Douglas, p. 333 (May 8, 1935); to FDR, p. 335 (June 4, 1935).
341 *"Increasingly, since last spring"*: Lippmann to Baker, ibid., p. 343 (Jan 22, 1936).
342 *"The record shows"*: "Draft of Declaration of Principles" in Lippmann to Douglas, April 16, 1936, Lippmann, ibid., pp. 348ff.
342 *Roosevelt's personal popularity*: Moley, *After Seven Years*, p. 318.
342 *"bluntly asked him"*: Ickes, *The Secret Diary*, vol. 1, p. 499 (Dec. 31, 1935).
343 *This approach had been questioned*: See Davis, *FDR*, pp. 603–604.
343 *"political diatribe"*: Ibid., p. 606.
344 *"He has been getting"*: Ickes, *The Secret Diary*, vol. 1, pp. 516–17.
344 *"a great distrust of the present administration"*: *NYT*, July 18, 1935.
344 *"Of course I believe"*: *NYT*, Aug. 31, 1934.
344 *"the best interests"*: The official text of Al Smith's speech as delivered on Jan. 25, 1936, is in *Vital Speeches of the Day*, Feb. 10, 1936.
345 *"I just can't understand it"*: Perkins, *The Roosevelt I Knew*, p. 157.
345 *"Every rat is out of its hole"*: Johnson to Hiram W. Johnson, Jr., Feb. 2, 1936, *Diary Letters*, vol. 6.
345 *"in the opinion of Republican"*: *NYT*, Jan. 27, 1936.
346 *"a certain controversy"*: *NYT*, Jan. 27, 1936.
346 *"Jammed elbow to elbow"*: Robinson broadcast, Jan. 28, 1936, *Vital Speeches of the Day*, Feb. 10, 1936.

17: NINE OLD MEN

348 *"a leader completely vindicated"*: Tugwell, *The Democratic Roosevelt*, p. 433.
349 *Over the following two years*: See Leuchtenburg, *The Supreme Court Reborn*, p. 102.
349 U.S. v. Butler: The decision is at 297 U.S. 1.
349 *"a magnificent structure"*: Howard Brubaker, "Of All Things," *The New Yorker*, Sept. 21, 1935.
349 *expected allotment checks worth $2 billion*: See Leuchtenburg, *The Supreme Court Reborn*, p. 98.
350 *"speculators are just as poor"*: Lilienthal, *The TVA Years*, p. 60.
350 *"I had completely resolved myself"*: Ibid., p. 59 (diary entry Feb. 17, 1936.)
350 Tipaldo: The decision is *Morehead v. New York ex. rel. Tipaldo*, 298 U.S. 587.
350 *"the power they thought"*: Leuchtenburg, *The Supreme Court Reborn*, p. 105.
350 *"the sacred right"*: Ickes, *The Secret Diary*, vol. 1, p. 614 (June 2, 1936).
351 *"'no-man's-land'"*: *PC*, vol. 7, p. 280 (June 2, 1936).
351 *"You know, boys"*: Rosenman, *Working with Roosevelt*, p. 131.
351 *"take off all gloves"*: Ibid., p. 133.
352 *the Court's 1937 docket*: See Leuchtenburg, *The Supreme Court Reborn*, p. 109.
353 *"Leave the whole thing very general"*: Rosenman, *Working with Roosevelt*, p. 141.
353 *"The President does not speak"*: *NYT*, Jan. 7, 1937.
353 *"made plain that he does not"*: Dean Dinwoodey of *United States Law Week*, quoted in Leuchtenburg, *The Supreme Court Reborn*, p. 127.

353   *"it is very plain"*: See Leuchtenburg, *The Supreme Court Reborn*, ibid.

354   *It was Roosevelt*: Rosenman, *Working with Roosevelt*, p. 142.

354   *"There was no doubt"*: Ibid., p. 144.

355   *"By this method there would be"*: Ickes, *The Secret Diary*, vol. 1, p. 495 (Dec. 27, 1935).

355   *"No one has yet"*: Leuchtenburg, *The Supreme Court Reborn*, p. 100.

356   *"ask it to instruct him"*: Ickes, *The Secret Diary*, vol. 1, pp. 529–30 (Jan. 27, 1936).

356   *"The President is really hoping"*: Ibid., p. 530.

356   *"pursuant to the Constitutional"*: Creel, *Rebel at Large*, p. 293.

356   *supplementing justices who had reached the age of seventy*: Leuchtenburg, *The Supreme Court Reborn*, p. 117ff.

359   *Rosenman could detect*: Rosenman, *Working with Roosevelt*, p. 146.

359   *he and Cohen participated in*: Corcoran, "Rendezvous with Democracy." See also Lasser, *Benjamin V. Cohen*, p. 154.

359   *"I had to skim"*: Corcoran, ibid.

360   *"hardening of the judicial arteries"*: Fireside Chat, March 9, 1937.

360   *"a matter of life-or-death importance"*: Ibid.

361   *They were scanning*: Ibid. See also Shesol, *Supreme Power: Franklin Roosevelt vs. the Supreme Court*, p. 298.

361   *"Whom did F. D. rely on"*: See Urofsky, *Louis D. Brandeis*, p. 715.

361   *In time the cheering news*: Alsop and Catledge, *The 168 Days*, p. 138.

362   *"fully justified"*: Ickes, *The Secret Diary*, vol. 2, pp. 64ff (Feb. 6, 1937).

362   *"we were all so stunned"*: Bascom N. Timmons, "John N. Garner's Story," *Collier's*, Feb. 28, 1948.

362   *"here's where I cash in my chips"*: Alsop and Catledge, *The 168 Days*, pp. 67–69.

363   *"Riding Circuit in those days"*: PC, vol. 9, p. 135 (Feb. 5, 1937).

363   *"Perhaps . . . he sees a chance"*: Ickes, *The Secret Diary*, vol. 2, p. 70.

363   *"If he can do it once"*: See HJ to Hiram W. Johnson, Jr., Feb. 14, 1937, *Diary Letters*.

364   *"This morning ex-President Hoover"*: Vandenberg diary, Feb. 6, 1937, cited in Leuchtenburg, *The Supreme Court Reborn*, p. 140.

364   *"subordination of the court"*: See Hoover, *Memoirs*, vol. 3, p. 373.

364   *"Who's trying to muzzle me?"*: Alsop and Catledge, *The 168 Days*, p. 98.

364   *accusing Roosevelt of plotting*: Hoover, *Memoirs*, vol. 3, p. 374.

365   *"The Republicans are as meek"*: Ickes, *The Secret Diary*, vol. 2, p. 93 (Mar. 6, 1937).

365   *"resounding bang"*: Wheeler, "My Years with Roosevelt," p. 203.

365   *Overtures in that vein*: For the machinations leading up to the Hughes letter, see Urofsky, *Louis D. Brandeis*, pp. 716–17.

365   *"I am not interested"*: Ibid., p. 204.

365   *"I went to the only source"*: Senate Judiciary Committee, Hearing, Reorganization of the Federal Judiciary, p. 487 (Mar. 22, 1937).

366   *"The Supreme Court is fully abreast"*: Ibid., p. 488.

366   *"The newsreels photographed it"*: Wheeler, "My Years with Roosevelt," p. 206.

366   *"certainly would not have joined in that part"*: Shesol, *Supreme Power*, p. 399.

366   *"as opposed to the Hughes-Brandeis intervention"*: Joseph L. Rauh, Jr., "A Personalized View of the Court-Packing Episode," *Journal of Supreme Court History 1990*.

366   *"did not shoot straight"*: Urofsky, *Louis D. Brandeis*, p. 718.

366   *"[thrown] all judicial discretion to the wind"*: TNR, April 7, 1937.

367   *"We abandoned this ground"*: Ickes, *The Secret Diary*, vol. 2, p. 104.

367   *a "brilliant and efficient Chief"*: Rauh, "A Personalized View."

368   *"in many ways one of the most disastrous"*: See Leuchtenburg, *The Supreme Court Reborn*, p. 168.

368   *"Let's let the Supreme Court"*: Ibid., p. 167.

369 *"the economic conditions that have supervened"*: West Coast Hotel v. Parrish, 300 U.S. 379.

370 *The purge of nationwide calamity*: Helvering v. Davis, 301 U.S. 619.

370 *"a pungent lecture from the bench"*: NYT, May 25, 1937.

371 *ruling for the government*: NYT, May 30, 1937.

371 *"I was taken for a ride"*: Johnson to FDR, April 13, 1937, *FDRL*, cited in Leuchtenburg, *Franklin D. Roosevelt and the New Deal*, p. 236.

371 *"Roosevelt largely accomplished"*: Hoover, *Memoirs*, vol. 3, p. 377.

371 *"I think the decisions"*: Lippmann to Willkie, May 28, 1937, Lippmann, *Selected Letters*, p. 361.

371 *Roosevelt had kept running*: Alsop and Catledge, *The 168 Days*, p. 154.

371 *"To tell you the honest truth"*: PC, vol. 9, p. 226 (Mar. 30, 1937).

371 *"chortling all morning"*: Ibid., p. 259 (April 13, 1937).

372 *"There are a great many things"*: Ibid., p. 391 (May 25, 1937).

372 *"confirm the Senate nomination"*: Ibid., p. 380 (May 21, 1937).

372 *"a political operative"*: Corcoran, "Rendezvous with Democracy."

373 *"off the reservation"*: Ickes, *The Secret Diary*, vol. 2, p. 140 (May 15, 1937).

373 *Roosevelt had it out with his vice president*: The anecdote comes from Ickes, who received a briefing from Roosevelt himself about a week later. Ibid., p. 143 (May 22, 1937).

373 *"I haven't read it"*: PC, vol. 9, p. 430 (June 15, 1937).

374 *"I confess I am worried"*: Johnson, *Diary Letters*, June 23, 1937.

374 *"No more questions today"*: See Leuchtenburg, *The Supreme Court Reborn*, p. 151; Alsop and Catledge, *The 168 Days*, p. 256.

374 *"not kill any more"*: Ickes, *The Secret Diary*, vol. 2, p. 162 (July 16, 1937).

375 *"in especially bad taste"*: Ibid.

375 *"Who lost the Supreme Court"*: Corcoran, "Rendezvous with Democracy."

18: ROOSEVELT'S RECESSION

376 *"A certainty, even an undesirable"*: Ickes, *The Secret Diary*, vol. 2, p. 173 (July 25, 1937).

376 *The economy was continuing to improve*: See Lauchlin B. Currie, "Causes of the Recession," *History of Political Economy*, April 1938.

376 *Over the first nine*: Industrial production figures are from Industrial Production Index, at Economic Research: Federal Reserve Bank of St. Louis, at http://research .stlouisfed.org/fred2/series/INDPRO (accessed Nov. 6, 2010); national income is from Federal Reserve, National Income Supplement, 1951, p. 150.

376 *"grave danger"*: Eccles, *Beckoning Frontiers*, pp. 296–97.

377 *"simply delighted"*: Blum, *From the Morgenthau Diaries, Years of Crisis: 1928–1938*, p. 381.

378 *"stopped priming the pump"*: TNR, Nov. 24, 1937.

378 *Yet the severity*: Roose, Kenneth D., "The Recession of 1937–1938," *The Journal of Political Economy*, June 1948.

378 *"the royalists of the economic order"*: Acceptance address, June 27, 1936.

379 *gross national product had grown*: Christina Romer, "What Ended the Great Depression?" *The Journal of Economic History*, Dec. 1992.

379 *"not because it did not work"*: E. Cary Brown, "Fiscal Policy in the 'Thirties: A Reappraisal," *The American Economic Review*, December 1956.

379 *"While things look"*: FDR to House, Apr. 5, 1933, in *F.D.R.: Personal Letters, vol. 3*, p. 342.

380 *"lacking in coherence and consistency"*: Lauchlin L. Currie, "Comments and Observations," *History of Political Economy*, Winter 1978. After World War II, Currie got

swept up in Washington's Red-hunting panic, becoming the target of accusations that continue to mar his reputation today. Shlaes, for example, identifies him as "a Soviet spy whose [economic] arguments won a good reception from naïve colleagues" (*The Forgotten Man*, p. 340; see also p. 418). The evidence for the categorical and oft-repeated charge of espionage against Currie is equivocal at best, and the insinuation that his economic thinking should be discredited because of it is unwarranted. For a different picture of this unedifying echo of the McCarthy era and a close analysis of the evidence against Currie, see Roger J. Sandilands, "Guilt by Association? Lauchlin Currie's Alleged Involvement with Washington Economists in Soviet Espionage," *History of Political Economy*, Fall 2000, and James Boughton and Roger J. Sandilands, "Politics and the Attack on FDR's Economists," *Intelligence and National Security*, Sept. 2003.

380   *Many other economists*: See, for example, Arthur Smithies, "The American Economy in the Thirties," *The American Economic Review*, May 1946.

380   *His calculations suggested*: Currie, "Comments and Observations." See also Currie, "Comments on Pump Priming," reprinted in *History of Political Economy*, Winter 1978, and Byrd L. Jones, "Lauchlin Currie, Pump Priming, and New Deal Fiscal Policy, 1934–1936," *History of Political Economy*, Winter 1978.

381   *"naked-eye observation"*: Eccles, *Beckoning Frontiers*, p. 132.

381   *"It will be through raising high the prestige"*: J. Maynard Keynes, "An Open Letter to President Roosevelt," *NYT*, Dec. 31, 1933.

381   *"I saw your friend Keynes"*: Perkins, *The Roosevelt I Knew*, p. 225.

381   *"The attempt to make a distinction"*: Annual Message to Congress, Jan. 4, 1935.

381   *Morgenthau was still stepping up*: Blum, *From the Morgenthau Diaries*, p. 382.

382   *"inquisitorial visits"*: *NYT*, Oct. 15, 1937.

382   *"a complete reversal"*: Ickes, *The Secret Diary*, vol. 2, p. 241 (Nov. 6, 1937).

382   *FDR, marginally less pessimistic*: Ibid., p. 232 (Oct. 22, 1937).

383   *"Certainly war with Japan"*: Ibid., p. 274 (Dec. 18, 1937).

383   *"he is punch drunk"*: Ickes, *The Secret Diary*, vol. 2, p. 182 (Aug. 4, 1937).

383   *after a cross-country trip*: Leuchtenburg, *Franklin D. Roosevelt and the New Deal*, p. 251.

383   *Yet when the session adjourned*: *NYT*, Dec. 22, 1937.

384   *"Nobody pays any attention"*: Ickes, *The Secret Diary*, vol. 2, p. 224 (Oct. 9, 1937).

384   *"very excited, very dictatorial"*: Blum, *From the Morgenthau Diaries*, p. 390.

384   *"You told the newspapers"*: Ibid., p. 391.

384   *"Of course, I am glad to hear"*: Ibid.

384   *"looked and acted like a spanked"*: Ickes, *The Secret Diary*, vol. 2, p. 242.

385   *"a steadily deepening indecision"*: Moley, *After Seven Years*, p. 373.

385   *"The emergency that we faced"*: *NYT*, Nov. 11, 1937.

385   *"There were indications"*: Eccles, *Beckoning Frontiers*, p. 304.

385   *"He looked bad"*: Ickes, *The Secret Diary*, vol. 2, p. 260 (Dec. 6, 1937).

386   *"When the business goes"*: Jackson, "Business Confidence and Government Policy," Robert H. Jackson Center, Jamestown, NY, at http://www.robertjackson.org/the-man/bibliography (accessed Nov. 7, 2010).

386   *"The blunt truth"*: Jackson, "The Menace to Free Enterprise," Robert H. Jackson Center, Jamestown, NY, at http://www.robertjackson.org/the-man/bibliography (accessed Nov. 7, 2010).

386   *"It is the old struggle"*: *NYT*, Dec. 31, 1937.

386   *"Nothing that I have ever"*: Ickes, *The Secret Diary*, vol. 2, p. 284 (Jan. 1, 1938).

386   *"I hope that he won't let us down"*: Ibid., p. 285.

387   *The policy drift*: See Moley, *After Seven Years*, p. 374.

388   *Donald Richberg had escorted*: Hawley, *The New Deal and the Problem of Monopoly*, p. 397.

388 *"It looks to me"*: Ickes, *The Secret Diary*, vol. 2, p. 326 (Mar. 2, 1938).

388 *"just treading water"*: Blum, *From the Morgenthau Diaries*, p. 415.

389 *"rarin' to go"*: Ibid., p. 417.

389 *"What you have outlined"*: Ibid., p. 420.

391 *After a conference committee*: O. R. Altman, "Second and Third Sessions of the Seventy-fifth Congress, 1937–1938," *The American Political Science Review*, December 1938.

391 *federal minimum hourly wage*: Leuchtenburg, *Franklin D. Roosevelt*, p. 262.

392 *marked the bottom*: Francois R. Velde, "The Recession of 1937—A Cautionary Tale," *Economic Perspectives*, Federal Reserve Bank of Chicago, Fourth Quarter 2009.

392 *"nine years of fiscal insanity"*: *NYT*, Dec. 11, 1938.

19: PURGATORY

393 *"The most exhaustive analysis"*: Jerome D. Cohen, "The Forgotten T.N.E.C.," *Current History*, September 1941.

393 *Hartford-Empire Company*: *NYT*, Dec. 13, 1938.

394 *"There will be no midgets"*: *Nation's Business*, September 1938.

394 *"the final expression of Roosevelt's personal indecision"*: Moley, *After Seven Years*, p. 376.

395 *"With all the ammunition"*: *Time*, Apr. 14, 1941.

396 *"Every time I ask"*: Farley, *Jim Farley's Story*, p. 130.

396 *"Mr. Dies seemed to have"*: "TRB," "Case History of a Red Hunt," *TNR*, Dec. 6, 1939.

397 *"From all over the country"*: Ibid.

398 *"a burly Congressman"*: Ickes, *The Secret Diary*, vol. 2, p. 455 (Aug. 27, 1938).

398 *"to be used in a flagrantly unfair"*: Roosevelt, "Statement on the sit-down strikes in Michigan," Oct. 25, 1938.

398 *"get down to the meat"*: HUAC hearings, vol. 1, p. 833 (Aug. 20, 1938).

398 *"consulting expert"*: Matthew Josephson, and Russell Maloney, "The Testimony of a Sinner," *The New Yorker*, Apr. 22, 1944, p. 30.

398 *"to have greater freedom to work"*: HUAC hearings, vol. 1, p. 880 (Aug. 20, 1938).

399 *"Before you shut me off"*: Ibid., p. 938 (Aug. 22, 1938).

399 *"not only is serving as a branch"*: *NYT*, July 27, 1938.

399 *"the outstanding zany"*: Ickes, *The Secret Diary*, vol. 2, p. 507 (Nov. 25, 1938).

399 *"It was the fashion at that time"*: Flanagan, *Arena*, p. 335.

399 *she was unmasked*: Quinn, *Furious Improvisation*, p. 79.

399 *"was known as far back"*: HUAC hearings, vol. 1, p. 777 (Aug. 19, 1938).

399 *"propaganda plays have been"*: Ibid., p. 784.

399 *"were so definitely propaganda"*: Ibid., p. 790.

399 *"We consider these plays"*: Ibid., p. 791, 799.

400 *"completely humiliated"*: Rosenman OH, *FDRL*.

400 *"The real fight"*: Raymond Clapper, "Roosevelt Tries the Primaries," *Current History*, October 1938.

400 *"a very, very strong animus"*: Rosenman OH, *FDRL*.

401 *"writing columns on whether"*: FDR to Early, Sept. 27, 1937, in *PL-III*, p. 713.

401 *A similar fiasco*: For Tydings's anti–New Deal record, see Leuchtenburg, *Franklin D. Roosevelt and the New Deal*, pp. 267–268.

402 *"they are in the panic"*: Quinn, *Furious Improvisation*, p. 250.

403 *"political affiliations"*: HUAC hearings, vol. 4, pp. 2733–34 (Dec. 5, 1938).

403 *"largest and most comprehensive"*: Ibid., p. 2737.
403 *"The Ethics of Living Jim Crow"*: Ibid., pp. 2743–44.
403 *"Could a few hours offset"*: Flanagan, *Arena*, p. 340.
404 *"un-American* inactivity": HUAC hearings, "Un-American Propaganda Activities," vol. 4, p. 2839 (Dec. 6, 1938).
404 *"definite propaganda"*: Ibid., p. 2851.
404 *"Every religious shade"*: Ibid., p. 2857.
404 *"The newest adventure"*: *NYT*, May 21, 1937.
404 *"very human and amusing"*: Flanagan to Davis, Nov. 8, 1936, cited in Matthews, *The Federal Theatre*, p. 117.
405 *"You are quoting from this Marlowe"*: Ibid.
405 *"I would like to make"*: HUAC hearings, "Un-American Propaganda Activities," vol. 4, p. 2885 (Dec. 6, 1938).
405 *"the most devastating attack"*: Ibid., p. 2887.
405 *"I said the last time"*: Ibid., p. 2903.
405 *"The chair wants to commend"*: Ibid., p. 2908.
406 *Alsberg's friends gave him*: Mangione, *The Dream and the Deal*, p. 320.
406 *"We are convinced"*: Flanagan, *Arena*, p. 347.
406 *Republican Congressman Everett Dirksen*: *Time*, June 26, 1939.
406 *"Who's in charge"*: Flanagan, *Arena*, p. 353.
407 *"These opponents were out to hang"*: Ibid.
407 *"Born December 23"*: Ibid., p. 365.
408 *"Only the extremists talk"*: Lindley, Ernest K., "The New Congress," *Current History*, February 1939.
408 *"This requires action"*: Rhodes, *The Making of the Atomic Bomb*, p. 314.
409 *"Under Joe the gains"*: *Time*, Oct. 11, 1937.
409 *On that Monday afternoon*: The exchange between Douglas and Jackson appears in De Bedts, *The New Deal's SEC*, p. 163, in a version Douglas certified as "substantially correct." See also Joseph Alsop, and Robert Kintner, "The Battle of the Marketplace-I," *Saturday Evening Post*, June 11, 1938.
410 *"on my face"*: Brooks, *Once in Golconda*, p. 261.
411 *"Did you expect me"*: Ibid., pp. 283–86.
412 *"part of the struggle"*: Arnold, *The Folklore of Capitalism*, p. 211.
412 *"professional smart aleck"*: Spencer Waller, "The Antitrust Legacy of Thurman Arnold," *St. John's Law Review*, August 2004.
412 "The New York Times": Ibid.
412 *"He is often"*: Fred Rodell, "Arnold: Myth and Trust Buster," *TNR*, June 22, 1938.
412 *"Years of disuse"*: Arnold, *Fair Fights and Foul*, p. 113.
412 *Before departing*: Ibid., pp. 51–52.
412 *He nearly quadrupled*: Corwin D. Edwards, "Thurman Arnold and the Antitrust Laws," *Political Science Quarterly*, September 1943.
413 *"idiot in a powder mill"*: Ibid., p. 115.
414 *Roosevelt brusquely upbraided*: Blum, *From the Morgenthau Diaries: Years of Urgency: 1938–1941*, p. 20.
414 *"We have tried spending"*: Ibid., pp. 24–25.
415 *The ranks of the unemployed*: Statistics are from Michael R. Darby, "Three-and-a-Half Million U.S. Employees Have Been Mislaid; Or, an Explanation of Unemployment, 1934–1941," *The Journal of Political Economy*, February 1976.
416 *"You had an opportunity"*: Eleanor Roosevelt to Mrs. Henry M. Robert, Jr., Feb. 26, 1939, *FDRL*.
418 *"the best speech"*: Ickes, *The Secret Diary*, vol. 2, p. 615 (Apr. 15, 1939).
418 *"There seemed to be people"*: Anderson, *My Lord, What a Morning*, p. 191.

Epilogue: Defining the New Deal

421   *The WPA produced*: Final Report on the WPA Program, Table XVI, pp. 131ff.
422   *536 school buildings*: *America Builds: The Record of PWA*, Public Works Administration, 1939.
423   *"They were happily agreeing"*: Tugwell, *Roosevelt's Revolution*, p. 45.
424   *"awkward and insufficient"*: Tugwell, "The New Deal in Retrospect," *The Western Political Quarterly*, December 1948.
424   *some 50 million Americans*: First Report of the Social Security Board of Trustees, Jan. 3, 1941, at http://www.ssa.gov/history/reports/trust/tf1941.html (accessed Jan. 15, 2011).
427   *"That Roosevelt could look"*: Moley, *After Seven Years*, p. 365.
427   *"humiliating compromises"*: Rexford G. Tugwell, "The Compromising Roosevelt," *The Western Political Quarterly*, June 1953.
428   *"for the first and only"*: Rosenman, *Working with Roosevelt*, p. 105.
428   *Moley was still nursing*: Moley, *After Seven Years*, p. 344.
428   *In recent years*: For the former approach, see Alter, *The Defining Moment*; Cohen, *Nothing to Fear* (both treating the Hundred Days); and Shesol, *Supreme Power* (the Court-packing scheme); for the latter, see Shlaes, *The Forgotten Man*.
429   *Exhibit A in this brief*: See, for example, Lee H. Ohanian, "Lessons from the New Deal," Testimony Prepared for the U.S. Senate Committee on Banking, Housing, and Urban Affairs, Apr. 4, 2009.
430   *Lauchlin Currie observed in a penetrating analysis*: Currie, "Comments on Pump Priming."
431   *That was 1936*: See E. Cary Brown, "Fiscal Policy in the 'Thirties: A Reappraisal," *The American Economic Review*, Dec. 1956.
431   *"not because it did not work"*: Ibid.
431   *rapid monetary expansion*: For a cogent discussion of monetary expansion in the mid-Thirties, see Christina D. Romer, "What Ended the Great Depression?" *The Journal of Economic History*, December 1992.
431   *blistering pace*: Ibid.
432   *The New Deal's most important*: See, for example, J. Bradford DeLong, "The New Deal: Lessons for Today," testimony before the Economic Policy Subcommittee of the U.S. Senate Committee on Banking, Housing, and Urban Affairs, Mar. 29, 2009; Eichengreen, *Golden Fetters;* and Stein, *The Fiscal Revolution in America.*

BIBLIOGRAPHY

Acheson, Dean. *Among Friends: Personal Letters of Dean Acheson.* Ed. David S. McLellan and David C. Acheson. New York: Dodd, Mead, 1980.

Alsop, Joseph, and Turner Catledge. *The 168 Days.* New York: Doubleday, Doran, 1938.

Alsop, Joseph W., with Adam Platt. *"I've Seen the Best of It": Memoirs.* New York: Norton, 1992.

Anderson, Marian. *My Lord, What a Morning: An Autobiography.* Urbana: University of Illinois Press, 1956.

Anderson, William. *The Wild Man from Sugar Creek: The Political Career of Eugene Talmadge.* Baton Rouge: Louisiana State University Press, 1975.

Arnold, Thurman W. *The Bottlenecks of Business.* New York: Reynal & Hitchcock, 1940.

———. *Fair Fights and Foul: A Dissenting Lawyer's Life.* New York: Harcourt, Brace & World, 1965.

———. *The Folklore of Capitalism.* New Haven, Conn.: Yale University Press, 1937.

Arsenault, Raymond. *The Sound of Freedom: Marian Anderson, the Lincoln Memorial, and the Concert that Awakened America.* New York: Bloomsbury Press, 2009.

Auden, W. H. *Prose: Vol. III 1949–1955.* Princeton, N.J.: Princeton University Press, 2008.

Badger, Anthony J. *New Deal/New South.* Fayetteville: University of Arkansas Press, 2007.

Barnard, Ellsworth. *Wendell Willkie: Fighter for Freedom.* Marquette: Northern Michigan University Press, 1966.

Barnard, Harry. *Independent Man: The Life of Senator James Couzens.* New York: Charles Scribner's Sons, 1958.

Bellush, Bernard. *The Failure of the NRA.* New York: Norton, 1975.

Berle, Adolf A., and Gardiner C. Means. *The Modern Corporation and Private Property.* New York: Harcourt, Brace & World, 1932.

———. *Navigating the Rapids, 1918–1971.* Ed. Beatrice Bishop Berle. New York: Harcourt Brace Jovanovich, 1973.

Bennett, G. H. *Roosevelt's Peacetime Administrations, 1933–41: A Documentary History of the New Deal Years.* Manchester, U.K.: Manchester University Press, 2004.

Bernanke, Ben S. *Essays on the Great Depression.* Princeton, N.J.: Princeton University Press, 2000.

Bernstein, Irving. *Turbulent Years: A History of the American Worker, 1933–1941.* Boston: Houghton Mifflin, 1970.

Biddle, Francis. *In Brief Authority.* Garden City, N.Y.: Doubleday, 1962.

Bindas, Kenneth J. *All of This Music Belongs to the Nation: The WPA's Federal Music Project and American Society.* Knoxville: University of Tennessee Press, 1995.

Bingay, Malcolm W. *Detroit Is My Own Home Town.* New York: Bobbs-Merrill, 1946.

Blum, John Morton. *From the Morgenthau Diaries: Years of Crisis: 1928–1938.* Boston: Houghton Mifflin, 1959.

———. *From the Morgenthau Diaries: Years of Urgency: 1938–1941.* Boston: Houghton Mifflin, 1965.

———. *Roosevelt and Morgenthau: A Revision and Condensation from the Morgenthau Diaries.* Boston: Houghton Mifflin Co., 1970.

Braeman, John, Robert H. Bremner, and David Brody, eds. *The New Deal: The National Level.* Columbus: Ohio State University Press, 1975.

Brands, H.W. *Traitor to His Class: The Privileged Life and Radical Presidency of Franklin Delano Roosevelt.* New York: Doubleday, 2008.

Brinkley, Alan. *Voices of Protest: Huey Long, Father Coughlin, and the Great Depression.* New York: Knopf, 1982.

Brooks, John. *Once in Golconda: A True Drama of Wall Street 1920–1938.* New York: Harper & Row, 1969.

Browder, Robert Paul, and Thomas G. Smith. *Independent: A Biography of Lewis W. Douglas.* New York: Knopf, 1986.

Brown, Douglas V., et al. *The Economics of the Recovery Program.* Freeport, N.Y.: Books for Libraries Press, 1934.

Callahan, North. *TVA: Bridge Over Troubled Waters.* South Brunswick, N.J.: A. S. Barnes, 1980.

Callow, Simon. *Orson Welles: Volume 1: The Road to Xanadu.* New York: Penguin Books, 1996.

Caro, Robert A. *The Power Broker: Robert Moses and the Fall of New York.* New York: Knopf, 1974.

Carpenter, Ronald H. *Father Charles E. Coughlin: Surrogate Spokesman for the Disaffected.* Westport, Conn.: Greenwood Press, 1998.

Carter, John Franklin ("Unofficial Observer"). *The New Dealers.* New York: Simon & Schuster, 1934.

Chase, Stuart, Robert Dunn, and Rexford Guy Tugwell, eds. *Soviet Russia in the Second Decade.* New York: John Day, 1928.

Chernow, Ron. *The House of Morgan.* New York: Simon & Schuster, 1990.

Cohen, Adam. *Nothing to Fear: FDR's Inner Circle and the Hundred Days That Created Modern America.* New York: Penguin Press, 2009.

Collier, Peter, and David Horowitz. *The Fords: An American Epic.* New York: Summit Books, 1987.

———. *The Kennedys: An American Drama.* New York: Summit Books, 1984.

Conkin, Paul K. *Tomorrow a New World: The New Deal Community Program.* Ithaca, N.Y.: Cornell University Press, 1959.

Creel, George. *Rebel at Large: Recollections of Fifty Crowded Years.* New York: G. P. Putnam's Sons, 1947.

Culver, John C., and John Hyde. *American Dreamer: A Life of Henry A. Wallace.* New York: Norton, 2000.

Cummings, Homer. *Selected Papers of Homer Cummings.* Ed. Carl Brent Swisher. New York: Charles Scribner's Sons, 1939.

Davis, Kenneth S. *FDR: The New Deal Years, 1933–1937.* New York: Random House, 1979.

Dawson, Nelson Lloyd. *Louis D. Brandeis, Felix Frankfurter, and the New Deal.* Hamden, Conn.: Archon Books, 1980.

De Bedts, Ralph F. *The New Deal's SEC: The Formative Years.* New York: Columbia University Press, 1964.

Dickson, Paul, and Thomas B. Allen. *The Bonus Army: An American Epic.* New York: Walker, 2004.

Douglas, Lewis W. *The Liberal Tradition: A Free People and a Free Economy.* New York: Van Nostrand, 1935.

Eccles, Marriner S. *Beckoning Frontiers: Public and Personal Recollections.* New York: Knopf, 1951.

Eliot, Thomas H. *Recollections of the New Deal.* Boston: Northeastern University Press, 1992.

Epstein, Pierre. *Abraham Epstein: The Forgotten Father of Social Security.* Columbia: University of Missouri Press, 2006.

Farley, James A. *Behind the Ballots: The Personal History of a Politician.* New York: Harcourt, Brace, 1938.

———. *Jim Farley's Story.* New York: McGraw-Hill, 1948.

Feis, Herbert. *1933: Characters in Crisis.* Boston: Little, Brown, 1966.

Final Report on the WPA Program, 1935–1943. Washington, D.C.: U.S. Government Printing Office, 1947.

Finan, Christopher M. *Alfred E. Smith: The Happy Warrior.* New York: Hill & Wang, 2002.

Flanagan, Hallie. *Arena: The Story of the Federal Theatre.* New York: Duell, Sloan & Pearce, 1940.

France, Richard. *The Theatre of Orson Welles.* Lewisburg, Penn.: Bucknell University Press, 1977.

Freedman, Max, ed. *Roosevelt and Frankfurter: Their Correspondence 1928–1945.* Boston: Atlantic Monthly Press, 1967.

Freidel, Frank. *Franklin D. Roosevelt: Launching the New Deal.* Boston: Little, Brown, 1973.

Friedman, Milton, and Anna Jacobson Schwartz. *A Monetary History of the United States, 1867–1960.* Princeton, N.J.: Princeton University Press, 1963.

Galbraith, John Kenneth. *The Great Crash: 1929.* Boston: Houghton Mifflin, 1988.

Gellhorn, Martha. *The View from the Ground.* New York: Grove/Atlantic, 1994.

Grant, James. *Bernard M. Baruch: The Adventures of a Wall Street Legend.* New York: Simon & Schuster, 1983.

Hargrove, Erwin C., and Paul K. Conkin, eds. *TVA: Fifty Years of Grass-Roots Bureaucracy.* Urbana: University of Illinois Press, 1983.

Harriss, C. Lowell. *History and Policies of the Home Owners' Loan Corporation.* New York: National Bureau of Economic Research, 1951.

Hawley, Ellis W. *The New Deal and the Problem of Monopoly: A Study in Economic Ambivalence.* Princeton, N.J.: Princeton University Press, 1966.

Hiltzik, Michael. *The Plot Against Social Security.* New York: HarperCollins, 2005.

Hoover, Herbert:. *The Memoirs of Herbert Hoover, vol. 2: The Cabinet and the Presidency, 1921–1933.* New York: Macmillan, 1952.

———. *The Memoirs of Herbert Hoover, vol. 3: The Great Depression, 1929–1941.* New York: Macmillan, 1952.

Hopkins, Harry L. *Spending to Save: The Complete Story of Relief.* New York: Norton, 1936.

Houck, Davis W. *FDR and Fear Itself: The First Inaugural Address.* College Station: Texas A&M University Press, 2002.

Houseman, John. *Run-Through.* New York: Simon & Schuster, 1972.

Hurd, Charles. *When the New Deal Was Young and Gay.* New York: Hawthorne Books, 1965.

Ickes, Harold L. *The Secret Diary of Harold L. Ickes, Vol. I: The First Thousand Days: 1933–1936.* New York: Simon & Schuster, 1953.

———. *The Secret Diary of Harold L. Ickes, Vol. II: The Inside Struggle: 1936–1939.* New York: Simon & Schuster, 1954.

Jackson, Kenneth T. *Crabgrass Frontier: The Suburbanization of the United States.* New York: Oxford University Press, 1985.

Jackson, Robert H. *That Man: An Insider's Portrait of Franklin D. Roosevelt.* New York: Oxford University Press, 2003.

James, Marquis, and Bessie R. James. *Biography of a Bank: The Story of Bank of America.* San Francisco: Bank of America N.T. & S.A., 1954.

Johnson, Hiram W. *The Diary Letters of Hiram Johnson, vol. 5 (1932–1933), vol. 6 (1934–1938).* New York: Garland, 1983.

Johnson, Hugh S. *The Blue Eagle from Egg to Earth*. Garden City, N.Y.: Doubleday, Doran, 1935.

Jones, Jesse H. *Fifty Billion Dollars: My Thirteen Years with the RFC*. New York: Macmillan, 1951.

Kennedy, David M. *Freedom from Fear: The American People in Depression and War, 1929–1945*. New York: Oxford University Press, 2005.

Kennedy, Joseph P. *I'm for Roosevelt*. New York: Reynal, 1936.

Kennedy, Rose Fitzgerald. *Times to Remember*. New York: Doubleday, 1974.

Kennedy, Susan Estabrook. *The Banking Crisis of 1933*. Lexington: University Press of Kentucky, 1973.

Kiewe, Amos. *FDR's First Fireside Chat: Public Confidence and the Banking Crisis*. College Station: Texas A&M Press, 2007.

Lasser, William. *Benjamin V. Cohen: Architect of the New Deal*. New Haven, Conn.: Yale University Press, 2002.

Leff, Mark H. *The Limits of Symbolic Reform: The New Deal and Taxation, 1933–1939*. New York: Cambridge University Press, 1984.

Leuchtenburg, William E. *Franklin D. Roosevelt and the New Deal*. New York: Harper & Row, 1963.

———. *The Supreme Court Reborn*. New York: Oxford University Press, 1995.

Lilienthal, David E. *The Journals of David E. Lilienthal, Volume I: The TVA Years of 1939–1945*. New York: Harper & Row, 1964.

Lippmann, Walter. *The Essential Lippmann: A Political Philosophy for Liberal Democracy*. Ed. Clinton Rossiter and James Lare. New York: Random House, 1963.

———. *Interpretations: 1933–1935*. New York: Macmillan, 1936.

———. *Public Philosopher: Selected Letters of Walter Lippman*. Ed. John Morton Blum. New York: Ticknor & Fields, 1985.

Lord, Russell. *The Wallaces of Iowa*. Boston: Houghton Mifflin, 1947.

Louchheim, Katie, ed. *The Making of the New Deal: The Insiders Speak*. Cambridge, Mass.: Harvard University Press, 1983.

Lowitt, Richard, and Maurine Beasley, eds. *One Third of a Nation: Lorena Hickok Reports on the Great Depression*. Urbana: University of Illinois Press, 1981.

Manchester, William. *The Glory and the Dream: A Narrative History of America: 1932–1972*. Boston: Little, Brown, 1974.

Mangione, Jerre. *The Dream and the Deal: The Federal Writers' Project, 1935–1943*. Boston: Little, Brown, 1972.

Mathews, Jane DeHart. *The Federal Theatre, 1935–1939: Plays, Relief, and Politics*. New York: Octagon Books, 1980.

McCraw, Thomas K. *TVA and the Power Fight: 1933–1939*. Philadelphia: Lippincott, 1971.

McKean, David. *Tommy the Cork: Washington's Ultimate Insider from Roosevelt to Reagan*. South Royalton, Vt.: Steerforth Press, 2004.

Michelson, Charles. *The Ghost Talks*. New York: G. P. Putnam's Sons, 1944.

Moffat, Jay Pierrepont. *The Moffat Papers: Selections from the Diplomatic Journals of Jay Pierrepont Moffat, 1919–1943*. Cambridge, Mass.: Harvard University Press, 1956.

Moley, Raymond. *After Seven Years*. New York: Harper & Brothers, 1939.

———. *The First New Deal*. New York: Harcourt, Brace & World, 1966.

———. *27 Masters of Politics*. New York: Funk & Wagnalls, 1949.

Myers, William Starr, and Walter H. Newton. *The Hoover Administration: A Documented Narrative*. New York: Charles Scribner's Sons, 1936.

Nasaw, David. *The Chief: The Life of William Randolph Hearst*. New York: Houghton Mifflin, 2000.

Nourse, Edwin G., Joseph S. Davis, and John D. Black. *Three Years of the Agricultural Adjustment Administration*. Washington, D.C.: Brookings Institution, 1937.

O'Connor, Francis V., ed. *The New Deal Art Projects: An Anthology of Memoirs.* Washington, D.C.: Smithsonian Institution Press, 1972.

Ogden, August Raymond. *The Dies Committee: A Study of the Special House Committee for the Investigation of Un-American Activities: 1938–1944.* Washington, D.C.: Catholic University of America Press, 1945.

Ohl, John Kennedy. *Hugh S. Johnson and the New Deal.* DeKalb: Northern Illinois University Press, 1985.

Parrish, Michael E. *Securities Regulation and the New Deal.* New Haven, Conn.: Yale University Press, 1970.

Partnoy, Frank. *The Match King: Ivar Kreuger, the Financial Genius Behind a Century of Wall Street Scandals.* New York: PublicAffairs, 2009.

Perkins, Frances. *The Roosevelt I Knew.* New York: Viking Press, 1946.

Perkins, Van L. *Crisis in Agriculture: The Agricultural Adjustment Administration and the New Deal, 1933.* Berkeley: University of California Press, 1969.

Pickett, Clarence E. *For More than Bread: An Autobiographical Account of Twenty-Two Years' Work with the American Friends Service Committee.* Boston: Little, Brown, 1953.

Quinn, Susan. *Furious Improvisation: How the WPA and a Cast of Thousands Made High Art out of Desperate Times.* New York: Walker, 2008.

Rhodes, Richard. *The Making of the Atomic Bomb.* New York: Simon & Schuster, 1986.

Richards, Henry I. *Cotton and the AAA.* Washington, D.C.: The Brookings Institution, 1936.

Richberg, Donald R. *My Hero: The Indiscreet Memoirs of an Eventful but Unheroic Life.* New York: G. P. Putnam's Sons, 1954.

———. *The Rainbow.* Garden City, N.Y.: Doubleday, Doran, 1936.

Rogers, Will. *Will Rogers' Daily Telegrams: Vol. 4: The Roosevelt Years: 1933–1935.* Ed. James K. Smallwood and Steven K. Gragert. Stillwater: Oklahoma State University Press, 1979.

Roosevelt, Eleanor. *This I Remember.* New York: Harper & Brothers, 1949.

Roosevelt, Franklin Delano. *F.D.R.: His Personal Letters, vol. 3 (1928–1945).* Ed. Elliott Roosevelt. New York: Duell, Sloan & Pearce, 1950.

———. *On Our Way.* New York: John Day, 1934.

———. *The Public Papers and Addresses of Franklin D. Roosevelt, vol. 1, The Genesis of the New Deal, 1928–1932.* New York: Random House, 1938.

———. *The Public Papers and Addresses of Franklin D. Roosevelt, vol. 2: The Year of Crisis, 1933.* New York: Random House, 1938.

———. *The Public Papers and Addresses of Franklin D. Roosevelt, vol. 3: The Advance of Recovery and Reform, 1934.* New York: Random House, 1938.

———. *The Public Papers and Addresses of Franklin D. Roosevelt, vol. 4: The Court Disapproves, 1935.* New York: Random House, 1938.

———. *The Public Papers and Addresses of Franklin D. Roosevelt, vol. 5: The People Approve, 1936.* New York: Random House, 1938.

Roosevelt, James, and Sidney Shalett. *Affectionately, F.D.R.: A Son's Story of a Lonely Man.* New York: Harcourt, Brace, 1959.

Roosevelt, Nicholas. *A Front Row Seat.* Norman: University of Oklahoma Press, 1953.

Rosenman, Samuel I. *Working with Roosevelt.* New York: Harper, 1952.

Roskolenko, Harry. *When I Was Last on Cherry Street.* New York: Stein & Day, 1965.

Ross, Alex. *The Rest Is Noise: Listening to the Twentieth Century.* New York: Farrar, Straus & Giroux, 2007.

Roth, Benjamin. *The Great Depression: A Diary.* Ed. James Ledbetter and Daniel B. Roth. New York: PublicAffairs, 2009.

Scheiber, Sylvester J., and John R. Shoven. *The Real Deal: The History and Future of Social Security.* New Haven, Conn.: Yale University Press, 1999.

Schlesinger, Arthur M., Jr. *The Coming of the New Deal: 1933–1935.* Boston: Houghton Mifflin, 1958.

————. *The Crisis of the Old Order: 1919–1933*. Boston: Houghton Mifflin, 1957.

————. *The Politics of Upheaval: 1935–1936*. Boston: Houghton Mifflin, 1960.

Schwarz, Jordan A. *The Interregnum of Despair: Hoover, Congress, and the Depression*. Urbana: University of Illinois Press, 1970.

————. *The Speculator: Bernard A. Baruch in Washington, 1917–1965*. Chapel Hill: University of North Carolina Press, 1981.

Sherwood, Robert E. *Roosevelt and Hopkins: An Intimate History*. Rev. ed. New York: Harper & Brothers, 1950.

Shesol, Jeff. *Supreme Power: Franklin Roosevelt vs. the Supreme Court*. New York: Norton, 2010.

Shlaes, Amity. *The Forgotten Man: A New History of the Great Depression*. New York: Harper-Collins, 2007.

Simon, Rita James, ed. *As We Saw the Thirties: Essays on Social and Political Movements of a Decade*. Urbana: University of Illinois Press, 1967.

Sinclair, Upton. *I, Candidate for Governor: And How I Got Licked*. New York: Farrar & Rinehart, 1935.

Skidelsky, Robert. *Keynes: The Return of the Master*. New York: PublicAffairs, 2009.

Slayton, Robert A. *Empire Statesman: The Rise and Redemption of Al Smith*. New York: Free Press, 2001.

Smith, Amanda, ed. *Hostage to Fortune: The Letters of Joseph P. Kennedy*. New York: Viking, 2001.

Smith, Richard Norton. *An Uncommon Man: The Triumph of Herbert Hoover*. New York: Simon and Schuster, 1984.

Smith, Rixey, and Norman Beasley. *Carter Glass: A Biography*. New York: Longmans, Green, 1939.

Spivak, John L. *Shrine of the Silver Dollar*. New York: Modern Age Books, 1940.

Stein, Herbert. *The Fiscal Revolution in America: Policy in Pursuit of Reality*. Washington, D.C.: AEI Press, 1996.

Sternsher, Bernard. *Rexford Tugwell and the New Deal*. New Brunswick, N.J.: Rutgers University Press, 1964.

Talbert, Roy, Jr. *FDR's Utopian: Arthur Morgan of the TVA*. Jackson: University Press of Mississippi, 1987.

Taylor, Nick. *American-Made: The Enduring Legacy of the WPA: When FDR Put the Nation to Work*. New York: Bantam Books, 2008.

Timmons, Bascom N. *Jesse H. Jones, the Man and the Statesman*. New York: Henry Holt, 1956.

Townsend, Francis Everett. *New Horizons (An Autobiography)*. Ed. Jesse George Murray. Chicago: J. L. Stewart, 1943.

Tugwell, Rexford G. *The Brains Trust*. New York: Viking Press, 1968.

————. *The Democratic Roosevelt*. Garden City, N.Y.: Doubleday, 1957.

————. *In Search of Roosevelt*. Cambridge, Mass.: Harvard University Press, 1972.

————. *Roosevelt's Revolution: The First Year—A Personal Perspective*. New York: Macmillan, 1977.

Tully, Grace. *F.D.R., My Boss*. New York: Charles Scribner's Sons, 1949.

Urofsky, Melvin I. *Louis D. Brandeis: A Life*. New York: Pantheon Books, 2009.

Vidal, Gore. *Point to Point Navigation: A Memoir*. New York: Doubleday, 2006.

Warburg, James P. *Hell Bent for Election*. Garden City, N.Y.: Doubleday, Doran, 1935.

————. *The Long Road Home: The Autobiography of a Maverick*. Garden City, N.Y.: Doubleday, 1964.

————. *The Money Muddle*. New York: Knopf, 1934.

Ward, Geoffrey C. *A First-Class Temperament: The Emergence of Franklin Roosevelt*. New York: Harper & Row, 1989.

Watkins, T. H. *The Great Depression: America in the 1930s*. Boston: Little, Brown, 1993.

———. *Righteous Pilgrim: The Life and Times of Harold L. Ickes, 1874–1952*. New York: Henry Holt, 1990.

Weinstein, Michael M. *Recovery and Redistribution Under the NRA*. New York: North-Holland, 1980.

Weiss, Nancy Joan. *Farewell to the Party of Lincoln: Black Politics in the Age of FDR*. Princeton, N.J.: Princeton University Press, 1983.

White, Graham, and John Maze. *Harold Ickes of the New Deal: His Private Life and Public Career*. Cambridge, Mass.: Harvard University Press, 1985.

White, Walter. *A Man Called White: The Autobiography of Walter White*. New York: Viking Press, 1948.

White, William Allen. *Selected Letters of William Allen White, 1899–1943*. Ed. Walter Johnson. New York: Henry Holt, 1947.

Willis, H. Parker, and John M. Chapman. *The Banking Situation: American Post-War Problems and Developments*. New York: Columbia University Press, 1934.

Wilson, Edmund. *The American Earthquake*. New York: Farrar, Straus & Giroux, 1958.

Witte, Edwin E. *The Development of the Social Security Act*. Madison: University of Wisconsin Press, 1963.

Young, William H., and Nancy K. Young. *The Great Depression in America: A Cultural Encyclopedia*. Westport, Conn.: Greenwood Press, 2007.

ACKNOWLEDGMENTS

M Y GRATITUDE GOES out to several distinguished institutions that provided me with access to their collections and other assistance with my research. The archives of the FDR Library are the starting point for any research into the Roosevelt administration. The Library of Congress manuscript collection granted me access to the Thomas G. Corcoran Papers, including his unfinished and unpublished memoir "Rendezvous with Democracy," as well as many other useful documents. The Oral History Collection of Columbia University is a repository of material of immeasurable value. The Young Research Library of UCLA and the Langson Library of the University of California, Irvine, were my research home bases for this project.

This book would not have been born without the enthusiasm of my agent, Sandra Dijkstra, who helped shape its initial conceptualization with the percipience on which I have come to rely. My editors at Free Press, Hilary Redmon and Martin Beiser, masterfully guided the development of this book and artfully shaped the final product. Without the support of my wife, Deborah, this book would not have been finished, and without her research contribution many aspects of the New Deal would have gone unremarked. As always, my sons, Andrew and David, provided me with the optimism for the future that makes efforts like this worthwhile.

INDEX

ABOUT THE AUTHOR

MICHAEL HILTZIK is a Pulitzer Prize–winning author and journalist who has covered business, technology, and public policy for the *Los Angeles Times* for three decades. Currently the *Times'* business columnist, he has also served as a financial and political writer, an investigative reporter, and a foreign correspondent. His most recent book is *Colossus: The Turbulent, Thrilling Saga of the Building of Hoover Dam,* published in 2010 by Free Press. His previous books are *The Plot Against Social Security: How the Bush Plan is Endangering Our Financial Future* (2005), *Dealers of Lightning: Xerox PARC and the Dawn of the Computer Age* (1999), and *A Death in Kenya: The Murder of Julie Ward* (1991). He received the 1999 Pulitzer Prize for articles exposing corruption in the entertainment industry and the 2004 Gerald Loeb Award for outstanding business commentary. A graduate of Colgate University and Columbia University, he lives in Southern California.